Religions in the Modern World

This is an unrivalled guide to contemporary religions. Comprehensive in its coverage, this completely revised and updated second edition of *Religions in the Modern World* considers the history and modern practices of the world's main religious traditions. It analyses trends in the manifestation of religion in the modern world, from secularization to the rise of new spiritualities, and is at the cutting edge of developments in the study of religion.

This second edition includes:

- new chapters on how to study religion in the modern world, spirituality, paganism, religion and violence, religion and popular culture, and secularization and secularism
- discussion of the strength of the Christian Right
- post 9/11 and 7/7 developments in religion and politics
- case studies and anecdotes, text extracts, chapter menus and end-of-chapter summaries, glossaries and annotated further reading sections
- a wide variety of photographs, figures, tables and maps.

Religions in the Modern World is the ideal textbook for those coming to the study of religion for the first time, as well as for those who wish to keep up to date with the latest perspectives in the field. Fully international in coverage, it is accessibly written by practising and specialist teachers.

The editors, **Linda Woodhead**, **Hiroko Kawanami** and **Christopher Partridge**, are all members of the Religious Studies Department at Lancaster University.

Religions in the Modern World

Traditions and Transformations

Second Edition

**Edited by Linda Woodhead,
Hiroko Kawanami
and Christopher Partridge**

Co-editors, first edition:
Paul Fletcher
David Smith

2009

Routledge
Taylor & Francis Group
LONDON AND NEW YORK

First published 2001
by Routledge
2 Park Square, Milton Park, Abingdon, Oxon OX14 4RN

Simultaneously published in the USA and Canada
by Routledge
270 Madison Ave., New York, NY 100016

Second edition published in 2009

Routledge is an imprint of the Taylor & Francis Group, an informa business

Typeset in Berling and Futura
by Keystroke, 28 High Street, Tettenhall, Wolverhampton
Printed and bound in Great Britain
by CPI Antony Rowe, Chippenham, Wiltshire

British Library Cataloguing in Publication Data
A catalogue record for this book is available from the British Library

Library of Congress Cataloging in Publication Data
Religions in the modern world / edited by Linda Woodhead, Hiroko Kawanami and
Christopher Partridge. – 2nd ed.
p. cm.
Includes bibliographical references and index.
1. Religions. I. Woodhead, Linda. II. Kawanami, Hiroko. III. Partridge,
Christopher H. (Christopher Hugh), 1961–
BL80.3.R443 2009
200--dc22
2008050733

ISBN10: 0–415–45890–0 (hbk)
ISBN10: 0–415–45891–9 (pbk)

ISBN13: 978–0–415–45890–0 (hbk)
ISBN13: 978–0–415–45891–7 (pbk)

IN MEMORIAM
PAUL FLETCHER 1965–2008

Contents

Illustrations

The following were reproduced with kind permission. While every effort has been made to trace copyright holders and obtain permission, this has not been possible in all cases. Any omissions brought to our attention will be remedied in future editions.

igures

Tables

Boxes

Notes on contributors

Cathy Cantwell holds research positions at Oxford University's Oriental Institute and at the University of Cardiff's School of Religious and Theological Studies. Her work centres on Tibetan tantric traditions, both textual and ethnographic studies. Recent joint publications with Robert Mayer include *Early Tibetan Documents on Phur pa from Dunhuang* (Austrian Academy of Sciences Press, 2008) and *The Kīlaya Nirvāna, a Tantra and the Vajra Wrath Tantra: Two texts from the Ancient Tantra Collection* (Austrian Academy of Sciences Press, 2007).

Douglas E. Cowan is Professor of Religious Studies at Renison University College, at the University of Waterloo, in Waterloo, Canada. He is the author or editor of several books, including: *Bearing False Witness? An Introduction to the Christian Countercult* (Praeger, 2003), *The Remnant Spirit: Conservative Reform in Mainline Protestantism* (Praeger, 2003); *Religion Online: Finding Faith on the Internet* (edited with Lorne L. Dawson; Routledge, 2004); *Cyberhenge: Modern Pagans on the Internet* (Routledge, 2005); *Cults and New Religions: A Brief History* (with David G. Bromley; Blackwell, 2008); and *Sacred Terror: Religion and Horror on the Silver Screen* (Baylor University Press, 2008). He is currently working on *Sacred Space: The Quest for Transcendence in Science Fiction Film and Television*, which will also be published by Baylor University Press.

Grace Davie has a personal Chair in the Sociology of Religion in the University of Exeter. She is a past-president of the American Association for the Sociology of Religion (2003) and of the Research Committee 22 (Sociology of Religion) of the International Sociological Association (2002–06). In addition to numerous chapters and articles, she is the author of *Religion in Britain since 1945* (Blackwell, 1994), *Religion in Modern Europe* (OUP, 2000), *Europe: The exceptional case* (DLT, 2002) and *The Sociology of Religion* (Sage, 2007); she is co-editor of *Predicting Religion* (Ashgate, 2003) and co-author of *Religious America, Secular Europe* (Ashgate, 2008).

Stephan Feuchtwang is part-time professor in the Department of Anthropology, London School of Economics. His current research interests include self-realization in different temporalities and the formation of a new concept of civilisation for comparative historical anthropology and archaeology. Recent publications include, as editor and contributor, *Making Place: State projects, globalisation and local responses in China*, (UCL Press, 2004); (with Wang Mingming) *Grassroots Charisma: Four local leaders in China* (Routledge, 2001); and *Popular Religion in China: the imperial metaphor* (Routledge/Curzon, 2001).

Charles Gore is senior lecturer in the History of African Art at SOAS and has conducted field research in Benin City and Edo state in Southern Nigeria since 1986 with particular focus on Edo ritual and religion at grassroots level. His publications include *Art, Performance and Ritual in Benin City* (International African Library and Edinburgh University Press, 2007) and a range of articles relating to religion, ritual, media and art in Edo state, Nigeria. Current interests are religion and ritual, African visual cultures, including mass media such as African photography, film, video and the internet; and approaches to popular culture and its relations to locality and the processes of globalization.

Wouter J. Hanegraaff is Professor of History of Hermetic Philosophy and Related Currents at the University of Amsterdam. He is president of the European Society for the Study of Western Esotericism and a member of the Royal Dutch Academy of Sciences (Koninklijke Nederlandse Academie van Wetenschappen). He is the author of *New Age Religion and Western Culture: Esotericism in the Mirror of Secular Thought* (Brill, 1996); (with Ruud M. Bouthoorn) *Lodovico Lazzarelli (1447–1500): The Hermetic Writings and Related Documents* (Tempe, 2005); and *Swedenborg, Oetinger, Kant: Three Perspectives on the Secrets of Heaven* (The Swedenborg Foundation, 2007). He has published numerous articles, and edited six collective works, including the two-volume *Dictionary of Gnosis and Western Esotericism* (Brill, 2005); and (with Jeffrey Kripal) *Hidden Intercourse: Eros and Sexuality in the History of Western Esotericism* (Brill, 2008).

Graham Harvey is Reader in Religious Studies at the Open University, UK. His research interests include contemporary Paganisms and indigenous religions, including revisiting animism, totemism, and shamanism, and the rituals by which people engage with the larger than human world. He is the author of several books, including: *Listening People, Speaking Earth: Contemporary Paganism* (Hurst & Co./Wakefield Press, 1997); *Animism: Respecting the Living World* (Hurst & Co./Columbia University Press/Wakefield Press, 2005); (with Robert Wallis) *Historical Dictionary of Shamanism* (Scarecrow Press, 2007). He has also edited several books, including: (with Charlotte Hardman) *Paganism Today: Ancient Earth Traditions for the 21st Century* (Thorsons, 1996); *Indigenous Religions: A companion* (Continuum, 2000); (with Karen Ralls) *Indigenous Religious Musics* (Ashgate, 2001); *Shamanism: A reader* (Routledge, 2003); (with Chas S. Clifton) *The Paganism Reader* (Routledge, 2004); (with Jenny Blain and Doug Ezzy) *Researching Paganisms* (Altamira, 2004).

Jeffrey Haynes is a professor of politics at London Metropolitan University. His research interests are: religion and politics; religion and international relations; comparative politics and globalization; democracy and democratization; and development issues. He is the author of 17 books. His most recent books are: *Comparative Politics in a Globalizing World* (Polity) and *Advances in Development Studies* (editor and contributor of three chapters, Palgrave), both published in 2005; *The Politics of Religion: A survey* (Routledge, 2006); *An Introduction to Religion and International Relations* (Pearson, 2007) and *Religion and Development: Conflict or cooperation?* (Palgrave, 2007); *Development Studies: A short introduction* (Polity, 2008) and *Handbook of Religion and Politics* (Routledge, 2008).

Hiroko Kawanami is lecturer in Buddhist Studies in the Department of Religious Studies, Lancaster University, UK. She has done research on the position of Buddhist nuns, Buddhist monastic education and dissemination of knowledge, and the relationship between politics and religion in Southeast Asia. Presently she is conducting research on how international relief organizations have affected the local communities in disaster-affected areas and Buddhist leadership in dealing with the aftermath.

Robert Kisala is former professor at Nanzan University in Japan and permanent fellow at the Nanzan Institute for Religion and Culture. He is currently on the General Council of the Society of the Divine Word, a Roman Catholic religious order in Rome. He is the author of *Prophets of Peace: Pacifism and Cultural Identity in Japan's New Religions* (University of Hawaii Press, 1999), and editor of *Urbanization and Mission in Asia and the Pacific* (Logos Publications, 2005).

Kim Knott is Professor of Religious Studies at the University of Leeds and Director of Diasporas, Migration and Identities, a strategic research programme funded by the UK Arts and Humanities Research Council. She is also General Secretary of the European Association for the Study of Religion. Kim Knott's recent research has focused on the development of a spatial methodology for locating religion, for examining its engagement with other social and cultural institutions, activities and issues, and for breaking open the 'secular'. In *The Location of Religion: A spatial analysis* (Equinox, 2005), she considered the application of socio-spatial theory to the study of religious, secular and postsecular relations. She won the SHAP Book Award for *Hinduism: A Very Short Introduction* (OUP, 1998) which since its publication has been translated into a dozen languages. She is currently co-editing books on *Diasporas: Concepts, Intersections and Identities* and on the geography of religions.

Seth Kunin is Professor in the Department of Theology and Religion at Durham University as well as being Pro-Vice-Chancellor and Head of the Faculty of Arts and Humanities. He received his PhD in Anthropology from the University of Cambridge, and his subsequent work has explored the use of anthropological approaches in relation to Jewish myth and culture. He is currently working on issues relating to identities at the boundaries, with particular reference to crypto-Judaism.

David Lehmann is Reader in Sociology at the University of Cambridge where he was Director of the Centre for Latin American Studies between 1990 and 1999. His main contributions have been on religion in Latin America: *Democracy and development in Latin America: economics, politics and religion in the postwar period* (Polity, 1990); *Struggle for the Spirit: popular culture and religious transformation in Brazil and Latin America* (Polity, 1996) and in Israel: *Remaking Israeli Judaism: the challenge of Shas* (Hurst, 2006), with Batia Siebzehner. He has also published extensively in the field of Development Studies and is the co-ordinator of a Religion and Secularism Network within the Religion and Society programme of the AHRC/ESRC Research Programme on Religion and Society.

Kenneth Mello (Passamaquoddy) is an Assistant Professor of Religion at Southwestern University in Georgetown, Texas. His areas of interest include contemporary Native American religious and cultural identities, myth and narrative as historical tools, sacred space and the environment, and the religious importance of music and sports in Native American cultures.

Christopher Partridge is Professor of Religious Studies at Lancaster University and Co-Director of the Centre for the Study of Religion and Popular Culture at the University of Chester, UK. His research and writing focuses on, first, religion and popular culture and, second, on new religions and alternative spiritualities. He has a particular interest in the relationship between popular music and religion. He is the author of *The Re-Enchantment of the West*, 2 volumes (T & T Clark/Continuum, 2004, 2006) and the co-editor of the series *Studies in Popular Music* (Equinox). He is the editor of several volumes on religious belief in the contemporary world, including *The World's Religions* (LionHudson/Augsburg Fortress, 2005), *Encyclopedia of New Religions* (LionHudson/ Oxford University Press, 2004), and *UFO Religions* (Routledge, 2003). He was also a founding co-editor of the journal *Fieldwork in Religion* (Equinox).

Charles Selengut is Professor of Sociology and Religious Studies at Drew University in Madison, New Jersey. He is the author of many scholarly studies on the rise of fundamentalisms and new religious movements in the Middle East. His books include *Sacred Fury: Understanding Religious Violence* (AltaMira, 2003), *Jewish Identity in the Post Modern Age* (Paragon House, 1999) and *Jewish–Muslim Encounters: History, Philosophy and Culture* (Paragon House, 2001).

Christopher Shackle FBA is Emeritus Professor of the Modern Languages of South Asia in the University of London at SOAS. His publications on Sikhism include *An Introduction to the Sacred Language of the Sikhs* (SOAS, 1983); *The Sikhs* (Minority Rights Group, 1983, revised 1986); *A Guru Nanak Glossary*, second edition (Heritage

Publishers, 1995); the co-edited *Sikh Religion, Culture and Ethnicity* (Curzon, 2001); and (with A.S. Mandair) *Teachings of the Sikh Gurus: Selections from the Sikh Scriptures* (Routledge, 2006).

David Smith teaches Hinduism and South Asian Art in the Department of Religious Studies, Lancaster University. He is the author of *Ratnakara's Haravijaya: An introduction to the Sanskrit court epic* (Oxford University Press, 1985); *The Dance of Siva: Religion, art and poetry in South India* (Cambridge University Press, 1996); and *Hinduism and Modernity* (Blackwell, 2001).

Giselle Vincett is a sociologist of religion and research fellow at the University of Edinburgh. Her research interests are in contemporary understandings and forms of religion, particularly emerging trends in the UK and North America. Most recently she has been researching the religiosity of young people in Scotland. Giselle co-edited the book *Women and Religion in the West: Challenging secularization* (Ashgate, 2008), and has papers published in *The Quaker Condition: The sociology of a liberal religion* (Cambridge Scholars, 2008) and *Feminist Spirituality: The Next Generation* (Lexington Books, 2009).

David Waines is Professor Emeritus of Islamic Studies, Department of Religious Studies, Lancaster University. He is the author, among other works, of *An Introduction to Islam* (1995; second edition, 2003) and has written extensively on medieval Islamic diet and medicine as well as on religious and political themes concerning the modern Islamic world.

Linda Woodhead is Professor of Sociology of Religion at Lancaster University, and Director of the AHRC/ESRC Research Programme on Religion and Society. Her research explores the role of religion in late modern societies. She is the author, with Ole Riis, of *A Sociology of Religious Emotion* (OUP, 2009). She is currently involved in an EU-funded research project on the Muslim veil and public policy. Recent publications include: *The Spiritual Revolution: Why Religion is Giving Way to Spirituality* (with Paul Heelas, Blackwell, 2005) and *An Introduction to Christianity* (Cambridge University Press, 2004).

Preface to the second edition

When the first edition of this book was sent to the publishers in early 2001, the subject of religion in the modern world was still considered marginal by many people. In the intervening years that situation has changed out of all recognition. Like it or loathe it, religion is back on the agenda again.

As the first edition showed, religion was a major force in the modern world well before 2001. Contrary to claims about recent religious resurgence, religion has not popped up like some jack-in-the-box. Rather, it has made itself known in ways which are harder to ignore. The attack on the World Trade Center on 11 September 2001 is the most obvious example, but other more incremental developments have also been important. These include global migrations which have brought religious pluralism to the heart of a supposedly secular Europe, the continuing growth of new forms of spirituality, and the reconfiguration of religion in a media culture.

What has changed the most is thus the way we look at religion, and how seriously we take it. Religion is no longer dismissed as a private pastime, but is taken more seriously as a public and political force. This change, in turn, impacts upon religion itself, often lending it new confidence and vitality, and increasing its range and power.

This new edition of *Religions in the Modern World* has been revised to take account of these changes. Each and every chapter is updated. In addition, new themes and topics are addressed, both within existing chapters, and in seven newly commissioned chapters:

- How to study religion in the modern world
- Spirituality
- Paganism
- New Religious Movements
- Religion and violence
- Religion and popular culture
- Secularism and secularization

The one thing which has not changed is the overall aim of the book, which is to present a full and up-to-date portrait of religion worldwide, authored by leading experts, accessible to new as well as more advanced students, offering basic information as well as new themes and perspectives.

In revising the book we have paid close attention to the extensive feedback provided by lecturers and students who had used the first edition. Their comments have helped make this a better book. We would like to thank them, and we hope they will be satisfied with the results.

Linda Woodhead
Hiroko Kawanami
Christopher Partridge
Lancaster University, 2008

Modern contexts of religion

Linda Woodhead

Modernity

Since the subject of this book is religions in the modern world, it is useful to begin by clarifying what we mean by 'modern world' and 'modernity'.

'Modernity' is an academic term used to refer to a distinctive era which breaks with what comes before, or 'pre-modernity'. Theories of modernity seek to isolate the distinctive characteristics of modern societies. Although different theories often single out different aspects of modernity, they tend to agree that Western, industrial societies typify what is meant by modernity, and that although modernization proceeds at a different pace in different parts of the world, when it occurs it follows the Western model. They also assume that modernization involves the loss of 'traditional' features of pre-modern societies; some theorists celebrate this change as progress, others see it as involving loss as well as gain. It is also common for theories of modernity to date the modern era from the time when science, technology and industry became powerful forces in the West, at some point in the eighteenth or early nineteenth centuries.

Taken together, the chapters in this book present a somewhat different picture of modernity. What they suggest is that the modern world comes in different guises and times in different parts of the world. Once one begins to look at religious change in a global perspective, easy generalizations about modernity begin to fail, and the assumption that all cultures and societies inevitably progress through uniform stages of development from the pre-modern to the modern, thus repeating the experience of the West, becomes less plausible.

In this book we allow each chapter to determine what counts as modernity for the particular tradition, region or form of religion with which it is concerned. For example, the chapter on Christianity considers the rise of the modern nation state to be decisive for Christian churches, and so dates modernity from around the time of the French Revolution in 1789. By contrast, the chapter on Chinese religions speaks of a 'long' modernity in China which has had a thousand years of slow emergence and is characterized by the growth of commerce, monetary economy, contractual and share-holding agreements, long-distance trade and banking, cities of manufacture and commerce and luxurious consumption. This is contrasted with a more recent political or 'republican' modernity, characterized by the institution of a nation state and mass politics, both of which have had a much more dramatic effect on religious practices. And, as a final example, the chapter on Sikhism distinguishes between a modernity which is in effect an imposition of colonialism, initiated by the British conquest of the Punjab in the 1840s, and a later postcolonial phase which begins with Indian independence in 1947 and in which many aspects of the older modernity of the colonial period begin to be questioned and discarded in favour of new forms of traditionalized modernity or modernized tradition.

This global perspective on modernization serves as a helpful reminder that:

1. the West (Europe and then America) only really became economically, technologically and possibly culturally dominant on the world stage after 1800, and before that time other civilizations including Chinese and Islamic ones were often more advanced and powerful culturally as well as politically;
2. modernization is not exclusive to the West, but can and has taken place in non-Western cultures, without Western stimulus;
3. modernization may be a process internal to a particular society, or may be imposed from outside, most notably by colonial intervention (or some combination of these two);
4. the Western experience of modernity and modernization is not a sole definitive model of 'evolution' and 'development' which all cultures and societies are destined to follow;
5. there are several varieties of modernization worldwide, and many different ways of being modern.

Instead of giving a single definition of modernity which implies that it is identical with the social and cultural changes experienced by Western societies in the last two hundred years or so, it is therefore more helpful to think of modernity in terms of a number of different processes, dynamics and societal characteristics which may operate together or in some combination, in different parts of the world and at different times. They may be characterized as a series of profound changes, or even revolutions, which operate at political, economic, social and cultural levels. On the basis of the evidence presented in the chapters which follow, five appear to be particularly significant as contexts for religion and spirituality worldwide.

1. The nation state

There are few religions which have not been profoundly affected by the rise of the nation state. Nations themselves are not new (ancient Israel was a nation, for example), but what is new is the rise of the secular nation state with its extensive apparatus of control over a huge range of aspects of social and political life. What is also new is the way in which the nation state has become the almost universal unit of territorial control worldwide. Increasingly, such states are constitutional, that is to say they exist to serve not those who rule but those who are ruled, and their power is checked in order to protect the freedom of their citizens. They are secular in the sense that they seek to keep religion out of politics.

Only in the course of the twentieth century have truly democratic states developed, in which government is by representatives elected by all adult citizens. Many chapters in this volume remind us that the twentieth century has also witnessed the rise of the one-party state, in which a single party is established to govern (most communist and fascist regimes, for example). The 'triumph' of democracy is very recent.

As the chapters which follow demonstrate, interactions between religions and nation states take many forms. Some states have been profoundly and violently hostile to religion: this is an extreme version of the 'secular' state. It has been particularly true of communist states – see, for example, Chapter 3 on the way in which China tried to eliminate Buddhism in Tibet. On the other hand, other communist states and regimes have tried to win the support of religious leaders and devotees in the attempt to legitimize their rule, as Chapter 3 also shows in relation to Buddhism in Laos, Burma and Thailand. (In the long run, the co-option of religion to support the state may prove a mixed blessing for religion, since to become 'established' by this process is to lose independence and so become tainted and compromised in the eyes of many.)

At the opposite end of the spectrum, religions may be antagonistic to the policies of nation states. Thus the Catholic Church in Poland played a key role in the overthrow of communism in the late 1980s (see Chapter 8). A more extreme example is provided by religious groups which organize themselves as religious alternatives to the secular nation state. The success of religious nationalism since the latter part of the twentieth century has surprised many commentators who believed that religion no longer had political significance in an era of nation states. In 1979, for example, the increasingly secular state in Iran was overthrown by Islamic nationalists. Religious nationalism is also a potent force in many other Islamic countries, as well as in India (Hinduism), Israel (Orthodox Judaism) and the former Yugoslavia (Roman Catholic Christianity, Orthodox Christianity, Islam).

In Western Europe and the USA, by contrast, religion (preponderantly Christianity) has come to accept the legitimacy of the nation state and democracy, and even to construct itself as the defender of democracy. Yet even so, religion remains capable of political opposition, as the rise of the Civil Rights movement, and more recently the Christian Right, in the USA has demonstrated. Even where it tries to ignore the nation state and keep out of politics, religion is inevitably affected by the state's creeping control of many areas of social life. The process which is called 'social differentiation' involves the state taking control not only of governmental matters, but of education, welfare and community organization, and thereby challenging religious activity in these areas. If the process is unchallenged, the secular state may succeed in turning religion into a cultural rather than a political force, which relates more to the sphere of private and domestic than public life. As many chapters show, however, religion in the modern world often resists such shrinkage, and the modern state is also capable of recognizing and supporting some of religion's public functions (for example, in education and social welfare).

2. Colonialism

Many chapters in this volume remind us that colonialism has been an extremely important dynamic of the modern world. Colonialism is a modern variant of imperialism. Empires have always existed, and imperialism refers to the general process whereby states extend their power and dominion by force (usually military, but also political and economic). Colonialism normally refers to something more specific: the modern European expansion whereby foreign territories were settled and ruled over by whites who controlled populations of indigenous peoples by military, legal and political means. (Arguably, non-Western forms of modern imperialism, for example Japanese, might also fit into the category of colonialism.)

Western colonialism can be dated back to 1500 and the expansion of Spain and Portugal, but its decisive phase began three hundred years later when modernizing Western nations like Britain and France rapidly expanded their territories. In 1800 Western nations controlled 35 per cent of the world's land surface; by 1914 they were in charge of 84 per cent. By the 1970s, the vast majority of these empires had been dismantled and new independent nation states created in their wake.

The fates of religion and colonialism have been bound up together in several ways.

First, colonialism has been aided by religion, most notably by Christian missions. In some cases missions explicitly legitimated colonialism, but more often Christian missionary work supported the colonial enterprise implicitly, and often unintentionally, by acting as the agent of a cultural imperialism. At the same time, however, Christianity provided cultural resources – not least education – which would, in time, serve as resources which colonized peoples could deploy to win independence from foreign rule.

Second, colonialism affected the religion of the colonizers. Not only was Christianity affected by its contact with other cultures (see Chapter 8), but it has been a major factor in what is sometimes called 'the easternization of the West', the process whereby oriental religions have been absorbed into the cultural life of the West, often giving rise to new forms of religion and spirituality (see the chapters on Buddhism, Spirituality, Paganism and New Religious Movements).

Third, religions carried by colonialism have affected the people and places to which they spread. For example, Christianity has been appropriated by many colonized peoples, most notably in Latin America and sub-Saharan Africa. Interestingly, widespread Christianization has only taken place in the post-colonial era, but its spread has been dramatic. Christianity is now the largest of the world religions, and there are more Christians in the Southern than the Northern hemisphere.

Fourth, colonialism had a profound effect on indigenous religions within colonized territories. Amongst elites, it often generated reforming and revisionist activity as they sought to modernize their religious traditions to conform more closely to Western models. For example, new forms of 'reformed Hinduism' came into being as Westernized intellectuals in India sought to interpret Hinduism as a text-based, ethical, universal religion (see Chapter 2). In other cases, religions were revitalized as they became markers of colonized peoples' identity, and were mobilized to oppose colonialism (see Chapter 4 on Sikhism).

As we will see throughout this volume, there has also been a widespread backlash against the West and Western culture in the wake of colonialism, a backlash which is often expressed in religious terms.

3. Capitalism and 'rationalization'

The rise of the economic system we call capitalism has both subtle and profound implications for religion. Capitalism is a flexible, varied and rapidly changing form of economic
organization which centres around:

1. a money-based economy with a developed banking system in which capital
   accumulation is possible, and in which a large proportion of capital is in the hands
   of institutions and corporations as well as private individuals;
2. the separation of ownership from control, and the development of complex
   managerial hierarchies;
3. the determination of individual and corporate activity by the overriding goal of profit;
4. a competitive and free market regulating supply and demand;
5. the division and specialization of labour (both between different trades, and within
   the manufacture of a single product);
6. the provision of labour by specialized and educated workers who are free agents, and
   the growth of a middle class;
7. the global expansion of markets, commerce and production;
8. the expansion of consumerism, such that consumption (buying things) becomes an
   important aspect of modern people's lives.

Although the capitalist form of economic organization was resisted in the modern
period by communist alternatives, the collapse of communism since the late 1980s has
left capitalism free to dominate the world order.

Capitalism is accompanied, and furthered, by what the sociologist Max Weber called
'rationalization'. Rationalization refers both to cultural and broader socio-economic
developments. At the cultural level it is associated with the Enlightenment movement
of the eighteenth century, and its successful championing of 'reason' and the scientific
method. More broadly, rationalization refers to the process by which more and more
aspects of social life are shaped by the aim of achieving their goals in the most effective
and efficient way, irrespective of other values, whether humanitarian or environmental.
This process involves the growth of bureaucratic arrangements. It is bound up with
capitalism, because capitalism dictates the overriding goal of profit.

In many ways capitalism and rationalization seem to exclude religion. Impersonal,
rational calculation in order to maximize profit overrides and excludes religious motives
and ends. This does not necessarily mean that capitalism undermines religion, but it at
least excludes it from huge swathes of life. Certainly, many forms of religion do not
attempt to interfere with or influence the economic sphere, and many religious people
work in capitalist enterprises, without feeling that this relates significantly to their
religious commitment, whether positively or negatively.

However, many of the chapters in this volume suggest that there are also important
two-way relations between religion and capitalism. Thus religion in the modern world
may:

1. aid and support capitalism. Max Weber himself pointed out the compatibility between the work ethic of Protestant Christianity and the spirit of capitalism. Evangelical and Charismatic forms of Christianity continue to sustain personal values necessary for success in a capitalist economy (see Chapter 8 on Christianity). There are many forms of modern religion which make explicit promises to help their followers achieve greater prosperity;
2. serve as a way of coping with the severe inequalities, disruptions, stresses and strains which capitalism generates;
3. resist and oppose capitalism. Many forms of contemporary Islam, for example, are highly critical of capitalism, and seek to replace or temper it with more egalitarian forms of 'Islamic' economic and social arrangement. Capitalism is seen as Western and secular. Other forms of religion serve as spaces in which people may retreat from capitalism and try to forge other forms of economic arrangement – for example, some New Religious Movements and some forms of paganism involve communal living and the abandonment of monetary exchange. Monasticism provides another example.

Religion has equally varied relations with science and technology. Most religions have been more than happy to appropriate modern technology to serve their own ends – for example, disseminating their teachings via the mass media. As for science, some have claimed that its findings are entirely compatible with their own beliefs and teachings (Buddhism, for example, often stresses its empirical credentials), whilst others have gone even further by claiming that their scriptures anticipated scientific findings (some forms of neo-Vedic Hinduism, for example). Another observable phenomenon is that whereby modern men and women compartmentalize their lives, living part of them in conformity with rational principles (in the laboratory, workshop or workplace), and others in conformity to non-rational or supra-rational beliefs and practices (asking invisible deities for worldly success, placing faith in alternative forms of medicine). Still other forms of religion resist and oppose certain aspects of modern science very fiercely. Many conservative Muslims and Christians, for example, remain firmly opposed to a Darwinian account of evolution, because it contradicts their scriptures, and undermines their values and way of life.

4. *Equality, human rights, and individualism*

Modern societies are characteristically committed to a set of cultural values which affirm the dignity, inviolable value, and equality of all human persons. This commitment is institutionalized in different forms, including legal codes. It is closely related to more egalitarian social arrangements and increased affluence.

All of the world religions have played some part in supporting and defending these values, with their 'liberal' wings being particularly associated with such commitments. Religion continues to serve as the moral conscience of many societies. But many other forms of religion – often within the same tradition – have also played a part in opposing these same values. In relation to the struggle for gender equality, for example, religion has served to support and motivate women to claim equality with men, as well as rein-forcing the idea that there is a sacred, God-given difference between the sexes, which dictates that women should be under the control of men (see Chapter 19, Religion and gender). Likewise, religion can serve to break down barriers between ethnic groups in the name of a common humanity and the brotherhood of man, or to mark and defend the distinctiveness of a particular people.

This cluster of modern values involves a commitment to the value of the individual which may be corrosive not only of the solidarity often required by religions, but of their commitment to tradition – to an authority which is considered external to and higher than the individual self. The authority of the past, of a clerical elite, of established religious institutions and practices, and even of a transcendent deity may all be called into question by the modern tendency to authorize individual reason and experience. Religions may resist such a 'turn to the self' and 'detraditionalization', or they may positively accommodate it. Thus at one end of the spectrum modern societies encourage highly traditionalized religions, often called 'fundamentalisms', which assert the absolute and literal authority of their sacred scriptures. At the other end we see the emergence of new forms of religion which draw on traditional authorities only insofar as they resource the individual self. Some move so far away from tradition that they reject the title 'religion' altogether, and prefer the language of 'spirituality'. Interestingly, this volume suggests that such religions and spiritualities are not confined to the West (as in the New Age movement and some New Religious Movements), but are also found in many other parts of the world (see, for example, discussion in Chapter 5 of Chinese religions, and Chapter 6 of Japanese religions).

5. *Secularism and secularization*

Secularization, or the decline of religion, has often been seen as an inevitable consequence of modernization. Chapter 21, Secularization and secularism, explains the reasoning behind this view. A good deal of evidence from Europe, where churchgoing has declined for well over a century, supports this idea. However, as many chapters in this volume reveal, secularization in Europe has not been matched elsewhere. Not only is religion flourishing outside the West, but even in the richest, most powerful, and arguably most 'modern' of all Western societies – the United States of America – religion continues to have a central place both in private and public life. Such examples of religious vitality cast doubt on the assumption that the decline of traditional forms of Christianity in modern Europe necessarily points the way to the inevitable fate of religion in all modernizing societies.

As the following chapters illustrate, just as modernization takes different forms in different parts of the world, so religion plays significantly different roles in the process in different contexts. In some, modernization may be corrosive of religion, whereas in others religion may itself be a modernizing force. One of the key variables is the extent

FIGURE 0.1 Face veiling

Across Europe the Muslim veil has become a symbolic focus of conflicts about the place of religion in modern 'secular' Western societies.
Courtesy Image Source.

to which 'secularism' gains support, and shapes the public life and institutions of a particular country. 'Secularism' refers to ideologies which seek to restrict, restrain or even destroy religion (see Chapter 21). Where there is active support for a 'secular state', for example, religion may be more likely to decline in influence than where religion retains close ties with politics and a political elite.

Late modernity

Most people today would accept the designation 'modern', and most of us would accept that we live in a 'modern world'. Yet twenty-first century societies are often significantly different from the earlier, industrial societies which were first called 'modern'. This has led some scholars to propose that we have actually left modernity behind, and now live in 'postmodernity'. Since most of the dynamics and trends characteristic of modernity are still clearly in evidence, however, it is more plausible to claim that societies may be entering a new phase of modernity, which may be referred to as 'advanced' or 'late' modernity. In addition to the dynamics listed above, late modern societies are characterized by processes of globalization and mediatization, and some can be described as entering a phase of 'postsecularism'.

1. Globalization

'Globalization' refers to increasingly important and extensive flows of people, capital, and culture across the world. Globalization is closely linked to advanced forms of capitalism, to new technologies including communication technologies, increased affluence, and new forms of political co-operation. Migrations of people, for economic and political reasons, have become increasingly significant since the 1950s, and have led to important ethnic and cultural changes in many societies. A major result has been a growing religious and cultural pluralism in many societies, which may challenge the secular nation state. Migrations, and associated diasporas, create new mixtures of religion in a single territory. Moreover, they create new transnational connections, since migrants in contemporary societies are more able and likely to retain strong connections with the places and cultures from whence they have come. On the one hand, globalization seems to perpetuate Western privilege, since Western societies remain economically powerful, and outsource to non-Western countries. On the other hand, globalization connects the world as never before, and challenges Western values and self-centredness by showing that there are other ways of being modern.

2. 'Mediatization'

The last few decades have witnessed the proliferating variety and increased effectiveness of media of communication, including television, the internet, and other digital technologies. It is now relatively easy to transmit and receive a vast amount of information and entertainment, and it has become virtually impossible to control and regulate such flows. Some people view such processes as corrosive of religion, not only because religion relies for many of its most important functions on face-to-face collective gatherings, but because traditional authority and knowledge is often highly regulated, and hostile to alternative influences. But whilst some forms of religion may suffer, others may make active use of new media to further their causes. As Chapter 20 on Religion and popular culture shows, for example, some new forms of religion not only make use of new media to spread their message and support their communities, they are actually reshaped as they are 'mediated' by new technologies and new forms of culture.

3. Postsecularism

Although modern societies are often characterized by a distrust or active hostility to religion, particularly on the part of powerful elites, such secularism is often challenged in late modern societies. The challenge comes from many sources, including migrations, and disillusionment with aspects of the modern project (for example, its failures to support human and environmental values, and its dismissal of tradition). Whereas in premodern societies religion was often a force by which majorities defended their interests, in late modern societies it is more likely to be a force by which minorities defend their interests and challenge secular majorities. This does not mean that secularism is dethroned, but that it has to defend itself, and that it can no longer assume that it is the only possible face of human progress.

A note on 'religion'

There is a vast, and ever-expanding, literature on the concept of 'religion', and there will never be an end to debates about the meaning of 'religion' and how the term can be defined. One way to approach the issue is to try to isolate distinctive characteristics of religion (what religion *is*) – such as belief in a higher power or powers, in a realm beyond this world, or in a God or gods. Another is to look for the distinctive functions of religion (what religion *does*) – such as gather people together in communities of solidarity, give meaning and purpose to life, and shape human emotions. Combining both approaches, we may say that religions are social forms which use practices, symbols and beliefs, usually in a collective setting, to orient people to a higher or ultimate level of reality, thereby providing them with a template for ordering social and personal relationships in this life.

Like any other definition of religion, however, this one must be treated with caution, because religion is not a 'thing' which can be captured and pinned down. Rather, 'religion' is just a useful word which helps us identify certain aspects of human life, but which is nothing more than a tool or framework of analysis and understanding (just like 'politics' or 'class'). We can always divide things up in a different way (including the many religious traditions considered in this book), and we always need to be wary of approaches which say that religion can only be this, not that. What counts as religion is always an open, empirical question, for religion is constantly being constructed in new ways. There is always an element of persuasion in a definition of religion, and there is often a power-play. For example, there may be political advantages in saying that one's own community is religious, whereas that one over there is not – or vice versa.

As well as addressing 'religion', this book considers 'spirituality'. Chapter 12 notes that significant numbers of people in contemporary societies prefer to describe themselves as 'spiritual' rather than 'religious'. What they often mean by this is that they are committed to the 'inner truth' of religion as it affects personal life, but not to the external, social manifestations of religion (like buildings, rituals, priests). Thus the term 'spirituality' can only be understood in terms of a particular, linked, sense of 'religion' (which it rejects). In this book we used religion in a much broader sense than this – a sense indicated by the working definition offered above. As such, we treat spirituality as one particular manifestation of religion in the modern world.

For more on 'religion' see the following chapter, 'How to study religion in the modern world'.

A note on the approach of this book

Rather than impose a single method or disciplinary framework in this book, we have allowed individual authors to pursue the approach which they believe to be most appropriate to the form of religion they are writing about. Some write from the perspective of Religious Studies, some from Anthropology, some from History, some from Sociology, some from Politics, and some from some mix of these and other approaches. The next chapter, by Kim Knott, explains these different approaches to the study of religion, and serves as a methodological introduction to what follows.

Further reading

Modernity

Stuart Hall and Bram Gieben (eds): *Formations of Modernity* (Cambridge: Polity Press in association with The Open University, 1992) is an extremely clear introduction to the topic in general rather than specifically religious terms.

On the future of modernity and the idea of postmodernity see another book in the same series: Stuart Hall, David Held and Tony McGrew (eds): *Modernity and its Futures* (Cambridge: Polity Press in association with The Open University, 1992).

Religion and modernity

Linda Woodhead and Paul Heelas (eds): *Religion in Modern Times: An interpretive anthology* (Oxford, UK, and Malden, USA, 2000) offers a framework and selected readings for thinking about the complex interactions between religion and modernity.

The concept of religion

For a useful review article see Jonathan Z. Smith, 'Religion, religions, religious', in Mark C. Taylor (ed.): *Critical Terms in Religious Studies* (Chicago: University of Chicago Press, 1998, pp. 269–84).

Chapter 1

How to study religion in the modern world

Kim Knott

As the Introduction to this book suggests, particular issues arise for religions as they engage with modernity; they cannot be treated separately from their contexts or indeed from one another. These points have consequences for how religions are to be examined in terms of the theories, approaches and methods to be used, all of which are subject to development as religion itself changes. After a general introduction to how religions are studied and researched, some key issues in the study of religions in the modern world will be identified and their theoretical and methodological implications considered. These include religious traditions old and new, the connections between religions and between the secular and the religious, religious identity, and the place of religion in public life. After that, attention will be turned to the question of how we study contemporary religion at a variety of different scales, from the body and objects to the world and globalization. But we will begin with a particular case, the Danish cartoons crisis of 2006 in order to see how a modern event generates a range of issues and methodological considerations for the study of religions.

On 30 September 2005 *Jyllands-Posten*, a major Danish national newspaper, published 12 cartoons of the Prophet Muhammad which were later reprinted in newspapers in various countries and on the internet. They were highly offensive to Muslims, partly because they breached the Islamic teaching that the Prophet should not be depicted, but also because they portrayed him as a terrorist. In February 2006 the publication of the cartoons became the subject of international protest resulting in more than 50 deaths worldwide. There were many political and diplomatic ramifications in Denmark and beyond. The popular and intellectual responses of Muslims, secularists and other interested groups and individuals were varied, often measured but occasionally strident and accompanied by verbal or physical violence, and the issues raised were complex, from debates about human rights, freedom of expression and incitement to hatred, to the clash of cultures, integration and the relationship of race and religion.

The crisis raised a great many potential issues for the study of religions. In terms of Islam, it revitalized the question of the Prophet and his depiction, in the *Qur'an* and *Hadith*, but also in later texts and contexts. Modern secular Denmark provided a new theatre for this age-old religious debate, and for the expression of religious versus liberal secularist positions and competing claims about human rights and ethics (including freedom of expression and the right to protection from religious hatred). The publication and its aftermath undermined community relations in Denmark and further afield as Muslims felt themselves to be ridiculed and vilified. The tension between national and religious identities, the place of religious minorities in secular nation states, and the integration and cohesion of faith and ethnic communities came to the fore. In addition, mass protests in countries round the world raised issues of the defence of religion and,

FIGURE 1.1 Danish cartoons crisis

Religion versus secularism. Muslim demonstrators in London in 2006 protest peacefully against Danish cartoons of the Prophet Muhammad and ask for justice for the Prophet and Islam. They question both the nature of the secular value of freedom of speech and its boundary with contempt and disrespect © Andrew Stuart/AFP/Getty Images.

at times, religion and violence. As we will see in the second part of this chapter, such issues are central to the study of religion in the modern world and invite a variety of theoretical and methodological responses. They require a range of scholarly methods, tailored to the particular case or problem to be examined, and raise complex questions about the standpoint of the student or researcher and the ethics and politics of their work. In the third part of the chapter, we will consider how religion can be the subject of investigation at the small scale (e.g. at the level of a cartoon or daily newspaper), at national and regional scales (e.g. in the Danish context and in subsequent developments across Europe), and at the global scale (in the media and on the internet, and in various transnational movements).

The study of religion as a discipline

The study of religion has developed substantially since the late nineteenth century in response to colonial expansion and interest in different places, peoples and religions, as well as the growth of new academic disciplines and the impact of the sciences on the study of individuals, societies and cultures. Prior to that, theology and philosophy were the pre-eminent disciplines; since then, historical, sociological, psychological, anthropological and phenomenological approaches have also contributed to our understanding and interpretation of religion and religions.

In the context of schools and universities and their academic pursuits, the term 'discipline' refers to the way in which natural, social and cultural phenomena are studied and theorized, and how knowledge about them is organized. A discipline – geography for example – normally has a focus of attention (the earth, its places and people) and a number of attendant theories and methods. It organizes its subject matter into categories (such as physical and human geography) and sub-categories (such as demography, migration, urban studies, sacred space and pilgrimage). The case of 'the study of religion', and some other disciplines or academic fields such as gender studies or postcolonial studies, is rather different. Like geography and sociology, it has a disciplinary focus, in this case, religion. Unlike them, it is poly-methodological in so far as it loosely includes a variety of different approaches to studying religion, such as those that I mentioned in the previous paragraph. The poly-methodological character of the study of religions is evident in books on the subject, for example, *The Routledge Companion to the Study of Religion*, edited by John Hinnells, in which chapters describe many of the different approaches that constitute the discipline.

Before going further, it is important to say a little more about religion itself, a topic which was briefly raised in the Introduction. Scholars are generally in agreement that 'religion' is a historical and scholarly construct. This is not intended to belittle people's experience of the sacred or to judge the veracity of their religious claims. Rather, it recognises that 'religion' is a concept used to identify, delimit and describe certain types of human behaviour, belief, organization and experience. It has a global history (matched by terms in other languages), and is capable of being separated – not without disagreement – from other concepts, such as 'society', 'economy' and 'culture', and studied independently. From the late seventeenth century in Europe when the term 'religion' and the idea of 'religions' in the plural began to be adopted, many beliefs, practices, individual and collective experiences, bodies, groups, artefacts, texts, works of art and performances have come to be associated with them. These provide data for the scholarly study of religion, all of which can be utilized in association with various approaches, theories and methods. When we study 'religion' in the modern world, we focus on its contemporary and recent historical facets, looking in particular at how they engage with and respond to the conditions, processes and issues of modernity. We look at what 'religion' means now and how religions differentiate themselves and interact in the broader context of science, secularism, capitalism, globalization and identity politics. The case of the Danish cartoons crisis above illustrates this.

Theory, methods, methodology

These are common terms used to denote the various tools used in scholarly study, whether in research or in the preparation of an essay or paper. 'Theory' is a term generally adopted to refer to concepts, laws, hypotheses and explanations used to make sense of the natural and social world. The nature and reality of 'the natural and social world' about which people theorize, the ability of theory to represent that world, and the politics of theorizing are all contested. One interesting perspective on theory is offered by the American scholar, Thomas A. Tweed. He presents the idea of theories as 'itineraries', and sees theories as journeys that scholars take from their own situated positions and then lay out as maps for others to use.

The theories in use in the study of religions are of different types. Some are meta- or grand theories which present an over-arching explanation for society, culture or religion as a whole, their origins and purposes. Émile Durkheim, in *The Elementary Forms of the Religious Life*, offered such a theory, and the work of Marx, Freud and Foucault among others has been used in this way. One book which reviews some of these grand theories is Seth Kunin's *Religion: The Modern Theories* (see Further reading). In most scholarly work on religion, such theories are not used as hypotheses capable of testing but rather as theoretical standpoints which locate researchers within scholarly traditions and explain their perspectives on such matters as the fundamental nature of society or religion, their origins, elementary forms and salience, social and economic relations, structure and agency, or power and discourse. Feminism and postcolonialism also offer theoretical and ethical stances which function in a similar way. Other broad theories can be used more directly in planning research on religion and have been developed, critiqued and amended in light of empirical evidence: globalization theory and secularization theory are good examples, as can be seen in the relevant chapters later in this book.

But theories can be useful in other ways too. In much scientific research theories function as starting points, often taking the form of research questions or hypotheses that can be tested. Two relevant examples, thinking back to the case with which this chapter opened, might be the hypothesis, 'Community relations in Denmark deteriorated as a result of the publication of the cartoons of the Prophet Muhammad', or the question, 'Were the causes of the Danish cartoons crisis religious?'. They can be used as starting points in a deductive approach to research. Is the hypothesis about community relations proven in an analysis of the data? Does an analysis reveal that the causes were religious or did they appear to be social, political, or a mixture of these?

Other scholars prefer an inductive approach which, instead of relying initially on a theory, begins instead with an examination of a wide range of data on a subject. Once data has been collected and analysed, it is then used in the development of theory for later use. For example, interviews could be conducted on the right to freedom of expression with a range of actors in Danish society – Muslim and other religious leaders, newspaper journalists and editors, representatives of government and civil society, writers, etc. – leading to the development of either a model of ideal types or a theory about the relationship between the nature of ideological commitment and attitudes to freedom of expression. These would be open to testing in other, similar cases.

A further way in which theory may be employed in research into the case of the Danish cartoons is to start with the views of a particular theorist, either one who has worked on a comparable but different case such as *The Satanic Verses* controversy in the late 1980s to early 1990s, or one who has already offered a useful theory on the case in hand, such as Tariq Modood or Randall Hansen who debated the liberal response to the crisis in the journal *International Migration* in 2006. The relevant 'micro theory' can be applied or modified and used on new data. This is a useful and common approach among students in dissertations or theses: Take a theory off the shelf and test it on new material in a different context.

Whether testing a theory deductively or conducting inductive research, the researcher must design her project, reflecting on what kind of methodology and methods to use to answer her research questions, what people or documents to research, and how to analyse the data that will be collected. Generally, she will have had some preliminary training in a particular methodology – the term 'methodology' refers to *how* we study, our way of doing things, the systematic approach we take to research – such as sociology or psychology of religion, history or theology, and will be familiar with its associated theories and methods. Increasingly, however, theories and methods have been cut free of their traditional disciplinary moorings and are used widely in an interdisciplinary way. The poststructuralist theory of Foucault, for example, has been drawn on by scholars in philosophy, sociology, linguistics, literature studies, healthcare studies, criminology, gender studies, and religious studies. Similarly, the interview method – and I'll say more about methods below – is now used in research across the disciplines despite having its origins in social science, particularly sociology and social psychology. Likewise, documentary methods that may once have been associated primarily with history or other text-based subjects are now used widely, not least by scholars researching websites and other electronic resources and those using visual documents such as photographs and video.

Different research problems and questions require different designs, methods and modes of analysis as is clear if we think about the two Danish cartoons crisis examples I gave earlier, the hypothesis, 'Community relations in Denmark deteriorated as a result of the publication of the cartoons of the Prophet Muhammad', and the question, 'Were the causes of the Danish cartoons crisis religious?'. Both of these could be addressed using existing primary and secondary sources of various kinds, but, equally, they are open to new research. Testing the first would require longitudinal social research (examining community relations before and after publication), though documentary research and discourse analysis may also be of value (looking at what people said about community relations in the media, for example). The notion of 'community relations' in the Danish context would need some examination, though it is likely in light of the centrality of Muslim and secularist voices in the crisis that ethnic and religious relationships would be to the fore. The researcher might choose to focus on one or more places in Denmark, on particular communities, and/or designated timeframes. Narrowing down the research in this way would make it more manageable. Several social research methods could be used for examining community relations. Opinions about past and present relationships could be collected using a questionnaire, interviews or focus groups. Current relationships could be researched ethnographically, with the researcher spending time in communities, talking to people, attending meetings, interviewing leaders and community workers. The question 'Were the causes of the Danish cartoons crisis religious?' would require an historical analysis of events and opinions leading up to the crisis, involving textual methods applied to relevant documents (e.g. religious and secularist texts of various kinds, government reports, bills and papers, newspaper articles and editorials, other media sources, etc.), though it would also be possible to conduct interviews with key public, civic and religious leaders to obtain their views. In both cases, which methods to use would depend on how the research was focused, what it was for (essay, thesis, policy recommendations or book) and how much time the researcher could dedicate to it. In both, a review of relevant literature would shed light on what research had been done already and would provide a context for the project.

Increasingly, for ethical reasons, the subjects at the centre of research are invited to contribute to its formulation and analysis. Research subjects are interested parties who have views about the value of research, the extent to which they are willing to be involved and on what terms, and on how the research should be presented and disseminated. 'Engaged research' and 'participatory methods' are a response to this. So, in the case of the Danish cartoons crisis and its impact in different contexts, Muslim or liberal secularist subjects might be involved in the research, not only as passive interviewees or questionnaire respondents but as diarists, photographers, interviewers or facilitators of focus groups. They might contribute to writing up the research or disseminating it in other ways, within their own communities or in public presentations.

Ethical issues more generally need to be borne in mind in planning research studies, particularly around gaining the consent of those agreeing to be involved, confidentiality, sharing results with research subjects and reporting their views fairly and with respect. Consciousness of one's own standpoint – ideological beliefs, class, gender, age, status and researcher role – is also important, particularly when analysing data and writing up results, but also in essay writing more generally. Reflexivity – the ability to be self-aware and knowledgeable about where we stand in relation to the subjects we write about and to use this awareness constructively – has become important in academic study, an area no less affected by power relations than other aspects of social life.

Having considered some general points about theory, methodology and methods, we move on now to consider these in relation to four key issues in the study of religion in the modern world.

Studying key issues in contemporary religion

1. Studying religious traditions, old and new

Religious traditions have been the principal pre-occupation within the study of religions since the 1960s. Key introductory books divided the territory of the discipline into major world religions, sometimes clustering these under different headings such as 'East' and 'West', 'Abrahamic religions', 'wisdom traditions', etc. The category 'world religion' of necessity demanded the production of other 'non-world' categories, such as 'primitive religions' (a term often criticised as orientalist and patronizing), 'nature religions', 'new religions' and 'indigenous religions'. Departments of Religious Studies, as distinct from Theology (though sometimes the two are combined), focused their programmes of study and staff expertise around different religions, and publishers and conference organizers often followed suit, with book series and conference panels on Islamic studies, Jewish studies, Buddhist studies, new religions and so on. To reflect scholarly interest in common dimensions, themes and comparative matters, the discipline was also divided into areas such as myth and ritual, beliefs, sacred texts, religious experience, sacred place and pilgrimage. Religions and their traditions, and the dimensions and themes that cut across them, formed the warp and weft of the study of religions in the second half of the twentieth century. One scholar whose work illustrates this is Ninian Smart (see Further reading).

Although this approach to organizing knowledge about religions continues, its limitations have been recognised. Scholars have questioned the tendency to treat all religions as if they were alike, often on the basis of the implicit model of Christianity, with religious traditions constituted by texts, words, beliefs, monotheism, priesthood, sacraments and so on. Timothy Fitzgerald, in *The Ideology of Religious Studies*, has criticised the 'family resemblance' model at work in Ninian Smart's dimensional view of religions, and suggested that a liberal, Christian ecumenical approach lay behind his categorization of religions. Some scholars have queried the difference between world religions and other religions and religious movements, some the adequacy of any single 'religion' to refer to and encapsulate the range of diverse phenomena within it, and others the categorization of religions as either 'traditional' or 'new'. Some have gone as far as proposing the abandonment of the category 'religion' and the use instead of 'culture' (though others have pointed out that this merely defers the problem of definition). A useful introductory discussion of some of these debates can be found in the first chapter of *Religion: The Basics* by Malory Nye.

Despite these critiques, there is no doubt that the concepts 'religion' and different 'religions' are widely used in everyday social situations and public discourse as well as academic study. They may have begun life as philosophical, social and political constructs in the work of early modern theologians and theorists such as Calvin, Zwingli, Bacon, Hobbes and Grotius, but their use and application is now widespread. People are asked to identify themselves by religion in surveys and population censuses. Books are classified by religion in libraries and bookshops, and pamphlets, articles and programmes on different religions are circulated in the media. Furthermore, Muslims, Hindus and Buddhists in other parts of the world debate the adequacy of the term 'religion' and its attendant dimensions for their own systems of thought, practice, organization and experience. Despite the exceptional case of Europe in which many identify as non-religious, the majority of people globally now think of themselves as having 'a religion', and see themselves as part of a community of religious believers and practitioners that is different from other religions, denominations, sects, churches or movements (or the equivalent terms in their own languages). In most cases they would be able to give examples of the things that distinguish them from others, and the 'traditions' they share – the practices, concepts, tenets, norms, values and social forms they received from others and that they live by. This does not necessarily constitute evidence of religion as an essential element of human experience (that there is such a essence is much debated), but it does suggest that the social construction of 'religion' and 'religions' is a global matter intensified by electronic communications, mass media, and the movement and travel of people and ideas.

In this sense it is important that religions and the traditions that constitute them continue to be studied, though contemporary contexts and new challenges raise different issues to those that were the focus of scholars half a century ago. That is why the authors who have written chapters in this book have considered how the traditions on which they focus interact with modernity. The appropriation by religious and non-religious groups of other people's religious traditions, for example, is discussed in the chapter on Native American religion. There is recognition too of the alternative ways in which religious practices, beliefs and impulses are now conceptualized, as 'new age', 'neo-pagan', 'NRMs' and forms of 'spirituality'. The ways in which these new movements and trends are seen by their adherents, sometimes as more fluid and less bounded than 'religions', and often as global networks rather than formal locally based organizations, raises issues about how 'religion' might best be defined and studied in the late-modern, global context.

In the past, religious traditions were generally studied by theologians, textual specialists, historians and phenomenologists of religion. Theologians explored their own traditions from within using various scholarly tools to build up a systematic approach, or to develop a particular sectarian perspective. Textual scholars with the appropriate philological skills examined sacred texts and their role in the development of religious traditions. Historians examined issues of continuity and change, of the movement, mission and growth of particular religions, and of the way in which traditions were interpreted to invoke claims of orthodoxy, heterodoxy and schism. And comparativists in the field of phenomenology of religions took on the task of describing and examining similarities and differences of belief, symbol, myth and ritual between religions and of building comparative models. Although these approaches continue to be used, there is now a greater awareness of the way in which class, gender and power operate to reify certain traditions and their associated texts, beliefs and rituals, and to require the consideration of multiple and alternative readings. Feminist and postcolonial approaches, in particular, have offered new resources to theologians, textual specialists and historians studying religious traditions.

Focusing today on religions as separate entities involves thinking about different issues and adding other methodological approaches. Understanding how religious traditions and their patterns of authority and legitimation, belief and belonging change, has become important. New research questions are appropriate for the study of religions in the modern world. How do contemporary religions distinguish themselves from one another and authorize themselves in the context of competition for resources and people, migration, and new forms of representation and communication? What effect has the late-modern 'turn to the self' had on the willingness of individuals to accept religious authority and thus on the way it is presented by leaders? Are people more interested in personal experience than collective discipline, and, if so, what effect is this having on the way religious traditions are mediated and presented, particularly to younger people? What new patterns of both belief and belonging are at work in different religious and social contexts, and how will this change the way in which religious traditions are transmitted? And what challenges do such questions pose for the theoretical and methodological resources of the study of religions?

The role of tradition and the process of traditionalization have come under scrutiny, with historians, anthropologists and political scientists reflecting on the way in which traditions are invented, invoked, manipulated and abandoned by people past and present as they make their religions fit for purpose, as they make them more inclusive or exclusive, and as they engage or disengage them from contemporary concerns. The process of 'de-traditionalization' has been theorized and debated by sociologists, but scholars have also noted a process of 're-traditionalization' taking place among diasporic communities, with migrants resisting change as a way of trying to secure their moorings and hold on to familiar beliefs and practices in a new context.

One scholar who offers both a critique and a new approach to researching religious traditions is Gavin Flood. In *Beyond Phenomenology: Rethinking the Study of Religion*, he states that traditions are subject to change as a result of processes of modernization, globalization and the condition of reflexivity and that, as such, they warrant an appropriate re-theorization and new methods. The phenomenological methodology once lauded within the study of religions is now unsuitable, he suggests, being too disengaged, rationalist and universalist for understanding contemporary religions and their traditions. He advocates a dialogical and narrative approach that engages seriously with the many voices within and beyond religions and that recognises both global context and local differences.

2. Studying the interconnections between religions, and between the religious and the secular

The new social, political and religious context that Flood recognises and for which he commends a new approach is one in which religious groups and their discourses are interconnected. It is still possible to study the traditions of a single group, but this must be done with awareness that the group may well have a global presence, and that it contains many different speakers who are in conversation with one another and with those outside the group. This need not imply that the boundaries between religious groups are any more porous than at earlier times. They may even be more firmly constructed and policed than before. Those groups that are often referred to as 'fundamentalist' are formed on strict principles based on what the group perceive to be original teachings contained in sacred scriptures. The boundary between those who accept these principles and outsiders may be rigid, but, despite this, debates and active struggles with outsiders continue to take place across the boundary. These outsiders may be the members of other, liberal religious groups who have different ideas about how to interpret scripture, or non-religious people for whom a religiously fundamentalist position may be anathema. The latter group may include those with staunchly held secularist views whose convictions lead them to preach against supernaturalism and the place of religion in public life, and for various liberal rights such as unequivocal freedom of expression. Contemporary controversies such as the Danish cartoons crisis or the debate around the teaching of intelligent design in schools (creationism versus evolution), fought out in the context of global media communications, bring people with opposing views into the same arena. They are interconnected despite their differences.

What theoretical and methodological resources are available for tackling these interconnections? The recognition by some religious people of the claims of others from different branches of the same religion or other religions has led to the development of ecumenical and inter-faith dialogue and encounter. Flood's dialogical approach, building on the theoretical contributions of Ricoeur and Bakhtin and based on the analysis of multiple, locally specific discourses, can be used to examine in depth the voices of all those involved and the understanding they have of their own religious traditions whilst taking seriously the dialogue between them, the linguistic devices by which they negotiate and the historical context in which their conversation takes place. The scholar – no less than the subjects – is part of this interpretive, dialogical process.

The nature of this issue – interconnections – itself suggests methodological strategies. Inter-religious and religious/secular connections, as well as being dialogical, are historical, social and spatial in type, inviting studies that focus on social relationships and the spaces in which they occur. Historical relations between the religious and the secular have become an important focus for interrogation in the work of Talal Asad and Charles Taylor. Social network theory, which has been used for analysing 'weak' religious relationships, the way in which religious beliefs and practices are communicated, conversion and personal influence, predictions of religiosity and the relationship between religion and ethnicity, is an obvious contender and has often been used in association with quantitative social science research. Charles Kadushin's work on network theory and informal social networks among Jews in the USA is just one example. But interconnections between groups and the positions they hold, as well as the boundaries they must cross in order to come into contact – positively or negatively – with one another, also take place in space. These physical, social and discursive interactions can be examined using spatial theory and method. I developed just such a methodological approach for locating religion in secular contexts which I have since applied to relationships and controversies between exponents of religious, secular and postsecular positions, including those present in an English medical centre around the doctor–patient relationship and the thorny subject of complementary and alternative medicine.

Contemporary approaches to spirituality, the sacred, and religious identity (see next section for discussion of the latter) are helping to bridge the gap between what for many decades were the separate territories of religious and non-religious ideologies and worldviews, with political scientists investigating non-religious claims and positions associated with nationalism, liberalism and secularism, and religious studies scholars, sociologists of religion and theologians investigating those associated with religion. But that is now changing. The argument for a 'spiritual revolution' has been made by Paul Heelas, Linda Woodhead and others, with Gordon Lynch proposing 'belief beyond religion' in his book on new spirituality. These authors offer useful theories on the ways in which spiritual matters have been taken up by people who are not formally religious. Another resource for examining comparable concerns on either side of the boundary between the religious and the secular is the concept of the 'sacred' which Veikko Anttonen has shown to be used in popular and public discourse, with reference to places, objects, events and times that matter to people, and about which they are unwilling to negotiate. The use of this concept and other terms related to it, whether in respect of God, love, freedom, equality or identity, provides data for those interested in examining and comparing religious and secular beliefs, practices and values in the modern world.

3. Studying religious identity

In late modernity, religion, gender, sexuality, ethnicity and nationality have become the focus of processes of identity formation and identification, in and beyond the West. How people see, label and represent themselves and each other, the work they do to fashion 'selves' and 'others', the way in which they identify with particular groups, communities and networks and sometimes stigmatize outsiders are matters of major social and political concern. In the Danish cartoons crisis many Muslims were concerned not only about the violation of the teaching against the depiction of Muhammad but the fact that some of the cartoons made a connection between Muhammad and terrorism. They felt that their Prophet, and indeed Muslims more generally, were being identified implicitly as terrorists. 'Islamophobia', the negative representation of Islam and Muslims, like anti-Semitism, stigmatizes a particular group and the individuals associated with it on their basis of their religious (and ethnic) identity. As a result of the publication of the cartoons, Muslims in many countries gathered to demonstrate their views in public settings, expressing and endorsing their common religious identity. Studying either Islamophobia or Muslim public demonstrations requires analysing discourse – what the media and Muslims say about identity issues and what linguistic and rhetorical strategies they use to make their case.

The 'politics of identity' has been recognised as a significant contemporary phenomenon which has come to the fore as identity groups have sought to find ways to be recognised, to compete for resources, to gain a public voice, to argue for their rights, and, in some cases, to win converts and friends. Religion has always played an important part in both identity formation and identity politics, at local, national and global level, and the study of religions – along with other disciplines – has responded by developing appropriate theoretical and methodological resources. Religions have often developed their own terms for signifying those who are acceptable 'insiders' and those who are deemed to be 'outsiders'. References such as 'heretic', 'fundamentalist', 'witch', 'devil-worshipper', 'apostate', 'heathen', 'kaffir', 'pagan' are all examples of religious slur. Examining how and when such terms have been used can itself be informative in revealing the boundaries between groups, and the way in which such boundaries come to the fore or recede as political, social and religious circumstances change.

Psychologists and sociologists of religion, in particular, have been interested in studying religious identity, its formation, engagement with other types of identity, and change. Psychologists, for example, have developed tools for looking at religious identity and identity changes among adolescents and students, and have considered conversion and stages of faith development. One well known study which has been widely used but also criticised is Lewis Rambo's *Understanding Religious Conversion* which offered a model that could be used and tested on conversions to a variety of different groups. How and why people choose religions has also been the subject of rational choice theory. First developed in the context of economics, it has been used to explain the need for religion and is associated particularly with the work of Rodney Stark. This approach, developed in part to challenge the widely accepted theory of secularization, has itself been criticised, for its focus on rationality and economic modelling and failure to take seriously emotional, historical and other social explanations of behaviour.

Sociologists have also studied the intersection of religious and other forms of identity, considering, for example, relationships between gender, ethnic, national and religious identities, and increasingly the clash over religious and sexual identities. In one piece of research, geographical, sociological, historical and theological approaches have been utilized to collect and analyse clerical and lay responses to homosexuality within African, British and American branches of global Anglicanism.

Although issues of religious identity and identity politics have come to the fore in public debate and scholarship since the 1980s, they are not entirely new issues. One area in which religious identity has been significant for more than a century is in public statistics, censuses and surveys. In India from 1871 those registering in the population census were asked to state their caste, tribal and religious sectarian identities. Despite the move in 1947 from British imperial rule to Indian independence, the collection of such data continued to inform national and regional decision-making. In Great Britain, on 30 March 1851, a religious census was conducted in which information on attendance at worship was collected. It did not ask for people's religious affiliation as such – political opposition prevented this – rather it considered their outward conduct (attendance) and the church facilities available to them. It was not until 2001 that the next national survey on religion was conducted in the UK when, after much consultation and political deliberation, a question on religious identity was included in the population census. Similar questions have been included in recent censuses in Australia and Canada. In the United States, religious adherence and identity have been the subject of large national surveys, the most recent being the US Religious Landscape Survey conducted in 2007 and analysed by the Pew Forum on Religion and Public Life in which 35,000 adults were interviewed about their religious affiliation. Changes in affiliation were analysed in relation to gender, age, ethnicity, education and income. Data from these censuses and surveys is available on-line along with various tools for the production of statistics, charts and cross-tabulations.

These national projects are large-scale examples of the use of quantitative methods for the collection of information about religious identity and adherence, but there are many smaller-scale studies which utilize similar methods, including student projects in which modest questionnaires are prepared, administered and their results analysed using a simple statistics package such as SPSS. At the other end of the scale are attempts to create global data-sets on religion from divergent national information. Co-ordinating and gathering together statistics for all countries and religions is a difficult task because approaches to collecting and holding information on religion vary from one country to another. Two major electronic resources are www.adherents.com, a collection of approximately 44,000 citations and statistics on religious adherence and geography, and http://worldchristiandatabase.org/wcd/, the World Christian Database, which holds statistical information on world religions, Christian denominations and ethno-linguistic groups. These resources provide useful background information for local, national and comparative studies on religious identity.

4. Studying religion in public life

We can surmise from the recent interest in collecting information on religious identity that such data are important for the conduct of government business and public life more generally. In addition to population censuses and surveys, ethnic and religious monitoring is increasing in public institutions and workplaces for the ostensible purposes of evaluating equal opportunity policies and responding to ethnic and cultural diversity, though such data can be used for a variety of other ends, some of which could be potentially discriminatory. Other evidence of the increasingly important place of religion in public life is found in references to religion, faith and belief in government policies, political speeches, legal decisions, and new acts, bills and directives on religious rights, religion in education, religious holidays and church-state relations. It is also reflected in media coverage of religious issues, the most prominent of which in recent years has been that of religious extremism in the context of terrorist activities conducted in the name of Islam from 9/11 in New York in 2001 to more recent events in the Middle East, South and South East Asia and Europe.

The place of religion in public life and the portrayal of religion in the mass media have provided new research opportunities and challenges for students and scholars of religion, and I have already noted some of these in relation to the Danish cartoons crisis. That public event and others in which religion plays a major role provide timely occasions for 'engaged research' when scholars and those directly involved beyond the academy can work together to answer questions, and design and conduct socially-beneficial research. Such projects might include journalists and academics getting together to examine how religious issues are portrayed in the media, how different groups are represented, and what language is used, or university researchers working collaboratively with those in government departments and representatives from religious communities on how young people become radicalized and open to recruitment by terrorist networks. The challenges involved in such projects should not be underestimated, however, because people outside universities understandably have different interests, motives and resources to bring to research from those within them. Negotiation is often required about the purpose, conduct, speed and writing-up of research, and about ethical issues concerning the people being researched and the publication of results and recommendations. When religious people are directly involved in research, questions often arise about their representativeness vis-à-vis the groups to which they belong, and how best to engage them in the research process given their working commitments and religious responsibilities. Some individuals and groups experience research overload, having been the subject of so many studies, questionnaires, interviews and visits that they close their doors to researchers. Others are unwilling to open their doors in the first place.

There are many areas in which religion now has a bearing on public life, one of the most widely discussed of which is education, particularly the relationship of state, religion and schooling. What sort of education on religion should be offered in state-funded schools and whether it should be confessional, multicultural or focused around the demands of citizenship is debated in countries all over the world with varying answers and solutions being agreed. Should the state fund faith-based schools? Should children be allowed to take religious holidays, wear religious dress or make religious claims on the school regarding provision of food and permission to be excluded from particular activities? These are normative questions for nation states, educational authorities, and religious and secular groups to debate; they are not research questions as such. *How* they are answered, however, forms the context for research on religion and education. Whilst research on the political and legal status of religion in state education may require the examination of public controversies and the changing legislative framework, research on religion *in* schools is often based on case studies. Such studies of one or more schools, which may well involve observing, interviewing or running workshops with children, raise ethical issues about safeguarding them from harm, and practical ones about how research can be conducted during the busy school day, bearing in mind the demands of the curriculum. Educational projects, for example on the role of children's religious identity or spirituality in curriculum development or on their school-based inter-faith encounters, sometimes take the form of 'action research', in which researchers – who are often themselves teachers – seek to bring about change, to develop the curriculum or improve social relationships in the classroom or playground. Finding ways to monitor and evaluate change is built into the research process.

Studying religion at different scales

Having examined some of the theoretical and methodological considerations of studying four important contemporary issues involving religion, we will change our point of view and look now at how to study religion at different scales. In the modern world religions play important roles at local and global levels. They affect individuals, communities, groups, networks and institutions. They have consequences for the body and for objects, for places and regions, for global communications and population movements. How we study religion differs according to the scale at which we operate.

1. Small-scale studies

I have always been interested in the way a small thing can encapsulate and tell the story of much larger events and processes. A similar idea is expressed in the title of a well known introduction to social and cultural anthropology by Thomas Hylland Eriksen: *Small Places, Large Issues*. It challenges the preconception that the study of small, local or particular objects, places or communities is parochial, small-minded or unrevealing. In fact, in methodological terms, the discipline of anthropology has traditionally been rooted in the principle of careful, detailed observation and inductive study of small social, cultural and geographical units leading to the development of social models and theories of, for example, the development and use of tools, patterns of kinship, ritual practice, hierarchy and status, and stages of life.

Some small things have been universally recognised as powerful, socially significant and worthy of study, such as the *totem*, the *gift*, the *symbol* and the *icon*. By their very nature they signify or stand in for a force, being or process greater than themselves, embodying a conception, relationship or action. The Christian cross is an obvious example. Marking buildings as places of worship, books as holy, and bodies as identified and disciplined by Christianity, it carries the weight of the story of the crucified son of God. It is recognised and shared by people across boundaries around the globe, but may also mark one group off from another – not only Christians from non-Christians, but types of Christian from each other. In so far as 'the sign of the cross' is a gesture and practice as well as an object, it separates Orthodox and Catholic Christians from most Protestants. However, in addition to the general meanings that can be attributed to the cross as a Christian symbol, every use of that symbol has its particular location, context, meaning and significance. Although these may in some cases be quite trivial, each tells a different story, one that is intimate, about the place of a cross in an actual landscape, the choice of a person to identify outwardly as a Christian, the struggle of an artist to be true to religious ideals in a world which may be hostile to them, or the commitment of a priest to his or her vocation. Placed alongside other symbols, the cross may speak of a shared inter-faith journey.

The in-depth investigation of a particular symbol in use can be a fruitful and often surprising study. I know this from my own experience of having chosen to focus on the *left hand* as a context for exploring religious and secular relationships. I was interested in examining the location and operation of religion at various scales, and wanted to start with the human body or one of its parts. A well known sociological essay on the right hand had been written in 1909 by Robert Hertz, one of Durkheim's circle. It was clear from this that the right was experienced and represented as the pre-eminent and favoured hand in most cultures, and commonly associated with the sacred. What then of the left hand? Was it associated with non-religion and the profane, or with deviant forms of spirituality? Reading contemporary electronic texts (identified by Google searches on keywords such as 'left hand' and 'left-handed'), I identified 'religious', 'secular' and 'postsecular' examples and analysed how their authors used the left hand to make their case, to self-identify and differentiate themselves from others. The key point here is that focusing on particular, small-scale examples can help us to see larger questions, movements and relationships.

What is striking, however, is that it is not only objects, persons, events and places with iconic, totemic or major symbolic status that have biographies or create memories with significance in people's religious lives; everyday things can have that power too. Ordinary things like shoes and spectacles in extraordinary places – such as holocaust memorial sites – can move visitors in ways that less intimate historical reportage cannot. But everyday objects can create strong emotions too because they can be the focus of memories or a stimulus for the imagination: a photograph of family members who have passed away, a stone from a beach once visited, the words from a hymn or popular song, a favourite blanket or cushion. The individual and subjective meaning of such things and the feelings they evoke may well be attributed with spiritual or sacred significance by those who experience them. They can be the subject of informative and original research. The rise in interest of material culture as worthy of study by scholars of religion and culture can be seen, for example, in the work of Colleen McDannell. Through an examination of American family bibles, gravestones, portraits of Jesus and holy water, she proposed that there is a relationship between experiencing physical religious representations and the development of Christian norms, values and beliefs.

Some of the methodological issues involved in researching at the small scale can best be illustrated by looking at a particular case. On 15 February 2003 a 'Stop the War' protest was held in London to demonstrate against US and UK plans for military action in Iraq. Somewhere between 750,000 and two million people participated, and it was just one of a number of similar events held around the world. The following questions might be posed for the study of religion: Where was religion located in this event, if at all? What role did it play? The first is a spatial and cultural question; the second an historical one with significance also for sociology and political science. How would we go about answering them? Tackling the first, we might look for signs of religion during the event itself. Did any acts of worship, prayer or meditation take place? Was there evidence of religious symbols in the paraphernalia of procession (banners, T-shirts etc), and of religious sentiments in the chants and songs? Who was involved? Had religious groups organized transport to the event, marched together and supported one another? Having gathered information by observing the event, examining media coverage, photographs and video footage, and by interviewing those involved, we might then consider the second question about the role of religion. In addition to asking leaders for their views, it would be necessary to consider the beliefs and attitudes of participating groups on war and non-violent protest, the significance of religion in events leading up to the protest (including public statements and pronouncements by churches and Muslim organizations, the mobilization of religiously inspired peace groups etc.), and the role of Islamic, Christian and Jewish groups or individuals in the organization and advertising of the march. We would also need to bear in mind that, for many participants, the event was not religious at all. Supporters of CND (Campaign for Nuclear Disarmament) and the Palestine Solidarity Campaign were involved some of whom were eager to join forces and share a platform with Muslim, Christian and Jewish groups whilst others were more dubious. A broader, cross-cutting consideration of the beliefs and values underlying the protest – whether religious or secular – would also be informative.

A third question then arises. What might be inferred from this event about the relationship between religion and anti-war protest that could then be tested elsewhere? This is a methodological question about how an inductive approach to gathering and analysing data in a case study can lead to the development of a 'grounded theory' that might then be used in later studies. A careful examination of available data on this event might produce a hypothesis, theory or model about the role of religion in non-violent protest that could be used in research on demonstrations held in other times or places.

FIGURE 1.2 Anti-war protest

Stop the War. A rainbow coalition of demonstrators protest in London in 2003 against US and UK plans for military intervention in Iraq. Evidence of the participation of religious as well as secular movements in the anti-war campaign can be seen in images and words on posters and banners. © Orhan Tsolak.

Apart from its high-profile, public nature, one reason for choosing this event as an example of a small-scale case for the study of religion in the modern world is its evident intersection with larger-scale issues, movements and protests and its role in the global production and circulation of anti-war rhetoric and representation. This is referred to as the presence of 'the global in the local', and can be taken as evidence of the relationship between globalization and localization in which not only do global processes affect what occurs in particular places, but those places and the events and ideas that occur there can be globalized and replicated elsewhere (see Chapter 16 on Religion and globalization).

Large-scale studies

Like the Danish cartoons crisis, the war in Iraq and protest against it are global issues that have had differential regional and national consequences. The formal relationship of religion and state, the role of Muslim organizations in political lobbying and public demonstration, and the expression of conscientious objection to war have been publicly visible in many countries since 2003, and it would certainly be possible to compare these issues in different national contexts. The comparison of different cases, whether within a single country or across national or continental boundaries, is one way in which research in a single location can be 'scaled up'. In the European Union, for example, many major research projects start life as national pilot studies and are then widened to include research in a variety of European countries. A huge research programme of research on welfare and values in 12 countries first began life as part of a project funded by the Swedish government on the relationship between individuals and the state. This was then widened into a comparative study in eight countries of the role of churches as agents of social welfare, and then still further into a project called 'WaVE' (Welfare and Values in Europe) in which in-depth qualitative research was conducted in 12 medium-sized towns on the values of majority and minority communities as expressed through the provision of welfare. Another example shows the scaling up of research using a quantitative and deductive approach. It involved the deployment of a multi-dimensional model for measuring diversity among organizations and adherents first developed by scholars in the sociology and psychology of religion during research on religious pluralization in the North Rhine-Westphalia region of Germany. It was then applied in three European locations with the aim of testing a rational choice hypothesis that 'pluralization leads to religious vitalization'.

Comparing religion in various national locations is rather different to examining its global presence. The first assumes the possibility of comparing broadly similar religious data in different contexts, the second, of examining the transnational circulation of religious organisations, people, ideas and practices, and the inter-relationships that develop as a consequence. It involves researching the historical processes whereby religion moves between and beds down in different places, societies and cultures, and the relationships and flows that help to sustain that religion as a global force as well as a multi-local presence. Simon Coleman's work on the globalization of charismatic Christianity, for instance, showed how one Swedish group, *Livets Ord* or 'Word of Life', used organizational, theological, iconographic, media, architectural and narrative resources to become a global movement working in many countries and 30 languages to spread the gospel of prosperity.

Such work needs to take on board the major issues and processes that have faced the world as a single scale made up of interconnected countries and regions in the last 200 years: the condition of modernity and the processes associated with it, the impact of colonialism and subsequent postcolonial developments, the economic, social and cultural aspects of migration and globalization, the impact of the ideology of western liberalism, democracy, human rights and the war on terror, the international development agenda, the rise of powerful multinational corporations, religious extremism, the anti-capitalist movement, and the women's movement. Although no single project can do justice to all of these, the study of religion at the global scale requires sensitivity towards such explanatory factors. For instance, making sense of the symbolic representations and personal meanings and values associated with the wearing of the *hijab* and other forms of head-covering and veiling by Muslim women in different social and religious contexts cannot be done without recognition of the way these broader issues are manifested locally.

Taking such issues seriously is not without its difficulties, however. Criticisms have been levelled at scholars who focus on universal rights, goods and responsibilities (on the grounds that they are exporting western norms and values and judging on the basis of them), as well as at those who have lent their weight to prioritizing local cultures and traditions (on the grounds that they are cultural relativists who have fallen under the sway of a locally dominant leadership at the expense of marginal voices). Studies of African 'female circumcision' or 'female genital mutilation' are a case in point with many writers sworn to expose both the cruelty of this ritual for the young women concerned and the complex issues of power which underlie the practice of tradition, but others inclined to defend the right of certain Muslim communities to produce sexual and gendered bodies in their own way, and to mark them with their own rites according to their established traditions. This debate raises the question of universal human rights and of the extent to which beliefs, practices and values from one culture should be the measure of what is acceptable in another. For the student or scholar it foregrounds questions about personal standpoint and the role of self-identity, subjective judgement and advocacy in writing about other people's religions. There are no definitive answers to such questions, and academics continue to debate the possibility and desirability of objectivity and the politics of research. However, being able to articulate and make reasoned judgements about these issues, and to be 'reflexive' about one's own position, is now considered to be essential for any kind of social research.

Whether large or small scale, focused on one or more religion or issue-based, the study of religion in the modern world offers rewarding opportunities for original projects. Being aware of the context of modernity, the complex historical, social, political and economic forces at work, the choice of potential approaches and methods, as well as the consideration of personal standpoint and ethics will produce an informed approach to researching and writing about contemporary religion.

Summary

■ The study of religion in the modern world calls for theories, approaches and methods that engage with the issues and processes that have affected the world within the last two hundred years, such as the impact of colonialism and subsequent post-colonial developments, globalization and the rise of global religious movements.

■ Theories can be used in various ways in the study of religion. They can be used to inform our theoretical approach to broad questions about such things as the nature of religion and non-religion, its relationship to society, class and gender, and its ability to discipline bodies and institutions. They can be used as starting points for research, for generating questions, hypotheses and propositions. The theoretical conclusions of other researchers can be put to the test on new data, and grounded theories can be developed through an inductive research process.

■ A range of methodological approaches continues to be used in the study of religion, including historical, sociological, anthropological, theological, geographical, psychological and discourse-based approaches. Contemporary problems and issues in the study of religion often require interdisciplinary research involving mixed methods.

■ Because of the interest in sacred texts and beliefs, the study of religions was traditionally associated with textual methods of various kinds, but social research methods are now commonly used, including questionnaires, interviewing and participant observation. The use of visual media such as photographs and video, participatory and dialogical methods that engage research subjects, and spatial methods have all been added to the toolkit of scholars of religion.

■ Certain key issues have come to the fore for the study of religions as a result of the challenges of modernity and the growing importance of religion as an important social force in the modern world. These include new questions about the significance of traditions, the interconnected nature of religions and of the religious and the secular, religious identity and the re-emergence of religion in public life, all of which have consequences for building theory, honing and developing methodology and the selection of research methods.

■ Religion in the modern world can be studied at different scales, whether through small-scale bodies, objects, places, events or communities, or large-scale nations, regions, global processes or the circulation of populations, ideas or movements. It is clear, though, that the local and global are interlinked and this needs to be reflected in the conclusions we draw.

■ As individual students and scholars, the way we study religion is affected by our own standpoint and background. Being self-aware and conscious of ethical, gender and power issues in how we represent and research other people's religions as well as our own is important.

Key terms

engaged research Academics working with those outside the academy on research in which they both have an interest; bringing the tools of academic research to bear on a non-academic problem or issue; using research to answer policy, business, industrial or other questions of public importance.

interdisciplinary research Collaborative research opportunities which bring scholars from different disciplines together; individual research projects which require a scholar to use tools from more than one discipline.

methodology How we study; the system of rules and methods we use; the disciplinary or interdisciplinary approach we adopt.

methods The tools and resources we use to gather and analyse data to answer a research question.

participatory methods Those methods that involve the research subjects or participants directly in all or part of the research process: devising and designing the research, gathering and analysing data, and writing up and presenting findings.

reflexivity Reflecting on the conduct of research and on the role and standpoint of the researcher; thinking critically about the way in these may affect research outcomes.

standpoint The theoretical, ideological, religious and wider social position of a student or scholar which may – intentionally or not – contribute to the research process, including how that person conducts research, analyses and interprets findings and writes them up.

scaling up Using the research process, findings or theoretical developments from an initial case study, pilot study or piece of research with a small sample to design a larger-scale project or set of case studies; bringing together previously dispersed sets of data or statistics to create a larger database or model.

theory A universal law or hypothesis devised to explain or make sense of the natural or social world; a map or model that has explanatory power and can be used and tested by others.

Further reading

On theory, methodology and methods

Alan Bryman: *Social Research Methods* (Oxford: Oxford University Press, 2nd edition, 2004). A comprehensive guide to the research process and the relationship of theory, methodology and methods.

Émile Durkheim: *The Elementary Forms of the Religious Life* 2nd edition (London: Allen and Unwin, 1976).

Thomas Hylland Eriksen: *Small Places, Large Issues: An Introduction to Social and Cultural Anthropology* (London: Pluto Press, 2nd edition, 2001).

Timothy Fitzgerald: *The Ideology of Religious Studies* (New York: Oxford University Press, 2000). Debates the nature, ideology and politics of the discipline of Religious Studies.

Gavin Flood: *Beyond Phenomenology: Rethinking the Study of Religion* (London: Cassell, 1999). A critique of the phenomenology of religion and presentation of a new dialogical approach.

John Hinnells (ed.): *The Routledge Companion to the Study of Religion* (London and New York: Routledge, 2005). Presents various methodological approaches and discusses key issues including insider/outsider perspectives, gender, postcolonialism, ethnicity, pluralism, and religion and science.

Kim Knott: *The Location of Religion: A Spatial Analysis* (London and Oakville: Equinox, 2005). Presents a spatial approach to studying religion and examines the relationship between the religious, secular and postsecular with reference to the left hand. See also introductory article on spatial approach in the study of religion in *Religion Compass* (2008).

Seth Kunin: *Religion: The Modern Theories* (Edinburgh: Edinburgh University Press, 2003). Includes accounts of key methodological approaches and theories of Marx, Durkheim, Weber, Freud, Jung and Otto.

Russell T. McCutcheon (ed.). *The Insider/Outsider Problem in the Study of Religion: A Reader* (London: Continuum, 1999).

Malory Nye: *Religion: The Basics* (London and New York: Routledge, 2003).

Jonathan Z. Smith: 'Religion, religions, religious'. In M. Taylor (ed.): *Critical Terms for Religious Studies* (Chicago: Chicago University Press, 1998, pp. 281–85). A landmark essay on the academic and historical construction of 'religion' in a useful book about key concepts.

Rodney Stark and William Bainbridge: *A Theory of Religion* (Bern: Peter Lang, 1987). A key work on religion and rational choice theory.

Thomas A. Tweed: *Crossing and Dwelling: A Theory of Religion* (Cambridge, MA and London: Harvard University Press, 2006). A spatial, movement-based theory of religion.

On issues and scales in the study of religions

Veikko Anttonen: 'Sacred'. In Russell T. McCutcheon and Willi Braun (eds): *Guide to the Study of Religion* (London: Continuum, 2000). Discusses the scholarly history and value of this concept for examining data from a wide range of religious and non-religious contexts.

Talal Asad: *Formations of the Secular: Christianity, Islam, Modernity* (Stanford: Stanford University Press, 2003). Anthropological theory of the relationship between religion and secularity in the West.

Simon Coleman: *The Globalization of Charismatic Christianity: Spreading the Gospel of Prosperity* (Cambridge: Cambridge University Press, 2000).

Laura Donaldson and Pui-Lan Kwok (eds): *Postcolonialism, Feminism and Religious Discourse* (New York: Routledge, 2002). Essays which bring together feminist and postcolonial approaches to the study of religion.

Paul Heelas, Linda Woodhead *et al.*: *The Spiritual Revolution: Why Religion is Giving Way to Spirituality* (Oxford and Malden, MA: Blackwell, 2005). Offers a theory of contemporary religious change based on a case study of spirituality in an English town.

Eric Hobsbawm and Terence Ranger (eds): *The Invention of Tradition* (Cambridge: Cambridge University Press, 1992). Ground-breaking collection of essays which shows that traditions are socially constructed, malleable and subject to change.

Darlene M. Juschka (ed.): *Feminism in the Study of Religion: A Reader* (London: Continuum, 2001).

Charles Kadushin and Laurence Kotler-Berkowitz: 'Informal social networks and formal organizational memberships among American Jews: Findings from the National Jewish Population Survey 2000–01'. (*Sociology of Religion 67*, 2006: 465–85).

Richard King: *Orientalism and Religion: Post-colonial Theory, India and the Mystic East* (London and New York: Routledge, 1999). Offers a postcolonial approach to the study of Indian religion.

Gordon Lynch: *New Spirituality: An Introduction to Belief beyond Religion* (London: I. B. Tauris, 2007). Contends that contemporary belief extends beyond conventional religious terrain into new spiritual forms.

Colleen McDannell: *Material Christianity: Religion and Popular Culture in America* (Princeton: Yale University Press, 1996). Major study of Christianity from the perspective of its popular material culture.

Tariq Modood: 'The liberal dilemma: Integration or vilification?' and Randall Hansen: 'The Danish cartoon controversy: A defence of liberal freedom' (*International Migration 44* (5), 2006: 1–16). Scholars debate liberalism in the context of the Danish Cartoons crisis.

Lewis Rambo: *Understanding Religious Conversion* (Princeton: Yale University Press, 1993). An influential theory about stages in the process of conversion.

Ninian Smart: *The Religious Experience of Mankind* (London: Fount, 1971), *The Phenomenon of Religion* (New York: Seabury Press, 1973) and *The World's Religions* (Cambridge: Cambridge University Press, 1989). Works by a renowned phenomenologist of religion that illustrate how 'world religions' were categorized and studied in the 1970s and 1980s.

Charles Taylor: *A Secular Age* (Cambridge, MA and London: The Belknap Press of Harvard University Press, 2007). A historical and theological approach to the relationship between the religious and the secular.

Web sites

http://www.adherents.com/, accessed 4 October 2008. A useful global statistical resource on religious adherence and identity that can be searched electronically.

The Pew Forum on Religion and Public Life: *US Religious Landscape Survey.* http://religions.pewforum. org/, accessed 6 October 2008. An excellent resource for research on contemporary American religion.

http://worldchristiandatabase.org/wcd/, accessed 4 October 2008. A useful 'World Christian database' which also includes data on other religions on a country-by-country basis.

Hinduism

David Smith

Hinduism, the primary indigenous religion of South Asia, claims to be the oldest living religion, and calls itself 'the eternal religion' (*sanatana dharma*). Its earliest scripture, the *Veda*, dates to approximately 1500 BCE; some features, such as Goddess worship, and perhaps yoga, might go back to the Indus Valley Civilization, around 2500 BCE. Traditionally it is held that the *Veda* is eternal and reappears at each new creation of the universe. At the beginning of the twenty-first century Hinduism has one billion adherents worldwide, making it the third largest world religion.

The term Hinduism has only recently been adopted by Hindus themselves, and the word 'Hindu' is also of external origin, coming from the Persian word for those who live on the other side of the river Indus, i.e. Indians. With its multiple deities – traditionally 33 million – Hinduism could be seen as a cluster of religions rather than a single religion, but it is now usually presented as an all-inclusive polytheistic system, encompassing myriad forms and levels. Its extreme intellectual openness – when viewed as a whole – contrasts with the restrictions on behaviour brought about by the caste system. Hinduism's most influential philosophy distinguishes between Brahman – the highest absolute, formless consciousness about which nothing else can be said – and deities which have form, such as Vishnu and Shiva. The strength and vitality of the myriad strands of Hinduism make any clear and simple definition of Hinduism impossible, though fundamentalist and right-wing Hindus in India today may be seen to be mirroring Islamic certainty and authoritarianism while emphasizing Hindu difference from Islam. The efforts of some contemporary politicians notwithstanding, Hinduism has never been under the control of any central authority.

Buddhism and Jainism originated as reform movements within early Hinduism; both continued in symbiosis with Hinduism for many centuries, beginning by challenging the caste hierarchy and inspiring the development of coherent Hindu metaphysical systems (see Chapter 3, Buddhism). A third major indigenous tradition, Sikhism, emerged in the fifteenth century out of an amalgamation of Hindu, Tantric Buddhist and Muslim ideas (see Chapter 4, Sikhism). Most of India was under Muslim rule from the fifteenth to the late eighteenth century, and there was some Islamic influence on Hinduism in north India; later there was some Christian influence during British rule (late eighteenth century until 1947).

Early in the first millennium CE Hindu traders took Hinduism to Southeast Asia, but there it was replaced by Buddhism and Islam by the twelfth century, except in Bali. Hinduism spread again in the nineteenth century as Hindus migrated round the world, first to British territories as indentured labour and then often as highly skilled professionals, with North America the favourite goal from the 1960s. Nevertheless, as can been seen from the table below, almost 95 per cent of Hindus still live in India.

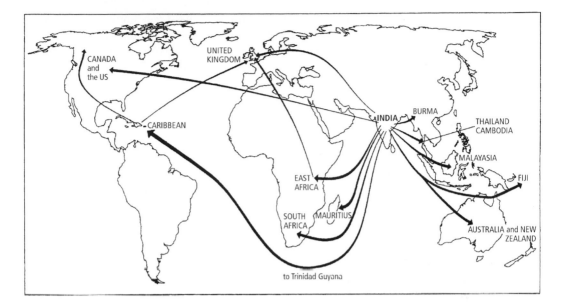

FIGURE 2.1 Map of Hindu migrations
Courtesy David Smith.

TABLE 2.1 Largest Hindu populations worldwide

Country	Per cent of population	Number
India	80	918,397,000
Nepal	80	23,615,000
Bangladesh	9	13,540,000
Indonesia	1.8	4,224,000
Sri Lanka	15	3,001,000
Pakistan	1.1	1,862,000
Malaysia	6.3	1,732,000
USA	0.4	1,218,000
Mauritius	48	607,000
United Kingdom	1	600,000
South Africa	1.3	568,000
Fiji	27	325,000

In many ways Hinduism is the prime example of traditional religion, with continuous traditions such as the oral transmission of the Veda going back 3,000 years, and animal sacrifice to goddesses perhaps far longer. Until the eighteenth century, under Islamic rule, the intellectual elite – the brahman caste – kept knowledge of Sanskrit religious and philosophical texts to themselves; little of Hindu thought was known to the West, and brahmans ignored both Western and Islamic thought. Paradoxically, the coming of British rule and British linguistic and archaeological investigations led to greatly increased knowledge about Hinduism not only in the West but also in India. British censuses of India led to an increased consciousness among Indians of the diversity of caste, and perhaps made caste into more of a system. Modernity came to India with the British, scientific education in English for the Indian elite being provided from the early nineteenth century. In the same period contact with the West prompted Hindu reform movements, influenced by Christianity and Western ideals of public service. Nevertheless, traditional Hinduism with its image worship and temple pilgrimage is as popular as ever, and greatly reinforced by modern media. Practices such as child marriage and even live cremation of widows (*sati*) persist in parts of India even today. At the same time, it must be recognized that rational argument and debate have always permeated Hindu thought, and its tolerance of alien viewpoints and its generally rational cosmology make it possible to argue that Hinduism has always had some of the features now claimed by modernity. This chapter will give a brief account of the historical features of Hinduism before turning to the present. We begin with the deities, rather than texts, for the deities have long been visually present in temple images, art, and many living incarnations, and do not depend solely on texts for their manifestation. A look at the many texts of Hinduism is followed by a summary of Hinduism in terms of self and society, concluding with consideration of gender. Much of this 'traditional' Hinduism is still alive today, but we next move into specifically modern times by inquiring into the special relation of modernity and India, noting also the traditional Hindu interpretation of modern times – the worst of times, the Kali age. The socio-economic condition of India today is then summarized. Modern Hinduism is discussed in terms of six aspects.

1.   traditional Hinduism and its divinities thrive;
2.   the 'reformed' forms of Hinduism produced by Western influence in the nineteenth century continue;
3.   gurus gain new importance and take Hinduism to the West;
4.   women's spirituality finds increased scope and expression;
5.   caste is still important, but the low castes gain influence, and the priestly caste declines;
6.   Hindu nationalism, the idea that India belongs to Hindus alone, comes to the fore.

Sources and resources

Deities

Traditional Hindus see themselves not as 'Hindu' but as Vaishnava ('worshipper of Vishnu'), Shaiva ('worshipper of Shiva'), or Shakta ('worshipper of the Goddess'), though each of these terms has many subdivisions. Vishnu has ten incarnations, of whom Krishna and Rama are major deities in their own right. But whatever deity or deities are worshipped, the rituals, texts, and beliefs usually have much in common. There is a common language of worship and practice within the branches of Hinduism. Each of the deities has its own iconography and mythology; but common to all is the fact that the divine reality has an explicit form, a form that the worshipper can behold – in images under worship in home and temple, and in dream and in states of possession. In addition to the three principal deities – Vishnu, Shiva and Devi, and the innumerable minor deities, regional and local, there is also Brahman the neuter absolute that is 'being, consciousness, and bliss', first mentioned in the *Upanishads*. The gods belong to a lower level of truth and are subsumed within Brahman along with everything else. Consciousness alone is the final reality, according to the Non-dualist school of Vedanta called Advaita. A distinction is sometimes drawn between popular and philosophical Hinduism, but the fact that Shankara, the great Non-dualist philosopher who commented on the *Upanishads*, is also held to have written fervent devotional hymns to a variety of deities shows that the distinction is easily bridged. The relative truth of the Hindu deities is readily seen by Hindus as shared by the gods of other religions, all of whom can be taken as aspects of the lower level of Brahman.

An essential notion in Hinduism is that of the chosen deity (*ishta devata*). None of the aforementioned deities is inherently supreme. The philosophically and mystically minded person might favour Brahman; most people will prefer to worship a tangible deity who can act upon the world. The deity a person chooses for him or herself is the supreme deity as far as he or she is concerned. Other than the universal Brahman, the deities are present in specific forms in specific locations. Their temples range from the vast city-temple of Shri Rangam in South India with its soaring gateway towers, to the pavement shrines of minor deities that flourish in every town. Every family has its home shrine with pictures or images of their deities, before which a lamp and incense burn. *Puja*, the loving offering of light, flowers, and water or food to the divine, is the essential ritual of Hinduism. For the worshipper the divine is visible in the image, and the divinity sees the worshipper. This interaction between human and deity, between human and Guru, is called *darshan*, 'seeing'. Whenever they can, people go on pilgrimage to notable temples, and bring back pictures or images of deities. Tirupati, difficult of access in the mountains of Andhra Pradesh, is one of the most popular temples in India, and the richest. From the river Ganges, water is everywhere brought back to be used in rituals on special occasions. India is covered with sacred sites; India itself is a goddess, and the map of India is the primary image in some modern temples.

Divinity is found in human form as well as in divine images and divine texts. All of life forms a hierarchy in Hinduism, and human beings range from divine incarnations to the worthless products of many previous lives of sin. This variety is explained by the notion of rebirth. Rather than brief instances of one short life span, Hindus see themselves as the product of an infinite series of previous lives, all of which can bear upon the present. It follows that the range of variation of human character and ability is itself infinitely greater than could be achieved in a mere single lifetime. Both theory and tradition support the widespread belief in 'Godmen' and 'Godwomen', as the highest instances of Gurus (religious teachers), are known. Most famous of all at present is Sathya

Sai Baba, who is an incarnation of both the God Shiva and his consort Shakti. Semi-divine powers are claimed by many practitioners of yoga; the first canonical text of yoga, Patanjali's *Yoga Sutras* (*c.* 400 AD), lists the *siddhis*, powers such as flying through the air and remembering one's past lives, that accompany the higher levels of yogic meditation. The priestly caste, the brahmans, intellectually and spiritually pre-eminent for many centuries, claim to be gods among men; their privileged position has been strongly contested by other castes, and saintly figures have figured among other castes since at least the coming of Islam to India. Deities also manifest themselves by possessing individuals. Possession may be voluntary, as in tantric ritual, or involuntary, as in festivals.

Texts

Hinduism's oldest text is the Veda, the earliest parts dated by scholars to approximately 1500 BCE, but held by the tradition to be eternal, seen anew by seers every time the world is recreated after its destruction. The variety of Hinduism relates to the variegated nature of the Indian social system with its many castes. A hymn in the oldest Vedic collection, the *Rig Veda*, describes the creation of the world from the sacrifice of a cosmic man: his mouth became the brahman or priest, his arms the warrior, his thighs the farmer, his feet the peasant. The great tradition of Hinduism, written in Sanskrit, the language of the Veda, is primarily the work of the Brahman caste. The religious literature in Sanskrit is enormous, flowing from the Vedas, through the mystical *Upanishads* (*c.* 700 BCE), the two epics – the *Ramayana* and the *Mahabharata* (texts finalized *c.* 400 CE), and the mythological 'Bibles' that are the *Puranas* (*c.* 400–1600 CE). Most texts in medieval Indian languages continue the earlier tradition; there are also the teachings of innovative saints, first influenced by Buddhism (the Siddhas) and then by Islam, e.g. Kabir (fifteenth century CE). All these texts, in varying degrees, are sacred and holy texts of Hinduism. The Vedas were learnt by heart by Brahmans and passed on as an oral tradition. Many gurus pass on their teachings only as oral tradition; it is standard practice for the initiatory sacred syllable to be whispered in secret to the disciple by the teacher. The *Bhagavadgita*, the teachings of the God Krishna on devotion and yoga, has become the best known text of Hinduism, partly in response to the expectation of followers of other world religions that a religion should have a single scripture; but the *Bhagavadgita* cannot be separated from the vast extent of the *Mahabharata* that contains it. In the *Bhagavadgita* Krishna gives the warrior Arjuna divine sight so that he can see his true divine form, which is brighter than a thousand suns. But in all the Hindu sacred texts the Gods make themselves known in visible form and are described by inspired sages (*rishis*).

The Vedas were the work of patriarchal pastoralists whose Gods were mainly warriors. However, from around 400 CE the Sanskrit texts give increasing space to Goddesses, and since the discovery of the Indus Valley civilization in the 1920s it is widely held by scholars that the agricultural society there from at least the third millennium BCE worshipped Goddesses and perhaps practised yoga. The religion of the Vedic texts seems therefore to overlay a different culture that is only gradually revealed to us by the historical progression of texts. Yoga and the notion of rebirth, elements held in common with the heterodox religions of Buddhism and Jainism, almost certainly had a non-Vedic origin, and first appear in the *Upanishads* at the close of the Vedic period.

The Sanskrit tradition continued with the Puranas, some of which formed a kind of Bible for particular sects. It is in one of these, the *Markandeya Purana* (*c.* 500 CE) that the ancient Goddess worship first resurfaces, in the section called the *Devimahatmya*. Here the Goddess (Devi/Durga/Kali) appears as the supreme deity. Most famous is the *Bhagavata Purana* (*c.* 900 CE), on which much Krishna worship is based. The rich mythology of the Puranas, itself of folk origin, is often omitted from formal presentations of their religion by Hindus, but nevertheless lives on, complemented by current folk and tribal mythology. From the Puranas arises the notion of the Hindu triad of Brahma the Creator, Vishnu the Preserver, and Shiva the Destroyer. However, the four-headed Brahma, modelled on the Hindu priest, has never received exclusive worship in his own right. As noted above, Devi, who finds expression in all Goddesses, is the third important deity, along with Vishnu and Shiva.

Also in Sanskrit is the extensive philosophical literature, principally in the form of commentaries on core texts. The qualified Non-dualist Vedanta philosophy of Ramanuja (1017–1137 CE), arguing that Brahman is Vishnu, and that the individual self finds salvation as a particle of that supreme reality, is more in accord with Hindu thought in general than the Non-dualist Shankara, though Shankara's is the most well known school outside India. Also of great religious significance are the systems of yoga, samkhya, and tantra.

The next oldest Indian literature is that in Tamil, going back to perhaps 200 BCE. Texts in other regional languages are later, and until modern times are mainly derivative of Sanskrit texts. But there are hundreds of vernacular texts rich in religious significance – the poems of Kabir (*c.* 1500) and the Hindi *Ramayana* of Tulsidas, *Ramcaritmanas* (*c.* 1600), 'the Bible of north India', to name but two. We should also note that the teachings of innumerable religious teachers (gurus) become the primary sacred text for their followers.

Self and society

Paralleling the profusion of divinities and texts, the caste system, which is an integral part of Hinduism, comprises thousands of different castes. One's caste (*jati*) has considerable influence on one's occupation and choice of marriage partner. The different castes form a hierarchy and are categorized under the four general caste categories (*varnas*) mentioned in the Veda, and in addition as a fifth category, the outcastes. Only relatively few castes are to be found in any one place. The dominance of the leading caste in any particular area does not necessarily relate to the *varna* hierarchy of brahman, warrior, cultivator, peasant.

From the time of the Buddha, reformers have sought to abolish caste, but without success. Caste is explained for Hindus by the doctrine of *karma*. From the time of the *Upanishads* (*c.* 700 BCE) Hindus have believed that one's actions (*karma*) determine one's future lives. One's condition in this life is thus morally justified because earned by previous actions. Caste is regulated by local caste councils, which have the power to set penalties for infringement of caste rules and even to exclude from a caste.

The *Laws of Manu* (*c.* 200 CE) and other texts which set out Hindu Dharma (the proper order of life) give detailed rules of life for the twice-born castes, so called because of the initiation or second birth that boys of the priest, warrior, and farmer castes received. For males, there are four life stages (*ashramas*): student, householder, forest dwelling ascetic, and wandering ascetic. For females, there are ideally only two: girl hood and wifehood, though inevitably many wives become widows. For humans, as for gods, the proper and normal state is to be married. Having produced sons, a man may then retire to the forest with his wife to devote himself to religion, and if he so chooses thereafter give up all possessions, leave his wife, undergo a funeral ceremony, and end his life as a homeless wanderer, as a renouncer. In fact, this last stage may be undertaken at any time. Its adoption as the last of four stages is an instance of Hinduism copying the successful practice of the reform movements of Buddhism and Jainism.

Hinduism sets out very clearly a hierarchy of four goals for human beings. These are 1. sensory gratification (*kama*); 2. material well-being (*artha*); 3. religious behaviour (*dharma*), which leads to heaven or higher rebirth; and 4. salvation, escape from rebirth (*moksha*). All four are legitimate goals. The fourth and highest (*moksha*) involves the fourth life stage, that of the renouncer, though, as has been said, this life stage can in fact be undertaken at any time of life. The more spiritually advanced the person, the earlier it will be done. The renouncer leaves the caste system, dies to ordinary life, and he alone is a complete individual, an autonomous self. The renouncer's view of the self is propounded by the Samkhya philosophy. In Samkhya the individual consciousness, which has the significant name Purusha ('the Male'), has as its true goal the separation of itself from Prakriti (Mother) Nature, and the analogy used for this liberation is that of a man who has been entranced by a female dancer but finally gets up and walks away.

In contrast to the spiritual self, the social self is enmeshed in society and family. A member of a caste, with duties and responsibilities to caste members, is usually also a member of a joint family, where parents and their married children share a single cooking fire. The social self necessarily has multiple roles, as son or daughter, husband, wife, daughter-in-law and so on. This multi-dimensional self, interlocked with many other selves, including its own previous existences, undergoes a series of life-stage rituals, that can begin with conception and continue even after death with the ritual feeding of dead ancestors. The self is polished and perfected by these rituals (*samskaras*) and ever more deeply embedded in Hindu culture (*samskriti*).

Gender

The biological difference of male and female is sometimes spoken of as the 'male caste' and the 'female caste'. Hinduism is patrilinear: families continue only in the male line. Daughters leave their natal families on marriage, and even as widows remain members of their husbands' families. Sons alone are required for the continuance of families. Daughters-in-law are not fully accepted family members until they have produced a son. At the same time, the mother of a son with her husband still alive is the most auspicious member of society. She nurtures and sustains not only her children but also her husband. Her status tumbles when her husband dies.

The auspicious married woman is a manifestation of divine power (*shakti*). A notable feature of Hinduism is the importance of Goddesses (*shakti*, *devi*, or 'mother'). Goddess temples, though generally very small, are more numerous than those of Gods. Goddesses are invariably seen as powerful, and when unmarried as dangerous. Despite the patriarchical nature of Hindu society, women too are held to be powerful and at times dangerous.

Within society, two separate polarities are important. There is the distinction between purity and impurity and the distinction between auspicious and inauspicious. Raw nature, matter out of place, such as bodily fluids, which have left the body but are of the body, are impure: blood, afterbirth, semen, menstrual blood, dead bodies, all are impure. Culture, that which as it were rises above dangerous nature, is pure, as for instance, Sanskrit language, vegetarianism, and abstinence from sex. Impurity applies to women more than to men. The menstruating woman does not cook, does not enter a temple. Nor indeed does the priest whose wife is menstruating. But Goddesses – in local or regional tradition – also menstruate. This fact of life is at the same time auspicious, for it means that the woman can give birth. Everything to do with birth and life is auspicious, whereas the barren woman and the widow are inauspicious.

According to the French anthropologist Louis Dumont, the caste system as a whole is to be explained by the opposition between purity and impurity. The brahman caste strives to maintain its purity by separating itself as far as possible from raw nature. The outcastes, who remove raw nature, impurity, from the higher castes by taking away their faeces, washing their clothes, dealing with dead animals and on, are in a state of permanent impurity. These extremes of the opposition between pure and impure demonstrate the hierarchy that runs through all the caste system, each caste pure to those below it, impure to those above it.

Interactions with modernity

The Kali yuga

Hinduism since the time of the *Mahabharata* has developed the notion of four world ages, going from good to bad. Dharma, visualized as the cow of righteousness, has four legs in the first and perfect age after creation, but then loses legs, so that at present she totters, notionally, on only one leg. The name of the current, and last of the four ages (*yugas*), is *Kali yuga*. Religious change from previous ages, and indeed anything detrimental, is explained by the fact of our being in the Kali yuga. This idea of deterioration, destruction of the world and then recreation in a continual cycle, is the exact opposite of the Western Enlightenment notion of the perfectibility of mankind and the gradual move from

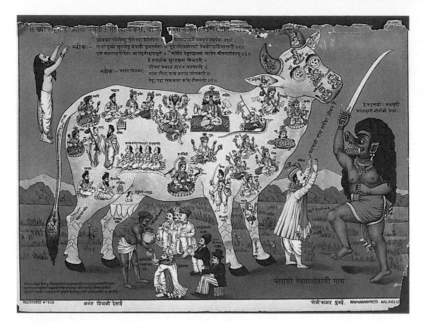

FIGURE 2.2 The personified Kali yuga

The personified Kali yuga attacking the cow of Dharma, *c.* 1915. The cow has long been a potent symbol for Hindus. Milk and clarified butter (*ghee*) are key elements in Hindu vegetarian diet, and beef-eating Muslims and Christians have always been liable to be perceived as Hinduism's foes. From the nineteenth century cow killing has provoked Hindu riots, and cow protection societies have been expressions of strong anti-Muslim feeling. Courtesy Chris Pinney.

superstition to rationality and from the pre-modern to the modern. It is important to note that Kali is the name of the worst throw of a dice, incarnate as Duryodhana, the villain of the *Mahabharata*, wherein the great battle marks the beginning of the Kali yuga. The name of Kali, the black Goddess of Destruction, is a different word and is spelt differently in Indian languages (Kālī). In pictures around the end of the nineteenth century, the Kali yuga is presented as a ferocious meat-eating demon threatening to assault Mother India who is represented as a cow giving milk to her children. In the Kali age, forms of religion change, the Vedas are neglected, and new easy forms of salvation such as the Tantras appear.

India in modern times

There are three key events in the history of India in modern times. The British takeover from Muslim rulers at the end of the eighteenth century, the formation of an independent and secular India, and the rise of Hindu nationalism. Colonial rule spearheaded by the British East India Company (a trading company) spread slowly at first from Calcutta, but the uprising in northern India in 1857, which used to be called the 'Indian Mutiny' by British historians, led in 1858 to the transfer of rule to the British government, and Queen Victoria became Empress of India. India gained independence on 15 August 1945, and was divided into India and Pakistan ('Partition'). Another notable date is 1992 when Hindu nationalists destroyed the Ayodhya mosque. Modern India has had to shake off the effects of long colonial rule, effects which include the exacerbation if not creation of Hindu–Muslim conflict.

Up to the eighteenth century India was prosperous, and enjoyed an important role in world textile trade. Europeans were impressed by the wealth and splendour of Indian cities. Conflict between rising Maratha power in the west of India and the crumbling Mughal Empire in the centre allowed the British to take control from the east, and Bengal became modernity's bridgehead into India. The brahman middle classes in Bengal enthusiastically adopted Western thought, and took up subordinate roles in the administration of the country. English literature was eagerly studied, and forms such as the novel were adopted in Bengali and other modern languages of India. This burgeoning of indigenous literature contributed to the rise of Indian nationalism. The nation is sometimes said to be the nearest thing to divinity in modernity, with nationalism being modernity's religion, but in India the modern notion of the nation happily co-existed with traditional Indian forms. Kali, the black Goddess of destruction, became the symbol of violent revolution. Bankim Chatterjee's novel *Anandamath*, 'The Abbey of Bliss' (1882), describes freedom fighters worshipping the Goddess Kali as an essential prelude to ridding India of the Muslims and – in the original serialized version, though later then removed – the British. The song *Vande Mataram*, 'I praise the Mother', from this novel became the anthem of the Independence Movement, but was not made the national anthem in 1947 because Nehru thought it too Hindu. The printing press, which did much to promote nationalism everywhere in the modern world, in India also served to spread traditional Hinduism, not only in texts but also in 'calendar prints', so-called from the addition of calendars to the brightly coloured pictures.

Vande Mataram

Mother, I bow to thee!
Rich with thy hurrying streams,
Bright with thy orchard gleams,
Cool with thy winds of delight,
Dark fields waving, Mother of might,
Mother free.

Mother to thee I bow,
Who hath said thou art weak in thy lands,
When the swords flash out in twice seventy million hands
And seventy million voices roar

---

continued

Thy dreadful name from shore to shore
In our hearts that conquers death.
Thine the strength that nerves the arm,
Thine the beauty, thine the charm.
Every image made divine
In our temples is but thine.
Mother, I bow to thee!

Thou art Durga, Lady and Queen,
With her hands that strike and her swords of sheen,
Thou art Lakshmi lotus-throned.

Mother, mother mine!
Mother sweet, I bow to thee
Mother great and free!

> Aurobindo's translation of the Sanskrit original
> of Bankim Chatterjee (verses 1, 3, 4, 6)

India's official national anthem is the first verse of the song *Jana Gana Mana*, composed by Rabindranath Tagore. Prime Minister Nehru objected to the popular choice *Vande Mataram* because of its reference to image worship. Aurobindo's response was that the Goddess Durga to whom *Vande Mataram* paid homage was none other than Bharata Mata (Mother India) symbolising Knowledge, Power, Greatness and Glory.

Sony Music in India celebrated India's fiftieth anniversary of Independence in 1997 by issuing a recording of *Vande Mataram* sung by the popular musician A. R. Rahman.

BOX 2.1   *Vande Mataram* ('I praise the Mother')

Hindus came to play a large part in the subordinate administration of British India, while Muslims stood apart, though praised for their martial ability by the British. Once it became clear that Independence was inevitable, there was increasing rivalry between Hindu and Muslim elites. M.K. Gandhi (1869–1948), the Mahatma ('Great-souled'), played an important role in reducing Hindu–Muslim conflict, and by his policy of non-violent action allowed the British Raj to end without violence between Britain and India. But Hindu and Muslim interests proved irreconcilable. Partition between Pakistan and India was hurried through by the British. Intercommunal murder took a million lives as Hindu/Sikh and Muslim crossed from one side to the other of the new border. Both countries, India and Pakistan, were deeply scarred by this traumatic event. India became a secular state, thanks to Nehru (Prime Minister 1947–1964), with a population 20 per cent Muslim and 80 per cent Hindu.

The subsequent political history of India is that of conflict with Pakistan and a gradual crumbling of the founding ideal of the 'secular state' which Nehru had cherished. Whilst refusing to recognise a 'state religion', Nehru gave a favoured role to minority religions, being especially concerned to make welcome those Muslims who had elected to remain in India rather than withdraw to Pakistan. A dynastic form of 'democratic' leadership evolved, with Nehru's daughter Indira Gandhi (1917–1984) becoming Prime Minister, followed by her son, Rajiv Gandhi (1944–1991). Rajiv's widow Sonia, Italian by origin, is currently head of the Congress Party. At Partition, Kashmir had a Hindu ruler and a mainly Islamic population. Pakistan attempted to seize control but secured only half the state. The border remains in dispute, and tension is constant. Both sides possess nuclear weapons and threaten their use. The position of Muslims within India is difficult. The Bharatiya Janata Party (BJP) formed the government three times (briefly in 1996 and 1998–99, and from 1999–2004), having come to power by supporting Hindu nationalism. In particular, the party urged the destruction of the mosque which it claims was built on the site of Rama's birthplace at Ayodhya, and the rebuilding of the Rama temple there. In the late 1980s the party organized a series of pilgrimages (*yatras*) across India in which the party's leader rode in a Toyota van adorned to look like the God Rama's chariot from the *Ramayana* – hence the term 'Toyota Hinduism'. Under BJP rule, the status of Islam in a majority Hindu country was particularly problematic, and so too the notion of a secular state in a country where religion shows no sign of decline or loss of vitality; and there was increasing antagonism to Christianity by rightwing Hinduism, in respect especially of externally funded Christian missions. President of India from 2002 to 2007 was Abdul Kalam, missile scientist, India's third Muslim president; his successor in 2007 was a Hindu woman, Pratibha Patil. From 2004 the Prime Minister has been Manmohan Singh, a Sikh.

Widespread poverty and corruption remain grave problems. But India is strong in natural resources, has a well-educated middle class, and the largest number of scientific workers of any nation. Many professionals go abroad but return to India bringing new skills with them. India is particularly strong in computer software personnel and companies. India remains open to all modern ideas, while preserving its rich cultural heritage.

It is not the British people who rule India, but modern civilization rules India through its railways, telegraph, telephone, etc. Bombay, Calcutta, and other chief cities are the real plague-spots of Modern India . . . India's salvation consists in unlearning what she has learnt during the past fifty years. The railways, telegraphs, hospitals, lawyers, doctors, and such like have all to go, and the so-called upper classes have to learn to live consciously, religiously, and deliberately the simple peasant life, knowing it to be a life giving true happiness.

from Mahatma Gandhi's *Confession of Faith* 1909

Gandhi's extreme position, product of his eclectic thought, has found favour neither with modern secular India nor with many traditional Hindus. Nehru declared that dams

continued

were to be the temples of the new secular India. Indeed, in his *Discovery of India* (1947) he admitted that the sculptures on South Indian temples made him 'feel uneasy'. Following the Soviet model, Nehru pushed the development of heavy industry and nuclear power. But the traditional Hinduism that Nehru hoped to move India beyond had no problem with science. Throughout the nineteenth century and up to the present there have been no lack of educated Hindus who claim that modern science is developed from, or even replicates, the ancient science that can, according to them, be found in the Veda. Nearly all Hindus believe that Hinduism can be rationally and scientifically proven. They take the view that, leaving mythology aside, Hindu sacred texts are based on a rational understanding of the universe, and that Hindu teachings are generally confirmed by the findings of science. There are ecological protest movements in India, e.g. the group opposed to the Narmada valley dam, but they are concerned with specific abuses rather than a general opposition to science and technology.

An important Government of India report on Hindu temples is typical in assuming the automatic efficacy of religious rites given properly qualified personnel, i.e. priests:

> [Temples are] occult laboratories where certain physical acts of adoration coupled with certain systematized prayers, psalms, *mantras* and musical invocations, can yield certain physical and psychological results as a matter of course, and if these physical processes are properly conducted, the results will accrue provided the persons who perform them are adequately equipped.
> *Report of the Hindu Religious Endowments Commission.* 1962.

BOX 2.2 Hinduism and modern science and technology

Modern Hinduism

The following strands may be discerned in contemporary Hinduism, and are explored in what follows.

1. First and foremost, traditional Hinduism continues to thrive. Rather than fading away, Gods and Goddesses have been invigorated by film, television, video, and cyberspace.
2. From the nineteenth century onwards various Western-inspired reform movements have developed, which combine a universalist Vedanta with humanitarian social work. These are often classified as Neo-Hinduism.
3. From the establishment of Islamic rule in thirteenth century north India, there has been a steady rise in the power and influence of Gurus, perhaps in compensation for the loss of Hindu kingship. New sects founded by Gurus from the eighteenth century onwards continue to flourish (whereas sects founded earlier have simply become part of traditional Hinduism). Many Gurus claim divinity for themselves, and some of these claims are widely accepted. Various forms of Yoga, including Tantra, have been strongly promoted in India and elsewhere by Gurus.

4. There is increased scope for the expression of spirituality by women, but women generally continue to be subordinate to men in public life; male and female remain differentiated domains. *Sati* (widow's self-immolation on husband's funeral pyre) finds fervent supporters and opponents.
5. The power of low caste Hindus, the Dalits, increases through their strength of numbers, and the status of Brahmans continues to decline. Whether or not Dalits are Hindus is an important question.
6. Hindu nationalism reached a peak in the late 1980s but is still powerful and influential, dominating public discussion of religion.
7. Hinduism continues to grow and change, while retaining a coherent unity. Hindus differ greatly in their religious practices, but make sense to each other however great the difference, and there is little scope for heresy.

Traditional Hinduism

> Rama incarnates in countless ways
> and there are ten millions of *Ramayanas*
> Tulsidas Ramcaritmanas 1.33.6

The television serialization of the *Ramayana* (1986–7, 91 episodes) and of the *Mahabharata* (1988–90, 94 episodes) strengthened the already secure position of the Hindu epics in public culture, for they have always been commemorated in festival and story-telling. Films about the Gods and demons, known as 'mythologicals', are as old as the Indian cinema, but the televising of the *Ramayana* struck a special chord in the nation. Televisions were treated as shrines, and airline schedules altered so that episodes were not missed. Another modern innovation is the combination of public recitation of sacred texts with the fire sacrifices (*yajna*) which have their roots in the Vedic sacrifice. Publishing and scholarship make ancient and medieval texts increasingly available. The practice of some Brahmans learning a complete branch of the Veda by heart has not completely ceased.

Traditional Hinduism also flourishes in the several monastic traditions claiming to date back to the original teacher Shankara (Adi-Shankara) (*c*. 700 CE), which continue to promote Non-dualist (advaita) Vedanta. The most famous of these Shankaracharyas, as the monastic heads are called, was Chandrashekharendra, Shankaracharya of Kanchi (1894–1994), who had been supreme pontiff from the age of 13. The celebration of his one hundredth birthday, when he was showered with gold coins, was a national event. The current Shankaracharya at Kanchi, Jayendra Sarasvati, makes full use of modern technology, offering automated telephone advice and an elaborate web site. On taking over as leader he said the new watchwords were 'culture of one's own land and technology from abroad' (*svadesa samskriti, videsa vijnan*). He has founded a university which offers advanced degrees in business administration, computer science, and Sanskrit. A similar persistence, though with a lower profile, is to be found among the institutions of other forms of Vedanta.

Hindu nationalist determination to build a temple to commemorate Rama's birthplace at Ayodhya is an extreme example of the continuing strength of the traditional Hindu temple religion. The Hindu diaspora aspires to build fully traditional Hindu temples. The Swami Narayan temple in Neasden, London, UK is an example in Europe of entirely traditional Hindu construction methods and materials. Traditional temples in India are renovated and expanded. In 1981 the temple of Dancing Shiva at Chidambaram in Tamilnadu was the first temple to allow dancing girls to perform since they were banned in 1947, but only on a concert platform in the courtyard, not before the deity. Apart from the exclusion of dance from forms of worship, the great Indian temples and their deities persist and thrive in modernity. On the local and regional front, animal sacrifice to Goddesses is reduced, and buffalo sacrifice is rare, but tradition continues.

Tantra

A major aspect of Hinduism that is also found in the Buddhist tradition is Tantra, the radical and often antinomian sets of ritual practices that increasingly permeated indigenous Indian religious culture from the fifth century AD (see Chapter 3, Buddhism). Summed up in the aphorism 'Pleasure is liberation (*moksha*)', this initially crude worship of sexual union and the feminine principle appealed to court culture and was soon developed in sophisticated texts. These texts are often in the form of conversations between Shiva and Shakti, the Divine Feminine who is his consort. Incorporating the physiological teachings of Hatha yoga, Tantra makes full use of the body to attain subtle and profound changes of consciousness. The body is said to contain centres of energy (*chakras*), from the base of the spine, to the top of the head. Energy, in the form of a internal coiled snake (*Kundalini*) rises up through the central subtle passage of the body to reach the thousand-petalled lotus at the top of the head, breaking through the *chakras* as it goes. The Tantric practitioner sees his own self as a manifestation of the ultimate divinity, and mentally goes through the ritual of *puja* (worship) within his own imagination directed towards his own self. We see here most fully what is described in other chapters as the turn to the self (see, for example, Chapter 12, Spirituality). Tantras were first made known in English by Sir John Woodruffe in the early twentieth century. The authentic tantric systems of Kashmir Shaivism were taught by Swami Lakshmanjoo (1907–1991), who had several eminent scholars as pupils. Ajit Mookerjee's book *Tantra Art* (1967) and the London Tantra exhibition of 1971 aroused interest in the west that continues today, as numerous web sites testify.

Modern traditional movements

Sikhism would be in this category had it not been so successful as to become a separate religion. Swami Narayan (1781–1830) founded the devotional (*bhakti*) movement in Gujarat that bears his name; and he is worshipped along with Krishna and Radha by his Gujarati followers around the world. Sikh elements including monotheism are present in another *bhakti* movement – the Radhasoami Satsang ('Association') founded by Swami Shiv Dayal (1818–1878). Here too Radha plays a part, a symbol of the individual soul in relation to God. A universal sound current carries the teaching of the living Guru to his worshippers. Modern only in its missionary zeal and rapid worldwide spread is the otherwise traditional sect known as the International Society for Krishna Consciousness, the Hare Krishna Movement. Founded by A.C. Bhaktivedanta (1896–1977), this devotional (*bhakti*) cult goes back to Chaitanya in the early sixteenth century and is based on the *Bhagavata Purana* and other texts of the great tradition. Western converts play a prominent part in the worldwide movement, adopting the dress and behaviour of orthodox Brahmans. An American, initiated as Satguru Sivaya Subramuniyaswami (1927–2001), founded the dynamic Shaiva Siddhanta Church based in Hawaii. Continuing to be led by American converts, this movement remains authentic – its members are mainly Tamil Shaivas – and an influential fund-raiser for Hinduism. It is most notable for its news magazine *Hinduism Today*, available on the internet, which since 1979 has provided well-informed news coverage of global Hinduism.

'Reformed' Hinduism

The term 'Neo-Hinduism' has been applied to reformed Hinduism by Paul Hacker and others. According to Hacker, the ethical values of Neo-Hinduism stem from Western philosophy and Christianity, although they are expressed in Hindu terms. Claims that Hinduism is a spiritual unity, that Hinduism is tolerant, that all religions are equal, are thus said to be the product of Hindu nationalism and are in fact the assertion of the superiority of Hinduism over all other religions. Hacker sees Neo-Hinduism as beginning in the 1870s, with Bankim Chattopadhyaya, Vivekananda, Aurobindo, Gandhi, and Radhakrishnan as its most famous proponents.

Of the reform movements of the nineteenth century, the Arya Samaj (founded 1875 by Dayanand Saraswati) is the most active today. Its aim is a purified Hinduism with a ritual and ceremony that somewhat resemble procedures of Protestant Christianity, but are justified as a return to an original purity of Hinduism said to exist in the Vedic hymns. Those aspects of Hinduism that aroused censure in Westerners, such as child marriage and the practice of widow burning (*suttee/sati*), were repudiated. Unlike the earlier Brahmo Samaj (founded 1828 by Ram Mohan Roy) the Arya Samaj vigorously rejected Christianity, reflecting the growth in nationalism in the intervening years.

Still significant today are two figures from early modern Hinduism. The first, Saint Ramakrishna (1836–86), a priest in the large Kali temple built at Dakshinesvar outside Calcutta in 1855 by a wealthy low-caste widow, is revered for his varied and intense mystical experience. He inspired the second, the charismatic organizer, Vivekananda. Vivekananda (1863–1902) founded the Ramakrishna order of monks, and preached a muscular Vedanta to India and the West. An important aspect of this movement came to be its taking up of social work, and this Western-inspired practical assistance thereafter came to be a feature of many new Hindu movements. The Ramakrishna Mission has centres round the world, and publishes many key Hindu texts.

Aurobindo (1872–1950), at first a freedom fighter against the British, was an independent thinker who claimed that his 'Integral Yoga' was the spiritual technique for the higher evolution of all mankind. India was the guru of the nations, and had been set apart by the Divine as the eternal fountainhead of holy spirituality. India was to send forth from herself the future religion of the entire world, the Eternal Religion which was to harmonize all religion, science and philosophies, and make mankind one soul. Although Mahatma Gandhi is still the most famous Hindu of modern times, his idiosyncratic views were of political rather than religious significance. His defiance of modernity by advocating the spinning wheel in place of modern technology and his favouring of the Christian cross above all other symbols, separated him from many Hindus. While alive his charisma was unparalleled, but his fame is dwindling away in India. The name he gave outcastes, Harijans, 'Children of God', is now rejected by them as patronizing, and in practice his doctrine of non-violence finds few takers.

Last in Hacker's list of proponents of Neo-Hinduism is S. Radhakrishnan (1888–1975), President of India (1962–67), author of *The Hindu View of the World*, who found many Western parallels to Vedanta.

These thinkers have received much more attention in the West than has traditional Hinduism, but the introduction of the term Neo-Hinduism is unfortunate in that it denies what is in fact the growth and change that has always been part of Hinduism, as well as undervaluing the part played by the natural development of non-dualist Vedanta. As Hacker admits, many educated Hindus have no problem in handling traditional and modern Hinduism simultaneously.

Gurus

Almost all Hindu spiritual teachers take from Neo-Hinduism the proud assertion of the universality of Hinduism and, to a certain extent, the belief in the importance of social work, but many continue in other respects to teach only traditional spiritual practices. The title *Swami*, 'Lord', is usually prefixed to their names, and they often maintain retreats called *ashrams*. A standard procedure is the process of initiation (*diksha*) in which a disciple is given a secret Sanskrit phrase (*mantra*). Some teachers have established outposts in the West, but remain centred in India. A good example of hundreds if not thousands of such teachers is Shivananda (1887–1963) who founded the Divine Life Society. His work is continued by his disciples Chidananda (1916–2008) and Krishnananda (1922–2001). There are also Western successors such as the Canadian woman Swami Radha (1911–1995). A traditional mystic whose ashram continues but who has no successors was Raman Maharshi (1879–1950), perhaps the best known and most respected of all Indian holy men in the twentieth century. The Ananda Marg founded 1955 by P.R. Sarkar (1921–1991) is one instance of the murkier side of spirituality: maintaining Tantric affiliations alongside welfare programs, its members have also been involved in gun running and murder.

Hindu Gurus in the West

Among many Gurus who brought forms of yoga to the West, important figures are Maharishi and Rajneesh. Maharishi Mahesh Yogi (1911–2008) founded Transcendental Meditation (TM). This technique of relaxed meditation on a personal *mantra* was especially popular in the 1960s, but TM centres are still found throughout the United States and Europe, where under the name of the Natural Law party the movement puts forward candidates in democratic elections. Rajneesh (1931–1990), later known as Osho, freely invented yogic and tantric practices; and the organization he started continues, sustained by videotapes of the master. Muktananda (1908–1982) promoted as 'Siddha Yoga' his ability to make other people's *kundalini* rise; his movement, which like the two above-mentioned organizations, enthusiastically adopts modern business practices, is now led by a woman, Gurumayi Chidvilasananda (1955–). A more straight-forward figure, and respected in India, was Satchidananda (1914–2002), a disciple of Sadananda, and founder of the ashram called Yogaville, in Ohio, who proclaimed Hinduism to America at the 1969 Woodstock music festival. Sri Sri Ravi Shankar (1956–), founder of the Art of Living Foundation, seeks to turn the world into a global family free of stress and violence; it is claimed that two million people with representatives from a hundred countries celebrated his Foundation's twenty-fifth anniversary in 2006 at a gathering in Bangalore.

The guru must be worshipped as God. He is God, he is nothing less than that. As you look at him, gradually the guru melts away, and what is left? The guru picture gives place to God Himself. The guru is the bright mask which God wears in order to come to us. As we look steadily on, gradually the mask falls off and God is revealed.

Vivekananda, 'Discipleship', *The Voice of India* November 1946, p. 170

BOX 2.3 Guru and God

Godmen and Godwomen

Divinity is readily seen by Hindus to be present in special human beings; and gurus are often worshipped as gods by their followers. Various explanations have been given for the phenomenon of Godmen. According to Max Weber the growth of guru worship, extreme forms of which can be traced back to the fifteenth century, relates to the replacement of Hindu kings by Muslim rulers, and the implication is that gurus took on the religious leadership role of the Hindu king. Another explanation is that where human relationships are organized by consideration of caste and family, choosing a guru is the only scope for free choice. The Neo-Hindu explanation for the prevalence of gurus and guru-worship would be that India is especially spiritual and the guru–pupil relationship is the primary expression of spirituality.

By far the most famous Godman today is Sathya Sai Baba (1926–), whose pictures, smiling under a round mass of hair, and clad in an ochre robe, are everywhere in India. He backs up his claim to be an incarnation of both Shiva and Shakti by a wide variety of well-publicized miracles. He produces sacred ash magically from his hands or at a distance from pictures of himself, and for the favoured few jewels and watches. Apart from his miracles, his teachings scarcely differ from those of the *Bhagavadgita*: one should be pure, one should do one's duty and dedicate one's actions to God in loving devotion. His divinity and miracles are accepted by many important Indians, and his charitable works are extensive, including hospitals and a university.

There are several instances of female gurus being accepted by their followers as manifestations of the Supreme Deity. Although veneration continues for medieval women saints such as Meera Bhai (late fifteenth century) who took nothing from their spouses, the first women gurus/saints in modern times tended to be wives of gurus who took over their husband's role after death or retirement, such as Saradamani (1853–1920), widow of Ramakrishna, and Mira Alfassa, 'the Mother' (1878–1973), wife of Aurobindo. A more modern phenomenon is women who are believed to embody the highest godhead. Instances are Anandamayi Ma (1896–1982), highly regarded by many important Indians; Ammachi, Amritanandamayi Ma (1954–) who touches and blesses individually vast crowds of devotees; and Meera Devi (1960–) who does the same on a much smaller scale in Germany.

Gender

A remarkable feature of Hindu life both in India and abroad is the continuation even among highly educated people of arranged marriages. Love marriages are not unknown, and romantic love is a key feature of the ever-popular Indian film industry; nevertheless most Hindus are content for their parents to find a marriage partner for them. Divorce is frowned upon: successful raising of children is the all-important goal of marriage. The family continues through time as a living entity. Parents are looked after in their old age, and live with their children.

Although many Hindu women work outside the home, and middle class women are well educated, Sita, wife of Rama – who as the *Ramayana* tells, faithfully followed her husband into the forest when he was banished by his father – remains a role model for many women. At the same time, many women play a vigorous role in public life, and the heroic goddess Durga also serves as a model. India has not only the late Mrs Gandhi, who at various times of crisis was identified with Durga in popular art, but also the female bandit Phoolan Devi (1963–2001) who worshipped Durga as well as identifying with her. After her surrender, having murdered the men who had raped her, she went on to become an MP (1996–99), and the film *Bandit Queen* (1995) told her story. India has a higher percentage of female members of parliament (the Lok Sabha) than does Germany.

Women play a leading role in domestic religious life. They usually tend the family shrine, and they maintain the well-being of their husband and children by undertaking vows, usually to fast or otherwise offer devotion to their favourite deities. Grandmothers teach religious stories and rituals to their grandchildren. The active women's movement in India and its many organizations tend to be secular in character, but women dominate the Brahma Kumari religious movement. Founded by a man, Dada Lekhraj (1876–1969), it is run by women, and while expecting the end of the world to be followed by the rule of the God Rama, its members are active in many welfare projects. Celibacy is advocated, and a form of yoga is taught.

Outside the home, men retain nearly all the leadership roles, whether in religion or politics. In the world of cinema, popular with the population at large, especially young men, scenes of attempted rape are a regular feature, revealing the vulnerability of women, and showing male power both in the attempted wrong and the punishment of the wrongdoer by the powerful hero. The attempted stripping of Draupadi in the *Mahabharata*, prevented by her prayer to the God Krishna, is familiar to all Hindu women, and they sympathize strongly with her.

Hindu society is changing, there are more nuclear families, more education for women, more high-level employment for women, and there is ever-greater exposure to Western social models through film and television. Nevertheless, the biological difference between male and female mediated by the difference between what is called the male caste and the female caste, remains as apparent in society as ever. In many fundamental ways, modernity appears not to have significantly affected the role of gender in religion.

Sati

A notable event in this connection was the death on her husband's funeral pyre of a nineteen-year-old woman called Rup Kanwar in 1987. Thousands flocked to see this death, and many more later to venerate the site, while at the same time thousands protested against what they saw as a barbarous murder. This sati took place in Rajasthan, a rural region with a long tradition of satis, along with female infanticide and child marriages. No notice had been taken of occasional satis in the preceding decade. Progressive thinkers denied that there was any legitimate tradition of sati, and said that it was murder by the in-laws. All the men in the village were arrested and detained. Incitement to commit sati was made a crime with heavier penalties than murder. Nevertheless, many families in the higher castes of Rajasthan claim to have a sati somewhere in the family history, the dead widow becoming a beneficent deity who looks after the welfare of future generations of the family. Suicide by fasting or self-inflicted wounds was a regular practice in the nineteenth century by the bardic caste of Western India, a tradition which Gandhi drew upon when he undertook his fasts to the death. In 1990 self-immolation by fire was a practice adopted by a dozen high caste protesters against the implementation of the proposals of the Mandal Commission Report on Backward Classes to extend reservation of government jobs and education for low castes and tribespeople ('scheduled castes and tribes').

The case of Rup Kanwar brought out into the open the gulf that separated traditional-minded Hindus from the Westernized urban elite. The Marwari merchant caste built dozens of Sati temples; progressive thinkers pointed out the connection between sati and the infamous 'dowry deaths', numbered by the thousands in the big cities of North India, where brides who bring too little dowry are burnt to death in kitchen 'accidents' brought about by husbands and in-laws. Sati is a rare event, and is now proscribed by very severe legislation. Nevertheless sati, which figured largely in early European accounts of India, was legislated against by the British, and attacked by the Hindu reform movements of the nineteenth century, continues.

Sati is the name given to a wife's immolating herself upon her husband's funeral. Though illegal in India, it has happened as recently as November 1999, in Mahoba, Rajasthan State. The event attracted far less publicity than the death of Roop Kanwar in the same fashion twelve years earlier, also in Rajasthan. But in both cases, reactions ranged from cries of "murder," to reverential awe at the widow's feat. In fact, police had to be posted at the Mahoba site to prevent a temple from being built upon it. The villagers protested the armed presence and, pointing to popular temples built in nearby areas to commemorate satis, demanded to know why they could not likewise honor their sati.

Hinduism Today May/June 2000

BOX 2.4 Sati

Caste

One of the features of Hindu society which sits most uncomfortably with modernity with its broadly egalitarian, 'humanitarian' ideals, is caste. The untouchable leader, B.R. Ambedkar (1891–1956), strove for the removal of caste privileges such as participation in public festivals, temple entry, Vedic wedding rituals, and the wearing of the sacred thread. In 1932 his proposal that untouchables to form a separate electorate, as was proposed for Muslims and Sikhs, led Gandhi to fast to the death until the claim was rejected. In 1935 Ambedkar declared that although he was born a Hindu he would not die a Hindu, and that untouchables could be free only outside the Hindu religion. Just before his death he converted to Buddhism, to be followed in this conversion by almost four million untouchables.

The caste system continues to be very important in respect of marriage, but the castes are no longer publicly admitted to form a hierarchy. People say that it is 'comfortable' to marry and socialize within their own castes; and caste associations have national political weight. The word 'community' is now sometimes used instead of caste. The former outcastes, the lowest castes, have given themselves the name Dalit, 'the downtrodden'. Numbering 200 million, their voice is growing. The tenth President of India (1997–2002) was a Dalit, K.R. Narayanan (1920–2005). Despite extensive government legislation, caste remains an important and often contentious part of life for most Hindus in India.

Nationalism

Regional 'nationalism'

India is made up of regions that are ethnically and culturally distinct. All are tinged to a greater or lesser degree by Brahmanic Hinduism, but that Hinduism is often rejected. To take one example: in the case of Tamilnadu, despite the strongly Hindu Chola Empire (ninth to thirteenth century CE) and post-Vijayanagara Nayak rulers (fifteenth to seventeenth century CE), Tamil language and literature both ancient and modern helped foster a strong sense of independent nationhood. An anti-Brahman independence movement was led by E.V. Ramaswami (1879–1973), who publically reviled Rama and took the demon Ravana as inspirational hero. Independence of India had meant the enslavement of the south by Hindu Delhi.

Hindu nationalism

A dominant part in Indian politics is played by Hindu Nationalism. The Bharatiya Janata Party's unstoppable rise to power from the mid-1980s was brought about by its demand for the destruction of the Babri mosque in Ayodhya and the rebuilding of the temple of Rama's birthplace. Although the secular Congress party seemed the natural ruling power in India for three decades from Independence in 1947, the rise of Hindu nationalism was almost inevitable. Hindu–Muslim tensions rose dramatically once it was clear the British Raj was about to end. While Gandhi attempted to form, or at least exemplify, a religion of love and sacrifice that ignored not only the realities of the modern industrial world but also the separateness of Hinduism, Islam, and Christianity, many Hindus and Muslims saw themselves as belonging to separate nations. The widely used Indian term for this religious nationalism is 'communalism'. Early Hindu nationalist thinkers were prominent in Bengal, the first home of the British Raj, and then in Maharashtra, the main industrial centre, and also the region of the last Hindu conquerors, the Marathas, who defeated the Moghuls and ruled much of India prior to the British. Among the Marathas, Brahmans were warrior kings as well as priests, and a succcession of Maratha Brahmans played a leading role in the development of Hindu nationalism. B.G. Tilak (1856–1920) promoted as a national figure the Maratha hero Shivaji (1627–1680) who initiated the defeat of the Moghuls, but while Tilak promoted the worship of Ganesha to strengthen the Hindu community in Maharashtra, V.D. Savarkar (1883–1966), terrorist and inspirational leader, made religion only one constituent part of being a Hindu. What counted for him was above all love of India, seen by him as Fatherland. All religions founded in India – Buddhism, Jainism, Sikhism – were Hindu. His nationalism was summed up in the new word, 'Hindutva', 'Hinduness'. Savarkar argued that violent action was required to remove the conquerors of India. In 1925 K.B. Hedgewar (1890–1940) founded the Rashtriya Svayamsevak Sangh 'National Volunteer Association' (RSS), a uniformed organization designed to correct all those faults of Indian character that the British pointed to in justifying their own rule; and making Mother India a deity above all others. A related organization, the Vishva Hindu Parishad (VHP), was started in 1964 to assemble and give a common voice to as many Hindu religious leaders as possible. The demand was formulated that three notable Hindu temples should be rebuilt. Just after independence it had been agreed by the government that the famous Shiva temple of Somanatha, many times destroyed by Muslims, should be rebuilt, though the rebuilding was not completed until 1995. But the new demand was very different, in that it called for the destruction of the mosques that had been built over the temple sites at Ayodhya, Mathura, and Varanasi. To further such aims, a youth wing of the VHP was founded in 1967. Named the Bajrang Dal, 'Mighty Hanuman's Army', the power and energy of the unemployed youth of North India was harnessed and given direction. In 1954 the RSS, though its own aim was the regeneration of the Hindu character rather than politics, had played a large part in the formation of the Jan Sangh political party. This party had not done well, but in 1980 it was repackaged as the Bharatiya Janata Party. This group of rightwing organizations took the overall title of the Sangh Parivar. Separate but analogous was the Shiv Sena, the Army of Shivaji, founded by the Bombay politician Bal Thackeray (1927–). All these groups converged on Ayodhya, where in 1992 the mosque – said to be built over the temple of Rama's birthplace – was destroyed, despite all orders of government and Supreme Court.

In this significant event many characteristics of modern Hinduism and modern India are thrown into sharp focus. Rightwing movements such as RSS, with their uniforms and their military discipline, are an after-effect of British colonialism, with its denigration of Hindu military prowess: these organizations want to demonstrate the strength of Hindus. Because of historical conflict and because of the ongoing dispute about ownership of Kashmir, Pakistan and all Muslims are perceived by Hindus of the extreme right as their enemy. The God Rama, *avatara* of Vishnu, already given new life by the televising of the *Ramayana*, is given a new iconography, as poised with his bow drawn ready to fire his arrow at the foe, at his feet the elevation of the temple of his birthplace, yet to be (re)built. Another innovation was a boy Rama, modelled on the much loved baby boy form of Krishna, a Rama who first showed himself, it is supposed, within the Ayodhya mosque in 1948. Using the resources of modern technology, television, film, audio tapes of incendiary speeches, Hindu nationalist forces swept aside the restrictions of the secular state.

Hinduism has gained much from Islam over the centuries, expressed in the rich tradition exemplified by Kabir and other saints, but it is also the case that the recent upsurge in Hindu fundamentalism has been influenced by instances of contemporary Islamic intransigence. Rightwing Hindu intolerance of Islam and Christianity in India today has also to be noted. Enmity with Pakistan, especially because of ongoing conflict over Kashmir, fosters enmity with Islam and ill-treatment of Muslims in India. At the same time, resentment of former British colonialism continues, sometimes generalized into hatred of the West and of Christianity. All this is summed up in a popular New Year card by the well-known artist Balraj showing a giant Mother India calling the Indian (Hindu) people to arms with her furious lion beside her already pawing at the multiple dragons that are India's enemies, dragons whose snake-like bodies are marked with the American dollar sign, the Islamic crescent, and the Christian cross.

Hinduism outside India

Hindu groups outside India build traditional forms of temples as soon as they can afford it, but new temples retain the quality of meeting place that is so important for new communities establishing themselves.

Hinduism tends to be vigorously affirmed by non-resident Indians (NRIs) who are Hindu and, especially in the USA, the question of who speaks for Hinduism has become of increasing importance. While study and teaching of yoga and other spiritual practices have long been carried out by non-Hindu Westerners, the teaching of Hinduism within university Religious Studies programmes outside India is increasingly questioned by middle class Indians. It is certainly true that discussion of sensitive issues by Western scholars is more robust in the case of Hinduism than it is in the case of Islam, partly no doubt because Islam tends to be more tightly defined than Hinduism. The identification of the convex-top pillar, the *lingam*, emblem of Shiva, with the erect penis is a typically contentious issue. On the one hand many Hindus are unhappy with this identification which is freely made by Westerners, preferring themselves to say that the *lingam* represents formless divinity; on the other hand, early textual and sculptural history provide irrefutable evidence to the contrary. Differing attitudes to sexuality often lie behind disputes over interpretation of Hinduism. Western understanding of sexuality in the second half of the twentieth century benefitted from the popularization of the *Kama Sutra* and the erotic sculpture of Khajuraho, but many Hindus today would disavow the more open sexuality of classical Indian culture.

Looking to the future

Most Hindus have not heard of the death of God. Hinduism's Gods and Goddesses are as alive as ever – in temples, in modern media, in human incarnations. It is impossible in a single chapter to do justice to the vigorous multiplicity of Hinduism. The controversial Indian novelist Salman Rushdie wrote: 'The selfhood of Indians is so capacious, so elastic, that it accommodates one billion kinds of difference.' This perfectly expresses the dynamic freedom that is the special heritage of India, despite all the constrictions that arise from communalism and caste.

Modern India has formed its own amalgam of tradition and modernity, indeed its own modernity. Indian government and Indian law are completely modern, fully 'rationalized', 'bureaucratized' and 'secular'. Hinduism likewise sees itself as modern and in accord with modern science, while at the same time accepting the plenitude and validity of human religious experience. The Gods and Goddesses are real because sacred texts describe them in detail and because people see, hear, and touch them. Religious practices like yoga and tantra, based on esoteric understanding of the mind and body, are experientially proven. Hindu thinkers long ago saw the universe in terms both of the infinitely large and the infinitely small. Rather like the present day Big Bang Theory, medieval Shaiva philosophers reasoned that the universe was produced in a split second from an infinitely small point, but went further, by positing an infinite series of such creations.

Hinduism has spread round the world with the Indian diaspora and the limited activity of Hindu missionaries. Yoga and spiritual disciplines stemming from yoga have had worldwide success. Innumerable Hindu spiritual teachers are active round the world, even if their activities are small-scale. Hindu art and culture from the second half of the twentieth century have at last begun to be understood outside India. From the perspective of modernity, Hindu Puranic myths plainly bear upon the realities of the human psyche rather than a special version of history, and thus retain value even if not fully believed.

Hindu fundamentalism aside, Hinduism is thus generally at ease in the modern world. For Hindus the traditional values of the family are self-evidently valuable in whatever world we find ourselves, and caste continues as groupings of families. Indeed, so at ease is Hinduism in the modern world that it may be argued that in certain ways Hinduism is not only modern, but even intrinsically postmodern. If the postmodern world is characterized as the late-capitalist, post-industrial world of the internet and cyberspace, a world of spectacle, sensation and simulation, then the Hindu view of the world as multilevelled, infinitely varied and infinitely coloured, as bewitched by Krishna's flute, as the projection of the divine light of Shiva upon the wall of his own consciousness, as the pure consciousness of Brahman, is a view that is easily adaptable to this ethos, and is not threatened by any of the promised and threatened developments of modern science.

Summary

- Traditional Hinduism continues into the modern world, and its rich complexity has to be understood for Hinduism today to be comprehended.

- Modernity has been mediated to India by British colonialism. Salient features include the nation state and the dissemination of scientific rationality.

- One effect of the Western impact on Hinduism (particularly in the nineteenth and early twentieth centuries) is the rise of different forms of 'reform' or 'neo' Hinduism. Generally small-scale and elite, such movements have nonetheless had a wider influence on Hinduism.

- At the same time traditional Hinduism persists in the modern world, in some cases revivified by new media such as film and television. Hindu Gods and Goddesses, in temple and in home shrine, are as popular as ever. Gurus have also become increasingly important in modern times, teaching a wide variety of yoga-based techniques in India and the west.

- Caste sits uneasily with modernity, and gender roles often continue to follow traditional stereotypes. Feminized divinity continues to give scope for female spirituality.

- Hindu concerns are important in Indian politics, but the ideal of India as a secular state has not been overturned.

Key terms

ashrama One of the four stages of life; the retreat or hermitage of a holy man or woman.

avatara 'Descent', the incarnation of the divine on earth, in divine or human form.

bhakti Loving devotion to a deity.

Brahma Four-headed male god, born from the lotus that arises from Vishnu's navel at the beginning of each cycle of creation.

brahman Priest, member of the highest caste.

Brahman Ultimate reality, the absolute that is pure consciousness; said by the *Upanishads* and the Non-dualist Vedanta philosophy to be identical with the individual self.

darshan Seeing, seeing a sacred image or person; also, philosophy, philosophical system.

Devi Goddess in general; or Supreme Goddess.

dharma The right way of life, in accord with cosmic truth. Hinduism is the eternal right way of life, the *sanatana* (eternal) *dharma*. *Dharma* in a more restricted sense is the third of the goals of mankind, meaning religious behaviour which leads to heaven or higher rebirth; in this sense it is inferior to *moksha*.

diksha Ritual consecration, initiation.

Durga Heroic saviour Goddess, who kills the buffalo demon.

guru Teacher, spiritual guide, godman.

jati Literally 'birth' – caste, sub-caste.

Kali The Black Goddess, fierce form of Parvati, destroyer of the universe.

kali yuga The fourth, worst, and final world age, endlessly recurring in the cosmic cycle of *samsara*. Kali here refers to the worst throw of a dice, sometimes personified as a male demon; and should not be confused with the Goddess Kali (spelt Kālī in Indian languages).

karma Action; the personal consequences that accrue from action.

Krishna The black or dark blue God, incarnation of Vishnu.

kundalini The female serpent coiled at the base of the spine, raised up by Tantric yoga.

Lakshmi Goddess of wealth and prosperity, wife of Vishnu.

mantra Sacred word or formula.

moksha Release, liberation of the self from rebirth.

Murugan Son of Shiva and Parvati, Tamil form of Skanda.

Parvati Goddess, wife of Shiva, mother of Ganesha and Skanda.

Prakriti Mother nature.

puja The act of worshipping a deity or holy person by offering light, flowers, food and water.

Purusha 'Male', the cosmic giant whose sacrificed body gave rise to the fourfold caste system; individual consciousness in the Samkhya philosophy.

Rama Hero of the Ramayana, husband of Sita, slayer of Ravana, incarnation of Vishnu.

Samkhya Philosophical system based on opposition of *purusha* and *prakriti*, consciousness and nature.

samsara The eternal cycle of rebirth.

Sanskrit The ancient language of the Hindu scriptures, still learned by some brahmans. Belonging to the Indo-European family of languages, with strong resemblances to Greek, Latin, Celtic, Old German. Sanskrit words form a large part of the vocabulary of modern Indian languages.

sati **(suttee)** Literally, 'a good wife' – a widow who joins the corpse of her husband on the funeral pyre and perishes in the flames; the act of so doing. After death, she is considered immortal and a family deity.

Shaiva Religion, philosophy or devotee of Shiva.

Shaivism The religion of Shiva.

Shakta Relating to Shakti, the religion of Shakti; Goddess worship.

Shakti Feminine force, feminine divinity.

Shiva One of the two great Gods of Hinduism, the Great Yogi, the King of Dancers, husband of Parvati.

Sita Wife of Rama, heroine of the *Ramayana*, ideal wife.

siddhi Magic power acquired through yoga.

svami **(swami)** Lord, master, usual title of a holy man.

tantra Doctrine and practice based on secret ritual worship of the female and magical sounds.

Vaishnava Religion, philosophy or devotee of Vishnu.

varna Literally 'colour' – the four caste groups of Priest, Warrior, Merchant and Peasant.

Vishnu One of the two great Gods of Hinduism, a kingly and warrior figure who periodically descends to earth to protect *dharma*.

yajna Fire oblation, sacrifice

yoga 'Joining' – self-mastery, union with the divine; meditational practice and philosophy.

yuga World age, of which there are four, endlessly repeating.

Further reading

Overviews of Hinduism

Sushil Mittal and Gene Thursby: *The Hindu World* (Abingdon: Routledge, 2004). Rich overview by eminent scholars, on key texts, sects, and concepts.

Hinduism in the nineteenth century

J.N. Farquhar: *Modern Religious Movements in India* (Repr. Delhi: Munshiram Manoharlal, [1914] 1967). Masterly survey up to 1913, but necessarily dated in treatment.

Hinduism and modernity

David Smith: *Hinduism and Modernity* (Oxford: Blackwell, 2003). A study of classical and modern Hinduism in relation to modernity.

Contemporary Hinduism

Nancy Auer Falk: *Living Hinduisms: An Explorer's Guide* (Belmont, CA: Thomson Wadsworth, 2006). Excellent overview, with plenty of personal fieldwork notes.

John Stratton Hawley and Vasudha Narayanan (eds): *The Life of Hinduism* (Berkeley: University of California Press, 2006). Essays on Hinduism today as lived practice.

Chapter 3

Buddhism

Cathy Cantwell and Hiroko Kawanami

Introduction

Buddhism, long established in Asia, has become a fast-growing religion in Western countries today. The number of adherents worldwide in 2005 was estimated at around 376 million, about 6 per cent of the world's population, and although it may not be easy to verify such estimates, these figures suggest that Buddhism ranks fourth amongst world religions today. In modern times, Buddhism has been affected by the impact of colonialism, capitalism, Marxism, and nationalism. Asian Buddhist countries have lost their traditional systems of government and in some cases experienced communist rule or other political upheavals and social changes. Challenges have also resulted from new technology, secularization, different world views and transportation of Buddhism to societies with different cultural traditions.

Buddhism remains dominant in Sri Lanka and several countries in mainland Southeast Asia and East Asia. It has survived or seen recent revivals in the Himalayan region, Tibet, China, Central Asia, pockets of east Bengal, south India and Indonesia. Late twentieth-century globalization has meant that the major Buddhist traditions all now have an international presence, and infringe on each other's territories. Buddhism has also become significant in North America, Latin America and Europe. Many texts have been translated into European languages since the nineteenth century, and Theravāda, Tibetan, Zen, Chinese Mahāyāna, and Japanese Nichiren Buddhist groups continue to mushroom in the West. Meanwhile, both in Asia and the West, new forms of Buddhism have attracted growing numbers seeking spirituality compatible with contemporary life.

For Asian Buddhists, 'modernity' may imply various experiences consequent upon their encounter with the West, their integration into modern economies and political systems, and the subsequent arrival of different world views and values challenging traditional outlooks and ways of life. In some cases, secular education, scientific knowledge, democratic and liberal ideas were introduced; all were a part of the modernity which stimulated local religious leaders to engage in reform or retrenchment. Secularization, mass literacy, urbanization, technological developments and growth in communications accelerated the process. Yet the timing of the Buddhist encounter with modernity, and the specific forms it took, varied significantly. In Sri Lanka, for example, modernity can be dated to British rule in the nineteenth century, whilst in Tibet it was postponed until the mid-twentieth century Chinese occupation.

This chapter focuses on southern Buddhism – South and Southeast Asian Theravāda (the way of the elders), and northern Tibetan Buddhism, concluding with a brief account of Buddhism in the West. Further discussion of East Asian Buddhism can be found in Chapters 5 (Chinese religions) and 6 (Japanese religions).

Sources and resources

Origins and fundamental tenets

Siddhārtha Gautama (*c.* 490–10 BCE), who became the Buddha, was one who had 'awoken' to the truth, and is regarded as the founder of Buddhism. Emerging from the Indian Renouncer movement, which emphasized the abandonment of worldly life for the pursuit of spiritual enlightenment, his teaching of the 'four noble truths' drew attention to the unsatisfactory nature of existence. According to early sources, everything is conditioned and subject to change; however, people ignorant of this become attached to impermanent things. The only cure is the 'noble eightfold path', a set of methods encompassing morality, wisdom and meditation. The ultimate goal is enlightenment (*nirvāna*), freedom from the cycle of conditioned existence.

Buddhism developed a universalist ethical system, unlike the Vedic traditions, which tended to situate ethics according to the status of the actor (see Chapter 2, on Hinduism), and held that there are universal values – especially that of the non-harming of living beings – which are equally valid for all people. In Buddhist thinking, rebirth in conditioned existence is dependent on laws of cause and effect (*karma*), which operate rationally and are ethical in nature – morally good actions lead to positive results while bad actions lead to negative results. While encouraging ethical discipline for all, renouncers of household life were to develop mindfulness and wisdom in order to exhaust ignorance and craving, seen as responsible for the conditioned existence, thus putting an end to the entire process of *samsāra* and attaining the unconditioned. This approach was partly shared with other Renouncer groups. Specifically Buddhist elements included:

1. The idea that it is intentional action that generates results in a being's consciousness. This had implications for both individual conduct and relations between monks and laity. For instance, an accidental taking of life might be seen as negative action influenced by confusion or carelessness, rather than entailing the full consequences of killing living beings. Thus, the stricter requirements for ascetics and lay folk in Jainism (a rival Renouncer movement which also had long-term success in India) were considered unnecessary in Buddhism.
2. The co-existence of perspectives that stressed the problem of ignorance and the corresponding need to develop wisdom, with perspectives stressing the problem of craving and the corresponding need to reduce emotional defilements. Many of the variations in Buddhist practice are related to the relative importance given to these two perspectives.
3. The development of meditation techniques for calming the mind and increasing mindful awareness, considered essential on the path to liberation; other elements of the Renouncer heritage, especially forms of asceticism, were comparatively neglected.

4.   A conceptualization of the Buddhist Path as a 'middle way' between the extremes of worldly indulgence and asceticism, combining a strong commitment to renunciation with a simple lifestyle without ascetic tortures or avoidance of the wider community.

Many of these early characteristics continued to be central in Buddhism, although the tradition diversified in time, and underwent complex developments in its practices and systems of philosophy during 1,500 years in India. The Buddhist scriptural heritage was transmitted orally by schools of reciters until texts were written down around the beginning of the Christian era. It was codified in the separate but parallel collections of the early Buddhist orders, including sections on monastic discipline (*Vinaya*), discourses (*Sutta*), and in the case of most (but not all) schools, Higher Teachings (*Abhidhamma*). The Mahāyāna (great vehicle) movement added a further set of *sūtras*, not recognized by all Buddhists. It was initially small in India, but had long-term historical significance.

Historical change and diffusion

Many Indian kings patronized Buddhism, but King Aśoka of the Mauryan dynasty played a crucial role in spreading Buddhism in the third century BCE to wider areas in Asia. Further diffusions of Buddhism were brought by the Mahāyāna teachings, which travelled to China and Central Asia from the early centuries CE, while large Mahāyāna scholastic centres thrived during the latter period of Buddhism in India, between the seventh and the twelfth centuries. In early Mahāyāna teachings, the actions of the compassionate *bodhisattva* were adopted as a religious path over spiritual endeavour focused on personal liberation.

The focus on compassion was combined with single-minded dedication to attaining wisdom, now summed up in the notion of emptiness. This complex teaching was elaborated at length in Mahāyāna philosophy, especially in the Madhyamaka school, which analysed the deceptive nature of all conceptual systems. On the other hand, the Yogācāra school in the fourth century integrated diverse Buddhist teachings, while emphasizing the centrality of the meditational experience of pure consciousness. More broadly, the Mahāyāna recognition of new *sūtras* as valid scripture, and the development of such philosophical and commentarial traditions in debate with the emerging Hindu philosophical schools, demonstrates the considerable dynamism and innovation in Indian Mahāyāna. In fact, the so-called Mahāyāna tradition was never a single school nor sect, but rather a spiritual movement or tendency. Its openness to creative developments later persisted to some extent, especially in Chinese Buddhism. In contrast, the later Theravāda, which firmly established itself in Sri Lanka, consolidated a more unitary outlook due to its conservative concerns.

A further development in Indian Buddhism was the Buddhist *tantric* or Vajrayāna tradition, using rich symbolic imagery and ritual practices, and based on the principle that the energies of aggression, passion, and delusion may be used to overcome themselves. Pure in their true nature when not afflicted by ignorance, these powerful forces may be co-opted for the Buddhist goal of enlightenment, although safeguards were considered necessary to preclude misinterpretation. New esoteric scriptures called 'tantras' were revealed, and in time, Vajrayāna became rooted in major monastic centres in northern India, and travelled alongside other Buddhist texts and practices to various Asian countries.

By the thirteenth century, Buddhism had been eclipsed in its Indian heartlands, but was firmly established through much of Asia, from Tibet to Japan. It spread not only in the form of religious scriptures but also in art, architecture and literature, which had profound impact on local cultures.

Most of the diverse forms of Buddhism which have survived into modern times can be categorized into three major groupings:

1. Southern Buddhism, practiced in Sri Lanka and countries in mainland Southeast Asian, especially Burma, Thailand, Laos and Cambodia. The main thread holding this group together is the Pali canon, common monastic rules and ritual practices. Theravāda tradition derives from one of the ancient Indian Buddhist schools, and preserves the only surviving complete corpus of early texts in an ancient Indian language, Pali. It also draws on later commentarial works, including those of Sri Lankan scholars during the first millennium CE.

2. Northern Buddhism, practiced in Tibet, the surrounding Himalayan areas, and wherever Buddhism spread from Tibetan sources, such as parts of Central Asia, principally Mongolia. The Buddhism of this branch derives from later Indian Buddhism especially of the Pāla dynasty (Bengal, eighth to twelfth centuries CE), incorporating Buddhist monastic scholarship, Mahāyāna and tantric traditions. It preserves large collections of scriptural and commentarial texts in Tibetan, including a comprehensive set of translations from Sanskrit sources as well as a vast indigenous literature.

3. East Asian Buddhism, practiced in East Asian countries such as China, Taiwan, Korea, Japan, and Vietnam, and in the diaspora with substantial ethnic Chinese populations. East Asian Buddhism mainly derives from the Mahāyāna traditions, which were established in China in the early centuries CE, although the textual heritage in Chinese includes earlier Buddhist scriptures and a few tantras.

Samantabhadra's aspirations, expressing the bodhisattva ethos, are well-known in Mahāyāna Buddhist countries. They conclude the Avatamsaka Sūtra, a Mahāyāna sūtra, which had a major impact on East Asian Buddhism. The extracts below follow Shenpen Hookham's translation from Tibetan.

> May offerings be made in reverence to the Buddhas of the past
> And those of the present in the worlds of the ten directions.
> May those Buddhas-to-be proceeding towards Enlightenment
> Quickly consummate all their wishes on the Path and become Buddhas.
> May all the realms that there are in the ten directions

continued

Become extensive and perfectly pure,
And each whole realm become utterly filled with Buddhas . . .

Throughout all my lifetimes as I pass from death to rebirth,
May I each time renew again my vow to live the life of renunciation. Following
the manner of training of all the Buddhas,
May I wholly complete the discipline of perfected deeds . . .
And never forget the aspiration of awakening to Buddhahood . . .
May I relieve the suffering of the beings in the lower realms,
Establishing them in happiness and acting for their benefit . . .

May I be able to see in a single atom Buddha realms numerous as atoms,
And then in each of these Buddha realms,
Buddhas in number beyond conception,
And each Buddha seated in the midst of his vast assembly of Bodhisattvas . . .
I pray I may be able to perform the discipline of perfected deeds
Before these endless Buddhas in the endless Buddha realms for endless
    aeons . . .

By the power of miracles, swift and all-embracing,
By the power of the universal gateway [the Mahāyāna],
By the power of the all-good qualities of the perfected deeds,
By the power of all-pervading love,
By the power of seeds of goodness from all wholesome states and actions,
By the power of unobstructed primordial wisdom,
By the power of wisdom, skilful action and concentrative absorption,
May I complete all the powers of Enlightenment.

The Samantabhadra Charyapranidhana, Shenpen Hookham
(Oxford: Longchen Foundation, 1997)

BOX 3.1 Samantabhadra's aspirations for perfected deeds

Organization and authority

Monasticism played an essential role in the consolidation and propagation of early Buddhism, viewed by most Buddhist schools as a superior way of life enabling its members to avoid worldly concerns and concentrate single-mindedly on their spiritual practice. The monastic code that governs the daily life of monks and their social relationships appears to have been codified at a very early stage in Indian Buddhism. Central to the Buddhist monastic code is the principle of combining aspects of the model of the other-worldly renouncer with that of the this-worldly householder *brahmin* priest. Monks, like ascetics, were to renounce household life, yet they were expected to serve the laity's religious needs by giving Buddhist teachings. The monastic community

(Sangha) in its classic form, emphasizing monastic and lay interdependence, was the long-standing ideal of Buddhist organization.

In early Indian Buddhism, a number of discrete monastic orders developed on the basis of separate ordination lineages, with minor variations in the list of monastic rules. These orders also came to be associated with certain doctrinal positions, but there was no insistence on adherence to these positions within each order. Rules governing the communal lives of monks seem to have derived from a model of republican government then current in parts of the region where Buddhism originated. Local Sanghas were autonomous, united by common adherence to the monastic rule and the Buddha's teachings, but not by hierarchical integration. Within each Sangha, ranking was based on seniority and gender, while decisions were made ideally by consensus, with provisions for majority voting. The small-scale, non-hierarchical structure of the Sangha persisted as an important feature, but it has frequently been modified by the integration of monasteries into wider political and socio-economic structures, generating increased cohesion and hierarchy in Buddhist monasticism.

Different models for religious practice stemmed from an early Buddhist opposition between town-dwelling and forest-dwelling monks. The alternative vocations of book duty and meditation duty are discussed in the fifth-century Pali commentaries written in Sri Lanka. The ideal type of bookish monk would be resident in a monastic institution, preserving and teaching the tradition as passed down, at first by oral transmission and later by written scriptures. Meditators, on the other hand, would be focused on gaining realization, often in reclusive forest retreats, wandering from place to place like the ancient ascetics. These two types can be seen as two distinct strands within the Buddhist tradition from the outset. Even before there were any books, the codified Buddhist monastic rule modified the strict ascetic codes for renouncers, encouraging the communal life of monasteries and association with the laity. These innovations appear to have been resisted by one faction of Buddhist monks; they won the concession that, although not binding on the whole community, various ascetic traditions would be accommodated.

Organization in Southern Buddhism

Southern Buddhism is fairly uniform in accepting the canonical Pali scriptures and commentaries as its textual authority. It has a solid monastic tradition with the ideal of renunciation accepted as a superior way of life. Although there is no orthodoxy as such, Theravāda Buddhists take pride in practicing a religious tradition seen by them as uncorrupted and close to the earliest forms of Buddhism. Conservative in outlook, the monks strive to preserve Theravāda doctrine and its monastic tradition with minimal change. As a Buddhist, one accepts and places one's trust in the Triple Gem: Buddha, Dhamma (the teachings of the Buddha) and Sangha. The formula of 'going for refuge' to the Triple Gem, publicly recited, is indispensable for any Buddhist ritual.

The Sangha specifically refers to the 'noble', spiritually advanced community, which might theoretically include nuns and lay people. However, the monks, pre-eminently, have come to symbolize the Sangha as the focus of people's worship. Their lifestyle is characterized by celibacy, detachment, and monastic discipline which, especially in the Southern tradition, and is valued above that of the ordinary lay person. The monks are thought to be in a privileged position to concentrate on the path to Nibbāna, whilst the laity's main task is to work for better rebirths through merit-making activities. Traditionally, whilst monks are encouraged to study and meditate, lay followers are expected to observe the Five Precepts, feed the monks and perform regular worship. Lay devotees also take additional vows such as celibacy, fasting in the afternoon, and not drinking alcohol or going to films on special days. In addition to such traditional practice, meditation is becoming an increasingly popular part of their spiritual training. In countries such as Burma and Thailand, the custom of becoming a temporary novice or a monk after 20 years of age, possibly for a week to three months, is regarded as essential in attaining an adult status for a man. For a woman, however, the most prestigious and meritorious act is to send her son into the Sangha; a monk repays his parents with spiritual merit. The monastic community also provides education and social mobility for the bright and ambitious, especially from rural areas.

In the political realm, Southern Buddhism has long upheld the ideal of a 'righteous king' (*Dhammarāja*) who defends Buddhist faith and its moral principles of non-violence, tolerance and compassion. The ideal is enshrined in the historically based legend of King Aśoka (268–31 BCE) who after his conversion, promoted Buddhism and governed in accordance with its moral law. It incorporated a theme arising from accounts of the Buddha's life: that a universal ruler and spiritual teacher may in some sense be equated. Southeast Asian kings, taking up this theme, were consecrated as rulers of extraordinary grandeur, such as the thirteenth-century Khmer King Jayavarman VII, depicted as Bodhisattva Avalokiteśvara, and King Bodawpaya in seventeenth-century Burma, identified with the Ariya Metteyya, the next Buddha-to-be.

The *Dhammarāja* model assumed that the king and monastic community were complementary, coexisting to maintain stability. The king patronized the Sangha, ensuring its purity and strength, while the monks provided the country with moral foundation. The king was expected to be righteous and administer the Sangha and society well. Failure justified his removal, at least in theory if not practice, and historically, religion was often subordinated to statecraft. To understand state control over the Sangha that has in some respects persisted to date, the following areas are important:

1.   Monastic discipline was enforced by the ruling power and corrupt monks were expelled.
2.   The state defined and enforced Sangha administration, appointing members to Sangha councils, and promoting monks supportive to the government.
3.   The state protected lines of monastic succession and ordination which would be, at least theoretically, traceable back to the Buddha, thus maintaining the Sangha's legitimacy.
4.   The state became responsible for the standards of monastic education, standardizing textbooks, and securing the quality of state-sponsored religious elite.

5. The state designated, regulated and controlled special areas for worship and religious constructions. Stūpas and pagodas containing relics of the Buddha were protected as symbols of kingship.

These provisions helped to ensure the moral behaviour of monks, popular support for the Sangha, and long-lasting political stability. However, the monks at times have been rebellious, manifesting their potential as an alternative power base. In the postcolonial period of Southeast Asia, monastic communities without traditional royal patrons have had difficulties; but political rulers have not always been able to undermine the religious authority of the Sangha.

Organization in Northern Buddhism (Tibet)

In early Buddhism, doctrinal variations did not necessarily imply separate organization. The Mahāyāna movement spread within rather than institutionally separating itself from the early monastic orders. The same is generally true of Tibetan Buddhist monasticism; the monastic code followed everywhere is that of the Mūlasarvastivāda, an ancient Indian order. Tibetan Buddhists also share Mahāyāna and Vajrayāna (*tantric*) practices and perspectives, while they are divided into monastic orders or loosely organized schools based on different lineages of teachers, and not, in most cases, on strictly doctrinal differences. The main four traditions are Kagyu (*bka' brgyud*), Sakya (*sa skya*), Nyingma (*rnying ma*) and Geluk (*dge lugs*), but each of these major schools contains groupings within it, which may be to a greater or lesser extent autonomous.

Certain doctrinal positions or specialisms in specific practices are associated with each school but, just as in the ancient Buddhist orders there are no rigid sectarian boundaries. Movement between monasteries and study within institutions of different affiliations has never been uncommon and there has also been constant cross-fertilization of teachings at the highest level, senior lamas sometimes receiving teaching lineages of lamas from different schools. An old tendency not to consider a lama's education complete without some training from lamas of other schools, became prominent through the impact of the nineteenth-century non-sectarian (*ris med*) movement, and even more so in the troubled contemporary situation. With the breakdown of formal mechanisms of social integration, there is increased concern for informal co-operation.

Cutting across the schools are three models of religious practice, each with precedents in Indian Buddhism: (1) the scholar monk; (2) the ascetic renouncer specializing in meditation; (3) the lay mantra practitioner, a tantric religious specialist. Frequently highly trained in Vajrayāna texts and meditation, lay mantra practitioners maintain a strict code of conduct distinct from the monks' code, and not entailing celibacy. Whilst different Tibetan schools have different emphases – some specializing in scholastic training, others on meditative retreats – the three types of practice are represented in each. There may also be movement from one pole to another at different stages of an individual's life, of a hermitage or even a monastic tradition. Meditators, responsible for exemplifying the goal, may repeatedly 'escape' from the world, only to find that they must cater for enthusiastic followers requesting the establishment of teaching centres, and the cycle begins again.

The third (lay) model of religious practice does not seem to have quite such ancient precedents in Indian Buddhism as the other two. Mahāyāna Buddhism introduced the theory that a lay person could work for, and even exemplify, the qualities of enlightenment, following the bodhisattva ethic to bring all beings to enlightenment. The idea that lay practice of bodhisattva virtues such as generosity and patience provides excellent potential for real spiritual progress is one which has persisted in lay traditions of practice in Tibetan Buddhism, but the model for the serious lay religious in Tibetan Buddhism is principally orientated to tantric traditions. Lay mantra practitioners may be considered to be of great religious stature, often preserving high status hereditary lineages, and in premodern Tibet sometimes inter-marrying with the aristocracy. Their religious training might include periods of retreat, pilgrimages and travel to visit religious masters, but the ideal mantra practitioner would marry and live within a lay community, frequently serving the population with ritual skills. Many mantra practitioners were not of renowned stock or high status, and there were some entire communities of lay religious specialists.

Different kinds of religious institutions are associated with each of the three models: respectively, scholastic institutes within large monasteries, mountain hermitages and lay mantra practitioner communities or yellow householder (*gser khyim*) villages. Just as it is often impossible to draw clear lines between practitioners – since individuals may combine or shift between each type – so these religious institutions were rarely entirely separate. A hermitage might become a settled monastery; large monasteries might support retreat facilities and lay practitioners might participate in local monastic ritual. A monastery's reincarnate lamas (*sprul sku*) may be found in mantra practitioner families, and hereditary and monastic lineages may coincide in one individual. The three kinds of exemplary practitioners and institutions were all supported by the large-scale funding of religion at state and local level in Tibet. There was a high proportion of monks, some recruited by government conscription as well as voluntary family donations of sons, and ordinary monks, who performed either ritual or administrative and other non-religious tasks, outnumbered trained scholar and meditator monks.

In premodern Tibet, there was often much stability in monastic institutions over generations, with long-standing local support backed by monastic land holdings and the political structure. Buddhist monasteries were almost everywhere central to socio-political organization in Tibetan speaking societies, although their exact role varied considerably owing to differences in social structure in different regions and at different historical periods. In politically centralized regions, large monasteries were part of the governmental administrative system. In contrast, in decentralized areas, monasteries helped to integrate local populations. Continuity of religious organization was provided by land-owning monasteries which in various ways were part of the political system, but at the same time the Tibetan Buddhist emphasis on the lama generated some dynamism. As in the followings of Indian Hindu gurus, there was some individual and community choice in religious patronage; monasteries and hermitages might rise or decline according to the reputation of their principal lamas. Within the overall monastic structure, then, we find a multiplicity of religious authorities, summed up in the proverb, 'every district its own dialect, every lama his own religious practice'. A monastery needed its lamas, but its lamas would not always conform to the practices favoured by the monastic order concerned, and they might occasionally fulfil the ideal spiritual life pattern more successfully by escaping from the confines of their monastery.

In the Tibetan context, secular authorities rarely entirely dominated religious authorities. The principle of the fusion of religious and secular authority (*chos srid zung 'brel*) was a powerful ideal in Tibetan society, drawing on pan-Buddhist symbolism of the righteous monarch. The strength of the religious vis-à-vis secular authorities, except in instances of national submission of Tibetan religious authorities to foreign powers (Mongol and Manchu) which had few implications for religious organization, often contrasts with the situation that pertained in Southeast Asia.

Gender

There is no single Buddhist approach to gender issues. One significant strand emphasizes that in terms of spiritual attainment, women and men have equal capabilities and that women not only can but also in many cases have attained liberation. Such a perspective is found in a number of sources of different periods, including early Buddhist literature, Mahāyāna *sūtras*, and tantric writings. Furthermore, Buddhist doctrines do not differentiate between men and women since everyone, regardless of gender, status or age, is subject to old age, illness and mortality, and the suffering and impermanence which mark conditioned existence apply equally to all. There are stories of women and even children who attained enlightenment during the time of the Buddha. Many early Buddhist nuns, called *therīs*, were also said to have attained liberation.

Contemporary Buddhists seeking more egalitarian gender relations within the tradition have found inspiration in these aspects of early Buddhism. Nonetheless, the picture is modified both by doctrinal elements, which appear to qualify or contradict the theory of spiritual equality, and by organizational features which formally relegate women to a subservient status and restrict them from taking part in the decision-making of the monastic community. There are also statements in Buddhist scriptures which appear to be misogynist, such as the presentation of women as obstructers of men's spiritual progress or the notion that a woman's birth is an inferior one with less opportunity for spiritual practice. These are open to other interpretations. In societies where men have access to authority and wider choices, a negative judgement of women's fate might be seen as simply reflecting empirical reality. Furthermore, the religious literature is more likely to address men and hence we find the Buddhist emphasis on renunciation of sensual desires and worldly concerns expressed in terms of the problems with attachment to women more frequently than we find the reverse. Yet the distinction between recognizing actual gender inequalities and commenting on women's innate nature might not be obvious and such statements have been used to justify acceptance of the situation.

Matters have been exacerbated by the organizational structure of the Sangha: the monastic community was stratified by seniority and gender, so that even senior nuns were junior to all categories of monks, and the autonomy of nuns was restricted. This formal structure may help to explain the relative smallness of the nuns' order and its inability to survive long-term in most Buddhist countries. Individual ability or attainment was irrelevant in the ranking system, and thus a low status did not necessarily imply a deficient spiritual practice. Yet, it is clear that both in the past and the present, the weakness of institutions for female practitioners, coupled with higher valuation of monks in Asian societies, resulted in the nuns having fewer opportunities to receive instruction, study the scriptures, or practice the Buddhist teachings.

Interactions with modernity

Southeast Asia

Modern Buddhist revival in Southeast Asia has been a response to a set of political events and historical developments since the nineteenth century. Buddhist countries responded to the forces of colonialism, foreign domination and modernization by reassessing their traditional religious identity and strengthening the foundation of their monastic institutions. In the twentieth century, monks in Sri Lanka and Burma were actively involved in the independence movements against British rule. After independence, many countries in mainland Southeast Asia were directly affected by the Cold War, and monastic communities became increasingly drawn into the ideological battle between communism and its alternatives. During the 1960s and 1970s, Buddhism in Laos and Cambodia sometimes became a vehicle for local political factions advancing their respective political agendas. As the nation state became increasingly dominant in these societies, education and welfare have ceased to be the exclusive preserve of Buddhism, while patronage by kings and religious patrons has been lost. Yet the Sangha – as the only organization to have retained its position equipped with a national network independent of state administration – has been expected to perform co-operative roles in nation building and social development. As monks sought new identities and roles in a fast-changing world, they came under increasing pressure to guide the public into a new era. Simultaneously, lay Buddhist activists have been gaining unprecedented importance in new Buddhist movements of a reformist and modernist hue.

The Dhammapada is an important and popular scripture in the Pali tradition. The second chapter, from which the extracts here are taken, is regarded to have special contemporary relevance.

The path to the Deathless is awareness;
Unawareness, the path of death.

They who are aware do not die;
They who are unaware are as dead . . .

Those meditators, persevering,
Forever firm of enterprise,
Those steadfast ones touch *Nibbāna*,
Incomparable release from bonds.

By standing alert, by awareness,
By restraint and control too,
The intelligent one could make an island
That a flood does not overwhelm.

Fame increases for the one who stands alert,
Mindful, and of pure deeds;
Who with due consideration acts, restrained,
Who lives *dhamma*, being aware . . .

Engage not in unawareness,
Nor in intimacy with sensual delight.
Meditating, the one who is aware
Attains extensive ease . . .

Among those unaware, the one aware,
Among the sleepers, the wide-awake,
The one with great wisdom moves on,
As a racehorse who leaves behind a nag.

From J.R. Carter and Mahinda Palihawadana (trans.): *Sacred Writings, Buddhism: The Dhammapada* (New York: Quality Paperback Book Club, 1992)

BOX 3.2 Awareness (Appamāda-vaggo)

Sri Lanka

Sri Lanka is geographically part of South Asia, but has clear cultural links with Southeast Asia. Compared with other countries in the region, Sri Lanka was subjected to foreign domination for much longer – ever since Portuguese traders arrived at the beginning of the sixteenth century. Although it remained independent during the earlier period of Portuguese rule and then Dutch in the seventeenth century, the royal Kandyan kingdom succumbed to the British rule in 1815. Christian missionaries challenged the status quo of Sinhalese (Sri Lankan) Buddhist monks and engaged them in a series of public debates. Although hampered by the absence of traditional state support, monks had some success in these debates with Christians, arguing that Buddhism was neither backward nor superstitious, but rather a rational, indeed scientific, teaching. Around the turn of the twentieth century, the urge to reassess and promote their revitalized religious identity became merged with strong aspirations for independence.

An important Buddhist reformer, Anagārika Dharmapāla (1864–1933), founded the Mahā Bodhi Society in 1891, and attempted to create a modern Sinhala-Buddhist identity. He was one of the main exponents of a reformed version of Buddhism often referred to as 'Protestant Buddhism', a term first coined by Obeyesekere in 1970, which referred to the 'protest' against Christian missionaries, coupled with the adoption by Buddhist revivalists of some of the traits and methods used by Protestant Christianity. Those sympathetic to this movement, came largely from the English-speaking urban middle class whose religious orientation was liberal and modernist. The reformed Buddhists manifested a puritan streak, emphasizing moral discipline and meditation, and there was a shift of emphasis from traditional ritual and merit making (through offerings to monks) to individual responsibility. There also emerged a new type of Buddhist activism, which considered social and even political engagement relevant for spiritual growth.

Involvement in the independence movement included scholarly monks such as Walpola Rahula (1907–97), who became openly active in the mid-1940s, promoting religious patriotism and arguing that monks had a duty to engage in national politics for the common good. The period after independence in 1948 saw renewed enthusiasm and pride in the Buddhist heritage. Sri Lankan monks travelled abroad to teach and instruct in meditation, while eminent Buddhist scholars published influential writings in Buddhist philosophy. The EBP (Eksath Bhikkhu Peramuna) was formed in 1952, a monastic political party which, alongside populist grassroot groups with lay and monastic leaders such as MEP (Mahajana Eksath Peramuna), became active in promoting Sinhalese Buddhist nationalism.

The first elected Sinhala-dominated government, led by Bandaranaike, forwarded a bill to privilege Sinhala, the language of the majority, and various nationalist campaigns promoted Sinhalese culture and Buddhism, which alienated the (Hindu) Tamils who had enjoyed certain privileges under the colonial rule. The upsurge of Sinhalese nationalism was not, however, supported by all Buddhists and monks. Some opposed the fusion of Buddhism and nationalism, fearing that it might fuel ethnic conflict with the Tamil population. Nonetheless, this was precisely what happened in the decades that followed. Triggered by the killing of government soldiers in 1983 by LTTE (Liberation Tigers of Tamil Eelam), the Tamil independence movement became increasingly militant, and with violence escalating, some monks have started to advocate war to maintain order.

Others have considered social development and politics a distraction from spiritual development. Forest monks have revived the traditional ascetic ideal, retreating from human habitation and secular activities to concentrate on meditation. Their followers include many modernist lay Buddhists attracted to their ancient spiritual ideal and stoical discipline. Meanwhile, the concept of *urumaya*, the Buddhist heritage, continues to associate Buddhism and Sri Lanka as a nation state, in its royal chronicles, historical narratives, and a large number of sacred archaeological sites believed to contain the Buddha's relics.

Laos, Cambodia, Burma

Buddhism in twentieth-century Laos, Cambodia and Burma demonstrates how relations with communist and socialist regimes have varied as each country struggled to maintain its autonomy through the control of the monastic community. In Laos, the Pathet Lao revolutionary movement had infiltrated the Sangha from the 1950s by propagating anti-imperialist slogans and appealing to monks from rural and poorer areas. Cambodia became independent in 1953, and King Sihanouk turned to Buddhism to steer a middle course between communism in Vietnam and American capitalism in Thailand. The Thai government in the 1960s began to actively recruit and train monks to provide leadership for rural development and become the vanguard of anti-communist propaganda. Divisions within the Sangha were exploited (Thommayut and Mahanikay, and later old and new Mahanikay orders in Cambodia, for example), representing a divide between urban elite and rural peasants, which added to the polarization process.

The 1970s saw Buddhism dragged even further into the revolutionary struggle. After Pathet Lao came to power in Laos in 1975, there were further efforts to find common ground between Buddhism and socialism. Monks were again used as propaganda agents to gain support for the communist regime, preaching that these two ideologies were compatible. Simultaneously, traditional Buddhist beliefs underwent scrutiny and those regarded as 'superstitious' (including much of the cosmology) were purged. Even the traditional notion of *karma* was rejected during this time. The custom of feeding monks and donating to monasteries was regarded as redundant, so the only option for monks in Laos was to become part of the political agenda. Young monks were encouraged to join the revolution as teachers and health workers. Yet, Buddhism was never targeted to the degree that it was in Cambodia; the party was relatively careful not to provide a focus for popular resentment.

In Cambodia, in contrast, after Sihanouk was deposed in 1970, the Khmer Rouge, a quasi-socialist group led by a despotic leader, Pol Pot, came to rule between 1975 and 1979. Advocating rural living and economic self-sufficiency, they targeted Buddhism as foreign, unpatriotic and valueless, and attacked it with devastating consequences. Monks were labelled corrupt parasites, and sent for re-education and forced labour. Villagers were discouraged from offering donations or inviting monks to officiate rituals, so monks came to be deprived of traditional sources of income. In the revolutionary excesses, more than 60,000 monks are said to have been killed or forced to disrobe. Buddhism went into considerable decline. Since the late 1980s, however, reconstruction of monasteries, and rebuilding of the ecclesiastical structure and monastic education have begun in both Laos and Cambodia. Especially in Cambodia, where Buddhism came near to extinction, religious rebuilding began in earnest with the support of international aid. In recent years, the monastic community seems to be reclaiming its place as an essential institution, uniting the torn country and people. Buddhist monks have been active in the restoration movement, and since 1992, a new non-partisan Buddhist activism has manifested in an annual peace march initiated by the monk Maha Ghosananda (1929–2007). This was in the tradition of Cambodian monks who led anti-colonial marches against the French rule in the 1940s.

Burma offers yet another example of close relations between state and religion. The Burmese Sangha remained relatively unified despite British rule and the demise of the kingship in 1853, notwithstanding its history of fragmentation into sects and branches. Christian missionaries were active from the early nineteenth century, but interfaith dialogue and rigorous soul searching were less evident than in Sri Lanka. Nor did Burma produce prominent religious activists such as Dharmapāla in Sri Lanka or social critics like Buddhadasa in Thailand to advocate new directions for modern spirituality. Yet the Sangha retained its traditional reciprocal relationships with the laity, commanding authority and respect, and providing a kernel for Burmese nationalism. It also maintained high standards of Buddhist scholarship among both monks and nuns, producing many famous *dhamma* teachers such as Mahasi Sayadaw (1904–82), instrumental in disseminating Vipassanā meditation to countries outside of Burma. Mingun Sayadaw (1911–93) became the first monk to memorise the entire canon of Tipitaka (7,983 pages) since the Tipitaka Selection Examination was introduced by the government in 1948. Both monks took prominent part in the Sixth Buddhist Council (1954–56) convened during the reign of U Nu.

The first Prime Minister of Burma after independence, U Nu (r. 1948–62) cast himself in the role of an ideal Buddhist ruler, applying Aśokan ideals to his political policies. He promoted a type of Buddhist nationalism by implementing moral policies and hosting the above-mentioned Sixth Great Buddhist Council to commemorate the 2,500th anniversary of the Buddha's enlightenment. However, his enthusiasm for reviving the Buddhist ideal proved unable to accommodate the political realities of the time. In 1962, he was removed in the military coup led by General Ne Win. His socialist government distanced religion from politics, whilst attempting to control the Sangha by compulsory registration and removing anti-government monks from positions of influence. During several decades of imposed isolation, monks withdrew or kept away from the political scene. Ironically, this period allowed the Sangha to consolidate their relationship with its lay congregation, providing them with a solid moral base, later to develop into a strong foundation to counter political oppression.

The Burmese Sangha has historically been an important rallying point for resistance and monks were prominent in political protests during the colonial 1930s, during the independence movements in the 1940s, and in support of the student activists during the last pro-democracy uprising in 1988. Although monks did not directly participate in violence, many were actively supportive of the pro-democratic movement and later of the NLD (National League for Democracy) led by Aung San Suu Kyi, which won the 1990 election. In the following years, however, the regime arrested hundreds of monk activists, forcing many to disrobe or escape to other countries. Monks showed their defiance by overturning their begging bowls and refusing food from the military regime, depriving ruling generals of the chance to acquire merit regarded essential for better rebirth.

Since the early 1990s, the government has tried to both control and cajole the monks and the Sangha has become invoked as a unifying force for the country. The regime has also attempted to lay claim to the traditional role of the state as 'protector of faith', restoring monasteries and sacred sites, offering senior monks and nuns special privileges to win back their support. Nevertheless, the monastic community has continued to serve as an alternative focus of defiance against the regime, using its wide moral influence that extends to the village level. In 2007, general unrest started against the backdrop of a sudden hike in fuel prices and exorbitant inflation, led by monks in a provincial town in Upper Burma. The protests were soon quelled, although they had spread across wide areas of the country, nevertheless, the active involvement of monks in demonstrations showed how faith embedded in the moral fabric of society continues to be a destabilizing adversary of an oppressive regime.

Thailand

Thailand is the only country in Southeast Asia that did not come under colonial rule, and it has been politically stable and prosperous since the late eighteenth century. The kingship has lent Thailand stability although it moved to constitutional monarchy and parliamentary government in 1932. The present King Bhumibol (r. 1946–) has exerted special authority at times of national crisis, and during the attempted coups d'état in the 1980s and 1990s, which failed to receive royal approval. In contrast to gradual development and social adjustment in Sri Lanka, Thailand has experienced rapid economic growth and major structural changes in the last half-century. With one of the world's fastest growing economies, the country has also reaped some of the consequences in social and regional dislocation, inequality, corruption and disenchantment with the establishment. There have been social protests, and inertia in the Sangha led to reformist Buddhist movements in the 1970s.

The state has played a major role in modernizing Thai Buddhism since the time of King Rama the Fourth (r. 1851–68), conducting Sangha reforms, founding the Thammayut lineage, and introducing a new form of monasticism. King Chulalongkorn (r. 1868–1910) continued his father's legacy in centralizing Sangha administration, uniting the sects and standardizing Buddhist education for monks. However, Buddhism seems to have changed most after Sarit Tharanat's government came to power in 1957, as he actively sought to strengthen national unity by bringing together traditional values associated with the king and Buddhism. Monks were trained for national programmes to promote community development in peripheral regions, and the government, perhaps fearing communist infiltration, sent them to minister to ethnic groups in the northern hills. The Sangha thus became part of the political programme for the promotion of national goals. In the process, monks who expressed opposition to government policies, such as the Mahanikay monk Phra Phimolatham, were labelled communists and expelled from the order.

Public regard for the Sangha in Thailand diminished as a consequence of the close relationship between the government, military, big business and the Sangha. Mounting disenchantment was expressed at the lack of spiritual direction provided by monks in a rapidly growing consumerist society. One consequence was that reformist Buddhist groups emerged in urban centres in the 1970s, representing a new social movement motivated initially by urban middle class activists and students hoping to force the Sangha to overcome corruption and assert strong leadership. One of the most important religious reformers in the twentieth century was the monk Buddhadasa (1906–93), who integrated modernist rationalism and a distinctive forest tradition. His liberal interpretation of canonical texts attracted an educated elite following and provided an ideological base for contemporary Buddhist activism. Although Buddhadasa was a 'career monk' who had received traditional monastic education, he was remarkably critical of the Sangha and of the contemporary social situation. He rejected ritual practice and merit-making, and interpreted traditional concepts such as not-self, *Nibbāna*, rebirth, and emptiness as moral principles for 'this' life. Although Buddhadasa's movement, Suan Mokkh (Garden of Liberation), which advocated social justice in the concept of 'Dhammic socialism', was not supported by mainstream Buddhists, he left an important legacy of new directions for cultivating contemporary spirituality and promoting 'this-worldly' Buddhism.

A group directly indebted to Buddhadasa is Santi Asok, started by Phra Bodhiraksa in 1970. It started as a sectarian protest movement that came to Thai people's attention by repeatedly criticizing the state-controlled Sangha. The Asok movement presented a new Buddhist vision, replacing traditional ritual with hard work and stoical discipline, frugal communal living and agricultural self-sufficiency. In short, the members presented a radical moral critique of contemporary Thai society and Sangha by living an alternative lifestyle. In contrast, other lay Buddhist groups attracted the rich and successful by embracing capitalist values and consumerist lifestyles. Dhammakaya (Dharma-Body), for example, led by Phra Dhammajayo and established in the 1970s, advocated a type of visualization meditation through which it claimed followers could become even more successful in reaping the fruits of the capitalist economy.

In recent years, Buddhist social activists in Thailand such as Sulak Sivaraksa have fought against social injustice and environmental degradation, and contributed to a growing lay activist movement by forming a wide network of non-sectarian grassroot activists. There are also activist monks, such as Phra Khru Man Nathipitak, who affiliated themselves with the Sekhiya Dhamma Sangha founded in 1989, and participated in education and community development. These monks, who address contemporary problems of deforestation, poverty, drug addiction and AIDS, have been criticized for their close involvement with worldly issues. However, many justified their involvement as duty to the community, but distinguished themselves from the so-called development monks involved in state programmes of development. By contrast, the forest monk tradition continues, especially in the northeast, concentrating on meditation and traditional practices of magical protection and ritual, whilst resisting the hegemonic influence of the state-controlled Sangha.

Gender and status in Southeast Asian Buddhism

In the Theravāda tradition, the ordination lineage of female monks called *bhikkhunīs* apparently disappeared in eleventh-century Sri Lanka and thirteenth-century Burma. Since then Theravāda nuns have been without official religious status. Therefore, although they shave their hair, fast in the afternoons and are celibate, contemporary Buddhist nuns in the Southern tradition are no more than 'pious lay women'. They observe eight to ten Buddhist precepts, which are equivalent to those observed by lay people on special religious occasions. Nonetheless, nuns have been integrally involved in the monastic community, actively supporting the monks and novices. In Southern Buddhist countries today, there are approximately 5,000 nuns in Sri Lanka, 8,000 in Thailand, 5,000 in Cambodia and Laos, and more than 40,000 in Burma. The fact that the number of nuns is so large implies that, in practice, they perform important religious functions in society.

Since the mid-1980s, the movement to restore the *bhikkhunī* lineage, initially instigated by Western Buddhist nuns and intellectuals, has been increasingly supported by local Buddhist activists. They assert that the female lineage has survived in the Dharmagupta Vinaya preserved in East Asian countries, and thus the ordination procedure for Southern Buddhist nuns could theoretically be revived. In 1996, the first higher ordination was conferred on ten Sri Lankan ten-precept nuns in Sarnath, India, who became the first batch of *bhikkhunīs* in the contemporary Theravāda tradition. A year and a half later, another higher ordination took place in Bodh-gayā, organized by Fo Guang Shan, an active Taiwanese Buddhist organization promoting humanistic Buddhism. In terms of technicality, this was considered to be the most complete *upasampadā* performed for Buddhist nuns in recent years.

Once ordinations began to be conducted on Sri Lankan soil, however, opposition grew vociferous, and proponents of the *bhikkhunī* restoration were criticized for creating disunity in the Sangha and violating the consecrated spaces in monasteries. Nevertheless, some monks supporting its revival, such as Inamaluwe Sumangala, since 1998, started to conduct regular higher ordinations for female candidates at his Dambulla temple. Nuns from Thailand, such as the Buddhist scholar Chatsumarn Kabilsingh, followed suit, and many have travelled to Sri Lanka to receive higher ordination. However, the controversy that erupted after a Burmese nun was ordained in Sri Lanka without the consent of the Burmese Sangha closed the debate regarding the *bhikkhunī* revival in Burma. The difficulty for newly ordained *bhikkhunīs* lies in the fact that their future remains in the hands of senior monks who influence the views of general public on whom they are materially dependent.

From a sociological perspective, women in Southeast Asian societies (even in Muslim-dominated Malaysia and Indonesia) have traditionally enjoyed high status and economic independence. They are visibly active and a large proportion of women engage in market trade as family breadwinners. The bilateral kinship system and lack of emphasis on the family as a collective unit seems to have supported flexibility in gender roles, in which marriage does not change women's status. The situation, however, is gradually changing. The growth of the Chinese population has brought Confucian values to the

FIGURE 3.1
Initiation as a nun

Temporary initiation has become increasingly popular amongst young girls in Burma. She stays in the nunnery to learn the prayers and observes monastic discipline, which includes sexual abstinence and fasting in the afternoon. Normally the length of stay is between a week to a month. Courtesy Hiroko Kawanami.

region, in which women are subordinate within their husbands' families. Even if traditional advantages persist, high social standing does not seem to generate authority for women in the religious domain. On the contrary, according to their self-perception and religious ideology, economic power is not seen as a source of spiritual potency, but more as a reflection of women's 'this-worldly' and materialistic nature. By the same token, motherhood is valued for Buddhist women, yet simultaneously depicted in vernacular texts as symbolizing attachment that binds them to the cycle of rebirth, and ultimately restricting spiritual progress. Nonetheless, opting out of marriage and childbearing as a nun brings opposition and hostility rather than moral support.

The presence of contemporary nuns in Southeast Asia seems to challenge the cultural and religious ideal that allows males to renounce their householder roles and become monks, whilst expecting females to look after the family and support the Sangha. A male is thought to have opportunities to steadily work towards enlightenment, whilst a female can only hope for a better rebirth. The nuns are anomalous in this scheme, yet remain supportive of the Sangha. In many Burmese monasteries, nuns are indispensable as treasurers and secretaries. They also cook for monks and look after their welfare and health. By taking on such subservient roles and merging their interests in the Sangha, however, nuns seem to have made their unofficial religious position acceptable. Whilst lay Buddhists are claiming more religious influence and questioning the traditional role of the Sangha, it seems crucial that the monks realize that the sustenance of the Sangha also relies on these nuns who protect the sanctity of monks from the encroaching influence of worldly corruption.

Tibet

The impact of Chinese Communism

In the first half of the twentieth century, Tibet was neither politically nor economically isolated. Lamas travelling to India arranged for religious works to be printed using modern printing presses, a development which would lead to wider readerships. However, the religious establishment as a whole, and especially the principal Gelukpa monasteries in the Lhasa area, exercizing a de facto veto over the government, strongly resisted socio-economic change, which they saw as threatening the dharma. Modifications to the socio-political structure were begun with the support of the thirteenth Dalai Lama (1876–1933), but the changes were limited by monastic interests.

Tibet's first large-scale encounter with modernity came with the Chinese communist invasion and occupation of Tibet from the early 1950s. Radical socio-economic upheaval, appropriations of wealth and attacks on monastic institutions were begun in eastern Tibet in the 1950s, and throughout Tibet after the abortive 1959 uprising, when about 100,000 refugees escaped to India and surrounding countries. Forcible political and economic reorganization was justified in terms of a Marxist ideology infused with an imperialist emphasis on allegiance to the Chinese state, and by notions of Tibetan socio-cultural backwardness and their need to be helped to progress by their Chinese masters. Matters were further exacerbated by the Chinese Cultural Revolution, in which even private religious expressions and Tibetan cultural traditions were suppressed. The entire monastic system and its socio-economic support structure was disbanded, many monks and nuns forced to disrobe, and even much of their textual heritage destroyed.

After the Cultural Revolution, which in the Tibetan case did not end until the early 1980s, the Chinese communist rhetoric of liberation from imperialism, feudalism and religion was toned down, and there were some liberalizations, permitting limited religious activities in recognition that outright oppression of religion had been counter-productive. The change of policy was also fuelled by the hope that further economic integration into the People's Republic of China (PRC) would undermine Tibetan religious belief and practice without the need for costly forcible repression. Different factions within the Chinese government today remain divided over policies towards 'minority' ethnic groups and religions. One approach favours toleration towards religion and different ethnic cultural traditions so long as they provide no threat to national unity, and accept institutional state control. The other, hardline approach points to the role of religion and ethnic traditions in resisting political and economic integration, and continues to see the outright suppression of religion as a necessity. This faction has been increasingly vocal and influential since 1995, and particularly in the Lhasa and central Tibetan areas, there has been some renewal of interference even in individual religious expressions.

Continuing aspirations for genuine autonomy and religious freedom have been witnessed in protests throughout the Tibetan plateau in 2008. As in the case of Burma, even severe repression by an authoritarian government has not altogether quelled the

Buddhist monastic voice, all the more so given the Chinese State's close regulation of the monasteries, which has undermined its claim to allow free religious expression.

From the outset, a major effect of Chinese persecution was to strengthen Tibetan concern to preserve their cultural heritage; Buddhism became a symbol of Tibetan ethnic aspirations. The remarkable success of the 'reconstruction' of Tibetan monasteries since the early 1960s by Tibetan exiles in the Indian subcontinent and beyond, and since the early 1980s by Tibetans in the PRC, must be related to the urgency of a people whose culture has suffered devastation. Yet while there is stress on recovering and preserving 'tradition', we are not dealing with conservatism. Indeed, a conservative rejection of modernity is not an option, given the loss of Tibetan political and economic autonomy and of the traditional system for monastic support. Of necessity, contemporary monasteries are organized within an entirely different legal and economic framework from that which existed in premodern Tibet, and lamas must attract patronage not only from traditional sponsors, such as Himalayan Buddhists in the case of the exiled monasteries, but also from wider international sources, especially East Asian and Western Buddhists. Thus the premodern pattern of a multiplicity of religious authorities and of various religious traditions cutting across monastic affiliations described above has become even more prominent in recent history, with neither the former Tibetan governmental apparatus nor the institutional centres of each monastic order retaining any effective socio-economic controls over individual lamas or monasteries. In the Indian subcontinent, the government-in-exile structure has brought some cohesion, but has had little effect on monastic organization. At the local level, Tibetans have attempted to keep alive some traditional connections between monasteries and communities.

In exile, some of the monasteries represent groups of refugees from specific areas who have worked to rebuild their own monasteries. In Tibet, in similar efforts to re-establish relations between local monasteries and lay communities, Tibetans resist Chinese policies defining religion in terms of individual belief, but their success is inevitably restricted in a political climate in which the state will still not tolerate any threat to its monopoly of power. In parts of Nepal and Ladakh, the effects of integration into the national economy and society has often reduced the political influence of traditional Buddhist institutions, while religious renewal has been encouraged by closer links with Tibetan exiled lamas and their new monasteries.

In terms of individual religious practice of the three types in Tibetan Buddhism (see p. 75), opportunities for each were curtailed by the devastation of Buddhism in Tibet. The scholarly institutes were affected most severely; in Tibet, an entire generation was denied the option of scholastic training, and by the 1980s there were few surviving scholar monk teachers. Now, however, there is some revival of scholarly institutes and training. Meditation teaching was also severely disrupted, although meditation traditions are more able to survive without institutional backing. While open practice of long contemplative retreats was only possible outside the PRC until recent years, some meditation masters have gained renown through stories of their seemingly miraculous escape from persecution during the Cultural Revolution. Although no one was unaffected by the radical change enforced on Tibetan society, it would appear that the lay mantra practitioner religious practices were not altogether eclipsed, since their integration with lay life made them less obvious targets for anti-Buddhist persecution.

Renewal of tradition and recent developments

The new international contexts in which Tibetan Buddhism must now survive, and indeed appears to thrive, coupled with weakening of traditional institutional regulation, have fostered an environment conducive to new and varied presentations of Buddhist teaching. Tibetan lamas now cater for Tibetans who receive modern education and may work in modern economies in the PRC, India and elsewhere. In some respects, Tibetan Buddhism has been rapidly catapulted from a premodern social context to one of postmodernity, missing out on some characteristic features of the encounter with modernity, such as gradual engagement with scientific rationality and modern nation states.

This does not mean that Buddhist doctrines are being radically reformulated or Buddhist practices changed beyond recognition. On the contrary, great efforts are put into the recovery of the scriptural heritage and the preservation of meditative and ritual traditions. Elaborate rituals with established written liturgies and ritual manuals remain central to monastic life, and there is considerable support for long contemplative retreats along traditional lines. Rather, creativity is evident in the ways in which tradition is interpreted to contemporary Tibetans and non-Tibetans, with variations in choice of practices, and an emphasis that teaching should relate to audience and situation.

In Tibet itself we currently find instances where either (a) Buddhist revival steers a careful path between enhancing Tibetan identity and co-operating with the Chinese authorities; and (b) more confrontational approaches in which modern ideas concerning human rights and democracy are blended with Buddhism in opposition to the restrictions and ideology of the Chinese state. In the diaspora community there has been involvement in conversations with Western sympathizers on contemporary issues such as war and peace, environmental degradation and feminism. The Dalai Lama has written extensively in English, combining quite traditional Buddhist ethical perspectives with modern concerns.

One international development is the transportation of Buddhist ritual symbolism into environments foreign to its traditional contexts – for example, *mandalas* constructed for cultural exhibitions, or monastic ritual dances performed in modern theatres. Tibetan lamas have encouraged the development of internet sites to propagate and advertise their teachings, monasteries and new-style Buddhist centres, and popular books on Buddhist practice have appeared, written in English and with international sales, frequently simplifying traditional Buddhist practices to make them accessible to non-specialists. At the same time, the centre of gravity in Tibetan Buddhism remains with lamas based in monasteries in the Indian subcontinent and Tibet; these lamas have reservations about the value of relatively superficial explorations of the religion, and work for the establishment of more serious supports for Buddhist practice, such as long-term retreat facilities.

FIGURE 3.2 The Dalai Lama

The fourteenth Dalai Lama addressing an audience of Tibetans, Dharamsala, India, 2000. Courtesy Shimon Lev.

In premodern Tibet, the Dalai Lama was the head of state, a role which did not always entail direct political involvement, but an active and politically skilled Dalai Lama could have a major impact on government. The Dalai Lama was an important figure of the Geluk tradition, which was politically and numerically dominant in Central Tibet, but his religious authority went beyond sectarian boundaries. While he had no formal or institutional role in each religious tradition, which was headed by its own high lamas, he was a unifying symbol of the Tibetan state, representing Buddhist values and traditions above any specific school. Furthermore, he was held in the highest esteem and treated with great devotion by Tibetans well beyond the political boundaries of premodern Tibet. This traditional function of the Dalai Lama as an ecumenical figure, holding together disparate religious and regional groups, has been enthusiastically taken up by the present (fourteenth) Dalai Lama, who has worked to overcome sectarian and other divisions in the exiled community, and has become a symbol of Tibetan nationhood for Tibetans both in Tibet and in exile. At the same time, the Dalai Lama has expanded his constituency even further and become a major international representative not only of the Buddhist tradition, but also of ethical values which he sees as going beyond Buddhism and even beyond particular religions. As such, he has actively participated in international forums, has become widely respected globally, and has attracted popular support in Asian and Western countries.

I am a comparative newcomer to the modern world. Although I fled my homeland as long ago as 1959, and although my life since then as a refugee in India has brought me into much closer contact with contemporary society, my formative years were spent largely cut off from the realities of the twentieth century. This was partly due to my appointment as Dalai Lama: I became a monk at a very early age. It also reflects the fact that we Tibetans had chosen – mistakenly in my view – to remain isolated behind the high mountain ranges which separate our country from the rest of the world . . .

In the past, families and small communities could exist more or less independently of one another . . . This is no longer the case. Today's reality is so complex and so clearly interconnected on the material level that a different outlook is needed . . . we cannot afford to ignore others' interests any longer . . .

Given today's reality, it is therefore essential to cultivate a sense of what I call universal responsibility. This may not be an exact translation of the Tibetan term I have in mind, chi-sem, which means literally universal (*chi*) consciousness (*sem*). . . . What is entailed . . . is . . . a re-orientation of our heart and mind away from self and towards others . . .

It is a matter of common sense . . . There is no denying that our happiness is inextricably bound up with the happiness of others . . . Thus we can reject everything else: religion, ideology, all received wisdom. But we cannot escape the necessity of love and compassion.

Ancient Wisdom, Modern World: Ethics for a New Millennium
(London: Little, Brown & Co., 1999)

BOX 3.3 H.H. The Dalai Lama

Authority in contemporary Tibetan Buddhism

Different traditional understandings of what constitutes 'authentic' Buddhism live on. A collection of Indic Buddhist scriptures, the Kanjur (*bka' 'gyur*), considered to be the historical Buddha's actual words (but now shown by modern scholars mainly to derive from later Indian developments) was compiled in the fourteenth century. Conservative Tibetan scholars saw this as the only authentic 'Buddha Word', a view which often dominated politically influential scholastic traditions. However, an important strand in Tibetan scholasticism emphasized the idea that the real essence of the 'Buddha Word' is to be defined in terms of its enlightening qualities, not in terms of historical authenticity. This was linked to a high valuation of the traditionally accepted works of interpretation and of Buddhist philosophy, which for many scholars were of greater value than the original scripture. Logic and reasoning were given greater worth than mere scriptural citation, which was considered to have limited use without interpretation. Thus, although some of the assumptions of Buddhist scholastics, such as those concerning the historical origins of scriptures, are being challenged in today's world, the scholastic emphasis on reasoned argument and debate, and the scope for re-interpretation of scripture, means that not even the conservative wing of the scholastic tradition is entirely closed to new approaches.

Scholar monks and lamas today receive broader education than would be covered in traditional curricula, and not only do they have some modern education and foreign language training, but there has been some reworking of scholastic syllabuses. At the Central Institute of Higher Tibetan Studies in Sarnath, traditional and modern scholarship are combined in an institution in the Indian university sector, where scholars from different Tibetan traditions are represented and Sanskrit learning has been revived. There is scholastic interest in debates with Western and Indian philosophy, and some traditionally trained scholar monks have joined Western academic institutions. While such exchanges may not be unproblematic for Buddhist scholarship, it seems likely that the traditions will be resilient enough to adapt and integrate more critical approaches to their textual heritage.

The alternative idea that new scriptures may be appropriate for different times was principally represented by the Nyingmapa (*rnying ma pa*) who follow tantric scriptures, which were rejected from the Kanjur because of non-Indic origins. The Nyingmapa still reveal new tantric scriptures (*gter ma*) today. These traditions were also popular in some Kagyupa and Sakyapa circles. New revelations by prominent mantra practitioner lamas are now playing a role in the dynamics of Tibetan Buddhist reconstruction. The meditative traditions which can be found across the different schools have also been resilient. The idea that direct realization of enlightenment is a fruit of meditative endeavour and not of book learning, remains powerful in Tibetan contexts. Today, it is also presented with some success to Western and other non-Tibetan spiritual seekers.

Gender and status

Institutional restrictions often co-exist with active informal involvement. In the Tibetan case, women were unable to penetrate monastic hierarchies, and scholarly training, centred in high-status monastic colleges, was not open to them. Despite limitations on their full participation in religious life, it would be a mistake to assume that women have entirely acquiesced in subservient roles in Buddhism. A small number of women from higher class and especially high status religious families were able to secure a good Buddhist education. But few nuns were well educated: nunneries, where they existed, were usually small-scale institutions, often junior partners to nearby monasteries. Nuns were generally expected to learn and recite prayers and rituals, not to study philosophy. Most of them lived full- or part-time with their families, rather than in nunneries, often having domestic duties. Yet, despite these impediments, vigorous nunneries were established or expanded thanks to the efforts at a local level of determined nuns. Such cases were dependent on the inspiration and involvement of high status lamas and local community support. Women were not so constrained in the meditation traditions as they were in the formal authority structure of the Sangha and in scholarship. Some nuns made great efforts to travel to receive meditation instruction, and there was widespread acceptance of both male and female itinerant practitioners, who might spend extended periods visiting lamas, making pilgrimages and doing retreat. There were examples of women meditation adepts, a few of whom became teachers in their own right. Women were also often significant in lay hereditary teaching lineages. While the official lineage bearers were invariably men, women had informal importance, a fact which is reflected in the scriptural heritage of these traditions, making a female consort necessary to the success of a *gter ston* (revealer of tantric scripture), not for her reproductive powers but for her spiritual inspiration and abilities to generate auspicious conditions for the new revelation of scripture. In other traditions too, a woman could secure a good religious training and gain respect by marriage to a high lama, and might eventually be able to teach, although her status was essentially dependent on that of her husband.

Since the radical break in institutional continuity which marked the Chinese invasion of Tibet, there has been some reassessment of the roles of women in Tibetan Buddhism, especially amongst the exiles, who have greater involvement in the international community. There have been moves (supported by the Dalai Lama) to reintroduce the full nuns' ordination from East Asian lineages (see above) and to improve the economic position, education and status of nuns. Women are still largely excluded from monastic educational institutions, although since the 1980s some nuns in Dharamsala (the seat of the Dalai Lama and the Tibetan government-in-exile) have started to study Buddhist philosophy, and elsewhere nuns' training has gradually improved. In contemporary Tibet, large numbers of nunneries have been re-established, and here too there appears to be some effort to provide nuns with reasonable training. Nuns in central Tibet have been in the forefront of political dissidence against the Chinese authorities, for which, like their monk counterparts, they have suffered imprisonment, torture and the closure of their institutions. Yet the rebuilding of nunneries continues.

While structural gender inequality in Tibetan Buddhism remains, many Tibetan nuns are cautious and unwilling to openly challenge monastic authorities. There is an awareness that more confrontational approaches might be counter-productive and that women may gain more by relying on their lamas to help them expand their informal role rather than attempting to make radical structural changes. Not all cases of contemporary influential Tibetan Buddhist women have been affected by modern liberal feminism. For example, a charismatic female meditation adept in 'Bri-gung, Tibet, has recently established herself in an apparently traditional position for a recognized emanation of the eighth-century female Buddhist saint Ye-shes mtsho-rgyal, and is active in recreating a nuns' community and revitalizing religious practice in the area.

East Asia

Buddhism in East Asia has co-existed with a number of religious traditions of the region such as Confucianism and Daoism in China, Shamanism in Korea and Shinto in Japan.

Moreover, a prevalent undercurrent of indigenous folk practices and ancestor worship has added to its diversity and pluralistic orientation.

Buddhism in Korea and parts of China were affected by Japanese colonialism in the 1930s and 1940s, as Buddhist missionaries advanced into the continent to spearhead the campaign for imperial Japan. Korean Buddhism had experienced an orthodox revival towards the end of the nineteenth century, and many lay Buddhist societies were established, rekindling an interest in the religion amongst ordinary people. Later, with the Japanese occupation and presence of Japanese Buddhist missionaries, Korean Buddhists began to modernize and reform their Buddhist practice and tradition. However, internal dissension intensified as the result of monastic movement to rid itself of 'married priests', a legacy of Japanese occupation, and confrontations between clerical groups led to an increased control of the state over the Sangha. In the 1980s, the ideology of *mingung Pulgyo* (Buddhism for the people) was promoted by younger generations of progressive monks who were initially anti-government, but later focused on social engagement in environmental protection and immediate issues that affected people's lives.

Although Buddhism in China declined since the thirteenth century, there were bouts of small-scale revival in the mid-nineteenth to the mid-twentieth century. Temples and monasteries were closed or destroyed, and monks and nuns suffered poverty under communist rule. And yet Buddhism survived the Cultural Revolution to a degree, and there has been renewed activity in certain regions since the late 1970s. In fact, the sense of revival seems to be the unifying factor in modern Chinese Buddhism after suffering a period of decline. The contemporary Chinese government is more tolerant of Buddhism, which tends to be seen as useful for promoting ties with other Buddhist countries in Asia, and state-sponsored reconstruction projects of temples and pilgrimage centres are aimed at attracting wealthy tourists from abroad. In contrast, post-war Taiwan, originally set up as an alternative power base by the defeated nationalist China, has seen the most vigorous revival of Chinese Buddhism. Freed from traditional constraints of monastic lineage and Confucian pressures, lay Buddhists and nuns have been active in promoting a new type of Buddhist movement emphasizing social welfare, education and meditation. Chinese modernist Buddhists see themselves as contributing to a modern revival of Buddhism through technological innovations, effective democratic management, and a 'humanistic' tone to make the *dharma* more accessible to society (see Chapter 5 on Chinese religions).

Meanwhile, in Japan, the twentieth century witnessed some reaction to Buddhist monasteries and priests who were seen as overtly commercial, concerning themselves purely with funerary rites for the dead. With rapid urbanization and other post-war developments, politically inclined lay Buddhist organizations developed, along with new religions catering for the needs of the individual in contemporary society (see Chapter 6 on Japanese religions).

Buddhism in the West

European intellectual curiosity in Buddhism dates from the mid-eighteenth century, but more general interest was initiated by scholars and philosophers who began translating Buddhist texts into European languages in the late nineteenth century. The Theosophical Society, founded in 1875 in New York, had some involvement in the Buddhist reformist movement in Sri Lanka. Contemporary Sinhalese Buddhists are sceptical of their influence in Asia, but Theosophists such as Henry Olcott certainly contributed to popularizing Buddhism amongst Western liberals and intellectuals, leaving a mark on the New Age movement in the West.

Buddhist teachings and traditions were brought to west coast America and Canada in the late nineteenth century along with immigrant labourers from China and Japan. Hawaii also became a major centre for Japanese Buddhism from the early twentieth century. Zen Buddhism gained particular popularity after the 1950s, partly due to the writings of D. Suzuki. The steady influx of refugees from Tibet after the 1950s, and from Vietnam, Laos and Cambodia in the 1970s, led to renewed interest in Buddhism, and the counter-cultural movements of the 1960s proved fertile ground for its diffusion. Almost all traditions of Buddhism were represented in America by then, as well as new Buddhist organizations such as Sōka Gakkai and other syncretic groups which became active in the latter part of the twentieth century.

Buddhism has seen its popularity rise as it has come to be transformed by exposure to liberal current of thoughts and become more acceptable to the values and modern living of the West. Specific ideals based on enlightenment values have permeated the self-identification of Western Buddhists and promoted a unique version of Buddhism as environmentalist, feminist, democratic, and socially engaged. More positive attractions of Buddhism have included an interest in its meditation traditions, its philosophy and psychological analyses of the human condition, as well as its empirical, experiential orientation. One significant strand in Buddhism is an emphasis on verifying the teachings for oneself, not only accepting them out of faith or respect for authority. In recent times, charismatic representatives of Buddhism, most notably the present Dalai Lama, have also been influential. Although Tibetan Buddhism was a late arrival on the Western scene, by the turn of the millennium it had became one of the most popular forms of Buddhism in the West.

Cultural differences between Western societies, together with the postmodern climate which favours diversity, have meant that successful Buddhist groups range from those focused exclusively on formless meditation to those promoting elaborate ritual symbolism; from those which stress the centrality of reasoning in Buddhist thought to those which stress faith and devotion; and from those rooted in the renunciatory values of traditional meditator strands to those combining Buddhism with social and political activism. Asian Buddhism has always had such variants, but it is more usual, even now, for certain strands to dominate in specific regions, and for affiliation to owe much to family and community involvements. On the contrary, in the West, most Buddhists are first or second generation converts, exercizing personal choice in affiliation, often after some spiritual exploration. The myriad types of Buddhist practice we now witness in Western countries also range from more explicitly liberal forms of Buddhism to branches of conservative Asian Buddhist traditions.

Even groups at the conservative end of the spectrum, however, such as representatives of the Thai Theravāda forest tradition who have established successful centres in southern England, cannot be entirely untouched by the radically different socio-cultural context in which they must operate. Furthermore, the lack of formal institutional controls on the part of traditional Buddhist authorities over the development of Western Buddhist groups, coupled with limited public knowledge of Buddhist traditions in Western countries, encourage a situation in which groups with little formal support in Asia may thrive, and innovative reinterpretation of Buddhism is common. Some early twentieth-century Western enthusiasts for Buddhism now appear to have retained vestiges of colonial arrogance in criticizing traditional Buddhists as corrupt and in advocating a 'Buddhism' purified of traditional Asian cultural practices. Some strands of contemporary Western Buddhism may be similarly ethnocentric, whilst others represent greater dialogue between Western and Asian Buddhist approaches. In a context in which Asian Buddhists are themselves re-evaluating their religious practices and responding to the challenges brought by modernity and postmodernity, some of the developments centred on the contemporary West may even in time have profound impact on Asian Buddhism.

Perhaps the general comment which can be made with the most confidence is that as yet the monastic Sangha does not have the central place in the West that it usually does in Asian Buddhist countries. While there are increasing numbers of Western monks and nuns, they are not always the main representatives of Western Buddhist groups, nor central to their organization. It is difficult to say how far the limited success of Buddhist monasticism in the West is a feature of limited resources for the support of those in full-time religious vocation (a feature which could change in time with the further expansion of Buddhism), or of cultural values inimical to the ways of life perceived as escapist or alien, or of urban lifestyles unsuited to monastic discipline.

Looking to the future

Buddhism, once largely a religion of agrarian Asian societies, has demonstrated vitality in surviving massive socio-economic change, contributing to the development of new ethnic and cultural identities in Asia, and adapting to numerous modern contexts internationally. Aspects of its heritage which fit well with postmodern environments include both its tolerance of diversity in social and kinship patterns and its teachings on the nature of mind, which underlie the Buddhist view that religious truth must be realized by each individual in a process of inner spiritual discovery.

The greatest challenge to Buddhism in modern times has undoubtedly been the loss of state and community support which were traditionally institutionalized in many Asian societies. Today, even where the Buddhist monastic Sangha retains an important place in society, it does not always represent the only or even the most influential voice on religious matters. Moreover, Buddhism has struggled to exist in the hostile environment of rapidly changing political regimes. Secular nation states in Asia, both communist and anti-communist, have alternately tried to control Buddhism, to eliminate it, or to harness it for the purposes of political legitimation.

Traditional Buddhist authorities have also had to cope with dramatic social change, increasing lay demands for involvement in religious practice, and various pressures as a result of political changes affecting monastic funding, organization, and education. And yet, despite adversity and rapid change, Buddhist monastic institutions have proved remarkably resilient. In some cases they have been revived in recent times, or taken the lead in religious and political developments. At times, as we have seen (most recently in Burma), they have been at the forefront of cultural and ethnic defence, and have even become agents of political action.

Buddhism's adaptability to postmodern conditions has been enhanced by a flexibility which stems in part from its own internal diversity. Buddhism's broad range of approaches to religious life stem from differences in the relative emphasis placed on morality, meditation or wisdom, and the contrasting models for religious practice. These variations characterized different traditions in the past, but today they facilitate flexibility, change and, increasingly, individual choice. Moreover, traditional attitudes of tolerance to alternative religious and philosophical viewpoints, so long as they promote well-being and reduce suffering, mean that contemporary representatives of Buddhist traditions have gained international respect by engaging readily in ecumenical dialogue.

Buddhism's survival in the modern world may also have been aided by the fact that, apart from its general ethical guidelines, it has little to say concerning 'correct' family or social relationships – these are 'worldly' matters, outside the proper scope of the religious tradition. Western cultural influences, together with socio-economic, environmental and political change in recent decades, have encouraged some rethinking of this approach. The new socially engaged movements within Buddhism are one result of this process. However, there seems little reason to anticipate the development of normative Buddhist teachings on family and social roles: not only would it be impossible to find agreement across different Buddhist schools, but the traditional flexibility seems a positive advantage in a world in which roles are continually being redefined in response to change. Equally, we find a number of quite different responses to political and environmental issues, ranging from withdrawal to activism – both can locate their authority in Buddhist scriptural sources.

At the same time, Buddhism does have well-developed perspectives on the psychology of individuals and methods for attaining liberation. There is the assumption that not only all humans but all living beings have much in common in terms of becoming attached to impermanent and unsatisfactory conditions as though they were stable and satisfying. Meditation techniques, many of which build on early Buddhist practices to generate tranquillity and insight, retain their traditional appeal, as well as seeming to fit with contemporary values stressing self-development and the cultivation of experience.

The twentieth century has witnessed meditation practice moving out of the confines of the monastery to be taken up by the laity, increasingly subject to the pressures of modern life. *Vipassanā*, a form of insight meditation that originally spread from Burma, has grown in popularity in Southern Buddhism and many meditation instructors have travelled to countries outside the confines of traditional Theravāda. Yet it is not only new lay urban forms of Buddhism which have been successful: the forest monk tradition with its overtones of ancient wisdom has attracted widespread support, including from the urban middle classes.

Buddhist scholarship, traditionally rooted in monastic learning, is increasingly challenged by the infringement of modern academic institutions and the perspectives of modern scholarship. Yet Buddhist philosophy has attracted some interest in global academic circles and there are instances of adaptations of the scholastic curriculum. A traditional assumption that the strength of Buddhism could be judged by the state of the monastic order may seem rather less relevant in today's world of lay meditation centres and the mass circulation of books on Buddhism, but it may be that it would be premature to dismiss it entirely.

Despite the very real setbacks which the Buddhist tradition has faced to its institutional position in Asia, far from witnessing the demise of a traditional religion uprooted from its socio-economic and cultural support systems, Buddhism has discovered both new and ancient sources of vitality on which to draw in its ongoing adaptations to modernity and postmodernity.

Summary

- For Asian Buddhism, modernity and postmodernity have involved radical socio-economic changes which in many cases have severed Buddhism from its traditional institutionalized support systems.

- There is continuity in some aspects of monastic organization in the modern world: in presentations of Buddhist doctrine in terms of morality, meditation and wisdom; in traditional models for the religious path; and in the range and flexibility of religious practices.

- Changes in socio-political, economic, technological and communication systems have engendered rethinking and reworking of the religious heritage, including reassessments of monastic and lay relations and roles, of Buddhist scholarship, gender relations and social and political involvements.

- Several new developments in Buddhism have been related to the internationalization or globalization of Buddhism: increased communication between Asian Buddhists as well as the expansion of Buddhism into Western countries.

Key terms

We have generally given the Sanskrit for Buddhist technical terms, although in specifically Theravāda or Tibetan contexts we have occasionally given the Pali or Tibetan respectively. (The following abbreviation implies S for Sanskrit, P for Pali, and T for Tibetan.)

Abhidhamma (P) / *Abhidharma* (S) Higher teachings, class of early Buddhist texts which systematized and expanded on the teachings given in the sutras.

bhikkhunī (P) / *bhikṣunī* (S) A Buddhist nun with full ordination almost equivalent to Buddhist monk (bhikkhu / bhikṣu).

bodhisattva One intent on attaining Buddhahood, in order to benefit all sentient beings and to bring them to enlightenment.

Buddha The awakened one, who has put an end to emotional defilements and attained enlightenment.

dhamma (P) / **dharma** (S) The teachings of the Buddha, the law, the true nature of reality.

dhammarāja The 'righteous king', who rules in accordance with the dhamma.

Geluk (T. *dge lugs*) One of the principal Tibetan Buddhist schools, whose followers are the Gelukpa (*dge lugs pa*).

Kagyu (T. *bka' brgyud*) One of the principal Tibetan Buddhist schools, whose followers are the Kagyupa (*bka' brgyud pa*).

Kanjur (T. *bka' 'gyur*) A collection of Indic Buddhist scriptures compiled in Tibet.

kamma (P) / **karma** (S) Laws of cause and effect, which according to Buddhist thinking operate rationally and are ethical in nature.

lama (T. *bla ma* / S. *guru*) A teacher in Tibetan Buddhism.

Mahāyāna 'Great Vehicle', a Buddhist movement which developed around the beginning of the Christian era.

Madhyamaka A philosophical school that analysed the deceptive nature of conceptual experience.

maṇḍala A representation of the tantric vision of reality in terms of an enlightened deity or circle of deities, abiding in a pure Buddha realm.

mantra practitioner (T. *sngags pa*) Lay tantric religious specialist.

Metteyya (P) / **Maitreya** (S) The coming Buddha.

mingung Pulgyo (Korean) Buddhism for the people.

Nibbāna (P) / **Nirvāṇa** (S) Enlightenment, the state of unconditioned existence and liberation from the cycle of rebirth.

Nyingma (T. *rnying ma*) One of the principal Tibetan Buddhist schools, whose followers are the Nyingmapa (*rnying ma pa*).

Pali An ancient Indian language in which the Theravāda scriptures are written.

reincarnate lamas (T. *sprul sku*) Tibetan teachers considered to be reincarnations of former Buddhist masters.

renouncer movement An ancient Indian movement of renouncers (S. *śramṇa*) who, in contrast to the Vedic tradition, stressed the renunciation of and liberation from worldly life.

ris med (T) An ecumenical movement in nineteenth-century Tibetan Buddhism which has had much effect on contemporary Tibetan Buddhism.

samsāra Endless rounds of rebirth.

sangha Monastic community.

Sakya (T. *sa skya*) One of the principal Tibetan Buddhist schools, whose followers are the Sakyapa (*sa skya pa*). The Buddhist community or order, often referring to the Sangha monastic order of monks and nuns. The noble Sangha consists of the spiritually advanced who are irreversibly established on the path to enlightenment.

sutta (P) / **sūtra** (S) A discourse; class of the earliest Buddhist scriptures containing teachings attributed to the Buddha, later expanded in the Mahāyāna.

Tantric Meditative and yogic traditions providing direct approaches to Enlightenment, often through the transformation of emotional and cognitive experience.

gter ma (T) Revealed tantric scriptures, revealed by discoverers called *gter ston*.

Theravāda 'Way of the Elders', the dominant tradition of Southern Buddhism.

therī Senior nuns in early Buddhism, many of whom were said to have attained liberation. Verses attributed to them were included in the early Buddhist corpus.

upasampadā Higher ordination.

urumaya (Sinhala) An ancient heritage, a sense of ownership.

Vajrayāna Tantric Buddhism.

Vinaya Class of the earliest Buddhist scriptures, monastic rules and regulation.

Vipassanā (P) A form of insight meditation, popularized in contemporary Theravāda Buddhism.

Yogācāra 'Practice of Yoga', named after one of its texts, it emphasizes the centrality of the meditational experience of pure consciousness.

Further reading

Introductory

For introductions to Buddhism, see P. Harvey: *An Introduction to Buddhism* (Cambridge: Cambridge University Press, 1990), a wide-ranging survey of Buddhist history, doctrines and practices, and R. Gethin: *The Foundations of Buddhism* (Oxford: Oxford University Press, 1998), which introduces the fundamentals of Buddhist thinking and practice underlying the mainstream Buddhist schools. For an illustrated collection on Buddhism's history and relationship with society, see H. Bechert and R. Gombrich (eds): *The World of Buddhism* (London: Thames & Hudson, 1984). On Mahayana doctrine, see P. Williams: *Mahayana Buddhism* (London: Routledge, 2008).

Early Buddhism and Theravāda

On early Indian Buddhism and Theravāda in Sri Lanka, including modern developments, see R. Gombrich: *Theravāda Buddhism* (London and New York: Routledge, 2006). On the revival of the forest monk tradition in Sri Lanka, see M. Carrithers: *The Forest Monks of Sri Lanka* (Delhi: Oxford University Press, 1983), and on late twentieth-century religious practice in Sri Lanka, see R. Gombrich and G. Obeyesekere: *Buddhism Transformed* (Princeton, NJ: Princeton University Press, 1988).

Gender

For early Buddhist nuns, see W. Pruitt (trans.): *The Commentary on the Verses of the Therīs*, by Ā. Dhammapāla (Oxford: Pali Text Society, 1988), and K. R. Blackstone: *Women in the Footsteps of the Buddha* (Richmond: Curzon, 1998). For an ethnographic study of nuns in the Tibetan tradition, see H. Havnevick: *Tibetan Buddhist Nuns* (Oslo: Institute for Comparative Research in Human Culture, Norwegian University Press, 1989). For a study of contemporary Thai Buddhist women, see C. Kabilsingh: *Thai Women in Buddhism* (Berkeley, CA: Parallax Press, 1991) and M. Lindberg-Falk: *Making Fields of Merit* (Copenhagen: NIAS, 2007). For a historical overview of modern Sri Lankan nuns, see T. Bartholomeusz: *Women under the Bo Tree* (Cambridge: Cambridge University Press, 1994).

Buddhism in Asia

S. C. Berkwitz (ed.): *Buddhism in World Cultures* (Santa Barbara, CA: ABC Clio, 2006) attempts to re-contextualize and understand Buddhism in the world today, following a volume with a similar aim by H. Dumoulin: *Buddhism in the Modern World* (New York: Macmillan, 1976). I. Harris (ed.): *Buddhism and Politics in Twentieth-Century Asia* (London: Cassell, 1999) examines the relationship between Buddhism and politics in the twentieth century. For a descriptive analysis of contemporary Buddhist practices, rituals and rites of passage in Buddhist societies in Southeast Asia, see D. Swearer: *The Buddhist World of Southeast Asia* (Albany, NY: SUNY, 1995).

Buddhism in Tibet

On Tibetan Buddhism, for historical developments and geographical variations, see G. Samuel: *Civilized Shamans* (Washington, DC: Smithsonian Institution Press, 1993). For an account of an early nineteenth-century meditator monk, see M. Ricard (trans.): *The Life of Shabkar* (Albany, NY: SUNY, 1994). For Buddhism and political protest in Tibet under Chinese rule, see R. Schwartz: *Circle of Protest* (London: Hurst & Company, 1994), and for religious practice in 1990s Tibet, see M. C. Goldstein and M. T. Kapstein: *Buddhism in Contemporary Tibet* (Berkeley, CA: University of California Press, 1998). More advanced reading on traditional Buddhist scholasticism can be found in J. I. Cabezón. *Buddhism and Language* (Albany, NY: SUNY, 1994). For a Nyingmapa perspective, see G. Dorje and M. Kapstein (trans. and ed.): *Dudjom Rinpoche: The Nyingma School of Tibetan Buddhism* (Boston, MA: Wisdom Publications, 1991).

Buddhism in the West

For a historical development of different schools of Buddhism in America, see R. H. Seager: *Buddhism in America* (New York: Columbia University Press, 1999). For a sociological study of the development of Buddhism in Western societies, see J. Coleman: *The New Buddhism* (Oxford: Oxford University Press, 2001). C. Prebish and M. Baumann (eds): *Westward Dharma* (Berkeley, CA: University of California Press, 2002) is a useful collection of essays that focus on various practices in Western forms of Buddhism. R. Bluck: *British Buddhism* (London: Routledge, 2006) offers a comprehensive survey of contemporary British Buddhism.

Chapter 4

Sikhism

Christopher Shackle

Introduction

The development of Sikhism over the five centuries of its history has always been closely tied to its homeland, the Punjab in north-western India (see map on p. 113). From an original context in which Hinduism and Islam were the opposed dominant creeds, Sikhism had evolved through one particularly significant internal change of emphasis and organization as the ethnic religion of a significant local minority when it was subjected to the impact of modernity caused by the British conquest of the Punjab in the mid-nineteenth century. Over the next century this colonial context therefore largely conditioned the pattern of Sikh responses to the modern world. Only more recently has that pattern itself begun to be questioned.

Although statistically one of the world's smaller religions, Sikhism's recognized status as a world religion is to be associated with the large diaspora established over the last fifty years through emigration to several countries in the English-speaking world. The Sikh diaspora, comprising about 1 million out of the world total of 16 million, is proportionately much larger than that of other recognized Asian religions, and in the ongoing articulation of responses to postcolonial modernity its voice has become increasingly significant.

TABLE 4.1 Estimated distribution of world Sikh population

Punjab	13,000,000
Rest of India	2,000,000
UK	450,000
Canada	200,000
USA	150,000
Rest of world	100,000

This chapter describes the evolution of Sikhism as falling into three overlapping phases, whose transitions are marked by the impact of two different kinds of modernity. Although itself marked by highly dynamic inner shifts of emphasis, the formative first phase lasting until the mid-nineteenth century is regarded as premodern. Initiated by the British conquest of the Punjab in the 1840s, the second phase is characterized by a largely successful set of redefinitions in the context of the notions of modernity and religious identity imposed by the dominant ideology of the colonial power closely associated with Victorian Christianity. Beginning after Indian independence in 1947, the third phase is the postcolonial age in which the more rigid formulations appropriate to the older modernity of the colonial period have come under growing internal question, particularly in the context of the very significant Sikh diaspora now increasingly acculturated to the acceptance of shifting fluidities characteristic of modern Western societies.

Sources and resources

Sikhism provides a striking illustration of the general rule that it is typically through the interstices between existing faiths that new religions emerge. The late fifteenth-century Punjab embraced not only the internal religious variety always characteristic of the Hindu world, but also a powerful Islamic presence associated with a long-established Muslim political authority. This dual context continued to the end of the premodern period to affect the evolution of Sikhism throughout its two formative phases, initiated respectively by the primary formulations of the First Sikh Guru Nanak (1469–1539), and the substantial redefinitions of authority and community effected by the Tenth Guru Gobind Singh (1666–1708).

The Nanak Panth

The broad alignment of Guru Nanak's teachings is with the *bhakti* movement of medieval north India. They are most nearly aligned with those of the Sants, the loosely associated group of teachers whose teachings were expressed in vernacular verse and are distinguished theologically by a soteriology based upon inward loving devotion to a formless divine principle rather than a personalized incarnation. Their social teaching is marked by an egalitarianism equally opposed to the qualitative distinctions of the Hindu caste hierarchy and to the value-laden religious differences between Hindu and Muslim. Guru Nanak is believed to have emerged from the direct experience of divine reality which initiated his mission with the words 'there is no Hindu, there is no Muslim' (na ko hindu, na ko musalman), signalling as a third way what was to become the Nanak Panth, the 'Path of Nanak', the community constituted by the Sikhs (literally, 'disciples') choosing to follow Nanak as their guide or guru, who were almost entirely drawn from Hindu backgrounds often similar to his own.

Powerfully organized in over 900 short verses, hymns and longer compositions of great beauty, Guru Nanak's teachings revolve around the path of salvation from the fate of unregenerate humanity, in which the domination of the psyche (man) by the impulses of the self (*haumai*) causes its subjection to the perpetual suffering of reincarnation. The key figure in the salvific path of alignment to the divine purpose is the guide, the true guru (*satiguru*), to whose inwardly heard voice God may graciously grant access in the case of those whose leading of a righteous life in this world allows the possibility of their being transformed from self-directed (*manmukh*) to guru-directed (*gurmukh*) beings, and thus of apprehending reality or truth (*sach*):

> If You bestow Your glance of grace, through grace we find the Guide
> This soul first passes many births, at last the Guide is heard
> No giver's greater than the Guide, all people mark this well
> The Guide once met imparts the Truth, to those who kill the Self
> The Guide who makes us grasp Reality.
>
> Asa ki Var M1 4, AG 465

While similar to the teachings of the other Sants in their primary emphasis upon a spiritual psychology directed towards transformation of the self, Guru Nanak's hymns express a notably more positive attitude towards women, as in the verse 'Why speak ill of her from whom great kings are born?' (AG 473). Their similarly marked emphasis on the need to balance the spiritual with the practical and the ethical is summarized in a key extra-scriptural formula which adds to the primary injunction to maintain a loving meditation on the divine attributes (*nam japna*) the necessity of leading a productive daily existence (*kirat karni*) and practising the charitable sharing of surplus goods (*vand chhakna*).

Around the primary focal point of the divine Word (*gurbani*) of Guru Nanak's hymns access to the divine was provided by private devotion and by the singing of hymns (*kirtan*) in the congregation of the faithful which is the earthly exemplar of the heavenly congregation of the saints. Separate temples, later called gurdwaras, with their communal kitchens (*langar*) whose encouragement of inter-caste commensality may have been inspired by the example of the similar kitchens attached to Muslim shrines, date from this early period, when the Nanak Panth was subject to the authority of a succession of gurus, each of whom composed further hymns under the signature 'Nanak'.

The guruship had become hereditary within one family by the time of the Fifth Guru Arjun (d. 1606), whose significant formalization and remodelling of the Panth included the construction of the Harimandir, the 'Golden Temple' at Amritsar which

ਛਾਰੁ ॥ ਗਿਆਨੁ ਨ ਗਲੀਈ ਢੂਢੀਐ ਕਥਨਾ ਕਰੜਾ ਸਾਰੁ ॥ ਕਰਮਿ ਮਿਲੈ ਤਾ
ਪਾਈਐ ਹੋਰ ਹਿਕਮਤਿ ਹੁਕਮੁ ਖੁਆਰੁ ॥ ੨ ॥ ਪਉੜੀ ॥ ਨਦਰਿ ਕਰਹਿ ਜੇ
ਆਪਣੀ ਤਾ ਨਦਰੀ ਸਤਿਗੁਰੁ ਪਾਇਆ॥ ਏਹੁ ਜੀਉ ਬਹੁਤੇ ਜਨਮ ਭਰੰਮਿਆ
ਤਾ ਸਤਿਗੁਰਿ ਸਬਦੁ ਸੁਣਾਇਆ॥ਸਤਿਗੁਰ ਜੇਵਡੁ ਦਾਤਾ ਕੋ ਨਹੀ ਸਭਿ ਸੁਣਿ
ਅਹੁ ਲੋਕ ਸਬਾਇਆ॥ਸਤਿਗੁਰਿ ਮਿਲਿਐ ਸਚੁ ਪਾਇਆ ਜਿਨੀ ਵਿਚਹੁ ਆਪੁ
ਗਵਾਇਆ ॥ ਜਿਨਿ ਸਚੋ ਸਚੁ ਬੁਝਾਇਆ ॥੪॥ ਸਲੋਕਮਃ ੧ ॥ ਘੜੀਆ ਸਭੇ

FIGURE 4.1 Gurmukhi text of *Granth* passage translated above.
Courtesy Christopher Shackle.

has ever since remained the spiritual centre of Sikhism. Guru Arjun was also responsible for the compilation of the Sikh scripture, the Adi Granth (1604), to which he is
the largest single contributor. The Granth is a massive collection written in the distinctive
Gurmukhi script of hymns composed in a mixture of Old Punjabi and Old Hindi by
the Sikh Gurus plus selected verses by other Sants. The following illustration shows the
original text of the verse by Guru Nanak from Asa ki Var quoted in translation above.
Although the Janamsakhis, the prose hagiographies of Guru Nanak compiled during
this period, have always remained central to devotional understanding, they have never
been accorded the special status enjoyed by the scripture as *gurbani*, whose canonization
as a sacred book would seem in part to derive from the unique status accorded to the
Qur'an in Islam.

The Khalsa

Following Guru Arjun's martyrdom by the Moghul authorities, much of the seventeenth
century was marked by political and military conflict, both within the Panth as each succession to the Guruship provoked the secession of unsuccessful claimants with their
followers and between Sikhs and the Moghuls, culminating with the execution in Delhi
on imperial orders of the Ninth Guru Tegh Bahadur (d. 1675).

His son Gobind, who became the Tenth Guru, instituted a major reorganization of
the Panth through his foundation in 1699 of the Khalsa. This was designed as an elite
brotherhood whose direct dedication to the Guru was formalized through initiatory
baptism (*amrit*), and whose internal equality was symbolized by the addition of the
Rajput titles Singh ('Lion') and Kaur ('Princess') to male and female names respectively.
The emphasis on masculine features naturally associated with the strongly militant
character of the Khalsa was underlined by the obligation on male members to bear the
well-known five Ks as outward marks of membership.

The verse compositions associated with Guru Gobind Singh, many with militant
themes, were gathered in a separate Khalsa scripture called the Dasam Granth, but
this has always been secondary in importance to the Adi Granth for whose final recension
he is believed to have been responsible. It was Guru Gobind Singh who before his death
proclaimed the end of the succession of living Gurus and the transfer of the Guruship
to the Adi Granth, thereafter given the honorific title of Guru Granth Sahib, whose
supreme status is underlined by the central position and numerous marks of ritual respect
accorded to copies of the scripture in a gurdwara. In the absence of a Sikh priesthood,
a parallel authority was considered to reside after the death of the last living Guru in the
whole community as Guru Panth.

Not all the Sikhs of the Nanak Panth chose to become members of the Khalsa, with
some choosing such alternatives as enrolment in one of the several Sikh ascetic groups
while many continued in the traditional patterns of observance, distinguished from the
Hindu co-members of their caste or family only by their devotion to the Gurus and
the Granth. But in the wars which accompanied the progressive collapse of Moghul
authority during the eighteenth century, it was the Khalsa which led the community, and

formal meetings of its leaders were invested with the power to issue resolutions binding upon all Sikhs. Recruited primarily from the farmer caste of Jats rather than the business caste of Khatris from whom all the Gurus and most early converts had been drawn, the Khalsa emerged as a major military and political force in the Punjab.

Prescriptive codes of Khalsa conduct (*rahit*), including a ban on smoking tobacco, were drawn up during this period, and an abundant literature of heroism and martyrdom reinforced a spirit of militant opposition to Islam. In this still influential literature, it is the martial characteristics of the armed male Sikh warrior with his beard and turban which are repeatedly exalted. Rival Sikh warlords were eventually conquered by Maharaja Ranjit Singh, whose reign over the Punjab (r. 1799–1831) in the name of the Khalsa marked the high point of Sikh political power, although Ranjit Singh's lavish patronage of Sikh institutions and religious specialists was never exclusive of other religions, and the absence of a proselytizing tradition accounts for the failure of Sikhism to expand with Ranjit Singh's territorial conquests beyond its traditional boundaries in the Punjab.

As in the case of all religions, understandings of the formative phases of Sikhism are themselves necessarily coloured by interpretations associated with modern viewpoints, but they may be understood as a process of evolution in which the kernel relationship of self to true guide leads from the living gurus and their gurbani to the scripture and the Khalsa. For this period at least, however, it would be misleading to conceive of the Khalsa as too tightly defined a community.

TABLE 4.2 Formative phases of Sikhism

	Nanak Panth	*Khalsa*
Authority	gurbani living gurus	Guru Granth Khalsa and Guru Panth
Community	loosely defined adherence Khatri prominence	baptismal admission Jat dominance
Self	permeable boundaries with Hindu society	emergence of separate definition by five Ks and *rahit*
Gender	relatively equalized status	powerfully masculine emphasis

Interactions with modernity

Sikhism in the colonial world

While Ranjit Singh had successfully prolonged his independence by reorganization of the Khalsa forces on modern European lines, the full impact of modernity was only felt after the two Anglo-Sikh wars of 1845–9 when the Punjab became the last major conquest to fall to British colonial expansion in India. The subsequent development of Sikhism is intimately linked to the new status of the Sikhs as one of the many colonized groups subject to British imperial rule. Moreover, as a relatively small local minority even within the Punjab to which they were largely confined, the Sikhs were faced not only with the familiar general pressures of the direct challenge of the values and institutions of European colonial states on so many Asian religious communities, but also by the secondary challenges posed to them by other religious groupings as a consequence of the latter's own responses to modernity, particularly by a revived neo-Hinduism. The quite profound modern remodellings of Sikhism are primarily the consequence of responses evolved to cope with these linked challenges.

Colonial challenges to tradition

The collapse of independent Sikh political authority left Sikh institutions variably well placed to cope with the challenges of the colonial state to traditional understandings. These challenges are best seen as having manifested themselves in the form of a whole set of linked category shifts, whose primary effect was upon definitions of community, but which in turn progressively influenced notions of authority, of the self and of gender. In the land settlements which followed the conquest, a number of leading Sikh landed families were confirmed in their estates, including the custodians of most major shrines and other religious leaders. The bulk of the Sikh population consisted of a rural population whose prime component was provided by the Jat farmer caste, from which the soldiery of the Khalsa had largely been drawn and who represented the British administration's ideal of the loyalist yeoman farmer.

Like most colonial powers governed by the divide and rule principle, the British were concerned with the mapping and definition of the peoples now subject to them and the determination of appropriate treatment for each group. As a religious minority with a demonstrable record of military prowess, the Sikhs were of particular interest to the imperial authorities. The British quickly defined them as a martial race whose loyalty was to be secured by privileged access into the army and whose separate status was to be rigidly underlined by making outward Khalsa observance a precondition of recruitment into the separate Sikh regiments.

Direct encouragement was thereby given to a shift from previous Indic patterns of highly permeable community boundaries to the operation of Western 'either/or' notions so characteristic of modernity. Later, access to the new economic opportunities provided by the colonial system, both in terms of internal emigration to new areas of the Punjab opened up for cultivation by canal irrigation or outside India to different parts of the empire again tended to be awarded along imperially defined community lines, and the Sikhs were well favoured in this process.

Simultaneously with this official reinforcement of separate definitions, all three indigenous religions of the Punjab were subject to the challenges posed by the modern and clearly successful Victorian Christianity of their new rulers, as particularly articulated by the missionary presence which was so prominent in the new educational system of the Punjab. These challenges provoked a series of responses ranging from conservative defences of tradition to more radical solutions which took on many of the concepts of modernity in order to reformulate new defences of tradition. One of the earliest and strongest responses of the latter type was the neo-Hinduism formulated by the Gujarati brahmin Dayanand Saraswati. Rejecting most of the features of traditional Hinduism condemned by its Western critics in the name of an absolutist scriptural authority quite newly conferred on the Vedas, his Arya Samaj gained rapid and longlasting support from the new Punjabi Hindu urban middle class. Initially its appeal extended even to some enthusiastic members of the much smaller Sikh middle class, but these rapidly became alienated by the characteristically aggressive line soon adopted by the Arya Samaj in its deprecation of the Sikh Gurus and its classification of the Sikhs as lapsed Hindus to be reclaimed for submission to Vedic authority.

Sikhism and colonial modernity

Intrinsically less bound by the elaborate orthodoxies and orthopraxies maintained by the religious specialists of both brahminic Hinduism and traditional Islam, the Sikhs with their emphasis upon lay reponsibility were in many respects well-placed to take advantage of the opportunities offered by a colonial system generally supportive of them as reliable soldiers and farmers. The inequalities of power between the British and Sikhs was however always going to ensure there would never be a perfect coincidence of interests between the British and the Sikhs, whose very lack of a centrally authoritative tradition of religious specialists was to condition the nature of their responses to the modernity introduced by the colonial system.

Thus a strongly hostile reaction to the colonial presence was formulated by Ram Singh (1816–85), the leader of the Namdhari sect, who combined calls for very strict observance of Sikh rituals with a boycott of the postal service and other colonial institutions. While exemplifying the heroic traditions of the Khalsa in his opposition to the British, his status was intrinsically discredited for most Sikhs by his claim to be the living Guru in direct descent from Guru Gobind Singh, in clear heretical contradiction to the central orthodox tenet of the latter's closure of the Guruship.

In accordance with the doctrine of the Guru Panth, it therefore fell to a lay leadership to articulate the main Sikh response to the general challenges of modernity while at the time mounting a defence against hostile takeover by the proponents of a revived Hinduism. Just like the Arya Samaj, the urban Sikhs who led this response adopted the modern forms of organization introduced by the colonial state, with the usual apparatus of elected officers, minutes and resolutions, in the formation of new lay associations. These were called Singh Sabha, the first being founded under aristocratic patronage in Amritsar in 1873, soon followed by the Lahore Singh Sabha (1879) whose more radical middle class membership's reformist agenda achieved the most successful articulation of a Sikhism adapted to modernity, which has until recently managed to dominate all subsequent understandings.

This reformulation was based on the ideal of the Tat Khalsa, the 'real Khalsa' as defined by the reformists to conform with the categories encouraged by the colonial state. This distinguished Sikhism from Hinduism as an ethical monotheism closely linked to a single scripture, the Granth as Guru Granth Sahib, whose unique authority un-equivocally guaranteed Sikhism's separate status as a fully scriptural religion. In the absence of any systematic codification of prescribed Sikh practice comparable to the Hindu Dharmashastras or the Muslim Sharia, a crucial further underpinning of separate identity was provided by continual reference to the line of Sikh Gurus, the foundation of the Khalsa and the subsequent achievements of the Sikh Panth. A strictly linear religious history thus became a principal means of giving absolute primacy within the existing wide range of Sikh–Hindu practice and allegiance to the full Khalsa identity as the only real kind of Sikhism.

Ever wider adherence to this norm was encouraged by the Singh Sabha reformists' continual emphasis upon the outward marks of male Khalsa identity as palpable symbols of an inner moral fibre whose closeness to Victorian values was to be guaranteed by maximal distancing from many types of previously current ritual and practice which were now stigmatized as degenerate and as Hindu. The consequent ideal is well-captured in the words of Max Arthur Macauliffe, an ex-official who left government service in order to become the leading English associate of the Sikh reformists:

> To sum up some of the moral and political merits of the Sikh religion: It prohibits idolatry, hypocrisy, caste exclusiveness, the concremation of widows, the immure-ment of women, the use of wine and other intoxicants, tobacco-smoking, infanticide, slander, pilgrimages to the sacred rivers and tanks of the Hindus; and it inculcates loyalty, gratitude for all favours received, philanthropy, justice, impartiality, truth, honesty, and all the moral and domestic virtues known to the holiest citizens of any country.
>
> M.A. Macauliffe, *The Sikh Religion*, 1909: 1, xxiii

Besides its core programme of enforcing unambiguous notions of religious authority and community, the Singh Sabha movement led to cultural, institutional and political consequences of great significance for the understanding of Sikhism in the modern world. Culturally, great emphasis was laid upon the local identity of Sikhs, who had historically always remained closely linked to their regional origins in the Punjab.

Thus in clear distinction from the Punjabi Muslims' espousal of Urdu as the chief cultural language of Islam in India and the Arya Samaj's strong support of Hindi, a core plank of the Singh Sabha programme was to encourage a congruence of religious and ethnic identity by for the first time developing Punjabi in the sacred Gurmukhi script as a vehicle for a modern literature. Since the Singh Sabha reformers were mostly lay activists lacking the specialist skills of professional theologians, their message was chiefly conveyed in writing by a few particularly creative figures like Vir Singh (1872–1957), whose imaginative works have been enormously influential in helping condition ideas of self and of gender.

It was however in the institutional and political spheres that the activist Singh Sabha programme was principally to work itself out. In the colonial period, the first major success in securing the validation of the Tat Khalsa agenda came with the passing of the Anand Marriage Act in 1909 which prescribed circumbulation of the Granth by Sikh bridal couples in place of the traditional Vedic fire. A longer and more violent campaign to gain Khalsa control over the Harimandir and other major gurdwaras, fiercely opposed by the traditional custodians inimical to reformist Sikhism, was mounted by a new generation of activists under the banner of the Akali Dal. This finally resulted in the Sikh Gurdwaras Act of 1925 which handed the administration of these gurdwaras and their great assets to the SGPC, an elected committee dominated by the Akali Dal which is the single most important modern Sikh institution, acting not only in secular matters but also claiming a religious authority on behalf of the Panth over all matters not covered by the Granth.

Well-equipped by his educated family background and a modern education in the Church Mission School of Amritsar, Vir Singh devoted 65 years of unremitting industry to the great task of conveying the message of revived Sikhism. Possessing private means and distanced from the political activism to which most of his fellow reformers were drawn, Vir Singh concentrated upon the development of his outstanding gifts as a scholar, propagandist and creative writer in Punjabi.

Besides editing many older Sikh texts and compiling a lengthy scriptural commentary, Vir Singh founded the Khalsa Tract Society to produce pamphlets on Sikhism in imitation and rebuttal of Christian missionary tracts and himself wrote over 1,000 of these. He also founded and for many years produced virtually single-handed the influential weekly newspaper *Khalsa Samachar*. A poet of considerable distinction, Vir Singh was the author of the first Punjab novels, beginning with *Sundari* (1898). This enormously popular tale set in the heroic age of the eighteenth century achieves a definitive portrait of idealized Khalsa womanhood in its eponymous heroine who is converted to Sikhism and helps a band of brave Sikh guerrillas as cook and nurse before dying of the wound inflicted by a treacherous Muslim warrior.

BOX 4.1 Vir Singh

Sikhism in the postcolonial world

As the modern world itself keeps changing, all processes of response to it must themselves necessarily be ongoing. The often troubled progress of reformist Sikhism in the postcolonial period since Indian independence in 1947 itself illustrates the rule that formerly very successful solutions may not always prove naturally adaptable to respond to altered questions. Definitions of authority and community were well devised by the Singh Sabha movement to maintain the independent development of a religion and its institutions in a colonial environment and to help lead these into the different circumstances of postcolonial independence. But they have proved less adequate to deal with the kinds of issues relating to self and to gender where pointers to a guided individual enrichment on the basis of a genuinely full equality of status for all humans are expected from religious thinkers in the Western societies where the Sikh diaspora is settled, as is also increasingly the case in a rapidly urbanizing and modernizing India.

Activist responses

When plans for Indian independence were seen to involve the partition of the Punjab on religious lines, there was some discussion of carving out a Sikh homeland to be called Khalistan. This came to nothing, but the massive transfer of Sikhs from areas awarded to Pakistan did result for the first time in a local Sikh majority population in some areas. This encouraged a determined Akali campaign disguised as a demand for a Punjabi-speaking state within the Indian Union for a Sikh-dominated Punjab. This was achieved by the separation of Punjab from Haryana in 1966.

In the early 1980s, a combination of these traditions of successful action campaigns with the economic disruptions caused by the agricultural revolution and the increasing questioning in a Hindu-dominated India of the privileged position perceived to have been derived by the Sikhs from the former era resulted in increasingly violent confrontation between the central government of Mrs Indira Gandhi and groups of

FIGURE 4.2 Map of Historical and Modern Punjab (shaded).

militant young Sikh activists. This culminated in 1984 with Operation Bluestar, the Indian army's sacking of the Harimandir, which had become the armed headquarters of the charismatic Sikh preacher Jarnail Singh Bhindranvale, the subsequent assassination of Mrs Gandhi by her Sikh bodyguards and the consequent Hindu mob violence against Sikhs in many Indian cities.

As violence continued in the Punjab throughout the 1980s, backlash support for the Sikh cause was widespread in the new Sikh diaspora established from the 1950s in the UK and North America, for whom the renewed demand for an independent Sikh Khalistan, for all its lack of any very plausible religio-political programme, proved temporarily to have a particular appeal as a powerful focus for displaced loyalties. While this appeal has receded with the later reimposition of government authority in the Punjab and growing realization among younger Sikhs abroad that Indian solutions may not always be best suited to the situation of increasingly well-established independent overseas communities, the Punjab remains the homeland of Sikhism, with the Harimandir as its perceived focal point.

Rethinking neo-orthodoxy

The Tat Khalsa's successful formulation of a neo-orthodox Sikhism is summarized in the *Rahit Maryada*, an official handbook first published by the SGPC in 1950 which has remained the standard authority. This deals at some length with the individual life, under three headings:

1. Study of the scriptures and meditation on God, including regulations for the prescribed daily devotions (*nitnem*) and the ritual of the *gurdwara*, with great emphasis on the centrality of the Granth.
2. Living according to the Guru's teachings, embracing both ethical teachings and life cycle rituals. Brief instructions on the duty of active service to the community (*seva*).
3. A much shorter final section deals with the disciplinary rules of the Panth and the penalties (*tankhah*) to be imposed on those who transgress them.

The apparent disproportion between the code's treatment of the individual and the Panth should be understood as a consequence of the difficulty of enforcing disciplinary rules in a religion without a hierarchy of authoritative specialists, and the self – a conspicuously masculine self – is here conceived very much as a unit of the community and fully subject to the authority by which it is defined.

This community identity continues to rely heavily on the authority of its history to maintain its distinction in the shifting world created by the continual process of Indic religious creativity. Even movements of charismatic renewal led by teachers of impeccable Khalsa orthodoxy are often liable to excite the suspicion that they challenge community authority. These suspicions naturally apply still more strongly to movements drawing more widely upon the bottomless well of Indic religious resource so as to appeal to non-Sikhs as well as Sikhs. A notable example of this is the Radhasoami

(Beas branch), with a Sikh leadership but owing a primary inspiration to the reinterpretations of yogic disciplines by the movement's Hindu founders.

Community boundaries are again called into question by the most significant modern proselytization movement, the Sikh Dharma or 3HO (Healthy Happy Holy Organization) founded by the Khatri Sikh known as Yogi Bhajan. Deliberately adapted to Western expectations, this has led to communities of American and Canadian Sikhs who have no intrinsic Punjabi background and differ from the standard pattern in such ways as their closer match with Hindu ascetic ideals in being practicing vegetarians and wearing white clothes, and in the abolition of gender differences symbolized by putting women in turbans.

Such radical reformulations border upon heresy for most Sikhs who continue to be guided by the Tat Khalsa vision. But in recent decades some of the underpinnings of that orthodoxy, which relies so heavily upon the authenticity of historical tradition and scriptural text, are themselves coming to be questioned by modern scholarship in the fashion successively experienced by most world religions since the critical questioning of Christianity in the nineteenth century.

Since the dominance of orthodoxy in Sikh institutions in the Punjab extends to the universities there, it is unlikely that they would originate such questionings, which have instead come from outside. Particularly strong reactions were evoked by the New Zealand scholar W. H. McLeod with the publication in 1968 of his *Guru Nanak and the Sikh Religion*, which drew on the familiar techniques of biblical scholarship to question the amount of reliable historical information to be gleaned from a careful examination of the classic hagiographies of Guru Nanak, hitherto regarded very much as the Gospels had been in pre-nineteenth century Christianity. An enormous amount of energy has subsequently been expended by Sikh academics and others in attacking the work of McLeod and his pupils on this and subsequent aspects of early Sikh history. But as the history of Christian studies shows, victories in such matters are ultimately hardly gained by either side.

Similar questions are starting to be raised about the even more sensitive issue of the text of the Granth, whose central place in Sikhism was carefully reinforced by the reformers' preference for scriptural commentary over textual criticism. This hitherto unquestioned status of the *textus receptus* has long been reinforced by the standard pagination of the Granth, so that all editions contain the same 1,430 pages, much facilitating scholarly reference across its intrinsic organization by the musical modes to which the hymns are to be performed. Those seen to question the orthodox account of its compilation are liable to the kind of concerted attack which resulted in McLeod's pupil Dr Pashaura Singh being summoned from Canada to perform ritual penance at the Harimandir. Meanwhile, however, the work being done by several other Sikh scholars in the diaspora in the collection and critical study of early scriptural manuscripts seems certain to raise issues which may be difficult for some to square with inherited notions of religious authority.

Looking to the future

Since Sikhism is so very much a religion of the book, if never in the sense that this definition would have had for the Islamic authorities of Moghul times, it is continually to the Granth that the ongoing process of responses to modernity returns. Somewhat paradoxically, given the increasing distance from the language of the scripture in an English-speaking environment, this is perhaps especially true in the diaspora where the other institutions of orthodoxy are weaker than in the Punjab. Since it was in Guru Nanak's hymns that the self was first directly addressed, it is indeed natural that it should be from the Granth that fresh inspiration is being sought for the reconstruction of self and gender within a Sikhism looking to different definitions of authority and community from those formulated during the colonial period.

Very much in the first phases of discussion and formulation, this process may be expected to result in a major reformulation in the first decades of the new millennium. In keeping with the spirit of the new age, there is a new emphasis upon the musical and inward character of the gurbani. A creative indication of the way in which this process might be expected to develop comes from the music inspired by the Granth, drawing upon both Eastern and Western sources, which is starting to be produced by such artists as the Canadian Sikh classical violinist Parmela Attariwala.

FIGURE 4.3
CD cover

CD cover of *Beauty enthralled: New music inspired by India.* Courtesy Parmela Attariwala and Hornblower Recordings.

TABLE 4.3 Challenges to neo-Orthodoxy

	Neo-orthodoxy	New expectations
Authority	justified by history	justified by truth
Community	defined by ethnicity	defined by choice
Self	externally fixed	internally chosen
Gender	dominantly masculine	gender neutral

As an indication of another very important area in which such altered attitudes might be expected to occur, attention may be drawn to the pioneering work of the American scholar Nikky Singh, who has drawn upon the insights of Western feminist theology to explore the implications of the Gurus' use of female poetic personae for the redefinition of understandings of gender in Sikhism, and who has produced the first gender neutral translation of gurbani.

Since it would be premature to forecast the exact direction of future changes, it is possible only to summarize the likely possibilities in diagrammatic contrast to the still dominant neo-Orthodox Sikhism of the Tat Khalsa.

Summary

- The dominant Sikh response to the modern world was conditioned by the need to enforce clear definitions of authority and community in the face of the double challenge of colonialism and of neo-Hinduism.

- The emphasis of this response, chiefly formulated by a lay Punjabi leadership and justified in terms of historic religious mission, was on securing institutional and political change in the Punjab.

- Further changes in the modern world, including the establishment of a very substantial Sikh diaspora in the West, are calling into question the adequacy of the earlier response and its underlying justifications, and are starting to provoke fresh responses.

Key terms

Akali Dal (lit. 'army of the Immortal's followers') The main Sikh political party.

five ks The five marks of Khalsa identity (*panj kakke*), whose Punjabi names are *kes* (unshorn hair, whose natural concomitant is the turban), *kangha* (comb), *kirpan* (sword), *kara* (steel bracelet), and *kachh* (undershorts).

Granth (lit. 'book') The Sikh scripture, especially the Adi Granth (Original Book) first compiled by Guru Arjun and subsequently invested with supreme authority as the Guru Granth Sahib.

gurbani (lit. 'Guru's Word') The Divine Word of the scripture.

gurdwara (lit. 'Guru's door') Sikh temple.

Gurmukhi (lit. 'Guru-directed') The script of the Sikh scriptures used to write modern Punjabi in India.

Janamsakhi (lit. 'birth-witness') Prose hagiography of Guru Nanak.

Khalistan (lit. 'land of the Khalsa') Ideal Sikh homeland.

Khalsa (Persian: khalisa, 'crown estate') The brotherhood founded by Guru Gobind Singh.

Panth (lit. 'path') The Sikh community.

rahit The Khalsa code of conduct.

SGPC Shiromani Gurdwara Committee which controls the historic gurdwaras of the Parbandhak Committee

Singh (lit. 'Lion') Rajput title affixed to names of Sikh males.

Singh Sabha (lit. 'Singh assembly') Sikh reformist association.

Tat Khalsa (lit. 'real Khalsa') The dominant definition of modern Sikhism.

Further reading

Sources and resources

The classic English study by a close associate of the Sikh reformers, M. A. Macauliffe: *The Sikh Religion* (Oxford: Clarendon Press, 1909) is a frequently reprinted and still valuable guide to the compositions and traditional lives of the Sikh Gurus. W. O. Cole and P. S. Sambhi: *The Sikhs: Their Religious Beliefs and Practices*, revised edition (Brighton: Sussex Academic Press, 1995) is a useful general introduction written from a religious studies perspective, including helpful charts and the full English text of the Rahit Maryada (pp. 200–8). Some of the key scriptural texts are introduced and presented in modern English verse translations in C. Shackle and A. S. Mandair (eds): *Teachings of the Sikh Gurus: Selections from the Sikh Scriptures* (London and New York: Routledge, 2006). Among the many general introductions, two are particularly recommended. W. H. McLeod: *Sikhism* (London: Penguin Books, 1997) is a comprehensive general account with very full annotated bibliography, while E. Nesbitt: *Sikhism: A Very Short Introduction* (Oxford: Oxford University Press, 2005) provides a lively and stimulating overview.

Sikhism in the modern world

J. T. O'Connell *et al.* (eds): *Sikh History and Religion in the Twentieth Century* (Toronto: Centre for South Asian Studies, 1988) is a bulky collection of stimulating papers relevant to many of this chapter's themes. H. S. Oberoi: *The Construction of Religious Boundaries: Culture, Identity and Diversity in the Sikh Tradition* (Delhi: Oxford University Press, 1994) is a pioneering study of the nineteenth-century reformist transformation of many traditional features of Sikh society and practice. D. S. Tatla: *The Sikh Diaspora* (London: UCL Press, 1999) provides an overview of the diaspora and its responses to the Punjab crisis of the 1980s, while some of the implications of the diasporic situation are explored in T. Ballantyne: *Between Colonialism and Diaspora: Sikh Cultural Formations in a Modern World* (Durham, NC: Duke University Press, 2006). Gurharpal Singh and D. S. Tatla: *Sikhs in Britain: The Making of a Community* (London: Zed Books, 2006) is an excellent introduction to its subject, while at a less academic level *The Sikh Messenger*, a London-based quarterly, offers a direct picture of many of the concerns of Sikhs in Britain.

J. S. Grewal: *Contesting Interpretations of Sikh Tradition* (New Delhi: Manohar, 1998) is a balanced account by a senior Sikh historian of modern scholarship's challenges to traditional understandings and the reactions these have provoked. Many contemporary issues are addressed in papers by leading diaspora academics in C. Shackle *et al.* (eds): *Sikh Religion, Culture and Ethnicity* (Richmond, Surrey: Curzon, 2001). N. G. K. Singh: *The Feminine Principle in the Sikh Vision of the Transcendent* (Cambridge: Cambridge University Press, 1993) is a pioneering study of Sikh scriptural and reformist texts from the feminist perspective which also informs her scriptural translations in *The Name of My Beloved: Verses of the Sikh Gurus* (San Francisco, CA: HarperCollins, 1995), and her provocative recent study, *The Birth of the Khalsa: A Feminist Re-Memory of Sikh Identity* (Albany, NY: SUNY Press, 2005). These books may be read alongside D. Jakobsh: *Relocating Gender in Sikh History* (Delhi: OUP, 2003).

Chapter 5

Chinese religions

Stephan Feuchtwang

Introduction

This chapter will include as religions all traditions transmitting revelations about the world that place everyday events in a time of greater scope – cyclical, ancestral, fateful, eternal, or providential – of both the living and the dead. Many of these traditions are written. Many others are purely ritual, handed down by experts and from elders to juniors, linked to but not dependent upon textual teachings and liturgies. But in cultures of writing, such as the Chinese, textual traditions dominate.

In the centuries of the modern era in China, the various textual traditions identified most closely with Chinese civilization have been grouped into three main teachings. They are those of Buddhism (Mahayana and Tantric), Daoism, and the ancestral, calendrical and life-cycle rituals prescribed in texts written by court officials or approved scholars and derived from writings attributed to Confucius and his followers. In chronological order they start with the textual record of Confucius (551–479 BCE) teaching the importance of ritual. Next come the earliest texts of philosophical Daoism attributed to the mythical authors Lao Zi and Zhuang Zi about a century after Confucius' death. Full-scale rituals of Daoist religion were first instituted some time in the last two centuries BCE. Buddhist texts and rituals were introduced in the third century CE. All three teachings accommodate household cults, such as making offerings to the Stove God before and after the turn of the year, or the handing down of cults of protectors of occupations and the even more numerous territorial protectors whose carnival-like fairs or festivals define every place in China.

The great majority of China's population of 1.3 billion takes part in rituals and festivals, many of them concentrated in the days around the turning of the lunar year, which belong to no particular teaching. In addition, there are the millions who belong to no religion and take part in no festivals at all. In part this is an effect of urbanization creating an environment without the pressure of local convention, and in part it is the effect of the spread of atheism during a century of republican revolution and its states which are ideologically above religion, as are most other modern states even when they are not as determinedly atheist as is China (or France). In China this spread has included strenuous campaigns of mass iconoclasm, particularly those of the Cultural Revolution of 1966–1976. But in the decades since the Cultural Revolution there has been an equally remarkable resurgence of religious activity. A small minority of the Chinese population adheres to what are now the dominant world religions of Islam and Christianity. But a minority in China is numbered in many millions, because it is so large a country.

551–479 BCE	Confucius
fourth to third century BCE	Lao Zi and Zhuang Zi (authors to which the first Daoist classics are attributed)
221 BCE	Unification of states under a single emperor
third century CE	Introduction of Buddhism to China
Tang dynasty (618–905)	A period of great openness during which all the main religions of the world entered China
	Consolidation of imperial bureaucracy
Song dynasty (960–1278)	A period of great commercial development. The Neo-Confucian orthodoxy was established, reinterpreting Confucius' ideas of ritual and self-cultivation
Yuan dynasty (1206–1260 in northern China, 1280–1341 over all China)	Mongol rule: incorporation of Muslim regions
Ming dynasty (1368–1628)	Emergence of syncretic sects and lay religious communities. Introduction of Roman Christianity
Qing dynasty (1644–1911)	Manchu rule. Protestant missions
Republican rule (1912–)	Institution of a secular state
Cultural Revolution (1966–1976)	Iconoclasm and suppression of all religious activities

BOX 5.1 Timeline of Chinese religions

Numbers of followers of any one tradition are difficult to estimate, and must in China as everywhere else rely on statistics compiled by the largest institutions, either those of the state – which tend to underestimate – or those of the religious institutions themselves – which tend to overestimate. If we include all the population of those designated 'national' minorities with an Islamic heritage in the territory of China then we can conclude that in 2004 there were 20 million Muslims in the People's Republic of China. In the case of registered and unregistered Protestants, estimates vary hugely, from 10 to 30 million in 1994, and 18 million in 2004, for example. But what everyone agrees is that there has been a remarkable growth, from some three million in 1982. There is a similar variation for Catholics, also growing to estimates in 1994 of between six and ten million and 12 million in 2004. For the religions of Buddhism and Daoism, official numbers are totally misleading for they are only of the ritual practitioners themselves, and even they are outnumbered by unregistered practitioners. The realistic estimates provided in *The State of China Atlas* (2005) by Stephanie Hemelryk Donald and Robert Benewick, is that in 2004 there were about 100 million Buddhists and about 250 million Daoists and followers of folk religion.

This chapter will concentrate on Chinese vernacular religious traditions and the textual traditions of Confucianism, Daoism, and Buddhism. The other religious traditions present in China are so much smaller in their following and they are too numerous, especially if they should include the religions of the many ethnic minorities partially or nearly wholly assimilated with the main Chinese traditions. The chapter will first provide more detail on the main traditions of religion and ritual in China. Then it will deal with the long process of modernization and of religious change during that time. The last part of the chapter will be on the fast process of change in the past century and a half, the politics of culture and the facts of religious revival.

Sources and resources

Indigenous traditions: Confucianism and Daoism

Chinese teachings are associated with their originating sages, such as Confucius or the legendary Lao Zi of Daoism. Many religions are similarly identified with a man or a woman said to be the first teacher, a prophet, a patriarch, or his mother. But usually there is an antecedent, which is the source of what they taught. That antecedent might be a force, such as Heaven or the Way in China or a divinity such as Buddha, or the Unborn Venerable Mother who comes before all other teachings according to millenarian sects popular in China from the sixteenth century onward. Shamanism and many other kinds of spirit possession and rituals of divination have also persisted in China, bound up with rituals and myths, but not confined to any of the named teachings. A number of cosmological terms, such as Tian (the celestial aspect of the cosmos, often translated as Heaven) and Yin and Yang (complementary forces of the universe), run through these *mantic* as well as the other Chinese religious traditions. Even so, there is serious debate about whether it is appropriate to write about Chinese religion in the singular.

Confucianism is the search for a middle way in order to preserve social harmony in accordance with the ordering principle of Tian. Its social universe is a patriarchy, which is a veneration of ancestors and descent in the male line. The Confucian emphasis on ancestral veneration and on Tian as the ordering and moral principle informs the construction of ancestral altars, within homes or, more communally, in ancestral halls of lineages and sub-lineages, and in the larger associations and halls of those who share the same family name. Within the family it stresses the core importance of filial, hierarchical father–son, elder–junior, male–female relations in the family. Beyond the family, it stresses reciprocity in personal relations of responsibility (*ren*), and the extension of filial duty (*xiao*) to the subjects of rulers. It is a prescription of family rituals, and in particular of weddings and death rituals. But it is important to note that death rituals performed in China also include major Daoist and Buddhist liturgies, along with those prescribed in the tradition associated with Confucius.

Confucianism in Chinese is called 'the teaching of scholars' (*rujiao*). It is both a teaching and a set of ritual practices. Its core textual canon consists of four books, only one of which – *The Analects* (Lun Yu) – is attributable to Confucius but all of which are said either to be the sources or the transmissions of the tradition in which he is at once the greatest sage and its chief transmitter. The canon was fixed during the Former Han dynasty (206 BCE–25 CE). Over the centuries since then this core and the texts added to it have become the basis of a learning that made those with the material resources and ability to master it into scholar-administrators, usually called the *literati* or 'gentry' in Western accounts of China.

Daoism was its complement as a teaching about various disciplines for achieving perfection. 'Perfection' is to achieve immortality by becoming one with the spontaneous, self-generating rhythms and forces of the universe called 'the Way' (*dao*). The Way is a philosophical and metaphysical conception equivalent to the ancient Greek *physis* or 'nature' in modern English, an idea of the processes of generation and regeneration underlying the existence of things and their moral order. Daoist sages emphasised the Way itself, while Confucius and Confucian sages emphasised the principles of celestial order.

Daoism generated a number of hermetic and lay liturgical traditions, the most widespread of which are traditions of exorcism and healing. Its textual corpus was turned into a canon by approved compilations under emperors who considered their regimes to be preordained by Daoist revelations. This canon is the result of inscriptions held to be revelations from past masters of the Way, ranging from metaphysics to instructions on how to control demons.

Emperors of China were themselves honoured as agents of Tian, communicating with Tian and sanctioned by the mandate of Tian. They could bestow royal and feudal titles upon mountains, rivers and the dead, acknowledging them as sage and powerful objects, to be venerated by offerings of food and precious objects, verbal and written address. When the Daoism of Celestial Masters (Zheng Yi Daoism) briefly became a set of local theocracies in the second century and then in the fifth century became a court religion, it denounced and sought to purify the carnal sacrifices and spirit mediums and gods of popular religion. But eventually it became the indigenous religion most closely associated with these gods, providing the liturgical services and textual offerings to them and to the superior beings of the upper heavens that Daoists still claim as their realm.

Selection of gods from the dead, similar to the cults of saints in medieval Europe, had its base not in the literati nor in Daoism but among the common people of China. Yet, for their own advancement as local leaders, Chinese literati sought imperial honour for gods already venerated in their home places. Now, long after the end of this system of imperial honour, local gods with imperial titles again proliferate in China's towns

FIGURE 5.1
Pantheon of deities

Domestic religion combines all three teachings of Confucianism, Buddhism and Daoism as well as vernacular deities, in this case Guan Di who is popular throughout China. This is a print of the pantheon of deities to be pasted up for the year at New Year above a household altar shelf in Hebei province (Qing dynasty). The main deities, from top to bottom, are the three Buddhas of past, present and future; the three Pure Ones of Daoism; the Jade Emperor, ruler of Heaven, and his six subordinates; and the red-faced God of War and Commerce (Guan Di), who is also a god of wealth. He is flanked by heavenly marshals and is seated behind a tablet inscribed with the characters for 'True rulers of the three realms and ten directions'. Similar prints are pasted up now in rural households all over China. Published in Po Sung-nien and David Johnson: *Domesticated Deities and Auspicious Emblems; The Iconography of Everyday Life in Village China* (Berkeley, CA: Chinese Popular Culture Project, 1992, p. 85). © Chinese Popular Culture Project, courtesy IEAS Publications.

and villages. They are deities whose human life energies and extraordinary deeds are considered to be effective after they have died, even though they are not associated with any particular teaching. Wealth gods, city gods, stove gods, door guardians and local temple gods can all be identified by a personal name and the history of the person bearing that name. Worship of the most popular deities has spread throughout China. Each has a centre and a temple in a place where the hero or heroine or their parents lived, and there are frequently disputes over which is the original place and therefore which is the source temple and main destination of pilgrimages. But the earliest recorded pilgrimages and festivals date from three years before the beginning of the common era and were dedicated to a female god of origin, the Queen Mother of the West (Xi Wang Mu), a celestial goddess with no historical legend as a person.

Imported teachings and heterodoxies

All the great religions of the world have existed in China at some time or other. In the past two thousand years Buddhism, Manichaeism, Christianity, Islam, and Judaism have entered China and been transformed. Manichaeism and an early Eastern Christianity were introduced in the seventh century by land from central Asia and by sea through south-eastern ports. They affected various syncretic movements, but have ceased to exist as separate traditions, though they could be revived. Similarly, Judaism has ceased to exist as a liturgical practice; just a few hundred people profess to be Jews and do not eat pork. By contrast, Roman Catholicism from the sixteenth century and Protestantism from the eighteenth century onwards have both spread and have increased dramatically in the last few decades. In addition, there are many Chinese-born Protestant movements.

Likewise, in every province there are Muslim families. But Islam entered China largely by the Chinese empire's western expansion into central Asia, particularly when it came under Mongol and Manchu rulers in the thirteenth and the seventeenth centuries. It exists mainly as the religion of non-Chinese people in its western provinces and as the descendants of immigrant Muslims who intermarried with locals everywhere else.

Of the introduced religions, Mahāyāna Buddhism (see Chapter 3 on Buddhism) has had by far the greatest influence. Its entry to China in the first two centuries of the common era, along the central Asian trade routes, began to have profound effects after it was adopted by emperors during a period of disunity between 311 and 589 CE. Asceticism and monastic organization were among its chief influences. But their slow spread throughout China was always in tension with the more persistent orthodoxy of family, lineal reproduction, worldly responsibility, the unworthiness of begging, and the imperial suspicion of the danger of vagrants to social order. Tantric Buddhism and its clergy, called lamas, were introduced to China in the seventh century. It took from Hindu religion an emphasis on ritual action, called *tantra*, which had something in common with the magical rites of Daoism, but it spread mainly with Tibetan influence in the south-western regions of China and as the religion of Mongol and Manchu rulers of China.

Some monarchs arranged disputations between the masters of opposed teachings. In addition, to enhance the cosmological power of their persons as well as the legitimacy of their reigns, several of them employed masters of one or another teaching – Daoist alchemists, Buddhist monks, or Roman Catholic scientists such as Matteo Ricci – and arranged for the collection of their teachings. Thrown together at court in this way, they influenced each other.

One of the greatest effects of this courtly presence has been the turning of what the Roman Christians learned at the imperial court into what Europe then learned to be the wisdom and religion of China. In particular the very idea of describing *rujiao* as 'Confucianism', as a religion among others, started in the writing of Christians and later returned to China as an aspect of its national heritage. It was also these court Christians who introduced into Chinese a translation of the word 'superstition' (*mixin*) by which to describe inferior religions, adding to the established vocabulary of condemnation of licentious sacrifices (*yinsi*) and errant sects (*xiepai*). Indeed, the suffix –ism (*zhuyi*) attached by European languages and later introduced into Chinese turned Chinese teachings and other ritual traditions into either lesser versions of the ultimate Truth or into one among many ideologies, which is now how an atheist government treats them. Possibly a more immediate effect of the manufacture of *rujiao* into Confucianism at the imperial court is the fact that from the seventeenth century onwards the dynasty founded by Manchu rulers, called the Qing dynasty, promoted the teachings of Confucius as the textual tradition superior to all others, made their laws more severely patriarchal than any previous dynasty and began the process of demoting both Daoist and Buddhist traditions. This was despite the fact that the Manchus like the Mongols before them were adherents of Lamaist Buddhism.

Many dynasties of rule in China, and many of the soldiers that overthrew these dynasties, have come from the margins of the empire, from the principalities or kingdoms or empires with which the Chinese empire had tributary and trading, diplomatic and warring relations, bringing with them their religious traditions. But then in power they have combined them with the Confucian tradition. Thus, tantric Buddhism can claim to have been the organization of both a spiritual and a political leadership through a small nobility in Tibet and through chiefdoms in the lands of the Mongols and the Manchus. But when the Manchu margin came to the centre, it relegated Buddhism to a means of controlling diplomatic relations with their former lands and the lands of the Mongols who had ruled over Tibetans as border regions. The Manchus as the Qing dynasty took each border region into an increasingly well-bounded empire or dealt with it, as with what is now the Tibetan autonomous region, as a region over which the dynasty claimed suzerainty in rivalry with the British Empire.

The negative result of the Manchu emperors' promotion of patriarchal Confucianism as its ruling ethic was the identification of Confucianism with the imperial rule of the Manchus and of the Manchus with the Western imperial incursions into China as the main targets of republican revolutionaries. This new national patriotism from the late nineteenth century onwards was strongly supported by Chinese living overseas in North America and Southeast Asia, but the republican governments nevertheless claimed the borders of the Manchu dynasty as their own.

Outside such authorized priorities there was a continual process of intermingling and a proliferation of teachings. At the same time, proliferation and mixing have been a source of political concern for all the regimes of China, including today's. Most unauthorized teachings were open and not rebellious, but some did purport to be a secret knowledge superseding all others, and this fuelled state suspicion of conspiracy with the result that there are many more records of secret societies with rebellious intent than actually existed. The best known is 'the White Lotus movement', which is still described as an extremely widespread teaching in the singular by those who rely too much on official records. 'White lotus' has in fact been shown to be a hostile official label for quite distinct syncretic teachings and rituals, combining Buddhist, Daoist and Confucian elements, from the fourteenth century to the present day and in northern China such syncretisms with their deities and ritual experts are the local popular religion of villages.

Most dangerous among heterodoxies were those in which a living person assumed an imperial title, ordinarily bestowed by the ruling emperor on humans-become-gods. Such heterodoxies were intrinsically rebellious and usually millennarian, promising a new age. They claimed a pedigree which was so often repeated that it can itself be considered a tradition without a text. In it, the world is seen as chaotic, a battlefield of demonic powers into which someone who can command them by secrets revealed through dream, vision or spiritual possession will bring about a new order. The secrets include treasures such as a peach and pennants coloured red and numbering nine, a sword, and a protective amulet that can be multiplied. The demon commander is a new emperor who has entered into a blood covenant with a bestowing divinity to save the world, in which humans are like hungry ghosts and are prey to the violent depredations of monster devils. The police in China have prosecuted several cases of such imperial impostors. They are haunted by the historical memory of how in the past some have become heads of great movements of rebellion, such as the syncretic Chinese Christian movement for Great Peace (Taiping) which conquered and ruled over many provinces of China from 1854 to 1864.

Human agency and the cosmos

In Chinese cosmology, human agency participates in the ordering of the universe through *Li* ('rites'). It is here that we come closest to being able to speak of a common Chinese religion.

One of the most common Chinese definitions of a rite is that it makes the invisible visible. Through the performance of rites at the proper occasions, humans make visible the underlying order. Performance of correct ritual focuses, links, orders and moves the social, which is the human realm, in correspondence with the terrestrial and celestial realms to keep all three in harmony. This procedure has been described as 'centring'. Centring was the duty of the Son of Heaven, the emperor, but it was also done by all those who conducted state, ancestral and life-cycle rites, and in another way by Daoists who conducted the rites of local gods as a centring of the forces of the universe upon a well-defined locality. Finally, centring was the issuing of texts, of exemplary history, of liturgical service, of the correct conduct of human relations, and of the arts of divination such as the earliest of all Chinese classics – the Book of Changes (Yi Jing) – joining textual learning to bodily practices for health and the harmonized enhancement of circuits of energy (*qi*).

All the different rituals conducted by officials of the Board of Rites, by Daoists, by local masters of ceremony or by local experts in the siting of graves and buildings according to the art popularly known as *fengshui*, convey a dynamic cosmology. In this cosmology the universe creates itself out of a primary chaos of material energy, organized into the cycles of Yin and Yang, and formed into objects and lives. Yin is the receptive and Yang the active principle, seen in all forms of change and difference such as the annual cycle (winter and summer), the landscape (north-facing shade, south-facing brightness), sexual coupling (female and male) and socio-political history (disorder and order). At the height of Yin, there is a growing nucleus of Yang, and similarly every state of Yang dominance harbours a reflux of Yin. Humans are merely one among the myriad things formed out of this primary organization of energies, or breaths, called *qi*. But since they can cultivate and centre them, human actors are themselves central.

The two cosmic principles of Yin and Yang are never personalized, but in a widespread usage they distinguish the invisible world of those who have died (Yin) from the visible world of the alive and corporeal (Yang). Dreaming and other kinds of communication with the dead have been described as meetings of Yin and Yang. The practical concept of force that establishes responsive communication between the Yin and the Yang worlds is *ling*. *Ling* is the magical power of gods or demons multiplied by their appearance in visions during trance, or by location through a ritual of inspiration into the objects which represent them. It is a power like that of the uncanny intelligence of great masters, of building or of healing, which is indeed one of the translations of the Chinese character for *ling* offered by dictionaries. *Ling* is a divine reciprocation for offerings and pledges of devotion to a deity or demon, an effective power sought to bring about such things as recovery from illness or success in gambling. At a more abstract level, it is a concept of the exemplary force of a sage, such as Confucius. Even more abstractly it has also been expounded as an attribute of the cosmological interplay between order and disorder.

Other forces could be conceived as universal or spontaneous, and at the same time personified and responsive. The state cults of the imperial dynasties included, at the highest and most elaborate level of sacrificial rites, not only temples for the veneration of the imperial ancestors but also open altars for offerings to Heaven, Earth, the heavenly bodies, Winds-Rain-Thunder-and-Clouds, Mountains and Rivers, Land and Grain. Like ancestors, they were represented by inscribed tablets and addressed with imperial titles. Similarly, in Daoism and Buddhism the most supreme and abstract concepts and positions in Chinese cosmology are also personalized. The Three Pure Points of the universe, the central one of which is that of primary origin, are personalized as Heavenly Worthies and as lords of the Three Treasures by Daoists. In Buddhism, Enlightenment, Salvation and post-apocalyptic Paradise are identified with three Buddhas: Sakyamuni, Amithabha, and Maitreya (whose Sanskrit names are transliterated into Chinese). And in sixteenth-century lay Buddhist and syncretic teachings, a myth and doctrine of the Unborn Venerable Mother was revealed as the personalization of the creative origin itself of the million things. She is the Matriarch of a heavenly realm of spirits from which humans have been exiled and to which they may hope to be returned in the new Maitreyan age.

Daoist recluses in monasteries or hermitages on mountains and other Daoist masters in their domestic altar rooms, which they treat as holy mountains, cultivate perfection by a discipline that concentrates cosmic forces. Their inner alchemy (*neidan*) takes them on a spiritual journey back to the original state of the cosmos transcending life and death and it gives them the power to sense both benign and malign energies and to ward the latter off by ritual techniques.

Buddhist recluses, particularly those in the Chinese Buddhist school of Chan Buddhism, similarly purify themselves in hermitages or monasteries by meditation and the reading of scriptures, and by work and other active exercises, including martial arts. But whereas Daoists seek to perfect their inner nature and thus attain oneness with the totality surrounding them, Buddhists seek to rid themselves of the emotional entanglement which is the self and to achieve enlightenment and the spiritual release described as Buddhahood. Transcendance in both cases is beyond the person, yet the states of immortality and Buddhahood are pictured as human bodies clothed and arranged in commanding and dignified postures.

At the more disorderly end of the cosmos, Daoist priests conduct rituals of adjustment for the refurbishing or opening of temples, which include dances with swords to command deities who are military heroes to bring demons under control. In lesser rituals they issue talismans of similar command to rid clients of malign influences. Daoists serving clients and communities as masters of purification, exorcising malign forces of ill-health and spiritual clouding both personal and territorial, invoke in their own bodies the Yin, the northern figure of the Sombre Warrior associated with water and the ancient hero Yü who first controlled the waters and channelled them. Below the Sombre Warrior are the female warrior of lightning and the male warrior of thunder, identified with the Daoist's feet with which he will stamp and hold down demons. Having invoked or rather identified himself with them by focusing on the appropriate part of his body and visualizing them, the Daoist master then dances with sword in hand the constellation of the dipper for the four directions from the centre, each time commanding the expulsion of filth. It is apparent that, although male, Daoist masters of purification rituals identify within themselves powerful female as well as male deities. The female principle can be warlike as well as maternal.

The fiercest and most malign demons are not human ghosts. They are monsters such as the Hound of Heaven, or the White Tiger, or another one of the 108 baleful stars. Exorcising them is not to destroy, but to control them, putting them in their places where their forces are no longer baleful. There is certainly non-human agency in Chinese religious cosmology, even in this demonic, most popular and vivid imagery. But command over it is human. This imagery of command over demons is most evident in the territorial guardian carnivals and processional pilgrimages to regional temples that define every place as part of a sacred landscape. It is the vision of an imperium as seen by commoners. On the other hand, those in positions of authority within the system of actual imperial or indeed republican rule decry the popular festivals, meat offerings and feasts as carnal, wasteful, and superstitious, and stress the more civil, ascetic and abstract nature of the cosmos. They scorn as wild and heterodox the vernacular spirit-mediums producing written or spoken voices of deities and the recently dead. The latter are demonstrative, theatrical productions in trances whose contents are not remembered by the medium, whereas elite inspiration occurs in solitude and is remembered by its medium.

Death rituals work the other way around, from personal to cosmological status. They deal directly with the demonic aspects of human being. All three textual traditions are involved. In rites of encoffinment, burial and commemoration, all human beings are treated as ghosts. If neglected or abandoned, they are hungry and trapped in the places where they met their death and can be very harmful to those who pass by. Death rituals deal with three aspects of human being. They seal off the demonic and corporeal aspects, by burying the body whose bones convey the forces gathered by the site of the grave. They honour and elevate what is conceived as an ancestor. Third, they intervene on behalf of a soul that needs salvation into the Buddhist Western Paradise. The ancestor is installed as a name onto the domestic altar of its descendants, to be honoured on its death-day and on standard occasions for the veneration of ancestors. The soul must be released from a purgatory pictured in both Daoist and Buddhist scrolls, prints, and temple murals. It is as lurid in its inventions of torment and torture as that of Christianity.

The gaining of merit, by virtue of the soul's children employing Buddhists or Daoists to recite scriptures and intercede on behalf of a soul, is solemn and repetitive. But attached to it is a much more theatrical enactment of the mythic stories of those who, like the filial son Mu Lian rescuing his dead mother or the merciful first emperor of the Tang dynasty, crossed from the Yang to the Yin world. The fact that they made the crossing shows the way to intercede on behalf of what would otherwise be an eternally trapped or forgotten soul. The performances of their crossings include comic enactments of the wiles of bribery and cajoling needed to find a way past guardian monsters and officious gatekeepers.

Many people have observed that the imperial imagery of the Yin world is an idealization of the bureaucracy and courts of Chinese

FIGURE 5.2 Hell Scroll (see note on page 133 opposite)

dynastic rule. But it differs markedly from the actual imperial administration in its gender and in its stress on military command. Imperial authority and the orthodoxy of ancestral veneration were strictly male and stressed descent in the male line, whereas the celestial pantheon included very important female deities. The most important and widespread god of intercession, for the dead, for women wanting children, and for the sick, was originally a Buddhist divinity who in Chinese history was transformed from a male into a female deity. This is the bodhisattva or *pusa* (one who has achieved buddhahood but chooses to remain in merciful attachment to the world) who in Sanskrit is called Avalokitesvara. In China he was merged with the legendary Miaoshan, a princess who incurred her father's rage by her choice of an ascetic, unmarried life until her death. She then returned to save him from severe physical and moral sickness by the sacrifice of her eyes and arms for him to eat as medicine. As a deity she is the female Guanyin, often known in English as the Goddess of Mercy. Her depiction is usually benign, but many Buddhist temples portray her other aspect as a much more majestic and commanding deity with a thousand arms and with her feet literally stamping authority on the monstrous dragon of the waters which is the realm of demons. Daoists honour her, as well as Buddhists. She is one of the gods whose worship has spread throughout China and epitomizes the mix of vernacular and textual traditions in Chinese religion and she brings even further to the fore than the Daoist cultivation of female warriors the figure of ambivalent female divinity, benign, commanding, unmarried and at the same time filial.

NOTE TO FIGURE 5.2

This is one of a set of scrolls that a family of Buddhists in northern Taiwan used in the 1960s for merit-making ceremonies after a death. The scrolls surrounded a provisional altar table before which the Buddhists read the scriptures and performed the rites to cross over into the invisible world of the dead in order to rescue the soul of the deceased from purgatory. Such sets of scrolls are quite standard, but allow local variations and when Daoists put theirs up the three Heavenly Worthies will hang at the centre behind their altar table, not the three Buddhas. The full set used by this Buddhist family includes the three Buddhas, scenes from the Journey to the West – a set of stories about the bringing to China of the first Buddhist scriptures, 24 scenes of filial piety in the family, and the ten courts of purgatory. At the top in the centre of the scroll shown here is the last, tenth court whose president is the Prince of Karma (the turning to new life through death according to a ledger of merit and misdeeds committed in each previous life). Everything is labelled, to help the mourning family and its neighbours familiarize themselves with the afterlife. To his left is the Gate of the Wheel of Karma of human ghosts or demons (*gui*), whose rebirth is shown in the incense smoke rising from the cylinders on the shelf. To his right is seated a benevolent old woman, the Buddhist Goddess Meng So. Below them are virtuous people being led up to rebirth as spirits (*shen*), or prosperous worthies, or good officials (another scroll shows the terribly killed victims coming out of the City of Victims of Official Injustice). The scroll of the first court depicts a similar scene, the Gold and Silver Bridge across which the meritorious are being led, but in their case straight to the Western Paradise – the end of the cycle of Karma. Below the meritorious figures are four hells, showing human ghosts tormented by demons and labelled by the misdeed for which they are there. Some of them are: in the upper two mountains, cruelty and plotting to injure others; in the Ox-goring Hell, killing oxen; in the Hell of the Tree of Double-edged Swords, again plotting against others, and harming their *fengshui* (the geomantic siting of ancestors' graves). Courtesy Stephan Feuchtwang.

Interactions with modernity

Modernity in the long term

The gradual modernization of China over a thousand years brought with it a synchronic development through mutual influence of the three teachings of Confucianism, Daoism and Buddhism, as we now know them.

By the tenth century, the increasing power of the imperial bureaucracy had reduced the privileges of a class of landed magnates and augmented those of the literati. The growth of commerce and manufacture was already providing new channels of social mobility and achievement of high status through mercantile wealth and the education of children so that the next generation could be admitted into the ruling class of literati.

After a series of introductions of different kinds of Buddhism from the fourth century onwards, two main schools of monastic Buddhism persisted. One is that of the Pure Land, both monastic and lay. It is a discipline of ascetic vows, learning what the patriarchs of the order said. For lay followers it is simplified into the practice of repeating the name of Amithabha (O-mi-to-hu) in greeting, parting and any other opportunity, in order to escape the cycle of rebirths and be born into the Pure Land as a place rather than as a state of mind. Gatherings of lay Buddhists for the recitation of Omitohu called themselves White Lotus meetings, after the floating bloom which symbolizes purity and transcendence from muddy underwater roots.

The other Chinese school of Buddhism is Chan, a monastic order that included productive labour, rather than begging for alms, and a highly ritualized discipline to induce sudden enlightenment. The state of enlightenment, provoked by the master's impossible paradoxes and quizzical gestures, is a non-activity, a plunge into the state of nothingness that precedes all distinctions.

Buddhist and Daoist monks earn material rewards as well as spiritual merit by performing scriptural readings and rites of sacrificial offering for the laity. Buddhist specialities are merit-making for the dead, as souls and as ghosts, and the charitable care of the forgotten dead in the seventh-month festival of the release of hungry ghosts to be fed and clothed by offerings transformed by rhetorical hand gestures (*mudra*) and the appropriate scripture of alms-giving. Daoists also perform these rituals, as well as their own speciality of the *jiao*, a great exorcism and offering for cosmic adjustment and harmonization of sacred places and their territories involving the whole population of the territory over a period of three or more days.

As the Chinese empire in the Song dynasty (960–1278) reached heights of commerce and civil culture unrivalled in the world, a version of *rujiao* became state orthodoxy. But it was very different from that of Confucius. It is for good reason called Neo-Confucianism, since it incorporated Buddhist and Daoist ideas and disciplines of the purification of self. Inner reality became a source of authority, but in relationship with the outer world of others. It was a relationship tense with the problems of not accomplishing the required calm and oneness with others. This tension of incompletion was to be covered over with decorum and strategies of indirection, the cultivation of face and good repute in human relations.

Emphasis on *Li* was always central to Confucianism. But Li had begun as a term for royal and noble sacrifices to ancestors and to deities and was then extended to all the manners and protocols of the court and nobility. Now the scope and meaning of Li was broadened to the whole population of China who were to be guided in the cultivation of their dispositions, inclinations, and emotions. To perform Li is to cultivate an ideal of human responsiveness, not only to other humans and their stations in the imperial and patriarchal order but also to the rest of the world and its harmony. This was the ideal and the ideology of the ruling literati of China. But their acts of cruelty, ruthless careerism and indulgence in the pleasures of eating, sex, and drugs led to accusations of hypocrisy.

Vernacular literacy and commerce spread and their networks of communication deepened from the fourteenth century onwards presenting many challenges to the moral authority of the literati and to the administration of the empire. The empire itself was going through a demographic explosion, putting extra strains on the comparatively small staff of the imperial civil service. Local gentry became increasingly powerful. They extended the notion of family and kinship to tax-protected clients. Many among the rest of the rural population, over-taxed and thrown into debt, had no alternative than to allow their land to be expropriated. They became bondservants and labourers for the commercializing gentry. Against this, replacing the disappointed expectations of local ties of benevolence and compassion, new kinds of association were created, under the patronage of reform-minded gentry. Among such new associations were syncretic religions bringing together Neo-Confucian teachings, the Buddhism of lay leaders independent of monasteries, and Daoist healing and meditational techniques. Many of their leaders were evangelists giving public lectures, publishing moral tracts, and keeping moral ledgers by which the merit and demerit of their followers' actions could be recorded and their prospects of salvation calculated. The Confucian priority of filial duty was retained but placed in a larger Buddhist context of karmic retribution. At the same time, the effort and discipline of classical learning and ritual were undermined by doctrines of spontaneous enlightenment.

Eventually, in the seventeenth century, against such popular moral cultivation, there was a Confucian reaction. High-ranking and disillusioned or dismissed officials and some of the highest degree holders in the lower Yangtze River region formed the Donglin Academy for reform of the literati and the practice of good administration. In order to deny authenticity to the many new sectarian associations, they demanded return to the canonized classics and the virtues they proclaimed.

The new stress on the original writings of a sage was accompanied by the development of an apparatus of careful textual scholarship to authenticate what was and was not written by the claimed master. In the same vein, empirical observation of astronomical and other changes, using whatever new instruments had been developed in China or brought to it, were another way of establishing authenticity and the superiority of the scholarly elite. In this way, the preservation of the authentically ancient came into tension with the observations of anomalies and irregularities. Great sophistication was required to justify ancient cosmology. Scholars themselves drew the parallel between the inevitability of corruption leading to the necessity for reform of the human heart-mind (*xin*), which includes rectification of social custom, and observations of anomalies leading to the necessity for a rectification of cosmology. Communications between the lowest and highest levels of the imperial bureaucracy maintained the prestige of this new metaphysics. They funnelled suspicion of every new movement of lay Buddhism and syncretic association. Conversely, corruption and extortion, large-scale persecution of peaceful associations, and the rebellions of millennarian sects against their persecution spread wide a sense of insecurity.

In this atmosphere, several bouts of mass fear flared, word passing like prairie fire of spells being posted on doors and weird shapes flying into people's houses and causing disaster. Such panics had occurred before, but in the sixteenth century for the first time they were attributed to individual magicians who were Buddhist monks, Daoist priests, carpenters, puppeteers, peddlers, or beggars, precisely the travelling objects of official suspicion and persecution. The internalization of agency and authority into magicians and imperial impostors paralleled the internalization of dignity, agency and authority in orthodox Neo-Confucianism.

Panics and mass fear indicated political crisis and growing numbers of those dislocated by debt and into beggary, refugees from flood, drought, banditry and the depredations of imperial troops. Another indication of political crisis was the increasing mobilization of local militia, organized as martial arts bands displaying the forces of the generals and soldiers of a local protective deity. Now they took part in uprisings to bring about a new age and to overthrow the rule and power of strangers, such as the Manchu dynasty or the missionaries of European business and religion, and any others branded as spies by local residents.

Lay communities

Buddhist monasteries and the imperial state together tried to bring under control one of these movements of new teaching, a movement whose followers took ascetic vows (*zhaijiao*). Their number grew into a proliferation of branches from the sixteenth century onwards. These lay Buddhists accused the tonsured Sangha of corruption, mocked them in popular stories, and declared themselves to be separate and better. They formed their own lay Sangha, combining married life with fasts, obedience to key precepts such as not to indulge in malicious or salacious talk, nourishing life in the Daoist and Chan way, cultivating the Neo-Confucian way of Heaven, and studying precious scrolls revealed and derived ultimately from the Unborn Venerable Mother. They met in congregations for the recital of memorized passages from both the orthodox *sutras* and the newly revealed precious scrolls and made donations for the printing and distribution of the scrolls and the building of assembly halls. Their congregations included both women and men, which was a scandal for Confucian orthodoxy. More scandalous yet, biographies of model women who had renounced marriage, and the stories of female deities who had done the same, encouraged one strand of this movement in which women formed communities equivalent to nunneries except that they earned their own livelihood by silk manufacture.

Religious communities for the less literate included meetings of the pupils of masters of meditation, the circulation of breaths that are also energies (*qi*) and other exercises to recover from illness, to nourish one's nature (*xing*) and strengthen one's destiny (*ming*), an inner visioning of the colours, directions, forces and processes of the cosmos. Often this strengthening had a martial character. The most famous of these networks of masters and pupils was centred on the Shaolin Buddhist monastery, but there were many others.

The most common 'religious' communities by far were, however, not these voluntary Buddhist and syncretic associations, but those formed by neighbourhood temples in cities, village ancestral halls and local, rural temples. Their endowments of land furnished the means to perform annual festivals, provide special meals and meeting places for the elderly, and in the case of ancestral trusts elementary schooling for lineage children. In many instances temples or halls were village corporations through which the use of such common property as land and inshore waters was distributed, or market concessions and standards of weight and measure were managed. In all instances, in addition to these sources of income, the collection of dues from households paid for the refurbishing of the local hall or temple, and for the procession and theatre of annual festivals. To donate to temple and festival was a work of public good by local residents along with the building of bridges and opening of roads. Rotation of responsibility for paying respects to the smallest Earth God could, for instance, carry with it responsibility for maintaining paths and bridges.

Republican modernity

Finally, though, it was not a millennarian uprising nor a combination of local temple militia but a republican movement for self-strengthening progress that did away with the imperial state, its cosmological rites, and its Neo-Confucian orthodoxy. The political parties and the new armies of the Nationalists and the Communists that rose through the republican movement fought a devastating civil war interrupted by the eight years of Japanese invasion and occupation (1937–1945). But they had two things in common: the profession of representing 'the people' rather than a celestial mandate to rule harmoniously, and the promotion of mass literacy and a scientific education. Both established a secular and constitutional definition of religion as an organized institution of beliefs and textual authority defined as an –ism. They also carried forward the imperial state's suspicion of lay religious communities and movements and condemnations of the carnal, theatrical and martial festivals of local temples. But of course the condemnation of superstition in twentieth-century China is implemented by governments with far larger apparatuses of policing than those of the imperial state. Among them in the People's Republic of China is the Bureau of Religious Affairs with which every religious institution has to register if it is to avoid the potential danger of being harassed or persecuted.

The new word *zongjiao* used to import the category 'religion' from Europe combines 'ancestral tradition' with 'teaching'. Institutions that fit this category, such as monasteries and churches, so long as they are patriotic, which means supportive of the state, are registered and granted the religious freedom pronounced by the state's Constitution. In the People's Republic (mainland China) everything else is liable to be 'superstition'. 'Superstition' appears in the 1997 Criminal Code of the People's Republic alongside older categories of legal prohibition on forming secret societies and using heterodox teachings to organize movements which cause unrest or cover other criminal and sexually licentious acts.

'Superstition' is a condemnation of aspects of popular culture that do not suit the ideals of a project of modernization. But since these modern governments claim popular legitimacy, compromises are made. Modernity's ideologues swing between condemnation and treating popular religion as a heritage and local custom to be preserved. Religious buildings and spectacles can be an attraction to tourists and to the nostalgia for their origins of urban and overseas visitors. In either case, religious activities are now legitimized by the agencies of a secular state.

In the middle of the twentieth century, the Communist state of the People's Republic on the mainland and the Nationalist state on the island of Taiwan redistributed the land, not only of private but also of corporate landlords. A main material foundation of religious communities was thereby removed. The building and repair of large and small temples and the holding of festivals were forced to rely only on subscription and donation, an appropriately populist basis for sacred communities. In any case, the main causes of decline in religious activities have been not the confiscation of land but two others. One is mass destitution – caused by war, civil war, and economic disaster; the converse is also true – prosperity has been the main spur to religious activity. The other is deliberate political action. Destroying local temples or turning them into schools began in the short period of an attempted reform by the Manchu dynastic court and then gathered pace in the Nationalist republican government from 1912 onward. But its pace accelerated from 1953 on the mainland when the collectivization of land and the state administration of industry created a monopoly for socialist political culture. First, it made religious teachings and practices private and marginal. Then, in the culmination of a series of campaigns against religion, the Cultural Revolution campaign against old habits, ideas, customs and culture in 1966 and 1967 destroyed or forced them underground.

Maoist socialism as expounded and recited during the Cultural Revolution eventually exhausted its ideological credibility as campaigns became too frequent and too patently used for personal vengeance and advancement by activists. It was replaced by the socialism of advancing the people's material livelihood. Religious buildings were returned and 'fevers' (*re*) of enthusiasm for various teachings occurred, particularly those of *qi* exercises promoted by various masters, some accepted by officials as 'scientific' (*kexue*, both natural and historical knowledge) others as dangers to society.

One lasting effect of the political rituals of mass mobilization is the habit of congregational participation with overtones of egalitarian comradeship and mutual support. This may be one reason for the increase in the numbers of Christian meeting places and churches. Indeed, the Cultural Revolution was often the period in which these meeting places and house churches started, secretly of course.

Looking to the future

In both Taiwan and the mainland, the intensity of material incentives and engagement in global economic competition has brought about a ruthless cynicism on one hand and a search for spiritual healing and justification on the other. Senses of moral regeneration in a chaotic and corrupt world are sought as before in local temples from responsive deities or in millennarian teachings and communities, and imperial impostors thrive among those left out of material advancement. But other, newer senses of religious community, not confined to a place or to traditional paradigms, have also emerged.

Freed from the assertion of imperial canonical, ritual and cosmological authority, religious traditions and movements in China now renew themselves under another kind of authority. With varying emphasis they present themselves and are presented as a national or a local identification under a compulsion, which is both externally imposed and internalized, to historicize themselves within a grand narrative of the Chinese people or peoples. At the same time they assert an alternative and transcendental authority. It may be an authority within the cosmology of the Way of *qi*, Yin and Yang and *ling*, or re-formulations of syncretic Buddhism and neo-Confucianism. It may be the joining of new transnational foundations of Buddhist, Christian and Muslim teachings. It may be the wish to escape all political involvement by withdrawal into communities of mutual spiritual support, such as house churches and meeting places. But none of them escape politicization, because they are always subject to governmental surveillance or supervision.

Meetings in parks and other open spaces for *qi* exercises increased with the increasing number of retired people, organizing themselves, helping each other, exchanging views of the world. But since they are not in regulated surroundings such as schools, they are looked upon with suspicion and anxiety by government agencies, because they hark back to the mass movements of the Mao era or even further back to the Taiping Kingdom of the nineteenth century. Many of the masters and mistresses of *qigong* – exercise techniques or methods – have been arrested and prosecuted for fraud or for creating disorder. A reduction in gatherings for *qi* exercise in public places occurred at the end of the twentieth century for one main reason, the popularity of one master, Li Hongzhi and his method. He turned the exercises into one of primarily spiritual accomplishment in which the world became a stage for an apocalyptic moral battle against demonic forces. Other masters did the same but none as well as he did. His was the Great Method of the Karmic Wheel – the literal English translation of the Falun Dafa or Falun'gong. It created a fixed line of division between itself and all other methods and rituals. The Method of the Great Wheel did not openly challenge the Chinese Communist Party and its state, but its practitioners protested by mass meditation against every publication or broadcast that questioned its validity, along with well-placed letters of protest and petition. Its members had the means to co-ordinate these peaceful protests. When one such protest gathered outside the residential and office headquarters of the Party in Beijing in 1999, Jiang Zemin as Party Chairman treated it as a political challenge to the Party on the same line of division. He ordered a massive and sustained crackdown, which brought all public gatherings for *qi* exercises under suspicion. His response became a self-fulfilling prophecy for the Falun'gong, whose practitioners were prepared to risk their bodies and suffer beatings and imprisonment and worse in continuing non-violent protests as a discipline that cultivates one of the three parts of their spiritual attainment – Forbearance. Followers of this spiritual leader, who lives in exile in the USA, exist all over the world and continue the Method of the Karmic Wheel, usually indoors and on their own, while also gathering in person or virtually on the web to protest the suppression of Falun'gong in its country of origin.

In Taiwan, where the government of the Nationalist Party has been transformed into a far more open, tolerant and multi-party regime, religious activities are far less strictly supervised. But culture, including religious culture, is the subject of intense rivalry between the main political parties, competing for community development and loyalty, and for establishing a sense of Taiwanese identity. Another new development is the rise of Buddhist foundations, enormously wealthy on the basis of donations. These new Buddhist teachings emphasise action in the world such as flood and earthquake relief, the building of hospitals, universities and museums. They result from reforms of the Buddhist Sangha led by monks on the mainland during the first fifty years of the twentieth century, influenced by and competing with imported Christian institutions of welfare, such as the YMCA. Now, in Taiwan many are led by nuns. Like Falun'gong, they too have a global diaspora, including a few non-Chinese adherents.

Nothing like this is yet possible on the mainland. There, selected Daoist and Buddhist seminaries are training a small, controlled number of monks and ritual experts. They are, as in imperial times, part of the system of religious control and supervision. But beyond their influence, Daoist and Buddhist families have revived their own traditions in several regions of every province by pooling resources, bringing out such manuscripts as they had managed to keep and sharing what they could recall of their liturgies. In all provinces of China, temples and ancestral halls have been rebuilt usually with the endorsement of local officials. New cults have been added, including for instance in southern Fujian province Che Gong, a protector of motor vehicles, and in the northern province of Shaanxi the Three Sages: Mao, his Premier Zhou Enlai, and General Zhu De. But in some regions and in most large cities, local cults and festivals have not been revived. This may be because of the presence and vigilance of officials convinced of the worth of the project of scientific modernization and Party atheism. It may also be because the destruction of religious institutions in these regions was so long ago that they are no longer in living memory. But in these places, as elsewhere in China, over and beyond the revival of local festivals, congregational religion (Buddhist or Christian) is growing, forming communities of followers of a faith which does sometimes coincide with a locality, but need not.

Gender

Gender considerations appear to have a bearing on the growth of congregational forms of religion. Local temple and rural domestic forms of rite and festival are not congregational and here males dominate public roles. Women do the everyday care of shrines, including domestic and temple offerings, and help prepare the offerings for the great public occasions. They also participate in the gatherings to watch theatre and processions, and they take part in pilgrimages. But Christian and Buddhist congregational meetings are public settings in which women have in recent centuries not only participated but assumed positions of leadership. This feminization may well turn out to be a feature of future religious practices in other traditions, as it is increasingly in town and city dance and *qi* exercise groups. Female drum and musical bands have also been formed in some villages and towns, whereas in the past they had been exclusive male preserves. The participation of young women in groups opposite groups of young men singing karaoke in towns and large villages is a parallel development.

Patriarchy, associated with Confucius, continues strongly to be associated with the veneration of ancestors. But on the other hand, the promotion of cremation instead of burial, the fast urbanization of Chinese dwellings, migration to cities, and increasing prosperity allowing couples to live separately rather than with the man's parents have all changed kinship and family patterns in favour of movement toward equal partnerships between man and wife, and reducing ancestor worship and gatherings at graves of distant common ancestors.

Ancestors are still revered in most households, particularly when families get together during the longest annual holiday at the turn of the lunar New Year, officially called the Spring Festival in partial denial of its traditional religious importance. When new houses are built for married sons ceremonies are performed for the breaking of the earth, the raising of the roof-beam, and completion, to ward off malign influences and bring blessings. The expertise of *fengshui* masters is sought for the orientation of houses in villages and graves in cemeteries. Recent studies indicate increased resorting to *fengshui* masters, other kinds of diviner, and spirit mediums for cures for ill-health, exorcising dwellings and other rites for changes of fortune.

On the other hand, the new, more congregational religious communities create environments for mutual care and transcendent principles of judging worldly conduct, including the self-centred exploitation of the world and its energies, and the conduct of political leaders and local officials. But as before in China, these new, less localized senses of transcendent self and community are not exclusive. Their followers often also participate in revitalized local cults and festivals, employ Daoist ritual experts and express a sense of national political pride.

Rather ambivalently, the heritage of Confucius, condemned to eradication in a campaign during the last years of the Cultural Revolution decade, is now officially spon-sored and recycled as the distinctively Chinese spirit of the remarkable growth of the Chinese economy, and as an encouragement of overseas Chinese to invest in China and renew their roots. Philosophical studies of Confucian thought are published, his home and the temple to him in Qufu, Shandong province, are well kept and visited by high officials for the annual celebrations of his birthday. Something similar but so far with less expense and propagation is growing around Daoist philosophical texts and the centres of religious Daoism in some of its sacred mountains. Buddhism has also been promoted, as has Islam, in a strictly controlled fashion as channels of diplomacy for international relations.

They have been promoted along with a number of national shrines and birthdays of legendary and historical figures of Chinese ethnic nationality. They start with the mythic founder of the Chinese 'race', the Yellow Emperor. But more numerous are the memorials to twentieth-century founders such as Sun Yatsen, leader of the first Republic in 1911, and the monuments, birth-places and dwellings during their military campaigns of Mao, Deng Xiaoping and other selected heroes of the Communist revolution. In the same spirit, minority nationalities in China have also built shrines to heroes of their own ethno-history, such as the great Mongol emperor Genghis Khan in Inner Mongolia. The revitalization of Islam among the north-western peoples of China, and the politico-religious reverence of the Dalai Lama among Tibetans in China participate in the same cycle of ethnic nationalism and global communication. But of course they are far more problematic to the leaders of the Chinese Communist Party than their own promotion of the cult of the Yellow Emperor.

Summary

- There are three main written religious traditions in China: 1. ancestral veneration, filial duty, reciprocity and the importance of rites, associated with the teaching of Confucius; 2. the disciplines and rituals of harmonization with the cosmic order, called Daoism; 3. Mahayana Buddhism and the rituals and disciplines of merit-making for reincarnation and salvation from purgatory.

- These traditions are eclectically mixed, and have influenced each other deeply in the course of the millennium of slow modernity from the tenth century under an established imperial bureaucracy and its literati.

- They are also mixed with a great number of vernacular traditions and local cults and festivals.

- Running through both written and vernacular traditions are a number of cosmo-logical principles and their personifications as deities. They include Tian (celestial order), the internal creativity of the universe out of its own origin, human agency in the harmonization of celestial and earthly orders, the complementarity of Yin and Yang, effective and communicative response beyond death between Yin and Yang, and the potential for both order and disorder in human demonic power and material energies, benign and malign, in a universal condition of constant change.

- The imperial state sought control through the authorization of religious orthodoxies and suspicion of what it had not authorized.

- Since at least the sixteenth century there has been a growth of lay religious communities, evangelical and syncretic, but the most common lay religious communities were those based on ancestral graves or halls and on local temples, a great many of which have been revived after their destruction in the Cultural Revolution (1966–1976).

■ Rule by secular, modernizing and atheist regimes in the twentieth century has established much stronger powers of supervision over religious teaching and activity.

■ At the end of the twentieth century this was accompanied by ethnic nationalization of Chinese and non-Chinese traditions, drawing local traditions into national narratives.

■ There has also been an increase in contrasting religious styles. One of them is congregational religion, Buddhist and Christian, in which women predominate. They may develop into large-scale non-governmental organisations of poverty relief, education and other kinds of charitable engagement in the world.

■ The other style is self- and family-centred consultation of spirit-media, or by *fengshui* and exercises to accumulate and strengthen *qi* to change luck and cure spiritual and physical sickness.

Key terms

cosmology A transcendental context of life, which places it in a universe of forces and an order of things.

fengshui The art of selecting an auspicious site for dwellings, graves and important buildings, and for laying out gardens and cities.

immortal One who has achieved perfection through inner alchemy and achieved unity with the Way (*dao*), transcending life and death. Stories of immortals, particularly those of a set called the Eight Immortals, tell of their funny, robust, licentious and heroic deeds.

li Rites, manners and protocol; observance of the right way of doing things; making the invisible visible.

ling The uncanny power to respond, of a sage, a deity or a demon.

literati Those who had been educated in the classics of the canon of scholars, whose greatest transmitter was Confucius, and who had passed at least the lowest level of the examinations testing their knowledge of these classics to qualify for entry into the imperial civil service.

mantic Of or concerning divination, spirit possession, or prophecy.

patriarch A Buddhist sage who has taken on the teaching of a previous patriarch, sometimes claiming to being his reincarnation.

patriarchy The senior male monopoly of public authority, including authority over a family.

qi Energies or breaths.

sage A person whose wisdom and teachings have been passed on and are paid the highest respect.

Further reading

General

Christian Joachim: *Chinese Religions; A Cultural Perspective* (Englewood Cliffs, NJ: Prentice-Hall, 1986).

Sourcebook

Gary Seaman and Laurence Thompson: *Chinese Religions: Publications in Western Languages, Volume 3: 1991–1995* (Ann Arbor, MI: University of Michigan Press, 1998).

Cosmology and divination

John B. Henderson: *The Development and Decline of Chinese Cosmology* (New York: Columbia University Press, 1984).
Richard J. Smith: *Fortune-Tellers and Philosophers: Divination in Traditional Chinese Society* (Boulder, CO: Westview Press, 1991).

Daoism

Judith Bolz: *Survey of Taoist Literature; Tenth to Seventeenth Centuries* (Berkeley, CA: Institute of East Asian Studies, University of California, 1987).
Vincent Goossaert: *The Taoists of Peking, 1800–1949: A Social History of Urban Clerics.* Harvard East Asian Monographs (Cambridge, MA: Harvard University Press, 2007).
John Lagerwey: *Taoist Ritual in Chinese Society and Tradition* (London and New York: Macmillan, 1987).
Kristofer Schipper: *The Daoist Body* (Berkeley, CA: University of California Press, 1993).

Confucianism

Chow Kai-wing: *The Rise of Confucian Ritualism in Late Imperial China* (Stanford, CA: Stanford University Press, 1994).
Patricia Buckley Ebrey: *Confucianism and Family Rituals in Imperial China: A Social History of Writing about Rites* (Princeton, NJ: Princeton University Press, 1991).
Lionel M. Jensen: *Manufacturing Confucianism: Chinese Traditions and Universal Civilisation* (Durham, NC and London: Duke University Press, 1997).

State cults

Angela Zito: *Of Body and Brush: Grand Sacrifice as Text/Performance in Eighteenth-Century China* (Chicago, IL and London: University of Chicago Press, 1997).

Buddhism

Holmes Welch: *The Practice of Chinese Buddhism, 1900–1950* (Cambridge, MA: Harvard University Press, 1967).

Holmes Welch: *The Buddhist Revival in China* (Cambridge, MA: Harvard University Press, 1968).

Christianity

K-k Chan and Alan Hunter: *Protestantism in Contemporary China* (Cambridge: Cambridge University Press, 1993).

Richard Madsen: *China's Catholics: Tragedy and Hope in an Emerging Civil Society* (Berkeley, CA: University of California Press, 1998).

Islam

Dru Gladney: *Muslim Chinese: Ethnic Nationalism in the People's Republic* (Cambridge, MA and London: Harvard University Press, 1991).

Popular religion

Stephan Feuchtwang: *Popular Religion in China: The Imperial Metaphor* (Richmond: Curzon Press, 2000).

Philip A. Kuhn: *Soulstealers: The Chinese Sorcery Scare of 1768* (Cambridge, MA: Harvard University Press, 1990).

David Palmer: *Qigong Fever: Body, Science and Utopia in China* (London: Hurst & Co, 2007).

Steven P. Sangren: *History and Magical Power in a Chinese Community* (Stanford, CA: Stanford University Press, 1987).

James Watson and Evelyn Rawski (eds): *Death Ritual in Late Imperial and Modern China* (Berkeley, CA: University of California Press, 1988).

Syncretic teachings and millennarianism

Thomas David Dubois: *The Sacred Village: Social Change and Religious Life in Rural North China* (Honolulu: University of Hawaii Press, 2005).

Barend ter Haar: *The White Lotus Teachings in Chinese Religious History* (Leiden: E. J. Brill, 1992).

David Johnson *et al.* (ed): *Popular Culture in Late Imperial China* (Berkeley, CA: University of California Press, 1985) [the chapters by Judith Berling, Susan Naquin and Daniel Overmyer].

The Cultural Revolution and its rituals

Richard Madsen: *Morality and Power in a Chinese Village* (Berkeley, CA: University of California Press, 1984).

Chapter 6

Japanese religions

Robert J. Kisala

Introduction

In contrast to the situation in many of the European countries and some other areas of the West, where we see relatively high levels of at least nominal religious affiliation and low levels of participation in religious rites, religion in Japan is marked by almost universal participation in certain rites and customs but low levels of self-acknowledged affiliation to a religious group. It has become commonplace to say that Japanese are born Shinto, marry as Christians and die Buddhists, a phrase that indicates both the high level of participation in religious rites of passage as well as the eclectic nature of Japanese religiosity. Note is also often made of the fact that nearly 90 per cent of the Japanese observe the custom of annual visits to ancestral graves, and 75 per cent have either a Buddhist or Shinto altar in their home. However, surveys consistently show that only 30 per cent of the population identify themselves as belonging to one of the religions active in Japan – this despite the fact that the religions themselves claim an overall total membership that approaches twice the actual population of 126 million. This is mainly due to the fact that much of the population is automatically counted as parishioners of both the local Shinto shrine and the ancestral Buddhist temple.

Although identified today as the major religious traditions of Japan, Buddhism and Shinto have been so closely intertwined throughout much of Japanese history that the forced separation of the two at the beginning of the modern period in the mid-nineteenth century resulted in a great upheaval in Japanese religious practice that, some have argued, continues to have repercussions today. In addition, these religious traditions have been combined with elements of Daoism and Confucianism from China, issuing in a kind of common or popular religiosity that is not easily contained in any one religious tradition. Christianity, introduced to Japan in the fifteenth century by the Catholic missionaries who accompanied the Spanish and Portuguese explorers, was actively persecuted throughout the early modern period (seventeenth century to mid-nineteenth century), and small groups of 'hidden Christians' continue to preserve a secret faith tradition that they trace back to the time of persecution. Reintroduced in the modern period, Christianity has had little success in attracting members in Japan, with less than 1 per cent of the population belonging to one of the Christian churches. Christian influence is generally acknowledged as greater than those membership numbers would indicate, however, especially in the fields of education and social welfare.

The modern period has seen the proliferation of new religious movements in Japan, to the extent that the country has sometimes been called a veritable religious museum and laboratory. Some of the new religions trace their roots to the end of the early modern period in the first half of the nineteenth century. Groups from this period are often based on folk religious practices and the experiences of a charismatic founder, and they can be described as attempts to revitalize traditional cultural elements in the face of the influx of Western influences during that century. Another wave of new religious movements emerged in the immediate postwar period, attracting much media attention in Japan as well as abroad. These movements were often Buddhist-based lay movements, and some of them have been successful in attracting followers numbering in the millions. Part of the reason for their success lies in the fact that they offered the increasingly urban population a means to perform the traditional ancestor rites in the home, independent of the Buddhist clergy and temples that they left behind in the move to the cities. Finally, a third wave of new religions has emerged since the 1970s, mirroring religious developments predominantly seen in the West. These movements emphasize personal spiritual development, and encourage the adoption of ideas and practices from a wide range of religions in order to contribute to that development.

Given this religious ferment, it is hard to describe Japan as a secular society. However, many Japanese would prefer to see themselves as secular or unconcerned with religion. In a recent survey, for example, only 26 per cent of the respondents in Japan described themselves as religious. In part this is due to the controversy surrounding some religious groups, particularly the new religions that have become so prominent in the modern period. The already poor image of these groups was further damaged by the terrorist activities of Aum Shinrikyō in the mid-1990s, contributing to the rise of an anti-cult movement in Japan. However, the attitude towards religion in Japan is also a function of fundamental differences in the understanding of 'religion' as compared to the West, differences that arise from the history of religion in that country.

FIGURE 6.1
The Great Buddha

The Daibutsu, or Great Buddha, at Kamakura, cast in the thirteenth century.
Courtesy Robert Kisala.

Modernity, as it is understood in Japan, is closely associated with the country's contact with the West. What is commonly referred to as the early modern period followed the arrival of Portuguese and Spanish explorers in the sixteenth century, and was marked by the attempt to limit contact with the West during the two-and-a-half century Tokugawa Shogunate (1603–1867). The modern period was ushered in by the collapse of that regime in the face of the forced opening of the country by American and other Western powers, leading to a mad rush to catch up with the West economically, technologically and militarily. The desire to build a nation strong enough to avoid Western colonization contributed greatly to the emergence of Japanese nationalism and Japanese colonialism, and impacted on religious developments during this period. Government attempts to separate Buddhism from Shinto and establish Shinto as the moral and spiritual basis for Japanese nationalism provided the background against which religion as a concept was debated and understood. In addition, the effects of industrialization, urbanization and the affluence of the postwar period are especially apparent in the emergence of new religious movements, where the changing face of Japanese society is reflected in the development of first rural movements that emphasized an egalitarian solidarity, then urban mass movements and finally a turn to the self in post-1970 movements. Despite the official attempt to identify a native Japanese religious tradition alongside various imported traditions, Japanese religious history is marked more by the eclectic use of religious elements from various traditions, a tendency that continues in the religious movements of the modern period.

Sources and resources

Buddhism was probably gradually introduced into Japan through Korea by means of migration from around the fifth century CE. The date usually given for the official introduction of Buddhist images and scriptures to the Japanese court is 552 CE, or perhaps 538 CE. This presentation was supposedly made by the ruler of a Korean clan allied to Japan, shortly before the loss of a Japanese colony on the peninsula. Prince Shōtoku, who administered the government of Japan from the end of the sixth century to the early seventh century, is credited with adopting Buddhism as the religion of the court, under the influence of the Soga clan, avid supporters of the religion.

The Buddhism introduced to Japan was predominantly Chinese Mahāyāna Buddhism, and from the seventh century groups of Japanese monks were sent to China for training. Of the myriad Buddhist texts, particularly important for Japanese Buddhism already from this period was the *Lotus Sutra*. Critical literary analysis indicates multiple authorship of the sutra, and the text was largely complete by the late second or early third century CE, although Chapter 12 was probably added in the sixth century. The sutra consists of 28 chapters, and purports to be the final teaching of Sakyamuni, the historical Buddha. It can be divided into two parts. The first half of the sutra, Chapters 1 to 14, expound the idea of the 'one vehicle', or the supremacy of Mahāyāna, the 'large vehicle', over monastic forms of Buddhism. Here use is made of the concept of 'expedient devices', or *hoben* in Japanese, to explain the limited nature of previous teaching as an attempt by all means to open humanity's eyes to Buddhist truth, but it is only now that the final teaching of universal salvation can be given. The second half of the sutra elucidates the idea of the eternal Buddha, existing from the eternal past and being born into this world to bring humanity to the truth of salvation. The historical Buddha preaching the sutra is just one of these appearances of the eternal Buddha.

This sutra has had profound influence not only on Japanese religious ideas, but also on Japanese art and literature. As the sacred text of some of the new religious mass movements in the postwar period, it continues to play a role in contemporary Japanese culture. Other sutras that have been particularly important in Japanese Buddhism include the *Garland Sutra* (*Kegon-gyō*), centring on the idea of the *bodhisattva*, one who seeks to attain Buddhahood by working for the enlightenment of all beings; the *Kannon Sutra* (*Kannon-gyō*, actually Chapter 25 of the *Lotus Sutra*) exalting the salvific grace of the bodhisattva Kannon; the *Essence of Wisdom Sutra* (*Hannya shin-gyō*) presenting the wisdom of the teaching of *ku*, or emptiness; the *Nirvana Sutra* (*Nehan-gyō* or *Daihatsu nehan-gyō*) explaining the eternal presence of the Buddha and the inherence of Buddha nature in every living being; the *Mahāvairocana*, or great illumination, *Sutra* (*Dainichikyō*) and the *Diamond Peak Sutra* (*Kongōchō-kyō*), both presenting esoteric teachings; and the three canons of Pure Land Buddhism, the *Buddha of Infinite Life Sutra* (*Muryōjukyō*), the *Meditation on the Buddha of Infinite Life Sutra* (*Kanmuryōju-kyō*) and the *Amida Sutra* (*Amida-kyō*), offering a means to rebirth in the Pure Land through faith in the name of Amida.

It was also under Chinese influence that the early histories of Japan, the *Record of Ancient Matters* (*Kojiki*) and the *Chronicle of Japan* (*Nihon shoki*), were compiled. Both of these works cover events from the mythical age of the native Japanese gods up to the late seventh century. Although they diverge on some details, together these works provide the mythical basis for the foundation of the nation as well as the imperial line, and thus they are central texts for the development of *National Learning* (*Kokugaku*) thought, a nativist intellectual movement in the eighteenth century, as well as state Shinto in the modern era.

Confucian and neo-Confucian texts are also sources for Japanese religion. Confucian learning entered Japan in much the same way as Buddhism, introduced through Korea from around the fifth century. The neo-Confucian revival reached Japan in the thirteenth and fourteenth centuries, primarily through Zen monks who had studied in China and made their monasteries centres for Chinese studies. While such study was largely limited to political, religious and military elites throughout much of Japanese history, Confucian and neo-Confucian teachings were popularized in the early modern period, largely through the efforts of itinerant preachers, and have had considerable influence on religious thought in the modern period. In addition to the *Analects* and the *Classic of Filial Piety*, prescribed as part of an official curriculum for members of the court in the eighth century, the *Book of Changes*, the *Elementary Learning* and the *Great Learning* have also been given a level of importance in Japan. Native Japanese Confucian works, such as *A Chronicle of Gods and Sovereigns* (*Jinnō shōtō*) and the *Chronicle of Great Peace*

The following is an extract from Chapter 10 of the *Lotus Sutra*, extolling the surpassing merit of this particular sutra. This passage is fundamental to the belief that faith in the power of the sutra is sufficient for salvation, central to Nichiren Buddhism and many of the postwar new religions.

> At that time the World-honoured One addressed the eighty thousand great leaders through the Bodhisattva Medicine-King (saying): Medicine-King! Do you see in this assembly innumerable gods, dragon-kings, *yakshas*, *gandharvas*, *asuras*, *garudas*, *kinaras*, *mahoragas*, human and non-human beings, as well as *bhikshus*, *shikshunīs*, male and female lay devotees, seekers after *śrāvakaship*, seekers after pratyeke-buddhahood, seekers after bodhisattvaship, or seekers after buddhahood? All such beings as these, in the presence of the Buddha, if they hear a single verse or a single word of the Wonderful Law-Flower Sutra and even by a single thought delight in it, I predict that they will all attain to Perfect Enlightenment.
> Translation by Bunnō Katō (Tokyo: Kosei Publishing Company, 1971)

BOX 6.1 Extract from Chapter 10 of the *Lotus Sutra*

(*Taiheiki*), both from the fourteenth century, emphasize the Confucian virtues of loyalty, benevolence and courage, important in the development of *bushido*, or the 'warrior ethic'.

In addition to these traditional texts, some of the new religions have developed their own scriptures, often based on the private revelation of their founder or some other charismatic personality within the group. Although believers of the particular groups are generally the only ones familiar with these texts, works of the founders of some of the earlier new religions, the *Ofudesaki* (*The Tip of the Writing Brush*) of Tenrikyō or the *Reikai Monogatari* (*Tales of the Spirit World*) of Ōmotokyō are somewhat more well known. In addition, despite the small number of followers that the Christian churches have been able to attract in Japan, the Bible is generally well known, and its teachings have clearly had some influence on the doctrine of some of the new religious movements.

Buddhist sects and Buddhist saints

Buddhism in Japan is organized around several major sects, most of which trace their development to Buddhist schools in China. Ritsu, Kegon, and Hossō are among the earliest of the sects, active in Japan during the Nara period (710–794 CE). Ritsu was established by Ganjin (Chinese *Chien-chen*, 688–763 CE), a Chinese monk who introduced procedures for the ordination of Buddhist clergy into Japan. As its name implies, Kegon takes as its text the *Garland Sutra* (*Kegon-gyō*), while Hossō is based on the Yogācāra tradition, offering the practice of yoga as a means to enlightenment.

Introduced during the Heian period (794–1185 CE), Tendai and Shingon have both played major roles in the development of Buddhism in Japan. Tendai, founded on Mount Hiei in present-day Kyoto by the monk Saichō (764–822 CE), is the Japanese expression of the Chinese T'ien-t'ai school. Both venerate the *Lotus Sutra* as the central Buddhist text, and teach the value of meditation as the means to enlightenment. A monk who had studied in both the Hossō and Kegon sects, Saichō retreated to a hermitage on Mount Hiei shortly before the capital was moved to present-day Kyoto. There he became familiar with the writings of the T'ien-t'ai founder, Chih-i, and in 804 travelled to China to study T'ien-t'ai doctrines. While in China he also became acquainted with Chan (Japanese *Zen*) meditation and esoteric tantric practices, which were incorporated in Tendai in Japan. Saichō emphasized the concept of a universal Buddha-nature inherent in all beings and a consequent egalitarian view of salvation. Later, under the influence of Kūkai, the founder of the Shingon sect, the idea of 'original enlightenment' (*hongaku*), the belief that all beings already exist in a state of enlightenment, also became a central tenet of Tendai doctrine.

Hongaku thought has played a major role throughout the schools of Japanese Buddhism, and remains an essential element of Japanese religiosity today. It is an egalitarian concept; there is a popular expression in Japanese that even the 'grasses and trees' possess Buddha nature. It is non-dualistic; particularly in religious discourse one will often see opposites combined with the word *soku*, meaning 'at the same time'. In recent years it has been the focus of controversy as a result of the work of so-called 'critical Buddhists', who blame the concept for an unreflective tolerance and inability to make moral judgement that they identify with Japanese Buddhism, and Japanese culture in general.

Kūkai (774–835 CE), more popularly known by the posthumous name of Kōbō Daishi, founded his sect on Mount Kōya, near present-day Nara. Kūkai was born into an aristocratic family on the island of Shikoku, and as a young adult took up the study of the Confucian classics prescribed for training as a government bureaucrat. After a conversion to Buddhism, however, he abandoned his studies and started practicing physical austerities on various mountains, with the aim of attaining extraordinary powers. Such ascetics were called *ubasoku*, indicating an unordained Buddhist priest; *hijiri*, a saint or holy man; *onmyōji*, a practitioner of Yin-Yang Daoism; or *shugenja*, a mountain ascetic. The mixture of Buddhist, Daoist and folk religious beliefs and practices exhibited by these men is one of the important streams of Japanese religiosity, and the belief that extraordinary powers can be obtained through the practice of physical austerities is another characteristic of Japanese religiosity up to the present day, as seen in the emphasis on the attainment of psychic powers in some of the latest new religious movements.

Like his contemporary Saichō, Kūkai also travelled to China in 804, but his study was more limited to the esoteric mantra tradition, the meaning of the Japanese word 'Shingon'. There he was initiated into several esoteric rituals as yet unknown in Japan, and ordained as a master of this tradition. Kūkai also emphasized the universally inherent Buddha nature, as well as the dissolution of dichotomies and oppositions through the awareness of the mutual relation and interdependence of all phenomena. One of the tenets of the Shingon school is the attainment of Buddhahood in this life, or in the body, just as it is (*sokushin jōbutsu*). In the belief that this was realized by Kūkai himself, his presence is still venerated on Mount Kōya.

Kūkai, or Kōbō Daishi, has become a legendary figure in Japanese religiosity, invoked not only within the Buddhist tradition, but also, for example, by some of the founders of new religious movements without clear Buddhist ties. In another form of popular religiosity, he is associated with pilgrimages in Japan, most famously with that to 88 temples on his native island of Shikoku. In his lifetime he was also favoured by the court. Although in the early years after the capital was moved to present-day Kyoto Saichō's Tendai school was in ascendancy with the court, from early in the ninth century it was Shingon esotericism that predominantly enjoyed the court's favour.

Both Saichō and Kūkai were open to the introduction of native Japanese religious elements into their schools of Buddhism, a trend that became increasingly noticeable in this period, and is yet another characteristic of Japanese religion. It became common to construct *jingūji*, or shrine-temples, where Buddhist rituals were performed within Shinto shrine precincts, often by the same clergy. Doctrinally, the idea of *honji suijaku* was promoted, identifying the Shinto *kami* as local manifestations of buddhas or bodhisattvas. Counter movements were also present, especially in the early modern period, but this Buddhist–Shinto amalgamation was dominant until the forced separation of the two at the beginning of the modern period in the mid-nineteenth century.

The twelfth and thirteenth centuries saw the emergence of several new Buddhist schools, one of them of native Japanese origin. Political and social instability towards the end of the Heian period ushered in an era of *de facto* military rule that was to last until the modern period. This instability contributed to the popularization of the Buddhist concept of *mappō*, or the final, degenerate age. In this final age former practices were deemed to be no longer effective, and thus new ways to salvation were sought. Although many of the schools that emerged at this time had their roots in Tendai, they differed from the older school in that they concentrated on one aspect of Tendai belief and practice rather than presenting a synthesis of varying Buddhist traditions.

The Japanese *Pure Land* school (*Jōdoshū*), whose founding is attributed to the monk Hōnen (1133–1212), illustrates these characteristics well. Orphaned as a youth, Hōnen was sent to a nearby Tendai temple, where his potential was noticed, leading to his acceptance at the main temple on Mount Hiei and ordination at the age of 14. Apparently dissatisfied with the political intrigues at the main temple, then deeply involved in the larger power struggles in the capital, Hōnen sought refuge in a small retreat at the foot of the mountain, a centre of Pure Land practice. Pure Land, also imported from China, had been popularized in Japan from the tenth century as part of the Tendai synthesis. It preached salvation by faith in Amida, a bodhisattva known for the *hongan*, or 'original vow', to postpone his own enlightenment until all beings had been saved. Through the invocation of Amida's holy name, the *nenbutsu*, the believer is assured of rebirth in the Pure Land, or Land of Bliss, there to await enlightenment. The *nenbutsu* was used as a means of meditation, or occasionally as a kind of charm to ward off evil, but in Hōnen's teaching it became the supreme act of faith, replacing attempts at attaining salvation through meditation or the study of Buddhist texts. In this way Honen introduced the distinction between salvation through one's own efforts (*jiriki*) or salvation by faith in Amida's mercy (*tariki*), and the latter was deemed to be the only effective means in the degenerate age of *mappō*.

Shinran (1173–1261), a disciple of Hōnen, was exiled along with his master in 1207, at the instigation of the Tendai establishment on Mount Hiei. A monk since the age of nine, Shinran married and fathered six children during his exile, finding religious meaning in the abandonment of monastic rules – the single-minded pursuit of salvation through faith in Amida rather than through one's own efforts. Following Shinran's example, clerical marriage had become all but the norm not only in the True Pure Land sect, which Shinran is considered to have founded, but throughout Japanese Buddhism by the early modern period, although the legal prohibition was only removed in 1872. With the exception of the True Pure Land sect, however, clerical celibacy continues to be the official norm, making the role of the priests' wives rather ambiguous; although accepted as a fact of everyday life, and even essential to the running of the temple in many cases, they are occasionally not even allowed a place in the family grave after death, since their marriage has not been recognized.

In contrast to the emphasis on salvation through faith alone in the Pure Land schools, other schools that emerged in this period continued to promote meditation as the means to enlightenment. The dominant Zen schools of Rinzai and Sōtō were both also founded by Tendai monks, Eisai (1141–1215) and Dōgen (1200–1253) respectively. Seeing the need for a religious revival on Mount Hiei, Eisai went to China in 1168, and again almost 20 years later, retracing the steps of the monks from the ancient period who had founded the established Buddhist schools. While he emphasized Zen, particularly after his second visit to China, he did not abandon the other Tendai beliefs and practices, but continued to preach devotion to the *Lotus Sutra* and perform esoteric rituals. However, his efforts still elicited opposition from the Tendai establishment, leading him to seek support from the military rulers in Kamakura who had gained ascendancy at the end of the twelfth century. Eisai is also credited with the introduction of the tea ceremony, and the Rinzai school that he founded is perhaps best known in the West for the use of kōan, cryptic statements or paradoxes used as an aid to meditation or the gaining of intuitive knowledge.

Born almost 60 years after Eisai, Dōgen also studied Tendai at Mount Hiei, but he was attracted to Zen at an early age. He travelled to China in 1223, where he attained awakening under a Zen master. He returned to teach the sole practice of *zazen*, sitting meditation. Establishing a monastery in the mountains near the Japan Sea coast, Dōgen instituted a rigid daily order for his monks, centred on the practice of *zazen*. After Dōgen's death, however, Sōtō Zen was popularized among the provincial samurai and the peasantry, especially through the development of funeral and memorial services for the dead, with which Buddhism is identified in Japan today.

The final school that emerged at this time was Nichiren, named after the monk who was its founder. Nichiren (1222–1282), the son of a fisherman from the area north of Kamakura, was ordained a monk at a nearby Tendai temple before making his way to Mount Hiei in 1242. Not limiting himself to the Tendai tradition, he also studied at Mount Kōya and ultimately became convinced that all of the Buddhist schools were incomplete and false. With a self-appointed mission to preach true Buddhism, he advocated faith in the *Lotus Sutra* alone, and promoted the chanting of the *daimoku*, a phrase in praise of the sutra. Attributing an increase in natural disasters and political unrest to the propagation of false faiths, in 1260 he presented a treatise to the military government in Kamakura entitled *Risshō ankokuron* (*Treatise on Pacifying the State by Establishing Orthodoxy*). As a result of this critique of the establishment, he was exiled the following year, and after a pardon in 1263 he was once again exiled in 1271. The only native Japanese school of Buddhism, the Nichiren sects are characteristically nationalistic and exclusivist, preaching that only faith in the one true religion can guarantee peace and stability. Through its popularization in the modern period, when it was linked with a rising nationalistic fervour, it has become an important religious resource for some of the mass new religious movements that emerged in the postwar period.

It is the monks and male mountain ascetics who have traditionally been highlighted in speaking of the Buddhist traditions in Japan. Ordained nuns, however, have played a role at key stages in the history of Japanese Buddhism. It was a nun by the name of Zenshinni who was the first Buddhist ordained in Japan, and it was nuns who first went to China to study. The first temple in Japan was a nunnery. In the early modern period, Soto Zen nuns did a better job of preserving the tradition of meditation while their male counterparts were largely engaged in the performance of funerals and memorial rites, and in this way they contributed to the Zen revival in the modern period.

The Japanese Buddhist traditions described here are perhaps more properly referred to as schools rather than sects or independent religious groups throughout much of Japanese history, for, as we have seen, it was not uncommon for monks to study several of these traditions. However, occasional rivalries, even conflicts, between the schools cannot be ignored, and despite an overall atmosphere of religious plurality – not only among the Buddhist traditions themselves but also with Daoist, Confucian and native Shinto beliefs and practices – the emergence of an exclusivist tradition in Nichiren Buddhism is also an important element of Japanese religiosity. It was in the early modern and modern periods that the Buddhist traditions increasingly took on the aspects of sects, as a result of government policies. In the early modern period, to enforce the prohibition against Christianity, everyone was required to be affiliated with a Buddhist temple for the purpose of funeral and memorial rites. This introduced a parochial system previously unknown to Buddhism, and served to institutionalize Buddhism as the purveyor of funeral rites, as well as the tool of government control. And in the modern period local temples were required to have clear affiliation with a major temple that served as headquarters for one of the Buddhist groups, further clarifying allegiance along sect lines. In present-day Japan, Pure Land groups (including True Pure Land) claim both the largest number of temples and believers, with Zen following in number of temples but Nichiren groups second in number of believers.

Interactions with modernity

The emergence of modern Shinto

Usually described as Japan's native religion, Shinto is a complex reality, reflecting in its concrete and historical expression several interwoven strands. Even today many Japanese would not consider Shinto a 'religion', but would rather describe it as a set of traditional customs without a doctrine, reflecting the official point of view in the prewar period, which has been upheld in court cases concerning the separation of religion and state in the postwar period as well. The term 'Shinto' itself was not in popular usage before the end of the early modern period. In the intellectual history of Japan, the term became important in the National Learning school, where it was used in contrast to Buddhism and Confucianism in order to legitimate it as a distinct, native Japanese religion. It would appear that the term Shinto was first used to refer to a distinct religious tradition in the fifteenth century at the earliest, when the Yoshida Shinto movement emerged to challenge the concept of *honji suijaku*, or the incorporation of the Shinto kami in the Buddhist pantheon.

Shinto incorporates belief in nature spirits, the veneration of clan ancestors, local and national cults surrounding heroes or warriors, as well as mythological beliefs in the foundation of the nation and the imperial lineage. Activities at local shrines centre around festivals to mark the seasons or to celebrate the particular kami venerated there. Some of the larger shrines, particularly those at Ise and Izumo, were better able to resist the trend towards amalgamation with Buddhism, thus providing some institutional continuity that indicates the preservation of an independent religious tradition. Clearly, however, it was in an atmosphere of Buddhist and Confucian thought, and in opposition to these traditions, that the organized Shinto traditions developed.

Both popular and intellectual influences led to the emergence, or perhaps more accurately the creation, of a Shinto institution in the modern period. From the early modern period pilgrimages to the shrine at Ise were popularized. Often local confraternities were formed to provide monetary support for a number of pilgrims annually, and the pilgrimages were occasionally raucous affairs. Intellectually, it was the development of the National Learning school that contributed greatly towards the establishment of the modern Shinto institution.

National Learning is at once a literary, political and religious movement whose foundation lies at least partly in a reaction to the increasing influence of Confucian ideas and scholarship in the early modern period. National Learning evolved from the philological study of Japanese classical literature and ancient writings whose purpose was generally to identify peculiarly Japanese cultural traits or a distinctive Japanese mentality. This study can be traced back to Keichū (1640–1701), a Buddhist monk of the Shingon sect who took up the study of the *Man'yōshū*, an anthology of eighth-century poetry. Keichū insisted that in order to understand the ancient classical literature one had to allow one's mind to become unfettered by intellectual concepts so as to come in touch with the naive emotions of a direct, human response, a primitivism that is reflected in later National Learning writings.

Another early influence on National Learning was Kada no Azumamaro (1669–1736), a descendant of a family of Shinto priests who focused his study on ancient documents as well as literary works. He opened a school for Japanese studies in Kyoto and had a direct influence on Kamo no Mabuchi (1697–1769), also from a family of Shinto priests. Like Keichū, Mabuchi took up the study of the *Man'yōshū*, finding there an honest and direct expression of emotion without the artificiality he thought had been introduced by foreign, specifically Buddhist and Confucian, influences.

Motoori Norinaga (1730–1801), usually acknowledged as the central figure of this movement, came to National Learning through a study of Keichū's work, later becoming a disciple of Mabuchi. Norinaga completed a study of the *Kojiki*, a foundational text of Japanese mythology from the eighth century, which had been started by his mentor. Continuing in the primitivist tradition of his teachers, Norinaga propounded his belief that in order to understand the text one needs a sensitivity to the appearance of objects and events in the human and natural world and the emotions that they arouse, unfettered by Confucian or Buddhist doctrinal interpretations. Norinaga believed that the *Kojiki* text was a factual record of the activity of the gods and people in ancient times, and that it reflected a natural moral sense. He maintained that ancient Japanese texts do not contain the word *michi*, or 'way' in the sense of a correct moral path, because the ancients had a natural feel for what was right, and were in this way superior to the Chinese, who were in need of the moral guidance supplied by Confucian principles.

In another work, the *Naobi no mitama*, Norinaga develops at length this idea of Japanese cultural superiority, identifying stability as the basis of that superiority. Relying on Japanese mythology, Norinaga states that Japan is the land of the appearance of Amaterasu Ōmikami, the central native goddess, and that the land is ruled by the emperor, the descendant of the goddess. For that reason, he argues that the rule of the emperor is in fact the rule of the gods, as it was, unchanging from ancient times, and that in turn is why Japan is referred to as the Land of the Gods. In foreign lands, namely China, there is no end to revolution and unrest, with people of lower status trying to seize power from those above. In Japan, however, the emperor's reign continues unbroken, and the people follow naturally that order as established in ancient times, resulting in profound peace. If there is unrest in Japan it is a result of the fact that people have tried to learn foreign ways and have allowed their spirit to become separated from the spirit of the emperor. This situation can only be corrected if people are loyal and obedient to their superiors and do what they know naturally to be right; they are endowed with this natural ethical sense because all share in the spirit of the gods that is the foundation of Japanese culture.

Although the ideas of cultural superiority based on the perceived presence of an unparalleled stability and innate morality did not originate with Norinaga or National

Learning, their codification in this school had a direct influence on important intellectual developments in the immediate early modern period. The Mito school, named after a domain north of present-day Tokyo where it was located, actually combined National Learning trends with Confucian thought to propose a plan for governing the nation in the face of increasing threats from abroad, based on the development of a common religious tradition to strengthen social cohesion. After Japan's self-imposed isolation was broken by the arrival of US gunboats in 1853, leading to the restoration of imperial rule in 1868 and the beginning of a rush to modernization in the mid-nineteenth century, the Mito synthesis provided a blueprint for the new government's religious policy. Buddhist elements were forcibly removed from Shinto shrines under the banner of *shinbutsu bunri*, or the separation of the gods and buddhas; a state agency for the administration of Shinto shrines was established, indicating the unity of ritual and government, or *saisei itchi*; a hierarchy of shrines was established, with Ise at the top, and new national shrines dedicated to the imperial family or war dead were constructed; a new set of national holidays, centring on imperial commemorations or dates associated with the mythical establishment of the nation, and commemorative rites to be performed by the emperor were prescribed; the official recognition of the Buddhist parish system, initially instituted by the early modern military government, was removed, and although the Buddhist temples were not directly targeted by the central government, widespread destruction of Buddhist statues and other treasures by mobs protesting against the temples' links with the previous government was allowed.

Devotion to State Shinto, as the new religious establishment was known, was made a duty incumbent on all citizens of the country. When a new constitution was promulgated in 1889, including the guarantee of religious freedom, State Shinto was defined as a set of traditions and rites that transcends 'religion', thus allowing for government patronage and the enforcement of universal participation in State Shinto rites. Formation of a civic creed was further enhanced by the promulgation the following year of the Imperial Rescript on Education, a succinct statement of the national myths surrounding the imperial establishment and a Confucian code of conduct that emphasized filial piety, harmony, benevolence, self-cultivation, obedience, and loyalty. The Rescript was committed to memory, recited by schoolchildren, and venerated alongside the portrait of the emperor and other Shinto symbols.

State Shinto was abolished by decree of the occupation forces in 1945, and many of the local as well as former national shrines are now independently affiliated with the Association of Shinto Shrines (*jinja honchō*). Since the 1970s, however, there have been repeated attempts to grant formal status to Yasukuni Shrine in Tokyo as a national memorial to the war dead. Yasukuni Shrine's predecessor was established in 1869 to enshrine the spirits of those who died fighting to restore imperial rule, and subsequently the spirits of those who fought in Japan's wars throughout the modern period have also been enshrined there. In 1978 the spirits of those executed as a result of the Tokyo War Crimes Trial were also added to the shrine. Other controversies have involved the use of Shinto rites to mark the construction of government buildings, visits to shrines by government officials and the use of public money to pay the customary fees on those

The Imperial Rescript on Education is a succinct summary of the official ideology promoted in the Meiji period as the moral and spiritual basis of the Japanese nation. It emphasizes the unbroken rule of the imperial line and the common Confucian morality of filial piety, right relationships, benevolence, and self-cultivation. The official translation of the rescript reads as follows:

Know ye, Our Subjects:
Our Imperial Ancestors have founded Our Empire on a basis broad and everlasting and have deeply and firmly planted virtue; Our subjects ever united in loyalty and filial piety have from generation to generation illustrated the beauty thereof. This is the glory of the fundamental character of Our Empire, and herein lies the source of Our education. Ye, Our subjects, be filial to your parents, affectionate to your brothers and sisters; as husbands and wives be harmonious, as friends true; bear yourselves in modesty and moderation; extend your benevolence to all; pursue learning and cultivate arts, and thereby develop intellectual faculties and perfect moral powers; furthermore advance public good and promote common interests; always respect the Constitution and observe the laws; should emergency arise, offer yourselves courageously to the State; and thus guard and maintain the prosperity of Our Imperial Throne coeval with heaven and earth. So shall ye not only be Our good and faithful subjects, but render illustrious the best traditions of your forefathers. The Way here set forth is indeed the teaching bequeathed by Our Imperial Ancestors, to be observed alike by Their Descendants and the subjects, infallible for all ages and true in all places. It is Our wish to lay it to heart in all reverence, in common with you, Our subjects, that we may all thus attain to the same virtue.

BOX 6.2 The Imperial Rescript on Education

occasions, as well as the use of Shinto rites in conjunction with the installation of the present emperor in 1989 and 1990. Japanese courts have consistently ruled in favour of the government on these occasions, arguing that these actions are more a matter of custom than religion. In a recent case, however, the court prohibited the use of public funds to pay for a Shinto service, and observers noted that the court in this case seems to be following public opinion, since there seems to be less support for such actions in recent years.

Although more than 80 per cent of the population will visit a Shinto shrine during the New Year holidays, smaller shrines have in recent years found it difficult to continue their festivals, because fewer young people, needed to carry the portable shrines that are central to these events, are either present or willing to participate. However, more famous festivals, such as the spring and summer festivals in Tokyo and the northern region of the country, or the naked-man festivals held in winter at various locales, continue to draw crowds in the tens of thousands.

New religious movements in the early modern period

The creation of a national religious ideology as a vehicle to promote cultural identity could only be maintained by the use of increasingly oppressive force, and ultimately failed when that force could not be sustained following the defeat of the nation in 1945. Other religious movements that emerged at the same time that State Shinto was being created ultimately proved to be more effective and long-lasting means to preserve cultural identity in the face of the massive importation of foreign cultural items. These movements can be identified as the first of three major waves of New Religious Movements that largely define the contemporary Japanese religious scene.

Tenrikyō, founded in 1838, is generally recognized as one of the oldest of the Japanese New Religious Movements. Its founding is traced back to the possession experience of Nakayama Miki, a farmer's wife living in the area of Nara, the ancient capital. Having already lost two daughters to disease, a *yamabushi*, or mountain ascetic, was called to cure the injured foot of Miki's son. Since the shamaness, or *miko*, who would normally accompany the *yamabushi* and acted as his medium could not come, Miki took her place. After falling into a trance, Miki was possessed by a god who revealed his name as Tsukihi, literally 'sun and moon'. Tsukihi declared through Miki that, 'I have come to save all of mankind. I wish to receive Miki as the shrine of God.' This incident was followed by numerous other possession episodes, subsequently without the aid of the *yamabushi*. At the direction of Tsukihi, later also called Oyagami, meaning 'God the Parent', Miki began to give alms to the poor, to the extent that the Nakayama family, once wealthy landowners, was left destitute. Miki took up sewing to support the family, and from the 1850s began to gain a reputation as a healer and miracle worker, after which time this new faith began to grow.

In 1869, the year following the institution of the new imperial government, Miki, who is supposed to have been illiterate, took up writing and composed the *Ofudesaki*, the record of Oyagami's revelation, one of Tenrikyo's scriptures. In the *Ofudesaki* the centre of the universe is revealed as lying precisely in the Nakayama residence, found in an area called Yamato, traditionally seen as the birthplace of Japanese civilization. Today Tenrikyō headquarters is located on this spot, and visitors to Tenri City are greeted with the words 'Welcome home!' indicating this is the place of birth for all humankind.

Tenrikyō teaches that it is the will of God the Parent that all human beings enjoy *yōki gurashi*, translated as 'joyous life'. The doctrine is based on the principle of fundamental equality, teaching that, 'All people of the whole world are equally brothers and sisters. There is no one who is an utter stranger' (*Ofudesaki* XIII, 43). Eventually all of humankind will partake in this 'joyous life' together here in this world, a paradise that is to be inaugurated after an indeterminate number of rebirths of those now living. All people are called to participate in the final establishment of this joyous life by reflecting now on the cause of their suffering, in order to understand their *innen* or karma. Karma – in Tenrikyō doctrine the good or bad effects of past actions, either in this life or previous lives – is the cause of all experience. Reflecting on karma should lead to a reform of life, to wipe away the dust that accumulates on the heart or spirit, in Tenrikyō's idiom. Tenrikyō teaches that there are eight 'dusts': miserliness, covetousness, hatred, self-love, grudge-bearing, anger, greed, and arrogance. The attitude of reform, or sweeping away this dust, is expressed through *hinokishin*, a word that is used to describe activity that ranges from service to the church to various volunteer activities, including international aid and development work.

The *Ofudesaki* is the written record of the revelation received by Nakayama Miki, the founder of Tenrikyō. The following text, from the opening passage of the book, describes God's purpose in making this new, and final, revelation: to realize the joyful life that has been ordained from the time of creation for all people.

Looking all over the world and through all ages, I find no one who has understood My heart. No wonder that you know nothing, for so far I have taught nothing to you. This time I, God, revealing Myself to the fore, teach you all the truth in detail. . . . When I, God, reveal Myself and teach you everything in detail, all people of the world will become equally cheerful. As I hasten to save all of you equally, I will set out to cheer up the minds of the world. If your minds become cheered up step by step, rich harvests will prevail all over the world, and every place will become prosperous.

From the *Ofudesaki*, Part I, 1–3, 7–9.
Translation by Tenrikyō Headquarters (Tenri: Jihōsha, 1971).

BOX 6.3 Extract from the *Ofudesaki*

Tenrikyō is representative of many of the new religions in its optimistic view of human nature, its emphasis on moral self-cultivation, the affirmation of benefits in the present world, and its use of elements common in Japanese religiosity in developing its own doctrine. The case of Nakayama Miki also illustrates one role that women have traditionally played in Japanese religiosity, that of a shaman-like practitioner, a role that has become more prominent in some of the new religions.

Tenrikyō and other new religions that emerged at this time in Japanese history served two social functions. First, their emphasis on solidarity within an essentially rural society – through the preaching of a universal equality, mutual help activities such as *hinokishin* in Tenrikyō, and emphasis on individual moral reform – helped to cushion the impact on the agricultural sector of the economic changes that had begun to occur already in the latter part of the early modern period. Second, they helped to preserve a sense of cultural identity in a rapidly changing society, as seen for example in Tenrikyō's belief that the centre of the universe lies precisely in the cradle of Japanese civilization. Indeed, many of the new religions emerging at this time were located in the area around Nara and Kyoto, the ancient capitals of the country. This sense of cultural identity sometimes took the form of xenophobia. This is perhaps most pronounced in Ōmotokyō, a group founded in the last decade of the nineteenth century by Deguchi Nao, a woman who, like Miki, was prone to episodes of possession. Nao is said to have proclaimed in a trance that, 'Japan is the way of the gods, but foreign countries are the lands of the wild beasts, ruled by devils, where only the strong survive.' She goes on to say that, under the influence of these foreign cultures, 'Japan is likewise becoming a land of wild beasts. Because the country can't survive like this, God has revealed himself and will reform the world.'

In this way Ōmotokyō perhaps possessed a stronger sense of mission that led it to openly oppose the central government, and as a consequence it was crushed completely by the authorities in the 1930s. Tenrikyō and the other new religions of this period were co-opted by the government, changing their doctrine in line with the official State Shinto ideology and eventually achieving recognition as Sect Shinto groups.

The urbanization of Japanese society and the postwar new religions

While it is difficult to give an accurate count, there are perhaps up to 1,000 New Religious Movements active in Japan. The vast majority are small, local groups; national, or international, movements like Tenrikyō, which has over one million believers, are relatively few. Nearly all of the mass movements, such as Sōka Gakkai with perhaps nine million members, or Risshō Kōseikai with over six million, are postwar urban forms of Buddhism, and they comprise the second wave of New Religious Movements in Japan.

Risshō Kōseikai was founded in 1938 but enjoyed a period of tremendous growth in the postwar years, like most of the religions in this group. The founder, Niwano Nikkyō, was himself born in a rural village in north-west Japan, and emigrated to Tokyo while still a teenager. In Tokyo he became engaged in various small businesses, and was exposed to a myriad of folk divination techniques before joining Reiyūkai, a lay Buddhist movement in the Nichiren tradition. He quickly made a convert of Naganuma Myōko, and in 1938 both of them broke with Reiyūkai to found their own group. Risshō Kōseikai incorporated some of the divination practices that Niwano had picked up, and Myōkō played a shaman-like role in the early development of the religion. Thus, while Risshō Kōseikai displays some elements of popular folk belief, in doctrine and practice it is a Buddhist-based group, revering the *Lotus Sutra*, chanting the *daimoku*, and encouraging daily prayers in front of the family Buddhist altar in the home.

Like its predecessor Reiyūkai, Risshō Kōseikai offers its believers a means to venerate the ancestors in the home, without the assistance of a Buddhist priest – an important religious development in reaction to the urbanization of Japanese society. Early in the twentieth century more than 80 per cent of the Japanese population was engaged in agriculture. By 1935 the urban population stood at 30 per cent, a figure that rose to 50 per cent by the end of the war. By 1977, however, more than 80 per cent of the population lived in cities, reversing the situation of only 60 years before. For many people this meant that their ties with the local Buddhist temple were completely severed by the move to the city. Interestingly enough, the observation can be made that Japanese

FIGURE 6.2
Naked man
festival

The naked man festival at Konomiya Shrine in Inazawa near Nagoya. The festival is held every year in February. Courtesy Robert Kisala.

urbanization has led to a considerable religious revival. Whereas in the past the main tie to the local Buddhist temple centred on annual memorial rites, for which a Buddhist monk was summoned and paid, the lay Buddhism that emerged in postwar urban Japan not only encouraged daily practice at home, but also resulted in more active and sustained participation in communal religious functions. A central practice here is the *hōza*, a combination of group counselling and faith witnessing carried out by the believers, often on a weekly or monthly basis.

The new postwar new religions serve a function in enhancing social cohesion comparable to that of the first-wave new religious groups. The postwar groups act as a bridge, both religiously and socially, between rural and urban Japanese society, providing an entirely new way to perform the requisite memorial rites for the ancestors, as well as becoming the focus of community for many people in the impersonal urban milieu. They also share much in common with the earlier new religions in terms of a doctrinal emphasis on moral self-cultivation and the enjoyment of benefits in the present world. Although women often play a major part in the establishment of these movements and in encouraging others to join the group, their governing structures continue to reflect the male dominance seen throughout Japanese society.

New Age religions

As in much of Europe and North America, in the last few decades in Japan one can see a new interest in mysticism and the occult that is sometimes summed up under the term New Age. This new religious ferment is often characterized as eclectic, individualistic and result oriented, as Wouter Hanegraaff points out in Chapter 13 on New Age religion in this volume. Through the use of certain techniques, either meditation or body work or some combination of the two, it is believed that one can achieve a personal transformation, resulting perhaps in a higher level of consciousness or the attainment of psychic powers (see also Chapter 12 on Spirituality). While one often participates in this movement by purchasing books that amount to training manuals at the local bookshop, or at best through a loose association or 'network' of fellow practitioners, in Japan a number of organized religious groups incorporating these characteristics have become popular since the 1970s.

Agonshū is representative of this latest wave of New Religious Movements. Although Agonshū was founded in 1978, it has its roots in a group called Kannon Jikeikai, founded by Kiriyama Seiyū in 1954. Kiriyama was born Tsutsumi Masuo in 1921, and came to religion after failing in business and an arrest for violation of alcohol tax laws. He was ordained a Shingon sect priest in 1955 and practised a religion based on fasting and cold water austerities, common to mountain ascetics in Japan. Around 1970 he abandoned these austerities and instead adopted the *goma* fire ceremony of esoteric Shingon Buddhism as his group's primary rite. He began to publish on spiritist and esoteric themes at about this time, and some of his books on the development of psychic powers became bestsellers. In late 1978 he came upon the *Āgama Sutra*, purportedly predating both Mahāyāna and esoteric Buddhism, and this became the basis of faith in Agonshū, as he renamed his religious group.

In Kiriyama's teaching, misfortune is caused by karma from previous lives, or by the curse of ancestors who have been unable to attain Buddhahood, a common belief in Japanese religiosity that encourages the performance of memorial rites in order to help one's ancestors achieve this goal. In Agonshū this was done especially through the practice of *senzagyō*, a 40-minute memorial service to be performed in the home for 1,000 days in succession. In 1986, however, Agonshū received a relic of the Buddha from the President of Sri Lanka, and thereafter *senzagyō* was declared unnecessary, replaced by simple veneration of the relic or its representative in the home.

Kiriyama has consistently shown a sensitivity to popular culture, moving from esoteric Buddhism through an interest in psychic powers to the discovery of early Buddhism as religious tastes changed through the 1970s. He was also the first religious leader to take up the prophecies of Nostradamus, which have enjoyed a high level of popularity in Japan since the publication of a volume interpreting the prophecies in 1973. Apocalyptic thought connected with the prophecy of some kind of disaster that was to occur in 1999 is one characteristic of many of the groups that emerged in this period, and contributed to the violent actions of Aum Shinrikyō, the group that released poisonous sarin gas on the Tokyo underground in 1995.

Asahara Shōkō, the founder of Aum Shinrikyō, was himself a follower of Agonshū in the late 1970s and early 1980s. He went on to found his own independent yoga school, teaching the practice of yoga for the purpose of attaining psychic powers. Incorporating elements of Hindu with Tibetan Buddhism, Aum Shinrikyō's faith and practice focused increasingly on the role of Asahara as the guru essential to the spiritual development of his followers. Vague ideas of a cataclysmic destruction, based on the Nostradamus prophecies, were present from early on in the group, and these were developed and played in increasingly important role as Asahara and some of his followers resorted to violence both within the group as well as directed at outsiders.

Movements from this period are at least in part a result of contemporary cynicism and ennui. In the 1970s and 1980s Japan achieved a level of economic development that would have been unthinkable a generation before. The 'oil shock' in 1973, however, introduced a period of relatively low growth, which made future advancement, for both the individual and society, less certain. This trend was further exacerbated by the collapse of the 'bubble economy', based largely on stock and land speculation, and the decade-long recession of the 1990s. With economic or social advancement thus stymied, individual spiritual development perhaps became more attractive. In addition, the failure of the 1960s student protest movement encouraged a turning inward: what could not be achieved through social protest was now sought through personal transformation, the reformation of society one person at a time.

The following is a promotional blurb taken from *Initiation*, published in English by Aum Shinrikyō in 1988. It identifies some of the religious elements that were incorporated in the group by its founder, Asahara Shōkō, promising the attainment of superhuman powers through the development of an innate spiritual capacity. The role of the guru in the training of the members is also emphasized. *Shaktipat*, for example, was a rite through which it was believed that Asahara transferred power by placing his hand on the forehead of the believer.

> AUM Supreme Truth, founded by Shoko Asahara, is an organization to promote one's spiritual growth, ultimately toward the state of absolute freedom and happiness, and the betterment of society. It provides the Yoga Tantra System to its members, which is a unique training method consisting of several Eastern practices: Yoga, Tantric Buddhism, Primitive Buddhism, and Daoism.
>
> Three Initiations are the core of the training method. They are *Earthly Initiation*, which purifies your *consciousness*; *Astral Initiation*, which purifies your *subconscious*, and *Causal Initiation*, which purifies your *super-subconscious*. Not only that, through these initiations you can develop various kinds of superhuman powers.
>
> Earthly Initiation is given through oral instruction of a secret meditative and breathing technique. Astral Initiation is the input of the master's divine energy into a trainee by such means as Shaktipat. Causal Initiation imprints the perfectly purified mind of the Guru into a trainee. These three initiations purify your mind and help you to realize your True Self.
>
> You can advance your practice in various ways, such as attendance at intensive seminars, on-going classes, weekly workshops, astral music meditation meetings, and home practice with our teaching materials. A free introductory lecture is provided every Sunday, and a free brochure is also available.

Shoko Asahara believes that it is quite rare for one to meet with the path to the truth, and hopes that you will seize this opportunity. The path to the truth is the path to supreme bliss and freedom.

Initiation (New York: AUM US Co., 1988, p. 231). [Punctuation and grammatical changes have been made to the translation where necessary.]

BOX 6.4 Promotional blurb from *Initiation*, Aum Shinrikyō (1988)

Women and religion

The role of women in religion in Japan, and the application of feminist critique to religious attitudes, doctrines, and practice is an increasingly important topic. Although women have numbered among the Buddhist monastics throughout Japanese history and have been instrumental in the emergence of new religious movements in the modern period, as pointed out above, the fact remains that women and their religious experience have largely been marginalized throughout the religious history of Japan, with perhaps the greatest outlet for this experience being a shamanistic presence in folk religion, especially in the southern islands of Okinawa.

The continuation of certain discriminatory practices, such as the closure of certain sacred mountains to women, or particularly to menstruating women, has been highlighted. Perhaps the clearest example of these practices in recent memory comes from the world of sports, from the sumo tournament held in Osaka in March 2000, when the governor of Osaka, Ōta Fusae, was not allowed to enter the ring, or *dohyō*, at the end of the match to present the traditional Governor's Prize to the winner of the tournament, but rather stood ringside while her deputy, a male, presented the prize on her behalf, because sumo is traditionally associated with Shinto and the *dohyō* is considered a sacred area where women are not allowed. Another focus of attention has been the practice of *mizuko kuyō*, a memorial service for aborted fetuses. While often seen as exploitation of women by religious establishments, recent research has also focused on women as the initiator of these rites, or women's interpretations of the practice.

Other studies have also focused on the subjectivity of women in religion in Japan, that is, studies of some of the New Religious Movements as well as some more traditional religious organizations from the perspective of women's religious experience and women's interpretation of that experience.

Looking to the future

In a recent survey, when asked about their confidence in 17 social institutions, only 13 per cent of the respondents in Japan indicated some level of trust in religious groups, putting religious institutions at the bottom of the list. This result reflects a high level of distrust towards religious groups across the board. Indeed, in popular discourse,

Buddhism is usually identified with the lucrative funeral industry, and its priests are criticized for their married state and meat-eating habits; Shinto suffers for its identification with the militaristic state; and new religions are seen as often dangerous frauds. In such an environment those affiliated with a religious group often feel that they have to hide their religious beliefs in order to be accepted.

Despite this low level of religious affiliation and considerable distrust of religious organizations, three-quarters of the population profess some kind of belief in a higher power, whether that be described as God, spirit or life-force. A similar number feel it is important to have a religious funeral service, and 80 to 90 per cent participate in annual rites such as the New Year's visit to a shrine or memorial services for the ancestors.

Religion is a difficult concept in modern Japan, because it is identified with religious organizations and is often divorced from religious sentiments and activities. In the wake of the Aum affair, one influential religious studies scholar, Yamaori Tetsuo, attributes these developments to the forced separation of Buddhism and Shinto at the beginning of the modern period and the introduction of the idea that one must choose an exclusive religious affiliation, an essentially Christian point of view. Yamaori argues that free participation in beliefs and rites of the various religious traditions present in Japan is the more proper expression of Japanese religiosity.

Thus we can expect that the Japanese will continue to be born Shinto, marry Christian and die Buddhist, all the while bearing a certain amount of reserve regarding all of these institutions. A certain number will continue to find meaning in some New Religious Movement, perhaps moving through affiliation with several movements in search of an answer to illness, discord or poverty. And New Religious Movements, drawing on diverse traditions that offer spiritual attainment and benefits in this life, will continue to emerge. The more difficult question, however, is whether these movements as well as the more traditional religious institutions will be able to find a moral voice in Japanese society and contribute positively to public discourse on important questions of ethnic and gender discrimination, individual rights and public ethics, war and peace.

Summary

- Japanese religiosity is characterized by low levels of self-initiated affiliation with a religious institution but high levels of participation in religious rites and practices.

- Throughout much of Japanese history, Buddhist, Shinto, Confucian, and other religious elements have been combined, forming a kind of common religion that is still characteristic of Japanese religion today.

- In the modern period, a large number of New Religious Movements have emerged, providing a means to express traditional religious beliefs and practices in ways adapted to the changing modern situation.

Key terms

bodhisattva One who seeks to attain Buddhahood by working for the enlightenment of all beings; the Buddhist model of compassion.

buddha nature A sharing in the state of enlightenment, inherent in all beings.

daimoku Chant in praise of the *Lotus Sutra*.

hongaku **thought** The concept of 'original enlightenment'; the belief that all things already exist in a state of enlightenment.

hongan The 'original vow' of Amida to bring all beings to rebirth in the Pure Land.

honji suijaku Buddhist concept that identified native Japanese gods as local manifestations of Buddhas or bodhisattvas.

jiriki Salvation through one's own efforts.

kami Native Japanese gods.

kōan Cryptic statement or paradox used in Rinzai Zen as an aid to meditation or the gaining of intuitive knowledge.

mappō Buddhist concept designating the final, degenerate age.

mizuko kuyō A memorial service usually associated with aborted fetuses.

Kokugaku Japanese nativist movement in the early modern period.

nenbutsu Chant in praise of the name of the bodhisattva Amida.

Pure Land Land of Bliss, for those awaiting enlightenment.

saisei itchi The unity of rites and government, expressed in the support of State Shinto by the government in the modern period.

shinbutsu bunri The separation of Buddhism and Shinto, enforced at the beginning of the modern period.

sokushin jōbutsu The attainment of Buddhahood in this life.

tariki Salvation through reliance on another power.

zazen Sitting meditation; Zen.

Zen Meditation practice common to many of the Buddhist schools, but emphasized especially in the Rinzai and Sōtō schools.

Further reading

General

For general works on religion in Japan see Tamaru Noriyoshi and David Read (eds): *Religion in Japanese Culture: Where Living Traditions Meet a Changing World* (Tokyo, New York, London: Kodansha International, 1996); Shigeyoshi Murakami (trans. H. Byron Earhart): *Japanese Religion in the Modern Century* (Tokyo: University of Tokyo Press, 1980); Winston Davis: *Japanese Religion and Society: Paradigms of Structure and Change* (Albany, NY: SUNY Press, 1992); and Ian Reader: *Religion in Contemporary Japan* (London: Macmillan Press, 1991).

Buddhism in Japan

On Buddhism in Japan see Koyu Sonoda and Yusen Kashiwahara (eds): *Shapers of Japanese Buddhism* (Tokyo: Charles E. Tuttle, 1994); George J. Tanabe, Jr. and Willa Jane Tanabe (eds): *The Lotus Sutra in Japanese Culture* (Honolulu: University of Hawaii Press, 1989); Richard K. Payne (ed.): *Re-Visioning 'Kamakura' Buddhism* (Honolulu: University of Hawaii Press, 1998); and Jacqueline I. Stone: *Original Enlightenment and the Transformation of Medieval Japanese Buddhism* (Honolulu: University of Hawaii Press, 1999).

State Shinto

Helen Hardacre: *Shintō and the State 1868–1988* (Princeton, NJ: Princeton University Press, 1989).

Japanese New Religions

On Japanese new religions, see the first chapter of Helen Hardacre: *Kurozumikyō and the New Religions of Japan* (Princeton, NJ: Princeton University Press, 1986). Several works are available on individual new religious movements: Winston Davis: *Dojo: Magic and Exorcism in Modern Japan* (Stanford, CA: Stanford University Press, 1980); Helen Hardacre: *Lay Buddhism in Contemporary Japan: Reiyūkai Kyōdan* (Princeton, NJ: Princeton University Press, 1984); H. Byron Earhart: *Gedatsu-kai and Religion in Contemporary Japan: Returning to the Center* (Bloomington, IN: Indiana University Press, 1989). See Mark R. Mullins: *Christianity Made in Japan: A Study of Indigenous Movements* (Honolulu: University of Hawaii Press, 1998) for a study of Christian-based new religions and discussion of some characteristics of Japanese religiosity. See Robert Kisala: *Prophets of Peace: Pacifism and Cultural Identity in Japan's New Religions* (Honolulu: University of Hawaii Press, 1999) for an analysis of postwar Japanese pacifism in several new religions and discussion of the role of religion in Japanese society.

Contemporary Japanese Religiosity and Practice

Robert J. Smith: *Ancestor Worship in Contemporary Japan* (Stanford, CA: Stanford University Press, 1974); Ian Reader and George J. Tanabe, Jr: *Practically Religious: Worldly Benefits and the Common Religion of Japan* (Honolulu: University of Hawaii Press, 1998); and Helen Hardacre: *Marketing the Menacing Fetus in Japan* (Berkeley, CA: University of California Press, 1997); Kawahashi Noriko and Kuroki Masako (eds): Feminism and Religion in Contemporary Japan (special issue of the *Japanese Journal of Religious Studies* 30, 3–4, 2003).

Aum Shinrikyō

Ian Reader: *Religious Violence in Contemporary Japan: The Case of Aum Shinrikyō* (Richmond: Curzon Press/Honolulu: University of Hawaii Press, 2000) and Robert Kisala and Mark Mullins (eds): *Religion and Social Crisis in Japan: Understanding Japanese Society through the Aum Affair* (Basingstoke, Hampshire: Palgrave, 2001).

Chapter 7

Judaism

Seth D. Kunin

Introduction

The Jewish people number some 15 million worldwide. Almost half of these, approximately 7 million, live in the USA. The majority of Jews both in the USA and the rest of the world are secular: they maintain some type of Jewish identity but have little or no strong connection to Judaism as a religion. Of the 5.7 million Jews who live in the USA, less than a third are members of one of the movements into which modern Judaism is divided. The memberships of the three main movements are: 355,000 Orthodox, 760,000 Reform and 890,000 Conservative. Some percentage of the remaining Jews will align themselves with the Reform movement, which is in some sense the default movement of American Jewry. Outside the USA, the number of Orthodox Jews outweigh those of the other movements, due in part to the fact that outside America Orthodoxy tends to be the default position taken by Jews who have no other strong alignment.

Judaism is a complex cultural system which in its modern incarnations can be viewed through a number of different, interrelated and sometimes contradictory categories: religious affiliation, ethnicity, nationality, (vague) secular identity, and civilization. Each one of these categories reflects a different way of categorizing groups in the modern world. None are mutually exclusive, though in most cases individuals or groups will emphasize one of the elements above the others. They reflect the fact that in the modern context 'Jewishness' constitutes only a partial aspect of individual and group identity that must compete or co-operate with other, often more dominant, cultural constructs.

During the last two centuries, the period in which a significant number of Jews began their encounter with the Enlightenment and modernity, there has been interplay between Judaism as religion, Judaism as a nation and the pressures of assimilation. All the modern Jewish movements are products of these forces, and represent attempts to respond positively or negatively to them. Each of these forces, at least in part, is distinctive of modernity. The compartmentalization of Judaism as a religion reflects the influence of the Enlightenment model of religion as something private and separate from other aspects of cultural and national identity. The development in the nineteenth century of political Zionism and the notions of race or peoplehood is a direct outgrowth of Romanticism and its notions of nationalism. The pressure for assimilation, although in part a response to living within increasingly dominant modern sociocultural frameworks, is also a reflection of the progressive development of liberalism and concepts of rational secularism (see Introduction to this volume).

Judaism in modern times can roughly be divided into five religious and two secular streams. The religious movements include: Reform (also called Liberal or Progressive), Reconstructionist, Conservative (also called Mesorati), Orthodox (also called Modern

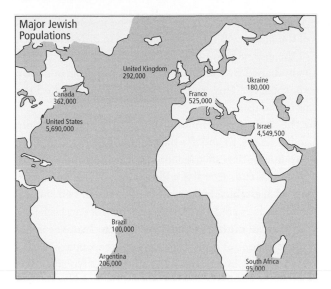

FIGURE 7.1
Map of the Jewish population

Map of Jewish population
distribution. Courtesy Seth Kunin.

or neo-Orthodox) and Ultra Orthodox (including the Hasidic communities). The secular streams include the various forms of political Zionism, many of which are or were antireligious, and secular Jews who sometimes have only vague ethnic associations with Judaism. In addition to these divisions, there is an additional divide between Ashkinazic and Sephardic Jewry. Ashkinazic Jews descend from the Jews of Central and Western Europe. Sephardic Jews descend from the Jews of Spain and Portugal and Islamic countries. This chapter focuses primarily on the Ashkinazic community as it is this community (as well as small pockets of Sephardic Jewry in the UK and the USA) which historically has most strongly responded to issues of modernity. In recent years, however, due to the role of Sephardic Jews in Israel, the Sephardic community has played an increasingly significant role in defining the State of Israel and therefore aspects of wider Jewish identity as well.

All of these streams can be seen as inheritors of a much less strongly defined and perhaps more heterogeneous historical tradition dating back to the first or second millennium BCE. Although some of the religious groupings might claim to be continuations of this earlier cultural form with little or no transformation, and thus the exemplar of authentic Judaism, it seems more likely that all the recent streams are products of or responses to modernity with roots going back to the Enlightenment. Each of these streams responds to the challenges of modernity by emphasizing or de-emphasizing the elements of religion, nationalism and assimilation.

Sources and resources

Judaism as a religious tradition has its roots in the second and first millennia BCE. The diversity of the traditions which ultimately developed into Judaism is reflected in the diversity of sources which were redacted to create the Torah, the first five books of the Bible, and the other sections of the Hebrew Bible. This diversity, in different forms, continued until 70 CE, the time of the destruction of the Second Temple in Jerusalem, after which Judaism was increasingly shaped by the Pharisees, sages or rabbis in a form which became to a large degree normative. This 'rabbinic' tradition established the foundation of all subsequent forms of Judaism.

The tradition established by the sages was primarily based on a legal tradition, halakhah, encapsulated in the Mishnah (200 CE) and the Babylonian Talmud (700 CE). This tradition worked through the interaction of models of interpretation with an authoritative set of legal sources. Although the sages also addressed non-legal questions, *aggadah*, they were primarily interested in establishing a context of accepted behavioural patterns. The legal tradition that developed covered a wide range of activities and spheres. It included, for example, discussions of ritual purity, family law and torts. Issues of belief and dogma – beyond certain basic conceptions of monotheism – were secondary, with a much greater degree of interpretation and individual or communal diversity. The emphasis on the halakhah remained the foundation of Judaism into the modern period, and the law continues to be debated and discussed.

The halakhah is divided into two main categories – the Written and the Oral Torah. The Written Torah includes the first five books of the Bible and was believed to have been given in written form to Moses on Sinai. The Oral Torah includes at the least the Mishnah and Talmud and at the most all halakhic discussions as an unfolding, expanding tradition. The Oral Torah was believed to have been given by God to Moses in oral form on Sinai. During the past centuries, it was encapsulated in several legal codes, culminating in the *Shulkhan Aruch* (1542 CE) which remains the cornerstone of traditional Judaism. The Orthodox and Conservative approaches to Judaism arise from differing interpretations of the possibilities of change within the halakhic system (see pp. 182–4). It should be emphasized that in spite of some traditions' view that the halakhah is unchanging, it has in fact constantly changed and developed and continues to do so today particularly in response to issues raised by Judaism's encounters with modernity.

Alongside the legal tradition, the *aggadic* tradition developed in many different directions. The most significant of these included mysticism and philosophy. These also laid the basis for some of the directions taken by Judaism in response to modernity – for example the Orthodox Hasidic community (established in the eighteenth century) emphasizes (alongside the halakhah) the mystical tradition and has its roots in the mystical response to the expulsion of the Jews from Spain in 1492. Likewise, the Reform movement can be viewed as a continuation into modern times of the philosophical tradition. It draws on philosophy, particularly that of Kant, as the basis of its under-standing of action and (in part) of God. The philosophical emphasis is even more important as the basis of Reconstructionist Judaism.

Several themes from the Biblical and historical tradition became major mythological motifs which shaped rabbinic Judaism and continue to shape all modern forms of Judaism. Historically, the most significant of these has been the concept of covenant, and the associated concept of redemption. These motifs are particularly encapsulated in the exodus narrative (recorded in the book of Exodus in the Bible) which tells of both the redemption from Egypt and the acceptance of the Commandments on Mount Sinai. This account became one of the significant paradigms for interpreting God's role in history. Its influence can still be seen – for example – in the way in which some Jewish communities and thinkers interpret the foundation of the State of Israel in the modern period.

A second motif of almost equal significance is based on the historical events surrounding the destruction of the Temple in Jerusalem. Here the motif is one of the power of God in destruction and punishment. Although this motif, which often focuses on punishment of Israel, has its roots in a biblical concept of reward and punishment and is first articulated in respect of the destruction of the First Temple by the Babylonians, it is most strongly developed in relation to the destruction of the Second Temple by the Romans and the diaspora (dispersion, migration) which followed. In modern times this motif has been used as a model for the interpretation of the periodic persecution of Jewish communities culminating in the Holocaust (the systematic persecution and extermination of Jews by the Nazi regime in Germany during World War II). Indeed, in many ways the Holocaust has become the prime exemplar of this motif in modern times, so much so that the latter has become a new lens for reunderstanding persecution and anti-Semitism.

The Holocaust has also become a significant motif in its own right. Its symbolic and theological effects have been felt throughout the second half of the twentieth century. As suggested, it has become symbolic of anti-Semitism and persecution of the Jewish people both linking into and surpassing or superseding past persecutions. It also has had a significant impact on all subsequent Jewish theologies. This is most clearly seen in respect to interpretations of evil and theodicy (explanations of evil and suffering). After the Holocaust many theologians could no longer accept older understandings of suffering as God's judgement, particularly as this would make Hitler and the Nazis God's tools.

Many new theodicies have thus been suggested. They have included: arguments about the 'death of God', denials that God acts in the world through miraculous intervention or even revelation, and an emphasis on the reality of unrestrained human free will. Other scholars have suggested that the Holocaust simply reveals the limitations of human understanding. In practical terms, the Holocaust has become for many the basis for a new emphasis on the importance of Jewish survival – often survival for its own sake. The theme may also be expressed in the terms of resistance to giving Hitler a 'posthumous victory'. Such ideas of survival, resistance and anti-Semitism often inform thinking about Zionism and the problem of diaspora. Their impact is various. As well as encouraging the formation of a separate Jewish state (Israel), they may challenge notions of messianic communal progress, or re-emphasize Jewish particularism.

A final historical motif that has been re-activated by particular pressures of modernity is that of the promised land – originally part of the covenant myth (in the Hebrew Bible God grants the promised land to Israel so long as they remain faithful to the covenant with God). For most of the last 2,000 years – during which time Israel has been dispersed, in diaspora – this mythological complex has played only a minor role, often associated with messianic speculations. But it was revitalized in the nineteenth and twentieth centuries, and developed in association with modern (Romantic) concepts of nationalism into Zionism. Although not all modern Zionists believe in a divine basis for the modern State of Israel, the biblical depiction of God's promise of the land clearly provided a strong religious and emotional tie to a specific geographic location, and continues to provide political and religious motivations for many Zionists.

Thus the events of the twentieth century have added new mythological ways of understanding past and present in Judaism. Zionism and the Holocaust (particularly a Zionist interpretation of the Holocaust) have been two essential shaping motifs. Some Zionist thinking sees the return of all Jews to the State of Israel as the culmination of Jewish history, and the return to normality as a nation. All events of the past, particularly those of the diaspora, are interpreted in this light. The model focuses on periods of persecution – culminating in the Holocaust – as the result of living in diaspora. It suggests that the only way to resolve this problem – the relation of Israel to the other nations – is to transform Israel, to make it a nation like any other nation, living in a land of its own.

This chapter examines how different forms of Judaism have attempted to respond to these motifs and the forces of modernity. Although the different movements reacted in various ways, some positive and some negative, all were forced to respond to modernity in some fashion. The political position of the Jews made this inescapable. Since most Jews prior to the foundation of the State of Israel in 1947 dwelt within host European societies, the rise of modernity in general and the modern state in particular was experienced at first hand. Equally, the migration of many Jews to American in the twentieth century placed them at the heart of the current leading society of the modern world. The chapter as it develops focuses most strongly on the Reform movement, not because it is the most significant, but because it most consciously and clearly articulates the issues raised by modernity.

Interactions with modernity

Moses Mendelssohn and the Jewish Enlightenment

The philosophy of Moses Mendelssohn marks the beginning of the Jewish encounter with the seventeenth-century Enlightenment, and may be regarded as the precursor of the Jewish encounter with modernity. Whilst it is true that Spinoza (1632–1677) was an earlier and more significant Enlightenment philosopher, his influence on Judaism was less direct. This was due both to the radical nature of his philosophical arguments and to his ultimate excommunication by the Jewish community of Amsterdam. Mendelssohn (1729–1786) marks the transition from a traditional Talmudic scholar to an Enlightenment philosopher; his work was influenced by that of Spinoza, Leibniz, Hobbes and Locke. His achievement also marks the beginnings of the wider integration of Jews into Western European culture, and the introduction of ideas from that culture into the wider Jewish community in both Western and eventually Eastern Europe.

In regard to the wider transformation of Judaism in the context of early modernity, the most significant of Mendelssohn's philosophical works is *Jerusalem, Or, On Religious Power and Judaism*. This work was intended both as an argument against compulsion within religion, and as a demonstration that allegiance to Judaism was compatible with full participation as citizens of European nation states. *Jerusalem* is divided into two parts. The first examines the relationship between the political and the religious and establishes the foundations of political philosophy. The second is a defence of Judaism. It argues that in terms of its core beliefs Judaism is a religion of reason; in arguing this Mendelssohn was situating Judaism within the Enlightenment search for the rational basis of all religion. For Mendelssohn the revealed and particular aspect of Judaism was its law, which was binding on Jews alone. As such Judaism was a religion of law rather than dogma. In arguing this, Mendelssohn drew a distinction between Judaism and Christianity. Unlike Christianity, which imposed a set of religious dogmas on its adherents, Judaism permitted its adherents freedom of belief. Its spirit was 'freedom in doctrine and conformity in law'. None of its laws, however, were coercive or dogmatic. In effect, Mendelssohn was arguing for the existence of the separate historical religions, thereby opposing the view that all religions should be merged into a homogenized form of Christianity presented as the universal religion of reason. His work thus presents a strong argument for the inclusion of Jews as citizens within European states, and laid the groundwork for the significant change in the social and political status of the Jewish people in Europe in the late eighteenth and nineteenth centuries.

Mendelssohn cannot simply be viewed as a reformer due to his arguments for the maintenance of Jewish law, and his commitment to the maintenance of the law. Yet in some respects his thought opened up cracks in the tradition. Amongst his innovations were the rejection of excommunication and of the right of the religious community to exercise force and compulsion, and his views about the laws of burial – these changes became touchstones for arguments between traditionalists and modernists. Mendelssohn's work also signals the beginnings of important changes within the Jewish community, and in the relation of that community to a new world of nation states. He can be seen as an exemplar of the possibilities of Jewish participation in modern European culture and thought. His contribution led to the development of the *Haskalah* or Jewish Enlightenment, which sought to introduce European thought and culture to the Jewish community. As such Mendelssohn became a symbol for reform and 'liberalism' – a new freedom of belief in religious matters.

The Haskalah: The Jewish Enlightenment

The *Haskalah* marked a change in many aspects of Jewish cultural life. At its simplest it was a movement of Jewish writers influenced by European literary forms. But it also had wider ideological goals, and sought to transform almost every aspect of Jewish life from education to communal organization. It viewed the Jews, particularly of Central and Eastern Europe, as remaining in a form of medievalism and challenged them to confront and absorb the best elements of modernity.

The initial period of the *Haskalah* was led by disciples of Mendelssohn. They championed a return to Hebrew and rejected Yiddish – the traditional language of the Jewish community of the time – as a degenerate form of German. They also respected biblical Hebrew rather than the later rabbinic Hebrew. This stance related to their rejection of traditional Jewish education which emphasized the study of rabbinic texts, particularly the Talmud, almost to the exclusion of any other subject. The reformers viewed rabbinic forms of Judaism as degenerate compared with the purer and earlier biblical form. Like liberal Christians, they sought a return to a purer, more historically authentic faith. Such a project ultimately became one of the building blocks for Reform Judaism as it developed in the nineteenth century. In terms of language the *Haskalah* initially emphasized Hebrew and subsequently emphasized the use of German – the emphasis on German and the vernacular language of the country of residence also became one of the hallmarks of Reform.

The *Haskalah* played a provocative and oppositional role in relation to the development of Orthodox Hasidism in modern times (the Hasidic community is discussed in greater detail below). As the *Haskalah* moved into Eastern Europe and Russia, its opposition to medievalism often translated into a rejection of Hasidism with its emphasis on mysticism and its charismatic leaders, the *tzadikim*. Its satires often singled out Hasidism for ridicule. One effect was to engender a fierce mutual opposition between the two tendencies in modern Judaism, and to precipitate Hasidic opposition to modernity. The opposition is reflected in many Hasidic tales in which the *Maskil* (disciple of the *Haskalah*) is depicted as an opponent.

Like the ideas developed by Mendelssohn, the *Haskalah* can be seen as transitional. It represented the beginnings of the transformation of the Jewish community through its encounter with modernity. It laid the foundation for many of the religious trends that came to fruition in the middle of the nineteenth century. On the one hand, as missionaries of modern values and culture the *Haskalah* influenced the early Reformers who sought to create a Judaism that was consonant with modern values and culture. On the other hand, by its opposition to traditional values and the Hasidic community, it helped create a strong association between modernity and the rejection of traditional Judaism and thereby strengthened Orthodox Judaism's suspicion and hostility towards modernity.

The beginnings of modern Jewish movements

This section of the chapter examines some of the developments in the eighteenth and nineteenth centuries that led to the rise of many of the movements which now constitute modern Judaism. It argues that all of the movements arose as responses, either positive or negative, to the Enlightenment and modernity. Each of the movements is examined in somewhat greater detail in later sections of this chapter.

Reform

In *Leviathan* Saul Ascher (1767–1822) laid the philosophical cornerstone of the Reform movement in Judaism. Unlike Mendelssohn, who saw Judaism as a revealed law, Ascher argued that the defining feature of Judaism was its religious faith, not its political or legal constitution. This emphasis on faith, in effect, made Judaism equivalent to other European religions – a theme constantly returned to by modern Reform Judaism. By separating it from its political and practical basis, Ascher placed Judaism among other 'religions', and saw it as compatible with the cultural and political life of modern Europe. Unlike traditional Judaism which treated all aspects of Jewish law and tradition as equally authoritative, Ascher selected or emphasized certain practices as essential while ignoring or de-emphasizing others. He focused on the subjective personal aspects of religion, emphasizing the importance of personal satisfaction and happiness. He saw the law as a means to these ends, thus opposing those who emphasized the communal aspects of religion and who saw faithful observance as the fulfilment of God's will and thus an end in itself. Ascher also emphasized a concept of history which underpins all modern forms of Judaism, that is, as a process of development with the implication of unfolding spiritual progress. Many of these themes, particularly the concept of religious subjectivity, underpinned the ideas of the Reform movement and are still significant features of it. Ascher's arguments also provided a philosophical basis for the changes which were subsequently introduced by both his contemporaries and successors.

The origins of the Reform movement lie not only in the cultural transformations associated with the dawn of modernity (notably the rise of the Enlightenment), but also in the political changes which characterized early modern Europe – most notably the rise of the nation state and individual freedoms. During the latter half of the eighteenth century and the first half of the nineteenth the Jewish community in Western Europe experienced a significant transformation in status. As this period progressed Jews were increasingly given political freedom – a transformation marked by the move from protected, semi-autonomous minority to citizen (or subject). The French Revolution and the Napoleonic period marked one of the key points in this transformation. With increasing access to political and cultural life and decision-making, Jewish communities, particularly in what was to become Germany, began to develop forms of Judaism more in keeping with their newfound status.

Although the process of reforming synagogue practice had been progressing since the late eighteenth century in Amsterdam, a more structured programme of reform did not occur until the nineteenth century, under the leadership of Israel Jacobson (1768–1828). It is perhaps significant that Jacobson was a lay rather than a rabbinic leader. The process began in Westphalia and continued in Berlin. Among the changes which were initially instituted was a transformation in the form of service, moving from one which was perceived to be less decorous, and thus out of keeping with wider cultural forms, to a form of service which was more highly structured and characterized by European ideas of decorum. Some of these changes included a reduction of physical rituals, for example the procession, and changes in the content and structure of the service, for example minimizing active congregational participation. After his move to Berlin, Reform services were held in the homes of Jacobson and Jacob Baer. These services added to the changes already instituted in Westphalia. The new additions included the use of German elements in the service alongside the Hebrew, removal of the partition between men and women and the removal of repetitions within the service. This process was also occurring in Hamburg, with the establishment of the first Reform Temple in 1817.

By the mid-nineteenth century the process of reform moved from a focus on forms of worship and life to include areas of belief and self-perception. Thus in the prayer book reforms of that period we find the removal of concepts of messianic ingathering, bodily resurrection and Zionist hopes. The removal of the messianic ingathering was tied to two separate concepts: (a) a transformation of the concept of messiah from the traditional model of an actual political and spiritual leader who would bring about a transformation in the world and gather all Jews back to Israel, to a concept of messianic age which would be brought about through the inexorable progress of humanity; and (b) the rejection of the notion that Jews would be returned to Israel as an end to the negative condition of diaspora. Reformers considered diaspora to be a positive state and wanted to emphasize their ongoing commitment to the European states in which they lived. These priorities led them to be hostile to Zionism. They saw Zionism as a statement of Jewish separatism and the desire for a nation set apart. The reformers chose to define Judaism as a religion, not a people or nation, and thus with no need of a national home or end to diaspora. Likewise, the concept of bodily resurrection offended their ideas of rationality. In many prayer books it was either removed or changed to reflect belief in the immortality of the soul.

Abraham Geiger (1810–1874) was another intellectual and rabbinic leader of reform during this period. He introduced or emphasized several themes which remain characteristic of the Reform movement. He emphasized the historical nature of Judaism and thus the contingent nature of its practices and beliefs. He also emphasized Judaism's universal message – a theme that also has been very influential in changes in the language of prayer. One of Geiger's most significant emphases was the ethical nature of Judaism and the concept of ethical monotheism. For him the key unifying theme of Judaism was not observance but morality. This concept was enshrined in the notion of prophetic Judaism – an emphasis on the ideals proclaimed by the prophets rather than the observances taught by the rabbis.

Orthodoxy

The self-consciousness of other parts of the Jewish community developed to a large degree in response to the rise of reform and the Reform movement. Thus, Orthodoxy came into existence as a self-conscious movement in opposition to the innovations that were being developed by the reformers. The two main early centres of Orthodoxy were Hungary and Germany, both areas in which the *Haskalah* and the reformers had made significant inroads. In Hungary the major figure in the development of the movement was Rabbi Mosheh Sofer (1762–1839). The form of Orthodoxy that he espoused rejected any changes in tradition. To some extent he also rejected any real accommodation with the wider culture. One of the key aspects of self-conscious Orthodoxy was the view of the past and tradition as unchanging and uniformly authoritative. The approaches to community and Zionism found in Hungarian Orthodoxy also reflected this rejection of modern values. Rabbi Sofer supported settlement of Israel with the hope of establishing a Jewish community that was separated from the corrupting secular influences of the modern world. The Hungarian community also expressed their separatist values through the maintenance of an autonomous communal structure – which continued and was legally sanctioned in the latter half of the nineteenth century.

A second model of Orthodoxy developed in Germany in the middle part of the nineteenth century. Samson Raphael Hirsch (1808–1888) was the leading figure of this approach. Although Hirsch, like Sofer, accepted the unchanging authority of halakhah (Jewish law) he took a different approach to modernity. His approach can be summed up in the statement: *Torah im derekh erets*, 'Torah [Jewish law] and the way of the world'. He believed that modernity and emancipation of the Jewish community could complement and enhance the Jewish mission, the core of which was leading a life according to God's will. The maxim was meant to suggest that Jews should take advantage of the modern world, especially its knowledge, but not allow this to undermine the commitment to Torah. The two worlds were not meant to be joined together or seen as equal partners, rather the two are meant to coexist, with Jewish values and traditions ultimately being the arbiter for participation and acceptance of modernity. Like other German Jews, Hirsch de-emphasizes aspects of Jewish nationalism or national aspirations. He saw exile as having a positive rather than a negative value.

Rav Abraham Isaac Kook (1865–1935) offered a third approach to Orthodox Judaism that was different from those proposed by both Sofer and Hirsch. Although he was aware of trends in modern philosophy, his approach was more inwardly focused and placed an emphasis on traditional Jewish mysticism. He emphasized that the world was in a state of spiritual disharmony which was mirrored by the exile of Israel from her land. He argued that the return of Israel from exile would bring about a transformation both in the human and spiritual realms, and result in the redemption of all humanity. Kook was very strongly associated with Jewish nationalist aspirations. He saw Zionism as a yearning of the Jewish soul to fulfil its spiritual destiny. Thus even secular Zionism was a sacred mission in spite of its own self-perception. On this basis Kook was more receptive and supportive of secular Zionism than other Orthodox leaders of his time. Kook prefigures some of the trends at the end of the twentieth century – this is most clearly seen in his synthesis of mysticism with aspects of modernity creating approaches that coexist with modernity and to some extent validate aspects of it.

To a degree the approaches of Kook, Hirsch and Sofer have all had a lasting impact on Orthodox Judaism. Hirsch's position became mainstream for the Orthodox movement, for example, particularly in the USA and the UK for much of the twentieth century. During the latter half of the century, however, there seemed to be a shift in focus among many Orthodox communities to a stance which is more similar to that of Sofer (see pp. 194–6).

Conservative Judaism

Like Orthodoxy, Conservative Judaism arose as a response to the process of reform. Unlike Orthodoxy, however, it had its roots among reformers both in Germany and the USA. The process of reform was not a unified one; it had both traditional and radical wings. Rabbi Zachariah Frankel (1801–1875) represented the traditionalist wing. He argued for a slower process of reform, with change focused on the less significant features of Jewish life and practice. The main split between Frankel and the reformers respected the use of Hebrew in religious services. Although both parties to the argument agreed that some German would be used as well as Hebrew, Frankel objected to the view that the maintenance of Hebrew was advisable rather than necessary. The argument over language was symbolic of a deeper argument over the nature and significance of tradition.

Frankel introduced a concept which was to become the cornerstone of Conservative Judaism: that of positive, historical Judaism. This concept included two, perhaps paradoxical, elements. It suggested that in order to understand Judaism one must examine the historical development of the tradition. Such historical consciousness was both modern and conservative. It forced an acceptance that the tradition had undergone a continuous process of change and development, and a recognition that this process of change would continue. It also, however, emphasized that Judaism is an organically integrated authoritative whole that develops over time. History and tradition should be a major element in shaping any decision for reform. Frankel also introduced a related concept – the wishes of the community. Change and tradition should reflect the needs of a community at a particular time; it should not run ahead of them due to the desires of individual reformers who embraced modern ideals and values wholesale. Through these two tenets Frankel sought to achieve a creative balance between tradition and reform with a strong emphasis on historical continuity.

The rise of Conservative Judaism in the USA was influenced by Frankel's approach. Like Frankel, the founders of the movement started within the reformist camp and found themselves uncomfortable with the pace and level of reform. Two rabbis, Alexander Kohut (1842–1894) and Sabato Morais (1823–1897) led the split in the USA. Both Kohut and Morais argued against many of the changes proposed by the radical reformers, while supporting a slower process of reform. The split in the USA led to the establishment of the Jewish Theological Seminary of America, which became the foundation of a distinctive movement. This process was completed and given final form with the appointment of Solomon Schechter to head the seminary in 1901. Schechter helped establish the institutional structures of Conservative Judaism and likewise gave the concepts fundamental to Conservative Judaism an intellectually coherent form. He emphasized the historical development of Judaism as both a reforming and conservative tool, and argued for the need to respond to the consensus of the community, which he called 'catholic Israel'. Schechter argued that it was this communal force throughout Jewish history that was both the motive force for change and for continuity. By community he was not referring to all Jews, but the core of committed Jews – who unconsciously kept, dropped or transformed practices through time.

Reform Judaism

The Platforms

Since the nineteenth century the Reform movement has responded to the changing faces of modernity at almost every level of practice and belief. Although in recent years there has been a trend back towards more traditional patterns, in general the trajectory has been towards transforming Judaism in line with Western cultural values and understandings. Many of these changes are highlighted in three main 'platforms' that have punctuated the history of the movement. Although all three are products of the American Reform movement, they have been reflected and have influenced trends in the Reform or Progressive movements worldwide.

The Pittsburgh Platform of 1885 marks the first self-conscious statement of the American Reform movement, and the point at which the American Conservative movement was born via those rabbis, particularly Kohut and Morais, who rejected the changes and values found in the platform. The platform reflects changes in beliefs and practices. Several significant changes or expressions in the statement indicate the reformers' attempted synthesis of Judaism with modernity. The first section of the platform speaks of God as the 'God-idea'. It is possible that this formulation reflects the influence of neo-Kantian thought. Although Hermann Cohen's (1842–1918) significant discussion of Judaism in neo-Kantian terms, *Religion of Reason out of the Sources of Judaism*, was not published until 1919, the Pittsburgh Platform does seem to be influenced by similar ideas. This is also seen in an emphasis on ethical monotheism which was also characteristic of Cohen's position. Moreover, the statement about the 'God-idea' reflects a universalist view of Judaism and other religions. While it recognizes the spiritual value of all religions' search for the infinite, it views Judaism as the highest expression of that search. The second statement of the platform affirms the value of the Bible as a record of Judaism's relationship with God and as a source of morality. It also, however, accepts the historically contingent nature of the text. It suggests that the Bible is a product of its own time – focusing primarily on the conflicts between modern science and the miracles and other non-scientific views found in the text. It argues that these forms are clothing for the message, but not the message itself. Another key change in belief is found in relation to the messiah. Rather than looking forward to an actual messianic figure, the platform looks towards a messianic age. One of the significant aspects of this change is an acceptance of nineteenth-century notions of progress. The platform views the modern era as the beginning of the messianic age. This change also reflects a general trend in reform which values the modern age as the acme of human progress. One additional change in belief is found respecting the fate of human beings after death. Traditional Judaism believed that there would be a bodily resurrection that would precede judgement. The platform rejects both bodily resurrection and heaven and hell. It argues instead for the immortality of the soul.

Several sections of the platform also reflect significant changes in both practice and the attitude towards Jewish law. The third section posits that the law was only binding during the period in which the Israelites lived in Palestine. During that period it served to prepare the people for their mission. Today, however, only the moral law – which was seen as being based on reason – remains binding. The other ceremonial aspects of Judaism should only be retained if they 'elevate or sanctify our lives'. Any rituals which are in conflict with modern values or aesthetics should be rejected. These themes are more specifically emphasized in the fourth section. It rejects food, purity and clothing rules as being obstructions rather than aids to spiritual elevation. These sections illustrate a key trend in reform thinking which emphasizes morality as being the heart of Judaism and sees ritual practice as being a means to that end, and to that of individual spiritual elevation, rather than being a significant end in itself. Yet the platform also emphasizes the sense of mission which was characteristic of the early stages of the Reform movement. It suggests that Judaism and its daughter religions of Christianity and Islam have the mission of spreading ethical monotheism. The platform concludes with a statement reflecting the liberal values which have been characteristic of the Reform movement. It specifically mentions the gap between rich and poor and the need to create a society based on justice.

The Pittsburgh Platform thus lays out many of the key themes that would remain central to the Reform movement during the twentieth century. In terms of belief it offered a rationalist and more transcendent view of the 'God-idea' and viewed all religions as coming from the same infinite source. It emphasized the notion of progress and encapsulated it in the concept of the messianic age. In terms of practice, it enshrined a more instrumental view of the law, seeing it as a means to a moral or spiritual end. It also enshrined the view that the law is historically contingent and that groups or individuals have the right to judge the law based on modern values and aesthetics, and that only the universal moral law was binding.

The Columbus Platform of 1937 reiterated and clarified many of these ideas. It, however, moves back from some of the more extreme positions taken by the earlier reformers, for example, that of the God-idea, critical discussion of the rabbinic tradition and the positive statement regarding Zionism. It does, however, retain the key trajectories of reform. This is particularly seen in the emphasis on morality, particularly twentieth-century liberal values. It also continues the rejection of the binding nature of Jewish law and emphasis on spiritual elevation and inspiration.

In 1976 the Reform movement celebrated 100 years of reform in America with a new statement of Reform principles, 'Reform Judaism: A Centenary Perspective'. One of the most significant changes indicated by the document was a change in attitude towards modernity. Due to the Holocaust, the movement no longer expressed the same attitude towards progress and modernity. The Holocaust also caused a new emphasis on survival, which found expression throughout the text. It expressed a much more positive attitude towards Zionism – this reflected a clear change in the Reform movement's attitude that initially occurred at the conclusion of World War II. Though the Centenary Perspective retained a universalistic emphasis on values and mission, the central focus on liberal values was also dropped. The text as a whole is much more inward looking and focused on the needs of the Reform Jewish community. It offers a new understanding of the relationship with modernity, emphasizing the uncertain nature of the individual's experience of the modern world, and using uncertainty as an explanation for the increasing diversity within the Reform movement. Arguing that the Reform movement is open to any 'position thoughtfully and conscientiously advocated', the Centenary Perspective reflects the increasing emphasis on individual conscience, choice and diversity which had developed during the course of the twentieth century.

One hundred years: What we have taught

We celebrate the role of Reform Judaism in North America . . . We also feel great satisfaction at how much of our pioneering conception of Judaism has been accepted by the household of Israel. It now seems self-evident to most Jews: that our tradition should interact with modern culture; that its forms ought to reflect a contemporary aesthetic; that its scholarship needs to be conducted by modern critical methods; and that change has been and must continue to be a fundamental reality in Jewish life. Moreover, though some still disagree, substantial numbers have also accepted our teachings: that the ethics of universalism implicit in traditional Judaism must be an explicit part of our Jewish duty; that women should have full rights to practice Judaism; and that Jewish obligation begins with the informed will of every individual.

(From *Reform Judaism: A Centenary Perspective*)

BOX 7.1 Extract from *Reform Judaism: A Centenary Perspective*

These three documents reflect several elements of continuity and development in the Reform project. There is a continued emphasis on universality and a positive attitude towards other religions, particularly Christianity and Islam. There is also a clear rejection of Jewish law as obligatory. Although the early documents do not highlight the mechanisms for change, the element of autonomy is clearly emphasized in the Centenary Perspective. It is not unlikely that this emphasis reflects a greater emphasis on the individual and individual spiritual needs and aspirations (a detraditionalization and 'turn to the self'), which has developed in the twentieth century. There are also several areas where the more recent documents reflect a retreat from the stances taken in the early stages of the movement, for example, a more positive revaluation of ritual and retreat from strong statements of liberal/individualistic values which reflect a more inward-looking movement, increasingly concerned for the survival of Judaism.

Authority and the Individual

As seen in the Centenary Perspective, Reform Judaism emphasizes the role of the individual – reiterating the position initially taken by Ascher. Religion is seen as serving both individual and communal needs, and though the importance of ritual gains fresh emphasis, it is left to each person to be responsible for their own ritual practice. The emphasis on autonomy means that there can be great diversity in practice within the movement based on individual choices and needs. In actuality, however, there is a greater degree of acceptance of authority in the movement. Most individuals do not exercise their responsibility to create their own Jewish life.

The degree of conformity found among Reform Jews was much more marked prior to the 1960s and 1970s. Until that time several factors combined to support conformity of ideas and practice rather than diversity: an acceptance of the value of a universal reason, social conformity and a greater sense of social cohesion and mission. In the 1960s this consensus began to break down with an increase in individualization and perhaps a broader relativization of values. It is also likely that the philosophy of Martin Buber (1878–1965), with its emphasis on the divine–human (individual) encounter and rejection of traditional forms of religion, also played a part in this process. Although the diversity found is still limited to a relatively small group of Reform Jews it plays a key role in challenging the movement's identity and in the 1990s led to a move towards various forms of spirituality and mystical practices.

Authority in the Reform movement is vested at several levels. Within most communities there are both lay and rabbinic structures. The lay leaders are primarily managerial, leaving most religious direction to the rabbis. The congregation elects the lay leadership. The rabbinic role is variously interpreted. Some rabbis emphasize the teaching aspect of the role, seeing themselves as facilitators rather than leaders, whilst others take a stronger role in shaping the ritual life of both the community and individuals within it. Most fall between these two poles. In all cases, however, it is important to note that the rabbi is an employee hired by the congregation and working for them on a contractual basis. This type of relationship shapes the interaction between the rabbi and congregation and may prevent the rabbi from moving in directions that are uncomfortable to the congregants or the congregational leaders.

The Reform movement in the USA is also highly organized in its institutional structures. Since the foundation of the movement in the nineteenth century three institutions have been dominant. The Hebrew Union College–Jewish Institute of Religion (HUC–JIR), with four campuses in New York, Cincinnati, Los Angeles, and Jerusalem – trains the rabbinic and other professionals for the movement. The Central Conference of American Rabbis (CCAR) is the organizational body of Reform rabbis. The CCAR has provided many of the communal aspects of religious input into the movement, publishing the prayer books used by Reform synagogues and making statements on aspects of religious practice and belief – the Columbus Platform and the Centenary Perspective were both produced by the CCAR. The third institutional body, the Union of American Hebrew Congregations (UAHC), is the congregational organization of the movement. Since its inception it has had both rabbinic and lay leadership. Of the three organizations in recent years the latter has tended to be the most influential in shaping religious policy. Similar structures are found in other parts of the Reform movement worldwide, though only the UK has a fully independent rabbinical seminary, the Leo Baeck College.

Gender

One of the most significant changes instituted by the Reform movement almost since its inception has been a move towards the equalization of the roles of men and women in Judaism. This change accelerated over time and reflected changes in the status of women in Western society during the course of the nineteenth and twentieth centuries (see Chapter 19). As in many aspects of the Reform approach to tradition, its decisions regarding women reflect the view that where modern values come into conflict with Jewish tradition, the tradition should be changed in line with the modern values.

In Reform temples today no distinction is made between male and female roles. Men and women sit together during all types of services and events – with the exception of some women's services, often regarding the new moon, which have been introduced by women in response to the desire to have rituals which reflect their particular needs. Rituals that were once limited to men such as Bar Mitzvah have been extended to women (Bat Mitzvah). Women can also fulfil all ritual roles within the community. These roles include both congregational participation in ritual and all professional roles. In 1972, HUC–JIR was the first seminary to ordain a woman as rabbi. Although the possibility of women rabbis had been debated and in principle accepted earlier in the century – and a woman, Regina Jonas, had served as a rabbi – it was only in the late 1960s that the college accepted a woman as a candidate for ordination. Today there are an increasing number of women rabbis, though none have yet been appointed as a senior rabbi of a flagship congregation. The other Reform seminaries followed the lead of HUC–JIR and women now serve as rabbis within all parts of Reform Judaism. Women are also found in other professional roles within the Jewish community including temple administrators, cantors and religion school directors.

FIGURE 7.2
Women with Torah

Women from the Jewish Community of Great Neck, New York, dance with a Torah specially commissioned and brought to the only existing synagogue in Oswiecim, Poland, where the Auschwitz death camp was built, during a joyful ceremony on 30 August 1999. The ceremony and the Torah restored the synagogue's religious character. Courtesy Leszek Wdowinski, Getty Images.

Recent developments

Reform Judaism, like other forms of liberal religion, is currently struggling to maintain its numbers and identity. During the past 30 years the movement has participated in many initiatives, some on its own and some in co-operation with other movements, to enhance Jewish practice and identity. It has also gone through many internal changes trying to fit the needs of a changing constituency. Many of the changes have been highlighted above. Thus, the shift in focus from liberal, social and political concerns to internal and spiritual concerns, which was seen in the Centenary Perspective, is even clearer in the most recent position statement of the CCAR. This change is seen particularly in the introduction of a wide range of forms of experience-based spirituality which have become increasingly common in Reform temples. The most visible of these are healing services which range from the calling out of names to the laying on of hands. The spirituality and the mystical elements which have been introduced also indicate a move away from the rationalism which was the hallmark of classical Reform.

In part some of these trends are a response to the challenges posed by New Age religion and the growth of spirituality (see Chapter 12 on Spirituality, and Chapter 13 on New Age religion). A New Age Judaism has arisen on the periphery of the mainstream movements. It tends to have weak boundaries and exhibits the modern phenomena of 'spiritual shopping' and 'networking' characteristic of the New Age. Such spirituality offers a more experiential or mystical form of Judaism. Many Reform and Conservative Jews, both as movements and more significantly as individual congregations, are responding to this external challenge by introducing similar practices and ideas. It will be interesting to see whether these changes alienate the parts of the Reform movement that still accept the notions of rationality which were fundamental to modernism rather than the more subjectivized experience which is fundamental to postmodernism.

Yet there is an additional trend in the Reform movement today which moves towards the opposite side of modern religious practice – a move towards the recreation of stronger religious structures. This is found in a move away from individual autonomy to a new Reform halakhah. While it is true that this pressure was present through much of the twentieth century, it made its mark primarily in the latter half of that century. This is seen in the increasing number of traditional practices followed by Reform congregations. The trend towards a neo-traditionalism was particularly highlighted in the preparatory documents, which led up to the CCAR's position statement of 1999. Although the final document watered the emphasis down, the trend towards a much more structured definition of Reform practice and ideology is clearly present. This trend is also found in the progressive movements of the UK. Both Reform and Liberal Judaism have become increasingly traditional and to some extent have tried to establish basic (sometimes extensive) sets of practices and beliefs that identify a progressive Jew. Very often this trend is accompanied by rejections of relativism and the need to re-establish baseline values.

Conservative Judaism

Conservative Judaism has responded to many of the same influences as the Reform movement – as well as to Reform itself. The key difference between Reform and Conservative Judaism, however, lies in their differing attitudes towards Jewish law. As mentioned above, the Reform movement has often been willing to set aside Jewish law if it conflicts with modernity. The Conservative movements, however, place greater emphasis on the significance and authority of tradition. Conservative Judaism, as suggested above, recognizes that Judaism undergoes a continuous process of change and thus accepts that modern values and norms will shape the Judaism of the future. It also argues for the importance of continuity and considers Jewish law and the legal processes which have shaped it as the key source of that continuity. This somewhat paradoxical dual emphasis has meant that the changes instituted by the Conservative movement have been introduced more slowly than in Reform and have required the validation of the Jewish legal process. Nevertheless, during the past century the Conservative movement has made many of the same changes to tradition as has the Reform movement – for example, equalizing the roles of men and women. Often the difference is one of process and attitude towards the law rather than one of final content and judgement.

The most recent and comprehensive statement of Conservative beliefs, *Emet Ve-Emunah*, was produced by the Conservative movement in 1988. The text was written by a commission and attempted to encapsulate a consensus of the beliefs found in the movement. As a consensus document it tends to attempt to present a moderate position which will satisfy the different wings of the movement. In those areas where consensus is impossible it presents the alternative positions. This type of process and result are characteristic of the Conservative movement as a whole. As the document covers a wide range of ideas, we will only touch on a few of them here. Many – such as the discussion of messianic expectations and a largely relativist understanding of the value of other religious traditions – are broadly similar to those found in the Reform movement. The document also mirrors the Reform concern for social values and includes a strong statement expressing the need for social change and justice.

The document opens with a discussion of Conservative theology, 'God in the World'. The first part of the section illustrates the diversity of belief within the movement. It offers two main divergent theological positions. The first presents a traditional depiction of the divine. It states that many people within the Conservative movement see God as being the supernatural power who controls and rules the world. It emphasizes, however, that there are many different reasons why people believe and many different ways in which human beings encounter God in experience. This position is in part shaped by the thought of Abraham Joshua Heschel (1907–1972) who argued for a more traditional, mystical or experiential understanding and relation to God. The second position is closer to the thought of Mordechai Kaplan (1881–1983), who argued for a non-supernatural and non-personal understanding of the divine. This position suggests that God is not a supernatural power who can be encountered, but rather a source of meaning or perhaps the moral–logical structure of being. This second position is perhaps even more extreme than would be found among most Reform Jews. The discussion concludes with a validation of diversity of belief. It ties the many different understandings of god to God's elusive nature.

The most important part of the first section of the statement, and perhaps the document as a whole, deals with the Conservative understanding of Jewish law. It emphasizes the importance of the law on several grounds: as an expression of God's will for the Jewish people; as a continuing way of encountering God; as a key feature of Jewish identity, and as an important means of preserving the Jewish people. There is also a discussion of tradition and development within the law. Both the need to maintain continuity with the past and the need to make appropriate changes as change in values and social contexts are highlighted, as is the necessity of change and of standing firm. Decisions need to be taken on a case-by-case basis and in dialogue with the legal tradition. It is asserted that the rabbi in a congregation is the primary source of religious authority – his authority derives both from training in Jewish law and the ordination process. Two further loci of authority are also identified: the Committee on Law and Standards and the Rabbinical Assembly. These two groupings of rabbis are viewed as the ultimate arbiters of Jewish practice within the movement (and are discussed on p. 197).

The State of Israel is a further topic that attracts extensive discussion in *Emet Ve-Emunah*. In general the text is very positive towards Zionism and highlights the importance of the role of Israel to Jews in the diaspora. Not surprisingly, the document particularly emphasizes the importance of religious pluralism in Israel, specifically focusing on the rights of non-Orthodox Jewish religious movements. This issue is increasingly significant to all non-Orthodox movements, none of which are recognized by Israeli law. To an extent the text presents the State of Israel as the cultural and religious hub for Jewish people in diaspora. In spite of this emphasis, however, it echoes the Reform documents in affirming the value of diaspora. Thus it offers a bi-polar model for Jewish life, which values both the diaspora and Israel as creative centres for the continuation of a creative Jewish spiritual and cultural existence.

The last section of the document covers a range of issues that relate to living a Jewish life. The two most significant of these are the section on women and the concluding section on the 'Ideal Conservative Jew'. While the statement on women strongly advocates the equality of men and women, there is also a degree of equivocation. It is emphasized that since the earliest days of the movement men and women have not been seated separately, and that the ceremony of Bat Mitzvah (Daughter of the Commandments) was instituted first by the Conservative movement. Yet the conclusion of the section highlights the ongoing debate in the movement regarding women's participation in ritual. It states that some believe that women should be allowed to participate fully in ritual and to become rabbis and cantors, while others believe that women can best express their spirituality in more traditional roles. It is emphasized that whichever position is taken, the Jewish law remains the necessary validation for views on gender roles.

The final section of the statement presents an image of the ideal Conservative Jew. The image is shaped by the challenges of living a Jewish life in the modern world. It is recognized that the holistic pattern of Jewish life, which preceded the Enlightenment, is no longer part of most people's experience. A return to this traditional pattern is impossible; what is advocated is a creative forum in which both Judaism and modernity can 'reshape each other'. Three elements are seen to be essential: first, a commitment to Jewish practices and concerns and the adoption of a Jewish perspective on all matters; second, the need for a continuous process of learning; third, a view of Jewish life as a constant process of open striving which is constantly enriched through engagement with the Jewish tradition.

Individual and Authority

As suggested in this discussion of *Emet Ve-Emunah*, Conservative Judaism places a stronger emphasis on rabbinic authority than is usual in Reform Judaism. This authority, however, is restricted to decisions regarding Jewish law, tradition and practice. Conservative Jews participate fully in modern life and accept the value placed on the individual and notions of individual choice. Nonetheless, due to its emphasis on the Jewish legal tradition, rabbis in their capacity as scholars (or students) of Jewish law are the primary source for information about halakhic practice. The traditional term used by the Conservative movement to describe this aspect of the rabbinical role is *mara d'atra*, 'master of the place', emphasizing that the rabbi is the primary authority for his or her community.

The hierarchy of legal authority, however, moves beyond the individual rabbi to the movement, or at least a committee of rabbis representing the movement, that is the Committee on Jewish Law and Standards. The committee represents all sections of the movement. Its voting members are all scholars of the Jewish legal tradition. It also includes lay members, chosen by the congregational arm, who participate in discussions but are not allowed to vote. A key feature of this process is that although it seeks consensus it will occasionally produce a range of opinions, reflecting divergence of views within the committee. Where there is a unanimous decision taken by the committee, the decision is binding on all Conservative rabbis and communities. If, however, there are several different opinions, it is left to the individual rabbi to select the position that he or she finds most convincing.

Women

Like the Reform movement, the Conservative movement has changed its attitudes on gender roles in line with changes in the wider cultural context. In the early part of the century the separation between men and women during services was removed – allowing them to sit together. As the century progressed the movement opened a greater number of doors to women's participation. Thus, in 1955 it allowed women to have *aliyot*, to participate in the rituals surrounding the reading of the Torah during a service; in 1973 it allowed women to be counted as part of the *minyan*, the quorum of ten needed for a public religious service; and finally, in 1983, the Jewish Theological Seminary decided to admit women to be trained as rabbis.

In many ways the current position taken by the Conservative movement is not dissimilar to that of the Reform movement. The key difference is one of process. The Reform movement viewed the status of women in tradition as going against modern ethical values; it therefore made the changes it saw as necessary to redress this problem. The Conservative movement saw the same conflict but needed to work within the Jewish legal system to make the necessary changes – this process meant that in some cases they were not able to go as far or as quickly as many would have liked. Due to its decision-making process, however, there is some diversity of practice with regard to women's participation. Several of the decisions that opened ritual participation to women also produced minority positions that opposed women being granted these rights and responsibilities. Thus there are communities that will not allow a woman rabbi to serve them. Outside the USA congregations in the Conservative tradition tend to be more traditional regarding women's roles in ritual life.

Orthodox Judaism

Orthodox Judaism is a much more heterogeneous grouping than the other movements discussed above. Indeed, there is really no such thing as the Orthodox 'movement', but rather many separate groups or alignments sharing some basic tenets and differing widely in other areas. The main ideas that bind Orthodox Jews together are the historicity of the revelation on Sinai and the acceptance that both the Oral and Written Law are eternally binding and essentially unchanging. Most Orthodox reject modernity where it impinges on or challenges aspects of Jewish tradition. Thus, most Orthodox rabbis will not accept the findings of archaeology or critical analysis of the Bible, particularly if they challenge the Mosaic authorship of the Torah.

Within the Orthodox community there are a wide range of responses to other aspects of modernity. These responses resemble those of the three Orthodox figures discussed above – Sofer, Hirsch and Rav Kook. Most Orthodox Jews accept the position presented by Hirsch. They find a creative synthesis between their Judaism and modernity, taking advantage of what modernity can offer them (such as technology) without compromising their heritage. Where there is a conflict between Judaism and modernity they accept the Jewish view rather than that of modernity. There were also an increasing number of Jews in the late twentieth century moving towards the position presented by Sofer. They were increasingly hostile to modernity, particularly to ideas of relativism and pluralism, and were looking for more authoritarian and clearly bounded forms of Jewish thought and practice. The term *Haredim* is sometimes used for this community. In Israel this form of Judaism has increasingly mixed with extreme forms of Zionist thought. This group is very strongly represented by settlers on the West Bank and among those Israelis who challenge any moves towards regularizing Israel's relations with her neighbours and the Palestinians. The mystical form of Judaism offered by Rav Kook is finding its way into many forms of Judaism today. It has its mainspring in the Hasidic community (which historically preceded Rav Kook) but is also found in other groups who are looking for more spiritual and less rational forms of Jewish expression.

The *Haredi* model of Judaism, in both its political and religious respect, has increasingly been that accepted by Sephardic Jews in Israel – particularly those who came to Israel after 1948 from countries in the Arab world. Many individuals from the Sephardic community have been attracted to the messianic aspirations of the *Haredi Yeshivot*. Due to its size, and to discrimination against Sephardic Jews by the secular Ashkinazic Israeli establishment, the Sephardic community has developed a strongly bounded identity which is increasingly powerful in Israeli politics. The agenda of the Sephardic parties and political blocs is often shaped by right-wing religious and political tendencies.

These *Haredi Yeshivot* have also been very attractive to large numbers of young Jews from Western Europe and more particularly from the USA. These Jews, often coming from secular or non-traditional backgrounds find in *Haredi* Judaism a clarity and surety which seems to have been lost in those forms of Judaism which have responded positively to modernity. These Jews reflect a growing trend in many Western countries, of individuals who reject the more liberal forms of Judaism in search of a firmer foundation against the tides of modernity and postmodernity. In an age of relativism these forms of Orthodoxy make strong claims to moral superiority and authority which are an increasingly loud voice within Jewish communities throughout the world.

Hasidic Judaism, which forms part of the right wing of Orthodoxy, develops the strongest opposition to modernity. It tends to take a strongly fundamentalist view of tradition and emphasizes the mystical aspects of religion as the most significant part of human experience. Over the last 300 years the Hasidic community has developed a wide range of methods for maintaining strong boundaries. These methods of boundary maintenance include particular forms of dress, highly centralized communal structures and an extreme emphasis on food rules. In addition, the Hasidic community refuses to participate in secular education and very few of its members, if any, participate in secular higher education. Some Hasidic communities also reject the use of television or other public media in order to control the flow of secular influences.

One of the most interesting trends in Judaism in the latter half of the twentieth century was the successful missionary activity undertaken by one of the major Hasidic dynasties, the Habad under its *rebbi* (leader) Rabbi Menahem Mendel Schneerson. This missionary activity was only aimed at the Jewish community; as the Habad saw it they were bringing Jews back to Judaism. The goal of this activity was primarily mystical. They believed that by bringing Jews back to Judaism they were causing transformations in the supernatural realm that would bring about the coming of the messiah. Many of the Habad Hasidim hoped that their *rebbi* would turn out to be the messiah. Non-Hasidic Jews were also influenced by this activity and a significant number became part of the Habad community or associated to related communities. Whilst this move towards traditionalism and rejection of modernity can be understood in part as a response to R. Schneerson's charisma, it also reflects a trend in many areas of modern religion towards more authoritarian structures with strong well-defined boundaries, combined with personal charismatic leadership (see Chapter 16). Like other fundamentalist groups, the Habad have made very effective use of television and other forms of media to carry their message to a wide audience.

Individual and authority

Although most modern Orthodox Jews participate in social, economic and cultural aspects of modern life, and thus accept something of the value placed on the individual in modern times, within their formal religious structures there is little or no place for individual autonomy. All aspects of religion are believed to be clearly stated in an eternal body of law which has a greater authority than individual choice. The authority to interpret the law is vested in the rabbis, who were traditionally seen as judges within the Jewish legal system rather than pastoral leaders. Although the pastoral aspect of the rabbinic role is also emphasized in Orthodox Judaism, it is this role of judge which has been reactivated.

In many Orthodox Jewish communities today, however, there are no formal hierarchical rabbinic structures – the exception being countries like the UK which has a Chief Rabbi of part of the Orthodox community. Certain rabbis who are recognized as being great scholars are looked to as the supreme arbiters of Jewish law. Different communities will look to different scholars. They will follow the scholar who reflects the part of Orthodoxy or the part of the Jewish community (for example, Sephardic or Ashkinazic) from which they come. The decisions made by these scholars are considered to be binding on their generation – future scholars may take different decisions that will then be binding on their generation.

The Hasidic Jews place the greatest emphasis on the authority of their leaders. Unlike other Jewish communities whose rabbis gain their position through education or selection by a community, the leader of a Hasidic community, the *rebbe* or *tzadik*, gains his position through birth. He is seen as being a spiritual conduit through which his followers, his Hasidim, gain a connection to God. His followers will look to him not only for decisions about Jewish law and practice but also for guidance on almost any aspect of their lives.

Women

Most modern Orthodox women are fully integrated into modern Western culture. Many have university degrees and work in a wide range of professions. Within their Jewish practice, however, they are excluded from most ritual activities. Essentially, women are excluded from any public ritual activity that might include men. In the synagogue women are separated from men, sometimes by a partition or a gallery. No Orthodox community allows women to become rabbis. Within traditional Judaism a woman's primary place of activity is the home and she is seen as being responsible for maintaining purity in the home and educating young children. Many women express the idea that men and women each have their own equally important sphere of activity.

In recent years some Orthodox women have been exploring ways in which they can participate more actively in ritual activities outside the home. One possibility that they have explored is having a religious service only for women – in which case they can do most of the necessary ritual activities. Although in the USA some Orthodox rabbis permitted this, in the UK it was ultimately forbidden.

Among the ultra-Orthodox and the Hasidim, women's participation in wider society is much more restricted. They tend not to have received higher education and usually do not work outside the community. In these communities women's activities are much more centred on the home than are those of the modern Orthodox Jews. Due to the emphasis on tradition and differentiated gender roles within these communities, such women are not publicly challenging the restrictions on their religious activity.

Zionism

Zionism emerged in the nineteenth century alongside the three main religious branches of modern Judaism. Like them it was equally a response to modernity, and its eventual culmination in the establishment of the State of Israel cannot be separated from its historical and social context. While Zionism arguably has its roots in an ongoing tradition of yearning for a return to land that stretched back to the Roman destruction of the Temple and the diaspora, the political variant only emerged in the modern period. Zionism as a nationalistic political ideology emerges in the context of the rise of Romanticism and nationalisms within European society. Perhaps the most important difference between the modern political form of Zionism and its purely religious predecessor is its view of human agency. Whereas the previous aspirations were closely associated with messianic hopes, thereby relying on divine rather than human action, political Zionism was firmly rooted in human action. Its hopes for the creation of Jewish homeland were rooted in the politics of the nineteenth and twentieth century as well as the neo-colonial settlement of Palestine; which was initially under Turkish rule and then a British mandate (via the League of Nations) until 1948.

Zionism provides a space for both secular and religious Jewish identities; with different Zionist movements expressing the differing aspirations of these communities. While the reality is much more complex, for the sake of discussion Zionism can be divided into five broad categories, each of which expresses a different aspect of Zionist ideology. Political Zionism is both a general and specific category. As a general category it encompasses all forms of modern Zionism (even the most ultra-Orthodox) as all forms engage in some degree of political action. As a specific category it refers to the largely secularized Jewish response to the social conditions of Jews in Western and Eastern Europe, particularly the perception of the rise of anti-Semitism. The goals of political Zionism were the establishment of a Jewish homeland through engagement in a political process in association with the great European powers. Although for some Palestine was the default position, others were willing to explore settlement of other locations – the important factor was the establishment of a Jewish state, not its specific location or religious/historical associations. Theodor Herzl (1860–1904) was the pre-eminent figure in political Zionism. His Zionism was born as a response to the rise of anti-Semitism in France, associated with the Dreyfus Affair and the perception that Jews would never be able to safely live and develop as a people in European society. Herzl brough activism and dynamism to Zionism; his political ideology was expressed in *The Jewish State* (1896), in which he argues for the establishment of a secular Jewish state modelled on modern European states – this state would not necessarily use Hebrew or be established in Palestine. For the rest of his life Herzl negotiated with the European powers of the time to fulfil this political dream. Although for Herzl and others the Jewish state could be separated from a specific location, for the majority Palestine was the focus of these aspirations and alongside the political work in Europe over the course of the nineteenth and twentieth century became the focus of settlement, primarily by Jews from Eastern Europe.

Cultural Zionism is the second form. Unlike Herzl's political Zionism cultural Zionism was firmly rooted in Jewish historical and cultural identity. The most significant spokesman of this tradition was Asher Ginsberg (1856–1927), who wrote under the name Ahad HaAm (meaning one of the people). Rather than focusing on the establishment of a national home for all Jews, he emphasised the creation in Palestine of a spiritual centre that would culturally and spiritually nourish the increasingly fragmented diaspora. While Ahad HaAm's agenda was not religious, it did focus both on the traditional land and the use of Hebrew as tools for creating the Jewish cultural and spiritual renaissance. Cultural Zionism became one of the key building blocks in the World Zionist Organization and shaped many aspects that were to become significant in the emergence of the State of Israel.

Labour Zionism, like cultural Zionism, focused on the problematic place of Jews within European society. Rather than emphasizing the need for spiritual revival, drawing on socialist ideology it argued for the importance of physical labour and the creation of a Jewish proletariat as the means of national salvation. Labour Zionism was one of the major forces in the settlement of the land, establishing communal settlements throughout Palestine. It also became the dominant political force in the establishment of the State in 1948 and was the dominant political party until 1977 with the election of Menachem Begin.

Revisionist Zionism became the primary opposition to Labour Zionism. Its most important leader was Vladimir Jabotinsky (1880–1940). Revisionist Zionism took up a much stronger view of nationalism, which in some of its later developments was closely associated with a right wing political agenda. Unlike the practical Zionism espoused by Labour Zionist leaders, Jabotinsky took up a more ideological nationalistic stance: his followers argued for the active and immediate establishment of a state on both sides of the Jordan River. Although initially working with the British, revisionist Zionism eventually led to the establishment of a number of terrorist organizations, most notably the Irgun and Lehi, which sought to use terror tactics as a way of forcing the British Mandatory authorities to abandon Palestine and allow the establishment of a Jewish state. After the establishment of the state, the Irgun transformed into the Herut and ultimately the Likud political parties, which was the main opposition party within the

Israeli Keneset (Parliament). These parties were characterized by hawkish and right wing nationalistic politics. Likud first took political power in 1977 with the election of Begin as Prime Minister.

Religious Zionism is the final branch of modern Zionism. Unlike the secular Zionists, its agenda was specifically Orthodox, and based on a traditional religious agenda. The term religious Zionism refers specifically to the more centrist aspects of Orthodox tradition, that is, those who argue for the political establishment and perpetuation of a Jewish State, and who participate fully in that political entity. Religious Zionism argued for the establishment of a state based on Jewish Law and emerging from Jewish history, and most specifically divine promises regarding the land and nation. Unlike some Orthodox or ultra-Orthodox Jews who saw Zionism as pre-empting divine or messianic action, religious Zionists saw political Zionism as part of a divine scheme. This view is specifically espoused by Rav Kook (1865–1935) who gave mystical meaning even to the apparently secular actions of labour Zionists. Religious Zionism is represented in the State of Israel by a number of political parties that can be grouped under the term *Mizrachi*. Although never achieving parliamentary majorities, due to the nature of the Israeli political system they have been part of most Israeli coalitions and have wielded political influence far beyond their size.

Gush Emunim (Block of the Faithful) and the closely associated *Haredim* are an outgrowth of religious Zionism that brings together both a right-wing political and religious agenda and an activist settlement policy. They take up a strong messianic stance, seeing the settlement of both sides of the Jordan as part of God's plan in hastening the coming of the messiah. Their stance has led them to oppose any negotiations relating to land – and at times has led to violent opposition to decisions made by the state, particularly the evacuation of Gaza and closing of some settlements in the West Bank. The *Gush Emunim* and *Haredim* are often portrayed as part of a fundamentalist aspect of modern Judaism, and in their opposition to certain aspects of a modern liberal political agenda and a literalist reading of specific aspects of scripture (particularly those with political implications), this term may be helpful.

In considering Zionism it is also important to touch on the relationship between the Jews in the diaspora and the modern State of Israel. The importance of Israel in the construction of modern Jewish identity cannot be overstated. For many secular Jews both Israel and the Holocaust are the cornerstones of their identity. While prior to the Holocaust there was a mixed response to Zionism, with, for example, some Reform Jews continuing to be anti-Zionist, afterwards Zionism became the default position for diaspora Jews, with all movements excepting of some ultra-Orthodox communities taking up a strongly pro-Zionist stance. This public consensus began to break down somewhat with the first *intifada* (1987) and has continued to weaken over the subsequent years. There are an increasing number of voices both in the diaspora and in Israel itself who question the nature of a Jewish state and challenge the relevance of Zionism today.

Looking to the future

This chapter has highlighted some of the responses, including acceptance or rejection, by Judaism to modernity.

- Within the Reform, Conservative and modern Orthodox communities most individuals have had to find some way of accommodating their religious beliefs and practices to modernity. Some type of synthesis is clearly necessary as all of these communities wish to participate to a greater or lesser extent in modernity.
- The Reform community has done this by privileging modernity over Judaism and modern Orthodoxy has attempted its synthesis by privileging Judaism over modernity.
- The Conservative movement has tried to find a balance. Although it changes and develops in response to modern values and norms it maintains continuity via the halakhic process.
- Only those communities that reject modernity, the ultra-Orthodox and the Hasidim, are able to try to develop patterns of life which exclude modern values and ideas.

It is appropriate to ask if these attempts at accommodation have succeeded in offering forms of Judaism which are meaningful in the twenty-first century. The demographic numbers presented at the beginning of the chapter suggest that they have not succeeded for the majority of Jews: more than 50 per cent of American Jews are secular. In the course of the twentieth century an increasing number of individuals rejected the mainstream forms of Judaism. They moved, in line with more general trends in modern religion, in two directions: some have moved to more authoritarian and structured forms of Judaism, and others have moved to a much more diffuse version of religion – a Jewish version of 'spiritual shopping'. These developments have begun to pull the mainstream movements in both directions. On the one hand, modern movements are learning from the spirituality movement and have added more individualistic, spiritual elements to their religious practice, on the other certain parts of the movements are moving in more traditionalist, authoritarian directions, publicly disavowing aspects of universalism and most clearly rejecting the notions of relativism which were characteristic of the modern period.

Summary

- Jewish legal and historical tradition have supplied many themes and motifs which are central in modern reconstructions of Judaism, not least those of law, covenant, exodus and redemption; divine destruction and punishment; the promised land; and the Holocaust.

- The three most important movements in modern (religious) Judaism are Reform, Conservative and Orthodox.

- The Reform movement has a particularly important place in the story of Judaism's interactions with modernity, not only because it was highly permeable to modern ideas and institutions, but because the other main movements of modern Judaism were often reacting to reform.

- Judaism's initial interaction with modernity begins in the eighteenth century with Moses Mendelssohn. Mendelssohn began the process of trying to recreate or rethink Judaism in response to the ideas and philosophies of the Enlightenment. Although he was seen by later movements as heralding the beginnings of reform, many of the issues which he addressed were fundamental to the other Jewish movements as well.

- The three major movements of Reform, Conservative and Orthodox Judaism are distinguished by their responses to many of the challenges posed by modernity, such as individualism, authority and the role of women. An underlying issue concerns identity, conceived in terms of Jewish particularism versus accommodation to Western philosophies and Western ways of living.

- Contemporary Judaism is as deeply divided as at any time in its history. Extreme Orthodoxy flourishes alongside a growing liberalism – the latter even showing some affinities with movements like New Age. Whilst the former tries to exclude modern values and ideas, the latter embraces them.

Key terms

aggadah Rabbinic texts discussing non-legal questions.

aliyot The rituals of being called up to the Torah during a religious service.

Ashkinazic This term is used to describe Jews of European origin other than Spain and Portugal – usually referring to Jews from Central or Eastern Europe.

assimilation The process through which a minority culture loses or merges its identity with the majority culture.

Babylonian Talmud The most authoritative text of Jewish law, written as a commentary or application of the Mishnah, edited in approximately 700 CE.

Bar Mitzvah Ceremony celebrating a boy becoming an adult; it occurs when the boy is 13 years of age.

Bat Mitzvah Ceremony celebrating a girl becoming an adult; it occurs when the girl is either 13 or 14. This ceremony was first introduced by the Conservative movement and is now also practised by Reform congregations.

diaspora This term refers to the settlement of Jews outside Israel. It is often associated with the concept of exile.

Enlightenment Western cultural movement of the seventeenth and eighteenth centuries which emphasized the importance of rationality. Often viewed as the dawn of modernity.

halakhah The Jewish legal tradition.

Hasidism A mystical, revivalist branch of ultra-Orthodox Judaism, which emerged from Eastern Europe in the eighteenth century.

Haskalah Eighteenth- to nineteenth-century movement of Jewish Enlightenment which sought to spread Enlightenment ideas to European Jewry.

intifada Palestinian uprising in Israel.

mara d'atra A Hebrew term which is used to indicate that a rabbi is the primary legal authority in his or her community. It is used by the Orthodox and Conservative movements.

minyan The minimum number of people needed to conduct a public religious service – ten men for Orthodox Jews and ten men or women for Conservative Jews.

Mishnah The first code of Jewish law, based on the discussions of the rabbis edited by Rabbi Judah HaNasi in approximately 200 CE.

mysticism An experience or knowledge of God based on experience rather than reason or tradition. Jewish mysticism is often encapsulated in the term *Kabbalah*.

Pharisee A member of a devout Jewish sect which flourished from the second century BCE to the early second century CE. Pharisees may have been the forerunners of Rabbinic Judaism.

rabbi Term meaning teacher, or leader, used to designate religious functionaries. Role is gained through education and ordination. Sometimes translated as 'sage'.

rebbe Term meaning 'my rabbi', used to designate the leader of a Hasidic community.

Reconstructionist Judaism A form of modern Judaism, which denies the existence of a supernatural God, it grew out of the Conservative movement based on the teachings of M. Kaplan.

sage See rabbi.

Sephardic Jews Believed to be descended from Jews from Spain and Portugal, the majority of whom were expelled in 1492. The term also includes Jews from non-European communities, for example, Yemen or Iraq.

Shulkhan Aruch A major code of Jewish law written by Joseph Caro (1488–1575).

Torah The first five books of the Hebrew Bible; also called the Five Books of Moses.

tzadik Term, literally meaning 'righteous man', used to describe the leader of a Hasidic community or sect. Equivalent to the term *rebbe*.

yeshiva Institution of higher learning for the study of Torah.

Yiddish Language related to German and Hebrew which was spoken by all Jews in Central and Eastern Europe.

Zionism The political movement established in the nineteenth century with the aim of building a Jewish homeland in Palestine.

Further reading

Judaism in the modern world

Robert Seltzer: *Jewish People, Jewish Thought* (New York: Macmillan, 1980) is one of the best one-volume histories of Judaism which includes both historical and philosophical analysis. It includes an extensive discussion of the response of Judaism to the Enlightenment and modernity. Arthur Cohen and Paul Mendes-Flohr (eds): *Contemporary Jewish Religious Thought* (New York: Free Press, 1987) presents a comprehensive set of essays examining modern Jewish concepts, movements and beliefs.

Reform Judaism

One of the best histories of the Reform movement is found in Michael Mayer: *Responses to Modernity: A History of the Reform Movement in Judaism* (Oxford: OUP, 1988). Eugene Borowitz: *Reform Judaism Today* (New York: Behrman House, 1983) provides a readable discussion of Reform Jewish thought by a major thinker within the modern Reform Jewish movement.

Conservative Judaism

Moshe Davis: *The Emergence of Conservative Judaism* (Philadelphia, PA: Jewish Publication Society, 1963) provides a comprehensive analysis of the early development of the Conservative movement. Neil Gillman: *Conservative Judaism* (West Orange, NJ: Behrman House, 1993) provides an approachable discussion of the history and theology of the Conservative movement. It includes a very useful selected bibliography.

Orthodox Judaism

Norman Lamm: *Torah Umadda: The Encounter of Religious Learning with Worldly Knowledge in Jewish Tradition* (New York: Aronson, 1990) presents a statement of Orthodoxy's response to modernity. Jonathan Sacks: *Tradition in an Untraditional Age* (London: Vallentine Mitchell, 1990) presents a view of modern Orthodoxy which is moving towards a more traditionalist inward-looking form of Orthodoxy, written by the Chief Rabbi of the United Synagogue in the UK. Jerome Mintz: *Hasidic People* (Cambridge, MA: Harvard, 1992) provides an anthropological account of the Hasidim.

Zionism

Walter Laqueur: *A History of Zionism* (New York: Schocken, 1972) provides a useful history of Zionism and Zionist thinking.

Chapter 8

Christianity

Linda Woodhead

Introduction

Christianity is the largest of the world's religions, and the most extensive across the globe. Estimates of the Christian population at the beginning of the twenty-first century put the total at around two billion, roughly a third of the world's population. Christianity's status as a truly global religion is fairly recent. At the beginning of the modern period it was largely confined to the northern hemisphere. Rapid expansion in Latin America, Africa and parts of Asia took place during the course of the twentieth century. At the same time, Christianity has also been declining in parts of the North, particularly in Western Europe. The net effect is a shift in numbers and vitality from North to South.

Christianity nevertheless remains the dominant religion of both Europe and North America. As such, it has been more intimately bound up with the rise of modernity than any other faith – so much so that some have argued that it has been an active force of modernization. Western modernity arose within Christian cultures, rather than coming to them from the outside. In some instances, as where Christian missionaries brought the religion to other cultures, Christians acted as agents of Western modernity. But Christianity has also been threatened by modernization, and some forms of Christianity have actively resisted aspects of the modern world. As this chapter will show, there is no single pattern of Christian interaction with modernity. Some types of Christianity (like 'fortress Catholicism') resisted; some (like liberal Protestantism) saw themselves as agents of modern progress; others (like Evangelicalism) came into being as traditional forms of Protestantism were reshaped by the forces of modernization; and Charismatic Christianity in the southern hemisphere represents an indigenous force of modernization which accepts some aspects of Western modernity whilst rejecting others.

Sources and resources

Although it was inspired by the figure of Jesus Christ, Christianity developed in many different forms in the first three centuries of its existence, and authority was located in many different sources, both written and unwritten. Although there have been important and partially successful attempts to impose unity on the religion from this time onwards, Christianity has always been a religion of immense diversity. Taken as a whole, it can be thought of as a vast reservoir of beliefs, stories, laws, symbols, rituals, practices, patterns of relating, and social institutions. Together these constitute the sources and resources of the religion. Different periods, contexts, circumstances, groups and individuals activate different resources from the Christian reservoir. This gives the religion immense vitality and flexibility. It means that Christianity displays both continuities and discontinuities in different places and different times. Over more than 2,000 years it has manifested such a variety of forms that it may be more helpful to think in terms of 'Christianities' rather than 'Christianity'.

Three clusters of resources are particularly important for Christians: the Bible, the figure of Jesus Christ, and the institutions of church and tradition. These are the key authorities in Christianity. As we shall see, different branches of Christianity are differentiated by the ways in which they understand and enact their relative importance.

The Bible and the Jewish connection

All forms of Christianity accept the authority of the Bible, though this may mean very different things in different types of Christianity. Like Christianity itself, the Bible is not simple or unitary. It does not have a single author, a single style, or a single message. Rather, it is a collection of different books and genres, including histori-cal chronicles, genealogies, stories, myths, prophecy, laws, poetry, proverbs, gospels, letters, and apocalyptic literature. The oldest documents of the Bible probably date back to the fifth century BCE, though they may contain traditions from as early as the eleventh or twelfth centuries BCE; the latest documents in the Bible date from the first century CE.

The diversity and richness of the Bible are partly explained by the fact that it is made up of not one but two collections of scripture: the Hebrew Bible (the Jewish scriptures, which Christians refer to as the Old Testament), and the New Testament. The former is in the Hebrew language, the latter in 'koine' ('common') Greek. The canon of the Christian Bible was not settled and closed until the late fourth century CE. Even so, there has been persistent disagreement among Christians about a number of disputed books, which some Christians regard as scriptural and others as apocryphal. Generally speaking, Roman Catholic Christians accept a greater number of books as canonical than do Protestant Christians.

For all its diversity, however, many Christians have read the Bible as having a certain narrative unity. It begins with the book of Genesis, which tells how the world and humankind were created, and it ends with the book of Revelation, which tells how God will bring creation to a glorious climax at the end of times. In between, the Bible tells of God's persistent attempts to reform and redeem the human race through his chosen people Israel, and of Israel's repeated failures to respond to the divine initiative. For many Christians, the turning point of this story comes with the sending of God's Son, Jesus Christ, to save the world and usher in the end times. Christians have thus tended to view themselves as the 'new Israel' and the heirs of God's promise to the Jews – this belief is one factor in the anti-Semitism which has been prominent in Christianity's relations with Judaism.

Jesus Christ

It was their belief that Jesus had been raised from the dead (resurrected) that convinced his first followers of his unique status. Many Jews in Jesus's day cherished the hope that God would send a messiah to save Israel. This savior would be raised from the dead as a sign that God's rule on earth had been inaugurated. Set in this context, Jesus's resurrection seemed to prove that he was the messiah, that God had decisively intervened in history, and that the end times were at hand. Just a few decades after Jesus's death the apostle Paul, some of whose letters are preserved in the New Testament, was articulating these beliefs, and ascribing to Jesus the unique status not only of 'Christ' (the Greek word for messiah), but the 'Son of God', 'Lord' and 'second Adam' sent to redeem the world. It was not only Jesus's resurrection, however, which made him special in the eyes of Christians. His life and teaching as recorded in the New Testament also have great authority. As we shall see below, some modern Liberal Christians have little interest in Jesus's resurrection or miracles, and emphasize his humanity and inspired teaching rather than his divinity. These represent just some of the many ways in which Christians have come to think about Jesus Christ.

In the attempt to secure unity, early Christianity attempted to articulate Jesus's status in a systematic way, particularly through its councils (meetings of bishops) and the creeds they produced. These statements of belief (such as the Nicene Creed of 325 CE) were designed to establish the limits of 'orthodoxy' (right belief), and those who disagreed with them were branded 'heretical'. By the time the process of credal definition came to an end in the eighth century CE, an understanding of God as Trinity had emerged as distinctive of Christianity. This doctrine enabled Christians to explain how the one God could be the omnipotent Creator, could take human form as Jesus, and could be present to his people at all times in the Spirit. The doctrine states that God is 'triune': Father, Son and Holy Spirit. According to orthodox doctrine, God is fully present in all three of these 'persons' of the Trinity – no one is any less divine than another. Nor are they separate gods ('tritheism'): the Trinity is one substance ('homoousios' in the original Greek), in three different instantiations ('hypostases'). In many ways the creeds have served to set the boundaries and limits within which Christian thought must work, though they have never been able to secure the unity which those who drafted them hoped they would secure.

The church and its diversity

The institution of the church dates from the time, shortly after Jesus's death, when Christians first began to meet together to worship, pray and reflect on their faith. It was a radical experiment in a new form of godly community. Christianity is thus a communal religion. Until modern times it would have been thought impossible for an individual to be a Christian on his or her own, without belonging to a community. Christians, like Jews, believe they are a chosen people, and wish to live as a new society. It is only in modern times that some forms of Christianity have become more individualized, as this chapter will illustrate. Christianity is also a universal religion. Unlike Judaism, which is tied to a particular people and locale, it aims to bring the whole of humanity into its ambit, and so into God's (universal) kingdom. Despite this universalism, Christianity has split into a number of different branches. Of these, the three largest groupings are: 1. Roman Catholic; 2. Orthodox; and 3. Protestant.

Jesus did not lay down any guidelines whatsoever for the formation of a church or a new religion. At first Christianity was composed of many competing communities and groups which took different forms and had different scriptures and beliefs. By the second century CE a dominant form of sacramental and sacerdotal Christianity was emerging, which claimed for itself the titles catholic (universal) and orthodox. It tried to suppress other forms of Christianity as heretical. It quickly spread from Palestine around the Mediterranean into Europe, Africa, the Middle East, and parts of Asia. (Despite this, some major churches, such as the Nestorian churches in Asia and the Monophysite churches in North Africa, split off from the main body of 'catholic' Christianity and remain separate to this day.) Historical circumstances, including the expansion of Islam, led to a separation between the church in the West (centred on Rome) and that in the East (centred on Constantinople). The latter evolved into the Orthodox (or Eastern Orthodox) church, and the former into the Roman Catholic Church. The split between the two was formalized in 1054, though it had developed for several centuries before that. The Roman Catholic church is monarchial with a single leader, the Pope, whilst the Orthodox church is made up of a number of autonomous churches with their own leaders, all of which are in communion with one another. Orthodox Christianity has always been marked by its sense of unchanging continuity with the past and its reverence for tradition.

The origins of the Protestant churches lie in dissatisfaction and 'protest' against the Roman Catholic Church in the West. This protest came to a head in the early sixteenth century, and eventually resulted in the creation of a number of churches or denominations which, despite their many differences, are grouped together under the Protestant label. The largest Protestant groups (in order of size) are the Lutherans (founded by Martin Luther), the Presbyterian or Reformed churches (founded by John Calvin), the Baptists, and the Methodists. Anglicans also constitute a large worldwide communion, but although it has its origins in the Reformation, the Anglican Church often emphasizes its Catholic as well as Protestant roots. There are also many smaller Protestant denominations as well as many independent Protestant churches.

One of the chief differences between these different groupings in Christianity lies in their understanding of authority. For the Orthodox churches, the tradition of the church – including its liturgy and its earliest writings and creeds – has primacy. For Catholics, the church, its sacraments and tradition are central, and these come to a focus in the figure of the Pope. By contrast, Protestants tend to attribute greater authority to scripture than to tradition, and to have a less hierarchical understanding of authority in the church. In modern times, both Protestantism and Catholicism have also developed Liberal versions, which emphasize the authority of individual reason and experience alongside scripture and the church. An even more recent development is Charismatic or

Pentecostal Christianity (again cutting across both Protestantism and Catholicism, though with more direct links to Protestantism), which attributes authority to both the Bible and direct experience of the Holy Spirit. The following tables indicate the primary locations of authority in traditional (premodern) and modern Christianity.

TABLE 8.1 Primary authority in types of traditional (premodern) Christianity

Type of Christianity	Authority
Orthodox	Church, tradition, liturgy, priesthood
Catholic	Church, tradition, Pope, priesthood
Protestant	Bible, church

TABLE 8.2 Primary authority in types of Christianity in the modern world

Type of Christianity	Authority
Orthodox	Church, tradition, liturgy, priesthood
Catholic	
a. conservative	Church, tradition, Pope, priesthood
b. liberal	Reason, Bible, church
c. charismatic	Holy Spirit, Bible
Protestant	
a. conservative	Bible
b. liberal	Reason, Bible
c. charismatic	Holy Spirit, Bible

Interactions with modernity

Roman Catholicism

Fortress Catholicism and the struggle with the modern state

Of all the transformations of modernity, the one which has had the greatest impact on Christianity has probably been the rise of the secular nation state. And of all the churches, the one which has been most radically affected has been the Roman Catholic Church. The reason is simple: for over a thousand years, the Catholic Church had attempted to maintain a political dominance in Europe. Even though it did not directly rule most of the region, it played a key role in giving legitimacy to the changing regimes which did. The church continually attempted to assert itself as the highest authority in political, economic and social matters. It believed it had the right and the duty to regulate every aspect of the lives of those who lived in Christendom.

The rise of the modern state was a direct challenge to the Church's assertion of political power. At the heart of the modern state lies the revolutionary idea that government should be not by God, nor by his clerical representatives, nor even by divinely appointed rulers – but by the people. Once this idea became established, the centuries-old link between state and church began to dissolve. No longer could a particular religion be imposed on a people by the state; rather, they must be free to practise the religion of their choice.

The threat which this posed for the Catholic Church became very apparent in France after the Revolution of 1789, when a new constitution subordinated both monarchy and Church to the state. The papacy reacted angrily, and continued to attack the rise of the modern state and the associated ideals of liberty and democracy throughout the nineteenth century, as the Syllabus of Errors (a list of the errors of the modern world condemned by the church) makes very clear.

The Syllabus of Errors condemns the modern state

Syllabus of the principal errors of our time . . .

15 Every man is free to embrace and profess that religion which, guided by the light of reason, he shall consider true.

. . .

24 The church has not the power of using force, nor has she any temporal power, direct or indirect.

. . .

44 The civil authority may interfere in matters relating to religion, morality and spiritual government.

. . .

77 In the present day it is no longer expedient that the Catholic religion should be held as the only religion of the State, to the exclusion of all other forms of worship.

. . .

80 The Roman Pontiff can, and ought to, reconcile himself, and come to terms with progress, liberalism and modern civilization.

Pope Pius IX, 1864. In Henry Bettenson (ed.):
Documents of the Christian Church
(Oxford: Oxford University Press, 1989, pp. 273–4).

BOX 8.1 Extracts from the Syllabus of Errors

One way in which the Roman Catholic church reacted to its loss of social and political power was by attempting to consolidate control over its own followers. From the mid-nineteenth century to the 1950s, Catholicism developed a fortress mentality, attacking modernity and setting its face against an increasingly secular world (hence the nickname 'Fortress Catholicism'). The declaration of papal infallibility in 1870 was part of this strategy. So too was the development of a particular style of Catholic piety centred around reception of the sacraments of baptism and the eucharist; regular confession; veneration of the saints, in particular Mary; devotion to the Pope; and reverence for the clergy and religious orders. More than ever before, the Catholic Church strove to maintain unity, even uniformity. Such unity was embodied in the person of the Pope who, in a world of rapidly improving communications, now became a figurehead for Catholics across the globe.

Unity and centralization were also achieved by the introduction of new rationalized forms of organization, training and bureaucracy (a case of the Church borrowing, and even pioneering, the tools of modernity). Thus Popes surrounded themselves with ever-larger staffs in the Vatican, and clergy training was organized and standardized across the world. The unity of the thought-world of Fortress Catholicism was achieved by elevating the medieval theologian Thomas Aquinas (1225–1274) to the status of official theologian of the church. In 1879 Pope Leo XIII gave official approval to this development. As a result, 'neo-Thomism' became the official theology of Fortress Catholicism, with all courses in Catholic colleges and seminaries based on Aquinas's teachings.

Despite their fundamental hostility to modern nation states, the modern Popes and their clerical advisers and diplomats worked tirelessly to achieve the best possible position for Catholicism in the modern world. The church entered into numerous agreements ('concordats') with modern rulers and governments designed to safeguard Catholicism's work and liberties within as many territories as possible. Such agreements often established the church's right to maintain Catholic schools and colleges, protected the status and property of the church and its clergy, and allowed Roman Catholicism to be practised freely and openly. The church was determined that the nation state should not squeeze it out of existence – the violence and repression suffered by the church in the French Revolution and its aftermath haunted the Catholic imagination.

Fortress Catholicism's efforts to protect its interests were not, however, confined to Europe and North America. It was also engaged in a highly active and influential drive to establish its presence across the globe. The missionary impulse in Catholicism was not new; from the sixteenth century onwards the church had sent missionaries to Latin America and Asia in order to win converts. Such mission developed hand in hand with the expansionist strategies of the powerful Spanish and Portuguese empires, and served the interests of both church and empire. The nineteenth century saw a revitalization and reconfiguration of this missionary impulse. In some cases Catholic mission went hand in hand with the new colonial enterprises of modern Catholic nation states (as, for example, in the Belgian Congo in Africa). Often there was competition with Protestant mission, which in turn was tied up with the empires of Protestant nations like Britain and the Netherlands. But Catholic missionary work was not confined to Catholic countries, and it was aided as much by new communications as by colonialism. In most cases the agents of Catholic mission were clergy or monks and nuns. Indeed the huge expansion of Catholic religious orders in the nineteenth century was often stimulated by the mission impulse – many orders were formed or reformed with world mission as their prime objective. Catholic missionaries worked in every part of the globe; their greatest impact was in Latin America, sub-Saharan Africa, China and the Philippines.

The Second Vatican Council and the liberalization of modern Catholicism

The end of Fortress Catholicism came with the Second Vatican Council of 1962–1965 ('Vatican II'). This council of almost 3,000 bishops and a number of theologians was set up to consider ways in which Catholicism could open itself to the modern world without losing its distinctiveness. When he summoned the council in 1959, Pope John XXIII spoke of his desire for *aggiornamento* ('bringing up to date') in the church. In his opening speech in 1962 he said that it was important to distinguish between the 'deposit of the ancient doctrine of the faith', and the way in which it is presented. Whilst remaining fairly conservative about many fundamentals of the faith, Vatican II thus opened the door to some significant changes including:

- a less hierarchical and clericalized understanding of the church;
- a new model of the church as the whole 'people of God';
- emphasis on greater participation by laity;
- use of vernacular/indigenous languages rather than Latin for the church's liturgy;
- greater openness to other churches and religions;
- an acceptance of every individual's right to freedom in matters of personal decision, including religion;
- acceptance of the legitimacy of the modern state and democracy.

In view of the Roman Catholic Church's bitter opposition to democracy and the nation state throughout the nineteenth century, the latter change is particularly significant. In many ways Vatican II overturned the Syllabus of Errors. What it had once regarded as error it was now prepared to revisit and, in some cases, rehabilitate. Both critics and supporters of the Council saw it as representing a partial liberalization of the church. The latter would have liked to see it go further; the former thought it had gone too far.

The radicalism of Vatican II can be overstressed. In many ways the council's conclusions were highly conservative – especially when contrasted with the new permissiveness of the time (the 'swinging sixties'). Whilst the Christianity which emerged from the lengthy deliberations of the Council made some adjustments to modern times, the adjustments were selective and qualified. The most complete adjustment was to the modern political revolution – the rise of the nation state and modern democracy (though it is worth noting that Roman Catholicism did not, and still has not, accepted the legitimacy of democracy in its own institutional arrangements). There was also some adjustment to the market economy – though Vatican II, like the so-called 'social encyclicals' which had preceded it, was also keen to criticize the harsh, destructive and anti-human tendencies of capitalism. Interestingly, the strongest resistance of Vatican II and official Church teaching since then has been to one important aspect of the modern social revolution – changed gender roles and sexual identities. Vatican II was followed swiftly by *Humanae Vitae*, Pope Paul VI's encyclical, which confirmed an absolute ban on the use of all artificial forms of contraception. The church has been equally adamant in its ban on abortion, its opposition to homosexuality and its refusal to entertain the possibility of women's ordination. These prohibitions are linked not only to an uneasiness about change to traditional masculinities and femininities (see Chapter 19 on Religion and Gender), but to a strong positive affirmation of the value of the 'traditional' nuclear family in which men and women have complementary roles, and women's responsibility for care and nurture is stressed.

Vatican II also represented a qualified accommodation to cultural changes associated with modernization. Its accommodation was most obvious, and most influential, in the way in which it affirmed the possibility of Catholics embracing modern scholarship and its methods – both historical and scientific. Roman Catholic New Testament scholars embraced the methods of historical criticism of the Bible, and Catholic theologians engaged with modern philosophy and social sciences and moved beyond the limits of neo-Thomism. The effect was a 'return to the sources' in Catholic theology which was guided by the idea that in order to tackle theological problems, whether they be old ones like the relationship between scripture and tradition, or new ones like the ethical problems of industrial society, the church needed to recover the wealth of its spiritual and intellectual heritage. The best-known exemplars of this trajectory are the theologians Henri de Lubac (1896–1991), Yves Congar (1904–1995), and Hans Urs von Balthasar (1905–1988).

De Lubac is most well-known for his work on the interpretation of scripture and on the nature of the church, but he also wrote on other topics, like modern atheism. Yves Congar was mainly interested in the theology of the church, understood in a broad sense, as including topics like the role of the laity and ecumenism. He is best known for his rehabilitation of the Holy Spirit in theology, and his trilogy *I Believe in the Holy Spirit* is the most substantial work on the Holy Spirit by any Catholic theologian of the twentieth century. Its production coincided with a revival of interest in the Holy Spirit among theologians of many different traditions, and also among many ordinary Christians (see section on Charismatic Christianity below). Like Congar, von Balthasar also wanted to mine the full riches of the Catholic tradition. The last decades of his life were devoted to three vast works, each in several volumes: *The Glory of the Lord*, *Theo-Drama* and *Theologik*. In each of them he emphasizes that theology must be rooted in prayer, the Christian life and the full richness of the available sources. Karl Rahner took a different theological direction by engaging more with the broad trajectory of modern thought which makes the self and its experience the starting point of reflection and action – as in the philosophy of Descartes and Kant. Rahner argues that human beings are self-transcending: i.e. that in their constant questioning, in their pursuit of truth and goodness, and in the humbler virtues of courage, hope and openness to the future, they are always going beyond where they are and reaching out. Rahner sees all this as a dynamism of the human spirit, directed towards God. In our self-transcending we are opening ourselves, whether we realize it or not, to divine grace (which, from the other side, is God's self-communication). Since all those who open themselves to God's grace are related to Christ, they may be described as in some sense Christian. This, in essence, is Rahner's famous idea of 'Anonymous Christianity'.

Liberation Theology and the globalization of Catholicism

Another trajectory of post-Vatican II Catholic thought takes us beyond the West. Liberation Theology is a movement which arose in Latin America in the late 1960s, and which has subsequently spread to other parts of the southern hemisphere. As such, it is just one symptom of the increasingly global nature of modern Catholicism. In the year 2000 it was estimated that 70 per cent of all Catholics were living in the southern part of the globe.

The emergence of Liberation Theology is often dated to a meeting of the Latin American bishops at Medelín in Colombia in 1968. The meeting was called in order to discuss the application of the teaching of the recently ended Vatican Council to Latin America. In the event it concentrated especially on social, political and economic issues. It denounced the oppression, injustice and institutionalized violence endemic in this part of the world, and it called on the church to endorse a 'preferential option for the poor'. This approach has been articulated systematically and became well-known through the work of Latin American Catholic theologians like Leonardo Boff, Gustavo Gutiérrez and Jon Sobrino. Liberation Theology does not regard itself as one branch of theology among many, but as a precondition for any theology. It also sees itself as an example of what all theology should be – i.e. contextual theology, a theology that is alive to the needs of a particular society at a particular time and uses the Gospel to answer those needs. It criticizes European and North American theology for being confined mainly to universities and seminaries, and cut off from the life of ordinary Christians and issues of political and social justice. Hence Liberation Theologians claim that praxis (i.e. practice guided by theory) is primary, and that theology is a 'second step'. Thus Gutiérrez argues that it is only if one has an open heart and a commitment to the welfare of the poor that one can truly come to know Jesus Christ.

Liberation Theology is more than merely an intellectual movement. Its aim is to become a grassroots movement of the poor who read the Gospels together and are struggling to realize the Kingdom of God here on earth. The institutional outworking of this ideal are the 'base communities' (CEBs – *communidad(e) eclesial de base*) which have developed in many parts of Latin America. Connected to Roman Catholic churches, and often facilitated by a priest, these are small groups of lay people who meet regularly to pray, talk and work together, with the aim of tackling oppression and changing society according to Christian ideals.

Whilst the Liberation Theology movement had considerable success, particularly in Latin America, it also faced serious challenges. Support from Rome was qualified, not least because of the fear that such theology owed too much to Marxism, and that its political agenda neglected core Christian teachings and values. In Latin America itself, the movement was also challenged by two powerful competitors – indigenous spiritualist and healing cults, and the rapidly-growing Pentecostal movement (see Global Charismatic upsurge, p. 227). In contrast to both these movements, and despite its emphasis on lay involvement, Liberation Theology can seem a somewhat elite movement led by academics and clergy and subject to control by a hierarchical church based in Rome.

In some respects then, Roman Catholicism in Latin America (as in Africa and Asia) may still be burdened by its colonial connections. Thus one of the most important debates in contemporary Catholicism concerns the 'indigenization' of Christianity in non-Western cultures. The debate centres round the question of the extent to which Catholicism can and should borrow from the non-Christian cultures it 'converts'. A major step in indigenization was the ordination of non-Western and non-white clergy and bishops, which took place from the beginning of the twentieth century (in advance of many Protestant churches). Another step has been the integration of indigenous elements of culture into church worship and life (for more on this tendency see Chapter 16 on Religion and globalization). But there are limits to how far the Catholic Church can go

FIGURE 8.1 Funeral of Pope John Paul II

The funeral of Pope John Paul II in 2005 was attended by royalty and heads of state from around the world; an indication of the global status of the modern Catholic Church. Courtesy AFP/Getty Images.

in these directions without losing its identity and undermining its control, and it has many competitors.

The most important competitor to the Roman Catholic church in the southern hemisphere is Pentecostal Christianity, a form of Christianity for which indigenization is not an issue, since (a) it has no old established, Eurocentric tradition to uphold, and (b) it has no formal, sacramental priesthood, being a movement not just for the people but of the people. Yet in recent times there are clear signs that Roman Catholicism is itself beginning to adopt Pentecostal features (see p. 227).

Despite being the 'Bishop of Rome', the modern papacy has endorsed and actively encouraged the shift in Roman Catholicism from being a Eurocentric to a global religion. The long papacy of Pope John Paul II (1978–2005) has been particularly notable in this regard. Building on the work of his predecessors, he carved out a new, truly international role for the papacy. From being the opponent of modern democracy at the beginning of the nineteenth century, the papacy became its defender on a world stage at the end of the twentieth. Polish by birth, his role in the opposition to and eventual overthrow of communism in Eastern Europe in the 1980s was considerable. Helped by his personal charisma and astute exploitation of the possibilities of modern mass media like television, John Paul II managed to win the Catholic Church considerable respect throughout the world, as was made clear by the number of heads of state who attended his funeral. Roman Catholicism remains by far the largest of all the Christian denominations in the world.

Orthodoxy

One of the many differences between Roman Catholicism and Orthodoxy concerns their understanding of church–state relationships. From the early medieval period onwards, Roman Catholicism developed an understanding of church and state as separate realms. Each had its own area of discretion, but ultimately the church had supreme authority. Thus church and the Pope both had the right and duty to legislate for affairs in the temporal as well as the spiritual realms – for economics and education as much as worship and doctrine. By contrast, the Orthodox churches accepted the supreme authority of the state – whether in the person of an emperor or an impersonal state apparatus.

Whilst Orthodoxy believes that church and state should work harmoniously together for the good of their people, it has therefore been more willing to accept the state's right to legislate in all matters including church belief and organization. This tendency has been reinforced by Orthodoxy's conciliar structure. Instead of having a single focus of authority like the Pope, Orthodox Christianity is composed of a number of autocephalous (self-governing) churches which run their own affairs and are identified with an empire or nation state. Historically four patriarchates had primacy in Orthodoxy: Constantinople, Alexandria, Antioch and Jerusalem. The largest autocephalous churches today are (in order of size) Russia, Romania, Greece, Serbia and Bulgaria.

These historic differences help explain the different pathways of Roman Catholicism and Orthodoxy through modernity. Given its tradition of supremacy over the state, it is not surprising that Catholicism was deeply threatened by the rise of the secular state, nor that it now adopts a critical, prophetic role in relation to politics. By contrast, Orthodoxy's long tradition of co-operation and subordination to the state helps explain why it has generally offered little resistance to the powerful and even tyrannical forms of secular power it has had to endure.

In the vast majority of cases – with notable exceptions like Greece and Cyprus – these regimes have been communist. Russia, for example, was the first communist state, as well as the largest Orthodox country. Faithful to Marx's teaching that 'religion is the opiate of the people', the Communist Party of the Soviet Union launched a sustained offensive against religion during the 70 or so years it was in power from 1918 until the late 1980s. The offensive against the churches was most brutal in the inter-war period: Orthodox property was seized, clergy and believers were persecuted, and the church was not allowed to elect a new Patriarch. In 1919 there had been some 46,000 churches in Soviet territory; by 1939 no more than a few hundred 'registered' churches were allowed to remain open. Significantly, however, the events of World War II led Stalin to realize how important the church could be in mobilizing support for the nation, and the church was once again allowed to exist – albeit as a de facto department of the state. After World War II, the state also made use of the church for propaganda purposes: clergy were used to spread a favourable image of communism abroad, and to promote the Soviet concept of peace in international gatherings. In 1961 the Russian Orthodox Church became a member of the World Council of Churches. Despite this, the Khrushchev regime launched a new antireligious offensive in the Soviet Union. From 1959 to the 1980s, institutional Christianity was allowed to exist only in a drastically limited and emasculated form.

Despite – or perhaps because of – its treatment at the hands of the Soviet regime, the Russian Orthodox church seems to have played little or no part in the collapse of communism in the late 1980s. The same is true of Orthodox churches in other communist territories, such as the Balkans and Eastern Europe, but cannot be said of Catholic or Protestant churches. Thus the Catholic Church was a powerful force in organizing resistance to communism in Poland, whilst the Lutheran Church in East Germany played a role in the overthrow of communism there, and the revolt against the infamous Romanian communist leader, Nicolae Ceauşescu, began in a Reformed Church.

For Orthodoxy then, modernity has been encountered as an almost entirely negative and destructive force. Partly because of its traditional form, Orthodoxy found itself lacking the resources with which to resist secular nationalism. The violent nature of the assault on Orthodoxy by secularizing states nipped in the bud a number of reforming initiatives which were beginning to take shape at the beginning of the twentieth century. The growing influence of Marxism had led to a quest to bring Orthodox values to bear on pressing social, cultural and even political questions, and to free the church from its long subjection to the state. But the revolution of 1917 brought such initiatives to an abrupt halt, and forced leading figures of the Russian religious renaissance of the twentieth century into exile in the West. Several, like Vladimir Lossky (1903–1958) and Georges Florovsky (1893–1979), championed the reinterpretation of the patristic (early Christian) heritage. Others, like Sergii Bulgakov (1871–1944), developed a sophiology (doctrine of Holy Wisdom), whilst Nikolai Berdyaev (1874–1948) blended Orthodox and modern Western philosophical themes to develop a widely influential and quasi-mystical account of human freedom and potentiality. The nature of the church, humanity, creation, and the Trinity have been key themes in modern Orthodox thought, whose influence has probably been greater in the West than in Orthodox lands.

The historical and political circumstances which prevented Orthodoxy from modernizing in its own territories also had the effect of enabling it to keep alive premodern traditions to a greater degree than Western churches. Most Orthodox churches remain hierarchical, patriarchal, worship-centred, deeply reverent of the past, and closely linked to a continuing and prestigious monastic tradition. As such, Orthodoxy now has appeal to some in the West who are disenchanted with modernity and the modernization of the churches and who seek a more traditional form of religion. There has been a small number of conversions to Orthodox churches in the West.

In formerly communist countries, Orthodox churches are also tending to revert to more traditional roles. In many cases they have been active in supporting the resurgent forms of sometimes xenophobic nationalism which have developed in the wake of communism. The most notorious example has been in Serbia, where the Serbian Orthodox church played an important role in legitimizing aggressive Serbian expansion. In Russia, the Orthodox church has also become a rallying point for many who wish to defend Russian identity against the whole range of threatening forces unleashed by the collapse of communism – economic and political instability, the breakdown of law and order, the incursions of Western culture and Western goods. The Orthodox Church has also become extremely defensive about the proselytizing activities of other religious groups in Russia – ranging from the Roman Catholics to the Baptists to New Religious Movements. The pluralism which is such a notable feature of most modern Western nations sits uneasily with the traditional ideals of Orthodoxy. In Greece there has been greater accommodation with pluralism, though the Orthodox church there is still the 'established' church. It is still unclear what accommodations Orthodoxy will make with modernity in the course of the twenty-first century. But given Orthodox churches' remarkable ability to survive the onslaughts of modernity, it will not be surprising that they remain wary of any easy accommodation or capitulation.

Liberal Christianity

Liberal Christianity serves as a reminder of just how diverse Christianity's interactions with modernity have been. In contrast to the conservative wings of the Roman Catholic and Orthodox Churches, which have generally tended to view modernity with suspicion and to accept its revolutions only partially, gradually and hesitantly, liberal Christianity not only embraced modernity more wholeheartedly, but viewed itself as integral to the process of modernization.

Unlike Roman Catholicism or Orthodoxy, liberalism is not a church or a denomination, but a movement within existing churches, both Catholic and Protestant. We have seen above, for example, that Vatican II represented a partial liberalization of the Roman Catholic Church. Supporters of the Council who wanted to implement and extend its reforms belong to the liberal wing of the church, whilst those who wished to limit its reforms belong to a more conservative wing. In many cases, liberals and conservative Catholics will worship together in the same church, though they may strongly disagree on theological, ethical and lifestyle issues. Liberal Protestantism is slightly different in that there may be whole denominations which have a liberal stance (Unitarians and Congregationalists, for example), but here too there are mainline Protestant churches (like the Anglican Church) which contain both liberal and more conservative members. In historical terms Protestantism has a closer connection with liberalism than Roman Catholicism, for it was within the Protestant tradition in Europe and North America that liberal Christianity first developed. Liberal Christianity remains a predominantly Western movement, and a relatively 'intellectual' one. In many ways liberalism represents a particular theological interpretation of Christianity, albeit one which often has a strongly activist agenda.

The first anticipations of liberal Christianity appear as early as the sixteenth century, when reformist Christians like Erasmus (*c.* 1469–1536) and the Deists (late sixteenth to seventeenth centuries) began to champion a purified version of the Christian faith which would strip Christianity of what they believed to be its superstitious, oppressive and divisive elements (rituals, dogmas, clericalism, for example), and leave only its essential teachings (rational love of God and humanity). These ideas later helped inspire the Enlightenment of the eighteenth century, and so played a significant role in the rationalist cultural revolution of modern times (see Introduction).

Liberal Christianity was also closely connected with the Romantic cultural revolution of the later eighteenth and early nineteenth centuries. The so-called father of Liberal Theology (or even of modern theology), Friedrich Schleiermacher (1768–1834), was an important figure in the German Romantic movement. The Romantics (artists, poets and novelists as well as philosophers and theologians) accepted some aspects of the Enlightenment project, including its suspicion of traditional religion and its exaltation of the freedom of the individual, but reacted against its belief in the authority of reason. In place of reason, the Romantics privileged feeling, sensibility and emotion. In this vein, Schleiermacher interprets the insights of the Christian religion so that it appears as that to which Romanticism aspires, but without knowing it. In *The Christian Faith* (1821–2, revised 1830–1), Schleiermacher presents religion as a determination of 'feeling', and defines it as a 'feeling of absolute dependence', over and against the feeling of relative dependence with which we are related to the world and to others. This feeling of absolute dependence is 'immediate self-consciousness', and it is 'God-consciousness' – for Schleiermacher the terms are equivalent. In this way he aimed to move the Protestant faith away from the cultural margins in modern Europe, and place it at the centre.

By the latter part of the nineteenth century it seemed possible that Schleiermacher's dream would be realized – especially in the world of Anglo-Saxon Protestantism, and in the USA in particular. The last decades of the nineteenth century up to World War I represented the heyday of liberal Christianity. Many Americans, particularly those belonging to the rapidly expanding and increasingly influential white middle classes, wove liberal Protestantism into their proud sense of national and self-identity. They saw America as leading the world in social, political and cultural terms, and liberal Protestantism as the religion which undergirded such progress.

One reason why liberalism could be viewed in this way was that it was so open to the revolutions of modernity. As its name suggests, it actively embraced the institution of the secular nation state which seemed to enshrine its ideals of political and religious freedom. Equally, it had no difficulty in accepting the findings of modern history and science, including the historical criticism of the Bible and the Darwinian theory of evolution which shook many more conservative Christians. Since liberal Christianity had always respected the rights and abilities of human reason and conscience, it was happy to follow where they led. Its strategy was not to reject or reinterpret science in the light of the Bible, but to reinterpret the Bible and Christian belief in the light of science.

The outcome tended to be a strongly humanistic reading of Christianity, which often focused on the historical figure of Jesus Christ. This religious humanism generally included the following elements: (a) a strongly ethical and activist concern (religion must be about deeds as much as beliefs); (b) a humanistic rhetoric and conceptuality (religion is about service of one's fellow humans); (c) an anthropocentric characterization of the Godhead (God as a loving Father); (d) a positive valuation of human ability, human worth and human potential; and (e) an optimistic belief in the natural progress of humanity and human society. Such humanism fitted an increasingly differentiated culture and society in which the church's functions were being taken over by the state and other agencies. As the church's ability to pronounce on the laws of the natural world shrank along with its activities in the public realm, so it began to emphasize its expertise in the more restricted realm of the 'human'. This emphasis was reinforced by a wider universalistic 'turn to the human' in modern culture which was reflected in secular and political liberalism and their discourses of human liberty and human rights. It was influenced by social and economic changes like the spread of capitalism and democracy which saw an increasing stress being placed on the equal value of each and every individual.

In some of its versions, nineteenth-century humanistic liberal Christianity appeared to lack any critical cutting edge. It seemed to be a religion that undergirded the comfortable aspirations of imperialistic Western nations, and legitimated the interests of the new middle classes. Yet the humanistic and activistic stress of liberal Christianity also generated a 'social gospel' teaching at the end of the nineteenth century which was often radical in its condemnation of social, political and economic complacency. Intellectually, the social gospel was inspired by the work of theologians like Albrecht Ritschl (1822–1889) who searched for the essence of Christianity and found it in ethical action directed to establishing the Kingdom of God which Jesus had proclaimed. It also developed as a response to changes and disruptions in the rapidly developing urban-industrial societies of the time.

It is thus no coincidence that one of the earliest versions of the social gospel – English Christian socialism – dates from 1848, a year of revolution, protest and unrest in many parts of Europe. In that year the Anglicans F.D. Maurice, Charles Kingsley and John Ludlow met to plan a Christian response to the Chartist agitations for democratic political reform. These European influences quickly fed into the developing social gospel movement in America. Here too the social gospel often commenced with an attack on individualism: individualism in existing Christianity and individualism in capitalist society. Against such individualism it set a new social vision which must transform both church and society. As the most influential American spokesman of the social gospel, Walter Rauschenbusch (1861–1918), put it: 'We are emerging from the era of individualism. The principle of co-ordination, co-operation and solidarity is being applied in ever-widening areas and is gaining remarkable hold on the spirits of men.' Rauschenbusch based his theology on Jesus's preaching of the Kingdom of God, a kingdom which Rauschenbusch believed could not be confined to another world but which must involve the 'harmonious development of a true social life' here and now. At an institutional level the social gospel's greatest success lay in the establishment of social agencies or commissions in many mainline Protestant denominations. The burgeoning ecumenical movement was also part and parcel of a new social concern stimulated by the social gospel, and the foundation of the (American) Federal Council of Churches played an important part in spreading its message – as, later on, did the World Council of Churches (founded in 1948).

The second half of the twentieth century witnessed a decline in the fortunes of liberal Christianity. Many liberal Christian denominations in the West declined, particularly after the 1960s. There are a number of reasons for such liberal decline, not least the increasing challenges faced by many of the ideas and causes which liberal Christianity had championed – not least, 'Western civilisation', progress, and the benevolent power of science and human reason. At the same time, liberal theology suffered a crisis of confidence in the wake of attacks by 'neo-orthodox' theologians like Karl Barth (1886–1968). In Barth's view Christian liberalism paid more attention to man than to God. It was a form of 'culture Protestantism' which baptized the socio-cultural status quo whilst losing sight of the radical message of the Gospel. Barth attacked liberalism's belief that there is a natural affinity between God and humanity by insisting on the total 'otherness' of God. As he put it in a commentary on *The Epistle to the Romans*:

> The Gospel is not a religious message to inform humanity of their divinity, or to tell them how they may become divine. The Gospel proclaims a God utterly distinct from humanity. Salvation comes to them from him, and because they are, as human beings, incapable of knowing him, they have no right to claim anything from him. The Gospel is not one thing in the midst of other things . . . The Gospel is the Primal Origin of all things, the Word which, since it is ever new, must ever be received with renewed fear and trembling.

Yet liberal Christianity is far from dead. A recent study of Christianity in the USA, for example, reminds us that Christians of a broadly liberal persuasion still constitute around half the members of American churches (Ammerman, 1997). Liberalism is not confined to Protestant churches; we have noted above the liberalizing tendencies of Vatican II, and the continuation of a liberal tradition in the Roman Catholic church (to some extent even in the Christian humanism of the otherwise conservative John Paul II and his successor, Pope Benedict XVI). Equally, it is hard to dispute the triumph of many liberal ideas even in fairly conservative Christian circles, ideals such as the ideal of free churches in a free state, the acceptance of the legitimacy of modern science and historical criticism of the Bible, a stress on the equal value of all human beings, male and female, and an emphasis on the overriding importance of love.

Liberal theology may have lost vitality, but its influence is still felt. Liberal Protestant theologians as diverse as Rudolf Bultmann (1884–1976), Dietrich Bonhoeffer (1906–1945), Paul Tillich (1886–1965) and Jürgen Moltmann (1926–) have attempted to bring the Gospel into conversation with modern culture and the experiences of modern men and women. Moreover, liberal theology has found new channels and forms. Perhaps most influentially, it has fed the rise and vitality of feminist theology, as well as being an influence within Liberation Theology. Both the latter take the concrete experiences of oppressed peoples as the starting point of theological reflection, and human dignity as a key principle. Feminist theologians have privileged women's experience, and criticized earlier theology as the product of male experience. Whilst some feminist theologians, including the early pioneer Mary Daly, eventually abandoned Christianity as irredeemably sexist, others, such as Rosemary Radford Ruether, have attempted to change theology and reform the church from within. Ruether's liberal credentials are evident in the way she uses the category of human liberation as a key interpretative tool, in similar ways to many Liberation Theologians.

Evangelicalism and fundamentalism

Evangelicalism is a broad movement within Protestant Christianity which has gathered up many of the most distinctive emphases of the sixteenth-century Protestant Reformation and developed them into a form of Christianity which has flourished in the context of modernity. As such it is not a church or denomination, but a widely influential current of Christianity (there are, for example, evangelical Anglicans, Lutherans and Presbyterians). An evangelical style of Christianity first emerged clearly in Europe and America in the eighteenth century in movements like Methodism, and it has staged periodic revivals ever since. Its identity as a pan-denominational movement became clearer and more self-conscious throughout the the twentieth century and into the twenty-first, partly in reaction to secular culture, and partly in reaction to what it regards as the easy accommodation to such culture by liberal Christianity. The most extreme anti-modern wing of evangelicalism emerged early in the twentieth century in North America under the banner of fundamentalism, and broke from the broader current of evangelical Christianity after 1957.

Evangelicalism grew directly from a number of movements in earlier Protestantism. From the Reformation it took its central doctrines of biblical authority, personal trust in God's saving work (Faith), and salvation through Jesus Christ. From Puritanism it took a concern with individual moral and spiritual development nurtured through self-examination and self-discipline and exemplified in thrift, hard work, self-control, independence, charity, and loyalty to family and church. The most immediate precursors of evangelicalism, however, were the revivals and awakenings of the eighteenth and early nineteenth centuries in both the Anglo-Saxon world and continental Europe. On the continent Pietism was the most important of the proto-evangelical movements, in Britain and North America Methodism emerged from the personal quest for holiness of John Wesley (1703–1791), his brother Charles (1707–1788), and like-minded university friends, most notably George Whitefield (1714–1770).

Like Pietists, the Methodists organized themselves into small groups in which they exhorted, examined, encouraged and disciplined one another; developed a strong missionary emphasis; encouraged Bible reading, personal devotion, and intense religious feeling; and attempted to renew existing Protestant churches from within. In a style which would become typical of Evangelicalism, Methodists also emphasized the importance of a deeply felt experience of conversion. In 1738 John Wesley recorded his own conversion in a now famous entry in his journal:

> In the evening I went very unwillingly to a society in Aldersgare Street [London], where one was reading Luther's Preface to the Epistle to the Romans. About a quarter before nine, while he was describing the change which God works in the heart through faith in Christ, I felt my heart strangely warmed. I felt I did trust in Christ – Christ alone for salvation; and an assurance was given me that He had taken away my sins, even mine, and saved me from the law of sin and death.

Wesley's conversion echoes the Protestant Reformer Martin Luther's experience, and the Lutheran influence is important. Yet Wesley developed the doctrine of justification by faith in a new way by placing much greater emphasis on the 'assurance' which accompanies it, and by insisting that it involves not merely an imputation but an attainment of righteousness. Methodism spread rapidly in both America and Britain in the eighteenth and early nineteenth centuries, and fed the growth of the broader evangelical current which emerged at the end of the nineteenth century and has flourished since then.

BOX 8.2 Methodism and the origins of Evangelicalism

Evangelicalism has a paradoxical relationship with modernity. On the surface it often appears hostile. Evangelicals are often sharply critical of the modern world, particularly in the area of personal morality. They stridently oppose the breakdown of the family, rising divorce rates, tolerance of homosexuality, and the abandonment of traditional domestic roles by women. Fundamentalists go even further, opposing any teachings and practices which they regard as contrary to Biblical teaching – even if these have the backing of science (the theory of evolution being the most obvious example). Instead of looking to the modern world for inspiration, evangelicals look back to Jesus and the early church (as portrayed in scripture). Yet evangelicalism came to birth in the modern era, and fits extremely well with other features of the modern world. Unlike Roman Catholicism or Orthodoxy, for example, it accommodates the modern secular state, for it is more concerned with winning individual souls for Jesus than with winning political influence. Likewise, evangelicalism makes an easy alliance with capitalism; indeed it actively promotes virtues which make capitalism, like hard work, honesty and frugality.

At the heart of evangelicalism lies a series of simple and straightforward affirmations. Two are particularly important: first, that salvation comes through a conversion in which the individual enters into personal relationship with God's only Son, Jesus Christ, and is saved through the latter's atoning work on the cross; second, that the Bible has a unique authority in human life. Evangelicalism, in other words, manages to hold together two very different elements. On the one hand, it recognizes a tangible and irrefutable source of authority in the Bible, and thus gives its followers clear rules for the guidance of their lives. On the other hand, it has a tendency to be experiential because of its stress on the importance of an overwhelming conversion experience. These two elements make evangelicalism attractive to many modern men and women, for it is able both to provide guidance in a pluralistic and rapidly changing world, whilst at the same time accommodating a modern turn to the self and experience (see the Introduction to this book). Evangelicalism also fits the modern context by virtue of being more individualistic and egalitarian than Roman Catholicism and Orthodoxy; it offers to bring each individual into relation with God without the mediation of church or clergy (though in practice membership of a church is important to most evangelicals).

These characteristics are closely bound up with a distinctively evangelical way of reading the Bible. Many evangelicals and fundamentalists read the Bible as a unified account of salvation history. According to this reading, scripture tells the story of God's work of creation from the beginning of time (the creation of the world in the book of Genesis) to its end (Christ's return to earth in the book of Revelation). The whole of history is seen as converging towards its climax – the sending of Jesus Christ to save the world by his cross and resurrection, followed by his final return to claim his chosen people (those who have been converted). Evangelicalism thus divides history into a number of divinely ordained periods or 'dispensations'. The contemporary world lies in-between the dispensation of Jesus Christ and his second coming. As a result, evangelicals tend to feel intense pressure not only to ready themselves for Christ's return, but to convert others. Nothing less than eternal salvation is at stake, for only those who have accepted Christ in their hearts and been 'born again' will be saved when he returns, whilst all others will be damned – hence the powerful evangelistic dynamic from which this form of Christianity derives its name. It was because Darwin's theory of evolution challenged this dispensational reading of history that many evangelicals were so troubled by it, and it was for the same reason that they reacted with hostility to historical criticism. Today some evangelicals accept both Darwin and historical criticism, whilst continuing to read the Bible as a unified narrative of a history focused on Jesus Christ. Fundamentalists distinguish themselves by their absolute refusal to accept either Darwinian science or historical criticism of the Bible.

In the nineteenth and first half of the twentieth century the two most powerful nations in the world – Britain and North America – affirmed and tried to export their 'Protestant' virtues of industry, sobriety, frugality, domesticity, sentiment, and order. In the pre-Darwinian era Protestant liberals and evangelicals had not clearly distinguished themselves, and they shared many core beliefs and values. The pulling apart of these two tendencies since the end of the nineteenth century has tended to favour evangelicalism and fundamentalism, for whilst liberal churches have declined, the former have shown greater vitality. Evangelicalism's success in the late modern world is related to the way in which it has shown itself able to adapt to changing conditions whilst maintaining its core affirmations. Evangelicals and fundamentalists have also shown themselves to be remarkably adept in utilizing new media in spreading the Gospel. All these tendencies have been evident in the career of the unofficial leader of twentieth-century evangelicalism, Billy Graham (born 1918). Yet traditional emphases have also remained, including reliance upon scripture and an emphasis on the importance of conversion, evangelism and the atoning work of Christ.

One of the most significant of all the shifts to affect evangelicalism since the 1960s has been the gradual absorption of Charismatic influence. The effect in the West has been a new emphasis not on the biblical pole of evangelicalism, but on the experiential pole. Many evangelicals have found a new place in their faith for the Holy Spirit and the exciting signs and wonders which accompany it. By the beginning of the twenty-first century, much evangelicalism in the West could more accurately be termed 'Charismatic-evangelical' than simply 'evangelical'. But it is outside the West that the Charismatic upsurge has been most dramatic (see below).

Evangelicalism has produced a huge literature for its highly literate audience, but much less academic theology than Roman Catholicism or liberal Christianity. It has tended to favour biblical commentaries and spiritual literature designed to meet the practical needs of ordinary Christians trying to conform their lives more closely to the teachings of Jesus Christ. The thought of Karl Barth (1886–1968) – the most influential of twentieth-century Protestant theologians – cannot be squarely located in the Evangelical camp, even though he was hostile to liberal Christianity and insisted that the Bible was God's word (though he did not accept a literal reading). The more important theological influences in twentieth- and twenty-first century evangelicalism have been more popular writers, such as John Stott, J.I. Packer, Alister McGrath, and Rick Warren.

The last quarter of the twentieth century, through to the start of the twenty-first, also saw evangelicalism and fundamentalism exercise an increasing right-wing political influence in the USA. The political critique has been selective. The 'new Christian Right' has tended not to criticise late capitalism, the collapse of welfare, the pursuit of personal wealth, or the 'War on Terror', for example. But it has campaigned vociferously on issues such as abortion, same-sex marriage, pre-marital sex, stem cell research, prayer in schools, and the teaching of evolution. With regard to the latter, there has been a widespread campaign to introduce teaching of 'Intelligent Design'. The influence of Christianity on American politics had become more rather than less visible by the start of the millennium, contrary to predictions of secularization (see Chapter 21, Secularization and secularism).

Global Charismatic upsurge

In the opinion of David Martin, one of the leading scholars of Charismatic Christianity, Charismatic Christianity and resurgent Islam represent the two most quickly growing forms of religion in the world today. Martin estimates that as many as a quarter of a billion people are involved in the Charismatic upsurge worldwide. Whilst Charismatic renewal has affected churches in the West, both Protestant and Catholic, its greatest impact has been in the Southern hemisphere, particularly in Latin America and sub-Saharan Africa. It is also influential in the Philippines, the Pacific rim (above all Korea), China, and parts of Eastern Europe, most notably Romania.

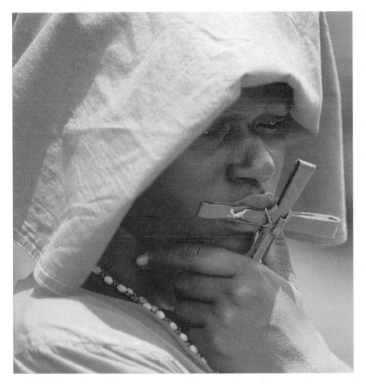

FIGURE 8.2
Christianity and gender

Early Christianity was accused by its detractors of being a religion for women and children. Its appeal may, if anything, have increased in modern times as the pressures of 'feminization' have affected a religion which already emphasized the importance of domestic life and 'womanly' virtues. Nevertheless, the church is often criticized by feminists for its patriarchal language, imagery, and forms of leadership. Courtesy C. Betty Press, Panos Pictures.

Pentecostal Christianity arose at around the same time as fundamentalism (the start of the twentieth century), and the two movements have much in common, including hostility to liberal Christianity, similar ways of reading scripture, belief in scriptural inerrancy, strict moral teachings, and belief in the imminent second coming of Jesus. What differentiates Pentecostalism, however, is the supreme importance it places on the gift ('charisma') of the Holy Spirit. Most Pentecostals agree that 'baptism in the Spirit' is the pivotal Christian experience which differentiates those who have been 'born again' from those who are still in slavery to the world, the flesh and the devil. The lives of those who have been saved in the Spirit are marked by powerful 'signs and wonders' including glossolalia (speaking in tongues, a humanly incomprehensible 'language' believed to be inspired by God), prophecy, healing and exorcism (casting out demons). Services of worship in which these gifts (charismata) are experienced lie at the heart of Pentecostal life, and greater weight is placed on them than on correct doctrinal belief, social action, reception of the sacraments, or obedience to church hierarchies. Much traditional Christianity is regarded by Pentecostals as a matter of empty ritual and dry 'externals' which lack the dynamism of the living Spirit of God.

Pentecostals trace their heritage back to the early Christian communities described in Paul's letters in the New Testament, and to the 'Pentecost' described in Chapters 1 and 2 of the Acts of the Apostles in the New Testament, when the Holy Spirit descends on the first Christians. They believe that they are restoring the pristine, primitive and powerful religion of the New Testament.

In many respects, Pentecostal Christianity is a religion of the margins. In the West it originally flourished amongst those who found themselves peripheral to the mainline churches and affluent white middle-class society. Elsewhere it flourishes in nations and societies which have experienced the marginalization which first accompanied colonization, and which now results from the pressures of participation as unequal partners in a rapidly evolving global market economy. Pentecostalism had several, near simultaneous points of origin. In 1906 the Asuza Street Apostolic Faith Mission in Los Angeles (a Western margin of the USA) became the centre of a Pentecostal movement which quickly spread to other parts of the world. Asuza Street was founded by the black Christian preacher William Joseph Seymour, and Pentecostalism owes much to the vibrant non-literary forms of Evangelical Christianity which had developed amongst blacks in America. At much the same time, Pentecostal-style Christian revival was also burgeoning in Wales – another western margin, though this time of Great Britain. In sub-Saharan Africa, Pentecostal-style independent churches were founded from the 1920s onwards by indigenous leaders marginalized by white-led colonial churches. They included the Zion churches in South Africa, the Aladura movement in Western Africa, and the Church of God on Earth through the prophet Simon Kimbangu in Central Africa. Pentecostalism was introduced to Latin America as early as 1910, but has grown most dramatically since the late 1940s. Pentecostalism is characterized by a huge variety of church styles, ranging from large denominations to small independent churches, some of the latter housed in tents, shops or garages.

Though the two terms may be used interchangeably, Pentecostalism generally refers to the first phase of Charismatic growth and the earliest denominations it spawned (the Pentecostal churches), whilst the label 'Charismatic' is more often applied to later, post-1960s developments. As has been noted above, this later Charismatic upsurge has not only given rise to a plethora of new churches, but has profoundly affected some of the mainline Christian denominations as Pentecostalism has moved from the margins to the mainstream. There are now Pentecostal Catholics as well as Charismatic Anglicans, Baptists and Methodists. Some scholars have linked Charismatic renewal in the West with the 1960s hippy counter-culture, since they share a common emphasis on the importance of personal experience in religion. The former differs, however, in having a much stronger social/institutional framework provided by a church, and much clearer and stricter moral rules and disciplines. As Chapter 17 shows, churches which combine the latter features with an emphasis on individual experience tend to be those which are currently displaying most vitality both in the West and elsewhere.

This ability to combine features of tradition with features of modernity is a major factor in the success of Charismatic Christianity. This late modern form of religion offers a remedy for the fears generated by a rapidly changing world in which social and moral order appears to be breaking down, whilst leaving behind those features of traditional religion which modern men and women find hardest to accept – hierarchies of power, formalized rituals, lack of participation. By offering the gift of the Holy Spirit to all men and women without distinction, Charismatic Christianity is also profoundly egalitarian and helps engender a new self-confidence in those who have previously been marginalized. Its lively and colourful services of worship do not demand high levels of literacy, education or culture, and its cohesive and mutually supportive congregations offer aid, education, care and welfare for all who participate.

By bringing the spiritual realm into such direct contact with the material world, Charismatic Christianity shares features with many indigenous religions in the areas it is successful (see Chapter 10 on Religion in Africa), and may take over some functions of the former, including exorcism and healing.

Charismatic Christianity appears to attract at least as many women as men, despite the fact that men are more prominent in positions of leadership (though there are growing numbers of women). One explanation may be that Charismatic Christianity offers the empowerment that matters most – the gift of the Holy Spirit – to both sexes, and in practice opens roles of considerable responsibility to large numbers of women, including healing and prophecy). Another reason may be that, like the evangelical tradition from which it flows, Charismatic Christianity affirms the pre-eminent value of the family and of the mother's role within it, and domesticates and tames men by affirming the womanly values of care, love and responsibility. (For more on women in Charismatic Christianity see Chapter 19 on Religion and gender).

Looking to the future

The most obvious way to think about the future is to extrapolate on the basis of present trends. In relation to Christianity, the following seem particularly significant:

1. Secularization

According to many sociologists, secularization is one of the most characteristic aspects of modernization, and Christianity, as the religion most closely involved with Western modernity, has been most affected. If we look at Western Europe in the modern period, the reality of secularization is apparent. In most cases secularization is quite recent, having gained pace throughout the twentieth century, but particularly since the late 1960s. Yet rates of secularization are very variable. In the USA, for example, rates of church-going are much higher than in Europe (some estimates put them as high as 40 per cent, whereas in parts of Europe they are lower than 5 per cent). There are other important variations too. In Europe some countries, like Sweden or the former East Germany, are much more secular than others, like Northern Ireland or Poland. And within different countries, some forms of Christianity, like evangelicalism, are doing much better than others, like liberalism. One conclusion must be that the strength or weakness of Christianity is very much a factor of particular circumstances, including its effectiveness in sustaining ethnic or national identity, aiding social and economic advancement, supporting wider cultural values, competing with other religions, and negotiating the changes associated with modernity.

2. Globalization and postcolonialism

Not only do rates of secularization vary within the West, they vary across the globe. In many parts of the non-Western world, Christianity has expanded rapidly since the second part of the twentieth century. This may be viewed as a second phase of Christian globalization. The first was associated with missionary activity and was bound up with Western colonialism. The second is postcolonial, and has seen much more rapid growth of Christianity. Unlike the first phase it is much more indigenous. Today few Western Christians continue to believe that they have a superior culture, or a superior form of Christianity, which they must impose on other nations. Non-Western Christianity is growing in confidence and in some cases exporting ideas and energy back to the West. This may well change the face of Christianity, as Western priorities become less and less determinative of the future of Christianity. We are also starting to see how alliances can be made between different parts of a world church, which can exercise great power. For example, in the Anglican church, conservatives in the USA and in Africa are uniting together against liberals, particularly over the issue of homosexuality, which they oppose.

3. *Opposition to secularism and the secular nation state*

Although Christianity has not challenged the legitimacy of the modern state, nor sought to replace it with a Christian state (unlike some forms of political Islam), there are recent signs that it is challenging the entrenched secularism of many modern states. In the USA we have noted the rise of Christian campaigning on issues like prayer and teaching of evolution in schools. In Europe too, Christians have challenged various aspects of state policy, and have sometimes united with other religions to oppose what they see as excessively secular measures which are dangerous to religion and/or to humanitarian and environmental causes. This area of ethical and religious campaigning activity is likely to grow, as opposition between religion and secularism grows in a 'postsecular' climate (see Introduction), and as religion acts as the moral conscience of nations.

4. *Conflict with other religions*

Although there are now many occasional, strategic alliances between different religions against aspects of secularism, there are also conflicts in many parts of the world. Conflict between Muslims and Christians is high in places like Pakistan, parts of the Middle East, and parts of Africa. Given that forms of resurgent Christianity and Islam both have ambitions to be universal religions, such conflict is likely to continue. Whether the churches in Europe side with or against the minority Muslim populations in their countries will be important for the future.

5. *The feminization of Christianity*

There are more female churchgoers than male, and women are often more actively involved in Christianity. Christianity often emphasizes 'feminine' values such as love, gentleness and relationship. Charismatic Christianity, the fastest spreading form of contemporary Christianity, has been very successful in attracting women. Both Islam and Christianity help many women outside the West to modernize without abandoning tradition or religion, and without becoming 'secular moderns'. Many Protestant denominations now ordain women, and women have become more active in Christian theology. At the same time, more conservative forms of Christianity are often hostile to more equal gender roles, and the breakdown of the 'traditional' family. The ways in which Christianity negotiates these different demands will be important in shaping its future.

6. *Subjectivization, individualization and the turn to experience*

The most successful forms of religion in the last half century have been those which have accommodated a modern emphasis on the unique value and dignity of each and every individual human being, and which have offered means of enhancing individual life and experience. By contrast, those which stress the authority of church, priests, and tradition over the individual have won less popular support, and in some cases have declined. Although there are some signs of a new appreciation of the value of tradition, this tendency towards 'subjectivization' is likely to continue. Traditional churches with heavy and expensive bureaucracies and clerical elites may have to make profound changes.

Summary

- The historical sources and resources of Christianity include the Bible, Jesus Christ and the institution of the church – each of which has been interpreted in widely varying ways over more than two millennia of Christian history.

- Most Christians accept the authority of Bible, tradition, and church but in varying combinations and with different emphases.

- Christianity in modern times may be divided into several types: Roman Catholic (liberal and conservative), Orthodox, liberal Protestant, Evangelical Protestant, Fundamentalist, Charismatic/Pentecostal. There is recent convergence between the Evangelical and Charismatic.

- Each of these types has interacted differently with modernity. Conservative Roman Catholicism and Orthodoxy have been most resistant, liberalism the most co-operative. Evangelicalism and Charismatic Christianity have both opposed some aspects of modernity whilst accommodating others.

- The centre of gravity of Christianity is shifting from the northern to the southern hemisphere.

- There has been a 'subjective turn' in late modern Christianity *and* a growing tendency to get involved in politics, particularly in opposition to secularism. These two trends towards the personal *and* the political appear to be compatible.

Key terms

anti-Semitism Hostility or prejudice against Jews.

apocalyptic A genre of literature which reveals things normally hidden, particularly things having to do with the heavenly realm and the world to come (the Greek word *apokalupsis* means 'revelation' or 'unveiling').

apocryphal Documents whose canonical status is disputed, i.e. which not all Christians accept as part of the canon of biblical scripture.

Atonement The work of God in Jesus Christ, which 'saves' humans by reconciling them with God (literally 'at-one-ment').

autonomy Self-regulation, independence.

canon From the Greek word meaning measuring rod or rule, the term refers to the books which were officially accepted within Christianity as authoritative.

Catholic/Roman Catholic The largest of the Christian churches whose leader, the Pope, resides in Rome.

Charismatic Christianity An offshoot of evangelicalism which has spread rapidly across the world throughout the twentieth century. Places particular emphasis on the gifts of the Holy Spirit. See Pentecostalism.

Christology The study of Christ; the attempt to articulate his nature and significance.

conciliar Concerning a council; ruled by an ecclesiastical council.

council An ecumenical or general council is a meeting of all the bishops of a church, advised by theologians, to formulate church teaching or to take measures to reform the church.

denomination A branch or grouping within Christianity (such as Methodism, Roman Catholicism).

ecumenical Seeking Christian unity, unity of all the churches.

evangelicalism A pan-denominational movement within modern Protestantism which emphasizes the authority of the Bible and experience of the Holy Spirit.

Fundamentalism The strictest form of Protestant evangelicalism which stresses the inerrancy and infallibility of the Bible.

heteronomy Opposite of autonomy; being regulated or governed by others or external duress.

monarchial Ruled by a single individual (like the Pope).

liberal Christianity A self-consciously 'modern' form of Christianity which stresses human goodness and freedom and is open to reform in the light of modern change.

liturgy Prescribed form of public worship and the formulas for it.

Orthodoxy The conciliar Eastern churches which separated from the Western (Catholic) church in the eleventh century. Sometimes called Eastern Orthodoxy.

Pentecostalism Often used interchangeably with 'Charismatic' Christianity. Used in a stricter sense, Pentecostalism refers to the first phase of the Charismatic movement (up to the 1960s/1970s).

Protestant The churches which split from the Roman Catholic church in the Reformation of the sixteenth century.

sacraments Historic Christian sacred signs and rituals which, for many Christians (especially Orthodox and Roman Catholic), are believed to convey God's grace directly (for example, the water of baptism, the bread and wine of the eucharist, and the rite of ordination).

sacerdotal Having to do with priests, the priestly hierarchy or the priestly office.

social encyclicals A series of official documents issued by the Roman Catholic church since the end of the nineteenth century which applied Christian teaching to the social conditions of the modern world.

Further reading

General

For an introduction to modern Christianity see Linda Woodhead: *Introduction to Christianity* (Cambridge: Cambridge University Press, 2002), the second half of which offers an introductory overview and interpretation of Christianity in the modern world.

For a detailed, multi-authored history of Christianity in modern times see Hugh McLeod (ed.): *Cambridge History of Christianity, Volume 9, World Christianities c.1914–c.2000* (Cambridge: Cambridge University Press, 2006) and Sheridan Gilley and Brian Stanley (eds): *Cambridge History of Christianity, Volume 8, World Christianities c.1815–c.1914* (Cambridge: Cambridge University Press, 2006).

On Christianity in Western Europe see Hugh McLeod: *Religion and the People of Western Europe 1789–1970* (Oxford: Oxford University Press, 1991) and Hugh McLeod: *The Religious Crisis of the 1960s* (Oxford: Oxford University Press, 2006).

For global Christianity see the relevant sections of Adrian Hastings (ed.): *A World History of Christianity* (London: Cassell, 1999), and Sebastian Kim and Kirsteen Kim: *Christianity as a World Religion* (London: Continuum, 2008).

Roman Catholicism

Although it is now dated, the collection edited by Thomas M. Gannon, SJ: *World Catholicism in Transition* (London and New York: Macmillan, 1988) offers an overview of the state of Catholicism in every part of the world in the 1980s, and contains a useful introductory survey article by David Martin. The *Cambridge History of Christianity* volumes listed above have several chapters on modern Catholicism.

Orthodoxy

Two useful surveys of modern Orthodoxy are: Sabrina P. Ramet: *Nihil Obstat: Religion, Politics, and Social Change in East-Central Europe and Russia* (Durham, NC and London: Duke University Press, 1998) and Nathaniel Davis: *A Long Walk to Church: A Contemporary History of Russian Orthodoxy* (Boulder, CO: Westview Press, 1995).

Liberal Christianity

There is surprisingly little literature on liberal Christianity, and no general introduction to the subject. Liberal Christianity in the latter part of the twentieth century is the subject of Robert Michaelsen and Wade

Clark Roof's collection of essays *Liberal Protestantism: Realities and Possibilities* (New York: Pilgrim Press, 1986). Wade Clark Roof and William McKinney's *American Mainline Religion: Its Changing Shape and Future* (New Brunswick, NJ and London: Rutgers University Press, 1987) also contains much relevant information.

See also: Nancy Ammerman: 'Golden Rule Christianity: Lived Religion in the American Mainstream'. In David D. Hall (ed.) *Lived Religion in America: Toward a History of Practice* (Princeton, NJ: Princeton University Press, 1997, pp. 196–216).

Evangelicalism

By contrast, there is no shortage of books on Evangelicalism. George Marsden's *Understanding Fundamentalism and Evangelicalism* (Grand Rapids, MI: Eerdmans, 1991) offers a classic introduction to the topic. There are a number of illuminating studies of contemporary evangelicalism including Christian Smith's *American Evangelicalism: Embattled and Thriving* (Chicago, IL: University of Chicago Press, 1998).

Charismatic Christianity

Vinson Synan's *The Holiness-Pentecostal Tradition: Charismatic Movements in the Twentieth Century*, second edition (Grand Rapids, MI/Cambridge, UK: Eerdmans, 1997) surveys the holiness movement, Pentecostalism and recent Charismatic renewal. David Martin's *Pentecostalism: The World their Parish* (Oxford, UK and Cambridge, MA: Blackwell, 2001) provides an analysis of the worldwide Charismatic movement.

Theology

David Ford's *The Modern Theologians: An Introduction to Christian Theology since 1918* (Oxford: Blackwell, 2005) is a comprehensive collection of essays that provides introductions to all the major figures and movements in modern Christian thought. Alister McGrath (ed.): *Blackwell Encyclopedia of Modern Christian Thought* (Oxford, UK, and Cambridge, MA: Blackwell, 1995) is a useful reference work.

Chapter 9

Islam

David Waines

Introduction

The number of Muslims worldwide is estimated to be in excess of one billion, making Islam the second largest faith community next to Christianity. Of this number the overwhelming majority would identify themselves as Sunni Muslims while about 15 per cent follow a variety of Shi'a Muslim persuasions (see p. 254). The Arabic word *islam* means the willing recognition of and active submission to the guiding command of the One God, Allah. Whoever acts in this manner is called a *muslim*, one who acknowledges and submits to the sole, unique God. The Islamic tradition or *din* (pronounced deen, a word which conveys the sense of 'obedience' closely related to *islam*) is founded upon the guiding command of Allah as contained in the Qur'an. Muslims hold the Qur'an to be the Word of God delivered to Muhammad (ca. 570–632 CE), God's elected messenger. The revelations were received in just over 20 years, first in Mecca, the Prophet's birthplace, and later in Madina where the first community was established. Both these cities are in present-day Saudi Arabia and are regarded by all Muslims as the central holy places of their faith.

From rather inauspicious beginnings in Arabia, Islam made a surprisingly rapid impact upon the contemporary map of the Middle East. Within a century of the Prophet Muhammad's death, Muslims governed throughout the Middle East and North Africa as far west as the Iberian peninsula (present day Spain and Portugal). In the east there were Muslim outposts in the Indus valley (north-west India) and expeditions which reached as far as the Great Wall of China. It naturally took much longer for mature, 'mass' Muslim societies to evolve in these areas. In regions such as Egypt some 300 years elapsed before Muslims became a majority displacing the previous majority Christian population through conversion. Significant Christian and Jewish communities nevertheless continued to exist and flourish in the Middle East throughout the premodern period. These traditional 'heartlands' of Islam remained fairly stable until about 1200 CE when a new phase of expansion commenced, although balanced to a lesser extent by territorial losses. By 1500 CE Muslims had been defeated and driven from the Iberian peninsula by the Christian reconquest supported by the Pope in Rome. By this same date Muslims under the banner of the Ottoman Turks had captured the capital of the Eastern Orthodox Church, Constantinople. The city was renamed Istanbul, and by its capture Muslims secured a foothold in Europe which subsequently included the Balkans and parts of Hungary and Austria. The Ottomans also absorbed Syria, Egypt and much of North Africa and became the guardians of the holy cities of Arabia. Another formidable Muslim dominion, the Mughal Empire, was about to emerge in India while Muslim traders, preachers and holy men during the years 1200–1500 CE

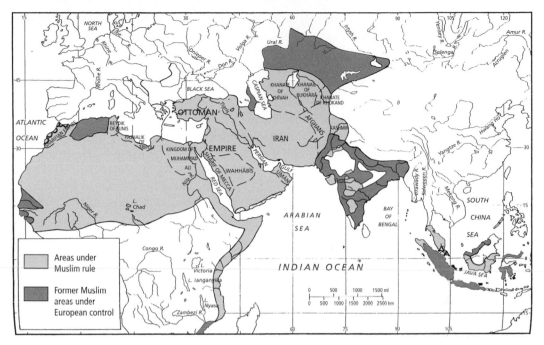

FIGURE 9.1 The Muslim world

The Muslim world in the mid-nineteenth century, showing areas under European control. Courtesy David Waines.

had been slowly spreading Islam eastwards from India to present-day Malaysia, Indonesia, and the Philippines. There even appeared a small and thinly scattered Muslim presence in China. During this same period Islam also became firmly established in parts of sub-Saharan and East Africa. Apart from the Ottoman and Mughal empires, a third great dominion emerged from 1500 onwards in Iran where, wedged between the two former Sunni powers, the Shi'a Muslim Safavid dynasty established itself. Shi'ism has since then grown into the predominant contemporary expression of Iranian Islam.

The worldwide Muslim community (*umma*) achieved its greatest territorial extent in the late seventeenth century. The most significant change in the *umma*'s pre-modern configuration has been the emergence in the twentieth century of Muslim communities throughout Western Europe and North America. As yet small, they are formed almost exclusively by immigrants from former European colonial territories. For example, the largest non-Christian religious minority in Britain today is comprised chiefly of Muslims from the Indian sub-continent. This phenomenon is the result of significant population movements from east to west. An even more recent development has been the emergence of independent central Asian Muslim republics, like Tajikistan and Kyrgyzstan, formed out of the collapse of the former Soviet Union.

'Modernity' is generally understood to refer to developments in Western Europe which commenced during the eighteenth century. It is also widely assumed that since such developments, especially those relating to science and technology and the challenge they posed to religious authority, did not occur elsewhere at this same time, non-European areas of the globe could therefore only truly 'modernize' once they adopted and followed European patterns. This model of modernity, however, can lead to important eighteenth-century religious developments in non-European cultures becoming obscured or ignored altogether. In the case of Islam, religious reform thought in the eighteenth century, while not entirely overlooked, has not been sufficiently appreciated for its influence on nineteenth-century Islamic movements which, consequently, have then been interpreted as simply 'anti-Western' and therefore 'anti-modern' developments since they occurred at the very time when much of the Muslim world was succumbing to overwhelming European political domination. On the other hand, Islamic thought and movements of the eighteenth-nineteenth centuries must be given their due as providing critiques of and tentative or partial solutions to clearly perceived problems of internal moral and spiritual decay in Islamic societies. With reference to the non-European world, one has often to become sensitive to observing and imagining 'modernity-as-tradition', or a specifically Islamic form of modernization (see the Introduction to this volume, and Chapter 19 on Religion and gender where it refers to Muslim women). These problems will be looked at in detail in this chapter following an initial discussion of the sources of the Islamic tradition.

Sources and resources

Scripture and tradition

The two major sources of the Islamic tradition are the Qur'an and a body of literature known as the Traditions of the Prophet (*hadith*) which contain the Prophet's *sunna*, his 'way' or 'path'. Described in its own terms the Qur'an appears in many ways distinct from the religious texts of other communities such as the Hebrew Scriptures of the Jews and the Christians' New Testament. The word *qur'an* means 'recitation' which emphasizes its essentially oral character, intended to be read aloud and listened to. Moreover, the Qur'an is seen as the literal and immutable word of Allah, the Arabic word *al-ilah* meaning 'the God' (Qur'an 18:27; also 10:15). Next, it is a guidance to all peoples, confirming the essential message of previous revelations (Q 6:92). Muslims believe these scriptures are either incomplete (Q 4:44) or had become corrupted by the earlier communities (Q 2:174) who distorted their original meaning (Q 5:16–18). The Qur'an is, therefore, the culmination and completion of God's guidance to the world.

> [The second Caliph] Umar ibn al-Khattab said: One day when we were with God's messenger [Muhammad], a man wearing very white clothing and black hair came up to us. No mark of travel was visible on him, and none of us recognised him. Sitting down before the Prophet, he said, 'Tell me, Muhammad, about submission [*islam*]'. He replied, 'Submission means bearing witness that there is no god but God and that Muhammad is God's messenger, that you perform the ritual prayer, pay the alms tax, fast during Ramadan and make the

pilgrimage to the House (in Mecca), if you are able to go there.' The man said, 'You have spoken the truth.' We were surprised at his questioning the Prophet and then declaring he had spoken the truth. He then said, 'Now tell me about faith [*iman*].' The Prophet said, 'Faith means that you have faith in God, His angels, His books, His messengers, and the Last Day, and that you have faith in divine destiny, both its good and its evil.' Again remarking that he had spoken the truth, he said, 'Now tell me about goodness and right action [*ihsan*].' The Prophet replied, '*Ihsan* means that you should worship God as if you see Him, for even if you do not see Him, He sees you.' When the man went away, I waited for a while and the Prophet asked me, 'Umar, do you know who the questioner was?' I replied, 'God and His messenger know best.' He said, 'That was (the angel) Gabriel. He came to teach you your religion.'

This famous Tradition describes the 'surrender to God' [*islam*] in terms first of the ritual 'pillars', then as the inner faith [*iman*] in God and His final judgement, and lastly as pious behaviour [*ihsan*] in all aspects of one's daily life as though acting in the presence of God.

BOX 9.1 Excerpt from the Gabriel Hadith

The relationship between the message and the messenger, the Prophet Muhammad, is often misunderstood. As the Qur'an is held to be the eternal word of God, the message is logically and existentially prior to an earthly messenger; hence the Qur'anic message should properly be viewed as the manifestation of the divine, somewhat in the manner as Christians regard Jesus Christ. As such, the Qur'an presents a kind of 'self-portrait' of God as lord of all creation, as lord of history, past and present, and as lord of the last judgement.

Through Muhammad God disclosed his will, nature and the purpose of creation. As a vehicle of the divine message, the Prophet became the second source of spiritual authority for Muslims. This was expressed in the *sunna* or 'way of the Prophet', the sum of his exemplary words and deeds. Unlike the Qur'an, a single volume about the length of the New Testament, the *sunna* is found in a large corpus of multi-volumed works. Six such works, compiled in the late ninth and early tenth centuries are considered as genuine, authoritative sources of information concerning all aspects of the Prophet's life. These works could be described as containing the early Muslim community's collective memory of the Prophet. The information is preserved in the form of stories, anecdotes, or simply personal observations, each called a *hadith*, or Tradition. These might be attributed either directly to the Prophet himself or to his close companions relating what they knew about him, about life in the early Muslim community or even about the days in Arabia before the Prophet's mission. The collections of *hadith* helped to clarify and extend Muslims' understanding of the Qur'an, since Muhammad was held to be the first interpreter of the revelations he had received. Moreover, they kept alive the memory of God's messenger who in turn became an exemplary model for Muslims to follow in their own daily lives.

In the generations following the Prophet's death an informal group of experts emerged, each specializing in one or more areas related to the relevance and application of the Qur'an and Traditions to the evolving life of the Muslim community. Collectively, this scholarly elite was known as the *'ulama* (singular, *'alim*) whose task it was to shape the religious ethos of the community based upon these twin foundations. Fields developed such as Qur'an commentary, *hadith* analysis, history, law, theology, ethics, grammar, lexicography, and medicine. Some of these early scholars were converts, or descendants of converts from Christianity, Judaism or other faiths, which explains the presence of influences from these sources in the early Islamic scholarly disciplines. Popular storytellers and preachers instructed and entertained audiences of ordinary folk with morality tales for their edification and guidance. The story of Joseph and his brothers, for example, is uniquely narrated in the Qur'an as 'signs for seekers after truth' (Q 12:7). The storytellers drew from the annals of all the ancient prophets, which included Adam, Abraham, Moses and Jesus, because they contained 'a moral for those of understanding' (Q 12:111). Some storytellers were later charged with inventing and disseminating false Traditions, albeit from the most pious of motives, in order to instil in their audiences the proper awe and reverence for the faith.

Community, authority and the self

The Sunni Muslim understanding of community (*umma*) and authority is reflected in its historical experience. The Prophet Muhammad founded the first Muslim community in Madina and guided it until his death after which leadership fell to a series of four caliphs (*khalifa*) from among his close companions, including his cousin and son-in-law, Ali. This period of nearly 40 years (622–661 CE) came later to be regarded as one in which the community was 'rightly guided', living in practice as closely in tune with the divine command as was humanly possible. Thereafter, rapid expansion and internal divisions endangered, according to some, the community's spiritual well-being. In response, they adopted a more ascetic style of life than common piety required which evolved into the spiritual expression known as Sufism.

God is the Light of the heavens and the earth. The similitude of His light is as a niche wherein is a lamp. The lamp is in a glass. The glass is as it were a shining star. (The lamp is) kindled from a blessed tree, an olive of neither the East nor the West, whose oil would almost glow forth (of itself) though touched by no fire. Light upon light. God guides to His light whom He will, and speaks to humankind in allegories, for God is the Knower of all things.

This verse, a favourite among Sufis, is seen as describing the immanence of God to His creatures.

BOX 9.2 Qur'an 24:35 'The Light Verse'

The notion of a pristine community comprising the first two or three generations of Muslims is reflected in Prophetic Tradition. Muhammad was reported to have said that after him the community would become divided into 73 sects, only one of which would be saved from eternal damnation. When asked which that would be he said: 'Those who follow me and my Companions.' This widely known Tradition was understood to mean that salvation, individual and collective, would be attained by following the guidance of the Qur'an and the Prophet's example expressed in the *sunna*. The Sunni (from the word *sunna*) community adhered to the *shari'a* (sacred law) as expounded in detail by the founders and their followers of four main schools of legal thought and practice. The law was derived from the material sources of the Qur'an and the *sunna*. Vigorous debates during the law's development were decisively resolved in favour of the experts in *hadith* who claimed the *sunna* had equal status with the Qur'an. In addition, legal scholars came to accept as binding the consensus of opinion on a legal matter arrived at within their own school or that of the broader community. Finally, decisions could also be made employing the rational tool of argument by analogy. The religious law covered two domains of activity, the relationship of the individual with God in worship, and the relationship of individuals with each other in social matters which included, among other fields, what today would cover family, commercial or criminal law.

One significant dissident group became known as the supporters of Ali, or the Shi'a. They held that legitimate leadership of the community had been designated by the Prophet to lie solely with the family of Ali and his male descendants, known as the twelve *Imams*. (Another dissident group, the Isma'ilis, held that the line of *Imams* ended with the seventh in the line.) The Sunni Caliphs, excluding Ali, were regarded as usurpers. The Shi'a would in time claim their *Imams* were divinely designated and possessed an infallible knowledge of the divine will expressed in the Qur'an. Shi'a understanding of the law is based upon the Qur'an and the Prophet's way as taught by the Imams, beginning with Ali. The twelfth and last Imam who 'vanished' around 900 CE, is believed by the Shi'a to be alive and his return is awaited to restore justice on earth prior to the day of judgement. The doctrine of the Imams is the key to the division between Shi'a and Sunni. This has led one modern observer to describe them as two parallel orthodox perspectives of the Islamic revelation which, in their formal, outward aspects, cannot converge. Conciliation is possible, however, both in daily life and at the inner spiritual level of Sufism. Differences notwithstanding, both Shi'a and Sunni Muslims base their sense of community upon acceptance of the Qur'an and his Prophet.

From this brief account, three levels of authority can be described: first, *ultimate* authority rests unquestionably with God who provides guidance for all humankind. Second, during Muhammad's lifetime, authority over his community was *derived* from his role as messenger of God (*rasul allah*). These two aspects are summed up in the Muslims' confession of faith, considered as the fundamental pillar of Islam, that 'There is no God but Allah and Muhammad is His Messenger'. To this the Shi'a add '. . . and Ali is the friend of Allah'. All Muslims would accept the Qur'anic injunction that 'if you have a dispute concerning any matter, refer it to Allah and the Messenger if you truly believe in Allah and the Last Day' (Q 4:59). The third level of authority is *social*, vested in those who possessed the requisite knowledge of the Qur'an and *sunna*, and a deep personal piety. This applied to the Sunni religious scholars and, following the disappearance of the twelfth and last Imam (ca. 900 CE), to those of their Shi'a counterparts who were expert in the law (*mujtahids*). According to the Sunni axiom 'scholars are heirs of the Prophets' and among the Shi'a the saying is that 'jurists are heirs of the Imams'. Thus religious authority in Islamic societies is diffuse and scattered, entrusted to individuals recognised within their own communities for the qualities mentioned, and at times for their aura of holiness alone.

The Muslim sense of community is reinforced by the other rituals or 'pillars' of the faith. For example, the daily prayers (*salat*) are performed in the direction of Mecca, the focal point of community worship. The annual pilgrimage (*hajj*) to Mecca, at least once in a Muslim's lifetime should conditions permit, brings together a microcosm of believers from around the world. Fasting (*sawm*) during the month of Ramadan is a time of spiritual renewal for the individual as well as the community and finally, the giving of alms (*zakat*) is a spiritual form of community welfare.

Each of these ritual acts also defines the status of the self, for every Muslim is ultimately responsible for his/her own salvation before God without resort to either intermediary or redeemer. Each individual possesses an innate sense of the divine and need for guidance and, therefore, must choose to follow or reject God's will and await his just dispensation at the last judgement. Unique in the order of creation, man and woman have been entrusted with building a moral social order on earth, a fearsome burden itself which can be achieved only by constant personal struggle (*jihad*) aided by God's mercy and compassion. Here the self and community are inextricably linked. The proper fulfilment of each is sought in an enduring 'remembrance of God'. The link is alluded to in the Qur'anic verse, 'The successful are those who can be saved from their own selfishness' (Q 59:9). Another approach to the Creator–creature relationship is that of the Sufi who strives, through various spiritual exercises, to live the words of the famous *hadith*, to 'worship God as if you see Him, for even if you do not see Him, He sees you'. Striving for a vision of the divine did not necessarily entail withdrawal from community concerns. Whether Sufi or not, every Muslim as *muslim* (one who has submitted to God) strives for a life of balanced, integrated moral action called *taqwa*, a term often rendered as 'piety' but is more properly understood as guarding oneself against the harmful consequences of one's own conduct.

The Muslim experience of community prior to the modern era was, in an interesting sense, never exclusively Muslim. As the youngest of the monotheist traditions, Islam's roots in the Jewish and Christian traditions were acknowledged insofar as Biblical figures like Adam, Abraham, Moses and Jesus were accepted as part of God's long prophetic chain culminating in the mission of Muhammad. Jewish and Christian minority communities of the Middle East, North Africa and the Iberian peninsula, therefore, lived in treaty relationship within Muslim dominions which allowed them generally peaceful pursuit of their own religious beliefs and practices. In India, Muslim rule confronted numerically superior Hindu communities which ensured the latter's continuing vitality despite conversions to Islam particularly from among the lower castes. Muslim experience of 'the Other' was, nevertheless, a unique premodern experiment in pluralism.

Interactions with modernity

Islam and the modern world: The eighteenth century

Following upon the ravages of the Mongol invasions of much of the Middle East and northern India in the thirteenth century and a series of plagues in the fourteenth century, the *umma* entered upon a phase of gradual recovery. As already noted in the introduction, the sixteenth and seventeenth centuries witnessed the rise and consolidation of formidable empires under Ottoman, Safavid and Mughal rule. By the beginning of the eighteenth century weaknesses had already begun to appear in these once impregnable dominions.

The story of Islam from 1700 CE onward has often been discussed in terms of the 'decline of Islam' versus the 'rise of the West' or as the struggle between 'tradition' and 'modernity'. The complexity of historical reality cannot easily be reduced to simple contrasting descriptive terms such as these.

It was evident that political corruption and military defeat were damaging the very core of these Muslim imperial structures allowing local, provincial authorities to rise to prominence. Moreover, weakness at their centres occurred at a time of increasingly aggressive commercial and trade policies of major private, international trading companies that had been established in Britain, France and the Netherlands a century earlier. In the long run European economic expansion overseas would be converted into direct political control over Muslim lands. This resulted from the need to protect their own rapidly growing economies at home which were increasingly dependent upon these overseas links. During the eighteenth century European economic penetration alone had little or no impact upon Muslim religious developments which were directed specifically at socio-moral revival of Muslim societies and reorientation of the Sufi tradition.

These internal Muslim developments arose out of local conditions but achieved notice well beyond the areas of their immediate influence. The dissemination of revival ideas occurred in traditional ways, first via the annual pilgrimage to Mecca and second in the practice of religious scholars (*ulama*) travelling over vast distances to gather knowledge from famous teachers elsewhere and exchanging views on current conditions within the *umma*. Moreover, the Holy Cities of Mecca and Madina were themselves centres of study for scholars from near and far. For example, of the dozen or so most prominent teachers between 1650 and 1750, apart from those born in Mecca and Madina, there were scholars who had come from as far away as India, Iraq and Morocco.

One of the greatest figures of the eighteenth century was the Indian Shah Wali Allah (1702–1762). He was born in Delhi and was accepted into the reforming Naqshbandi order of Sufis by his father who had undertaken his son's early education. While on pilgrimage to the Holy Cities of Arabia, he became immersed in the study of *hadith*. On returning to India his chief concerns were the decline of Mughal power and disunity within the Indian Muslim community. Over the centuries Sufism in the Indian context had acquired un-Islamic accretions and superstitions derived from Hindu influence. Wali Allah condemned practices like auto-hypnotic visions, orgiastic rituals and saint veneration bordering on worship. Drawing upon the work of his great predecessor Ahmad al-Sirhindi (d. 1648) he attempted to 'purify' Sufism and then to reconcile the various strands of contemporary practice into one that reflected both the Indian spiritual environment and the need to regenerate Islamic forces. A profound study of the *hadith* (Prophetic Traditions) led Wali Allah to highlight points of agreement between the four Sunni schools of law and to insist that blind imitation of the teachings of any single school damaged community welfare. In effect, the only unquestioned sources of authoritative guidance were God and his messenger.

A second important figure was Muhammad ibn Abd al-Wahhab (1703–1792). He was born in central Arabia, at the time nominally under the suzerainty of the Ottoman sultan. Like his contemporary Wali Allah, he studied in Mecca and Madina where he too underwent a rigorous study of *hadith*. This forcefully brought home to him the gulf between the ideal community expressed in the Traditions and the sorry state of Arabian society he saw around him. His thought was also influenced by a major puritan of an earlier era, Ibn Taymiyyah (d. 1323). Between Abd al-Wahhab and Wali Allah there were points of agreement but, more profoundly, points of difference. Both accepted the Qur'an and *sunna* as binding sources for a Muslim's faith and law. Moreover, each rejected blind imitation of generations of medieval legal scholarship which, over the centuries, had thoroughly examined these sources. But whereas Abd al-Wahhab insisted that there was no human guide for a Muslim other than the Prophet, Wali Allah allowed, within proper limits, the guidance of a Sufi master so long as the relationship did not involve the disciple's veneration of his teacher. Abd al-Wahhab also stressed the transcendence of the One, Unique God, while Wali Allah accepted the possible vision of a more accessible, immanent God. Their greatest point of disagreement was over Sufism, although each had studied with prominent Sufi masters. Abd al-Wahhab roundly denounced practices including the seeking of intercession with God from the 'spirits' of dead holy men and women and the excessive devotion at their tombs since prayer *for* the dead could easily degenerate, he thought, into prayer *to* the dead. Wali Allah, on the other hand, strove to purify Sufism, bringing those practices broadly agreed as acceptable and its individualist form of spirituality more firmly into the domain of the sacred law (*shari'a*).

In brief, these revivalist programmes attacked the world negating attitudes and superstitions of medieval Sufism. Reformed Sufi orders shifted the emphasis away from popular ecstatic practices and stressed as well the need for the social and moral reconstruction of Muslim societies. The significance of the study of *hadith* was a renewed focus upon the role of the Prophet as a model for moral conduct at both the individual and collective levels. Revivalists challenged the acceptance of the opinions of the medieval legal schools as fixed and final. Instead they insisted on *ijtihad*, or the effort to rethink for oneself the meaning of the original message contained in the Qur'an and *sunna*. They intended also to reflect the moral dynamism of early Islam, thereby attacking the debilitating burden of a pre-deterministic, fatalistic outlook produced by popular religion. Political involvement, therefore, was a logical corollary of their religious views as they vigorously assailed social and economic injustices. For example, the Wahhabiya became the dominant religious force in Arabia when it allied with the political forces of the Sa'ud family and established the first Sau'di polity in 1773. Shah Wali Allah was himself not directly involved in the Indian political scene but his influence was evident in the activities of his son and grandson in the early nineteenth century. Militant revivalist movements emerged elsewhere across the *umma* from west and north Africa to Indonesia and China. The chief weakness of the revivalist programmes, it has been observed, was the belief that the sacred law could (and, of course, should) be more or less *literally implemented* in all ages. This presented an obstacle to creative rethinking of the social content of Islam. Nevertheless, revivalist groups did represent an important expression of self-analysis and criticism of contemporary Muslim societies.

Meanwhile, in Shi'a Iran, the power of the Safavids came to an end in 1722. By the end of the eighteenth century they had been replaced by the Qajar dynasty which ruled until 1925. An unsettled interregnum during which the new ruler, Nadir Shah (1736–1748), attempted for political reasons to transform Shi'ism into a fifth Sunni legal school proved a passing episode without lasting consequence. Despite the political instability witnessed throughout the century, the Shi'a tradition preserved its vitality and, ultimately, its predominance. An important, ongoing controversy between two groups, the Akhbaris and Usulis, ended in victory for the latter. The core of the dispute was about whether scholars could exercise their independent judgement (*ijtihad*) in deriving fresh insights from the Qur'an and the Traditions of the Prophet and the teaching of the *Imams*. The Akhbaris denied this, claiming solutions to all questions could be found solely within these sources alone. The Usuli position, emphasizing *ijtihad*, stressed the *mujtahids'* role as spiritual guides in helping the community to cope with changing times in the absence of the last *Imam*. In effect, the *mujtahids* became agents or representatives of the last, vanished or hidden *Imam*. The Usuli triumph helped religious scholars consolidate their social position in Iranian society, with their own financial resources and a growing sense of independence from all central political authority. Among Sunni reformers, as we have seen, *ijtihad* was also urged, although in their societies this never had the consequence of the *'ulama* securing a collective role independent of political power.

Examination of the eighteenth-century Islamic experience has shown vigorous revival movements emerging within contexts of weakening political and social structures. These movements significantly established an Islamic agenda which influenced future reform strategies in an era of the increasingly direct impact of Western ideas, values and institutions upon Muslims throughout the *umma*.

The 'long' nineteenth century: Colonialism and modernity

The nineteenth century in modern Islamic history was an unusually long and troubled one. Symbolically it begins with the invasion of Ottoman Egypt by Napoleon Bonaparte in 1798. The French occupation, although shortlived, was a clear signal of the Ottoman Empire's waning fortunes. The symbolic end of the period is 1920 when Britain and France divided the remaining Ottoman territories of Iraq, Syria and Palestine between themselves. Throughout the 'long century' European colonialists managed to occupy or directly influence almost the entire Islamic world. Of the three great medieval Muslim empires, the Ottoman and Mughal were totally dismembered; only Iran emerged relatively intact but subject nevertheless to pressure from both Britain and Russia. Muslim-inhabited territories in sub-Saharan Africa and in modern-day Malaysia and Indonesia also fell under European control.

Set in this framework, 'modernity' and Muslims' responses to it raise problems in significant ways different from the course of modernity in Europe itself. Understood as a cluster of social, political, economic and cultural institutions and values, modernity was experienced in Europe and North America as an internally generated transformation. As part of that process some European nations, notably Britain, France and the Netherlands, built vast imperial networks overseas. These nineteenth-century imperial structures enjoyed advantages possessed by no premodern empire. Developments in science and technology, transport and communications, together with commercial and industrial transformation of the home economies, gave these countries unprecedented power of expansion overseas. 'Modernity', therefore, was experienced in Muslim lands within a power relationship between themselves and their new non-Muslim rulers. Even territories which did not come under direct European control, like modern day Saudi Arabia and Turkey, were nonetheless confronted with the same powerful challenges of the modern era.

The experience was by no means all negative. Until the 1880s, thoughtful Muslims who had acquired firsthand experience of European countries, admired those features which were most conspicuously lacking in their own societies. These observers recognised that parliamentary governments stood in stark contrast to their own despotic, dynastic regimes. They also acknowledged that European charitable societies, dedicated to ameliorating the plight of the poor and disadvantaged, were superior to the equivalent traditional Muslim institutions which had fallen into widespread neglect. At the same time the implications of secularization for religion in their own societies were not grasped.

Gradually the mood in educated Muslim quarters changed. A new sentiment of nationalism arose and the desire for independence from European rule. This goal was fed in part by growing Muslim resentment at the double standards exercised by the European 'civilizing missions' towards their colonial possessions. Enlightenment values of equality, democracy and human rights were often distorted and devalued in their application by European imperial rulers to subject peoples. A complicating factor was religion. In Europe, modernity was experienced as the challenge by the secular nation state to the traditional religious authority of the church. But for their part, Muslims experienced Europe's power over themselves as Christian power. This was exercised most clearly in the expansion of Christian missionary activity encouraged by European governments. Missions provided education in the 'new European knowledge' and health care. These provisions were widely welcomed. The explicit missionary objective to convert Muslims was, on the other hand, stiffly resisted. Muslims drew parallels with the era of Christian Crusades against Muslims in the middle ages. Missionary propaganda attacked the character of the Prophet as sensual and violent and dismissed the Qur'an as his own incoherent composition. Apart from the crudity of such methods, the major obstacle to the missionary programme was the Muslims' own understanding of Jesus as one of God's great prophets and exemplary model of love, but not as the evangelists' Son of God or Redeemer of humanity. Nonetheless, Protestant scripturalist views influenced modernist Muslim thinking as we shall see below.

The legacy of European colonial rule was mixed: Muslims willingly accepted the real material benefits of modernity such as science and technology but were more suspicious of and ambivalent towards certain values like individualism and democracy. Individualism went against the Muslim sense of community and family, while democracy compromised the sovereignty of God. Moreover, in a few notable cases the violent end of colonial rule contributed to the subsequent politicization of Muslim religious movements. Three such traumatic examples of the colonial end-game were in Algeria, Palestine and India. In Algeria, France had implanted a huge colony of French settlers on vast tracts of prime agricultural land, dispossessing the local population. Only a bloody eight-year war brought about Algerian independence in 1962, but left the country on the verge of economic ruin. Britain promoted the idea of a Jewish National Home in Palestine against the wishes of its inhabitants. The creation of the State of Israel in 1948 was built upon the destruction of Palestinian society and the creation of hundreds of thousands of refugees. Finally, in the wake of Britain's hasty retreat from India in 1947 two nations, India and Pakistan, divided the subcontinent in bitterness and enmity at the cost of hundreds of thousands of lives and the displacement of as many more.

The association of colonialism with Christianity had further consequences. In the minds of modern Muslim reformers, social change could not entail secularization or the trivialization of religion manifested in the removal of its interest in politics, economics or social problems. The policies of the colonial powers promoted secular institutions in their overseas domains. Two key institutions were education and the law. While private mission schools were allowed to flourish, colonial governments' overall control of education further encouraged the marginalization of Islamic knowledge. Likewise, Muslim legal systems were reformed and largely replaced by the introduction of European codes (especially, French, Swiss and German) lock, stock and barrel. In both cases it meant that those trained in traditional Islamic knowledge, the *ulama*, were disenfranchised and replaced socially by a new secularized Muslim elite. This process occurred earlier in India than in the Middle East, although in Iran the *mujtahids* maintained their social and economic base for a longer time. Politically, the new secularized elite formed the governing circle in all the independent nation states of the postcolonial period.

On the question of the place of religion in modern society, a gulf by then existed between the visions of the *ulama* and the secularists. Towards the end of the nineteenth century there slowly emerged an unco-ordinated group of modernist reformers – they could hardly be called a 'school of thought' – who were at once acutely aware of their society's modern needs and also for a public debate about Islam's present and future role. They built upon the work of their medieval and early modern predecessors, but rather than seeking to recapture an ideal past looked to a better, modern future. Their impact touched both the more culturally sensitive secularists and the enlightened wing of the *ulama*.

Muslim responses: Tradition and modernity

Religious debate and controversy throughout the twentieth century have been fluid, a good example, perhaps, of 'tradition-in-modernity'. Some religious movements viewed over time seem to defy simple labelling, making analysis more complicated and terminology meaningless when applied rigidly. An example may help illustrate the problem.

The Deobandi movement began in India with the foundation of its first school in 1867. Some of its founders had close connection with *ulama* linked to the family of Shah Wali Allah and to Delhi College established and run by the British. The goal of the Deobandi school was to provide instruction in the faith and graduates to carry on the work at a moment when traditional support for Muslim education in India had collapsed. British policy was openly hostile to the Muslim community, holding it responsible for the Indian uprising against imperial rule a decade earlier. The six-year curriculum emphasised the study of Traditions (*hadith*), individual responsibility for correct belief and practice together with spiritual transformation along sober Sufi lines. The school, however, borrowed many institutional features from British example, including formal exams, an annual convocation, and a system of raising public contributions through mail and money orders. Students from all India, Central Asia and Afghanistan were attracted to the school whose members remained politically quiescent until just before the outbreak of World War I. This apolitical strand has given rise since the 1920s to a significant international movement which today is well established among Muslim communities in Europe and North America. Among the various available labels, how may one best characterize this many-sided movement: traditionalist, fundamentalist, modernist, or secularist? While inevitably described as fundamentalist, in fact it shares features with all four categories. The application of any single label can be misleading, as important features may otherwise be overlooked. In the Deobandi movement, tradition and modernity seem in league with one another. Recent studies on Islam in the modern world employ a number of designations for different movements. While the term 'fundamentalist' seems to lack rigorous analytical power when used of Islamic contexts, in a very broad sense, 'modernist' Muslims may be said to seek to modernize Islam while more radical reformers sometimes called 'Islamicists' (another unfortunate term) seek to Islamize modernity.

Given the structure of this chapter and the four-fold scheme of themes it covers, it is not possible to deal with every twentieth-century development across the vast breadth of the Muslim world. In what remains of the story, the question of religious authority and its implications for Muslim society will be highlighted. Debates on this issue have occurred in many countries and contexts but it is those in India (and latterly Pakistan), Egypt and Iran which will be dealt with.

Modernist reform: nineteenth and twentieth centuries (Sunni and Shi'a)

Sunni developments

Two figures stand out as the major Sunni reformers in the Muslim world, the Indian Sayyid Ahmad Khan (d. 1898) and the Egyptian Muhammad Abduh (d. 1905). Both confronted direct British imperial rule over their lands, of India from 1857 and of Egypt from 1882. Abduh supported a proto-nationalist uprising in the Egyptian army which led to British occupation and as a result he spent some years in exile. Ahmad Khan was employed in the British East India Company. In the wake of the revolt against British presence in 1857, he strove to reconcile the Indian Muslim community with British rule and assure the British of Muslim loyalty to them. He was knighted in 1888. Each received a traditional Islamic education, and had early, close relations with Sufi spirituality, while in their middle years each became acquainted with Europe first hand. All these influences informed their efforts toward social reform focused especially upon education. Ahmad Khan founded the Muhammedan Anglo-Oriental College; it would become the first secular university for Muslim students in India. Abduh, from his position as the highest religious authority in Egypt, strove to reform the religious courts, religious endowments and the 1000-year-old al-Azhar university. He also conceived the idea for a complementary secular university, eventually founded after his death. Both men also conveyed their ideas through the modern medium of newspapers which they founded or edited themselves.

The modernist agenda set out two inter-related goals. The first was to provide a way forward out of Muslims' current spiritual malaise and material decadence by demonstrating the compatibility of Islam with the values of the modern world. Second,

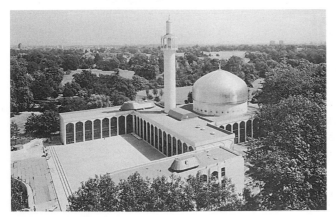

FIGURE 9.2 Central mosque

Central Mosque, London.
Courtesy *Saudi Aramco World*/PADIA.

was to counter the Western perception of Islam as destructive and irrelevant to the modern world, and to challenge assertions like that of Lord Cromer, onetime governor of Egypt, that 'Islam reformed is no longer Islam'.

Traditionally, the state of contemporary life had been judged on the basis of norms which were, in theory, ultimately grounded in the Qur'an and *sunna*. Modernists, on the other hand, approached the Qur'an and *sunna* from the rational norms of ninteenth-century natural science. Like their eighteenth-century predecessors, modernists argued that fulfilment of their task entailed returning to Islam's original sources. But where the revivalists had tended to read the sacred texts in a literal fashion, modernists sought to capture their essential spirit and to distinguish a universal, immutable core from features deemed valid only for a particular time or place.

The modernist position implicitly involved a reassessment of the authority of the past. Like their eighteenth-century predecessors, they rejected *taqlid* (the authority of the medieval law schools), and advocated *ijtihad* (independent re-thinking) and *hadith*-based reform. Modernists, however, were far more radical in their reassessment of the *hadith* and *sunna*. Ahmad Khan expressed his view of Islam in the following revealing aphorism: 'the Qur'an is the Word of God, nature is the Work of God'. No modernist ever questioned the fundamental precept of Islam that the Qur'an was the eternal word of God. It provided the principles by which the individual and society were governed just as nature followed its own laws also created by God. From here Ahmad Khan was led to deny miracles as they contravened God's natural and immutable order. The Qur'an, he argued, did not support the view that some events could violate the laws of nature. Therefore, incidents recorded in the Qur'an which traditionally had been accepted as miraculous needed to be rationally reinterpreted: Moses' escape across the Red Sea (Q 26:63) by smiting the waters with his staff meant simply he had found a fordable path across it at low tide. Abduh fully upheld the natural order of cause and effect but argued more cautiously that miracles could not rationally be demonstrated to be impossible.

The nature of the Traditions (*hadith*) was quite another matter. Ahmad Khan questioned and finally rejected the supposed authenticity of almost the whole corpus. He dismissed the classical methods of *hadith* criticism and argued for new, rational methods of assessment, allowing only a handful of Traditions dealing with spiritual matters as relevant and binding on contemporary Muslims. For his part, Abduh expressed a slightly more cautious scepticism toward the Traditions but did open the way for personal judgement to determine which Traditions to accept or reject. Significantly, their positions meant that rather than interpreting the Qur'an in the light of Traditions, revelation could be understood solely on its own terms. In other words, Tradition literature and the *sunna* it contained no longer held equal status with the Qur'an but were subordinate to it. This approach did not belittle the stature of the Prophet in modernist eyes, but meant that the large amount of *sunna*'s minute detail which touched upon worldly matters was now judged to have been relevant only for the lifetime of the Prophet. Moreover, in a somewhat 'Protestant' fashion, the modernists implicitly proposed that each Muslim could search for scripture's meaning for him/herself.

Neither thinker worked out the implications of his position for the traditional understanding of the religious law (*shari'a*) and its application to public life. If the authenticity of *hadith* were questioned, severely affecting the scope of the *sunna*, the second most important foundation of the law was placed in peril. Both Abduh and Ahmad Khan appeared to be saying that rather than blindly adhering to the accumulated medieval corpus of the law, 'pure' and 'pristine' Islam had to be rediscovered by seriously adopting the Qur'anic proposition that 'God does not alter what is in a people until they alter what is in themselves' (Q 13:12). This verse became the banner of all modernist thought. It meant that rather than indiscriminate, literal acceptance of the past, Muslims had to shape their future based upon what might be called the public interest or welfare in order to meet the dramatically new circumstances of the modern era. The concept of 'public interest' or 'equitable preference' was known and discussed in the medieval legal literature. Critics of the modernist position represented by Ahmad Khan and Abduh and their followers, argued that its application in modern times was still subject to traditional legal norms and had to be supported and applied according to the four legal sources including the *sunna*. For example, both men concluded from close examination of the Qur'an *alone* that the traditional practice of polygamy was unjustified and monogamous marriage had always been God's clear intention. A more recent application of the principle has been in the banking system which is based upon the giving and taking of interest, a practice forbidden in Islamic law. The notion of Islamic banking rationalizes 'interest' as 'dividends' received by an investor from joint participation with the bank in its investment schemes.

The early unsystematic body of modernist ideas expounded by Ahmad Khan and Abduh may appear to have an air of unreality about them. Discussion over the nature of the *sunna* and prophetic authority was unlikely to affect the current reform of law along European lines in India and Egypt. British policy and secularist Muslims alike opposed building the modern state upon the medieval *shari'a*. Debate continued nonetheless. The supporters and detractors of *sunna* endorsed contrasting views of the purpose and scope of revelation. If the *sunna* was a form of revelation, it was eternal and immutable, embracing every area of individual and communal life in a fixed pattern of norms. Opponents of the *sunna* asserted that God revealed only the general principles of guidance in the Qur'an, leaving mankind to work out the details by reason themselves; hence each generation must draw its own conclusions from the Qur'an in tune with the circumstances of its day. Underlying this controversy is a contest over who possesses the proper authority to interpret the Qur'an. The traditional religious leadership (*ulama*) claimed their expertise in the *sunna* was indispensable to true Qur'anic interpretation while the more technocratic, modern, educated Muslim held that his understanding of the world best enabled him to make the Qur'an relevant to modern conditions. Even secularists have attempted to justify the separation of the spheres of religion and politics by referring to the Prophet's model Madinan community as secular.

In the climate of debate stimulated by modernist ideas over a 'return to the sources' and their relative authority, one writer, thinker and activist took the controversy onto new terrain by advocating an Islamic state. Sayyid Abu al-Ala Mawdudi (d. 1979) was born in India and moved to Pakistan after the partition of the subcontinent in 1947. Educated by his father at home and then largely by his own efforts, his career was dedicated to writing, especially as editor of a religious journal, the main instrument for dissemination of his views, from 1933 until his death. He also set out his teachings in a six-volume commentary on the Qur'an; together with his many other publications, he became one of the most widely read Muslim authors of the late twentieth century. He was founder and head of a political-religious movement from 1941 for the promotion of Islamic principles. He initially opposed the creation of Pakistan as he believed it would be run along secular European lines rather than built upon an Islamic foundation. His radical movement subsequently campaigned for Pakistan to become an Islamic state subject to sacred law.

Mawdudi attempted to steer a middle course between those who rejected *hadith* altogether and their opponents who held that *sunna* was part of revelation. He defended the necessity of the *sunna* for the stability of Islam, but demanded flexibility which would allow for adaptation to change. Simply put, he adopted the jurist's approach to the Traditions by closely examining their content and relevance to a given context rather than the technique of *sunna* experts who stressed the vital importance of the good character and reputation of the transmitters of *hadith*. Critics charged that Mawdudi's method was arbitrary by introducing an excessive degree of subjectivity to *hadith* criticism leading, in effect, to an unrestrained freedom in Qur'an interpretation. Secularists dismissed his blueprint for an Islamic state and society as puritan and totalitarian. Mawdudi described it as a 'theo-democracy' in which God remained sovereign but the people elected a temporal ruler who, like everyone, was subject to the divine law. His views influenced those of his Egyptian contemporary, Sayyid Qutb (d. 1966). Both men held a deep conviction that Muslims should conduct their entire lives according to God's law.

Traditional Islamic notions of authority are associated with the understanding of community (*umma*) as we have seen in an earlier section. The ideal triad of one God, one law and one community may have long since ceased to be historical reality but Muslims everywhere still retain a sense of belonging to the domain of Islam where Muslims control their own affairs. European colonial encroachment seriously challenged this sense of belonging. Calls to revive Islamic unity and solidarity to withstand European pressures have been widely popular but short lived and ultimately ineffective. The modern era introduced the powerful symbol of the secular nation state as competitor to the traditional informal view of the *umma*. A response characteristic of the modern era was the creation in 1962 of the Muslim World League based in Mecca. Its purpose is to co-ordinate affairs affecting Muslims throughout the *umma*, develop missionary work, and to discuss matters of Islamic jurisprudence and social welfare.

Shi'a Iran

Iran witnessed the most spectacular development anywhere in the modern Islamic world in the 1979 Revolution led by religious leader Ayatollah Khomeini. Out of the collapse of the Pahlavi regime of Muhammad Reza Shah the Islamic Republic of Iran was born, the most evident contemporary example of 'modernity-as-tradition'.

Shi'a scholars (*mujtahids*) had gained in power throughout the nineteenth century, consolidating their claim that certain experts among them could act as deputies of the last Hidden Imam who had 'vanished' a thousand years earlier. Although some scholars chose to remain politically quietist others threw their moral authority against attempts at European intervention in Iran and the corrupt misrule of the Shahs. Between 1906 and 1911 many became involved in, both for and against, the social movement known as the Constitutional Revolution. This raised the fundamental problem of whether authority rested in a humanly created law or the *shari'a* and whether sovereignty ultimately resided in the people rather than God. The same dilemmas had confronted the Sunni modernists treated above but their responses were muted and ineffectual in comparison to those of their Shi'a counterparts. This was due to the *ulama*'s historically less assertive role before political authority and their inability to build independent financial resources coupled in more recent times with the more controlling presence of a colonial power, as in India and Egypt.

The Constitutional Revolution ended the days of the Qajar dynasty to be replaced by the rule of a military leader who styled himself Reza Shah, founder of the new Pahlavi dynasty. His aim was Western-style modernization in the spirit of the secular reforms of his neighbour Kemal Ataturk in Turkey. These involved wholesale legal changes, the importation of European criminal, civil and commercial codes, and administrative centralization along French lines. Reform, however, went in tandem with political repression and a frontal attack on the influence of the *mujtahids*, policies also pursued by his son and successor Muhammad Reza Shah. Leading scholars wrote and preached against rising secularism and the growing climate of nationalism but remained aloof from direct political combat until the early 1960s when Khomeini called for the overthrow of the Shah. He was arrested and exiled in 1963 where he remained until his triumphant return in 1979.

Khomeini's radical interpretation of one strand of Shi'a thought produced his thesis for an Islamic government. In the absence of the Twelfth Imam and uncertainty as to the date of his return and further given the present state of corruption and despair in Iran, responsibility for its affairs could not be entrusted to tyrannical rulers like the Shah. Citing passages from the Qur'an and Prophetic Traditions he concludes that only those with knowledge of the sacred law, the jurists (*mujtahids*), could regulate Muslims' daily affairs and ensure the community's salvation. In other words, the jurists would assume all the tasks the Prophet Muhammad had performed. However, Khomeini's views provoked dissension among the *mujtahids* when he proposed that only one, the leading jurist or 'the source of emulation' (i.e. himself) was owed obedience by everyone including all other jurists. Khomeini's own interpretation of supreme spiritual and political leadership survived in practice until his death in 1989, although changes were introduced into the Iranian Constitution before that time.

Observers' fears, Western and Muslim alike, that Iran's example would spill over and ignite revolution in other Sunni countries have proved unfounded. Whether the regime

FIGURE 9.3 Faisal mosque

Worshippers on the steps of Faisal Mosque, Islamabad, Pakistan. Courtesy *Saudi Aramco World*/PADIA.

survives and adapts or is overthrown, it nevertheless sets a challenge in one sense for all developing, modernizing Muslim countries. The challenge is to what extent and in what ways Islam will be and remain authoritative as divine guidance in the lives of Muslims into the new millennium.

Gender and present trends

Earlier it was noted that the Muslim understanding of community and the self are closely related, even intertwined. This is illustrated by the daily prayer when Muslims around the *umma* worship in the direction of Mecca. Individually each Muslim worships alone before God while collectively prayers are offered from the community's spiritual heart, the birthplace of the Prophet. All Muslims, men and women, pray as equals in the eyes of God. Men and women congregate as equals to perform the annual pilgrimage in Mecca. The Qur'an (33:35) describes this spiritual relationship: 'Those who surrender themselves to God and are believers in the faith; who are devout, sincere, patient, humble, charitable, and chaste; who fast and keep constant remembrance of God – on these both men and women, God will bestow forgiveness and a rich reward.' Or again, God's promise to all is the same in that 'I will deny no man or woman among you the reward of their labours. You are the offspring of one another' (Q 3:195). The spiritual equality of men and women has been traditionally agreed and accepted. Questions of social equality, on the other hand, have throughout this century been a deeply contested field. The complexity of the issues is nowhere more evident than in debates on laws affecting family life and the role of women within it.

The family is the microcosm of society. A medieval view of Islamic society proposed that harmony and stability could be achieved ideally through the ruler's holding together the disparate but unequal segments of society in just and equitable balance. Likewise a harmonious and stable family can contribute to the greater good of the whole when the relationship between its parts (comprising adult males, females and children) is based upon equity. The goal was sincere while nevertheless frankly acknowledging the patriarchal dominance of the husband within the family, thereby privileging male power. Traditional legal doctrine and thought upheld a system of roles and rights in matters of marriage, divorce and parental responsibilities based on gender. Jurists agreed that the Muslim marital relationship was one of complementarity but not of equality. As recent studies of some pre- and early-modern Islamic societies have shown, the interpretive ability of the jurists and the discretion of the judges allowed them to respond flexibly and with independent judgement to concrete cases brought before them. They worked to prevent or correct abuses when male privilege threatened the harmony and stability of the family. The legal process they oversaw was one of negotiation and judicial discretion. With no conscious sense of paradox, they strove to uphold the gendered social system, but attempted to modify it in part, always from their sense of responsibility to dispense justice for all, men, women and children, under God's law.

Modernist thought has sought in several ways to reduce customary male privilege within the family: by arguing that the Qur'an's true intent supported monogamous marriage, not polygamy; by raising the minimum age of marriage for young men and women and thereby abolishing child marriages; by restricting the male right of divorce and increasing the grounds upon which women may sue for termination of marriage and by adjustment to the traditional laws affecting the custody of children in the event of dissolution of marriage. Profound structural changes in modern Muslim societies – among them the promotion of equal education for girls and boys and economic pressures forcing women onto the job market, male migration in search of better work opportunities – have further eroded the age-old patriarchal edifice. Positive results in practice, however, have been very unequal from one country or region to the next throughout the *umma*. Debates about the place of religion in the modern state, the very nature of that state, the place of the family in modern society and the very nature of the family, the role of men and women within life's private and public spheres, all are being conducted along a spectrum ranging from pure secularists at one end to advocates of religious purity at the other. All engaged in these debates today seek answers to the same two questions: first, 'How does God speak?' (through the Qur'an and *sunna* or by His Word alone), and second, 'Who may speak for God?' (that is, who is best equipped to interpret His will and command for the modern era).

Postscript to 9/11

In the West – before the tragic events of 11 September 2001 – these questions were of little interest except to academics engaged in the study of Islam. Indeed, the 'how' question continues to be confined chiefly to scholarly concern: the Muslim secularist reads the Qur'an alone for guidance in his or her personal life while the so-called 'fundamentalist' examines scripture and the *sunna* as a divine blueprint for the construction of a Muslim utopia. The vague slogan 'Islam is the solution' became popular among groups with commitment to a variety of faith-based programmes and, if political, for the most part non-violent. In the wake of 9/11, however, a sense of urgency swept through the corridors of government in North America and Europe and the question 'who speaks for God?' became of immediate relevance.

The shadowy menace of al-Qaeda, led by the video-phantom Osama bin Laden, seemed to provide a straightforward answer. Both had been linked to criminal attacks against American interests in Africa and Arabia during the 1990s. Shortly after the events of 9/11 Bin Laden declared in a taped broadcast that, 'events have divided the world into two camps, the camp of the faithful and the camp of the infidels . . . Every Muslim must rise to defend his religion.' That same evening, the American President, George W. Bush, spoke on national television. He announced that, 'In this conflict, there is no neutral ground. If any government sponsors the outlaws and killers of innocents, they have become outlaws and murderers themselves.' The conflict, therefore, involved each side in a cosmic struggle in which all must join one or the other side while a possible middle ground of reasoned moderation and reflection was explicitly rejected. In the United States, critics of the government's invasion of Iraq in 2003 were intimidated from voicing their views for fear of being labelled unpatriotic towards the so-called 'war on terror'. In Britain, massive public demonstrations against the war were possible, if ultimately ineffective. Nonetheless, criticisms that the invasion and occupation of Iraq would encourage the spread of terrorist acts were brushed aside by government ministers, despite contrary warnings from their own security services.

In these circumstances – viewed from the West's perspective of its 'war on terror' – the chief Muslim culprits formed a group of criminal extremists, namely al-Qaeda and its sympathisers. From the attacks on New York and Washington (2001) through those on the commuter trains in Madrid (2003) and the London underground (2005) to the assassination of former Pakistan Prime Minister Benazir Bhutto (2007), the bloody hand of al-Qaeda was readily discerned. Al-Qaeda supplied an easy answer to the question of who spoke for God. Without dispute, Muslims were the perpetrators of these and other crimes whether or not they were directly the work of al-Qaeda. Nonetheless in every case Muslims, too, were among the innocent victims, a fact not lost upon Muslim commentators although generally overlooked by their Western counterparts.

The United States' 'war *on* terror' was ironically characterized and defined by its own 'war *of* terror'. The carpet bombing of Afghanistan employing the latest lethal technology was followed by the invasion of Iraq where a link between al-Qaeda and Saddam Hussain had been declared but never demonstrated. The major claim justifying the invasion, vigorously pressed by the USA and Britain, was that Saddam possessed weapons of mass destruction ready for immediate deployment. This also proved totally false. The Iraq operation was named 'Shock and Awe' after a US military doctrine developed in the 1990s designed to create 'fears, dangers and destruction that are incomprehensible to the people at large . . . or to the leadership'. In addition, evidence slowly emerged of the torture and humiliation of Iraqis in the Abu Ghraib prison in Baghdad and of hundreds of other Muslims held in Guantanamo Bay. In these American-run prisons torture to extract information seemed secondary to the attempt to break the personalities of those under detention. Well-known techniques such as sensory deprivation and overload and simulated drowning known as 'water boarding' were supplemented by insults specifically aimed at the prisoners as Muslims. These ranged from the forced shaving of beards, being wrapped in the Israeli flag, to the desecration of the Qur'ans they were allowed to read. Symptoms of regression to childlike behaviour were reported among many of these prisoners. The practice of extraordinary rendition is strongly believed responsible for Muslims seized illegally by American agents being sent to foreign-run jails for interrogation. Israel's own contributing war of terror against terrorism, sanctioned by Washington, witnessed the destruction of the Palestinian Authority's infrastructure on the West bank in 2002 and the similar devastation of Lebanon in 2006.

A consequence of the crude 'us versus them' war was to broaden the identity of the enemy by the re-emergence of an older suspicion in the West. Often dormant but never dead, Islam itself was viewed as essentially antipathetic to core Western values, and inherently violent in nature; conflict with Muslims was seen as inevitable, not because of any particular grievances Muslims held against the West, but rather owing to its very existence and nature. The views of the overwhelming majority of moderate Muslim thinkers on the West's war on terror were easily ignored as they, too, became regarded a potential, if not a present, threat to Western civilization.

Since Bin Laden was seen as a dangerous, fanatic religious leader, many Western observers failed to grasp how his political message might be received by Muslims. When he called for the gratuitous death of Americans and their Jewish allies wherever they may be found, mainstream Muslims knew this command ran counter to the very letter and spirit of their historical faith. On the other hand, Bin Laden's repeated stress upon political flashpoints such as Palestine, Chechnya, Bosnia, and Iraq resonated with these same Muslims. In these situations, Muslims were under occupation or caught in ethnic conflicts where Western governments had either been slow to seek their resolution (Bosnia), or were seen as applying double standards to the parties in conflict (Palestine/ Israel) or had violently overthrown one dictator (Iraq) while actively supporting others (Egypt, Pakistan, Uzbekistan). Possibly the most provocative political decision by the European Union and the United States was to sideline Hamas when it had resoundingly won the elections for the Palestine Authority, a process which foreign observers agreed was fair and free. It should come as no surprise that thinking Muslims question many Western government policies, while at the same time they seek many of democracy's positive benefits, denied them in Muslim countries.

So, who does speak for God among Muslims today? The answer may at first appear to be 'almost anyone and everyone'. There are, however, in the broadest sense, two discrete tendencies, within each of which several strands may be discerned. The first tendency owes much to the spirit of debate within the medieval Islamic jurists' culture. It will be recalled that in Sunni Islam, there are four main schools of legal thought, each with its own methods, legal injunctions and rules, all considered appropriate. Working with the material sources of the law, the Qur'an and *hadith*, jurists acknowledged their task was to uncover the divine purpose behind each question brought to them. God's will could be known only through the jurist's subjective interpretation. Hence no specific, correct solution to each problem was possible, only a careful balancing of all the evidence. Crucial was the jurist's faithful and diligent effort to reach a preponderance of belief on a particular issue. As certainty could never be achieved, all legal responses were held to be equally valid. Contemporary Muslim scholars, influenced by this tendency, men as well as women, have written and spoken publicly on matters they regard as urgent concerns to their societies, such as democracy, pluralism, human rights and gender issues.

Scholars who follow the second tendency approach the Qur'an and *hadith* in a literalist fashion. They adhere to a medieval juristic view that every legal problem does have a correct solution but that it is known only to God who will reveal the true response on the Final Day. Jurists of this tendency in practice appear to find themselves in the same position as those above inasmuch they cannot know for certain whether they have found the correct solution to a problem, although they are also commended for their effort in the search. A key difference is that their position does not entail recognition that all legal responses are in practice equally valid. In the hands of modern literalists the complex and contested nature of the medieval jurists' culture is effectively reduced to unequivocal religious commands and prohibitions. This is achieved by simply declaring – without an accompanying methodology to demonstrate the claim – that the sacred sources are themselves clear and unambiguous so that disagreement could scarcely arise. And since no disagreement should arise on the fundamentals of religion, literalists proceed to enlarge the scope of these basics so as to reduce debate further to a very few marginal issues. The result is a rigorous authoritarian system, illustrated today by important strands within legal circles in Saudi Arabia, justified simply on the grounds that religious truth is what literal interpretation claims it to be.

The contrasting ethos of these two approaches is profound. In the first, historical change is acknowledged, as is the fact that the divine law, the moral sovereignty of God, stands alongside political sovereignty that belongs to the citizens of the modern state. In the authoritarian version, God is the only legitimate legislator and the divine will revealed during the Prophet Muhammad's lifetime remains valid for all time. This latter approach can lead in extreme cases to an adherent's assertion that he speaks in God's name because he knows the mind of God. Tensions between these two tendencies are expressed in ideological and sometimes political conflict, whereas the spiritual strand of Sufism which has achieved renewed vigour in recent decades views the other tendencies, particularly their politicization, with a certain indifference.

To sum up. Well before 9/11 some Western intellectuals had warned of a 'clash of civilizations'. They explicitly identified the protagonist as the West and its chief antagonist, Islam. 9/11 itself was the act of an extremist criminal gang which successfully exploited known weaknesses in American airport security systems. The atrocity, while not confirming the 'clash' thesis, did present the opportunity for a group of American analysts and their political supporters in Washington (backed by London) to push a policy for the political and economic transformation of the Middle East through violent military means, or 'shock and awe', all in the name of the war on terror. Among that campaign's living victims have been Muslims everywhere of good conscience and moderate political persuasion, whatever their religious tendency, who condemned 9/11 just as earlier they had roundly condemned the now almost forgotten Srebrenica massacre of Muslims in Bosnia in 1995. The efforts to bring the perpetrators of this latter atrocity to justice pale into insignificance against the billions of dollars (not to mention the accompanying massive destruction) poured into the as yet unsuccessful defeat of al-Qaeda. There are signs that moderates everywhere, both Muslim and other, are starting to exercise a new political influence, but the extreme positions on either side remain powerful.

Summary

- Although Islam is today spreading in Europe and North America, Muslims historically have belonged overwhelmingly to the non-Western world. The experience of 'modernity' for Muslims, therefore, was bound to differ from that of Christians in the West.

- Islamic revivalist movements in the eighteenth century set the tone of later modernist developments in a call for a 'return to the sources' and the use of independent judgement towards them.

- Modernist reformers confronted European colonialism and the modern values and institutions which it brought; the debates in response throughout the twentieth century reflect historical change on the patterns of 'tradition-in-modernity' and/or 'modernist-as-tradition'.

Key terms

din Faith tradition, used in the Qur'an to refer to the beliefs and practices of a people.

hadith A Tradition or report, being the source for the *sunna* of the Prophet.

hajj Pilgrimage to Mecca once in a lifetime if a believer is able; one of the obligatory religious duties for all Muslims.

ijtihad The use of one's personal effort to arrive at a legal decision not found in the Qur'an or *sunna*.

Imam Title of each of the line of twelve religious leaders of the Shi'a who are the source of authority in the community.

jihad Internal, personal struggle in the faith; in a more general sense, 'holy war'.

Khalifa Caliph, leader of the Sunni community.

mujtahid Used among both Sunni and Shi'a communities to mean a jurist qualified to exercise his individual effort (*ijtihad*) in arriving at legal decisions.

Rasul Allah Messenger of God; referring to the Prophet's role as deliverer of the Qur'an.

salat One of the five daily prayers required of all Muslims.

sawm Fasting during the month of Ramadan, one of the obligatory duties for all Muslims; according to tradition, the Qur'an was revealed in this same month.

shari'a The sacred law in Sunni Islam based upon four sources, **Qur'an**, *sunna*, consensus and analogy; the major law schools are known as Maliki, Hanbali, Hanafi and Shafi'i.

Sufism (or *tasawwuf*) The way of inner spirituality in Islam, generally referred to as 'mysticism'.

sunna The model behavior of the Prophet collected and recorded in **hadith** reports; one of the sources of the four Sunni schools of law together with the Qur'an, consensus and argument by analogy.

taqwa Piety, or guarding against the consequences of one's behavior.

'ulama (sg. *'alim*) Learned class of scholars in religious matters.

umma Community; worldwide community of Muslims.

zakat Alms or purification tax, one of the obligatory 'five pillars' for Muslims.

Further reading

K. Abou el Fadl: *Islam and the Challenge of Democracy* (Princeton, NJ: Princeton University Press, 2004). An important discussion and debate of this crucial subject.

D. Brown: *Rethinking Tradition in Modern Islamic Thought* (Cambridge: Cambridge University Press, 1996). Excellent discussion of modern Muslim debates on authority.

J. Esposito (ed.): *The Oxford Encyclopedia of the Modern Islamic World* (Oxford: Oxford University Press, 1995). The leading reference work on Islam in the modern world.

D. Eickelman and J. Piscatori: *Muslim Politics* (Princeton, NJ: Princeton University Press, 1996). Explores how the politics of Islam unfold in the daily lives of Muslims.

W. Hallaq: *A History of Islamic Legal Theories: An Introduction to Sunni Usual* al-Fiqh (Cambridge: Cambridge University Press, 1997). Contains a very good chapter on modern developments.

M.Z. Husain: *Global Islamic Politics* (New York: Harper Collins, 1995). Deals with various categories of Muslim revivalists.

G. Nonneman, T. Niblock and B. Szajkowski (eds): *Muslim Communities in Europe*, (London: Ithaca, 1996). Covers communities in both Eastern and Western Europe.

F. Rahman: *Islam and Modernity: Transformation of an Intellectual Tradition* (Chicago, IL: Chicago University Press, 1982). The now classic work by a leading Muslim thinker.

A. Rippin: *Muslims: Their Religious Beliefs and Practices*, vol. 2: *The contemporary period* (London: Routledge, 2001). A useful introduction to the impact of modernity on Islam.

C. El-Solh and J. Mabro (eds): *Muslim Women's Choices; Religious Belief and Social Reality* (Oxford: Berg, 1994). Presents a cross-cultural perspective of Muslim women's experiences and choices.

J. Voll: *Islam: Continuity and Change in the Modern World* (Syracuse, NJ: Syracuse University Press, 1994). Attempts universal coverage of Islam from the eighteenth century.

Mai Yamani (ed.): *Feminism and Islam: Legal and Literary Perspectives* (London: Ithaca, 1996). Muslim women and their efforts to improve their status through a re-reading of their rights in Islamic law.

Chapter 10

Religion in Africa

Charles Gore

of influence in claiming such territories. However, it needs to be noted that many African economies were already linked to Europe through prior mercantile capitalism in complex ways, the most tragic and inhumane example being the mass-trafficking of Africans across the Atlantic Ocean.

These colonial partitions engendered radical changes in political organization, territorial demarcations, and the development of social and economic infrastructures that articulated new but unequal linkages with the European colonizing nations, together with the imposition of bureaucracies that managed these new territorial units. An imperialist desire for monopolistic economic control and increased exploitation of commodity resources (required by the manufacturing processes of European industrialization) allied to the ideological justifications of spreading Christianity and 'European civilization' fostered an intense competition between the European powers. This colonial partitioning of Africa is commonly described as 'the scramble for Africa' and took place in the last two decades of the nineteenth century.

Once territory was seized – despite armed resistance in many instances – the major administrative structures of the European colonies were gradually put in place. These developed differently in relation to territories used for permanent European settlement that allowed for direct control of all resources, and territories that were not settled by Europeans. Large areas of Africa, particularly in west and equatorial Africa where environmental health conditions were seen as particularly inimical to Europeans, were not utilized for settlement, and in these a policy of rule through existing African political hierarchies was developed – most explicitly by the British in the colonial doctrine of Indirect Rule codified by Lord Lugard in 1906 and further validated in the 1920s. However, European administrators lacked detailed knowledge of pre-colonial forms of governance, were subject to manipulation by competing local African interests, and imposed hierarchial colonial orderings that suited their imperialist and bureaucratic interests rather than corresponded to precolonial conditions.

Although territorial partition of Africa had for the most part been completed by 1904 (with some readjustments at the end of World War I), consolidation was uneven and varied greatly between colonies. In general terms, colonialism centred on the expropriation of labour and land in order to extract the economic resources of the colonies. In more concrete terms, colonialism involved the introduction of standardized currencies regulated by the colonizing nation; development of new transport links; and the emergence of new or expanded urban centres that attracted migrants from rural areas. It was accompanied by the emergence of new social groups and formations equipped with the skills required by the colonial enterprise. Although locked into unequal political, economic and cultural relations with the dominant colonizing nation, these relations also linked the African colonies to the processes of modernity, albeit along trajectories specific to African contexts.

The 1940s saw the rise of nationalist movements in Africa, and decolonization commenced with Ghana (the former Gold Coast) gaining independence in 1957. However, in many of the settler colonies throughout Africa the tide of nationalism was resisted, often encouraging armed struggle such as the Mau Mau uprising in Kenya against the British in 1952. Independence was conceded to most colonies by the mid-1960s, although the Portuguese colonies remained obdurate until the mid-1970s. Zimbabwe and South Africa remained notable exceptions shored up socially by their large European settler communities and economically through their greater integration into the world economy – here democracy was not gained until 1980 and 1994 respectively. With decolonization came an increased drive for modernization as planned programmes of national economic self-development were implemented in many of the newly independent African nation states. However the economies of these new nation states were still structured by their origins as dependent colonies fashioned to extract the maximum resources for the benefit of the colonizer. One consequence has been the perpetuation of often unequal economic relations to the world markets as part of the postcolonial experience.

This chapter opens with a look at the three main forms of religion present in sub-Saharan Africa: Indigenous religions, Islam and Christianity. It also considers the significance of the Western missionary movement in Africa. In its central sections it explores the most salient features of indigenous African religions in the modern world, highlighting how 'indigenous' religious beliefs and practices have been transformed or shaped by the impact of modernity. The chapter then considers the place of Islam and Christianity in modern sub-Saharan Africa and the ways in which both religions have been aligned to their African contexts, before turning to a consideration of recent changes and innovations in religion in Africa.

Sources and resources

Indigenous religions

In the localized forms of indigenous religion found in sub-Saharan Africa, there is an emphasis on participation in religious or ritual activities which usually precedes the acquisition of religious knowledge. The specialist esoteric religious or ritual knowledge is often restricted in access and gained only by induction into long apprenticeship or initiation. In contrast to the world religions that are exclusive in terms of affiliation (one cannot be a Christian *and* a Muslim), indigenous religious frameworks are often open-ended, allowing individuals to acquire and accumulate various and different forms of religious experience according to need and inclination. Moreover, few indigenous religions separate out material from spiritual experience (unlike Judaeo-Christian traditions which often draw a contrast between the material and spiritual). In indigenous African religions the two spheres are considered interdependent, such that events in the material world are predicated on relations to the spiritual world – but open to individual, and sometimes contested, interpretation. As a consequence much 'indigenous' or 'traditional' religion centres on the well-being of the community or social grouping through explanation, prediction and control of events. Although it is possible to extrapolate coherent or systemized doctrines and cosmologies of a particular community (such as the classic example of the anthropologist

Griaule's exploration of the religion and cosmology of the Dogon peoples of Mali in conversations with Ogonmetilli [1965]), this emphasis on the experiential means that such abstractions or rationalizations of cosmology are not necessarily shared by all members of community (although there may be the insightful reflections and interpretations of a particular individual). Analysis that gives undue emphasis to such systematized abstraction overlooks the dynamism, creativity and innovation available within African religious processes.

Many of these localized indigenous forms of religion and ritual rely on oral traditions, which makes it difficult to chart their historical trajectories and the ways in which change has taken place. But this feature gives much flexibility in adapting to changing social circumstances, migration and diverse physical environments. Religious ideas and practice can vary from adjacent community to community, but others spread over wide geographical areas and cross social, linguistic and ethnic divides. Similarly, even where religious ideas differ between communities and different societies, many of the assumptions upon which they are based are shared over wider regional areas. What varies is the way in which they are articulated within different societies that can range in organization from kingdoms and empires to petty chiefdoms to less hierarchical and non-centralized communities. But a defining characteristic in the twentieth and early twenty-first century is that all these different socio-political formations are now situated within postcolonial African nation states with their hegemonic bureaucratic infrastructures.

Islam and Christianity

Historically the geographical barrier of the Sahara did not preclude the diffusion of the world religions of Christianity and Islam. Islam spread southward along the trans-Saharan trade routes from the eighth century CE onwards, with conversion taking place on a reciprocal basis between trading partners (a process whereby an individual conversion to Islam occurred as a personal choice within a primarily non-Islamic society as a means of securing trust and economic credit with an external Islamic trading partner). But by the fourteenth century CE the rulers of the empire of Mali in the northern savannah (that stretched between the upper regions of the rivers Senegal and Niger) had embraced Islam. A record of a stay in Cairo in the fourteenth century CE during a pilgrimage to Mecca by one of its greatest rulers Mansa Musa describes how his lavish expenditure in gold caused a devaluation in the value of money at that time. Christianity spread from lower Egypt, reaching Meroe and Axum by the fourth century CE, and then to Ethiopia in East Africa where it has maintained a historical continuity up to the present day with the orthodox Ethiopian Coptic church as the official state religion. Christianity was also disseminated by European mercantile traders and missionaries from the fifteenth century CE onwards; they followed the Atlantic sea routes along the West and Central African coast, occasionally gaining an insecure and temporary purchase in some societies. A notable success was the adoption of Christianity by Mbanza Kongo, the ruler of the Kongo kingdom in Central Africa in 1491, along with many of his elite followers. Despite the political disintegration of the kingdom in 1665 and the disappearance of Christianity by the beginning of the eighteenth century CE, Christian iconographic elements such as the crucifix were incorporated into local religious practices and are evident up to the present day.

Along the East African coast there arose a series of trading centres incorporating a mix of Arabian, African and Indian populations that linked eastern Africa to the Indian Ocean with the importation of iron goods in exchange for gum, spices, ivory and horn. These trading centres became a conduit for the spread of Islam from the eighth century CE onwards resulting in the emergence of a relatively homogenous mercantile coastal corridor up to the present day (that did not preclude political and social diversity). By the eleventh century CE this corridor stretched from the Somali coast in the north to what is now Mozambique in the south, having in common shared social and economic ties underpinned by Islam and the Swahili language.

The missionary impact

Though Islam and Christianity have had a longstanding presence in certain areas of sub-Saharan Africa, the nineteenth and twentieth centuries saw an intensification and expansion of their influence. In relation to Christianity this expansion was initiated by European missionary activity. In 1787 a Christian settlement was established on the coast of Sierra Leone for Africans liberated from slavery as well as, among others, loyalists of Afro-American descent who had fought on the side of the British in the American War of Independence. This founding of a Christian settlement inspired the modern missionary movement to evangelize among the indigenous peoples of sub-Saharan Africa. Various mission societies were set up by different Christian denominations including the prominent Protestant Church Missionary Society (CMS). Christian missionaries (who were prominent in the successful drive to abolish the slave trade in the nineteenth century) were active along the coasts of Africa throughout the nineteenth century, following in the footsteps of the coastal trading enclaves of the European nations that had developed in their pursuit of trade for commodities from the interior such as rubber and palm oil. Much of the program of conversion of peoples of the interior was left to African missionaries – the most notable example being Bishop Samuel Ajai Crowther of the CMS who travelled extensively into the interior of what is now Southern Nigeria to proselytize. At least initially, successful conversion mainly began with the marginalized or outcast in indigenous societies.

In many ways colonialism and mission went hand in hand. In the drive for conversion missions imparted education as part of the Christianizing process. Education offered many useful skills relevant to the colonial state which gave an added momentum to conversion to Christianity. However the concomitant hierarchical imperialist ideologies that accompanied the establishment of the colonies also saw the replacement and subordination of African ministers by European missionaries as Christianity was institutionalized as a religion allied to the colonial state. In time this exclusion would precipitate the establishment of independent African churches headed by

Africans. Such churches attracted congregations drawn from the growing urbanized African populace that had acquired literacy and the attendant clerical skills required by colonial bureaucracies. These congregations embraced the modernity expressed in the 'innovation' of Christian religion, while at the same time rejecting European churches and developing Africanized forms of worship which subsequently dispersed to rural populations.

However, the relationship between mission and colonialism was often complex. The agendas of the European missionaries who wished to recreate African society within the framework of the Christian faith did not always coincide with the colonial project. The high costs of imposing martial law on African societies meant that colonial administrators in the interests of civil order, where expedient, supported indigenous political hierarchies such as those based around the institution of sacred kingship. In effect colonial administrations, utilized and co-opted such indigenous institutions to govern, even where the latter were legitimized by indigenous religious ideas and practices abhorred by missionaries. But other religious leaders, not recognized by the colonial authorities as part of traditional kingship or chieftaincy, were carefully monitored for the threats they posed to civil order. In more extreme instances they were dealt with through military interventions (as, for example, in the British suppression of the charismatic prophets of the Nuer indigenous religion in the Sudan during the 1920s). Similarly, the emergence of African-led Christian and Islamic institutions which successfully recruited through mass conversions were also closely monitored. Missionaries, particularly from non-conformist denominations, were sometimes placed in an ambiguous position in relation to colonial authority when they defended the interests of their converted communities against the depredations of state or other opportunist exploitation. A striking example is found in the brutal atrocities and exploitation of populations in the Congo Free State in central Africa controlled as a personal dominion by King Leopold of Belgium: these abuses were highlighted in print by the Afro-American Presbyterian missionary William Sheppard from 1900 onwards. Their exposure would ultimately precipitate a Congo mass reform movement in Europe and its handover to the Belgium nation state in 1908.

Further evidence of the important link between Christianity and colonialism is provided by the fact that the colonized in some areas, such as in Senegal, adopted Islam as a means to assert alternative forms of identity. Islam provided access to different resources of moral power and legitimacy that had long been a component of their societies, and challenged the coercive colonial hierarchies of secular power and authority. In colonies where rapid mass conversion to Islam took place, the colonial authorities often discouraged Christian missions as a direct threat to civil order. Indeed the Islamic emirates which developed in the Hausa-speaking areas of what is now northern Nigeria in the first half of the nineteenth century as a result of the great reformist movement (which sought to purify Islam of elements deemed pagan) led by the Islamic cleric Sheik Uthman Dan Fodio, were held up by Lord Lugard and the British colonial administrations as an ideal exemplar of an indigenous political hierarchy that the colonial Indirect Rule policy could utilize.

Islam and Christianity continued to make inroads in the conversion of the populations of Africa in the twentieth century, penetrating all areas of the continent. Islamic and Christian missionaries generally sought to undermine local indigenous religious ideas and practices and aspired to provide 'universal' religious frameworks for adherents in their place. In their conjunction with the particular historical trajectories of the colonial enterprise their effect was also to help implement major social reorderings. In the postcolonial order they became key institutions within the new secular nation states of sub-Saharan Africa. None of these developments, however, have meant the disappearance or exclusion of localized forms of 'indigenous' or 'traditional' religious experience, nor resulted in the syncretization or merging of local 'indigenous' beliefs with the world religions. Much more common has been a compartmentalized positioning of individuals in relation to both indigenous religions *and* Christianity or Islam. This overlapping accommodation and dialectic with the world religions underlines the dynamic and creative qualities of religious experience in Africa.

Interactions with modernity

The modern period in sub-Saharan Africa has witnessed the transition from precolonial forms of social organization, to their subjection within colonial structures of domination, to the emergence of autonomous nation states. Although independence has been achieved, these nation states are still locked into capitalist economic formations shaped by the needs of Western societies and their transnational corporations. As a result sub-Saharan nation states are often unable to control economic flows out of their territories, and any consequent political instability can engender conflict and political violence as well as the accumulation of debt in relation to the international banking community. Such factors in turn contribute to a weakening of the state and its bureaucracies as the principal means of organization of these nation states. However this retreat or transformation of the state provides a postcolonial space for the emergence and shaping of alternative and multiple identities that draw on the diverse histories and cultural resources available from the post-independent, colonial and precolonial periods, including religion. Religious repertoires in sub-Saharan Africa establish continuities with the past as well as positioning themselves as part of the processes of African modernity.

In considering such religious repertoires here, themes and topics are selected to highlight key characteristics associated with 'indigenous' or 'traditional' religious ideas and practice – although it needs to be noted that many of these are innovations of the twentieth century and do not necessarily have the historical continuity with precolonial Africa that they may claim, even though seemingly legitimized in this way as 'traditional'. Exploration of these themes begins in relation to the individual and kinship, and then moves outwards to take account of the social orderings of institutions as they articulate and shape relations of power and authority within contemporary society. Account is also taken of some of the major studies and debates relating to the interpretation of these phenomena.

Ancestors, elders and community

In many African societies, but not all, conceptualizations of the ancestors play an important role in structuring religious experience and social life – so much so that African kin groups are sometimes described as communities of both the living and the dead. Ancestors are distinguished from other cults of the dead by virtue of being named forebears with specific genealogical relations to a particular grouping of descendants that is mediated by collective rituals. They can reward and punish the living lineage members, a power that underpins the authority of elders who ritually mediate on behalf of the ancestors through their closer proximity in terms of age.

The role of the ancestor can vary considerably from society to society. One example of the way in which ancestor worship relates to social organization comes from the classic study by Fortes (1989) of the Tallensi-speaking people of Northern Ghana. Their society is organized without forms of centralized authority, and they practise subsistence farming focused on a family unit of a father, his wives and the adult sons and their wives. These family units are organized into patrilineages descended from a single common ancestor. There is little material wealth and consequently little differentiation in material terms between one individual and another. However ritual and jural authority is vested in the men who have the status of fathers and during their lifetime their offspring have no independent economic, jural or ritual rights except through the father. The relationship between father and sons is marked out with ritual prescriptions of behaviour that ameliorate the conflictual tensions between the generations, which also tend to increase as the sons marry and become fathers themselves. Fortes observes that in Tallensi society all events are dependent on the ancestors to whom shrines are established and suggests that the ancestors encapsulate an idiom of 'parental' relations of absolute authority over the succeeding generations which can only be accessed through the father.

However, this is mediated by the capability of individuals to discover through divination and dreams knowledge of their pre-natal destiny, which is given by special relations with particular groupings of ancestors unique to each individual. Prior to birth the individual appears before a remote supreme being to choose certain ancestors who provide guidance throughout life. Fortes suggests that this plurality of ancestors, both in their absolute relations of power and in their individuated configurations, provides complex and resourceful means for individuals in Tallensi society to negotiate success and adversity as they pass through the succession of rigidly ascribed statuses during the course of their lives.

This theoretical model was taken up by Horton (1983) who develops it further to argue that there is a correlation between the spiritual agencies available in a society and the forms of social organization of that society. He compares the near-exclusive control of the ancestors in Tallensi society (linked to its rigidly ascribed statuses) with the wider range of roles available in other societies, including the Kalabari of the Nigerian riverine delta where he conducted most of his research. Kalabari society depends on fishing along the swamps and creeks which are accessible to all male members within a community's domain. In each community there are a variable number of lineages of differing size organized on the basis of a dual system of marriage, whereby high bride price affiliates the children to the father's group, while low bride price affiliates the children to the mother's group. As a consequence descent can be traced through the male and female lines from a lineage founder. However the different lineage founders within the community are considered to be unrelated so that village unity is organized through territorial isolation, political autonomy, an age-grade system that shapes collective identity, and a shared cultural repertoire centring most notably around masquerade displays (Horton, 1963).

Some settlements such as New Calabar historically expanded as a series of canoe houses. These consisted of closely knit trading and war-canoe teams that ruled through an elected head who was often comparatively young and chosen for his abilities in trade and war. The heterogeneous diversity of recruited members (some were slaves purchased from the Atlantic trade) of these expanded houses was overcome by creating fictitious descent that represented its organization in notional terms of a lineage with the founding ancestor. As houses expanded, successful and ambitious traders could apply to establish their own canoe-houses. In Kalabari society, whether fishing settlement or city state, there was and is considerable scope for self-advancement of individuals by using an advantageous choice of economic trading partners and networks. Women are able to trade equally successfully and, although not able to intervene directly in the public political arena, gain much influence through the profession of divining, in which they are possessed by water spirits.

The individual in Kalabari society can thus choose among a diversity of roles and routes to economic and social success which, according to Horton are represented in the spiritual agencies available. In Kalabari society there are both the founding heroes of the community that protect the entire community, as well as the founding ancestors who sustain the unity and prosperity of the lineages. These ancestors are able to reward harmonious living with success, and punish disruptive conduct that endangers the lineage with sickness and misfortune. However, in Kalabari society individuals can also draw on the powers of the water spirits that reside in the creeks who bring economic success in return for human devotion. These water spirits are sited in the natural world rather than in the human community (such as the ancestors and founding heroes), and engage in particular relations with an individual. As among the Tallensi, Kalabari individuals are considered to appear before a remote supreme being prior to birth to make prenatal choices. Here, however, there are more options open to individuals from which to choose a particular course for their future life with a greater variety of spiritual agencies to assist them. Moreover, if they fail in their personal life there are rituals through which they may revoke their choices and replace them with a new set of goals. In contrast to the Tallensi where only men chose guardian ancestors, both men and women in Kalabari society chose and developed relationships with spiritual agencies emphasizing the wider spectrum of social and economic possibilities available for both genders. These spiritual agencies, rooted in the social world and also the natural world, are thereby linked to the achieved statuses of Kalabari society where individual initiative, skill and effort play a crucial role in their successful attainment.

In the late twentieth century such conceptualizations of the ancestors still form an important part of individual and collective identity. They define and validate particular corporate kin groups who are obligated to mutual support (with the threat of punitive sanctions from the ancestors) in relation to wider social groupings. The often predatory nature of the nation state in the late twentieth century, with little or no provision of social security for its citizens, underlines the necessity of this mutual support provided by the kin group (however constituted) in order to guarantee personal security. The delineation of the ancestors within the social environment also contributes to collective claims to ownership of land in precedence to later incoming migrant groups and is often utilized in maintaining particular ethnic identities. Furthermore, claims to ownership of land, buttressed by ancestral claims, often shape and mediate the ways in which the nation state regulates and distributes land resources in relation to local communities (a contentious political and social issue in resource-rich areas – as is demonstrated in the civil disturbances of the oil bearing regions of the delta areas of Nigeria in the 1990s).

Masquerade, spirits and embodiment

In many societies in Africa relations between the living and the spirit world are enacted through masquerade performance. Here relations with the spirit world are embodied in the masquerade figures. Masquerade performances usually, but not always, entail some form of masking and, through whatever means, establish a social or dramatic distancing of the masquerade performer. A convention of most masquerade is that the identity of the individual performer remains secret and participation in masquerade usually requires access to restricted or initiated knowledge that marks out the boundaries of a collective membership.

Throughout most of sub-Saharan Africa masquerade is differentiated on the basis of gender, being a male organization from which women are excluded – although representations of women often appear among the masquerade forms. The masquerader is recognised as an embodied agency from the spirit world vested with the appropriate social, political and spiritual powers. Masquerade often enacts a collective as opposed to personal authority within the community that can be used beneficially or punitively. But in some contexts it is also used to criticise those in power without the fear of retribution. This is possible because such commentaries emanate from the collective authority of the spirit world and not from identified, and therefore vulnerable, individuals in the community.

One of the most well known masquerade complexes is the Poro secret society cluster which is found in various forms throughout the petty chiefdoms of Sierra Leone and Liberia. All boys are taken into the bush to be initiated at puberty by the great spirit Poro, who originated deep in the forest and is assisted by lesser spirits who appear masked among the community (unlike the spirit of Poro which is only heard and always remains unseen). The boys spend two or three years in the bush removed from village life (although this period of time has now become greatly reduced to coincide with public holiday periods). During this seclusion they are circumcised and instructed into the social skills necessary for adult life. At the end of the initiation period they return to the community as newly born male adults with a new status within their households. The Poro society structures social life in the community but also provides arbitration in disputes and regulates trade both within and between communities and chiefdoms. It provided a focus of resistance to the imposition of colonial rule and facilitated the organization of widespread opposition to its regimes.

Dispersed over a smaller area within the Poro cluster area is the Sande secret society for women which complements the Poro society. Sande initiates girls into women's life, such that there is an alternating cycle of ritual time constituted between the Poro and the Sande. For three or four years the Poro society manages the initiation of all the boys of appropriate age and publicly regulates the community and land. However after an interval the Poro society formally withdraws into the forest and the women's Sande society emerges to initiate the young girls who are removed to the Sande forest groves. It similarly regulates the community and land, albeit for a somewhat shorter period of time of about two or three years. The Sande secret society to which all women belong originates through a mythological charter between the first founders of the community and the autochthonous nature spirits whose land they occupied. This co-operation (which guarantees the fertility of the land and the safety of the community) was secured by ritual marriage of women of the founding lineages to these nature spirits. The members of each Sande lodge are characterized as the wives of their particular nature spirit. These spirits appear as masquerades in the community to enforce the social relations with which they are concerned. Exceptionally these masquerades are performed by women, both masked and unmasked, in contrast to most other areas of Africa (d'Azvedo, 1973). Gender differentiation is still assiduously maintained but in this context it is the men who are excluded from women's affairs and the women are patrons and performers of the Sande masquerade.

Masquerades and other local cultural forms such as art and dance have been adopted by the nation state and utilized in secularized presentations in national and regional sponsored festivals that outline local variations of identity within the processes of nation building. They have also been appropriated for international presentation of 'African Heritage' in national sponsored projects of tourism. However the forms of legitimacy and power embedded in the constitution of masquerade ideas and practice have also been, on occasion, more overtly co-opted to support the repressive politics of authoritarian regimes. In Malawi in central Africa the one-party regime of the Malawi Congress Party (MCP) led by life President Dr H. Kamuzu Banda (which lasted some three decades until the beginning of the 1990s) utilized Nyau, the male secret society of the Chewa-speaking people to political ends (Englund, 1996). The Nyau society and its masquerades which feature public displays of animal masquerades within the rural communities had dispersed and been adopted by the other ethnic groupings throughout Malawi. At the national level the Nyau was used as a cultural display during public political rallies and was directly associated with President Banda as a Chewa-speaker. In the one-party state of President Banda party membership was mandatory and fees were collected by the Malawi Young Pioneers, a paramilitary arm of the MCP. Where resistance was encountered it would be collected by Nyau masqueraders in the middle of the night. The significance of the Nyau spirits as predatory animals and their role in mortuary rituals inspired fear in villagers. It was used both in the coercion of party membership and also as a means of enforcing attendance at local and regional political rallies where, prior to commencement, Nyau masqueraders would round up the community to ensure full attendance and participation. The legitimacy and authority of the MCP was thus embedded at village level both in the overt politics of the party and also in the shared religious traditions of the rural communities where the political hierarchies of the one-party system were expressed in local idioms of power, even though the majority of the community were Christian. Though Christianity is dominant throughout Malawi, active membership of Nyau masquerade does not exclude participants from practising as Christians.

Masquerade can have a more ambiguous relationship with the governing elite as Nunley (1987) shows in his research on the Ode-lay masquerades of Freetown, Sierra Leone. Freetown has a diversity of social groupings in part due to its initial founding as a settlement for liberated slaves as well as a coastal cosmopolitan metropole. Many of these social groups have their own forms of masquerade and at the appropriate times these parade about the town in procession. These include many forms of Yoruba masquerade introduced by resettled Yoruba-speakers such as Egungun ancestral masquerades and the hunting societies, as well as (among others) Poro, Sande and Kono masquerades introduced from the interior of the country. However there also developed urban forms of masquerade from the 1950s and 1960s onwards known as Ode-lay. These were organized along the lines of Egungun masquerade and Yoruba hunting societies that provide access to the powerful spiritual and medicinal protections of the society. Membership was drawn from the marginal and socially excluded youth within the urban environment.

FIGURE 10.2 Youth masquerade

Youth masquerade at Enugu, a twentieth-century town in eastern Nigeria; a New Year and Easter ceremony where youths learn contemporary traditions of urban masquerading. Courtesy Charles Gore.

Members of Ode-lay societies often occupied squatting settlements illegally and sometimes engaged in criminal and semi-criminal activities, including drugs and robbery. Their masquerades drew on local and international sources such as urban gang identities (reflected in their names, such as Bloody Mary or Firestone). They appropriated selective tenets and music of Rastafarianism in order to fashion an urban and cosmopolitan identity that cut across the markers of ethnic identity with which the more 'indigenous' masquerades are associated. The Ode-lay masquerades adopted contemporary forms and materials in their physical appearance, although they still drew on the aesthetic and religious conventions of masquerade. They used an eclectic repertoire of imagery drawn from futuristic films (such as in the robot masquerade) as well as international films from Hollywood and India. They also employed modern materials (including gas masks) with which to construct the masquerades, while vinyl records were included among the sacrifices made at the beginning of masquerade processions. These youthful urban societies were often sponsored by members of the political elite as a means of identifying with particular areas and their constituencies. But the sometimes violent conflicts that occurred between rival societies during parades – as well as their marginality and association with criminality outside the bounds of society – has led to their public banning within Freetown.

The civil war that started in Sierra Leone in 1991 curtailed many of the urban masquerades. However insurgents, in their abduction of boys and girls to military training camps in inaccessible forest, continued to utilize concepts of initiation marking the transition from childhood to adult maturity, whereby the Poro or Sande masquerade seizes the uninitiated child. The child disappeared into the forest to re-emerge with a new social identity as part of a rebel army, often wearing eclectic adornment associated with masquerade and its associated protective medicines which highlighted their new means of enforcement over civil populations.

Spirit possession and cults of affliction

It is not only through the effacement or transformation of an individual's identity in masquerade that spiritual agencies are made visible in the social world. In many parts of Africa individuals develop personal relations with such agencies and are possessed directly by them. Among the Tonga in the Zambezi valley in Zambia authoritative spirits, Basungu, appear as important deceased men within the community. They possess chosen individuals who become prophetic diviners and rainmakers able to mediate between the spirit and material worlds and their shrines become an important focus of community worship. Tonga women who are restricted to a domestic environment, on the other hand, are possessed by marginal non-ancestral spirits known as Masabe who demand and are satisfied with gifts bought out of the wages of their husbands in a cash economy from which they are excluded (Lewis, 1971).

However in other societies such as among the Yoruba- and Edo-speaking peoples in Southern Nigeria, a pantheon of deities possess male and female devotees of their respective cults. In Benin City individuals can set up shrines to particular deities who intervene in their lives through initiation, with each deity having its own distinctive set of knowledge that remains exclusive to those that have initiated (Gore, 2007). Some charismatic individuals are recognized to have particularly strong relations with the deities, and develop large public followings of devotees and clients. They are possessed by the deities who are encouraged to manifest through music and dance in the course of worship. During such possession devotees and clients are able to consult directly with the deity who is able to advise them in speech or song about the difficulties they face. These public performances also provide the possibility for the recruitment of new devotees; on occasion uninitiated onlookers will be possessed by a particular deity under the guidance of the chief priest or priestess, indicating which deity has possessed them through the form of dancing and music to which they respond. Onlookers who become possessed are encouraged to initiate, as the deities are considered to be calling them.

There is a reciprocal relationship between the deity and devotee such that the devotional impulse to glorify the deity increases its fame which in turn reflects back on the devotee. Moreover, among the Edo, a devotee can acquire different deities and, if one proves inadequate, is able to rely on others. This empirical validation or rejection enables innovation and creativity in the range of possibilities of religious experience. Priests and priestesses in Benin City have developed their personal shrines through their own charismatic capabilities. The expanding population of Benin City combined with the cash economy in the twentieth century enable these priests and priestesses to sustain their full-time activities with the establishment of large-scale followings that support them economically. Moreover the economic independence provided by the urban cash economy has created a framework in which women, who in precolonial times were excluded on account of their gender from many areas of religious ritual, have been able to take up roles as full-time priestesses and assert their religious authority underpinned by the legitimacy provided through possession by the deities.

Possession often has political significance. In pre-liberated Zimbabwe, for example, the royal ancestral spirit-mediums associated with particular regions of the country played an important role in the liberation struggle conducted from neighbouring countries (Lan, 1985). Liberation forces moving through regions of Zimbabwe had to contend both with the security forces and the political difficulties of relating to areas with which they had no social or ethnic connection. Regional spirit mediums in Zimbabwe publicly recognised the liberation fighters as spiritually legitimated representatives of the ancestral owners of the land. They conferred various ritual injunctions on the fighters within the borders of Zimbabwe including abstinence from sex, prohibitions on the killing of wild animals in the forest, and the eating of certain foods. These marked them out as contemporary agents of the ancestors who therefore must be supported by rural communities rather than excluded as unknown strangers. This made a powerful contrast with the European colonizers who had taken most of the land but had none of the legitimacy that derived from the moral order that these spirit mediums underpinned. The liberation forces successfully positioned themselves as part of this moral order to mobilize support from local populations. In the Independence parades at the end of the war the ancestors who had helped secure victory in the liberation struggle were displayed prominently in banners and referred to in political speech. The legitimacy of these ancestors was now mobilized to endorse the new nation state of Zimbabwe.

Personal adversity or misfortune experienced by the individual is often interpreted in terms of the intervention of deceased human or spiritual agencies. One means of resolving such adversity is through induction of the afflicted individual into cults that venerate the particular spiritual agency involved. These interpretations of affliction and healing situated within frameworks of cults, specialized communities and networks, usually accompanied by a therapeutic dimension, are found throughout central, southern and eastern Africa. In seeking to understand their range and variation, this categorization of 'cults of affliction and healing' is used by Janzen (1994) as a model for extended regional and historical comparisons. Many, but not all, of these cults are known as Ngoma, a linguistic term distributed from the Atlantic coast of Angola and the Congo to the Indian Ocean coast of Kenya and Tanzania. Ngoma describes the single-membrane wooden drum which is a central feature in the music and dance in such rituals, often in conjunction with other musical instruments (although in Southern Africa Ngoma refers exclusively to the singing, divining and the diviners of these cults). Cults of affliction provide a therapeutic redress for afflicted individuals through which social situations are mediated and notions of personhood reconstituted by the ritual processes of affiliation to the cult, often entailing such individuals becoming diviners and healers themselves. In colonial and postcolonial Africa these cults with their emphasis on redressing affliction and adversity have proliferated as sources of revitalization and renewal within the constraints of the nation state, which has tended to limit their regional spread through the maintenance of national boundaries.

Sacred kingship

In many kingdoms in Africa the principles underlying relations between the living and the ancestors underpin the constitution of kingship where the ruler's ancestors represent the ancestors of the entire kingdom. In South Africa with the emergence of the Zulu kingdoms in the eighteenth century, it was through the king and his ancestors that all the Zulu-speaking members of the kingdom were united as members of a single polity. The king officiated on behalf of his ancestors at the great first fruit ceremonies and in war rites or during exceptional circumstances such as at the advent of drought. He possessed important exclusive therapeutic medicines and controlled all the rainmakers of the kingdom.

Other parts of Africa developed similar forms of ritual-political authority. Benin City is the urban centre of the Edo kingdom in southern Nigeria ruled by the Oba of Benin, the descendant of a dynasty dating from at least the fourteenth century onwards. In the Edo kingdom rights of inheritance pass from father to eldest son upon the accomplishment of funerary rites during which the son incorporates his father into the ancestral shrine. The ritual relations of the Oba of Benin to the spirit world are exercised not only on behalf of his family but also for all the various groupings of the kingdom and so encapsulate the relationship between the living and the dead as defined within the idiom of the family and its ancestors.

The king's ritual and political authority is based not only on his office and the institutions that underpin it but also is vested in the actual person of the Oba. He is regarded as the reincarnation of previous Obas and embodied with their spiritual attributes. During the coronation the new Oba undergoes a series of ritual events which redefine him as a unique and singular social category separate from all his subjects (including his close kin) over whom he has the sole power of life and death. Similarly, in the many court rituals that surround the Oba of Benin his actual person is ritually sanctified as the embodiment of the kingdom – as can be seen during the annual festival of Igue when his body is physically fortified with medicines (during the ceremony an attempt is made to ritually shake him but he remains immobile demonstrating the strength of the kingdom). However in the twentieth century, after an interregnum of 17 years lasting until 1914, the Obaship has been articulated within the infrastructures of first the British colonial administration and then the Nigerian nation state. It acquired a strategic importance during the years of military rule of the 1980s and early 1990s as the sole representative of legitimate rule drawing on precolonial traditions shared by the local Edo-speaking population. The military regime ensured that their actions were publicly endorsed by traditional rulers such as the Oba of Benin.

While such metaphysical and political kingship is often described as 'divine kingship' this shorthand term of reference does not indicate the complex ways in which an exclusive and unique social category is vested in the singular office and person of the ruler. It is through the articulation of sacred kingship that a hegemony of seamless political and ritual power centred on the ruler is constituted as an organizational principle under-pinning a kingdom (albeit that the ways in which it is configured varies from kingdom to kingdom). In the twentieth century these precolonial antecedents are often utilized to inscribe a local ethnic identity within the context of the nation state.

Witchcraft and the ambivalence of power

Veneration of ancestors as spiritual beings is unknown in some African societies, as among the Tiv of central Nigeria. In many such societies ancestors are simply deceased forebears through which lineage is traced. It is the living who are able to act in the world through their physical efforts but also through spiritual prowess. In certain contexts, however, this prowess is considered ambiguous in that the benefits it provides can also be detrimental to others, causing physical and spiritual harm which is often defined in terms of an illegitimate use of power. This is characterized as witchcraft, although how it is defined can vary from society to society.

Among the Tiv all individuals who have exceptional talents or skills are presumed to have this spiritual prowess or power. This is accompanied by a physical analogue known as Tsav which grows in the heart region as individuals become older. However it can also grow unnaturally through the harming and killing of other human beings. In these cases it is believed that malign individuals meet at night in order to eat the human flesh of kin offered up by members of these covert groups. Consequently Tsav is used to describe powerful individuals who act legitimately on behalf of the community as well as witches organized for clandestine and evil purposes who act illegitimately for private gain at the expense of the community. As such it becomes an idiom for describing the ambivalence of power.

An important contribution to the understanding of witchcraft was made by Evans-Pritchard's seminal analysis of witchcraft in the Azande kingdoms of the Sudan (Evans-Pritchard, 1937). In this society witchcraft is hereditary, although when a guilty witch is discovered he or she is always considered (for one reason or another) not to have been part of the patrilineage. As with the Tiv, there is also the concept of a physical analogue (in the body, located near the liver) for witchcraft activities which is sometimes revealed at postmortems. Both men and women can be witches (as well as certain categories of wild animals) and witchcraft usually works through close proximity to the victim. Evans-Pritchard suggests that witchcraft plays an important part in understanding the causes and consequences of events that occur in Azande society, especially misfortune. As an example he describes how granaries often collapse due to the predations of termites. This is a commonplace event which needs no further explanation. However, if people were sitting underneath it at the time of collapse and suffer injury, the intersection of two events (the people sitting and the collapse) is explained through the malign actions of witchcraft rather than in terms of random chance.

In order to identify and counter the effects of witchcraft the Azande use different forms of divination. The most well-known of these is the poison oracle operated by married men in which poison is administered to a fowl and questions are asked while its movements are closely observed prior to its death or survival. Usually two fowls are used and a clear verdict on a situation depends on one fowl surviving in response to the questions posed and the other dying. Women are excluded from using the poison oracle which is considered a key resource for married men in discovering their wives' adultery. Moreover, bridewealth offered in marriage alliances resides with the senior men of a narrow group of patrikin (brothers and their offspring) and it is these groups who own poison oracles. As a consequence the poison oracle plays an important role in concentrating political power, controlling marriage alliances and structuring gender relations. The poison oracles of princes and rulers are extremely prestigious and decisions that affected the entire kingdom were often based on the outcome. Though an important means of political and social power, colonial and postcolonial rule has removed much of the judicial aspect of the poison oracle except in localized situations.

Conceptualizations of witchcraft can be applied in varied social contexts within a society. Among the Maka of the Cameroons in West Africa, for example, witchcraft at village level is a powerful means of levelling inequalities between villagers through the pressure it exerts to share communally the fruits of individual success rather than risk witchcraft attacks (Geschiere, 1997). Witchcraft is also used in the client–patronage relations that villagers seek to maintain with successful members of the urban elite who control the resources of the nation state and to whom they are connected through kinship and a common place of birth. There is constant pressure on elite members of a village to redistribute wealth and employment opportunities through the conduit of client–patronage relations with the ultimate sanction of witchcraft if they prove recalcitrant.

The urban elite are unable to sever their relations with their close kin in the village setting even though they often regard their natal villages as hostile environments because of this potential threat of witchcraft. As a result they often redistribute a large proportion of their income and use the state apparatus to provide roads, schools, hospitals and other state provisions for their local communities.

Similarly the political contestation between members of this urban elite within a one-party system leads to sudden and extreme shifts of political fortune for individuals, which is also couched in the idiom of witchcraft. The successful elite claim personal skills of witchcraft in order to survive the intense political competition – and these assertions increase their prestige. The forms of witchcraft they have control over are popularly represented as urban and modern with powerful abilities garnered from other ethnic groups and ritual specialists rather than simply relying on the more local and rural village forms of witchcraft articulated in their own communities. This reflects the capacity of the ruling elite to order the hierarchy of unequal power in patron–client relations. Witchcraft provides a potent mode of discourse about the acquisition of power, legitimate and illegitimate, and a means to critique the ways in which it is exerted within a moral economy. Witchcraft is a fluid category dependent on the context in which it is applied and the variable ways in which it is configured within different societies.

Africanization of the world religions

The consolidation of the colonial territories in Africa at the beginning of the twentieth century underpinned the development and spread of institutional frameworks of missionary Christianity, although for some colonized peoples Islam afforded an alternative identity with which to contest European colonial hegemonies. Mass conversion to both Christianity and Islam began to take place among many peoples in Africa where the world religions had not been much in evidence before. Such conversion was often related to the emergence of new social groupings which were responsive to conversion. They developed in the urban areas with the clerical skills required for administering the colonial enterprise. They were also linked to social change among rural populations where the introduction of new transport infrastructures accompanied changing modes of production (such as the introduction of commodity crops for export) and expansion of various mass communication media.

Although mass conversion can be linked to social change engendered by the processes of colonization, other complex – and much debated – factors were also at play. In an influential analysis, Horton (1983) notes that mass conversion to Christianity and Islam took place in relation to the changing boundaries of social life. He describes precolonial African cosmology as two-tiered between a remote supreme being and lesser but more active spiritual agencies. He suggests that the lesser agencies underpin events and processes in the microcosm of social life within the local community and environment whereas the supreme being underpins events and processes in the wider world. Horton's analysis, sometimes described as 'Intellectualist', argues that where the way of life of a community is restricted to the local boundaries of the microcosm far more emphasis is placed on the lesser active spiritual agencies whereas the remote supreme being remains in the background. When these boundaries of the local microcosm weaken or shift to include events and processes of the wider world (because of trade, enclosure within colonial administrative systems or other reasons) the supreme being comes to feature more prominently. Horton argues that in these weakening circumstances of the microcosm where there is already a shift in emphasis towards the supreme being, this provides a catalyst for mass conversion where the dissemination of Christianity and Islam is already taking place (with their emphasis on a universal God). However the differentiation necessary between the social worlds of the microcosm and macrocosm for this model of explanation is questioned by examples of some local shrines and cults with their emphasis on lesser spiritual agencies (both prior to and during the twentieth century) which have extended beyond the local microcosm to include large regional areas within their influence, often providing networks of personal security and trade for diverse social groupings.

Missionary Christianity and orthodox Islam both emphasize salvation achieved in the next world and so present a contrasting model of religious experience compared to the processual emphasis of African 'indigenous' or 'traditional' religion with its focus on explanation and control of events, utilizing an open-ended range of spiritual resources. The contrast is sometimes described as between salvational and structural modes of religion; however with the Africanization of these world religions, these distinctions become blurred and interpenetrate. The processes of mass conversion to Islam and Christianity at the beginning of the century led to new and dynamic forms of religious innovation and organization that developed to meet African concerns and contexts, leading to the 'Africanization' of the world religions. Among the Yoruba-speaking areas in south-western Nigeria, for example, conversion to Christianity contributed to the formation of a new regional Yoruba ethnic identity coalesced from the heterogeneous cluster of city states and dialects in the region. The dissemination of the Bible as a textual resource translated into an indigenous language by converts fostered the regional acceptance of a 'standardized' Yoruba language over its range of dialects, some of which are mutually unintelligible (Peel, 1989). As happened in many parts of Africa however, conversion to Christianity was followed by disillusionment with the control maintained by European mission churches which marginalized African clergymen, who had often been at the forefront of the drive for conversion. Many left the mission churches to form separate churches.

In southern Nigeria the new administrative subordinate class with the literate skills acquired from the mission schools and inculcated in Christianity utilized the text of the Bible to mediate the often acute tensions and evident contradictions generated by colonization. They initially formed prayer bands in the Yoruba-speaking areas, which developed into the Aladura churches, and began to articulate radical religious innovation through the use of visions, prayer, and healing rituals in comparison to the mission and more orthodox African churches (Peel, 1968). The development of such 'indigenous churches' occurred elsewhere in Africa as in the case of the Zion churches of southern Africa. Such churches were not simply a form of resistance to colonial hegemonies but rather created an autonomous space in which to form sacred communities that were aligned to what might be called the modernities of contemporary life. There was a rejection of what was now defined as pagan worship as a prior religious form that was no longer appropriate although the problems it mediated were still relevant. For example, notions of witchcraft and its effects within the community were still salient but the modes of action through which such concerns were addressed were situated within a new radical Christian context, such as the Aladura churches and now the Pentecostal churches. Though the dependence on charismatic religious leaders led to fission and the formation of new churches up to the present day, these processes provide a means of renewal and revitalization that aligns itself with modernity.

Conversion to Islam under the European colonial regimes in the twentieth century also led to new adaptations. In Senegal in western Africa, for example, the charismatic Islamic religious leader Cheik Amadu Bamba became a focus for religious resistance to the French administration at the beginning of the twentieth century. He was educated in the traditions of the longstanding Sufi brotherhood of the Qadiriyya prevalent in West Africa. Although his religious teachings always advocated peaceful resolutions to conflict, some of his followers supported more forceful political action that resulted in the French authorities exiling him first to Gabon and subsequently to Mauretania. This merely increased his charismatic appeal as a martyr and attracted increasing numbers of adherents who formed the independent Islamic brotherhood of the Mouride with its own litany and clerical hierarchy. With the introduction of peanuts as a commodity crop by the colonial regime, the Mouride brotherhood further increased its power and political influence through its development of new farming communities in the semi-arid and more remote regions of Senegal. They comprised impoverished adherents who cultivated the new crop and contributed a tithe of their earnings to the brotherhood. The Mouride brotherhood underpinned the agricultural transformation of the rural economy in Senegal and its making into a modern nation state, as reflected in the close ties maintained between the Mouride clerical hierarchy and the governing elite after independence.

However the introduction of Christianity and Islam into new areas of Africa in the twentieth century did not curtail or hinder innovations in other forms of religious experience that are usually described as 'indigenous' or 'traditional'. Often there is an affiliation with one or other of the world religions as well as an overlapping participation in these other forms of religious activity. Janzen (1994) describes how the city of Dar-es-Salaam on the Indian Ocean coast of East Africa lies within the Swahili regional corridor that runs along the coast with its longstanding traditions of Islam. Yet Ngoma cults of affliction and healing are also found here and are patronized by the coastal Islamized peoples as well as by migrants from the interior. However, Ngoma in Dar-es-Salaam can be utilized for therapeutic or entertainment purposes and this provides an ambiguity in defining it in relation to Islamic doctrine. Janzen gives an example of two Islamic healers to demonstrate this ambiguity; the first uses Ngoma rituals as a medical healing rite which consequently does not compromise his Islamic devotion whereas the second, a Sufi adherent (with an alternative repertoire of prayers, singing and dancing that is therapeutically available), considers it a pagan religious ritual and therefore unacceptable.

Recent renewal and innovation

Indigenous: Bwiti and Mami Wata

In the twentieth century new religious movements have developed that appropriate elements from the world religions but also creatively maintain continuities with 'indigenous' or 'traditional' beliefs and practices. They are reconfigured and transformed so as to mediate or incorporate the localized conditions of modernity as they impact on their community or society. A notable example is the Bwiti religious movement researched by Fernandez (1982) among the Fang-speaking peoples in the Gabon in central Africa. The Fang are an uncentralized patrilineal society that trace descent from founding ancestors of clans and are organized into segmented lineages. The smallest unit in Fang society is the family household of the father, his wives and children living in villages with a number of other families. As a people they had slowly migrated southwards from the savannah to the tropical rainforest with a history that in different contexts read either as conquering newcomers or fleeing refugees. With French colonization these villages which had tended to relocate periodically became fixed spatially within its bureaucratic infrastructures (for which they supplied a flexible labour force). Prior to colonization the focus of religious activity was the ancestor cult with the reliquaries of bones and skulls of its deceased male members located in the men's council house where all important matters of village life took place, watched over by the benign protective guardianship of the ancestors. Although the cult had become discredited by the impact of mission Christianity as 'uncivilized', these ideas still had a powerful influence in the lives of villagers. Anti-witchcraft cults periodically swept through the Fang-speaking region, in part a response to a perceived divisive individuation engendered by access to the cash economy of the colony that undermined the communal egalitarian basis of village life. Among these cults was one known as 'Mademoiselle of Ndende' who was a white female spirit originating in the river and was equated with the Virgin Mary of Christianity. Her devotees offered protection against witchcraft on condition reliquary bones (described by them as 'fetish' objects) were dug up and destroyed to be replaced by a shrine devoted to her. However the impact of her cult was, in the main, transient in the village communities.

From the 1920s onwards a new and innovative religious movement of renewal started to develop. Known as 'Bwiti' among the Fang peoples, it sought to reconstitute an egalitarian but communal social life through the organization of chapel houses, which formed by a constant process of fissioning rather than the establishment of a hierarchy. Leading members of Bwiti were often mission-educated and literate. During initiation into Bwiti, large quantities of eboga, a psychotropic drug derived from the rainforest, are ingested causing vivid hallucinations and psychomotor disturbances. These experiences are structured through what Fernandez describes as the religious imagination of the Bwiti movement as an enactment of creation – a journey which resonates with their mythic history of migration. In the course of this journey initiates encounter the supreme being and Jesus Christ, who is represented as an indigenous healer, as well as ultimately the ancestors who impart to them experiential but esoteric knowledge of communal 'one heartedness' that restores an egalitarian understanding through which to relate to all members of the chapel house and the wider community. These experiences are integrated within Bwiti into complex rituals of worship using dance and song. They take place during the night, focused around a central post that is a conduit between the physical and spirit world. Although there is considerable adoption of Christian liturgy and imagery, members do not consider themselves Christian. Bwiti is a renewal and revitalization of the ancestral cult articulated within the modern world, of which Christianity is a feature. Bwiti and many similar prophetic movements in Africa dynamically appropriate Christian motifs to indigenous idioms and discourses to obtain a legitimacy similar to that perceived in the orthodox Christian hegemony from which they are marginalized.

However not all religious innovations draw on the past. Mami Wata is a 'new' riverine deity found throughout West and Central Africa and depicted as a fair-skinned female with long flowing hair, often represented with a fishtail (to underline her links to the water spirit world). The term Mami Wata derives from pidgin English, which is used as a common language over wide areas, and was initially used to describe and compare differing riverine female deities from different localities. In the twentieth century she has developed as an autonomous female deity who is able to bestow great wealth and riches on her devotees or wreak severe suffering on those who displease her. She is represented as seductive, and associated with notions of irresistible female sexuality, often maintaining a sexual relationship with her devotees in the spirit world. She is considered cosmopolitan and characterized as fast-living and independent. She has all the consumer goods of this urban lifestyle, including sunglasses and fast cars. When possessed by her, devotees sometimes smoke cigarettes and play popular musical instruments such as the harmonica or guitar instead of the traditional musical instruments appropriate to other deities. Mami Wata is prominent in popular discourses featuring in books, films and songs in describing the qualities of independent urban women. Similarly she is utilized through her association with extreme unexpected riches in discourses on the illegitimate acquisition of unexpected wealth, especially relevant where patrimonialism is often exercised by the political elite who are able to extract extreme wealth from government resources.

Evangelical and Pentecostal churches have vigorously attacked the followers of 'indigenous' or 'traditional' forms of worship as pagan idol worshippers. They single out Mami Wata in particular as exemplifying all paganism's demonic evils and dangers through her lure of uncontrollable female sexuality that destroys the spiritual community which these churches seek to create. However these church communities often marginalize single and divorced women who are seen as a potential threat to the spiritual harmony of married life. Mami Wata offers an empowering autonomous role model for such women. It underlines and legitimates control of their own individual sexual, reproductive and economic capacities and frees them from being dominated through

FIGURE 10.3 Priestess

Priestess playing the harmonica while possessed by Mami Wata. Courtesy Charles Gore.

kinship or marriage, while at the same time sanctioning the personal pleasures of modern urban consumption.

Evangelical and charismatic churches

Evangelical and Pentecostal churches (see Chapter 8 on Christianity) have spread rapidly throughout Africa in the late twentieth century. They have promoted themselves using mass-media techniques, inspired by the example of similar churches in the USA. They often aspire to an international programme that reflects the global possibilities of conversion for their organizations through building up a network of associated branches – although their dependence on charismatic leaders leaves them prone to a certain amount of fission. These evangelical and Pentecostal churches are distinguished by a common set of religious ideas and practices that include baptism in the Holy Spirit, speaking in tongues and healing through personal prayer. The use of exorcism from the devil and demonic forces is central to their concept of personal deliverance afforded through the intervention of the church and its spiritual community which shields the individual from the malign forces that pervade wider society. These churches place an emphasis on situating themselves as modern and vigorously oppose what they consider the idolatrous customs of the pagan past, albeit that they share many of the same concerns such as witchcraft which is articulated in terms of these demonic forces. It is through this positioning against demonic forces that they distinguish themselves from the more orthodox churches from which they attract many of their followers to offer a more radical approach in addressing an individual's spiritual and material needs.

The 'prosperity gospel' many churches disseminate aspires to the success and material benefits of the consumer world brought about through the personal intervention of God on behalf of the individual. Consumption is consequently valorized as the reward of the individual who has achieved deliverance within the spiritual community of the church. The success of these churches is reflected in the size of congregations, the conversion rallies held, and the use of the latest technologies to promote their church. This emphasis on material success in the modern world also provides the ideological framework for worshippers to redefine and reduce the collective obligations (and economic costs) of extended kinship. The community of the church substitutes for kinship and they are able to focus on a more individuated sociality. (For more on the Charismatic upsurge see Chapter 8, Christianity, and Chapter 16, Religion and globalization).

Islamic renewal

Islam has undergone dynamic renewal and revitalization from precolonial times to the present day, through processes of reform and purification in which elements of Islamic practice deemed idolatrous are rejected. Islam provides a religious context underpinned by the legitimation of a new orthodoxy through which to challenge established hierarchies of authority and transform them into a new social and religious order. With the emergence of independent nation states from the colonial states a renewal of international links within the Islamic world has taken place, particularly between sub-Saharan, northern Africa and the Middle East. The pilgrimage to Mecca which all Islamic adherents are encouraged to take has now been mobilized in sub-Saharan Africa through modern means of mass-transportation. Links have been further strengthened with the core centres of Islam through the establishment and sponsorship of Islamic institutions including schools and hospitals.

The dominance of the Wahhabi Islamic movement founded in the eighteenth century by Muhammed ibn' Abd al-Wahhab in the Arabian peninsular, and in particular Saudi Arabia, has resulted in the dissemination of Wahhabi-inspired teachings. These advocate a return to the primary teachings of the Koran and a rejection of the longstanding culturally mediated interpretations of it found in the Islamic Sufi brotherhoods in sub-Saharan Africa (see Chapter 9, Islam). Furthermore, the successful resistance of Islamic nation states to the encroachments of Western capitalism and its attendant secularization has served as a model for Islamic activist groupings who wish to turn the secular nation state into a religious theocracy under the guidance of Islamic law. These diverse reformist Islamic movements challenge the longstanding Islamic institutions of sub-Saharan Africa and resort to the use of the mass media of print and cassettes to pass on their teachings, especially effective when met with hostility or repression. Such Islamic renewals and the means by which they disseminate their messages align them as modern religious mass movements which attract a broad grassroots base of support that includes radical intellectuals and Islamic scholars as well as both the urban and rural disenfranchised, among whom the young feature prominently.

In Northern Nigeria from the 1970s onwards, the reformist Yan Izala movement has spread rapidly. Emphasizing doctrinal understanding, Arabic literacy and strict ritual practice, it rejects Sufi or Islamic brotherhood-derived influences as non-Islamic. In addition it criticises these brotherhoods for endorsing the high expenditure involved in marriage and other social customs which reinforce the economic and status divisions in society. This movement has recruited poorer farmers, the socially disadvantaged and young men who are keen to limit these expenses which they find financially onerous (Loemeier, 1997). The adoption of Yan Izala also provides a means to limit socially necessary costs by restricting the boundaries of sociality to other adherents of the movement and thereby excluding the fulfilment of social obligations of distant kin affiliated to other forms of Islam which are categorically rejected as non-Islamic. It advocates better (if separate) education for Muslim women and modern schools and aligns itself as a progressive movement that offers a modernity with which to challenge the status quo of the longstanding Sufi brotherhoods. It has been castigated by the latter for the ways in which its teachings have created deep-seated divisions and conflicts within communities and families. These movements have attained a further political dimension with the adoption of Sharia law (initially adopted in Zamfara state in 1999) to regulate Muslim populations in many states in northern Nigeria and, despite occasional outbreaks of sectarian violence, established an accommodation with a secular but federal nation state.

Looking to the future

The capacity of religion to renew and innovate in sub-Saharan Africa means that it continues to be an important resource in associational life, generating new forms of community that provide a means for local empowerment even in the most marginalized of social contexts. It provides dynamic ways of redefining and transforming gendered roles within civil societies in Africa, in some instances enabling women to adopt and adapt male patterns of leadership through their own charismatic religious legitimation, while in many others religion advances new orderings of gendered roles. Where military rule or government elites control the resources of the nation state, the religious imagination at the grassroots level can offer alternative visions of society. Often this is a positive force. As Gifford (1998) has argued, for example, Christianity in Africa can offer the possibility of democratization by offering a vision of an alternative social order as well as by generating its own institutional frameworks to structure local social community in more democratic ways. However religion can also have a negative impact where it is adopted to empower conflict such as in the case of the Lord's Resistance Army in northern Uganda which has waged an unwinnable war on the nation state (with the potential threat of its fragmentation), which is led by the charismatic Joseph Kony who organized his army as a form of cult guided by his possession by spirits. In the oil-rich delta region of southern Nigeria an indigenous war cult, Egbesu, has been adopted as part of the modes of resistance to the nation state in the twenty-first century by local militias campaigning for more of the wealth earned by oil production on behalf of disenfranchised communities who bear the costs of oil and gas expropriation, including environmental degradation that destroys local livelihoods. However religion can also mediate the articulations of the grassroot communities to the institutions of the nation state. An example of this is the way in which the South African government in its AIDS awareness programmes has also made use of the Ngangas, local cult healers, to give advice on AIDS prevention during their divination and healing consultations, thereby creating local idioms for the communication of information.

Both the Pentecostal and radical Islamic movements have deployed the mass media technologies to proselytize through videos, music and sermons as they advance transnational agendas of conversion exploiting these modes of communication, including the worldwide web. By this same means localized indigenous religions have also participated in these technologies of modernity. An example is the video CD disc productions of the celebrated Ikeji (new yam) masquerades festival of the Arondizuogu village cluster in south-eastern Nigeria that circulate to Igbo speaking diasporas worldwide and even more recently user-generated video content of the festival can also be accessed via the internet. These localized religious forms enable their revitalization and renewal through the presentation of cultural spectacle that promulgate their own modernity (alongside claims to precolonial trajectories) rather than agendas of conversion.

The striking trend in religion in Africa is the way in which it continues to be exported to other continents, especially the Americas and Europe, as part of the processes of globalization. It travelled historically with the dispersion of the African diaspora through the Atlantic slave trade up to the end of the nineteenth century. The varied religious resources drawn from the heterogenous slave social groupings, articulated in differing ways with the dominant Christian system, often led to translations between the African spiritual agencies and the saints of Christianity in religions such as Santeria of Cuba, Candomble and its variations in Brazil, and Vodou of Haiti, among other examples. With continued migration from these societies (particularly to the USA) throughout the latter part of the twentieth century, African religions have dispersed further. Moreover the rejection of a eurocentric Christianity and the adoption of African religion by Afro-Americans has seen a massive increase in affiliation to these religions, supplemented by its spread to other communities in both South and North America who have no claims to it by descent, literal or figurative. Arguably diasporic religions characterized under the rubric of 'traditional' African religion have now attained an international status that qualifies them as members of the world religions.

Similarly, the Africanization of Christianity with the emergence of independent churches and their dynamic forms of worship which energize and personalize ritual are currently being exported to both the USA and Europe. The methods of recruitment through conversion rallies are gaining worshippers outside their African migrant groups and helping reshape the practices of western evangelical churches. Likewise 'orthodox' or mainstream denominational Christian constituencies in Africa (both Protestant and Catholic) with their rising numbers of followers are becoming an increasing influence in determining the directions of Christianity as a religion in the twenty-first century (see Chapter 8, Christianity).

Summary

- There is a great diversity of indigenous religions in sub-Saharan Africa but there has also been the longstanding presence of Christianity and Islam in particular areas since the fourth century CE and, at least, the ninth century CE respectively.

- Indigenous religions found in sub-Saharan Africa include a complex and variable range of social phenomena that do not easily correspond to western institutional categories of the religious, political, economic, judicial and social.

- Indigenous religions emphasize participation and are also open-ended in that they allow individuals to acquire alternative forms of religious experience from different sources and according to need and inclination. They focus on the well-being of the community or social grouping and for this reason often emphasize explanation, prediction and control of events.

- Mass-conversion to Christianity and Islam took place at the beginning of the twentieth century in response to the consequences of colonialism and the impact of missionaries, although at this time in some areas Christianity was embraced as a resource associated with the 'modern' benefits of colonialism whereas in other areas peoples converted to Islam (which often already had a longstanding presence) as a means of resistance to these hegemonic colonial encroachments.

- Mass-conversion to the world religions of Christianity and Islam did not result in the disappearance or exclusion of indigenous localized forms of religion nor a syncretization of indigenous and world religions; but rather there is often a compartamentalized positioning of individuals in relation to both indigenous religions and either Christianity or Islam.

- The dynamic and creative forms of religious experience deriving from sub-Saharan African social and cultural contexts, characterized by renewals and revitalizations, has resulted in the Africanization of the world religions in sub-Saharan Africa.

- The Africanization of Christianity is helping to shape its worldwide forms both in its orthodox Protestant and Catholic denominations and also its more radical evangelical modes, while sub-Saharan African forms of Islam are engaged in closer international links with the rest of the Islamic world, especially northern Africa and the Middle East.

- Indigenous religions of sub-Saharan Africa, which were carried across the Atlantic to the Americas with the African diaspora to develop new forms, have expanded enormously (and contrast with an eurocentric Christianity); they also attract new adherents who have no claims to it by descent, literal or figurative.

Key terms

Aladura churches Independent African churches formed in Yoruba-speaking areas from the beginning of the twentieth century onward that emphasised the efficacy of prayer and healing to directly effect change in the spiritual and material circumstances of individuals as well as introducing African religious practices such as the use of drumming that had been previously rejected by the European missionaries.

Church Missionary Society (CMS) Anglican missionary society founded in 1799 to spread the Christian gospel overseas, specifically to lands where Christianity was not present. The first CMS missionaries reached Sierra Leone in 1804.

Griaule, Marcel One of the most prominent French anthropologists working principally in Francophone Africa between 1928 and 1956; famous for his long-term project to understand the complex culture of the Dogon peoples of Mali, particularly under the tutelage of a Dogon elder Ogotemmeli.

Lord Lugard British administrator who developed and codified the British system of colonisation which utilized the precolonial authority and hierarchies of chieftaincy and kingship to rule the colonies.

Ngoma Linguistic description of drumming that plays a central part in the range of cults of healing and affliction that have a wide regional currency in Southern and Eastern Africa.

patrilineage Kinship group tracing descent through the male line.

Wahhabi Islamic groupings, associated with the contemporary ruling elites of the Arabian peninsular, that follow the eighteenth-century teachings of Muhammed ibn' Abd al-Wahhab which advocate a direct return to the teachings of the Koran with condemnation of all innovations and religious practices, such as venerating saints' tombs or the mystical aspects of the Sufi religious orders which are classed as non-Islamic.

Further reading

Introductory

Thomas D. Blakely, Walter E.A. van Beek, and Dennis L. Thomson (eds): *Religion in Africa: Expression and Experience* (New Haven, NJ: James Currey/Heinemann, 1994). A series of indigenous, Christian and Islamic case studies that suggest how wideranging and diverse religious experience is in sub-Saharan Africa.

Louis Brenner: '"Religious" Discourses in and about Africa'. In K. Barber and P.F. de Moraes Farias (eds): *Discourse and its Disguises: The Interpretation of African Oral Texts* (Centre of West African Studies Series 1: Birmingham: University of Birmingham, 1989, pp. 87–105). An important discussion of how to understand the framings of religious ideas and practices in sub-Saharan Africa.

Peter Geschiere: *The Modernity of Witchcraft: Politics and the Occult in Postcolonial Africa* (Charlottesville, VA and London: University Press of Virginia, 1997). An explanation of the persistence of witchcraft as a key idea for conceptualizing social and political relations among the Maka in the Cameroon as a response to the exigencies of modern-day life.

Christianity and Islam in Africa

Paul Gifford: *African Christianity: Its Public Role* (Bloomington and Indianapolis, IN: Indiana University Press, 1998). A survey of the ways Christianity has emerged in relation to the state and civil society in the late twentieth century.

Rosalind Hackett: 'Charismatic/pentecostal Appropriations of Media Technologies in Nigeria and Ghana'. (*Journal of Religion in Africa* 28(3): pp. 258–277).

Robin Horton: 'On The Rationality of African Conversion: Part 1'. (*Africa* 45(3), 1975: pp. 219–235). A seminal discussion of why mass conversion to the world religions has taken place in sub-Saharan Africa.

Donal B. Cruise O'Brien: *Saints and Politicians: Essays in the Organisation of a Senegalese Peasant Society* (Cambridge: Cambridge University Press, 1975). In-depth analysis of the processes of conversion to Islam in Senegal in opposition to the imposition of French colonial hegemonies.

John D.Y. Peel: *Aladura: A Religious Movement among the Yoruba* (Oxford: Oxford University Press, International Africa Institute, 1968). A comprehensive study of the rise of the Aladura movement in Nigeria and its relations to mission Christianity.

John D.Y. Peel: 'The Cultural Work of Yoruba Ethnogenesis'. In M. Chapman, M. Mcdonald and E. Tonkin (eds): *History and Ethnicity* (ASA Monograph 27. London: Routledge, 1989, pp. 198–215). An analysis of the interaction between emerging articulations of ethnic identity and the missionary project.

David Westerlund and Eva Evers Rosander (eds): *African Islam and Islam in Africa: Encounters between Sufis and Islamists* (London: Hurst, 1997). An important discussion of the Islamic reformist movements in Africa and their interaction with the more longstanding forms of Islam already present with case studies.

Indigenous religions in Africa: General

Edward E. Evans-Pritchard: *Witchcraft, Oracle and Magic among the Azande* (London: Oxford University Press, 1937). Evans-Pritchard's seminal discussion of how the Azande use witchcraft, oracle and magic to structure and order events. He demonstrated the importance of such concepts in helping to explain the chains of causality by which fortune and misfortune occur (where no other explanation is available) and how this provides an alternative model to Western models of random chance in accounting for events.

James W. Fernandez: *Bwiti: An Ethnography of the Religious Imagination in Africa* (Princeton, NJ: Princeton University Press, 1982). An in-depth comprehensive study of the development of an indigenous religion in central Africa in the twentieth century which makes accommodations with the presence of Christianity to reshape and restructure the precolonial cosmology.

Meyer Fortes and Robin Horton: *Oedipus and Job in West African Religion* (Cambridge: Cambridge University Press, 1983). A cross-cultural comparison and exploration of the relations between religious cosmologies and social organization in selected societies in West Africa.

John M. Janzen: 'Drums of Affliction: Real Phenomenon or Scholarly Chimaera?' In Thomas D. Blakely, Walter E.A. van Beek, and Dennis L. Thomson (eds): *Religion in Africa: Expression and Experience* (New Haven, NJ: James Currey/Heinemann, 1994, pp. 160–181). A review of how cults of affliction and healing can be used to understand religious movements regionally and historically.

Ian M. Lewis: *Ecstatic Religions* (London: Pelican, 1971). Overview of how spirit possession is articulated in a wide range of societies including sub-Saharan Africa.

Various case studies

Warren d'Azvedo: 'Mask Makers and Myth in Western Liberia'. In Anthony Forge (ed.): *Primitive Art and Society* (Oxford: Oxford University Press, Wenner-Gren Foundation, 1973, pp. 126–150).

Karen Barber: 'How Man Makes Gods in West Africa: Yoruba Attitudes Towards the Orisa'. (*Africa* 51(3), 1981: pp. 724–745).

Harri Englund: 'Between God and Kamuzu: The Transition to Multiparty Politics in Central Malawi'. In R. Werbner and T. Ranger (eds): *Postcolonial Identities in Africa* (London: Zed Books, 1996, pp. 105–135).

Meyer Fortes: *Religion, Morality and the Person: Essays on Tallensi Religion* (Cambridge: Cambridge University Press, 1987).

Charles Gore: *Art, Performance and Ritual in Benin City* (London: International African Library and Edinburgh University Press, 2007).

Marcel Griaule: *Conversations with Ogotemmeli* (Oxford: Oxford University Press, International Africa Institute, 1965).

Robin Horton: 'The Kalabari Ekine Society: A Borderland of Religion and Art'. (*Africa* 33(2), 1963: pp. 94–114).

Robin Horton: 'Social Psychologies: African and Western'. In M. Fortes and R. Horton (eds): *Oedipus and Job in West African Religion* (Cambridge: Cambridge Press, 1983, pp. 41–82).

Igor Kopytoff: 'Ancestors as Elders in Africa'. (*Africa* 41(2), 1971: pp. 129–142).

David Lan: *Guns and Rain: Guerrillas and Spirit Mediums in Zimbabwe* (London: James Currey, 1985).

Kenneth Little: 'The Political Function of the Poro: Part 1'. (*Africa* 35(4), 1965: pp. 349–365).

Roman Loemeier: 'Islamic Reform and Political Change'. In David Westerlund and Eva Evers Rosander (eds): *African Islam and Islam in Africa: Encounters between Sufis and Islamists* (London: Hurst, 1997, pp. 286–307).

Joseph N. Nevadomsky: 'Kingship Succession Rituals in Benin. Part 3: The Coronation of the Oba'. (*African Arts* 17(3), 1984: pp. 48–57).

John W. Nunley: *Moving with the Face of the Devil: Art and Politics in Urban West Africa* (Urbana and Chicago, IL: University of Illinois Press, 1987).

John Parker and Jean Allman: *Tongnaab: The History of a West African God* (Bloomington, IN: Indiana University Press, 2005).

Chapter 11

Native American religions

Kenneth Mello

Introduction

This chapter seeks to examine Native American religions as adaptive, flexible, culturally-localized traditions which have shaped native responses to historical and cultural changes across a broad spectrum of both time and space. One of the first things we should realize is that the term 'religion' is elusive in terms of its definition (see Introduction and Chapter 1 How to study religion in the modern world). What might be considered religion or religious activity within one group, community, or culture would not have the same consideration among other groups. Rather than looking for 'truth' in the study of religion, then, we should be looking for an objective understanding of how a tradition or faith might function, from the inside, according to its followers. This chapter will examine Native American religions as not just sets of beliefs, but calls to action and agency, based on long-held cultural values and experiences.

Historically, Native American religions (it is relevant to note here that there is no term that connotes the concept of 'religion' in any Native American language, as it was not and is not understood as a concept separate from daily life) have not fared well in competition with mainstream, Western religious traditions. They have been seen as polytheistic, paganistic, and sometimes as 'devil worship'. Yet these understandings reveal little more than a misunderstanding and misconception of how religious and spiritual activity functioned and was understood within native communities.

What does it mean to say that Native Americans have a unique way of looking at the world? Vine Deloria Jr., probably the pre-eminent scholar in the study of Native American religions, has noted that there are two types of philosophies which orient human societies: there are those types of people who orient their lives around the 'idea of history', and there are those who orient their lives around 'the idea of nature'. This chapter will attempt to clarify these terms, and then examine the ways in which such a localized, culturally contextualized relationship with place has shaped native agency right up to the present.

If we believe that religion has a presence in human societies in any fundamental sense, then we can no longer speak of universal religions in the customary manner. Rather we must be prepared to confront religion and religious activities in new and novel ways.

(Deloria, 2003: 64)

Western religious traditions, such as Christianity and Judaism, are understood to be linear in their orientation – they place all of human history on an established timeline, and trace important events, including creation, back to that timeline in order to make sense out of them. Native American religious traditions, on the other hand, are understood to be spatial in their orientation – they place greatest emphasis on the places where things have happened, and tend to devalue the need to define events and activities according to a specific timeline. We need to begin to understand exactly how these concepts of linear and spatial function to both define traditions and shape the ways in which peoples view the world and their place in it. This will be critical to understanding Native American religions and how they have functioned to define groups of people and their understanding of the larger questions of life.

The first goal of this chapter, then, is to begin to unravel what exactly Native American religions were and are about – how they function within communities and cultures, how they are similar to and different from other types of religions, what is distinctly unique about them, and how they continue to adapt, change, and function within the lives of contemporary native peoples today.

Linear and circular orientations

Although somewhat simplistic, one of the best ways to see what is unique about the philosophical underpinnings of Native American religions is in comparison to other 'types' of religions. The common markers of distinction which have been drawn have been between religious systems which are linear, historical and temporal in nature, and those which are local, contextual, and spatially oriented around a relationship with a defined physical place.

Linear traditions typically focus on time, and assume that time proceeds in a logical, linear fashion. As such, people and institutions are judged according to their progress over time, an idea which traces its origins back to various realms of both science and philosophy, including Enlightenment environmentalism and Darwinism. In its application to religion, such a philosophical orientation leads to traditions which place near absolute value on both time and human history, but which tend to devalue or denigrate the role and value of the natural world, and the places where events occur. The 'divine plan' is thus worked out through a series of historical events, which can be neatly plotted along a linear timeline, each one progressing from the event before it. In such a view, revelation is historical, and the present is focused on cementing and transmitting dogma.

Oppositionally, spatial traditions, like those of Native Americans, are those in which advocates see a unique value and power in the natural world, and orient themselves and their cultures to it. Spatial traditions typically look to experience, rather than dogma, and are religious systems that are triggered by long-standing relationships with places, typically among small cultural groups within defined geographical areas. They are local in context, do not purport to have any type of universal, historical message, and see revelation as a continuous process occurring in the world around them to which the individual and group must both attune themselves.

In circular philosophy, all things are related and involved in the broad scope of Indian life. As part of their life ways, the indigenous peoples of the Americas have studied the Earth, observed the heavenly bodies and contemplated the stars of the universe. The Mayans recorded a calendar based on the number of new moons in a year. The Lakota completed an astronomy about the heavenly bodies, and the Muscogee Creeks incorporated the stars and galaxies into their ethos of the universe . . . Native peoples looked for the constants in life as a part of the universe. They understood life to occur in cycles and those powers of nature formed definite patterns that occurred, repeating themselves.

(Fixico, 2003: 42–43)

As an example of these two ways of seeing the world and placing the human in it, let us think about the variety of creation narratives which exist. The Biblical creation is understood by many to be a true, historical event – the beginning event of a linear time sequence in which the divine plan is to be worked out. The natural world is seen as corrupted, and man is given authority to rule both animals and nature in whatever way suits his needs and desires. This monogenetic creation narrative then lays out a series of historical events, each linked in linear progression, in which what is important is human beings and their events, and what is not is nature and everything else.

Native American creation narratives are typically not concerned with pinning down, in terms of time, the beginnings of anything, but rather tend to be more concerned with explaining how a given group of people have come to inhabit the place that they do, and what their relationship with this place is meant to look like. These traditions view all of creation as good, as having their own roles and functions, which are often separate from human needs and desires, and locate the human within the larger web of natural systems, not outside of it. They are flexible and adaptive to both cultural and historical changes, and thus resistant to strict dogma. They also typically blur the lines between past, present, and future, and instead use experiences and lessons from the past, applied to contemporary situations, with an eye on the future, to shape actions and ideas.

Native American religions and Western colonialism

In both missionization and the various Native American responses to it, native people employed agency and their spiritual and cultural flexibility to respond to colonialism and to survive it. History is not simply victors and victims, but rather action and reaction, and native people fell back on their spiritual beliefs and values in order to know how to respond to their changing world, both pre- and post-contact.

Missionization

Almost from the moment of contact, Europeans began the effort to force Native Americans to give up their own religious traditions and beliefs and to adopt European models (particularly Christianity) instead. Many of the early explorers of the 'New World' were accompanied by religious missionaries, and missionization quickly became part of the larger process of 'civilizing the Indians' which would drive much of the activity focused towards Native Americans in the early days of European and American colonization.

> Prior to contact Native people had their own cultural and religious systems that sustained their physical and spiritual well-being for centuries. However, with the arrival of European colonizers came the suppression and prohibition of traditional Native religious practices. In an attempt to 'civilize' the Indians the colonizers sought to undermine traditional ways of worship. Europeans challenged the authority of religious leaders and banned Native worship, penalizing and/or jailing those who continued their traditional ways.
>
> (Vernon, 1999: 76)

It was these early missionaries who began to negatively label Native American religious traditions as childish, simplistic, and primitive (these were the kinder labels) or pagan, demonic, and devil worship (these were some of the harsher labels). These ideologies would frame the ways in which average Euro-American colonists and settlers would view Native Americans, and would lead to missionization and Americanization moving from the realm of ideology to national policy. Missionaries often blurred the lines between messages of faith and messages of colonization and acculturation, and typically sought to achieve conversion through the larger process of forced cultural change. They actively worked to promote religious, economic, political and social change in Native American communities, and often bought into the ideology of cultural and religious superiority which drove colonization as a whole.

Luckily, a great deal of primary source material remains from these missionaries (journals, diaries, church writings, etc.) which allows us a view into what missionaries were thinking and saying about Native American traditions, and how natives were responding to this effort to wipe out their traditions and replace them with new ones. Many native people accepted missionization, but we want to look closer at the reasons why, for they are varied, and sometimes have little to do with actual beliefs or acceptance of faith. In fact, historically, it is safe to say that missionization failed in its efforts to provide complete conversion and the elimination of Native American religious systems. Despite their flexibility and willingness to incorporate some of this 'new religion' into their already well-established traditions, most Native Americans were unwilling to accept a singular, abstract deity, but rather sought to incorporate this new god into the gods they already accepted in the world around them. Many Native Americans also actively resisted the 'global truth' of Christianity when it did not make sense in comparison to their own cultural beliefs, thus enacting agency in choosing the parts they liked, and rejecting the parts they didn't, rather than wholeheartedly rejecting one for another. This would be typical of native responses to religious change from the contact period to the present.

> The question that the so-called world religions have not satisfactorily resolved is whether or not religious experience can be distilled from its original cultural context

and become an abstract principle that is applicable to all peoples in different places and at different times. The persistent emergence of religious movements and the zeal with which they are pursued would seem to suggest that cultural context, time and place are the major elements of revelation and the content is illusory. If not illusory, it is subject to so many cultural qualifications that it is not suitable for transmission to other societies without doing severe damage to both the message of revelation and the society which receives it.

(Deloria, 2003: 65)

Prophecy and prophetic movements

Prophecy has always played an important role within Native American spiritual communities, and has served, historically, as one of the ways in which native people responded and adapted to colonialism and the changes that came with it. In times of great social, political, and economic distress, great prophets have often arisen within native communities to try to help their people to reorient themselves, to overcome hardship, and to move forward and survive, blending new ideas and established cultural traditions. Prophets performed similar functions long before contact, as both social critics and as harbingers of great social and cultural change. Within many native communities and traditions there are narratives in which prophets foretell the coming of Europeans, the great social and cultural changes that would be forthcoming, and the potential end of the world.

> Full-fledged prophetic movements almost never occurred in the initial encounter between Native Americans and Europeans. Rather, they emerged after several generations of either direct or indirect contact. They emerged most often within the kind of unequal and exploitative relations that characterized full-fledged colonialism . . . they not only reacted and rebelled against colonialism, they also innovated tradition and initiated new ways of life within the world created by contact.
>
> (Martin, 1991: 683–4)

Some prophetic movements have also been associated with times of warfare. The Pueblo Revolt of 1680 is associated with the great Pueblo prophet Popé, who foresaw the defeat of the Spanish by the Pueblo peoples. During the American Revolution, great prophets such as the Shawnee Prophet, Pontiac, and Handsome Lake also rose to prominence among their peoples in times of great social distress. But the majority of religious prophets in native communities functioned as arbiters of social activity and change, and offered a way for communities to respond to great social, political and spiritual changes, within a cultural framework that would make sense within their communities.

Prophets incorporated traditional ideals, while also borrowing freely from both other native groups and from non-natives. This often led to the creation of new dances, new songs, and new stories meant to represent the transforming reality of a given place and time. Prophets, in their criticism, attacked specific social and cultural practices within their own communities, and tended to focus on practices that endangered the community rather than just the individual. The things they attacked, such as alcohol use, changes in family structure and kinship relations, and the incorporation of Christian ideals, were not seen as inherently bad in and of themselves, but rather specifically in terms of their negative threats and consequences to the community. Prophecy should thus be understood as an internal system which had existed long before contact with Europeans, focused on reorienting a people within a changing historical and cultural framework.

> In almost all these revolts, the critique of colonialism began at home with self-critique. This self-critique brought to consciousness major ways in which the people had collaborated with colonial forces . . . the internal struggle, which sometimes became civil war, demonstrated once again that transformative movements were movements in which Native Americans reclaimed their power to shape their own future as they saw fit, in accord with their understandings of power. For participants in these movements, history was understood not from the perspective of passive victims confronting a monolithic and inevitable invasion. Rather, they affirmed that their situation was partly their responsibility by asserting that their situation resulted from the action of *traitors within*, traitors who had neglected tradition. . . .
>
> (Martin, 1991: 686–88)

Ceremonialism and ritual activity

Despite the changes wrought by colonialism, Native American religious systems survived, partly because of their ability to adapt and change as conditions changed and opportunities arose. New, pan-Indian religious movements, such as the Ghost Dance, arose during the nineteenth century, and centuries-old traditions, such as the Potlatch in the Pacific Northwest and the Sun Dance on the Plains, changed dramatically in response to significant cultural changes. The common link between them, however, is the fact that in each instance, native communities sought to assert and maintain cultural uniqueness, both in how they interpreted change, and how they applied these ideas to their own traditions to make them relevant to the specific time and place they were practised. Once again, we see agency being very strongly asserted from within Native American religious traditions.

The Ghost Dance movement

Probably the most well known religious movement among Native Americans in the nineteenth and twentieth centuries has been the Ghost Dance movement. Started in Nevada in the late 1800s and stemming from a series of spiritual visions received by the Paiute Jack Wilson (Wovoka), the Ghost Dance became a nation-wide movement which connected Native Americans across the country around common issues of poverty, destitution, despair, and hopelessness. This spiritual movement was able to offer varied people hope in times of great despair, despite their cultural differences, and functioned as a catalyst for many future changes in the relationships between Native Americans and the larger political entities which were overseeing them during this period.

The Ghost Dance also brought severe rebuke, however, from missionaries, from Indian agents, and from the government as a whole, who all greatly feared a spiritual movement which was banding Native Americans together and causing them to question their current conditions and call for drastic changes. Ultimately, this conflict over the Ghost Dance led to the greatest single massacre of unarmed Native Americans in US history – that of Wounded Knee (South Dakota) in 1890, where hundreds of Native Americans were gunned down, left to die in the snow, and buried in unmarked mass graves. This landmark event signalled the determination of the government to subdue Native American religious activities and identity, to the point of being willing to kill people to make it happen.

Where we see native agency in the Ghost Dance movement is in the ways in which different groups interpreted the message of the prophet Wovoka. Rather than a static, generalized message meant to fit all people and all situations, the message was reshaped, moulded, and changed by communities to fit their own needs and situations. What was considered a peaceful spiritual endeavor by the Paiute was interpreted as a call to activism and resistance by the Lakota. Much like with missionization and the ideals of Christianity, the message had to make sense, within a given cultural and spiritual framework, or it would be rejected. Native people sometimes syncretized cultural ideals, elements of Christianity, and new ideas from pan-Indian movements like the Ghost Dance to come up with whole new, locally and culturally specific religious movements, through which they responded to their current situations and made decisions about their futures.

> References to the Great Father, Jesus and the Bible attest to the influence of Christian missionaries. The presence of Christian syncretisms in Ghost Dance rituals suggests that the Kiowa adopted concepts from Christianity that accommodated their needs. Belief or disbelief in Christianity was founded in the Kiowa notion of *dwdw*, or power, which has remained intact since the collapse of the horse and buffalo culture. Kiowa individuals merely chose the religion they felt was most powerful.
> (Kracht, 1992: 463)

Potlatch and Sun Dance

The Potlatch is a ceremonial complex distinct to the Pacific Northwest, Western Canada and Alaska. Originally, it served a variety of functions in different communities: as an initiation ritual, used to mark important life events such as the birth of a child, or marriage; as a validation of social status within a community; or as reverence and awareness of supernatural power in the world. However, with the influx of European trade goods like blankets and copper items, the ceremony changed and evolved into a means of maintaining and observing social hierarchy, community values, and a sense of cultural identity. The Potlatch, or 'give away' ceremony as it is sometimes called, became a way to balance wealth within the community, by ensuring a more even distribution of material items, but also became a way for people to validate their status within the society through gifting and exchange.

> The ability of the potlatch to serve as the key link between the 'thought of' and the 'lived in' socio-cultural order explains its centrality in nineteenth-century Tlingit life, as well as its survival into the present, despite years of criticism from missionaries and government officials and significant changes in the native culture and society.
>
> (Kan, 1986: 207)

The Potlatch has economic, social, legal and spiritual dimensions, and as such, offers a good example of the lack of separation between what is 'sacred' and what is 'profane' within Native American communities. With the influx of new materials in the region, such as the Hudson Bay blanket, and the removal of groups from specific geographical areas, Potlatch served as a logical response mechanism through which to filter new cultural situations and economic realities. It synchronized social reality with cosmology and spiritual beliefs, and also allowed these native communities to participate in two economies at once: the capitalistic economy being forced on them by outsiders, and the traditional spiritual economy of exchange (through the development of items like the Button Blanket). Native people were able to act out and express their spiritual ideals and cultural values through the incorporation of new social structures, political ideals, and material objects.

In the late nineteenth and the early twentieth century, Potlatching was outlawed and, in some cases, actually made illegal, as part of the effort to subdue Native American religious activity and force conversions to Christianity and acceptance of the process of Americanization and Westernization. Despite these efforts, however, the Potlatch continued to be practised, in a more clandestine fashion, and continues to function within Native American communities in these areas today. The Potlatch continues to include important ceremonial feasts, the exchange of gifts and commodities, and revolves around their concepts of cultural balance and identity.

The Sun Dance, typically practised in the Great Plains region of the United States, but sometimes seen to have extended into other areas and communities as well, has always been one of the most controversial Native American ceremonial activities. Typically involving the ritual piercing of practitioners as part of their ritual offering, missionaries, Indian agents, and outsiders have held the ritual up as a prime example of Native American paganism and savagism, and have misunderstood the ceremony to be some sort of horrific ritual to the Sun or Sun-god.

Yet the Sun Dance is in fact a highly ritualized, deeply ceremonial, community-based activity, meant to cement the relationship between the individual and the Creator, but also meant to ensure the health, safety, and continuity of the entire community by the individual giving of their own flesh for the sake of others. From the preparation of the location to the choosing of the Sun Dance pole to the actual ceremony itself (which sometimes lasts as long as four days) the Sun Dance stands out as a distinct example of American Indian spiritual activity, which was often community-based or -oriented and which was often directed at healing, health, and maintenance of a people and a way of life.

Because of the impact that colonialism has had on native communities on the Plains, the Sun Dance has undergone various changes over time. There are many varieties of the ceremony, some considered to be more 'traditional' than others, some of which have incorporated elements of Christianity and other beliefs, and some of which bear little resemblance to their historical predecessors. Again, I would suggest that we read this as cultural and spiritual flexibility, and as a tool that works both to help a community and a religious complex survive, and to make spiritual activity make sense in a specific time and place. To fall into arguments over what is and isn't 'traditional' is in part to miss the point. Tradition is what people *do*, now, in the contemporary, not what they *did* in some distant, ill-defined past. Plains people have maintained and grown their traditions in large part because of their cultural tenacity and ability to adapt their beliefs and values to current experiences rather than abstract dogmas, and native people will continue to do so into the distant future. This, again, is part of that larger process of spiritual agency and strength.

Environmentalism and religious freedom

As we have noted, Native American religions are place-based, and inasmuch, their maintenance and continuity requires continued access to important, spiritual places at specific times of the year. This relationship to place has led to the stereotype of Native Americans as 'simpler' people, and has brought them sometimes undue and unwanted attention from groups like the environmental movement, for whom native people and their traditions have become almost mascots. It has also caused significant legal issues, particularly around the issue of religious freedom, access to places and religious materials, and the control and use of native remains. Native religions have resisted simplification of their conceptions of the world, and have actively sought to maintain their social and cultural distinctness, despite such external intrusions.

The environmental Indian

The stereotypes of the 'environmental Indian' or the 'Indian as natural man' have plagued Native Americans since the time of earliest contact, and continue to be employed by various outside entities such as the modern environmental movement, the Boy Scouts of America, and the New Age movement. Today, people are encouraged to treat the world as the Indians did, to walk on the earth like the Indians, and to be more nativistic in their overall orientation to the natural world. Is such a thing possible? In our contemporary, materialistic society, how can we connect with the world around us, and does it make sense to try to mimic another culture, and really, another religious system, in order to develop or maintain such a relationship? Despite efforts to do so, is it possible to mimic another culture from within one's own?

What we have here is a native cosmology that is so fundamentally different from ours as to make even comparison very difficult. To suggest that we might adopt such an Indian world view is preposterous . . . surely we deluded ourselves when we imagined that the Indian could teach us his peculiar land ethic; we did not understand that it is not just a land ethic but a comprehensive way of life. Anyway, as far as the Indian is concerned, it isn't he who does the teaching, but rather the land . . . We are not presently in a position to understand culture and humaneness in discourse with the land – or with the Indian for that matter. Both, unfortunately, are inarticulate in the world as we presently define it.

(Martin, 1981: 250–51)

Traditional native relationships with place are based on close observation of both nature and natural phenomena. Native people, in spending generation after generation in the same place, developed a deep knowledge – what we might call a scientific knowledge – of the world around them, and attuned themselves to this world. They recognize that all things exist on their own terms, and that there are webs of inter-action and power in the world, with which the human must align himself. Native Americans thus managed their environments accordingly, and through this specialized environmental knowledge, developed ceremonial activities directed toward maintaining relationships with powerful, non-human persons all around them. If we understand that the word culture, in its root form, means basically 'to inhabit and care for a place' we begin to see the inherent connection between the development of a culture and the place in which that culture develops. No culture develops in a vacuum, and therefore, in inhabiting a place and cultivating it for a long period of time, Native Americans were, and continue to be, developing cultural practices which would be actualized through the body (through actions) into specific places. Sound ecological ideals converted into religious terms and ritual became the physical representation of social values, creating kinship with place.

With this in mind, is this notion of the environmental Indian a valid one? Native Americans certainly had, and continue to have, specialized ecological and environmental knowledge and philosophies, but these are not inherent racial, social, or cultural traits. Instead, they represent hundreds if not thousands of years of relationships with specific places, and may only seem foreign to most of us because most Americans, as fairly new residents of the 'New World', lack this length of relationship with and experience of place. Native Americans are active in environmentalism and ecological movements today, but perhaps for very different reasons than most Americans, and likely for reasons which are much more religious and spiritual in nature than the average.

Religious freedom

The First Amendment to the United States Constitution notes that, 'Congress shall make no law respecting an establishment of religion, or prohibiting the free exer-cise thereof'. If this is the case, and we take this text on its face value, why is religious

FIGURE 11.1 The Black Hills

Devil's Tower in the Black Hills region of Wyoming. Sioux tribe members continue to fight the US government over the rights to this picturesque region more than a century after the discovery of gold forced the Sioux tribes to give up the Black Hills and enter reservations. Courtesy Getty Images.

freedom such an important issue for Native Americans today? The reasoning lies in the wording of the amendment, and how it has been understood through the development of American policy towards American Indians and their religious activities and identities. In this case, 'free exercise' has been interpreted to protect beliefs, but not actions. What is clear is that the First Amendment has been understood to make a clear distinction between a religious belief and a religious activity, which is troubling for Native American religious followers, who don't make such a distinction, and whose traditions are less focused on maintaining a text or set of religious dogma, and more focused on the continued performance of religious ceremonies and activities in both daily life and according to ritual cycles. In as much, native religions have come into direct conflict with environmental groups, who wish to maintain the sanctity of natural places for very different reasons, and who fail to understand native religious ideologies or needs, or, more likely, simply choose to ignore those needs for the sake of others that are considered more valid or pressing.

Historically, the battle over religious freedom was fought between Native Americans and agents of the government, including missionaries, Indian agents, and educators. After centuries of oppression, many native religious activities 'went underground' as a protective mechanism, and therefore seem to have disappeared to the general public. Yet they are still active and vibrant within communities, but also now held very secretively, away from the public eye.

The list of indigenous practices prohibited by federal regulations promulgated in 1883, 1892, and again in 1904 included: 1) all dances and 'any similar feast', 2) all plural and polygamous marriages and those not 'solemnized' by an appointed judge, 3) all practices of medicine men and the prevention of Indian children from attending religious schools, 4) the destruction, injury, taking or carrying away of any personal property without reference to its value, particularly in the case of the death of an Indian, 5) immorality, particularly the exchange of gifts between families when negotiating marriages, 6) intoxication, and 7) the failure to 'adopt habits of industry, or to engage in civilized pursuits or employments'.

(Gooding, 1996: 161, taken from 'Rules for Indian Courts', 1892)

Various legal battles are underway today in America to clarify this issue, and also to get the US government to recognize that Native American religions are just as valid as other religions, and deserve equal protection under the law. Most of these legal battles centre around access to and use of specific places on the natural landscape – so-called sacred spaces, which are critical to the maintenance and function of native religious traditions. Places such as Devil's Tower in Wyoming, the Medicine Wheel in the Bighorn Mountains and Mount Graham in Arizona have become hotbeds for arguments about religious freedom, and what it really means to practise religion in America today.

One of the other significant contemporary religious freedom issues Native Americans are dealing with is the issue of repatriation. With the passage of the Native American Graves Protection and Repatriation Act (NAGPRA) in 1990, a door was opened to discuss the history of the collection of all things materially Indian, the pilfering of graves, and the violation of ceremonial activities and sites by geologists, anthropologists, grave robbers, and collectors of all kinds. NAGPRA has opened the door for tribes to attempt to re-obtain important ceremonial, cultural, and individual material goods which have long been lost to them, housed in universities, museums, and private collections throughout the United States and the world.

Yet this law has also created new challenges to tribes. How do they go about 'proving' that things belong to them without invalidating the sanctity of their spiritual activities and beliefs? How do they handle these powerful and sacred items in an appropriate and respectful manner, and what is to become of these things once they are repatriated? This has created very different, and sometimes conflicting, ideas both within native communities and between them in terms of whether such powerful items should be repatriated, what to do with them if they are, and how to address their original loss to outsiders. It has also created great tension between tribes and the institutions which are currently in possession of these materials, including some of the largest and most important museums in the country, as these organizations do not wish to give up these artifacts, and have actively fought to prevent tribes from repatriating ceremonial and cultural artifacts, out of fear of those artifacts being lost or destroyed.

Native American religions in the contemporary context

This section focuses on two important developments in Native American spiritual traditions today – the development of new, more globalized religious movements such as the Native American Church, and the subsequent rise of movements intent on spiritually appropriating Native American religious ideas, including the New Age movement and 'hobbyism'. Ironically, the spiritual appropriators are often operating on the assumption that Native Americans have disappeared, or are at least no longer culturally 'authentic', and therefore their religious traditions are up for grabs, while new, pan-Indian religious movements suggest exactly the opposite – that Native Americans are still alive and well, and still actively engaging their spiritual lives and practising cultural and spiritual agency in the contemporary world.

Spiritual appropriations

Native American religions are facing a relatively new challenge in the contemporary period – the appropriation of their spiritual systems, practices, and beliefs by outsiders, particularly non-native individuals and groups functioning as part of the modern New Age movement. This is an ironic twist, considering that not a century ago, native traditions were outlawed in the United States, and seen as Paganism by most Americans. The New Age movement is a relatively new movement on the American religious scene, and has been interested in culling ideas from a wide variety of religious systems and beliefs in order to create an individually-centred religious system which is acceptable to those who feel lost or disenfranchised by mainstream religious systems (see Chapter 12 on Spirituality and Chapter 13 on New Age religion). The New Age movement has often framed Native Americans as somewhat 'mythical and magical' and many within the movement have sought to profit from native rituals, ceremonies and knowledge through the selling of books, hosting of workshops, and the sale of religious ceremonial participation, which is particularly distasteful to Native Americans today. Their basis for doing so is the idea that contemporary natives are 'corrupted', and they challenge notions of native religions being culturally affiliated and not open to anyone. America has always been more about individual rights than responsibilities, and many, though not all, New Agers have expressed this 'right' in their appropriation of all things native.

> Commercial exploitation of Native American spiritual traditions has permeated the New Age movement since its emergence in the 1980s. Euro-Americans professing to be medicine people have profited from publications and workshops. Mass quantities of products promoted as 'Native American sacred objects' have been successfully sold by white entrepreneurs to a largely non-Indian market . . . New Age interest in Native American cultures appears more concerned with exoticized images and romanticized rituals revolving around a distorted view of Native American spirituality than with the indigenous people themselves and the very real (and often ugly) socio-economic and political problems they face as colonized peoples.
>
> (Aldred, 2000: 329–333)

Hobbyism has become another way in which native spiritual practices are being appropriated by those outside the cultural bounds of the traditions. Hobbyists are those people who 'play Indian' on the weekend, dressing up in what they consider to be 'authentic' Indian garb and performing a wide variety of generic 'Indian' ceremonies. These groups typically have no connection with actual native communities, and have actively bought into the stereotype of mimicking natives to 'get back to nature'. 'Indian clubs' have become very popular in Europe, and are beginning to infiltrate America as well, as non-natives take to wearing Indian garb, practising Indian ceremonies, and imitating Indian cultural and social activities, typically in weekend gatherings at clandestine locations.

Yet this type of 'religious borrowing' has been actively resisted by many American Indians, who see such spiritual appropriation as simply another step in the long history of cultural loss and assault. This has led to some outright conflicts between individuals, tribes, and New Age groups, and raises important arguments about what religion really is, who has control over it and rights to it, and what to make of those who take freely from other traditions and cultures without actively participating in or contributing to them.

The Native American Church

One of the ways in which Native American religiosity is playing out in the contemporary world is through the proliferation of the Native American Church (NAC), sometimes also called the Peyote Church or Peyote Religion, both within communities and across community bounds in a larger, pan-Indian context. The NAC is built around traditional religious values and activities, such as the use of purification and the sweat lodge, as well as healing and community-building, but has also incorporated elements of Christianity into its rituals, making it a more syncretic faith, and signalling a more common adaptation among native people today – the joining of faith ideas into new religious ideologies and movements.

Religious use of peyote, a hallucinogenic cactus, is said to have begun in indigenous communities in Mexico thousands of years ago. Through both travel and trade, peyote made its way into various Native American communities, where it was incorporated into religious ceremonies and rituals. The Native American Church, as an established movement, is said to have started around 1890, and incorporated significant Christian elements. It is still very actively practised in native communities across the United States, and is said to be the largest religion practised by Native Americans today.

The NAC recognizes two roads to contemporary native life. The first road is known as the 'profane road'. It is wide and paved, but also full of temptation and trouble. It is easy for an individual to go down this road, but it is rarely fulfilling. The second road is the Peyote Road. Visualize it as being narrow, unpaved, and weaving back and forth through the natural world, rather than straight over it. It is a journey that one must, at its core, make alone, and the journey is often challenging, and uphill. It is peyote that will help the individual crest that hill, and then begin moving downhill, which will be much easier.

FIGURE 11.2
Peyote ceremony

Navaho Indians at
Peyote Ceremony
in Hogan, near
Pinyon, holding a
special ceremony
for a sick boy.
Time & Life Pictures/
Getty Images.

Summary

- Native American religions are adaptive, flexible, culturally localized traditions that are based more on experience than dogma, and more 'spatial' than 'linear'.

- Linear traditions are those focused on time and its linear progression, focused on the working out of the 'divine plan' at the expense of the natural world, spatial traditions are those which arise from a relationship with a specific geographical location, and which orient themselves around that relationship. Place is more important than time.

- Missionization functioned as part of the larger process of colonialism in the United States.

- Missionaries saw native religions as childish, archaic, simplistic paganism.

- Native Americans practised agency in their relationships with missionaries, accepting parts of their religions, but rejecting others, based on their ability to correlate them with the beliefs they already had.

- Prophets and prophetic movements function as social critique, evaluating changes that occur, and devising new responses based on the syncretism of old and new ideas.

- The Ghost Dance movement, probably the best known Native American religious movement, was adapted by each group that practised it, in order to make it culturally relevant.

■ Changes in the Potlatch ceremony were a logical response that allowed natives in the Pacific Northwest to participate in the market economy while also maintaining cultural and spiritual traditions.

■ Native Americans have been stereotyped as being more 'in touch with nature' when in fact their environmental knowledge has been cultivated over long cultural and spiritual relationships with places.

■ Religious freedom is a critical issue for Native Americans, who do not separate religious beliefs from religious actions.

■ The issue of repatriation centres around issues related to Native American burial remains, particularly those in museums and collections.

■ Participation in the New Age movement and hobbyism are ways that non-natives have appropriated Native American spiritual traditions.

■ The Native American Church is one of the largest religious movements among natives today, and shows integration of traditional ideas with Christianity.

Key terms

agency The exertion of power or influence to promote ideas or desires.

Button Blanket New cultural materials, constructed by Native Americans in the Pacific Northwest, made from Hudson Bay blankets. A good example of the integration of traditional symbols and motifs with an imposed material object.

dogma A settled, authoritative doctrine that is rarely open to change.

Ghost Dance A national religious movement among Native Americans which began in the late nineteenth century and which predicted a return to traditional ideals and values.

hobbyism A movement typified by non-Native Americans who dress and act like 'Indians' and who appropriate native spiritual ideals and rituals.

Indian agents Government agents assigned to oversee Native American reservation communities and impose government ideals and values there.

linear traditions Traditions oriented around the progression of time and the historical value of human events.

missionization The process of attempting, sometimes forcibly, to convert individuals from one religion to another.

monogenetic creation The idea of a single act of creation, out of which all peoples can trace descent.

Native American Church Also known as the Peyote Religion, a contemporary religious movement in Native American communities that syncretizes native and Christian ideals.

New Age movement A self-help spiritual movement often associated with the appropriation of Native American spiritual ideals, sometimes for financial gain.

Pan-Indian A term used to describe ideas, concepts, music, religions, etc., which are not culturally bounded within specific native groups, but rather are more general and universal.

peyote A hallucinogenic cactus plant used in ceremonies by the Native American Church.

Potlatch A ritual complex from the Pacific Northwest focused on exchange, cultural standing, and the maintenance of cultural ideals.

prophecy The act of foretelling future events, but also the act of self-critique and criticism practiced by Native American religious figures.

religious freedom Legal protection from religious persecution, this concept is important for Native Americans because it has legally been interpreted to protect only religious beliefs and not actions.

repatriation The return of material objects and funerary remains, including human remains, to Native Americans from museums, universities and other collections.

ritual piercing Part of the Sun Dance ritual, individuals are pierced on the chest, legs, and/or back with bones and offer their flesh for individual and community health.

sacred spaces Places on the land where religious activity occurs, these are often contested in religious freedom cases in the United States.

spatial traditions Traditions oriented around a long-developed relationship with a geographical location. Religious ideals and values spring up from this relationship with place.

spiritual appropriation The practice of religious traditions by those who are not actually members of that tradition.

Sun Dance A ritual complex typically found in the Great Plains which focuses on ritual piercing and sacrifice to obtain individual and community health.

sweat lodge A Native American domed structure often used for purification rituals, either alone or as part of another ritual complex.

syncretism The blending of ideas from multiple traditions, cultures, etc., to form a new set of beliefs, ideals, etc.

traditional ecological knowledge A term used to describe Native American environmental knowledge, formed over a long time in a particular place.

Wounded Knee The site of a massacre in 1890 associated with followers of the Ghost Dance movement. It is the largest massacre of non-military individuals in US military history.

Wovoka Also known as Jack Wilson, the Paiute prophet whose visions became the foundation of the Ghost Dance movement.

Further reading

Linear and circular orientations

Vine Deloria Jr.: 'Thinking in Time and Space'. In *God is Red: A Native View of Religion*, thirtieth anniversary edition (Golden, CO: Fulcrum Publishing, 2003, pp. 61–75). A critique of Christianity and its linear focus, which also addresses issues of civil religion and its relationship to Native American spatial traditions.

Donald Fixico: 'American Indian Circular Philosophy'. In *The American Indian Mind in a Linear World: American Indian Studies and Traditional Knowledge* (New York: Routledge, 2003, pp. 41–61). An examination of the notion of circularity as it pertains to Native American ideologies and religious systems.

Winona LaDuke: 'What is Sacred?'. In *Recovering the Sacred: The Power of Naming and Claiming* (Cambridge, MA: South End Press, 2005, pp. 11–15). A brief examination of the ways in which the notion of 'sacred' functions in Native American belief systems.

M. Jane Young: '"Pity the Indians of Outer Space": Native American Views of the Space Program'. *Western Folklore* 46, (1987: pp. 269–279). An examination of what is unique about Native American ideology through an examination of ideas about outer space, space exploration, and the continuation of frontier ideology.

Native American religions and Western colonialism

Michael D. McNally: 'The Practice of Native American Christianity'. *Church History* 69(4), (2000: pp. 834–859). An attempt to look at the religious actions resulting from Missionization, focusing specifically on Ojibwe hymn singers and their syncretism of Ojibwe and Christian concepts.

Joel W. Martin: 'Before and beyond the Sioux Ghost Dance: Native American Prophetic Movements and the Study of Religion'. *Journal of the American Academy of Religion* 59(4), (1991: pp. 677–701). Looks at the historical function of prophecy in Native American communities, and the ways in which prophets help communities to accept change and integrate new ideas.

Irene S. Vernon: 'The Claiming of Christ: Native American Postcolonial Discourses'. *MELUS* 24(2), (1999: 75–88). Examination of the consequences of Missionization in Native American communities, particularly the notion of syncretism and how Christian ideals have been adapted to fit native realities.

Elizabeth Vibert: '"The Natives Were Strong to Live": Reinterpreting Early Nineteenth-Century Prophetic Movements in the Columbia Plateau'. *Ethnohistory*, 42(2), (1995: pp. 197–229). An examination of the role and function of prophecy on the Columbia Plateau, particularly focusing on the existence of prophetic movements before contact with Europeans.

Ceremonialism and ritual activity

Arthur Amiotte: 'The Lakota Sun Dance: Historical and Contemporary Perspectives'. In Raymond DeMaille and Douglas Parks (eds), *Sioux Indian Religion: Tradition and Innovation* (Norman, OK: University of Oklahoma Press, 1987, pp. 75–89). An examination of the history and function of the Lakota Sun Dance, as well as some of the contemporary changes which have occurred within the complex.

Raymond Bucko: 'The Contemporary Lakota Sweat Lodge'. In *The Lakota Ritual of the Sweat Lodge: History and Contemporary Practice* (Lincoln, NE: University of Nebraska Press, 1998, pp. 59–96). Shows the role and function of the Lakota sweat lodge, both as a stand-alone ritual and as a cleansing ceremony often used before another ceremonial complex.

Thomas Lewis: 'The Contemporary *Yuwipi*'. In Raymond DeMaille and Douglas Parks (eds), *Sioux Indian Religion: Tradition and Innovation* (Norman, OK: University of Oklahoma Press, 1987, pp. 173–187). Examines Yuwipi as it is practised in the contemporary world, and looks at some of the changes which have taken place within it over time.

Sergei Kan: 'The Nineteenth-Century Tlingit Potlatch: A New Perspective'. *American Ethnologist* 13(2), (1986: pp. 191–212). Suggests that Potlatch moves from being a religious complex to being an economic one due to the imposition of capitalism and the subsequent cultural change that occurs.

Benjamin R. Kracht: 'The Kiowa Ghost Dance, 1894–1916: An Unheralded Revitalization Movement'. *Ethnohistory* 39(4), (1992: 452–477). Examination of the Ghost Dance among the Kiowa, its cultural relevance for them, and its continuation beyond the more well known versions of the complex.

Joseph Masco: '"It is a Strict Law That Bids Us Dance": Cosmologies, Colonialism, Death, and Ritual Authority in the Kwakwaka'wakw Potlatch, 1849 to 1922'. *Comparative Studies in Society and History* 37(1), (1995: 41–75). Examines the historical functions of the Potlatch in this native community, and the historical and cultural changes/adaptations which have occurred within the complex over time.

Thomas W. Overholt: 'The Ghost Dance of 1890 and the Nature of the Prophetic Process'. *Ethnohistory* 21(1), (1974: pp. 37–63). Looks at the ways in which the message of the Ghost Dance was transmitted through middle men, and subsequently adapted to fit the needs and cultural values of different communities.

William K. Powers: *'Sun Dance' in Oglala Religion* (Lincoln, NE: University of Nebraska Press, 1975, pp. 95–100). A brief overview of the process of the Sun Dance, including some of the ritual activities leading up to the dance itself.

William Powers: *Selected Readings from Yuwipi: Vision and Experience in Oglala Ritual* (Lincoln, NE: University of Nebraska Press, 1982, pp. 38–72). An extremely detailed explanation of the Yuwipi ritual, its processes, and its function in native communities.

James R. Walker: *Selected Readings from Lakota Belief and Ritual* (Lincoln, NE: University of Nebraska Press, 1980, pp. 176–191). A collection of first-person descriptions and narratives about the meaning and function of the Sioux Sun Dance.

Environmentalism and religious freedom

Vine Deloria, Jr.: 'Secularism, Civil Religion and the Religious Freedom of American Indians'. In Devon Mihesuah (ed.) *Repatriation Reader: Who Owns American Indian Remains?* (Lincoln, NE: University of Nebraska Press, 2000, pp. 169–179). A brief overview of the history of the issues of religious freedom, as well as its relevance and impact for Native Americans.

Roger C. Echo-Hawk: 'Ancient History in the New World: Integrating Oral Traditions and the Archaeological Record in Deep Time'. *American Antiquity* 65(2), (2000: pp. 267–290). An attempt to elucidate ways in which Native American oral narratives can be used as 'evidence' in issues of religious freedom, where other written evidence does not exist.

T.J. Ferguson, Roger Anyon and Edmund Ladd: 'Repatriation at the Pueblo of Zuni: Diverse Solutions to Complex Problems'. In Devon Mihesuah (ed.), *Repatriation Reader: Who Owns American Indian Remains?* (Lincoln, NE: University of Nebraska Press, 2000, pp. 239–265). An examination of the issue of repatriation as it applied to a specific repatriation effort undertaken by the Zuni tribe in order to return religious objects to tribal control.

Susan Staiger Gooding: 'At the Boundaries of Religious Identity: Native American Religions and American Legal Culture'. *Numen*, 43(2), Religion, Law and the Construction of Identities, (1996: pp. 157–183). An overview of the American legal system and its dealings with Native American religions.

Ira Jacknis: 'Repatriation as Social Drama: The Kwakiutl Indians of British Columbia, 1922–1980'. In Devon Mihesuah (ed.), *Repatriation Reader: Who Owns American Indian Remains?* (Lincoln, NE: University of Nebraska Press, 2000, pp. 266–281). A historical examination of a lengthy effort by the Kwakiutl tribe to return important artifacts to the tribe, and the result of such repatriation.

Shepard Krech III: 'Reflections on Conservation, Sustainability and Environmentalism in Indigenous North America'. *American Anthropologist* 107(1), (2005: 78–86). An attempt to counter ideas of Native American environmentalism by showing ways in which Native Americans acted counter to environmental ideals at times.

Calvin Martin: 'The American Indian as Miscast Ecologist'. *The History Teacher* 14(2), (1981: 243–252). An examination of the stereotype of the Native American as natural ecologist, and the issues associated with the promulgation of such a stereotype.

Robert S. Michaelsen. 'The Significance of the American Indian Religious Freedom Act of 1978'. *Journal of the American Academy of Religion* 52(1), (1984: pp. 93–115). An examination of the significance, or lack thereof, of the American Indian Religious Freedom Act, and its inability to effect real protections for Native American religious traditions.

Raymond Pierotti and Daniel Wildcat: 'Traditional Ecological Knowledge: The Third Alternative (Commentary)'. *Ecological Applications* 10(5), (2000: pp. 1333–1340). A complex piece which attempts to elucidate ideas about Native American environmental knowledge and the notion of being native to a place.

Native American religions in the contemporary context

Lisa Aldred: 'Plastic Shamans and Astroturf Sun Dances: New Age Commercialization of Native American Spirituality'. *American Indian Quarterly* 24(3), (2000: pp. 329–352). Shows the history of New Age spiritual appropriation, especially as it concerns commercialization and the sale of books, rituals, and ceremonies to non-natives, by non-natives.

Phil Cousineau and Gary Rhine: 'The Peyote Ceremony'. In Huston and Reuben Snake (compiled and eds), *One Nation Under God: The Triumph of the Native American Church* (Santa Fe, NM: Clear Light Publishers, 1996, pp. 77–101). An inside examination of the role of the Peyote ceremony, and more specifically, of the meaning of the different elements of the ritual as a whole.

Rayna Green: 'The Tribe Called Wannabee: Playing Indian in America and Europe'. *Folklore* 99(1),

(1988: pp. 30–55). An examination of the history of hobbyism among a variety of groups, both in the United States and Europe.

Emerson Spider Sr.: 'The Native American Church of Jesus Christ'. In Raymond DeMaille and Douglas Parks (eds), *Sioux Indian Religion: Tradition and Innovation* (Norman, OK: University of Oklahoma Press, 1987, pp. 189–209). A description of one faction of the Native American Church that rejects traditional Native American religion and ideals and uses almost wholly Christian ideals to fashion its rituals and ceremonies.

Chapter 12

Spirituality

Giselle Vincett and Linda Woodhead

'Spirituality' can mean many things. Originally it was a term which referred to a mystical stream within mainstream religious traditions. Books on 'Christian spirituality', for example, dealt with practices integral to that tradition which foster personal piety and devotion to the Christian God. By the mid-nineteenth century, however, 'spirituality' was being used in a different way: it was being contrasted with mainstream, traditional forms of religion and presented as a preferable alternative. The latter usage has persisted to the present day, and explains why some people still speak about 'alternative' or 'complementary' spirituality, or say they are 'spiritual not religious' or 'spiritual and religious'. They are drawing a contrast between 'religion', understood as having to do with external, dogmatic authority set over the individual, and 'spirituality', understood as having to do with the deepest experiences of the individual as he or she comes in touch with that which is most sacred, or of ultimate concern. Thus the term 'spirituality' is value-laden from the start, and it enshrines a key conflict at the heart of modern religion.

The fact that 'spirituality' is an 'emic' (insider) term, rather than an 'etic' (outsider) term does not mean that it cannot be used in the study of modern religion, but that it must be used critically. Critical distance is lost if spirituality is taken at face value as the true, subjective essence of religion in contrast to 'religion' understood as the external husk of dogmatic beliefs and empty rituals. But critical distance can be maintained if we understand spirituality as a movement which arises in the nineteenth century in conscious reaction against existing forms of traditional religion, particularly the more conservative Christian churches. As such, spirituality positions itself as preferable to religion and more in tune with key modern values – and thereby positions religion as inferior. This sort of spirituality, which will be the main focus of this chapter, can be distinguished by its possession of all or some of the following features:

- a value-laden contrast between spirituality and religion;
- emphasis on the importance of inner, subjective, ineffable experience;
- authorization of the individual to be the final arbiter of spiritual truth;
- high valuation of 'seeking'; open and tolerant attitude towards other spiritual 'paths';
- promotion of practical, often embodied, means and techniques for attaining spiritual insight – e.g. meditation;
- tendency to embrace 'progressive' and 'anti-establishment' causes, including liberalism, equality, democracy, self-development (though it can also take right wing and elitist forms);
- universalistic or 'holistic' emphasis (i.e. an emphasis on the interconnectedness of things).

In practice spirituality demonstrates considerable diversity, and has changed significantly over time. Diversity has intensified as spirituality has matured and grown in influence, not only in the West, but across the globe. 'Spirituality' is thus a label for many different types of practice rather than the name of a single variety of religion. This chapter offers an overview and introduction to the most important contemporary varieties of spirituality, several of which are investigated in more detail in the chapters which follow. Far from being a realm of harmonious co-operation, differences between the several kinds of spirituality – like New Age and Paganism – often run deep. Even within a single form of spirituality, like Paganism, there can be deep inner divides between different groups and tendencies.

Go placidly amid the noise and haste and remember what peace there may be in silence.

Be yourself. Especially, do not feign affection. Neither be cynical about love; for in the face of all aridity and disenchantment it is perennial as the grass.

Do not distress yourself with imaginings. Many fears are born of fatigue and loneliness. Beyond a wholesome discipline, be gentle with yourself.

You are a child of the universe, no less than the trees and the stars; you have a right to be here. And whether or not it is clear to you, no doubt the universe is unfolding as it should.

Therefore be at peace with God, whatever you conceive Him to be, and whatever your labors and aspirations, in the noisy confusion of life keep peace with your soul.

BOX 12.1 Extract from *Desiderata* by Max Ehrman (1927), a text which has remained popular down the centuries within many different forms of spirituality

Institutional forms

Some forms of religion maintain a balance between individual members, the religious community and its leaders, and its sacred texts and symbols. The authority of each one balances the other. For example, the authority of individual judgement should not outweigh that of scripture, and the demands of the community must temper the demands of the individual. More authoritarian forms of religion tip the balance, giving sacred scripture, symbols or leaders authority over the individual. For example, a believer must follow the official teaching even if he or she disagrees with it. Spirituality tips the balance the other way, by giving individuals the ultimate authority, and holding that neither a religious community nor its sacred teachings and symbols should override the authority of individual experience. For example, although it may be considered valuable to venerate certain sacred symbols, it is ultimately for the individual to decide which symbols are most meaningful for his or her spiritual journey.

This does not mean that spirituality is necessarily individualistic in the sense of self-centred or narcissistic (concerned only with 'me'). For a start, most spiritual practitioners recognise the authority of many sacred symbols and teachings. There is a common core of teachings widely accepted by most forms of spirituality. There even seems to be an informal canon of sacred documents which are widely accepted by those involved in spirituality – such as the Desiderata, quoted in Box 12.1. Likewise, there are certain sacred symbols, gods and goddesses which are widely venerated, and others which are never associated with any form of spirituality.

Neither is spirituality individualized in the sense that it is practised by isolated individuals entirely on their own. Although a premium is placed on forging one's own spiritual path, and realizing the sacred in the depths of one's own experience, spiritual practitioners connect with others in various ways. Most belong to informal networks, which may connect by way of media like magazines and the internet as well as in occasional face to face gatherings. Such gatherings take place at the local, national, and international levels, for example, in centres of spiritual activity like the town of Glastonbury in England, or at the annual Burning Man Festival in Nevada, which attracts tens of thousands from across the world. There is enormous cultural interchange within spirituality, and those who are involved tend to be highly literate, devoting a great deal of time and money to buying books and other cultural products. In addition, many participants will engage in one-to-one activities, such as visiting a practitioner who will perform healing, usually for a fee, and many also belong to small groups which meet regularly and are dedicated to the mental, physical and spiritual advancement of their members.

What different forms of spirituality tend not to have, however, are forms of authority which override the choices and preferences of individuals. They have no Bible or Qur'an, no single set of noble truths or pillars, no one God, no priesthood or monastic elite whose authority is recognised by all members. This means that it is rare for a form of spirituality to have the power to enforce unity, mobilize 'members' as a unified body, or represent the views of 'followers' to political authorities. Nor can beliefs and behaviour be directed and monitored by a higher authority. In some ways this makes spirituality less powerful than, say, a church. On the other hand, the fact that spirituality is continually produced and reproduced by individuals bound by loose ties of loyalty and fairly close ties of mutual influence gives it great flexibility and adaptability. Change does not have to be imposed from above, but can flow directly from the grassroots. Anyone can set up shop as a provider of new spiritual services or set up a new group, and can tailor their offerings to fit current needs and demand.

It is a mistake to think that the fact that spirituality does not co-operate with political (state) power, in the way many of the world religions do, means that it is politically insignificant, and even 'privatized' (i.e. confined to the sphere of private life). Spirituality has political influence in other ways and through other channels, for example by inspiring and directing commitment to 'progressive' causes and movements like feminism, the environmental movement, pacifism, and so on. Spiritualities are also increasingly located in a wide variety of public spaces, not merely in the home. For example, some forms of spirituality are influential in education, in healthcare, in the marketplace, and even in some workplaces (for example, selective shamanic or 'New Age' practices are sometimes used to train managers in corporate settings).

Although spirituality has its origins in attempts to reform or move beyond what were viewed as the unsatisfactory aspects of Western religion, spirituality also owes a great deal to the interchanges which took place in the colonial era between 'East' and 'West'. It also borrows from various indigenous religions, like Native American and Australian aboriginal religions. Its flexible institutional forms make it adaptable to many different contexts and needs. Spirituality is to be found right across the globe, particularly amongst literate middle classes. It is often popular with those who dissociate themselves from traditional roles, and with those who associate with progressive social and political causes – although historically it has also proved adaptable to right wing causes, including fascism.

There is ongoing debate about the numbers involved in spirituality. Research carried out so far in Europe and America suggests that:

1. the number of active, highly committed, regular participants stands at around 2–5 per cent of the population;
2. the level of adherence/affiliation (indicated by those claiming to be 'spiritual not religious') stands at around 10–20 per cent;
3. agreement with beliefs characteristic of spirituality – such as belief in 'some sort of a spirit or life force' or 'God as something within each person rather than something out there' – lies somewhere between 20 per cent and 40 per cent.

Generally speaking, involvement in spirituality is higher in the United States and northern Europe than in southern Europe. As for the gender and age of participants in spirituality, several studies indicate that most forms of spirituality attract more women than men, and that people are most likely to become involved in spirituality from middle age onwards.

Varieties of spirituality at the start of the twenty-first century

Although interest in spirituality has grown over the course of the twentieth century, there have been periodic explosions of interest and activity. The 1960s was one such period, but there also seems to have been a period of explosive growth from the late 1980s through to the present. In the West, growth has been particularly significant in North America and northern and western Europe, and there has been an increasing diversification within the world of spirituality during this time. Surveying the contemporary scene, we can see a spectrum of different forms of spirituality, ranging from those which attract the most casual interest amongst participants and are most individualized, to those which attract the greatest commitment from their adherents and have more tightly organized social forms, as shown in Figure 12.1 below.

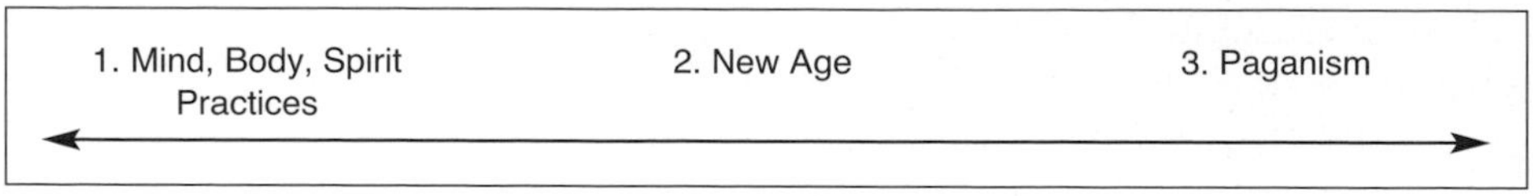

1. Mind, Body, Spirit Practices	2. New Age	3. Paganism

FIGURE 12.1 Spectrum

A spectrum of contemporary forms of Spirituality.

Here we give a brief description of these three main varieties of contemporary spirituality, as well as looking at 'theistic' forms of spirituality. More information about New Age and Paganism can be found in Chapters 13 and 14.

1. 'Mind, Body, Spirit' practices

The forms of spirituality which can be categorized together under this heading pay particular attention to the physical, mental, and spiritual well-being of the individual. 'Well-being' and 'holistic well-being' are key terms. Mind, Body, Spirit practices are typified by one-to-one meetings where a 'client' visits a provider and, for a fee, participates in the practices on offer. Such practices are enormously diverse, and ever-changing. They include, for example, Reiki healing, aromatherapy, reflexology, and various forms of massage. Mind, Body, Spirit practices may also take place in groups with a leader or facilitator. Currently popular group practices include yoga, Tai Chi, Qigong, and various forms of meditation. Clients and group members sometimes participate on a casual and occasional basis. They may use the practices solely for medical/physical purposes – for example, to bring down high blood pressure by relieving stress. There is a close connection between CAM (Complementary and Alternative Medicine) practices and Mind, Body, Spirit practices, with each shading into the other. Broadly speaking, CAM deals only with issues of the body and mind, whilst more spiritual practices 'go deeper' by also addressing spiritual issues. In some cases individuals may come to Mind, Body, Spirit practices seeking only bodily health, but may find themselves attracted to the full holistic approach, and start to pay more attention to their spiritual life. They are thereby drawn deeper into spirituality. This can be an effective mode of recruitment.

Mind, Body, Spirit practices are particularly influential within the area of healthcare and in the beauty and leisure industries. Even state-provided medical care may direct patients to CAM activities in some cases (for example, recommending meditation to deal with anxiety), and individuals who are dissatisfied with 'conventional' medicine often turn to CAM and Mind, Body, Spirit practices. The latter are also influential in the burgeoning leisure and spa 'well-being' industry, which often draws on practices like yoga, aromatherapy and massage to enhance 'inner' as well as 'outer' beauty, and to foster relaxation. Thus Mind, Body, Spirit practices can now be found in an enormous

FIGURE 12.2 Woman meditating
©iStockphoto.com.

range of locations, catering for clients with a very diverse range of social backgrounds and very different levels of wealth. It is possible to partake of practices in private homes or shops for a relatively small sum; or to enjoy similar wellbeing techniques in the most expensive spas in the world.

Mind, Body, Spirit practices are regularly criticised for being individualistic in the sense of selfish, narcissistic and navel-gazing. Because such spirituality can be easily commercialized, it is often depicted as shallow and even deceitful. According to this line of criticism, its proponents con their clients by offering irrational, magical practices for large sums of money. Such criticisms often overlook two important aspects of such practices. First, the vast majority take place in relatively humble surroundings, and are offered by dedicated workers who believe in what they are doing. Many come from caring professions, like teaching and healthcare, and wish to extend their work of care in new directions. Second, although such spirituality is indeed focused upon improving individual well-being, such 'individualism' often has a relational, other-regarding dimension to balance it. This is true of those who provide such practices, who are extending care to others. It may also be true of the largely female clientèle who avail themselves of such practices. One explanation of the enormous popularity of such spirituality with women is due to the fact that it helps them negotiate the conflicting roles and demands which have been placed upon them since the 1960s: to be competitive individuals forging their own career paths, and to continue in traditional roles of caring as mothers, wives, and daughters. Mind, Body, Spirit practices can be used to help find some balance between these conflicting demands and identities.

Mind, Body, Spirit practices currently seem to be most popular with women in their forties and fifties. It may be that they are most attractive to the Baby Boom generation, or it may simply be that the sorts of problems which they deal with are problems which emerge in middle age – for whatever generation. At the moment such practices seem to be proliferating, and there is no sign as yet of any decline in popularity. They may well be the most popular of all the contemporary varieties of spirituality, in part because such varying levels of commitment are possible, and such tangible, health-related outcomes with immediate benefits are promised.

2. New Age

'New Age' is a term which refers to a widespread but diffuse movement. Although its roots stretch as far back as the nineteenth century, it experienced greatest growth and influence in the 1970s, 1980s and early 1990s. There are early signs that 'New Age' is now falling out of fashion, partly because of ridicule in the media. Those involved in Mind, Body, Spirit practices rarely use the term 'New Age' these days, even though they may borrow many elements from the movement, and Pagans actively distance themselves from New Age.

Despite its close connections with other parts of the spectrum of spirituality, key elements of what distinguish many forms of New Age are (a) focus on the individual self and its potential; (b) universalism; and (c) optimism and evolutionary progressivism.

Paul Heelas, one of the most influential scholars of the New Age movement, captured its distinctive individualism when he characterized it as a 'self-spirituality'. Its basic message, he argued, is that 'your life is not working', because you have identified too strongly with 'outside' social pressures and expectations and a false ego. In order to find and free the true self, New Age prescribes that people should become more not less individual, by throwing off social conditioning and discovering their true, authentic, subjective reality. In so doing they can touch with the genuinely sacred, the 'god within', one's 'higher self'.

Different forms of New Age are distinguished by the wide variety of means – mental and physical – which they offer to destroy the 'ego' and allow the true self to shine through. Spiritual seekers are free to borrow from many traditions because of a widespread sense that all religious traditions are built upon common insights (a 'perennial philosophy'). New Age participants locate the authority to select from different traditions firmly within their own self-experience; the ultimate test for the truth of a tradition, philosophy or practice is whether it rings true to oneself. New Agers tend to question external authorities, and to be strongly detraditionalized. Though practitioners often come together on workshops or courses, and though there are some well-known examples of communal forms of New Age (the Findhorn community in Scotland, for example), the dominant discourse is one of individual seeking and experience.

New Age is not narrowly individualistic, however, because it balances its focus on autonomy and individuality with a universalistic philosophy. According to this, difference and individuality is ultimately illusory, since every being is part of a larger whole. The New Age has many cohering themes, and one of the most important is that everything and everyone is connected (holism). As well as emphasising the underlying unity of religions, New Agers discern a unity of connection between all life forms. Further, they see the world as populated by much more than simply what may be seen or touched, and they speak of various spirits and mysterious beings abroad in the world. These beings are generally helpful to the individual (as with spirit guides or guardian angels), and New Agers may try to cultivate relations with such beings, and 'channel' their wisdom so that others can benefit from it as well. New Age practices thus tend to promote both knowledge of self *and* knowledge of the underlying connections between self and the world, particularly its spiritual dimension.

Though New Agers may speak of 'God', they are more likely to talk about ultimate reality in impersonal terms, for example as the 'One', or 'the Universe'. The latter is conceptualized as radically immanent (i.e., the self contains or even *is* God) and transcendent (i.e., something with which one can unite, as the self dissolves into an ocean of Being). It is the experience of unity of self and God (or self as God) which New Agers seek, and they maintain that it is through knowledge of self that they come to know and experience Unity. There is a general optimism in New Age which maintains that all things, and the course of history itself, move inexorably towards a point of culmination, fulfilment and 'Oneness'. Some forms of New Age develop schemes to show the different 'ages' through which we are progressing towards the final state of unity, harmony and realization. Evil, suffering and apparent meaninglessness are considered ultimately illusory. They are stages on the path of spiritual evolution, and when seen in the wider perspective of the unfolding of Oneness, they can be understood to have their own meaning and goodness.

Scholars are divided as to whether the New Age as a movement is continuing to grow or if it is now in decline. It may be that the New Age is a movement which has been particularly important for the Baby Boom generation who were shaped and formed by the cultural revolution of the 1960. Others argue that the New Age has only become less visible because many of its concepts have been absorbed into the general culture of the West; it is a victim of its own success (for more on New Age see Chapter 13).

3. Paganism

Nurture life.
Walk in love and beauty.
Trust the knowledge that comes through the body.
Speak the truth about conflict, pain and suffering.
Take only what you need.
Think about the consequences of your actions for seven generations.
Approach the taking of life with great restraint.
Practice great generosity.
Repair the web.

BOX 12.2 'Nine Ethical Touchstones', Carol Christ (1997) (Carol Christ is an influential writer on goddess spirituality/paganism.)

Although some scholars have presented contemporary paganism as part of the New Age, the differences between the two, and a growing mutual suspicion, mean that it is better to treat them as separate varieties along the spectrum of spirituality. Paganism can also be referred to as 'neo-paganism' in acknowledgement of the fact that what we are dealing with is a recent development in Western religious history. Although it traces its roots back to premodern pagan traditions, it nonetheless has many modern preoccupations. Like all forms of modern spirituality, it has roots in the nineteenth century, but like New Age and Mind, Body, Spirit practices, it came to prominence as a popular movement in the West only in the last decades of the twentieth century. Some of its defining marks include (a) a focus on, and reverence for, 'Nature' (itself a modern construct); (b) interest in Occultism and spiritual beings, including 'spirits' and 'ancestors'; and (c) a concern with ancient pre-Christian cultures, their gods and goddesses, and their revival. Paganism generally differs from New Age not only by its greater respect for (some) traditions, but also by being less focused on the self at the expense of community, less optimistic (death, destruction, and evil have their own reality), and affirming not only 'Oneness' but plurality and difference. It demands a greater commitment from its followers than most Mind, Body, Spirit practices, and is often less easy to access.

Contemporary paganisms are sometimes referred to as 'nature religions' because they are rooted in celebration of natural, this-worldly cycles, places and powers. Thus pagans celebrate the turning of the seasons (often in eight seasonal festivals), the cycles of earth, sun and moon, and the cycles and stages of human life. Pagans cultivate relations with the spirits or powers of particular places, including animals, trees, and rivers. There is a growing belief in paganism that it is important to be rooted in one's own traditions, which are the traditions of the particular place in which one is located, and many pagans are consequently hostile to a New Age-style eclecticism whereby people select from different traditions, and use different spiritual symbols solely on the basis of personal preference. Eco-spirituality and politics are also increasingly important in many pagan traditions.

Western paganism has a strong tradition of celebrating embodied life, without separation of body and spirit, and bodies are treated as the location in which people explore reality. A stress on the importance of embodied and ritual experience often go together in contemporary paganism. Many pagans regularly participate in communal and personal rituals – often tied to natural cycles – which are thought to teach participants more about the world, deities, spirits, and their own lives and relations. Pagans who call themselves 'reconstructionists' cultivate ritual relations with the ancestors and deities of particular places and cultures, and attempt to be strict in observance of past traditions and practices. Pagan stress on positive embodiment means that bodily processes such as menstruation and ageing are celebrated. This emphasis has contributed to the formation of feminist forms of paganism, and feminism has been highly influential on most forms of paganism, especially in North America. Some feminist paganism focuses strongly on the Goddess, or many goddesses, but goddesses are important in most forms of paganism, although they may take their place alongside male deities as well.

Paganism is similar to the New Age in its emphasis on an individual, experiential, spiritual journey, but it differs in its strong group traditions (though many pagans are solitary practitioners). Further, an individual's authority to explore is mediated by the authority placed in nature, spirits, ancestors and certain common pagan ethics. Though many pagans are universalist in the sense that they speak of many 'aspects' of One deity, for example, polytheism is increasingly stressed. The holism of New Age and Mind, Body, Spirit practices is worked out in paganism by special emphasis on the interconnection of the natural world. Whereas the New Age concept of 'the One' tends to be rather abstract, pagan deities are highly personalized and located, and may be seen and touched through experience of the world. Compared with Mind, Body, Spirit practices and New Age, paganism appears to have significant numbers of younger practitioners. Pagans have no expectation of a New Age, and reject any ideal of transcendence of this world (for more on Paganism see Chapter 14).

4. *Theistic spirituality*

Although spirituality often retains its historic opposition to 'religion', there are increasing signs of a crossing of the boundaries between new forms of spirituality, and aspects of traditional theistic religious practice.

Theologically, one of the points of incompatibility has been that theistic religions conceived God as a personal, often male, being with authority over the individual. Another has been an exaltation of the 'Creator' over the creation as a whole, which may imply a hierarchy of value in which the natural world comes at the very bottom. How then can the two come into closer contact and rapprochement with one another?

One way is by highlighting the mystical tradition within theistic religions. Christianity, Judaism and Islam all have mystical strands, often with distinctive teachings, traditions and rituals. In some cases these downplay the 'hierarchy' of God, and emphasise the unity between God and the believer. They may also present God as ineffable (beyond name), and unknowable. Another way is by emphasising the extent to which theistic religions venerate the whole creation, which is understood as brought into being and upheld by God. For example, the sacramental emphasis of Roman Catholicism views the natural world as a sign and gateway to the divine, and 'Celtic' Christianity (the Christianity of parts of the early British Isles before it was Romanized) has some features which resemble a nature-mysticism. In addition, the more feminine aspects of theistic faiths may be emphasised – for example, veneration of the Virgin Mary or Fatima or Wisdom.

There are indications that some people involved in spirituality are actively combining elements from theistic religions, with new 'fusions' taking place. For example, there is now a network of 'Quagans' (Pagan Quakers), and some Goddess worshippers have made veneration of Mary central to their practice. Similarly, a number of ancient religious sites have even become meeting points for both Christians and pagans (for example, several sites in Glastonbury, and St Brigid's fire pit in Kildare, Ireland). The ancient sites, rituals and buildings of theistic religions are attractive to forms of spirituality seeking greater rootedness in place and time. Equally, some kinds of theistic religion draw closer to spirituality by changing their institutional forms to become more participatory; for example, the small 'cell group' has become increasingly important in many theistic religions, and provides a setting in which participants can explore their inner, subjective lives and experiences. Similarly, traditional embodied and holistic practices of theistic religions may be revived and re-emphasised (for example, meditation, walking the labyrinth, postures of praying, rituals centred around sacred foods).

Theories and explanations

Many factors must be taken into account in explaining the rise of spirituality, and understanding why it takes the characteristic forms outlined above.

1. *Processes of modernization*

Equality, human rights and individualization

These linked values, discussed in more detail in the Introduction, may favour spirituality over some traditional forms of religion in at least two ways. First, spirituality's characteristic stress on primacy of personal choice can be understood as being closely linked to the way in which modern societies, constitutional political systems, and systems of law and human rights emphasize and enshrine the value and the right of individual freedom of choice ('liberty'), and freedom of religion. A strong stress on traditional authority is replaced by a stress on the authority of individual choice and experience. Second, a modern focus on the equal value of each and every individual may favour forms of spirituality which share these commitments, and undermine more hierarchical and non-democractic forms of religion.

Privatization?

As was noted in the Introduction to this book, the process of modernization can change the position of religion in society. Instead of being an important part of public life, it becomes confined to private life. Social functions in which religion was once involved – such as education and healthcare – become more autonomous. Spirituality is often said to be the best example of a fully 'privatized' religion. As we noted above, however, it is a mistake to over-stress the privatized nature of spirituality. Whilst it is true that it no longer has the extensive social functions which established churches had in Europe in medieval and early modern times, spirituality has come to have an influence not just in the domestic sphere, but in education, healthcare, and other 'public' spheres.

Colonialism

The growth of spirituality is simultaneous with that of Western colonialism, and there are clear links between the two. One, which has already been mentioned, is the borrowing of many elements of 'Eastern' religions, especially Hinduism and Buddhism. This was reinforced as spiritual teachers from colonized parts of Asia – like Vivekananda and Krishnamurti – came to the West to spread 'Eastern wisdom'. Also important is the way in which opposition to 'religion' and embrace of 'spirituality' could be an effective protest against Western culture and colonialism.

2. *Processes of late modernization*

Globalization and pluralization

The pluralization of modern societies and cultures is due to a number of factors, including urbanization (the growth of cities as people move from rural to industrial occupations), and globalization (see Chapter 16). Greater mobility, and higher levels of movement and migration, lead to different cultures coming into contact with one another, often in urban settings. This is reinforced by a growing range of electronic media, from TV to the internet. The resulting pluralization can have a decisive impact on traditional religion by undermining what were once presented as universal truth-claims. Pluralization brings knowledge of alternate religious possibilities. This may lead to the weakening of old beliefs, as well as established family and community ties, but also to a search for new truths, new forms of community and a new sense of place. There may also be new cross-overs between religious boundaries, and borrowings between different forms of religion.

Capitalism, consumerism and the market

Late modern societies are characterized by unprecedented levels of affluence, and by a situation in which consumption or 'shopping' becomes central to people's sense of identity. In many ways spirituality is very well adapted to consumer society. It offers a wide range of different spiritual goods, which the individual seeker can peruse and buy. Because they are freely chosen, they enhance a sense of unique personal identity. The flexible institutional form of spirituality also makes it relatively easy for 'suppliers' to find a niche in the market, set out their 'stall', and try to create a monopoly. Since it is a free market, other suppliers may set up in competition, but the system as a whole is likely to ensure that the market is able to predict, drive and satisfy demand efficiently. On the other hand, the presentation of spirituality as a mere 'commodification' of religion can overstress the importance of the profit motive, and understress the way in which many theistic forms of religion are also oriented towards consumption – for example, American and Asian 'prosperity' Christianity (see Chapter 8).

Subjectivization and 'post-materialism'

The social and political theorist Ronald Inglehardt argues that as late modern societies become more affluent, so their members are freed from the necessity of having to shape their lives around securing the basic material necessities of life. Instead, they can focus on 'post-materialist' concerns, such as gaining experience and enhancing the quality of life. This involves a 'turn to the self' or 'subjectivization', whereby individuals become concerned with their 'inner' lives and subjective experience. A new premium is placed on cultivating one's subjective life, which easily leads to a concern with the 'spiritual' dimension of the self, and with the sorts of spirituality we have described above.

3. Cultural influences

Romanticism

The Romantic movement of the late eighteenth and early nineteenth centuries was a direct reaction to urban, industrial modernization. Romantics rejected reason, rationalism and science in favour of the emotions and artistic creativity. They yearned for an idealized rural existence spent in contemplation of 'Nature' and humanity's place within nature. Writers like Wordsworth stressed the immanence of the divine, and found God *in* nature. There are close links between Romanticism and the rise of spirituality. The ideas of Romantics like Henry David Thoreau (1817–1862), Ralph Waldo Emerson (1803–1882) and Walt Whitman (1819–1892) in America, and William Blake (1757–1827) and William Wordsworth (1770–1850) in Britain are important in the origins and development of spirituality.

Occultism

The nineteenth century also witnessed a proliferation of secret ritual magic societies. Most of these societies' adherents were Christian, especially in Britain and North America, though they drew upon a long history of European magical thought. Despite studying, and in some cases practising, magic, most of these societies were discernibly modern in their emphasis on human will and mind. Movements such as Freemasonry, Rosicrucianism, and Theosophy flourished. Occult societies such as the Hermetic Order of the Golden Dawn drew upon Eastern traditions and helped to fuel an 'Easternization of the West'. Many of these societies influenced the development of contemporary spiritual traditions, particularly paganism. For example, the common pagan association of certain elements (air, earth, fire, water) with directions on the compass derives from nineteenth-century occultism, as does pagan emphasis on the importance of ritual.

Therapeutic culture

The growing importance of therapy in twentieth-century societies helped feed the growth of spirituality, and prepare the climate for its wider acceptance. More than any particular therapeutic school, what was influential was the idea that it was possible and even desirable for individuals to seek personal growth through a one-to-one encounter with a professional, in whose presence they would explore their innermost feelings and experiences (their 'subjectivity'). The link with many Mind, Body, Spirit practices is clear. There has also been a direct influence on spirituality by some key figures in the movement, including Carl Jung (particularly on New Age), and Karl Rogers (particularly on the idea that there is an authoritative inner self who is the individual's best guide). In the nineteenth century spirituality was also intertwined with proto-therapeutic movements of mind and bodily healing, including mesmerism, New Thought, and Christian Science.

Feminism

Feminism is also tied into the origins of spirituality. Feminism and spirituality have contributed to the way women have questioned gendered social expectations and traditional institutions. Many feminists rejected the churches as 'patriarchal', searched for new ways to be Christian, or left the churches seeking new forms of spirituality. Spiritual feminists have sought to create new forms of spirituality which can affirm women's full humanity, for example by focusing on a female divine rather than a male God. The latter part of the twentieth century saw the rise of some radical spiritual/ feminist movements, including revivals of 'Wicca' (witchcraft), and Goddess Feminism (see, for example, the work of Starhawk). Spiritual feminists were also active politically, for example in the protests against nuclear weapons at Greenham Common in the UK.

FIGURE 12.3 Cauldron

The cauldron is a richly symbolic ritual tool popular in some forms of paganism.
©iStockphoto.com/Amy Chipman.

Environmentalism

Much contemporary spirituality is characterized by an eco-discourse or an eco-consciousness, and this has increased as concern about the state of the environment has grown. Spirituality's blurring of the boundaries between sacred and profane allows nature and the body to be sacralized, whilst its stress on interconnectedness leads to a quest for a more harmonious relationship between human beings and the rest of the planet. Theistic spirituality has also been characterized by a growing eco-discourse, particularly in feminist theology (for example, in the work of Rosemary Radford Ruether). Likewise, certain forms of theistic spirituality like Celtic Christianity place a strong emphasis on the sacredness of the earth and its creatures.

4. Generational change

Some scholars have tried to explain the rise of spirituality in the modern world by looking at the formative conditions which shaped the particular generations which have been most involved, especially the Baby Boom generation which came of age in the 1960s.

Factors which can be singled out as conducive to the growth of interest in spirituality include: the rise of a youth culture which was able to set its own cultural and religious agenda independently of adults; birth in an era of economic stability and growth; unprecedented access to higher education; the 'sexual revolution' which involved a rejection of 'puritanical' sexual attitudes and growing equality between the sexes; the Cold War, the Vietnam war, and government scandals which led to widespread disillusionment with the established order of things, and in some cases, open rebellion against it. Many of these developments encouraged Baby Boomers to be hostile to established religion, which was viewed as too puritanical, too tied up with the establishment, too patriarchal, too 'square', too boring, too 'adult' and old-fashioned. At the same time, they facilitated and encouraged the growth of spiritual alternatives.

Generation X (born c.1961–1981), the generation after the Boomers, and Generation Y (born c.1982–2000), may have a somewhat different relation to spirituality. They have participated in increasing rates of higher education, and have grown up reaping the benefits of affluence and the growth of information and communications technologies. However, they experienced greater instability and insecurity than the Baby Boomers. Generation X grew up in an age of AIDS and nuclear threat, and both generations have experienced economic booms and busts and fears about climate change. In Europe at least, Generation X was the first generation in which a large majority had little or no church family background. Despite many of Generation X having little interest in Christianity, they have also become known for their pluralistic, spiritual eclecticism, and for reshaping and experimenting with traditions. Generation Y is even more truly a generation of the technological revolution, and their experience is fully 'mediatized'. They may be more influenced than ever before by events and phenomena on a global scale, and more are migrants or children of migrants with cross-cultural experience. They also have the ability to create a plethora of new subcultures and 'virtual worlds'. We can expect that defining characteristics of Y spirituality will be plurality, stress on identity construction through a wide range of personal choices, and sophisticated use of many media. Instability and change may render spirituality – and religion – increasingly valuable resources for creating new meaning systems, and defending and empowering minority identities.

Conclusion

Spirituality, in all its variety, shares a common desire to move away from what it sees as the authoritarian aspects of traditional religion, in order to give more space for personal exploration of the sacred. As such, spirituality allies itself with some central dynamics of modern and late modern societies, including the affirmation of the unique value of the individual, and the stress on the centrality of consumer choice. In its 'holistic' emphasis it also responds to growing concerns about human relationship with the environment. Spirituality has become increasingly prominent in many societies since the nineteenth century, and an explosion of growth in recent decades has seen it differentiated into several main varieties. Although spirituality arose out of opposition to 'religion', there is some evidence of the two growing closer together, as each begins to appreciate certain features of the other. Although some forms of spirituality are currently dominated by the Baby Boom generation, others appear to be attracting younger generations in greater numbers. This suggests that spirituality will remain influential for some time to come.

Summary

Spirituality:

- arose in the nineteenth century from a value-laden contrast between 'religion' and 'spirituality';

- emphasises the importance of inner, subjective, ineffable experience over the 'externals' and 'formalities' which are said to characterize traditional forms of religion;

- authorizes the individual to be the final arbiter of spiritual truth;

- is characterized by a 'holistic' emphasis on the interconnectedness of the self and all things, and an emphasis on self-in-relation;

- emphasizes the immanence of the sacred, which is often understood to manifest itself in and through nature and the body;

- places value on 'seeking', and tries to maintain an open and tolerant attitude towards other spiritual 'paths';

- promotes practical, often embodied, means and techniques for attaining spiritual insight;

- displays a tendency to embrace 'progressive' and 'anti-establishment' causes, and a discourse of 'freedom' or 'liberation' (though there can also be right-wing forms of spirituality);

- takes an increasingly wide variety of forms, including 'Mind, Body, Spirit' practices, New Age, and paganism;

- has been showing some recent signs of rapprochement between some forms of spirituality and some forms of theistic religion;

- although the percentage of the population highly active in Spirituality may be as low as 2 per cent, it exercises a much broader cultural influence.

Key terms

consumerism A focus upon consumption (buying things).

holism A stress upon the 'wholeness' or interconnectedness of things, including the self (seen as a 'whole' of body, mind and spirit), the self in relation to others, and all aspects of life viewed in connection with one another. Sometimes holism posits an underlying unity or 'energy' which is manifest in many forms.

immanence In religion, a stress on the sacred as found within life and the world, rather than on the sacred as 'transcendent' over life and the world.

Mind, Body, Spirit practices Currently, a popular variety of spirituality typified by its focus upon well-being, and upon the use of a range of bodily techniques to improve well-being. Takes many different forms, e.g. yoga, aromatherapy, Reiki.

mysticism A tendency within all major religious traditions, which places emphasis upon the nearness of the divine and the human, and on the possibility of human experience of the divine.

New Age A variety of spirituality which came to prominence in the 1980s and 1990s, and which is characterized by its stress on the importance of freeing the self from constraints which prevent it from realizing its own sacred, limitless potential. Characteristically optimistic, such spirituality looks forward to a 'New Age' of enlightenment and harmony.

occultism The occult is that which is hidden and secret. Occultism normally refers to societies which offer forms of secret, often magical, knowledge to their members.

paganism A variety of contemporary spirituality which is growing in popularity. Although there are many different forms of paganism, many of them share a concern for close relationship with nature, a stress on the importance of ritual and of a ritual community, and a pluralistic tendency which stresses the plural nature of reality, and the polytheistic nature of the sacred realm.

polytheism Belief in many divine beings.

subjectivization A process characteristic of late modernity, whereby the individual's 'inner depths' of experience, feeling, memory, etc. become increasingly valued, and considered worthy of exploration and cultivation.

theism Belief in a God, a personal divine being.

therapy Short for 'psychotherapy', a practice which treats mental and emotional problems by way of a 'talking cure', whereby a client and a therapist talk through emotional issues in regular one-to-one therapy sessions.

Further reading

History of Spirituality

Leigh Eric Schmidt: *Restless Souls: The Making of American Spirituality* (New York: Harper Collins, 2006).

Spirituality, including Mind, Body, Spirit practices

Paul Heelas and Linda Woodhead: *The Spiritual Revolution: Why Religion is Giving Way to Spirituality* (Oxford, UK and Malden, USA: Blackwell, 2005).

Gordon Lynch: *The New Spirituality: An Introduction to Progressive Belief in the Twenty-first Century* (London and New York: I.B. Tauris, 2007).

New Age

Wouter J. Hanegraaff: *New Age Religion and Western Culture: Esotericism in the Mirror of Secular Thought* (New York: State University of New York Press, 1998).

Paul Heelas: *The New Age Movement: The Celebration of the Self and the Sacralization of Modernity* (Oxford: Blackwell, 1996).

Paganism

Graham Harvey: *Listening People, Speaking Earth: Contemporary Paganism* (London: Hurst & Company, 1997).

Helen Berger, Evan A. Leach and Leigh S. Shaffer: *Voices from the Pagan Census: A National Survey of Witches and Neo-Pagans in the United States* (Columbia, SC: University of South Carolina Press, 2003).

Carol Christ: *She Who Changes* (New York: Routledge, 1997).

Generations

Wade Clark Roof: *The Spiritual Marketplace: Baby Boomers and the Remaking of American Religion* (Princeton NJ: Princeton University Press, 1999).

Richard W. Flory and Donald E. Miller: *GenX Religion* (New York, NY and London: Routledge, 2000).

Chapter 13

New Age religion

Wouter J. Hanegraaff

Introduction

New Age is not so much a religion as a buzzword that achieved popularity chiefly in Europe and the US during the 1980s. The wide and often vague use of the term, and the amorphous nature of the phenomena it refers to, make it impossible to gain any accurate impression of the numbers involved. For reasons which will be explored below, it is most influential in modern (industrial and post-industrial) societies, particularly North America, Europe, Australia and New Zealand – though pockets of influence may also be found in cosmopolitan cities worldwide, from Rio de Janeiro to Mumbai.

As a buzzword, New Age refers to a wide array of spiritual practices and beliefs which share as their most common denominator the fact that they are perceived as 'alternative' from the perspective of mainstream Western society. To many observers during the 1980s, the increasing visibility of its representatives in the media and popular culture conveyed the impression of something radically new: the birth of a grassroots movement of social and spiritual innovation, prophesying a profound transformation of Western society that should, in due course, culminate in a vastly superior culture – 'the Age of Aquarius' (Ferguson, 1980). Actually, what came to be known as the 'New Age movement' has its immediate roots in the counter-culture of the 1960s and some of its immediate predecessors, but its fundamental ideas can be traced much further back into history. As will be seen, New Age religion is neither something completely new, nor just a revival – or survival – of something ancient. Its basic ideas have ancient roots, which need to be taken into account in order to understand the movement that grew from them; indeed, from one perspective New Age may be seen as merely the contemporary manifestation of Western esotericism. But perceived from another perspective, New Age religion is radically new: a manifestation *par excellence* of postmodern consumer society, the members of which use, recycle, combine and adapt existing religious ideas and practices as they see fit. In order to understand the New Age movement and its role in the modern world, we therefore need to understand its historical foundations as well as its specific modernity.

The chapter will proceed by first distinguishing two senses of New Age – a wide and a strict sense – before going on to consider its historical roots in esoteric and occult traditions in Christian culture. The impact of modernity is considered in two stages: first, the impact of Enlightenment and early post-Enlightenment modernity (the rise of the natural and psychological sciences being particularly important); second, the impact of later capitalist, consumerist modernity.

New Age in a wide and in a strict sense

Flying saucers and utopian communities

The immediate roots of the New Age movement may seem surprising at first sight. Shortly after World War II, popular curiosity was attracted by unexplained phenomena in the sky referred to as Unidentified Flying Objects (UFOs). In various places in Western Europe and the USA, study groups were formed by people who wanted to investigate these phenomena, and some of those groups rapidly proceeded to take on 'cultic' characteristics. Typically, such groups believed that the UFOs were in fact spaceships inhabited by intelligent beings from other planets or other dimensions of outer space. Representing a superior level of cultural, technological and spiritual evolution, they now made their appearance to herald the coming of a New Age. The earth was entering a new evolutionary cycle that would be accompanied by the emergence of a new and superior kind of spiritual consciousness. However, since the present cultures of humanity were thoroughly corrupted by materialism, they would resist this change. As a result, the transition to a new cycle of evolution would necessitate the destruction of the old civilization, by violent causes such as earthquakes, floods, diseases and the like, resulting in global economic, political and social collapse. Those individuals whose consciousness was already in tune with the qualities of the new culture would be protected in various ways, and would survive the period of cataclysms. In due course they would become the vanguard of the New Age, or Age of Aquarius: an age of abundance, bliss and spiritual enlightenment when humanity would once again live in accordance with universal cosmic laws (Spangler, 1984). These beliefs were inspired by occultist teachings of various provenance, but especially by the writings of the Christian Theosophist Alice Bailey (1880–1949) and, in some respects, the anthroposophical metaphysics of the German visionary Rudolf Steiner (1861–1925). In 1937, Alice Bailey 'channelled' a spiritual prayer known as 'The Great Invocation', which is still being used by New Age adherents to invoke the New Age.

THE GREAT INVOCATION

From the point of Light within the Mind of God Let Light stream forth into the minds of men. Let Light descend on Earth.
From the point of Love within the Heart of God Let Love stream forth into the hearts of men. May Christ return to Earth.
From the centre where the Will of God is known Let purpose guide the little wills of men – The purpose which the Masters know and serve.
From the centre which we call the race of men Let the Plan of Love and Light work out. And may it seal the door where evil dwells.
Let Light and Love and Power restore the Plan on Earth.

BOX 13.1 'The Great Invocation', Alice Bailey (1937)

FIGURE 13.1 David Spangler

David Spangler was born in Columbus, Ohio, in 1945. He spent much of his childhood in North Africa where he had a number of spiritual experiences which led him to an awareness that humanity is entering a new cycle of evolution and stands at the threshold of a New Age. In 1964 he began lecturing on human and planetary transformation in the United States and Europe. He was co-director of the Findhorn Foundation community in northern Scotland for three years before returning to the United States and becoming a founder-director of the Lorian Association. Courtesy David Spangler.

These lines illustrate the pronounced Christian elements that still informed the occultist millennarianism of the early New Age movement. These elements would remain prominent during the second, counter-cultural stage of its development. During the 1960s, the basic belief system and millennarian expectations of the UFO groups were adopted by various utopian communities, the most famous of which is the Findhorn community in Scotland. The members of these communities were trying to live in a new way, in tune with the universal laws of nature and the universe. They were trying, in the spirit of the 'Great Invocation', to be 'centres of light' or focal points in a network from which spiritual illumination would eventually spread out and encompass the globe. In the attitude of these early New Agers, represented by popular spokesmen such as David Spangler (b. 1945) or George Trevelyan (1906–1996), an important change took place compared with the perspective of the UFO groups of the 1950s. Whereas the pronounced apocalypticism of the latter entailed an essentially passive attitude of 'waiting for the great events' that would destroy the old civilization and usher in a New Age, utopian communities of the 1960s, such as Findhorn, increasingly emphasized the importance of an activist, constructive attitude: 'Instead of spreading warnings of apocalypse, let Findhorn proclaim that the new age is already here, in spirit if not in form, and that anyone can now cocreate with that spirit so that the form will become manifest' (Spangler, 1984: 34–35). This became the perspective typical of the New Age movement of the 1960s and its sympathizers in later decades.

The cultic milieu

This early New Age movement, born in the context of the postwar UFO cults and flowering in the spiritual utopianism of the 1960s and 1970s, was only one particular manifestation of the counter-cultural ferment of the times. More generally, this ferment found expression in a widespread 'cultic milieu' (the term comes from Campbell, 1972) in Western society: a diffuse phenomenon consisting of individuals who feel dissatisfied with mainstream Western culture and religion, and are looking for alternatives (see also Chapter 12 on Spirituality). This cultic milieu proved to be fertile soil for a plethora of New Religious Movements of various provenance. Some of these movements took the form of relatively stable social entities, including an internal hierarchy of power and authority, definite doctrines and rules of conduct, clearly defined boundaries between members and non-members, claims of exclusive truth, and so on (see Chapter 15 on New Religious Movements). Other movements were more ephemeral and fluid, functioning as client cults with relatively few demands on members, and an inclusive and tolerant attitude. The latter type of cultic group may come into existence quickly and vanish as quickly again, and its membership may sometimes be very small. Members may participate in several such groups at the same time – displaying an activity known as 'spiritual shopping' – without feeling committed to making a choice in favour of the one at the expense of the other. This type of spiritual activity is most characteristic for the development of the 'cultic milieu' that spawned and supported the New Age movement of the 1980s.

It is helpful to distinguish the latter movement from the original New Age movement described above. The spiritual perspectives associated with the UFO cults of the 1950s and the utopian communities of the 1960s and 1970s may collectively be referred to as the 'New Age movement in a strict sense'. This movement is characterized by a broadly occultist metaphysics (with special prominence of the deviant forms of Theosophy founded by Alice Bailey and, to some extent, Rudolf Steiner), a relatively strong emphasis on community values and a traditional morality emphasizing altruistic love and service to humanity, and a very strong millennarian emphasis focusing on the expectation of the New Age. This New Age movement in a strict sense still exists, but its membership is rather strongly dominated by the baby boomer generation and tends to be perceived as somewhat old-fashioned by new-generation New Agers. By the end of the 1970s, this New Age movement in a strict sense came to be assimilated as merely one aspect within the much more complex and widespread phenomenon that may be referred to, by way of contrast, as the 'New Age movement in a general sense'.

The New Age movement

This New Age movement in a general sense may be defined as the cultic milieu having become conscious of itself, by the end of the 1970s, as constituting a more or less unified movement. (As indicated above, it is not a New Religious Movement in the normal sense of that word, since it lacks a tightly bound organizational structure.) In other words, people who participated in various alternative activities and pursuits began to consider themselves as part of an international invisible community of like-minded individuals, the collective efforts of whom were destined to change the world into a better and more spiritual place. The American sociologist Marilyn Ferguson referred to this phenomenon as the 'Aquarian conspiracy': a 'leaderless but powerful network' working to bring about radical change (Ferguson, 1980); and the physicist Fritjof Capra saw it as the 'rising culture' destined to replace the declining culture of the modern West (Capra, 1983). But eventually what they were referring to came to be known as the New Age movement:

by the late 1970s and early 1980s the term 'New Age' was adopted from the specific occultist-millennarian movement known under that name, and came to be applied as a catch-all term for the much more extensive and complex cultic milieu of the 1980s and beyond. This is how the New Age movement in a strict sense was absorbed by the New Age movement in a general sense.

This development has been a cause of concern for some representatives of the original movement, who perceived in it a cheapening of the idea of a New Age. While the original New Age movement had been carried by high-minded idealism and an ethic of service to humanity, the movement of the 1980s quickly developed into an increasingly commercialized spiritual marketplace catering to the tastes and whims of an individualistic clientèle. While the original movement had espoused a reasonably coherent Theosophical metaphysics and philosophy of history, the movement of the 1980s seemed to present a hotch-potch of ideas and speculations without a clear focus and direction. While the excited expectation of a radical New Age dominated the earlier movement, this expectation ceased to be central to the movement of the 1980s which, in spite of its name, tends to concentrate on the spiritual development of the individual rather than of society. The development might also be described in terms of cultural geographics: while the original movement was England-based and relied upon occultist

FIGURE 13.2 Shirley MacLaine

Shirley MacLaine was born in Richmond, Virginia, in 1934. She wrote autobiographies during the 1980s describing her spiritual quest. Her website (www.shirleymaclaine.com) discusses her views on topics as broad as spirituality, health and stress reduction, UFOs, prophecy and psychics, reincarnation, transformational travel, karma, divination, ageing, relationships and dreams. Courtesy Getty Images.

traditions that had long been influential there, the new movement was dominated by the so-called metaphysical and New Thought traditions typical of American alternative culture. The move from community-oriented values to individual-centred ones is a reflection of that development.

Indeed, the New Age movement in a general sense has been dominated by American cultural and spiritual ideas and values, and the most important spokes(wo)men have been Americans. While many names could be mentioned, two stand out as symbolic of the 1980s and the 1990s respectively. During the 1980s, the most vocal representative of the New Age idea may have been the film actress Shirley MacLaine. Her autobiographies published between 1983 and 1989, in which she describes her spiritual quest, and the television miniseries 'Out on a Limb', based upon the first of these books, encapsulate the essential perspective of the New Age movement of the 1980s. For the 1990s, the same thing may be said of the bestsellers of James Redfield: *The Celestine Prophecy*, with its accompanying *Celestine Workbook*, and a succession of follow-up volumes capitalizing on the success of the first one. While MacLaine's autobiographies were certainly easy to read, Redfield's books carried the New Age perspective to a new level of simplicity, thereby broadening the potential market for New Age beyond the audiences already reached by earlier authors. It may still be a bit too early to point out a typical representative for the first decade of the twenty-first century, but among various candidates, Neil Donald Walsch and his enormously popular books of 'Conversations with God' might not be a bad choice.

These developments contributed to the fact that, by the beginning of the 1990s, more and more people attracted to alternative spirituality began to distance themselves from the label New Age, perceived by them as loaded with unwanted associations. During the 1980s it was still possible to investigate the New Age movement (in a general sense) simply by questioning people who identified themselves as involved in New Age; during the 1990s, participants have increasingly refused to identify themselves as such, preferring vague and non-committal terms such as 'spirituality'. It is a mistake to conclude from this, as has sometimes been done, that the New Age movement is declining or vanishing. Rather, the movement is showing signs of moving away from its traditional status as a counter-culture that proclaims the New Age in a gesture of rejecting the values of the old culture. Attempts to replace the term 'New Age' with a term such as 'spirituality' fit within a new strategy of adaptation and assimilation instead of rejection and confrontation, as a result of which the New Age movement is now securing its place as an increasingly professionalized 'spiritual' wing within the cultural mainstream. Within that general context, new developments can, of course, be noted all the time. For example there is an increasing interest in various types of (neo)shamanism, including its original psychedelic variety, which receded into underground culture after the new drug laws of around 1970, but has become much more visible again since the spread of the internet. Partly connected to New Age shamanism, one may also note the emergence of new types of millennarianism and apocalypticism, mostly focused on the year 2012 (Braden *et al.*, 2007; Hanegraaff, 2009).

Sources and resources

Origins: Esoteric currents in Jewish and Christian culture

We have been referring to various occultist movements that provided the early New Age movement with its basic metaphysics, as well as to the metaphysical and New Thought movements in American culture that were equally important to the New Age movement in a general sense. These various expressions of an alternative and popular Western spirituality have a long history. While earlier scholarship tended to interpret them in exclusively sociological terms, as an irrationalist and essentially regressive reaction to the secularization and rationalization of society (for example, Tiryakian, 1974), more recent generations have come to consider such an approach unhistorical and misleading (Bednarowski, 1989; Hanegraaff, 1996). The occult in contemporary Western society is merely the most recent manifestation of a complex of religious currents and traditions that existed long before the processes of secularization and rationalization began to have their impact, and which should be taken seriously as religious movements in their own right. Furthermore, it turns out to be simplistic to imagine the more recent representatives of these currents as irrationalists and conservatives who are fighting a rearguard battle against secularization and rationalization. Rather, historical research demonstrates that their attitude to modernity has always been highly complex and ambiguous: occultists have typically been adapting and reinterpreting ancient traditions so as to make them relevant to the modern world, while simultaneously hoping for a transformation of society along occultist lines. In order to understand the co-existence of 'tradition and modernity' in modern occultism and New Age religion, we first need to take a look at their historical foundations.

Hermetic gnosis

Human thinking and behaviour is far too fluid and complex to be caught in neat theoretical categories; but provided that this fact is clearly recognized, such categories can nevertheless be of service for providing some rough orientation through the jungle of history. It is useful to distinguish between three general strategies which have been followed in Western culture in order to find truth. The first one relies on human reason, observation and argumentation: this is the strategy of rational philosophy and scientific research. The second one relies on the authority of divine revelation, which transcends merely human wisdom: this is the approach of established religion and doctrinal theology. The third one, finally, relies on the authority of personal spiritual experience or inner enlightenment: this approach may conveniently be referred to as gnosis, and has always had a problematic relationship to the first two approaches. The fact that its adherents look for truth 'beyond reason' has made them look like obscurantists in the eyes of rationalist philosophy and science; and the fact that they believe to have personal access to divine revelation has evoked the suspicion that they are bypassing the authority of established religion and its collectively recognized sources of revelation. In short: the representatives of this third approach tend to be suspected of irrationalism and excessive individualism, while they in turn blame their opponents for relying on religious authoritarianism and excessive rationalism.

Undoubtedly the most famous manifestation of this third perspective in antiquity is known as Gnosticism. But far more important for our present purposes – although less important from the perspective of early Church history – is a second movement relying on gnosis, and known as Hermetism. This religious current has its origins in Hellenistic Egypt, and flourished in the second and third centuries CE; its name refers to a mythical and quasi-divine founder, Hermes Trismegistus (the 'thrice-greatest Hermes'). Among the many writings attributed or linked to Hermes, most important and influential are the collection known as the *Corpus Hermeticum*, and a longer text entitled *Logos Teleios* but known in its Latin translation as *Asclepius*. The *Asclepius* was known in the Latin West throughout the Middle Ages; but the *Corpus Hermeticum* only became widely known after it had been translated by the Florentine neo-Platonic philosopher Marsilio Ficino in 1463 (printed in 1471).

Renaissance Hermeticism and Western esotericism

Ficino's translation proved to be of pivotal importance for the development of alternative 'esoteric' spiritualities in modern and contemporary Western society. Renaissance thinkers such as Giovanni Pico della Mirandola and Ficino himself saw in Hermes one of the earliest and hence most authoritative sources of a *prisca theologia* or ancient theology. This primordial wisdom had supposedly been revealed by God to Adam, but had declined after the Fall. It was kept alive, however, by a succession of divinely inspired sages, beginning with Zoroaster and Hermes Trismegistus. Since this primordial wisdom had been revealed by God himself, it was necessarily consistent with the most profound mysteries of the Christian faith and could be seen as a prophetic announcement of it. This in itself accounts for the great spiritual authority attached to the *Corpus Hermeticum*, and that authority was enhanced further by the suggestion that the teachings of the Egyptian Hermes had been a source for Moses as well as for Plato: accordingly, the Hermetic philosophy might be seen as a means to reconcile philosophy and Christianity, reason and faith. An important corollary of the authority attached to 'Hermes' was a new appreciation of the so-called 'occult sciences': magic, astrology and alchemy. The *Corpus Hermeticum* contains a spiritual philosophy with very little reference to occult sciences; but since these sublime teachings were supposedly written by the same author to whom had long been attributed a wide array of magical, astrological and alchemical writings, the latter were bound to be perceived in a new and more positive light. As a result, the 'Hermetic philosophy' of the Renaissance came to be linked from the very beginning with a revival of the occult sciences. In the writings of authors such as Cornelius Agrippa, Francesco Giorgi da Veneto, Giordano Bruno, Paracelsus, and many lesser figures, the outlines appeared of a new type of religious syncretism: a mixture of Christianity, neo-Platonism, Hermetism, Magic, Astrology and Alchemy, as well as an important new phenomenon: Christian reinterpretations and adaptations of the Jewish Kabbalah.

During the sixteenth century, a basic 'referential corpus' of writings came into existence which, in spite of variations and divergences, clearly displays a common direction. While the Hermetic writings are certainly not its only source, the authority attached to 'Hermes' is sufficient to refer to this new syncretism as 'Hermeticism' in a general and encompassing sense (as distinct from 'Hermetism', which refers specifically to the teachings of the *Hermetica* and its commentaries). This phenomenon of Renaissance Hermeticism is the foundation of what is commonly referred to as 'Western esotericism': a distinct current of 'alternative' religion and religious philosophy, the history of which can be traced from late antiquity, and more specifically from the Renaissance through the succeeding centuries, and indeed up to the New Age movement. As the main modern and contemporary representative of the 'third component' referred to above, its representatives emphasize the importance of personal religious experience or gnosis.

More specifically, its world view has been defined in terms of four intrinsic characteristics: a belief in invisible and non-causal 'correspondences' between all visible and invisible dimensions of the cosmos, a perception of nature as permeated and animated by a divine presence or life force, a concentration on the religious imagination as a power that provides access to worlds and levels of reality intermediate between the material world and God, and the belief in a process of spiritual transmutation by which the inner man is regenerated and reconnected with the divine (Faivre, 1994: 10–15; for more recent perspectives on the nature of Western esotericism, cf. Hanegraaff *et al.*, 2005).

In 1614, the Swiss scholar Isaac Casaubon provided conclusive proof that the *Corpus Hermeticum* dated not from a remote antiquity but from the first centuries after Christ, thereby exploding the Renaissance myth of Hermes Trismegistus. However, while this discovery eventually weakened the authority of the Hermetic writings among intellectuals, it did not prevent religious currents originating in Renaissance Hermeticism from continuing during the seventeenth century and beyond. Most important in this respect is the so-called Rosicrucian furore caused by the anonymous publication, in Germany and beginning in the very same year as Casaubon's book, of several manifestos claiming to be messages from a mysterious brotherhood of the Rose Cross. The brotherhood in effect announced a transformation of society and the coming of a 'New Age', in the context of a religious ideology wholly founded on Western esoteric (and particularly Paracelsian and alchemical) premises. Due to the excited discussions caused by these pamphlets, the image of a 'Rosicrucian brotherhood' took hold in the popular imagination, and eventually (from the eighteenth century on) actual movements were founded that claimed to be its representatives. Side by side with the Rosicrucian manifestos, the writings of the great visionary philosopher Jacob Boehme (1575–1624) laid the foundations for another highly influential Western esoteric current, known as Christian Theosophy, the influence of which would continue through the seventeenth and eighteenth centuries and into the heart of the German Romantic movement. The existence and influence of a popular and learned Hermeticism during the Age of Reason, partly linked to Freemasonry and the general surge of secret societies in this period, has recently begun to receive more attention from historians, and challenges received ideas about the nature and history of the Enlightenment (see Neugebauer-Wölk, 1999).

Interactions with modernity

The impact of modernity

Western esotericism emerged as a syncretistic type of religiosity in a Christian context, and its representatives generally were Christians until far into the eighteenth century. From about the middle of that century, however, the complicated historical processes that may be referred to under the general heading of 'secularization' began to have their impact on Western culture and religion generally, and they naturally affected esotericists as well. If we understand the term 'secularization' as referring not to a process in which religion declines or vanishes but, rather, to a process of profound change and transformation of religion under the impact of a combination of historically unprecedented social and political conditions, we may speak not just of a 'secularization of religion' but also, more specifically, of a 'secularization of esotericism' during the nineteenth century. The result of this process was a new type of religiosity that may be referred to as 'occultism', and that comprises 'all attempts by esotericists to come to terms with a disenchanted world or, alternatively, by people in general to make sense of esotericism from the perspective of a disenchanted secular world' (Hanegraaff, 1996).

Occultism

The first signs of a secularization of Western esotericism may be perceived in the perspectives of the Swedish visionary Emanuel Swedenborg (1688–1772) and the German physician Franz Anton Mesmer (1734–1815), both of whom have exerted an incalculable influence on the history of esotericism during the nineteenth and twentieth centuries. Theurgical practices, spiritual manifestations and psychic phenomena of a type already present in some esoteric societies of the later eighteenth century as well as in the popular practice of 'magnetic healing' achieved mass popularity in the second half of the nineteenth century, in the occultist movement *par excellence* known as Spiritualism. Spiritualism provided a context within which a plethora of more or less sophisticated occultist movements came into existence. Among these manifestations of alternative religiosity, the Theosophical Movement founded in 1875 by the Russian Madame Helena P. Blavatsky (1831–91) is certainly the most important in terms of its influence, and the basic metaphysical system of modern Theosophy may be considered the archetypal manifestation of occultist spirituality at least until far into the 1970s. In addition, popular practices of 'magnetic healing' also referred to as 'Mesmerism' reached the USA as early as 1836 and spread widely in the following decades, eventually providing a popular basis for the emergence of the so-called 'New Thought' movement of the later nineteenth century. Each one of these various currents – Spiritualism, modern Theosophy, and the American New Thought movement – has taken on a multitude of forms, and their representatives have mingled and exchanged ideas and practices in various ways. The result of all this alternative religious activity was the emergence, during the nineteenth century, of an international cultic milieu with its own social networks and literature.

Relying on an essentially nineteenth-century framework of ideas and beliefs, this cultic milieu continued and further developed during the twentieth century, eventually to provide the foundation after the World War II for the emergence of the New Age movement.

Secularized esotericism

The occultist milieu of the nineteenth and twentieth century differs from traditional Western esotericism in at least four key respects, and these are of crucial importance for understanding the nature of New Age religion (for further discussion of these areas of difference see Hanegraaff, 1996). First, esotericism was originally grounded in an 'enchanted' world view where all parts of the universe were linked by invisible networks of non-causal 'correspondences' and a divine power of life was considered to permeate the whole of nature. Although esotericists have continued to defend such an enchanted holistic view of the world as permeated by invisible forces, their actual statements demonstrate that they came to compromise in various ways with the mechanical and disenchanted world models that achieved cultural dominance under the impact of scientific materialism and nineteenth-century positivism. Accordingly, occultism is characterized by hybrid mixtures of traditional esoteric and modern scientistic-materialist world views: while originally the religious belief in a universe brought forth by a personal God was axiomatic for esotericism, eventually this belief succumbed partly or completely to popular scientific visions of a universe answering to impersonal laws of causality. Even though the laws in question may be referred to as 'spiritual', nonetheless they tend to be described according to models taken from science rather than religion.

Second, the traditional Christian presuppositions of modern Western esotericism were increasingly questioned and relativized due to new translations of oriental religious texts and the emergence of a comparative study of the religions of the world. Oriental religions began to display missionary activities in Western countries, and their representatives typically sought to convince their audience by using Western terms and concepts to present the spirituality of religions such as Hinduism and Buddhism. Conversely, since occultists had always believed that the essential truths of esoteric spirituality were universal in nature and could be discovered at the heart of all great religious traditions East and West, it was natural for them to incorporate oriental concepts and terminology into already existing Western occultist frameworks. One excellent example is the concept of 'karma' that was adopted by Blavatsky from Hinduism, as a welcome alternative for Christian concepts of divine providence, whereas Blavatsky's essential understanding of reincarnation depended on Western-esoteric rather than oriental sources.

Third, the well-known debate between Christian creationism and the new theories of evolution became highly relevant to occultism as well, and in this battle occultists generally took the side of science. But although popular evolutionism became a crucial aspect of occultism as it developed from the nineteenth into the twentieth century, and although this evolutionism was generally used as part of a strategy of presenting occultism as scientifically legitimate, the actual types of evolutionism found in occultism depended less on Darwinian theory than on philosophical models originating in German idealism and Romanticism. The idea of a universal process of spiritual evolution and progress, involving human souls as well as the universe in its entirety, is not to be found in traditional Western esotericism but became fundamental to almost all forms of nineteenth- and twentieth-century occultism.

Finally, the emergence of modern psychology (itself dependent partly on Mesmerism and the Romantic fascination with the 'night-side of nature') has had an enormous impact on the development of occultism from the second half of the nineteenth century on. While psychology could be used as an argument against Christianity and against religion generally, by arguing that God or the gods are merely projections of the human psyche, it also proved possible to present Western-esoteric world views in terms of a new psychological terminology. Most influential in this respect was the Swiss psychiatrist Carl Gustav Jung (1875–1961), whose spiritual perspective was deeply rooted in the esoteric and occult currents of German Romantic *Naturphilosophie* but whose theories could be used to present that spirituality as a 'scientific' psychology. Apart from Jung, the 'pop psychology' of the American New Thought movement has been a major influence on the mixtures of occultism and psychology typical of New Age spirituality.

Postmodern spirituality: The religion of the self

To the four main aspects of the 'secularization of Western esotericism', perhaps a fifth one may be added that became dominant only after World War II, and is fully characteristic of the New Age movement at the end of the twentieth century and start of the new millennium: the impact of the capitalist market economy on the domain of spirituality. Increasingly, the New Age movement has taken the shape of a spiritual supermarket where religious consumers pick and choose the spiritual commodities they fancy, and use them to create their own spiritual syntheses fine-tuned to their strictly personal needs. The phenomenon of a spiritual supermarket is not limited to the New Age movement only, but is a general characteristic of religion in (post)modern Western democracies. Various forms of New Age spirituality are competing with more traditional forms of religion (including the Christian churches as well as other great religious traditions such as Islam or Buddhism) and with a great number of so-called new religious movements, popularly referred to as 'cults'. However, in this universal battle for the attention of the consumer, the New Age movement enjoys certain advantages over most of its competitors, which seem to make it the representative *par excellence* of the contemporary 'spirituality of the market'. Whereas most other spiritual currents that compete for the attention of the consumer in modern society take the form of (at least rudimentary) organizations, enabling their members to see themselves as part of a religious community, New Age spirituality is strictly focused on the individual and his/her personal development. In fact, this individualism functions as an in-built defence mechanism against social organization and institutionalization: as soon as any group of people involved with New Age ideas begins to take up 'cultic' characteristics, this very fact already distances them from the basic individualism of New Age spirituality. The stronger they begin to function as a 'cult', or even as a 'sect', the more will other New Agers suspect that they are becoming a 'church' (i.e., that they are relapsing into what are considered old-fashioned patterns of dogmatism, intolerance and exclusivism), and the less acceptable they will be to the general cultic milieu of New Age spirituality. Such a group then takes up a life of its own as a 'new religious movement', which may share many basic beliefs with the New Age movement but should no longer be considered a typical representation of it. Within the present social context of a democratic free market of ideas and practices, the New Age's strict emphasis on the self and on individual experience as the only reliable source of spiritual truth, the authority of which can never be overruled by any religious dogma or consideration of solidarity with communal values, thus functions as an effective mechanism against institutionalization of New Age religion into a religion. This essential individualism makes the New Ager into the ideal spiritual consumer. Except for the very focus on the self and its spiritual evolution, there are no constraints *a priori* on a New Ager's potential spiritual interests; the fact that every New Ager continually creates and re-creates his or her own private system of symbolic meaning and values means that suppliers of the New Age market enjoy maximum opportunities for presenting him or her with ever-new spiritual commodities.

> You never knew how beautiful you were, for you never really looked at who and what you are. You want to see what God looks like? Go look in a reflector – you are looking God straight in the face.
>
> (J.Z. Knight, *Ramtha: An Introduction* [back cover])

J.Z. Knight is one of the most famous channelling mediums of the 1980s. She channelled Ramtha, an 'entity' identifying himself as a warrior from ancient Atlantis who achieved enlightenment during his first and only life on earth.

As indicated above, that New Age as a spiritual supermarket caters to an individualistic clientèle primarily interested in personal growth and development is not only a fact of social observation but also reflects beliefs that are basic to the movement. At the symbolic centre of New Age world views, one typically finds not a concept of God but, rather, the concept of 'the (higher) self', so that New Age spirituality has indeed sometimes been dubbed 'self religion' (Heelas, 1996). The basic symbolism of the self is linked to a basic mythology, that narrates the growth and development of the individual soul through many incarnations and existences in the direction of ever-increasing knowledge and spiritual insight (Hanegraaff, 1999b). Strict concentration on personal spiritual development rather than on communal values is therefore not considered a reflection of egoism but, rather, of a legitimate spiritual practice based on 'listening to your own inner guidance': only by following one's inner voice one may find one's way through the chaos of voices that clamour for attention on the spiritual supermarket, and find one's personal way to enlightenment.

Looking to the future

For quite some time now, it has been claimed by scholars and critics that the days of the New Age movement are numbered, that the New Age is over, or that the movement has already yielded to a follow-up phenomenon sometimes referred to as the 'Next Age'. Whether this is true depends very much on one's definition. There are indeed clear signs that New Age religion is losing its status as a counter-cultural movement and is now increasingly assimilated by the mainstream of society. Such a development is anything but surprising: rather, it may be seen as the predictable result of commercial success. From one perspective, the fact that New Age is developing from a distinct counter-culture to merely a dimension of mainstream culture may indeed be interpreted as 'the end of the New Age movement as we have known it'; but from another perspective, it may be seen as reflecting the common-sense fact that New Age is developing and changing, just as any other religious movement known from history.

In any case, we should beware of optical illusion. There are indications that the phenomenon of specialized New Age bookshops is declining; but at the same time one notices a substantial increase of spiritual literature on the shelves of 'regular' bookshops. Likewise one may predict that specialized New Age centres for 'healing and personal growth' will become less necessary to the extent that at least parts of their therapeutic services are becoming more acceptable in mainstream medical and psychological contexts. One might well interpret such developments as reflecting not the decline of the New Age movement but, precisely, its development from a counter-cultural movement set apart from the mainstream to a significant dimension of the general spiritual landscape of contemporary Western society.

One thing is clear: whether or not the label 'New Age' will eventually survive, there is no evidence whatsoever that the basic spiritual perspectives, beliefs and practices characteristic of the movement of the 1980s and 1990s are losing popular credibility. Quite the contrary: all the evidence indicates that they are becoming more acceptable to many people in contemporary Western society, whether or not the latter choose to identify themselves as New Agers. Again, the phenomenon is anything but surprising, for the highly individualized approach to spirituality traditionally referred to as 'New Age' simply accords too well with the demands of contemporary consumer culture in a democratic society where citizens insist on their personal autonomy in matters of religion.

Finally, that the social dynamics of postmodern consumer society happen to favour a particular type of religion (referred to above as 'secularized esotericism') is a fact of recent history, but once again it is not a surprising one. That traditional forms of religion – the Christian churches and their theologies – are in decline at least in the contemporary European context is a generally known fact (see Chapter 21, Secularization and secularism). The vogue of postmodern relativism indicates that the 'grand narratives' of progress by science and rationality are losing credibility as well. If more and more people feel that traditional Christianity, rationality and science are no longer able to give sense and meaning to human existence, it can be expected *a priori* that a spiritual perspective based on personal revelations by means of gnosis will profit from the circumstances. As long as the grand narratives of the West fail to regain their hold over the population and no new ones are forthcoming, and as long as Western democratic societies continue to emphasize the supreme virtue of individual freedom, the type of 'self religion' traditionally known as New Age will remain a force to be reckoned with.

Summary

- New Age in a strict sense is the movement born in the context of the post-World War II UFO cults and flowering in the spiritual utopianism of the 1960s and 1970s.

- New Age in a wide sense is the general 'cultic milieu' of alternative religion which flourished after the 1970s and has become increasingly 'mainstream' since. Dominated by American spiritual values and ideas, it is more individualistic and 'self' focused than New Age in a strict sense.

- The roots of New Age are to be found in (a) Renaissance Hermeticism and Western esotericism, which themselves draw on earlier pagan, Jewish and Christian sources; and (b) occultism, which represents the early 'secularization' of esotericism under such pressures as the Enlightenment and the rise of science.

- Recent New Age has been influenced by a consumerist, market-led cultural economy, leading to a focus on 'spiritual shopping' and spiritual self-development.

- The success of the New Age lies in its rapid assimilation into more mainstream culture, and its congruence with the values of the latter.

Key terms

alchemy A practical and speculative tradition focusing on the transmutation and spiritual purification of material substance, whether or not interpreted in a mystical sense.

apocalypticism The expectation of a cataclysmic event that will radically change the world.

counter-culture The 1960s movement of young people revolting against the values of the Western establishment.

gnosis Greek term for 'knowledge', referring to personal spiritual experience or inner enlightenment leading to true knowledge of God and the self.

Gnosticism Movement of late antiquity characterized by a reliance on gnosis and a negative view of the created world as a 'prison of the soul'.

Kabbalah Medieval Jewish mysticism.

Millennarianism The traditional hope for a 'thousand year' reign of peace.

Paracelsianism A Western-esoteric tradition referring to the ideas of the sixteenth-century physician Paracelsus (1493–1541).

secularization The historical processes by which the Christian churches and their theologies have lost their central position in Western religion and have been reduced to the status of competitors in a pluralistic religious market. (See Chapter 21).

syncretism The phenomenon of two or more religions or religious traditions intermingling so as to produce new religious syntheses.

theosophy Has two primary meanings. It refers to an important Christian-esoteric current represented by the Silesian mystic Jacob Böhme (1575–1624), his followers and later traditions inspired by them. It also refers to the perspectives of the Theosophical Society (founded in 1875) and its offshoots.

theurgy A type of ritual practice in late antiquity (particularly in the context of neo-Platonism), by means of which the soul was believed to be raised to the divinities.

Utopianism The hope for an ideal society.

Further reading

Sociological approaches

Early publications have mostly emphasized a sociological approach at the expense of a historical one; a representative example is E.A. Tiryakian (ed.): *On the Margin of the Visible: Sociology, the Esoteric, and the Occult* (New York: John Wiley and Sons, 1974). Of fundamental importance for later research has been a classic article by Colin Campbell: 'The cult, the cultic milieu and secularization'. (*A Sociological Yearbook of Religion in Britain* 5, 1972: pp. 119–136). Probably the most influential sociological study of New Age is Paul Heelas: *The New Age Movement: Celebrating the Self and the Sacralization of Modernity* (Oxford and Cambridge, MA: Blackwell, 1996).

Historical approaches

For a historical rather than a sociological approach, pioneering work has been done by Robert S. Ellwood: *Religious and Spiritual Groups in Modern America* (orig. 1973), revised edition with Harry B. Partin (Englewood Cliffs, NJ: Prentice-Hall, 1988), and J. Gordon Melton: see especially James R. Lewis and J. Gordon Melton (eds): *Perspectives on the New Age* (Albany, NY: SUNY Press, 1992). One of the first authors to emphasize the importance of analysing New Age beliefs and their context in intellectual history was Mary Farrell Bednarowski: *New Religions and the Theological Imagination in America* (Bloomington and Indianapolis, IN: Indiana University Press, 1989). An encompassing analysis and interpretation of New Age beliefs from the perspective of the history of ideas is Wouter J. Hanegraaff: *New Age Religion and Western Culture: Esotericism in the Mirror of Secular Thought* (Leiden: E.J.Brill, 1996) [US paperback: Albany, NY: SUNY Press, 1998]. In two later articles, the same author has proposed additional frameworks for interpreting the relation between New Age and the secularization of religion in contemporary Western society: 'Defining religion in spite of history'. In Jan G.Platvoet and Arie L.Molendijk (eds): *The Pragmatics of Defining Religion* (Leiden: E.J. Brill, 1999a, pp. 337–78) and 'New Age spiritualities as secular religion: a historian's perspective'. (*Social Compass* 46(2), 1999b: pp. 145–60).

Religious Studies approaches

Recent monographs on New Age tend to be written from a Religious Studies perspective that seeks to integrate rather than separate sociological and historical approaches. Examples of such recent work are Steven J. Sutcliffe: *Children of the New Age: A History of Spiritual Practices* (London & New York: Routledge, 2003), (problematic as concerns its theoretical approach, but recommended for its discussion of the English 'New Age in a strict sense'); Sarah M. Pike: *New Age and Neopagan Religions in America* (New York: Columbia University Press, 2004); Nevill Drury: *The New Age: The History of a Movement* (New York: Thames & Hudson, 2004), focused on a popular rather than academic market, but informative and well written; Christopher Partridge; *The Re-Enchantment of the West* (2 vols.; London & New York: T&T Clark, 2005 and 2006), a comprehensive study that also pays attention to various aspects of 'alternative spirituality' which were ignored or marginalized by earlier scholars; Daren Kemp: *New Age: A Guide. Alternative Spiritualities from Aquarian Conspiracy to New Age* (Edinburgh: Edinburgh University Press, 2004); and Daren Kemp and James R. Lewis (eds.): *Handbook of New Age* (Leiden and Boston, MA: Brill, 2007). On psychedelic shamanism and 2012 millennarianism, see Wouter J. Hanegraaff: 'And End History. And go to the Stars: Terence McKenna and 2012', in: Carole Cusack and Christopher Hartney (eds) *Religion and Retributive Logic* (Leiden and Boston, MA: Brill, 2009).

Primary sources

For primary sources of New Age up to and including the first half of the 1990s, see numerous references in Hanegraaff op.cit. (1996). The authors and books specifically mentioned in the text are: Marilyn Ferguson: *The Aquarian Conspiracy: Personal and Social Transformation in the 1980s* (orig. 1980) (London: Granta, 1982); Fritjof Capra: *The Turning Point: Science, Society, and the Rising Culture* (London: Fontana, 1983); David Spangler: *The Rebirth of the Sacred* (London: Gateway Books, 1984); Shirley McLaine: *Out on a Limb* (Toronto: Bantam Books, 1983); James Redfield: *The Celestine Prophecy* (New York: Warner Books, 1993). For many additional references since 1995, see in particular Partridge, *Re-Enchantment* (details above). For New Age millenarianism focused on 2012, see Gregg Braden *et al.*, *The Mystery of 2012: Predictions, Prophecies and Possibilities*, (Boulder, CO: Sounds True, 2007).

Sources and antecedents of New Age

For the historical roots of New Age religion in Western esotericism and the emergence of a 'secularized esotericism', see Hanegraaff, op.cit. (1996). On Western esotericism generally, see Antoine Faivre: *Access to Western Esotericism* (Albany, NY: SUNY Press, 1994); Kocku von Stuckrad: *Western Esotericism: A Brief History of Secret Knowledge* (London, and Oakville, CT: Equinox, 2005; and Wouter J. Hanegraaff *et al.* (eds), *Dictionary of Gnosis and Western Esotericism* (Leiden and Boston, MA: Brill, 2005). Groundbreaking research on the relation between Western esotericism and the Enlightenment is presented in Monika Neugebauer-Wölk (ed.): *Aufklärung und Esoterik* (Hamburg: Felix Weiner Verlag, 1999).

Chapter 14

Paganism

Graham Harvey

Introduction

Paganism is an increasingly popular religion that is often described as a 'nature religion' and as a revitalization or reclamation of pre-Christian traditions. It first became well-known in the mid-twentieth century in Britain, but draws on ancient and modern ideas and practices to engage with some of the major concerns of today (see Chapter 12, Spirituality, for an introduction). Although few Pagans are frontline environmental activists there is certainly a resonance between Pagan celebration of the natural world and the need to respond swiftly to global climate change and other pressing ecological issues. Similarly, although not all Pagans identify themselves as feminists, few Pagan groups are dominated by male leaders and many are non-hierarchical. Certainly, the pluralist and non-dogmatic tendencies of Pagans have been influenced by feminism.

Paganism is practiced in many countries in the world, in most continents, in a variety of loosely related movements, usually called 'traditions' or 'paths', including Druidry, Goddess Spirituality, Heathenry, Wicca, a number of 'ethnic Paganisms' (e.g. Celtic, Hellenic, Lithuanian, Norse), and the increasingly significant Eco-Paganism. All these draw on regional ancestral traditions, archaeology, ecology, folklore, and history, as well as anthropological and esoteric writings. The precise mix of sources and a range of personal and group preferences in ways of performing rituals and narrating important ideas determines the style of each tradition and the evolution of the whole religion.

This chapter begins by addressing the question of what 'nature religion' means. It then surveys the origins of Paganism before introducing the sources and resources that Pagans draw on. An overview of some key features of the main Pagan traditions is followed by short vignettes of typical Pagan events and activities. The chapter ends with a discussion of Paganism's interactions with modernity.

'Nature religion'

Paganism is often labelled a 'nature religion' by scholars who wish to point to its central concerns, link it with similar religions, and distinguish it from other kinds of religion. The term does not mean that Paganism is the only religion interested in nature, or that Pagans do nothing but celebrate nature, still less that they 'worship nature'. Rather, 'nature religion' typically contrasts Paganism with religions that are particularly focused on divine beings or transcendent realities rather than on the ordinary, physical world, i.e. that which is often called 'nature'. Pagan organizations often have trouble gaining tax exemption in the United States or charity status in the United Kingdom because those who decide such matters frequently define religion as systems of belief and practice focused on beings (e.g. gods and angels) or realms (e.g. heaven) that are thought to be beyond the physical – supernatural rather than natural. While much Pagan ritual is devoted to deities (gods and goddesses), the intimate involvement of such beings in the processes (e.g. the weather) and places (e.g. springs or forests) of nature is often used to exclude Paganism from the category of religion. However, Paganism is similar to some indigenous religions in which the pursuit of well-being, happiness and responsible living in this world is more important that any supernatural idea or transcendent afterlife.

In addition to the contrast between 'nature religions' and 'transcendent religions', there are also religions that have been called 'self religions' (Heelas, 1996). In New Age spiritualities, for example, there is a central concern with the authority of the 'self', understood as the innermost reality of each individual. Pagans agree with New Agers that individual preferences are important, but they insist that people are thoroughly relational beings: unavoidably part of other people's lives. The Pagan 'self', like that of most indigenous religions, is best understood as that aspect of persons (human or otherwise) that enables relationships, communication, participation and belonging. Pagans might meditate (especially using guided visualization techniques) and seek to be aware of their desires, intentions and motivations (all aspects of the inner 'self') but attempts to understand and enhance their relationships and contribution to the well-being of other beings is more definitive of Paganism. This has led Michael York, a sociologist of religion, to define Paganism as 'an affirmation of interactive and poly-morphic sacred relationship by individual or community with the tangible, sentient and nonempirical' (York, 2000).

In addition to these questions of the focus of religions (transcendent or earthy, individual or relational), the term 'nature' in 'nature religion' points to the popular perception that Paganism is all about nature. The most common Pagan events are celebrations of seasonal festivals (see below – particularly 'Vignettes'). But Pagans are no more likely than anyone else to romantically idealize the countryside or wilderness. Many do prefer to perform their rituals outdoors or in rural places. Others, however, insist that urban spaces are also part of the planet and deserve celebration and care. Neither do all Pagans think that they ought to be permanently involved in frontline environmental activism. In fact, many Pagans are involved in local, regional and global organizations and activities that seek to protest ecological harm or protect threatened environments. Pagans are likely to recycle or compost, and few participate in extravagant consumerism. Many, though certainly not all, are vegetarian or vegan on the understanding that such ways of life are more ecologically responsible and less damaging to the wider community of life. So, while few Pagans imagine that 'nature' is a pure realm unaffected by humanity and offering nothing but joyful festivity, the centrality in Paganism of the encouragement to live as respectful citizens of the natural world cannot be exaggerated.

In short, Paganism is a 'nature religion' because it is defined by practices that root people in 'nature' – the physical, sensual world within which humans are embodied participants. Belonging and behaving appropriately are prioritized rather than, as in some other religions, anticipating a postulated alternative spiritual reality.

Origins

There have been many claims about the original meaning of the term 'Pagan'. It is more useful to understand the role these ideas have played than to insist on an historically accurate interpretation.

In the mid-twentieth century, when increasingly large numbers of people openly identified themselves as Pagans for the first time, it was generally understood that 'Pagan' derived from Latin words for the countryside and those who lived there. Pagans, according to this view, were country-dwellers, living close to the land, celebrating the seasons, uncorrupted by either the excesses or the constraints of urban life. Even today, dictionaries propagate the ideas that the Latin word *pagus* first meant a place marker, then expanded to label a rural district, and that while *paganus* may once have neutrally referred to rural people, it took on the pejorative connotation that country-dwellers were backwards or even refused progress. This allegedly set the scene for Christian usage of the term to refer to people who wilfully refused to join the new religion, preferring to maintain their ancestral superstitions and festivities. Mid-twentieth century Pagans contested the denigration of the countryside and rural life and religion. They followed a path set out by late-eighteenth- and nineteenth-century writers and poets who found industrial cities to be inhospitable and inhuman, while they claimed that in remote places it was still possible to encounter the awe and majesty of the cosmos. These ideas encouraged Pagans to proclaim the virtue of the natural world and the value of pre-Christian veneration of deities intimately related to the changing seasons.

The idea that country-dwellers conservatively maintained old traditions was asserted with a particular vigour by scholars who interpreted the mediaeval and early-modern witch trials as a Christian assault on the last surviving Pagan religions of Europe. Out in the woods and secluded places, it was claimed, people continued to honour the old deities and festivals until they were betrayed to Christian authorities, accused of devil worship, and condemned to death. The most detailed expression of such arguments was in the works of Margaret Murray, an Egyptologist who wrote the entry on 'witchcraft' for the *Encyclopedia Britannica* (Murray, 1929). These ideas about ancient Pagans and more recent witches inspired Gerald Gardner and his companions in the 1940s to actively construct a Pagan Witchcraft that they came to call 'Wicca'. The popularity of the movement was aided by the publication of books like Gardner's *Witchcraft Today* (1954).

The rejection of this Murray/Gardner-style origins story by most Wiccans and other Pagans today – largely following a positive response to academic criticism by, for example, Ronald Hutton (1999) – has not undermined the movement or diminished its numerical growth. Instead, Pagans have welcomed more careful research about both ancient, pre-Christian religions and about the precursors to the 'Pagan revival' of the twentieth century. The European esoteric tradition that has also resulted in New Age religion (see Chapter 13) has been influential, providing a structure for most ceremonial events in Paganism and, in particular, for initiations in Wicca. Conducting rituals in circles marked out by the participants with ritual tools such as daggers and bowls of salt and water, and the introductory invocation or welcoming of elemental beings (air, fire, water and earth) associated with the cardinal directions (east, south, west and north) are only the most obvious aspects of this inheritance.

In addition to this blend of nature veneration and esoteric ritualism, Pagans often emphasize their affinity with ancestral religions. Their ceremonies address deities known from the literatures of ancient Assyria, Egypt, Greece and Rome, alongside deities referred to in Icelandic, Scandinavian, and Anglo-Saxon sagas, poetry and histories. Christian missionaries too provide resources for reconstructing the stories, calendar feasts and rituals of pre-Christian times. More recent regional folklore and folk-music is sometimes utilized by those who stress the importance of locality and ethnicity. Various 'ethnic Pagan' movements (e.g., Celtic, Lithuanian, Hellenic, Ukrainian and Norse Paganisms) pay particular attention to whatever they can find out about particular styles of ancient or historical practice, insisting on the value of literal inheritance from ancestors and places. Some argue that their religious practices are parallel to revitalization movements among indigenous peoples which reclaim as relevant to today the practices of earlier generations living in specific locations. These 'ethnic' emphases add another strand to the understanding that Pagans are members of a 'nature religion': nature here meaning that which is natural to a location and a people who trace genetic and cultural descent from particular ancestors.

Despite these assertions of linkages to ancestral, pre-Christian religions, most Pagans are happy to acknowledge that Paganism is a new religion. Whether they emphasise a particular kind of tradition or merrily borrow whatever idea or practice serves their purposes, most Pagans consider their religion to be a thoroughly contemporary one. The term 'reconstruction' rather than 'revival' is gaining in popularity as a way of expressing the dynamic link between old and new origins. If the intensely contemporary desire to link religious practice with environmental concerns draws many of these strands together, the influence of feminism is similarly evident. Pagan organizational structures, participative rather than hierarchical ritual practices, and activist engagements are often rooted in feminism. The influence of the ideas and activities of women of the Greenham Common Peace Camp (initially opposing a cruise missile base) have been enormously influential – even though rarely made explicit – in a wide range of more recent movements working for social justice.

Sources and resources

It is already clear that academic writings about ancient religions and witchcraft have been drawn on in the creation and development of various kinds of Paganism. Similarly, collections of regional folklore, the writings of esotericists, environmentalists and feminists have also been useful. *The Paganism Reader* (Clifton and Harvey, 2004) offers examples of all these. It includes excerpts from classical texts: e.g. Biblical references to rituals for a goddess, Greek hymns and a Roman novel about other goddesses, Pliny the Elder's thoughts about Druids, a letter from a Roman emperor about the organization of Pagan congregations, a Norse wisdom poem, an evocation of an Icelandic shamanic séance, and medieval Welsh and Irish tales. These are followed by examples of esoteric, evocative, poetic and polemical texts (including Murray's 'Witchcraft' article) that were clearly inspirational for the first generation of openly self-declared Pagans. The florescence of writings by Pagans of all kinds is also exemplified in the *Reader*, illustrating the rapid diversification and maturation of Paganism once people felt confident about building networks and publishing ideas and practices.

None of the literature used by Pagans has been elevated to the status of sacred scripture. Whether it is ancestral wisdom like the *Havamal* – purporting to represent the wisdom of the god Odin and his statement about how he achieved that wisdom – or the writings of the founders of new Pagan traditions (e.g. Gerald Gardner, Raymond Buckley or Starhawk), everything is open to question, and available for use in new ways. Explicitly fictional novels can be as inspiring as guides to ritual practice. Indeed, many Pagans assert that if you want to read a book about Paganism it would be better to read something fictional rather than any of the 'How do to it' manuals. Marion Zimmer Bradley's *Mists of Avalon* (1984), Terry Pratchett's Discworld series (e.g. his 1988 *Wyrd Sisters*) and re-tellings of the mediaeval Welsh *Mabinogion* tales (e.g. Alan Garner's *The Owl Service*, 1967) are frequently cited. Indeed, some fictional works are treated almost as manuals: Brian Bates's historical novel, *The Way of Wyrd* (1983) seems to have played this role more popularly than his manual, *The Wisdom of the Wyrd* (1996).

All of this academic and popular, ancient and recent literature is read avidly and responded to both negatively and positively as resources for developing Pagan theory and practice. Still, if not even the *Havamal*'s record of a divine epiphany has become scripture in over six decades of Pagan development, it is unlikely that anyone will now produce a text that will gain such a status. For a highly literate community, Pagans tend to treat publications as adjuncts rather than ultimate authorities.

In contrast, the chief source of authority about how to be Pagan (or how to be Wiccan, Druid, Ukrainian Native Faith, or Goddess Devotee) is experience. People are invited to reflect on the experiences that led them to identify as Pagans, or to affiliate with a particular tradition, and then to develop those existing affinities and expectations. Each person is more or less free to contribute to the development of Paganism – although some are recognised as expert writers, speakers or ritualists and thus as being worthy of emulation. As in any idealistic movement, there are individuals who attempt to impose themselves as leaders with more right to be heard than anyone else. Pagans, however, tend to make poor followers and frequently satirize and reject overweening individuals. The authority of Pagan leaders is curtailed by the pervasive understanding that each person is responsible for the development and expression of their relationship with the world, their spirituality, their Paganism. Simultaneously, the growth of the worldwide web alongside the growth of Paganism makes it impossible for anyone to claim to be the only source of knowledge. The ease with which ideas and practices can be disseminated by anyone with internet access contributes to the democratization and popularization of all varieties of Paganism.

While Pagans, like New Agers, have inherited and popularized originally esoteric meditation and inward-looking imaginative practices that aid self-awareness, the most valued Pagan experiences are those of intimacy with the world. Sensual knowledge of the self, 'nature', and the relationship between them, rather than otherworldly 'spirituality', is the key. The matter may be put somewhat humorously with reference to an element of the legends of the Holy Grail (even if such legends arose within Christian circles): the appearance of the Grail is always accompanied by the provision of 'that which one most desires' in the way of food or drink. In contrast with the insistence of the Grail legends that only the unworldly and chaste could find the Grail and, eventually, reach Heaven, there is at least this one suggestion that sensual pleasure can be rewarded. In Monty Python's less reverent version of the legend, *Monty Python and the Holy Grail*, the decisive question the seeker has to answer is 'what is your favourite colour?'. It is unlikely that the more moralistic and mystical Christian Grail legends could have accepted this to be the key question. But if they are to achieve their heart's desire, shape their life and their world according to their truest intimations of what is good, and – not incidentally – be offered the kind of food and drink they most desire, a person has to be able to celebrate something as simple as their favourite colour. This is not to assert that Pagans regularly cite Monty Python as an authority, however much some enjoy this style of humour. It is, rather, to indicate that amusing stories can sometimes convey truths that some consider profound. Here, encapsulated in an amusing moment, is the idea that it is good, proper and indeed necessary to enjoy the world and the senses in order to recognise the authority of embodied experiences as authoritative.

Pagans are also like New Agers, and members of many other new religions, in being accused of being like consumers in a spiritual supermarket. Rather than recognising the pervasive tendency of all lived religions to adapt what seems helpful and complementary, the assertion that new religions are eclectic often implies a negative criticism. However, it needs to be recognised that people do not select ideas and practices randomly. Just as people enter hardware stores, bakeries, clothing stores and even supermarkets to acquire goods that fit with their existing self-understanding and their future intentions, so Pagans and other religious people adopt that which 'fits' their existing religious framework. Pagans read widely and draw on a disparate range of sources and resources, but do so according to their desire to develop traditions that celebrate participation in the living world.

Pagan traditions

A number of Pagan traditions have already been mentioned, including various reconstructionist and ethnic movements (Celtic, Norse, Ukrainian, Hellenic and others), various popularizations of esotericism built around a 'nature'-venerating core (Wicca and Druidry), and at least one specifically feminist tradition (Goddess spirituality). More should be said about these to indicate both what is specific to them and what they have in common.

Witchcraft

It is not possible to be certain how many Pagans there are because some belong to more than one tradition while others do not openly identify themselves as Pagan. Some Pagans subscribe to many of the Pagan magazines that are available internationally, and some actively participate in internet lists and chat-rooms. Many others, however, remain almost invisible to any survey. Knowledge of the existence of Pagans in some countries is hard to come by, and it is far from rare to hear Pagans say that until recently they thought that no one else shared their ideas or practices. However, judging by the number of publications by and for Witches, and by the predominance of Wicca in academic publications about Paganism, it is clear that Wicca, Witchcraft, or the Craft of Witches, is among the best known Pagan traditions. It may also have the most members.

Actually, things are a little more complex: some Pagans see Wicca as one type of Witchcraft, which is one type of Paganism, while others treat all three terms synonymously. In the UK, 'Wicca' is always reserved for a tradition that requires members to be initiated into small groups, called covens, with a high priestess and (usually) a high priest who can trace their initiatory lineage back to Gerald Gardner, Alex and Maxine Saunders, or others identified as founders or leading figures of particular groups. Wiccans may also call themselves 'Witches' and identify their tradition as 'Witchcraft', but there are many who identify as Witches but not Wiccans. Similarly, many Pagans have not been initiated into covens and, whether they belong to another tradition or not, do not identify as anything but Pagans. In contrast, in the USA 'Wicca' can refer to such initiatory groups but it is also used more broadly and often embraces members of non-initiatory groups of Witches, sometimes referring to people who would call themselves only 'Pagans' in the UK.

The difference between these two uses of 'Wicca' is indicative of part of the range within Paganism. To British Pagans Wicca is initiatory: it is closer to the trajectory of esoteric traditions in which people present themselves to groups for membership on the basis that they wish to acquire knowledge and skills in the practice of magic. Initiatory groups, under high-ranking leaders, offer training packaged in a series of 'degrees', each marked by ceremonies that grant access after the initiates have demonstrated their increasing ability. Part of the attraction of Wicca is that it simplifies what can be a cumbersome and hierarchical structure. The magic in which initiates are trained can be described as either 'the art of causing change according to will' or 'the art of changing consciousness according to will' – in practice, both the attempt to bring about changes such as healing and the attempt to raise one's own consciousness are entwined. It involves learning correspondences and associations between, for example, colours, deities, elements, directions, seasons, magical implements and gestures. Once these are mastered, the adept can use one of the corresponding items to implicate others: they might chose a particular colour associated with a specific deity to aid their healing efforts. A related attraction of this type of Wicca is that it braids such practices into the celebration of festivals timed to honour the changing seasons and the lunar cycle. Wiccans seek empowerment from deities, particularly the Goddess – who is visible in the moon and experienced in lunar influences – and the God, experienced in another series of natural changes through the year.

The broader USA usage of 'Wicca' draws on these same traditions of esotericism and seasonal festivals, but further democratizes its practices so that self-initiation is a fairly simple matter of self-declaration. Lineage groups are far from rare, but they are out numbered by groups in which 'Wicca' principally refers to the attunement of people's lives to the natural seasons. The most open style of Witchcraft, perhaps, is the increasingly popular movement called 'Teen Witchcraft'. Research by Helen Berger and Douglas Ezzy (2007) shows that a growing number of teenagers are identifying as Witches, sometimes networking with one another through web-based sites, sometimes sup-ported by books specifically aimed at them, but often carefully selecting ideas and practices by trial and error from less sensationalist and more careful literature. They blend their own adaptations of seasonal celebrations with experiments in magic with which they seek to make the world better for them and those they love at the same time as seeking personal development. Many see themselves as outsiders, different from their peers, but typically value and even enjoy their sense of difference, moulding it into enriching experiences of reflexivity and responsibility. Quite where this growing trend will lead is difficult to say, but some of the more articulate young Witches are likely to make significant contributions to the further evolution of a religion open to the push and pull of all adherents' wishes.

Druidry and Celtic Paganism

Pagans who identify as Druids or as Celtic Pagans draw on archaeological and literary evidence of what the religions of pre-Roman Celts and the Iron Age priestly/political leaders were like. Many of them also draw on the inheritance of the esoteric traditions and the result can be similar to Witchcraft, especially in the structure of rituals and the use of correspondences. But another historical resource feeds Druidry: the revival of interest in Celtic culture in Wales, Brittany, Cornwall, Ireland and Scotland from the late eighteenth century onwards. Religiously, most of those who called themselves Druids until around 1950 were nonconformist Christians. It is their celebration and elabora-tion of the bardic arts of musicianship and story-telling that they have passed on to contemporary Pagan Druids. Some observers have claimed that the major difference between Witches and Druids is that the former are mostly women who perform rituals privately by moonlight, while the latter are mostly men whose rituals are held publicly in daylight. In fact, both Witches and Druids hold both private and public rituals at night and during the day. While the majority of Druid leaders were male until recently, it is now increasingly rare for any Pagan ceremony to be conducted or led only or even primarily by men. In fact, the chief difference between Witchcraft and Druidry is that the latter lays greater emphasis on bardic performance.

The difference marked by identification as Celtic Pagans rather than Druids can involve either a more radical attempt to reconstruct the local polytheistic prac-tices of the non-priestly pre-Roman inhabitants of northwest Europe or, conversely, a more romantic notion of Celticity that has also given rise to the 'Celtic Christianity' movement.

Ethnic Paganisms

Most of the countries of central and eastern Europe have given rise to movements that claim to reconstruct the pre-Christian religions practised by their ancestors in those lands – if they do not claim to simply continue an unbroken tradition that had survived underground during the Christian and Communist eras. While they share a focus on the celebration of seasonal festivals, ancestral and folk traditions, the performance of magic, reverence of pre-Christian deities, and an affirmation of vital importance of ritual, they clearly understand 'nature' in a way that distinguishes them from most Western European Pagans. Adrian Ivakhiv (2005) demonstrates that 'Native Faith' Ukrainians are commonly energized by an emphatic insistence on human relatedness to particular lands. Unlike most Western Pagans, they do not tend to mean that individuals 'come home' to the pleasure of respectful relationship with places with which they find or form an affinity. Rather, they stress a fundamental and inescapable relationship between ethnic groups and particular lands that, it is argued (sometimes vociferously), ought to be reciprocally formative. That is, particular people are made by particular lands and vice versa. Particular religions belong to particular places, and those that practice such religions are being true to their ancestral and located identities. Some of the exponents of such movements are undoubtedly passionately involved in racist and right-wing political activism. Many, however, are more vocal about the value to all inhabitants of places of the celebration of belonging, utilizing folklore and local performance traditions to reinvigorate distinctive local cultures.

Goddess Spirituality

According to Margaret Murray's vision, witches were led by male priests who venerated a male deity who could be mistaken for the Christian devil. Gardner and his companions swiftly raised the profile of a Goddess whose path to fame may have begun in the ancient world but was promoted by Victorian and Jungian theories of the pre-eminence of lunar and mother goddesses among the earliest humans and in the collective unconscious. Wherever she came from, most Pagans now speak of 'the Goddess' even when, in response to further questioning, they indicate that this is a shorthand reference to 'all the deities' or even to 'all of life'. Among some Pagans, however, the female divine takes absolute precedence over all other possible manifestations of divinity. Allied to feminist emphases on the liberation and empowerment of all people from the inequities of masculine dominance and misogyny, the Pagan form of Goddess Spirituality reveals further implications of the call to celebrate 'nature'. Where the gendered reality of human and other lives has been the excuse for hierarchy and male-supremacy, and the validation of 'ecocidal' assaults on female 'nature' by male rationality, it is now countered by an invitation to celebrate complementarity, difference, and diversity.

Sexuality has played significant roles in the lead up to the rebirth of Paganism, and was an important aspect of the early Wiccan idea that Paganism was a fertility religion that would enhance the vitality of the earth. But in Goddess Spirituality, sexuality is honoured as a further self-revelation of a passionate and sensual female divine. Asphodel Long (1994) summed up much of this in her affirmation that, 'In raising Her we raise ourselves; in raising ourselves, we raise Her'. A particular blend of Goddess Spirituality and Witchcraft is particularly associated with Starhawk and the Reclaiming tradition that she inspired. Her books (e.g. *Truth or Dare*, 1990) are widely read among Pagans of all kinds, and have increased the importance of activism supported by public ritual performances that inspire hope even as they contest military, ecological and economic injustices.

Reconstructionist Heathenry and Ethnic Paganisms

The religious traditions of Iceland, Scandinavia, Germany and Anglo-Saxon Britain inspire a number of related but distinct movements that are more commonly called 'Heathen' than 'Pagan'. Some of these position themselves as reconstructions of ancient cultural practices, others as the direct heirs to ancestral or 'ethnic' religions.

In *Nine Worlds of Seid-Magic* (2002), Jenny Blain discusses the reconstruction of a shamanic practice based on historical, archaeological and anthropological sources but made relevant to the needs of contemporary Heathens. She traces the creation of communities not only in relation to specific deities, but also according to choices in styles of trance performance. People consult someone skilled in entering trance states who is understood to travel to other dimensions to seek wisdom and information from deities and ancestors. The séances of *seid*-workers are one aspect of the interaction between Heathens and the deities and other beings known from pre-Christian texts. Not only is veneration offered but aid is requested as relationships evolve between all these living beings.

Heathenry also connects to a wider context of the revival or resurgence of ethnic religions. For some Pagans there is a 'natural' connection between the religious traditions of a person's ancestors and the compulsion they feel towards rediscovering such practices. Some debate whether ethnicity alone is sufficient: is it enough to be of Norse, Saxon or Ukrainian origin to venerate Norse, Saxon or Ukrainian deities and/or ancestors? Can these religious traditions be practised in North America or anywhere but their native lands? In fact, the phrasing of such questions begs the further questions: Are the deities of Saxon people 'Saxon deities' themselves? Do deities have an ethnicity? Not surprisingly, there are divergent answers, some insisting that the label 'ethnic Paganism' or 'Native Faith' is only appropriate in the place of origin, while others insist that deities and traditions are as mobile as humans and that it makes perfect sense to honour one's ancestors and origins wherever one lives.

Eco-Paganism

In many surveys that have asked people to name the Pagan tradition with which they most associate, nearly half of respondents say that they prefer to be identified only as Pagans, not as Witches, Druids, Asatruar or any of the other possible labels. Among this large and increasing number, some are identifiable as Eco-Pagans. Unlike the other names this is not always one that people use for themselves, indeed it is a novelty to many Pagans. It is a term that usefully points to a growing trend towards environmentally active (but not necessarily full-time frontline activist) Paganism. It includes people who work as environmental educators, the inhabitants of camps that seek to protect threatened ecosystems from developers, as well as Pagans who might also call themselves 'animists' to indicate their attempt to live respectfully among all the living beings of the greater-than-human world. Some Eco-Pagans are, or have been, members of the more organized Pagan traditions, but many prefer to not to join formal groups. Some are disappointed with, or even disaffected from, the larger Pagan movement, seeing it as missing the key point that 'Pagan' requires active engagement with 'nature' and not only occasional visits to the countryside or wilderness for brief rituals focused on human well-being. This may not be an entirely fair assessment of other styles of Paganism, but it indicates that Eco-Pagans emphasize the active prioritization and explicit enactment of respectful relationships between humans and other living beings. Elaborate costumes and ritual regalia may be deemed unnecessary (although dramatic events may attract other celebrants, or enhance eco-education by drawing people in as participants) and simplicity may be valorized. Alternatively, many Eco-Pagans actively participate in large ritual festivals but insist that these must meld with ecologically responsible everyday lifestyles.

One or many?

It has become increasingly popular among academics to write about 'Paganisms' in the plural. This correctly indicates that the differences between some of these groups are now clear enough to cast some doubt on whether Paganism is one religion or many. Nonetheless, much the same could be said of Christianity and other religions: is there one Christianity or many Christianities? Are Roman Catholics and Charismatic evangelicals members of the same religion? (See the discussion of this issue in Chapter 8, Christianity). In fact, all that is new here is the increasing recognition that religions are not enclosed realities, neatly boxed, separate from one another. They are always diverse phenomena. The key question then is whether there is enough common ground shared between different kinds of Pagan to allow acceptance of the shared use of the name. Since few Pagans insist that their way of being or doing Paganism is the only correct way, it is not difficult to use 'Paganism' as a large umbrella term beneath which a range of diverse movements coexist. What they have in common is a desire to celebrate life in the material, sensual world as relational, embodied people. They all seek, to one degree or another, to learn lessons from pre-Christian or other-than-Christian religious cultures and to find ways to use the insights gained to enhance contemporary life. The differences between, for example, Wiccans and Heathens, or Eco-Pagans and Ukrainian Native Faith members, are significant but do not (as yet) indicate the separation of Paganism into entirely separate religions.

Vignettes

The most typical Pagan events are seasonal festivals celebrating the relationship between the earth, sun, moon and stars. A wheel of eight annual festivals – some originating in ancient Ireland but almost certainly brought together as a cycle by Gerald Gardner and his colleagues in conversation with Ross Nichols (one of the Druids responsible for the eventual re-emergence of a new Pagan Druidry) – structures the way in which most Pagans experience and honour the changing seasons. They also mould them as citizens (alongside all other living beings) of the places where they live and celebrate. The solstices and equinoxes mark the middles of seasons, and four further festivals mark their beginnings and ends. The cycle of the moon's growth and decline adds to the complexity of many Pagans' festive calendar. Pagans who draw on Norse or other ancestral traditions may also celebrate these moments of relationship between the earth, sun and moon, but draw on relevant literature and other sources in the development of calendars fitting to their tradition. In all such events Pagans find resonances with the seasons of their personal lives and relationships. Paganism contests any separation of humanity from the world, culture from nature, and mind from matter. Most but by no means all Pagans acknowledge the existence of deities, but insist that only deities who are intimately involved with the world are worthy of veneration. The following short vignettes are only intended to suggest some of the flavours of some typical Pagan events. (These are fictional but based on recorded events.)

A coven gathering

After a temporary sacred space is formed by the use of purificatory water and salt, and the coven members take their places around the circle, the Four Quarters are greeted. For example, the entire company follow one selected to greet North as she turns to face north, raises both arms, and intones 'Hail, Guardian of the North, element of Earth. We invoke you and call you . . . Be with us now'. After these initiatory preliminaries, the heart of the ritual takes place, often including the dramatizing of the lifecycles and relationship between the Goddess and the God (e.g. honouring their procreative powers or their ageing through the year). Priestesses and priests not only represent but are perceived to become manifestations of the divinities. Most Wiccan events entail the raising of 'energy' to aid the working of magic by which the world is made a better place. Energy may be raised by chanting, drumming or by energetic circle dances accompanied by the visualization of power from the earth and divine and human participants blending in a cone that can be directed, for example, to heal or protect someone or some place. Ceremonies end with the saying farewell to those powers invoked in the opening, the opening up of the temporary sacred circle and by the sharing of food and drink both as celebration and as an earthing back into everyday reality.

Druids celebrate Beltaine

The beginning of May is celebrated as the coming of summer in Britain and Ireland. Pagan Druid gatherings at ancient circles of standing stones (such as Avebury in southern England) celebrate not only the season but also its association with love, vitality and fecundity. They have drawn on folklore to form a ceremony focused on dances around a maypole (explicitly and joyfully recognised as a sexual symbol) but they also blend entertainment and the serious business of honouring the seasons by adopting a 'Jack

FIGURE 14.1 Stonehenge

A woman communicates with a Bluestone, Stonehenge, Summer Solstice 2008. © Mika Lassander.

in the Green' and an 'Oss' – someone dressed in a frame covered in foliage, and an unruly 'hobby horse' with a wide skirt over a circular frame and a mouth that clacks as it dances around the circle. Marriages, or 'handfastings' as many Pagans call them, are often performed as part of the festival of Beltaine. In Britain these are not legally recognised – indeed, there is little desire and considerable objection to any attempts to gain legal recognition for an official Pagan clergy. As with Wiccan coven events, Druid ceremonies are commonly conducted in circles (both temporary and of ancient, permanent manufacture). The beginnings and ends of Druid ceremonies are also marked by greetings to the directions and associated elements.

Heathen seidr

A Heathen hearth (as some local groups prefer to be called) gathers to honour the various deities of the Anglo-Saxon pantheon. After expressions of honour and the offering of libations to these deities, one of the company takes her place in the High Seat otherwise reserved for the god Woden. Indeed, as she becomes entranced she becomes Woden. She appears to change physically so that later people will swear that she was dressed as a traveller in a cloak and brimmed hat, and even that she somehow lost an eye – just as the legends say of the travelling and wise god Woden. Once in a trance (which these people prefer to call *seidr* although they disagree about exactly how to translate the term), the seated traveller is asked questions about issues of importance to individuals, the group and their tradition. Some answers seem to take ages to be brought back to the company, others are immediately answered, not always in ways that the questioner or companions immediately understands. After some time, the trance state begins to diminish and Woden is thanked and bid farewell.

Teen magic

Having consulted a few of the many popular books aimed at young witches, and asked a few questions of friends only met in internet chat rooms, a teen witch performs magic to raise his chances of passing an exam. He put some mood music on his CD player, lit a candle, and imagined what it would be like to receive a glowing report from a successful exam. Later he told his internet friends that this may have only made him feel more confident and relaxed, but he recognised that these may be good enough reasons for averring that his magic worked and aided him to pass his exams.

Ethnic Pagans protect a burial site

Threats to burial mounds by road builders and land developers express contempt towards ancestors and reveal an ignorance of one's heritage according to some Russian ethnic Pagans. In addition to mounting a physical defence of the mounds similar to direct actions common in Western Europe, members of a closeknit group conducted ceremonies to address the ancestors. Libations are poured, flaming torches are kept burning all night, songs affirming ethnic and cultural pride are sung, vodka is consumed, and speeches are made to the ancestors. A leader among the group is recognised as an adept in listening to the dead, and he is given time to seek knowledge from those buried in the mounds. While archaeologists cast doubt on whether there was any direct cultural, ethnic or genetic link between these burial remains and those seeking to defend their integrity, the group are adamant that conversations with the dead have aided their understanding of their heritage and what needs to be done in adjusting the traditional religion to the contemporary world.

Interactions with modernity

Paganism is a new religion. All of its traditions were initiated in the twentieth century after about a century of foment and anticipatory rumours among poets and esotericists. All the ancient and historical sources that are undoubtedly of vital importance to particular Pagans – from Palaeolithic cave paintings to Celtic legends and Lithuanian folklore – are utilized creatively to mould and evolve a religion that arises from and addresses key issues of the contemporary world. The individualism, eclecticism, mass dissemination, and relatively egalitarian social structures are almost unthinkable in any previous age. Even the various understandings of 'nature' that are the heart of Pagan celebration and activism are framed in modern ways. Moreover, Pagans are catered for by a large industry of publishers of books, magazines, desk diaries, calendars and car bumper stickers. Even if few of these publishers thrive by supporting only Pagan requirements, they provide incontrovertible evidence that Pagans participate in the contemporary global culture of consumerism. To this we might add the providers of conference, meeting and festival venues; the musicians, storytellers and those who record and disseminate their CDs; the designers and retailers of costumes, jewellery, ritual tools, and incense; and others whose services and goods are evidently necessary to the practice of the contemporary styles of Paganism.

If Pagans are embedded in modernity both ideologically and materially, they are also the focus of considerable attention by scholars, journalists and other observers. Almost every university department of Religious Studies will include some coverage of Paganism – whether it is a single lecture in a course on new religions or the possibility of conducting PhD research. There are conferences and journals devoted to the study of Paganism (especially noteworthy is the journal *The Pomegranate: The International Journal of Pagan Studies*).

What then of the claims that many Pagans make that they and their religion are counter-cultural, different, or even a radical alternative that anticipates a more ecological and egalitarian future? Such claims are not silenced by the obvious point that they too arise within modern culture and are a common theme of internal cultural critique. There are aspects of Paganism that do present a radical face to modernity. Increasingly during the rapid and continuing evolution of Paganism, ideas and practices have arisen that either do not fit in the wider culture or demonstrate significant disjunctions and challenges. Right from the beginning of the Pagan revival in the mid-twentieth century Pagans adopted ritual as their primary activity. They did not adopt preaching to disseminate their ideas. None of the books (academic, fictional, classical or contemporary) has achieved the status of scripture. It is telling that some of the most frequently cited works (i.e. fictional literature) is closer to the style of story-telling around a campfire than to the formal educational discourses of lecture theatres. Perhaps there is something surprisingly radical about a religious movement that celebrates fiction and story-telling and refuses to produce a scripture (but in fact this would look more normal were it not for the dominance of the Protestant Christian insistence on the authority of scripture as a model for what is expected of religions). Nonetheless, elevating ritual rather than discourse to pre-eminence was a radical move in that it counters a long tradition of opposition to ritual as 'meaningless repetition' in Western culture. Admittedly, some Pagans are keen to ensure that participants understand what is happening – and many Pagan books produce lists of correspondences from which people can construct meaningful rituals. However, the maturation of Paganism as a distinctive religion is often marked by the celebration of rituals that do not pause to explain each step. People are caught up in the performance, become participants, and find their Pagan lives inspired, energized and authorized. Giving priority to ritual and only secondary place to ideas and

FIGURE 14.2 Glastonbury

The Goddess procession climbing Glastonbury Tor, August 2007. © Mika Lassander.

discourse is part of a process identifiable as an indigenization of Paganism. It is one way in which the religion is becoming more like the traditional religions of indigenous peoples.

Another aspect of indigenization is the growing insistence on the importance of locality and belonging. While Paganism is globally present (and globally resourced), there is an increasing counter-cultural trend to seek integration with particular locations, to express local rather than universal truths, and to work for the well-being of local communities (human and larger-than-human). In such localization processes, Pagans invigorate the intimation that the heart and guts of their religion is about relationships. The implications of this rooted, localized relational emphasis are likely to lead to further challenges to the contemporary global culture of consumerism.

A final consideration of Paganism's interactions with modernity must note the challenge all these ideas and practices offer to the notion that modern people are disenchanted and live in an increasing rational (or rationalist) world. The choice to attend to the possibilities that we share the world with faery beings, that it makes sense to read fantasy fiction religiously, that environmentalist activism can be conducted with colourful and carnivalesque rituals, and that humans and divinities can meet intimately – these are not disenchanted views or activities. They are part of a wider current in contemporary culture that insists that the modern project is unsatisfactory not only in its gifts but also in its goals: people do not want disenchantment and they do not work for the regimentation of the world.

Conclusion

Paganism is a new religion, a spirituality of the contemporary world. It draws on ancient resources to address major issues of the day, especially concerning human relationships with one another and with the living world. While it owes many debts to modernity, it challenges contemporary Western culture by conducting colourful seasonal and environmentalist rituals, seeking inspiration in imaginative meditation and literature, and by insisting that everybody can participate in making the world a better place.

Summary

- Paganism is a new religion, initiated in the mid-twentieth century.

- Paganism is a 'nature religion'.

- Paganism draws on historical information about ancient religions.

- Paganism is expressed in many different sub-movements or 'traditions'.

- The trend towards localization and indigenization, expressed in the centrality of ritual practice, offer a challenge to the disenchanting project of modernity.

Key terms

enchantment The sociologist Max Weber theorized that modernity is defined by processes of disenchantment, especially secularization and rationalization, so that religion, myth and magic would decline in the face of science. The resurgence of religion as an authoritative aspect of many people's lives challenges the ubiquity of disenchantment, while widespread attraction to imaginative films and literature suggests a continuity of enchantment. Even where religious institutions have become marginal, diverse forms of spirituality contest the empiricism of modernity.

environmentalist religion Since many religions contrast 'spirituality' with the mundane physical world and embodiment, those religions in which 'nature' is celebrated are often identified as 'nature religions'. Some practitioners and traditions encourage radical contests with the dualist separation of humanity from the world by inciting public eco-activism (sometimes expressed in rituals).

imagination An ability to conceive of and develop ideas about alternatives and possibilities that might enhance a person's abilities to thrive or to aid others. Often expressed in deliberate efforts to picture internally what might result from practical or ritual physical actions. The use of imagination (e.g. in exercises of guided visualization) can be a core element in the practice of magic.

magic Commonly defined as either 'the art of causing change according to will' or 'the art of changing consciousness according to will', magic is a core element of various religious and/or esoteric traditions.

nature A polyvalent term bearing contradictory implications. In forms of dualism, 'nature' can mean everything other-than-human, especially non-urban countryside or wilderness. Such 'natural' domains may be esteemed or denigrated in particular worldviews, e.g. 'nature' can be either integral or opposed to 'spirituality', and indicates the division of academic disciplines between 'social' and 'natural' sciences. In contrast, 'nature' can refer to the unity of all that exists, rooting humans in the wider cosmic community and sometimes requiring humans to relinquish separatist ambitions.

ritual Ceremonial practices, especially in religions, that are treated as traditional by performers and are usually differentiated from the habits of everyday life.

tradition The complex of ideas and practices that are accepted as, or asserted to be, authoritative because they have been inherited from previous, respected generations or teachers. As received ways of doing things 'tradition' is used to indicate particular styles of religious practice, e.g. 'the Wiccan tradition', functioning somewhat like 'denomination' in Christianity.

Further reading

Paganism defined

M. York: 'Defining Paganism'. (*The Pomegranate: The International Journal of Pagan Studies* 11, 2000: pp. 4–9).

Scholarly introductions

B.J. Davy: *Introduction to Pagan Studies* (Lanham, MD: Altamira, 2007).

G. Harvey: *Listening People, Speaking Earth: Contemporary Paganism*, second edition (London: Hurst, 2007).

Recent research and methods

J. Blain, D. Ezzy and G. Harvey (eds): *Researching Paganisms: Religious Experiences and Academic Methodologies* (Walnut Creek, CA: AltaMira, 2004).

The Pomegranate: The International Journal of Pagan Studies published by Equinox, URL: www.equinoxpub.com.

History and origins

C.S. Clifton: *Her Hidden Children: The Rise of Wicca and Paganism in America* (Lanham, MD: AltaMira, 2006).

R. Hutton: *The Triumph of the Moon: A History of Modern Pagan Witchcraft* (Oxford: Oxford University Press, 1999).

P. Jones and N. Pennick: *A History of Pagan Europe* (London: Routledge, 1995).

Primary sources (including fiction)

B. Bates: *The Way of Wyrd* (London: Century, 1983).

B. Bates: *The Wisdom of the Wyrd* (London: Rider, 1996).

M.Z. Bradley: *The Mists of Avalon* (London: Sphere, 1984).

C.S. Clifton and G. Harvey: *The Paganism Reader* (London: Routledge, 2004).

G. Gardner: *Witchcraft Today* (Secaucus, NJ: Citadel, 1973 [1954]).

A. Garner: *The Owl Service* (London: HarperCollins, 2007 [1967]).

J. Gantz (translator): *The Mabinogion* (Harmondsworth: Penguin, 1976)

T. Gilliam, and T. Jones: *Monty Python and the Holy Grail* (DVD CDR14164, 2002 [1975]).

M. Murray: 'Witchcraft'. (*Encyclopedia Britannica* 23, 1929: pp. 686–688. Reprinted in C.S. Clifton and G. Harvey: *The Paganism Reader* (London: Routledge, 2004: pp. 90–94).

T. Pratchett: *Wyrd Sisters* (London: Gollancz, 1988).

Traditions

P. Carr-Gomm: *The Druid Way* (Shaftesbury: Element, 1993).

C. Christ: 'Why Women Need the Goddess: Phenomenological, Psychological and Political Reflections'. In C. Christ and J. Plaskow (eds): *Womanspirit Rising* (New York: Harper & Row, 1979, pp. 273–287).

H.A. Berger and D. Ezzy: *Teenage Witches: Magical Youth and the Search for Self* (New Brunswick, NJ: Rutgers University Press, 2007).

J. Blain: *Nine Worlds of Seid-Magic: Ecstasy and Neo-shamanism in North European Paganism* (London: Routledge, 2002).

G. Harvey: *Listening People, Speaking Earth: Contemporary Paganism*, second edition (London: Hurst, 2007).

A. Ivakhiv: 'In Search of Deeper Identities: Neo-Paganism and Native Faith in Contemporary Ukraine'. (*Nova Religio* 8(3), 2005: pp. 7–38).

A. Long: 'The Goddess Movement in Britain Today'. (*Feminist Theology* 5, 1994: pp. 11–39). Reprinted in Chas Clifton and Graham Harvey (eds): *The Paganism Reader* (London: Routledge, 2004: 305–325).

Starhawk: *Truth or Dare* (New York: Harper & Row, 1990).

Paganism and New Age

P. Heelas: *The New Age Movement: Religion, Culture and Society in the Age of Postmodernity* (Oxford: Blackwell, 1996).

M. York: *The Emerging Network: A Sociology of the New Age and Neo-Pagan Networks* (Lanham, MD: Rowman & Littlefield, 1995).

Enchantment

B. Latour: *We Have Never Been Modern* (New York: Harvester Wheatsheaf, 1993).

C. Partridge: *The Re-Enchantment of The West* (London: T & T Clark, 2004)

Chapter 15

New Religious Movements

Douglas E. Cowan

Introduction

Many commentators argue that new and alternative religions, often pejoratively and incorrectly lumped together as 'cults', are a phenomenon peculiar to late modernity, that they require the kind of open religious economy one finds among technologized nations in the latter half of the twentieth century, and that they are marked by distinctive characteristics that set them apart from more dominant traditions. Certainly, for some kinds of new religions – UFO groups, for example, such as the Raelians, Heaven's Gate, or the Unarius Academy of Science – this is the case. But as a social phenomenon new, alternative, or controversial religions are hardly new, and cataloguing what detractors believe to be their errors is a practice extending back hundreds of years, arguably to early Christian apologists like Tertullian and Irenaus.

Put differently, as a cultural constant, alternative religious movements, whether they are innovative or renovative (a distinction some scholars have used to generalize between 'cults' and 'sects'), are as much an historical and theological problem as they are sociological or social psychological. In 1742, for example, Thomas Broughton (1704–1774) published *An Historical Dictionary of All Religions from the Creation of the World to This Present Time*. A generation later, responding to what she considered Broughton's 'hostile treatment' of his subject, Hannah Adams (1755–1831) published *A Dictionary of All Religions and Religious Denominations: Jewish, Heathen, Mahometan, Christian, Ancient and Modern* ([1784] 1992). Pagans, wrote Adams, for example, are 'heathens, and particularly those who worship idols', while pantheists are 'sort of philosophical atheists, who consider the universe as an immense animal' and 'Sintoos' (i.e., Shintoists) were 'the ancient idolaters of Japan'. Though modern readers may consider Adams's treatment no less hostile than Broughton, hers was a stunning achievement for the time and her book went through a number of popular editions in both the United States and Britain (Tweed, 1992). In the nineteenth century, the emergence of new religions such as the Church of Jesus Christ of Latter-day Saints (Mormonism), Christian Science, Jehovah's Witnesses, Theosophy, and New Thought generated an active countermovement literature among more traditional religious groups who felt threatened by what they regarded as dangerous theological interlopers. From Eber Howe's *Mormonism Unvailed* [*sic*] (1834) to George Hamilton Combs's *Some Latter-day Religions* (1899) and Gaius Glenn Atkins's *Modern Religious Cults and Movements* (1923), from various contributors to *The Fundamentals* (1910–1915) to William Irvine's *Heresies Exposed* (1935) and Jan Karel van Baalen's *The Chaos of Cults* (1938), which went through four editions over three decades, those who feel threatened by new religious movements have been quick to docket their concerns, a practice that in no small measure still accounts for the opprobrium with which these groups are often met today. However, as historian Philip Jenkins (2000) points out trenchantly, 'the United States had Buddhists before it had Pentecostals, just as American Rosicrucians and alchemists predate its Methodists'. New religions, it seems, have always been with us in one form or another.

However we rubric them, whether we consider them positive, negative, or inconsequential, new, alternative, and controversial religious movements are a fascinating and important feature of the human religious landscape. In this chapter, we will explore a number of aspects that make them so. First, we will consider the basic question, 'What is a new religion, and is that different than a "cult?"'. Second, we will look at who joins new religions and why, how long they tend to stay, and what happens when they leave. Next, we will discuss two of the principal controversies that have come to define new religions in late modernity: the social panic over 'brainwashing', and the rare times when new religions and violence intersect. This leads to a consideration of the reasons and the methods by which different social groups have tried to control new religions. Finally, we will consider the significance of new religions. Put simply, since they form such a relatively small part of the global religious landscape, why are they so useful for understanding religion as a human and a social phenomenon?

Understanding New Religious Movements

Put bluntly, there is no such thing as a 'new' or 'alternative' religious movement, at least not in any ideal, Platonic sense. This is even more so for the common media label, 'cult', which is often underpinned by specific political or theological agendas and deployed as little more than cultural shorthand for 'bad religion'. Rather, religious groups are labelled 'new', 'alternative', or, more pejoratively, 'cults' both as a function of their relationship to the shifting patterns of religious dominance and marginalization in the societies within which they emerge and in terms of the particular agendas at work in the groups by which they are so labelled. Thus, what is a well-known part of an ancient religious tradition in the East, say Buddhism, is considered a 'new religion' when it is transported to the West and begins to be adopted by Westerners. While indigenous religions have existed for so long that it is difficult to propose a time when they were 'new' or a tradition to which they were 'alternative', when non-indigenous people begin to appropriate indigenous religious teachings and practices, incorporating them into innovative religious forms, they take on a novelty unknown heretofore. Thus, in one sense, 'newness' is a temporal and a spatial category, a function of time and place. Perhaps the most obvious example of this is Christianity, a tradition now shared in some way by one in every three people on the planet. Yet, it was not always this way. As a missionary faith, at some point in time Christianity was a 'new religion' everywhere it went, an alternative that challenged incumbent faiths in a number of ways. What changed over time was its position of social dominance.

Though scholars have struggled valiantly in the effort, nearly half a century's worth of research has not generated a 'one size fits all' definition of either cult or new religion, something that makes the field of new religion studies both fascinating and frustrating in almost equal measure. On the one hand, different stakeholder groups disagree both on what constitutes a 'new religion' and on what that means. Clearly, for an active member, being a Scientologist means something very different than for an anti-Scientology activist. For one, the Church of Scientology is the touchstone of transcendence and the guarantor of salvation; for the other, it is a principal locus of social betrayal and religious fraud. Since Maharishi Mahesh Yogi (1917–2008) brought Transcendental Meditation to the West in the early 1960s, it has been marketed as a therapeutic science and practitioners often reject the claim that it is a religious movement at all. Yet, relying on its derivation from Advaitic (non-Dualist) Hinduism, social scientists have always considered it among the new religious movements that exploded in popularity during the counterculture of the 1960s and 1970s. Although it seems clear that Wicca owes much of its systematization and late-modern popularity to Gerald B. Gardner (1885–1964), many Wiccans feel they are an integral part of a religious tradition extending back hundreds, if not thousands of years.

On the other hand, countermovement groups such as the secular anticult or the evangelical Christian countercult often rely on categorical templates in their efforts to stigmatize and control new religions. Thus, for American anticult activists such as Janja Lalich and Michael Langone, a group is a 'cult' when it meets social psychological criteria such as having a leadership toward which members display 'excessively zealous, unquestioning commitment', 'a polarized us-versus-them mentality', or preoccupation with recruitment or fundraising. Conversely, for evangelical countercult apologists, cults are a function of theological differentia. Walter R. Martin (1928–1989), one of the most prominent countercult apologists of the late twentieth century and founder of the first dedicated countercult ministry, the Christian Research Institute, defined 'cultism' as 'any deviation from orthodox Christianity relative to the cardinal doctrines of the Christian faith'. Indeed, following in the footsteps of the Reformation, a number of fundamentalist Christians label Roman Catholicism the 'largest cult in the world'. Obviously, members of the groups attacked by both the anticult and the countercult disagree with these assessments, and many are mystified and horrified to learn the religion in which they have been raised or to which they have converted is considered by others a dangerous cult. Indeed, with only a very few exceptions, 'cult' is a label applied by others, not a name taken by religious groups themselves.

Over the past several decades, scholars have generated a variety of definitions and typologies intended to frame the problem of new religions in analytically useful ways. Some began by adding the concept of cult to Ernst Troelsch's venerable church-sect dichotomy. In *The Future of Religion* (1985), for example, sociologists Rodney Stark and William Sims Bainbridge consider both sects and cults to be religious movements that are in varying states of tension with the surrounding culture. Where the former maintains some kind of tie to a larger parent tradition in that society, however, cults represent deviant traditions that 'occur by mutation or migration'. Not dissimilarly, sociologist Roy

Wallis understood new religious movements in terms of their orientation to the dominant society. Are they 'world-rejecting', 'world-affirming', or 'world-accommodating'? A few years later, in *A Theory of Religion* (1987), Stark and Bainbridge located 'cult movements' as part of a more complex network of religio-social exchange relations, defining them as 'social enterprises primarily engaged in the production and exchange of novel and exotic general compensators based on supernatural assumptions'. Sociologist Susan Palmer, on the other hand, describes them more lyrically as 'beautiful life forms, mysterious and pulsating with charisma. Each "cult" is a mini-culture, a protocivilization' (2001), while sociologist Lorne Dawson (2006) suggests that 'cults share the following cluster of traits': they 'are almost always centered on a charismatic leader'; they 'usually lay claim to some esoteric knowledge'; they 'often display no systematic orientation to the broader society'; and, drawing on the thought of sociologist Bryan Wilson, they tend to 'offer a surer, shorter, swifter, or clearer way to salvation'. While each of these offers some insight into the problem, clearly none is comprehensive or exhaustive. Indeed, though Dawson retains it, many scholars consider the word 'cult' to be too tainted by media usage, too heavily freighted with negative baggage to be analytically useful, and so opt for the even more ambiguous 'New Religious Movement'. But, even that is not without its problems.

Putting the 'new' in new religions

As I have indicated already, some religions are new in the sense that they are newly arrived, they are newly appropriated by practitioners different from those traditionally associated with the group, or they are perceived and labelled as 'new' by dominant social or religious groups. Thus, despite its long history in China and Japan, Zen Buddhism became something of a new religion when Westerners popularized it in the 1960s and 1970s. Despite its millennia-old roots in India, when A.C. Bhaktivedanta Prahbupada (1896–1977) brought Krishna Consciousness to the United States and Great Britain in the 1970s, the bhaktic Hinduism of the Hare Krishna movement became, for several years, synonymous with the brainwashing cult. When, though, does a religion stop being 'new'? After all, broadly speaking, there was a day before Christianity and a time when the followers of Jesus were considered a dangerous new religion, both by the state and by more dominant religions of the day. Since its inception, the Church of Jesus Christ of Latter-day Saints has faced pressure from social and religious authorities, many of whom to this day refer to it unapologetically as a cult. Scholars still regularly include it under the broad category of 'new religion', yet it was founded nearly two hundred years ago and counts many of its members among the highest levels of American government.

Rather than look for a particular set of characteristics, as both the secular anticult and Christian countercult are wont to do, historian of religions J. Gordon Melton makes the case that what are often lumped together as 'new religions' are really the religious residua of a society once all the other religious groups, movements, and traditions have been accounted for. That is, they are 'a set of religions assigned an outsider status by the dominant religious culture and then by elements within the secular culture'. This approach to the problem has the advantage of foregrounding the reality that a group's religious position in society is a function of sociocultural relationships and the manner in which those relationships are framed, for example, by government, mass media, and more dominant religious traditions. Though the beliefs and practices of a specific group have not changed, what is a well-known (if minority) religious tradition in one place is considered a 'dangerous cult' in another. Melton's proposal, however, does not address the issue of 'newness' that so many stakeholder groups in the study of culturally alternative religions consider central to the debate.

Thus, on the other hand, sociologist Eileen Barker argues for keeping the quality of novelty, of 'newness', in academic discussions. While she points out quite rightly that there is nothing really new under the sun, there are aspects of these groups that are new in particular sociocultural contexts, aspects that allow us to see them (and ourselves) in new light. 'An NRM', for example, 'may be *new within a particular tradition*, involving some sort of innovation or novel interpretation of an ancient rite or Scripture' (Barker, 2004). Though she uses the example of the Children of God (now The Family International), this insight could easily be extended to include such groups as the Mormons, Jehovah's Witnesses, and People's Temple within Christianity, American Zen and Insight Meditation as innovations within worldwide Buddhism, and, as noted, Transcendental Meditation and the Hare Krishna movement within Hinduism. New religions, obviously, 'may be *new to a particular society* although they had thrived for centuries, even millennia, in another society' (Barker, 2004). When a traditional religion changes social contexts, it may adopt a new '*institutional organization*' (Barker, 2004). While Transcendental Meditation evolved directly out of the Advaitic Hinduism of its founder, in an effort to present the practice to what Maharishi Mahesh Yogi regarded as the far more worldly West, it was reorganized as a scientifically validated therapy, as secular rather than religious. Further, Barker contends that these dynamics push new religions to 'undergo transformations and modifications far more radically and rapidly than the vast majority of older religions under normal circumstances'. In less than 50 years, for example, Latter-day Saints went from a divine decree instituting the religious practice of polygamy (or 'plural marriage') to the renunciation of polygamy as part of the price of statehood for Utah. From its beginnings as a form of psychotherapy, it took only a few years for the practice of Dianetics to evolve into the new religion of Scientology.

Finally, Barker points out that those who join new religious movements – who convert – are different in significant ways from those raised in a particular faith. On the one hand, they 'tend to be considerably more enthusiastic about their new beliefs and practices', but, on the other, 'converts tend to be more vulnerable than "born into" members'. That is, while converts are often more zealous in their new beliefs, they require considerably more socialization in order to maintain those beliefs in the face of challenge. Contrary to the most extravagant claims of countermovement groups – that everyone is at risk of brainwashing or that original sin means anyone can be led astray by the wiles of Satan – NRMs do not appeal to converts of different ages and generations. Contrary to the stereotypes almost ubiquitously employed by the secular anticult and the Christian countercult, new religious adherents cannot be categorized as mindless drones, stripped of agency and ready for deployment by unscrupulous religious leaders. Men and women join new religions for a wide variety of reasons, many of which – at least initially – have little to do with the actual beliefs taught by the group. It is to this phenomenon that we now turn.

Membership careers

Historically, religious conversion is relatively rare. Of course, conversions happen, sometimes spectacularly so, as in the case of an Indian neo-Buddhist movement founded by B.R. Ambedkar (1891–1956), which saw upwards of six million initial conversions in the mid-1950s. Such instances are exceptional, though, and most people grow up and remain in the faith tradition into which they were born. Roman Catholics remain Christian, Vaishnavite Hindus remain Hindu, Pure Land Buddhists remain Buddhist, and so forth. There may be some intrareligious movement or syncretic practice – according to their preference Catholics seek out more conservative or liberal parishes; depending on circumstance Vaishnavites may participate in Shaivite rituals; Pure Land Buddhists engage in Zen meditation, often as an adjunct to their own practice – but the complete, voluntary exchange of one religious identity for another, especially when the new demands the renunciation (and occasionally the denunciation) of the old, is comparatively infrequent.

When it does happen, then, especially in the context of religious groups that are regarded as socially deviant or otherwise at odds with dominant cultural mores, the dynamics of conversion, membership, and disaffection are of particular interest. Indeed, the processes of affiliation and disaffiliation, of conversion and exit, are among the most closely studied aspects of new religious belief and behaviour. Who joins new religions and why? What does 'membership' mean, since it is not the same for all groups and the conception of membership may differ greatly between group leaders and rank-and-file adherents? Why do members leave a group and what are the costs associated with exit? Indeed, rather than a particular event that can be located in time and space, conversion is often better understood as a process, as some scholars have labeled it a 'career'.

Just as there is no one definition of 'new religion', so too the concept of 'conversion' is itself fraught with problems. Many groups and movements that are regularly included among the new religions either do not require conversion in a traditional sense or understand the process of affiliation in very different terms. Practitioners of Transcendental Meditation, for example, can remain active members of other faith communities, as can those who take basic auditing courses at local Scientology organizations. Only at the more advanced levels of each is more exclusive commitment required. Many modern Pagans prefer not to speak of converting to Wicca or Witchcraft, but of 'realizing' that they have been Pagan all along, of 'waking up' to the spiritual reality of their lives that had been heretofore hidden by social and family expectations (see Chapter 14 on Paganism). Other groups, however, make the complete renunciation

FIGURE 15.1
Contemporary Pagans

Contemporary Pagans dance around a ritual fire. Courtesy Time & Life Pictures/ Getty Images.

of former religious ties either an explicit or implicit condition of membership. Socially encapsulated groups such as Heaven's Gate or The Family International (at least in its early years) make the prospect of partial membership problematic. Theologically encapsulated groups, the exclusivity of whose beliefs preclude participation in competing faith communities – the Unification Church, for example, or the Church of Jesus Christ of Latter-day Saints – require a level of commitment that far exceeds that of many other new religions.

In 1998, despite the fact that the 'great American cult scare' (Bromley and Shupe, 1981) was largely over by this point, though following in the wake of the Heaven's Gate suicides in 1997, an article in the otherwise relentlessly cheerful *Homemaker's Magazine* warned readers that everyone was at risk of cultic involvement and, more-over, 'anyone could be in a cult without knowing it'. Quoting anticult activist Margaret Singer, the article hearkened back to the popular stereotypes of the 1970s and 1980s: the belief that new religions specifically target those who are most vulnerable, but that their tactics are so insidious that we are all vulnerable after a fashion. But, is this an accurate understanding, or does it radically oversimplify what is in reality a complex set of social negotiations in which different people participate for different reasons? While it is the case that some new religions have used extraordinary tactics to win over converts – the Unification Church originated the practice of 'love-bombing' to make potential new members feel needed and wanted, while for several years members of the Children of God engaged in 'flirty-fishing', overt sexual advances made in the cause of evangelism and recruitment – across the spectrum of new religions these too are relatively uncommon.

Who joins and why?

Very early in the post-World War II efflorescence of new religions, years before the brainwashing hypothesis took hold of public imagination, scholars struggled to understand why men and women would leave the relative security of one tradition for the uncharted religious waters of another. In the early 1960s, for example, sociologists John Lofland and Rodney Stark studied a group of converts to what was then 'a small, millennarian cult' – the Unification Church. In their now classic statement of the problem, they theorized that a number of factors must come together to effect conversion. That is,

> a person must: 1. Experience enduring, acutely felt tensions 2. Within a religious problem-solving perspective, 3. Which leads him to define himself as a religious seeker; 4. Encountering the [*Divine Principle*, the Unification Church scripture] at a turning point in his life, 5. Wherein an affective bond is formed (or pre-exists) with one or more converts; 6. Where extra-cult attachments are absent or neutralized; 7. And, where, if he is to become a deployable agent, he is exposed to intensive interaction.
>
> (Lofland and Stark, 1965)

While the essential nature of many of these elements have been questioned in the intervening decades, others have been added, and though Lofland and Stark both revisited and refined their theory, three aspects remain particularly salient and are worthy of mention here: (a) the importance of in-group ties, (b) the significance of meaning-making structures, and (c) the agency of what they call the 'religious seeker'.

While many retrospective conversion narratives are structured to highlight the theological aspects of a decision to leave one religious tradition for another – to reinforce in hindsight the ontological validity of the new religious worldview – the fact is that few people wake up one morning believing in *The Book of Mormon* over the Bible or deciding to replace God the Father with the Great Mother Goddess in their lives. Put differently, theology is rarely the prime mover behind conversion. Far more important in the early stages of the affiliation process are the relationships that are established with group members. Latter-day Saints may remember their moment of conversion in terms of a 'burning in the bosom' that confirms for them the teachings and the truth of the Church, but their conversion stories almost inevitably reveal the profound effect of personal contact: the Mormons who invite a neighbour family to church, who help out in a moment of crisis, or who model particularly admirable behaviour. The same is true for other traditions: Jehovah's Witness pioneers who faithfully visit a shut-in seemingly forgotten by her own church, for example, or the undeniable effect of dating and marriage on religious choice and commitment. This makes sense since a particular group's exoteric and esoteric teachings, its religious ritual and devotional practice, its organizational structure, as well as its ethical concerns and moral dicta are often confusing to new-comers and require considerable effort to negotiate. In-group social ties help facilitate membership, often bridging the gap between old beliefs and new, guiding new members in the intricacies of ritual and practice, and, perhaps most importantly, modelling and reinforcing what are presented as the benefits of continued membership and increased involvement.

In terms of religious preference and commitment, one theory that has gained popularity in recent years is 'rational choice theory': adherents base their commitments on a reasoned analysis of the costs and benefits of involvement (on rational choice theory see Chapter 21, Secularization and secularism). Although both the explanatory power and the logical foundations of rational choice theory have been challenged by other scholars, implicit in it is a very important aspect of new religious conversion and commitment: there are tangible benefits that new adherents recognize and want for themselves. These benefits can be cognitive and ideational, in that the new religion provides a plausible explanation for questions that have placed the adherent in the 'seeker' category, or devotional and affective, in that they fulfill emotional or spiritual voids. They can be practical and mundane, meeting the everyday felt needs of the adherent when other traditions could not – friendship or community involvement. Many who have left Christianity for modern Paganism, for example, express their delight at finding a religious tradition that 'fits' them emotionally, that makes sense to them intellectually, that explains the world and their place in it in a way their former tradition could not. Converts to the Church of Jesus Christ of Latter-day Saints report that the principle of the nuclear family that grounds Mormonism both theologically and experientially fills a gap in their lives. Whether abstract or concrete, the conversion process is an exploration of meaning for potential adherents that takes place on multiple levels. Whether consciously or subconsciously, seekers measure what they are looking for against what they receive. They evaluate whether continued involvement will add meaning to their lives or reduce it. This highlights the issue of agency in the conversion process.

One of the principal arguments on which both religious and secular counter-movements base their opposition to new religions is the claim that unscrupulous religious leaders use insidious or deceitful recruiting tactics to target socially 'abnormal' or particularly vulnerable individuals, thus stripping potential members of their ability to make informed choices about conversion and commitment. Claiming that this significantly reduces the agency prospective recruits can exercise, this was one of the primary arguments made in the 1970s when parents of new religious believers sought to establish legal conservatorship over their adult children on the grounds that they had been brainwashed. Decades of social scientific research, however, have uncovered little if any empirical evidence to support these claims and few courts recognized the validity of the legal arguments. Beyond the broad concept of 'seekership', there is no one class of person who is more susceptible to new religious involvement than another – although beginning in the 1970s, many NRMs saw the advantage of recruiting well-educated, middle-class young adults. People enter into the seekership process for vastly different reasons and want vastly different things out of their religious commitments. Some want to establish more control over the contours of their faith and so may gravitate to modern Paganism, in which personal authority over one's spirituality is a paramount virtue; others may desire more structure in their religious lives and be willing to surrender a measure of control in order to achieve that. Still others want the relative security of answers supplied once-and-for-all and find themselves seeking out any one of a number of emergent fundamentalisms. Even the choice to give up control is a choice – different in degree, perhaps, but not in kind for those who join traditional religious groups than new religions.

How long do they stay?

How long new adherents stay with a group is a much more difficult question to answer, largely because new religions rarely keep exit statistics and those that do even more rarely release them. Some new religions have been more effective than others at retaining members – either through organizational restructuring that allows for an expanded recruiting pool or aligns the group more closely with dominant cultural traditions – but most last for time then wither away for lack of new blood. Social scientists have long recognised that the two more important hurdles to generational advance of new religions are the death of the founder and the socialization of the second generation. If the group cannot successfully negotiate the former or administer the latter, the likelihood of survival is slim.

Notwithstanding these rather significant events, what we might call everyday defection or disaffiliation is a serious problem for new religions. In her research on the Unification Church, for example, which was one of the first longitudinal studies of new religious affiliation and disaffiliation, Eileen Barker (1984) found that less than 5 per cent of those who made contact in some way remained in the group after just one year. In a similar study, Marc Galanter (1989) found similar results: just 6 per cent of new members remained in the Unification Church a mere four months after initial contact. Synthesizing the available literature, though recognizing that 'no systematic data on leave-taking exists for most contemporary NRMs', sociologist David Bromley (2006) estimates that 'the rate of defections varied between 50 and 100 per cent annually during the NRMs' high growth periods' – that is, the 1970s and 1980s. Two things are particularly important to note here: (a) the challenge these defection rates present to the membership claims of many new religions, and (b) the contradiction they pose to popular notions of new religions as a clear and present social danger.

Consider first the issue of membership claims. A number of new religions profess to be among the fastest growing religions on Earth: the Church of Scientology; Jehovah's Witnesses; modern Paganism, most notably Wicca; and even the tiny United Nuwaubian Nation of Moors – all have laid claim to this title. Clearly, certain advantages accrue to such pronouncements, principally, the social legitimacy and existential validity implied by cultural popularity and belief in the willingness of people to commit to one's cause. The logic is simple (if fallacious): It must be working for so many people to be involved. In the vast majority of its promotional material, for example, the Church of Scientology declares itself unequivocally 'the fastest growing religious movement on Earth' (Church of Scientology International, 1998) and 'the most vital movement on Earth today' (Church of Scientology International, 2002). Claiming now ten million members worldwide, it presents itself as 'arguably the only great religion to emerge in the twentieth century' (Church of Scientology International, 1998). If most people know about Scientology, however, it is more likely through its high-profile association with celebrities such as Tom Cruise, John Travolta, and Kirstie Alley, or through occasional media exposés that often challenge Scientology's claims to be a religion and question the benefits it promises adherents. Since membership numbers are popularly equated with social status and religious efficacy, it is possible that the Church arrives at this figure by counting as a member anyone who takes a basic course in auditing, purchases goods or services from a local Scientology organization, or signs up to take its perennial 'Free Personality Test'. Thus, membership – and the attendant questions of affiliation and disaffiliation – become a contested discourse. While many Scientologists may make the claim to ten million members, believing it to be true, others look around puzzled, wondering where all the Scientologists really are. Popular fear of new religions, on the other hand, is often exacerbated by hyperbolic claims to membership numbers. During the late 1970s and early 1980s, for example, at the height of popular cult panic in Canada it was commonly believed that as many as ten thousand Hare Krishna devotees had descended on major cities across the country, most notably Toronto. However, when these claims were actually 'investigated by Daniel G. Hill for the Ontario Government he could only find 80 members' in the city (Hexham, Townsend and Poewe, 2008). Similar disparity between membership claims and membership realities could be presented across the new religious landscape.

What both of these circumstances indicate is that while many thousands of people may develop a level of interest in new religions – indeed, as religious seekers many may explore a variety of different alternative faith paths – only a tiny fraction will entertain seriously the prospect of conversion, and only a small fraction of those will affiliate in any lasting or meaningful way. This brings us to the issue of disaffiliation.

What happens when they leave?

There are as many reasons why someone might choose to leave a new religion as there are for joining in the first place. Potential benefits are not realized or the spiritual answers one hoped for are not found. Interpersonal difficulties, either with fellow members or with group leadership, can lead to significant social strain and a decision to leave, while an inability to conform to the norms of group behaviour can precipitate being asked to leave. Many find the cost of continued membership too high – either financially (as in Scientology) or personally (as in groups that require members to move from place to place). From the 1970s to the early 1990s, many new religious members were compelled to leave when deprogrammers hired by friends and family removed them from the group by force.

However it occurs, what happens when new religious adherents leave a group depends on a number of factors, including membership career, mode of exit, and post-exit socialization. First, are those who leave converts to the group or have they been raised in it? Leaving the Church of Jesus Christ of Latter-day Saints after a brief membership career, a flirtation almost, is vastly different than for someone who is, say, third- or fourth-generation Mormon, for whom all their family and probably most of their friends are Latter-day Saints. For the former, disaffiliation may involve nothing more traumatic than not going to church on Sunday, while for the latter, it could mean the dissolution of one's entire social and cultural network. Second, research indicates that those who control when and how they disaffiliate are far more likely to move on with their lives in positive fashion. In addition to its criminal nature, one of the scandals of forced exit and coercive deprogramming was its astonishingly low rate of success, the significant incidence of recidivism, and the mental and emotional trauma experienced by its victims. Indeed, of those who leave voluntarily the majority continue to regard their new religious experience as positive and meaningful. Finally, the character and level of post-exit support one receives can significantly influence one's reflexive interpretation of the experience. Does one, for example, simply become a 'former member', perhaps retaining ongoing relationships with current adherents, or does one assume the role of 'apostate' and develop an antagonistic relationship with the group and one's former co-religionists? Though the latter is considerably less common than the former, apostate testimony has carried significant and arguably disproportionate weight in the cultural debates over new religions and has contributed significantly to the controversies by which they are all too often framed.

Cult controversies

Although the phenomenon of new religions far predates their emergence into popular consciousness in the 1960s, awareness of them since then has been largely crisis-driven. Much of the scholarly literature on new religions has considered groups that emerged in the West, especially those that rose to social notoriety through some crisis event or the perception of crisis – allegations of brainwashing in the case of the Unification Church or Hare Krishna, of sexual abuse of children in the case of the Twelve Tribes or The Family International, of fraud in the case of the Church of Scientology, or of violence in the case of Peoples Temple, the Branch Davidians, Aum Shinrikyo, and Heaven's Gate. In all these cases, scholars have tried to understand whether the perceptions of crisis were supported by the empirical data available, and, if they were, how the crises developed, or, if they were not, how the perception of crisis shaped the situation. Since the popular advent of late modern new religions, two issues particularly have galvanized our attention: the question of brainwashing and the potential for violence.

Brainwashing hypothesis

Although there is no one demographic that is, by definition, always more likely to investigate new religious participation than another, new religions that emerged in the 1960s and 1970s did make a concerted effort to recruit young adults from the educated middle class. Suddenly, or so it seemed, parents watched as their children rejected the staunch Presbyterianism in which they had been raised and claimed the

Reverend and Mrs. Moon as their 'True Parents', or traded traditional Sunday attire for the saffron robes of the Hare Krishna, or joined David Berg as itinerant evangelists with the Children of God. As much as anything else, distraught family and friends needed a way to explain what had happened, to understand why their loved ones had abandoned them.

Aided by anticult activists such as Ted Patrick, who performed some of the first forced deprogrammings, and psychologists such as Margaret Singer and Richard Ofshe, who for a time lent a measure of academic credibility to the hypothesis, parents of new religious adherents rejected the authenticity of the conversion choice and instead held tight to the belief that their children had been 'brainwashed'. Through a variety of insidious processes – allegedly including sleep deprivation, poor diet, and forced indoctrination – parents and anticult activists argued that the ability to make rational faith choices had been taken away from their loved ones. However fallacious, the logic of this was alarmingly simple: since no one in their right minds would make these kinds of religious choices, they must not be in their right minds. Buttressing this belief was the nascent anticult's adamant insistence that what was happening to American youth at the hands of these sinister new religions was similar to the so-called brainwashing suffered by Chinese inmates in 're-education' camps following the Communist revolution and by American prisoners of war in North Korea.

Use of the concept, however, became a textbook exercise in confirmation bias – the cognitive process by which we filter information according to what most supports our preconceptions. Among other things, for example, it was pointed out early on that new religions did not torture adherents in order to gain either conversion or continued affiliation, nor did potential members face death as the cost of non-adherence. Rather than invalidate the brainwashing hypothesis, however, for its proponents this simply meant that a far more insidious process was at work than either the Chinese or North Koreans could muster. Indeed, the concept of 'cultic brainwashing' was sensationalized, institutionalized, and attained almost a mystical status, as though some dark, irresistible supernatural force were in play.

Significant scholarly research has been conducted into the brainwashing hypothesis, both on its efficacy and its effect on the social construction of new religions, and though members of the anticult movement remain committed to it in principle, though in a modified form – anticult activists now refer to it variously as mind control, coercive persuasion, or thought reform – little evidence has been found to support it. Indeed, a number of points mitigate against it as a satisfactory explanation for new religious conversion and adherence. Among these, the most salient are that:

■ as brutal as they were, the North Korean and Chinese programmes on which the brainwashing model was initially based were largely unsuccessful, which means that the anticult model itself is predicated on failed experiments;

■ despite the high pressure recruiting tactics deployed by some new religious movements, both the attraction and retention rates of these groups are extremely low. Thus, if there is such a thing as 'brainwashing', it is startlingly ineffective;

- over time, as groups became more experienced at recruiting, the brainwashing process should have become more effective. This did not happen and many groups, such as the Unification Church, the Hare Krishna and the Children of God, abandoned the kind of tactics the anticult most clearly associated with the concept of brainwashing;
- research into behavioural reform and coercive social control indicates a relatively poor success rate in a number of different cultural domains – prisons, for example, or mental institutions – many of which are staffed by highly trained professionals with an array of sophisticated resources at their disposal. As Bromley and I note, 'it seems implausible that neophyte members of nascent new religions, operating without such knowledge and training, would succeed where these professionals had failed' (Cowan and Bromley, 2008).

FIGURE 15.2 Sun Myung Moon

Sun Myung Moon, founder of the
Unification Church. Courtesy Getty Images.

Founded in 1954 by Sun Myung Moon (b. 1920), the Holy Spirit Association for the Unification of World Christianity is known more commonly as the Unification Church and its members colloquially as 'Moonies'. Presenting himself as the 'Lord of the Second Advent', Moon's theology mixes a variety of Christian belief and practice with elements of Korean shamanism, Confucianism, and Taoism. He believes that Jesus's death on the cross was a mistake, that it was never intended by God, and that the salvation of humankind was left unfinished as a result. Thus, it has fallen to him and his wife, Hak Ja Han (b. 1943), to complete the work of salvation as the True Parents of humankind. Since Moon teaches that only families may enter the Kingdom of Heaven, the most significant Unificationist ritual is the Blessing, mass weddings in which hundreds of couples chosen by Moon are married and become part of his new, God-centred human family. National Blessing Committees now facilitate this complex process, matching prospective partners on the basis of information submitted by candidates. In the early 1990s, Moon expanded the Blessing in two significant ways. For the first time since the movement began, non-Unificationists were eligible to be considered as marriage partners, and, in the Heaven and Earth Blessing, the physical and spiritual realms are brought together as living spouses are reunited with their dead loved ones.

Though initially unsuccessful in the West, during the 1970s and early 1980s, fears of brainwashing made the Unification Church one of the principal targets of the emerging secular anticult movement. Young men and women were leaving more established

continued

religious traditions and joining Moon's movement at what parents, media and those opposed to new religions felt was an unprecedented rate. Moon's controversial fundraising methods, his authoritative control over the movements, and the Blessing all convinced anxious parents that something dire was afoot. To counter this alarming trend, many turned to deprogrammers, anticult activists who used techniques ranging from confrontation to kidnapping and forcible confinement to convince new religious adherents to renounce their allegiance.

In the late 1970s, at the height of brainwashing hysteria, sociologist Eileen Barker conducted systematic research intended to answer a question surprisingly few outside the academy had asked: why *did* people join the Unification Church? Are they, in fact, brainwashed, or was it something else? Using a variety of means, Barker studied the group for six years and found no evidence of brainwashing. Indeed, contrary to the extravagant claims made by the anticult movement, that the mysterious power wielded by religious leaders like Moon made groups like his a clear and present social danger, Barker determined that the Unification Church's retention rate was extremely low. Only 30 per cent of those who attended an introductory workshop chose to explore the movement further and, of those who did, only 10 per cent joined the Church and remained more than a week. After two years, only 5 per cent were still involved in any way (Barker, 1984).

BOX 15.1 Case study: The Unification Church

New religions and violence

Part of the fear of brainwashing was that unscrupulous religious leaders could create cadres of deployable agents who would then carry out all manner of mayhem on their behalf. Indeed, because of the basic principles governing newsworthiness – 'If it bleeds, it leads' – when a new religion breaches the threshold of media awareness, it is usually because something has gone wrong. When that happens, media inevitably resort to a handful of episodes in the history of late modern new religions to serve as a metonym for all new, alternative, or controversial faiths. The names are familiar to most: Peoples Temple (1978); Branch Davidians (1993); Aum Shinrikyo (1995); Order of the Solar Temple (1995, 1997); Heaven's Gate (1997); and, perhaps less familiar to Western audiences, the Movement for the Restoration of the Ten Commandments of God (2000). While most of the violence in these incidents was confined to group members, all involved significant loss of life and are regularly deployed by media, secular and religious countermovements and the state as presumptive evidence of the new religious threat. They are, as it were, seen to be all of a piece. Two important questions, however, must be considered: (a) are these, in fact, comparable incidents? and (b) are they in any way representative of new religions writ large? Put simply, the answer to both is: No.

First, comparatively speaking, incidences of new religions and violence are extremely rare and what the media routinely group together under the rubric of 'cult violence' or 'cult death' often reveal themselves as very different circumstances. The murder-suicides at Jonestown in 1978, for example, were a desperate response to what Peoples Temple members saw as a completely untenable position. With the death of Congressman Leo Ryan, the world as they knew it was about to end, and more than 900 men, women, and children died in the grips of that belief – some willingly, others not, all violently. Nearly 20 years later, on the other hand, the ritual 'exit' of 39 Heaven's Gate members presents a radically different situation. Rather than a response to the failure of their utopian dreams, the suicides of the Heaven's Gate 'Away Team' facilitated the realization of those dreams. By shedding the corporeal containers they considered of no further use, participants believed they would ascend to TELAH, The Evolutionary Level Above Human, and rejoin those who had gone before them. The differences between the two events are striking: No children were involved; there is no evidence that anyone was forced to commit suicide; and all the evidence suggests that considerable care and compassion surrounded the exit process. In February 1993, when agents of the Bureau of Alcohol, Tobacco, and Firearms raided the Branch Davidian residence near Waco, Texas, they set in motion a series of events that ended in the deaths of more than 70 Branch Davidians, including 23 children, and four federal agents. While scholars remain divided on the proximate cause of the fire that engulfed the Branch Davidian buildings on 19 April, few contest that the tragedy could have been avoided in a number of ways. Two years later, however, though they were under significant government scrutiny at the time, the attack ordered by Aum Shinrikyo leader Shoko Asahara on the Tokyo subway system was entirely pre-meditated and intended to inflict a significant number of civilian (i.e., non-member) casualties. On 20 March 1995, during the morning rush hour when millions of people ride the metro, group members released a form of sarin nerve gas on five separate subway lines, killing twelve people and injuring hundreds more. But for the ineptitude of the delivery system and the poor quality of the chemical, the result could have been much, much worse. Once again, though, the two events are very different and have in common only that new religions were involved. Both, however, are regularly used as examples by media, government, and countermovement groups intent on demonstrating what they regard as the danger inherent in all new religions.

Second, these few cases indicate that the range of violence and the motivations for it differ drastically across the history of new religions in the late modern world, and violence in any social situation is rarely the result of only one or two causal factors. More to the point, though, is that of the thousands of new, alternative, or contro-versial religions around the world that emerge, flourish for a time, then fade away into obscurity or institutionalization, only a tiny fraction ever approach the levels of social and internal conflict demonstrated by these few examples. Indeed, some new religions have demonstrated far more forbearance in the face of popular oppro-brium and systemic cruelty than many dominant traditions. Throughout their history, for example, Jehovah's Witnesses have been the subject of intense persecution in a number of countries: sentenced to concentration camps by the Nazis for their refusal to fight in the war; declared a seditious organization in Canada during World War II for their refusal to take part in 'patriotic exercises'; banned even today in nearly 30 countries around the world.

For many people in North America, events in early 1993 on a ranch near the small town of Waco, Texas, define the image of the dangerous cult. On 28 February, acting largely on the advice of a disgruntled former member and members of the secular anticult, nearly 100 heavily armed agents of the US Bureau of Alcohol, Tobacco, and Firearms (ATF) attempted a 'dynamic entry' at Mount Carmel, the residence of a reclusive breakaway group of Seventh-day Adventists – the Branch Davidians. Five Branch Davidians and four ATF agents were killed in the initial assault, and the next day the Federal Bureau of Investigation (FBI) began a siege that lasted 51 days. On 19 April, a disastrously executed tactical plan resulted in a fire that engulfed the buildings and killed more than 70 Branch Davidians, including 23 children. Throughout this, despite the fact that they had little knowledge of the group itself, mainstream media consistently portrayed this as a law enforcement story: duly authorized agents of the state attacked by criminal cultists while in the lawful performance of their duties. The Branch Davidians, on the other hand, were routinely caricatured as dangerous cult members led by a megalomaniacal would-be messiah. Most of the 70-year history behind the movement, including their Adventist heritage, their beliefs about the End-times, their life at Mount Carmel, were ignored. Throughout the siege, Branch Davidian pleas for direct contact with the media went unanswered. This is not surprising, however, given that the FBI maintained a strict cordon around the property and kept journalists at least three miles away from the site. The vast majority of information about the situation came through FBI media liaisons.

While it is clear that journalists face considerable pressure in crisis situations like this – deadlines that require them to communicate the story with clarity and concision, editorial policies that often predetermine the direction stories will take, and, as at Waco, proactive interference and misinformation from government sources – the conclusion is unavoidable that the media's willingness to reduce complex situations to their most easily digestible elements contributes significantly to the ongoing stigmatization of new religious movements. Residents of Waco knew of the Branch Davidians, to be sure, but relatively few had much interaction with them. Indeed, when the FBI siege began, local opinion polls showed considerable sympathy for the residents of Mount Carmel. Because one of the principal components of newsworthiness is the negative or violent nature of the event, however, new religious movements such as the Branch Davidians rarely make headlines except when something has gone terribly wrong. Because media are in constant competition for advertising revenue – the bottom line beneath audience share and ratings performance – more nuanced representations of tragic events are rarely possible. Thus, the real people involved in crisis situations, the men, women, and children of Mount Carmel, for example, are reduced to vague media cyphers, interchangeable symbols for conflicts few outside the immediate situation could hope to understand.

BOX 15.2 Case study: Branch Davidians

New religions and social control

Because they often exist at varying levels of tension with the surrounding society, and often challenge many of the principles upon which the society rests, New Religious Movements throughout history have experienced a wide range of attempts at social control. In some cases, new or alternative religions have been declared anathema and measures taken to eliminate them. In others, the threat of prosecution forced the migration of different religious groups from one place to another. Broadly speaking, three groups have mobilized efforts to control the emergence and evolution of NRMs: religiously motivated countermovements; the secular anticult movement; and the state. Although there is often overlap between these countermovements, each relying to greater or lesser degree on the insights of the other, there are distinct differences in the way each understands the problem of New Religious Movements, its motivation in addressing that problem, and the solutions it proposes.

Christian countercult movement

It is often thought that dedicated movements opposed to new religions arose in the 1970s in the wake of the social panic over brainwashing and the Peoples Temple murder-suicides in Jonestown, Guyana. As I pointed out at the beginning of the chapter, however, this is incorrect. Religious opposition to new faith practices and traditions has a long history in North America, dating back at least to the emergence of Mormonism in the early 1830s. Organized religious countermovements, though, are largely a reaction to the efflorescence of new religions in the 1960s and 1970s. For those who consider themselves part of the Christian countercult movement, new religions are basically a theological problem, trespassers on their particular religious preserve.

For many evangelical Christians, new religions are empirical evidence of what they regard as the ongoing battle between God and Satan, and one's rightful place in that cosmic conflict is determined by adherence to evangelical beliefs. Writing about the loose amalgam of self-directed meditation practices, human potential movements, and miscellaneous spiritualities that are collected under the broad rubric of the New Age movement, for example, conservative Christian Douglas Groothuis declares that 'whatever good intentions New Agers may have, it is Satan, the spiritual counterfeiter himself, who ultimately inspires all false religion' (1988). Like most (arguably all) evangelical countercult apologists, Ron Rhodes, who worked for many years with Walter Martin's Christian Research Institute, believes that since 'Christianity rests on a foundation of absolute truth', a 'cult' or 'false religion' is any religion that does not conform to his vision of evangelical Christianity, a category that includes, for example, Roman Catholicism (1994). Indeed, Rhodes succinctly articulates the understanding of the countercult in response to the perceived 'culting of America': 'If Christians do not act, the cults will. The war is on – and you as a Christian will either be a soldier in the midst of the conflict or a casualty on the sidelines' (1994). What does it mean, however, to be involved in this battle?

'The only reason for becoming familiar with other religions and other religious writings', declares Dave Hunt, a prolific evangelical countercult apologist, 'would be in order to show those who follow these false systems wherein the error lies and thereby to rescue them' (1996). Rescue, in this instance, though, does not mean simply encouraging or persuading new religious adherents to leave their faith communities. If a young man leaves the Hare Krishna movement and joins the Mormon Church, apologists like Hunt, Groothuis, and Rhodes would consider that as much a failure (if not more) than if he had not left at all. Rather, the intention is to convince new religious participants that their current path is spiritually dangerous (invasion and epidemic metaphors are extremely common in countercult literature) and their souls are at risk if they do not convert to conservative Christianity. Indeed, a prominent subgenre within countercult literature consists of books and pamphlets designed explicitly to guide conservative Christians in evangelizing new religious adherents. Less often, new religious venues are the site of conservative Christian protest. Anti-Mormon apologists, for example, are a common fixture at the opening of Latter-day Saint temples and the Hill Cumorah Pageant in upstate New York, an annual festival that commemorates Mormon origins. Handing out anti-Mormon tracts and leaflets, holding signs decrying the LDS church, members of the countercult see this as a proactive means of counteracting the influence of the Latter-day Saints.

Though relatively few conservative Christians take part in any such direct action, far more are influenced in their opinions about new and alternative religious movements by the seemingly endless supply of books, pamphlets, tracts, audio and video materials and internet resources that are designed to do nothing more than portray new religions in the worst possible light relative to Christianity. In this we see an excellent example of the point Melton (2004) stresses in his understanding of new religions: they are defined less as a product of particular characteristics, but exist as a function of competition among religious groups and the various methods of social control different groups can bring to bear. Since conservative Christians see this competition as an integral part of the battle between good and evil, there is little reason to believe that time and familiarity will ameliorate their antipathy toward new religions.

Secular anticult movement

Unlike religious opposition to new faith alternatives, the secular anticult movement did emerge as a direct reaction to new religions in the latter half of the twentieth century. Distraught over what they considered their children's disastrously irrational choices, families came together for support and intervention in ad hoc groups, among the first of which was FREECOG (Free the Children of God) and which came to include such organizations as the Cult Awareness Network (CAN) and the American Family Foundation (now the International Cultic Studies Association). While religious countermovements have been in existence far longer than their secular counterparts, the latter's coercive deprogramming led to a much higher media profile during the 1970s and 1980s. Indeed, some scholars came to see religious countermovements as little more than a subset of the secular anticult. This is not the case. Several significant differences distinguish them, most notably their definition of the new religious problem and their solution to it.

Unlike the evangelical countercult, the anticult came to regard any extraordinary religious or quasi-religious choice as problematic and, over time, the brainwashing hypothesis on which its understanding of new religious adherence was based evolved into an ideology that framed both its organizational development and behaviour. Most notoriously, it became known for the practice of deprogramming, the forcible removal and confinement of new religious adherents against their wills in an effort to coerce renunciation of their beliefs and membership. More accurately known as kidnapping, anticult activists rationalized this criminal activity on the grounds that they were, in fact, rescuing those who had fallen under the manipulative sway of the cult leaders.

New religions and the state

As I have indicated throughout this chapter, state response to new religions has varied widely, from official recognition as a religion (e.g., the coveted 501(c)3 tax exempt status in the United States) to state censure (e.g., the nearly 200 groups declared a danger to society in 2000 under France's About-Picard Law), from the criminalization of new religious involvement (e.g., the Jehovah's Witnesses in Canada during World War II) to direct state intervention (e.g., the ATF/FBI siege of the Branch Davidian residence in 1993). Indeed, depending on the country involved and the historical period, the same group is often treated in vastly different ways. In the early 1970s, for example, the Church of Scientology lost its 501(c)3 status in the United States and fought a 20-year battle to regain it. In Canada and Britain, on the other hand, Scientology has never been (and is still not) recognised officially as a religion and can claim none of the perquisites that would normally obtain. In 1998, with the release of '*Die Enquete-Kommission Soganannte Sekten und Psychogruppen*' (the Commission of Inquiry into So-called Sects and Psychocults), the German government identified the Church of Scientology as one of a number of groups it considered a threat to the security of the constitution. Scientologists were forbidden to join certain political parties and were subject to a regime of government surveillance. Though some of these strictures have been relaxed in recent years, tensions have not eased between the state and the new religions.

Even in countries with more progressive laws regarding freedom of belief, new religions are often the target of state intervention, most particularly when children are rumoured to be in danger. In 1984, for example, acting on information provided by anticult activists and disgruntled ex-members, Vermont authorities raided the home of the Twelve Tribes, a group that emerged from the countercultural Jesus Movement, and removed all the children. Though the case was dismissed later that day and the children returned, the memory of this event is so strong its remembrance has been woven into the group's ritual year. Similar efforts at social control have plagued The Family International in many jurisdictions around the world, and were even introduced as part of the post hoc justification for FBI action during the siege at Waco. Indeed, as I write this chapter in mid 2008, law enforcement and child protection agencies in Texas, acting on an uncorroborated (and, as it turned out, entirely spurious) report, entered the Yearning for Zion ranch, home of a polygamous sect of fundamentalist Latter-day Saints, and removed several hundred children on grounds of suspected sexual abuse. As has been the case with numerous similar incidents involving new religions, state actions were found to be without merit and the children eventually reunited with their parents.

The significance of New Religious Movements

Although modern readers may regard Hannah Adams's *Dictionary of All Religions* (1784) as biased and slightly retrograde in its presentation, the acclaim it received in its day is testimony to the popular awareness and social influence of new religious phenomena. Two hundred years later that interest has not waned, and while sensationalized media reporting and the alarmism that marks both the secular anticult and the Christian countercult could lead people to believe that new religions are more numerous, more populous, and more dangerous than they are, across the landscape of human religious belief and practice new religions continue to occupy relatively little ground. That said, though, whether they survive beyond the first generation or not, whether they build on dominant religious traditions, import belief and practice from other sociocultural contexts, or invent what appear to be entirely new religious forms, beside their inherent fascination two aspects highlight their significance for all students of religion: the ongoing challenge they represent to the concept of secularization and the continuing opportunity they present for understanding how human religious phenomena emerge and develop.

In the 1960s and early 1970s popular wisdom insisted that the technological and scientific advance of late modern society was inevitably displacing religion as the dominant force in human life. No longer did we need 'the God hypothesis' to explain the world, and what remained of religion was little more than a rapidly fading echo of our less enlightened past. Judging by the declining condition of the mainline Protestant churches in North America and Western Europe, this seemed a reasonable hypothesis. Three things, though, were wrong with it. First, it ignored the larger religious world beyond those churches, the Muslim and Hindu worlds, for example, which saw significant development in those decades. Second, in North America at least, it failed to notice that conservative Christian churches – Southern Baptists, the Salvation Army, Assemblies of God, to name just a few – were growing at an astounding rate. Third, it all but completely failed to take into account the irruption of New Religious Movements. Those same decades saw the rise of most of the new religions popularly associated with the phenomenon: the Unification Church, the International Society for Krishna Consciousness, Transcendental Meditation, the Divine Light Mission, Peoples Temple, the Children of God, and many others. In reality, people were not becoming *less* religious, but they were becoming *differently* religious – and the new religions were a significant part of that difference.

The origins of most religions in the world are shrouded in 'mythistory' and we do not know with certainty how they began nor why they survived when so many others have vanished from the stage, this is not the case for new religions. With them, we have the opportunity to observe the processes of religious emergence and development in real time, as it were, and this has remarkable potential for the study of all religion. How do religious believers cope with the failure of prophecy, for example, when the great expectations turn to great disappointments? When social psychologist Leon Festinger learned in the early 1950s that a small group of UFO believers was expecting an imminent apocalypse – but one from which they would be miraculously spared – he and his colleagues arranged to observe the group as the fateful night progressed (Festinger, Riecken, and Schachter, 1956). From these observations, Festinger developed his theory of cognitive dissonance, a landmark in social psychology. Though it has been challenged and refined in the half century since he first proposed it, the ability to see a new religion struggle with the failure of prophecy laid the groundwork for theoretical understandings that are still essential to new religions studies today. Rodney Stark (1996), on the other hand, has used research on the Mormon Church and the social scientific models of religious development it helped generate in an effort to answer a number of questions about the early Christian church: how and why it was able to survive; whether its growth rate and rise to social prominence required the kind of miraculous mass conversions recounted in the Book of Acts; and, if not, then what could account for its success? My own work on modern Paganism allowed me to observe an emergent religious tradition's creative interaction with internet technology and hypothesize many of the ways religions can (and cannot) replicate their offline lives online (Cowan, 2005).

Summary

■   New Religious Movements have always been a part of the social landscape, though we are just now beginning to realize the potential they represent for understanding larger aspects of the human religious impulse.

■   New religions embody the same hopes and dreams that have animated religious consciousness around the world for millennia. Although we often see them as strange or fear them as deviant, new religions exhibit the same innovative theological impulse that has marked religious evolution throughout history.

■   New religions suffer the same failures and disappointments as their more culturally dominant cousins, and they are no less prone to abuse and exploitation than many other human institutions – and only rarely more so.

Key terms

apostate A former member of a new religious movement, often one who adopts an antagonistic stance toward their erstwhile co-religionists through involvement with either the evangelical Christian countercult or the secular anticult movement. This label is not often chosen by the former member, but is applied pejoratively by members of the new religion.

brainwashing A putative process of radical personality change that has been used to stigmatize new religious movements since the early 1970s and has given rise to the secular anticult movement. Though very little empirical evidence exists for it, and most social scientists reject it as an explanation for new religious conversion and affiliation, it is still a popular metaphor for unpopular religious choice.

cognitive dissonance First theorised by Leon Festinger (1919–1989) in the mid-1950s, the theory of cognitive dissonance holds that when expectation is at odds with experience – failure of prophecy is the classic example in Festinger's case – a variety of social and psychological mechanisms will act to resolve intragroup and intrapersonal conflict.

cult In late modern parlance, 'cult' is most often used pejoratively, as media shorthand for 'dangerous religious group'. Aware of the popular negative connotation, scholars have suggested a variety of value-neutral alternatives, including New Religious Movement, alternative religious movement, and emergent religious movement.

deprogramming Invasive and often criminal process adopted by the secular anticult movement in which new religious members are forcibly removed from the group, often held against their will, and required to undergo an intense regimen of pychological conditioning designed to convince them that their membership in the group is misguided and that they should leave. Data indicate that deprogramming is often more harmful to the individual than new religious membership.

exit counselling A less invasive form of intervention into new religious affiliation and involvement. Less coercive than deprogramming, but some data indicate that it is also harmful.

Family International, The Founded in the late 1960s by David Berg (1919–1994) as the Children of God, but known now as The Family International, this is one of many so-called Jesus People movements that emerged in the midst of the counterculture. Rejecting what he called 'churchianity', Berg called his followers to a life of communal living, radical discipleship, and constant evangelism. Most notorious for sexual practices that deviated significantly from social norms, the Children of God was the target of one of the first organized anticult organizations, FREECOG (Free the Children of God). As The Family, it has been the target of numerous governmental control attempts in a variety of countries.

millennarianism Belief that history is moving forward to a time of peace, prosperity and collective salvation, though there is significant difference among proponents in terms of how this will occur, who will participate in the millennium, and whether there will be a prior period of significant tribulation.

New Religious Movement A common term used to denote those groups more pejoratively known as 'cults'.

Raelians A UFO religion founded by Claude Vorilhon (Raël), a French race car driver and journalist, in the mid-1970s. Raelians believe that humans are the product of extraterrestrial genetic engineering and that the Old Testament of the Bible actually recounts the history of human relationships with extraterrestrials, whom Raelians know as the Elohim. Proponents of advanced cloning research, in 2002 a Raelian organization named Clonaid announced that it had successfully cloned a human being, though no evidence was ever produced to support this claim.

Unarius Academy of Science A small UFO contactee movement founded in 1954 by Ernest L. Norman (1904–1971) and his wife, Ruth Norman (1900–1993). Acting as mediums for what they consider communications from extraterrestrial beings, Unarians believe that Earth is on the cusp of an age of global peace and will soon be invited into a vast interplanetary confederacy.

Further reading

Understanding New Religious Movements

H. Adams: *A Dictionary of All Religions and Religious Denominations: Jewish, Heathen, Mahometan, Christian, Ancient and Modern* (1784; repr. Atlanta, GA: Scholar's Press, 1992). An eighteenth-century compendium of religious diversity around the world.

G.G. Atkins: *Modern Religious Cults and Movements* (New York: Fleming H. Revell, 1923). Concentrates primarily on Christian Science, Theosophy, and Spiritualism.

E. Barker: 'What Are We Studying? A Sociological Case for Keeping the 'Nova'. (*Nova Religio* 8(1), 2004: pp. 88–102). Good discussion of what is 'new' about new religions.

D.G. Bromley and A.D. Shupe, Jr.: *Strange Gods: The Great American Cult Scare* (Boston, MA: Beacon Press, 1981). An early study of the response to new religions in the 1960s and 1970s.

T. Broughton: *An Historical Dictionary of All Religions from the Creation of the World to This Present Time* (London: C. Davis and T. Harris, 1742). An eighteenth-century compendium of different religions around the world.

Church of Scientology International: *What is Scientology?* (Los Angeles, CA: Bridge Publications, 1998). Principal primary source explaining the practice of Scientology.

Church of Scientology International: *Scientology: Theology & Practice of a Contemporary Religion* (Los Angeles, CA: Bridge Publications, 2002). Principle primary source explaining the religion of Scientology.

D.E. Cowan and D.G. Bromley: *Cults and New Religions: A Brief History* (London: Blackwell Publishing, 2008). Intended as a case-based textbook for undergraduate courses on New Religious Movements.

D. Daschke and W.M. Ashcraft (eds): *New Religious Movements: A Documentary Reader* (New York: New York University Press, 2005). A very useful collection of primary source documents.

L.L. Dawson: *Comprehending Cults: The Sociology of New Religious Movements*, second ed. (Oxford and New York: Oxford University Press, 2006). An excellent introduction to the study of new religions.

M. Galanter: *Cults: Faith, Healing, and Coercion* (New York and Oxford: Oxford University Press, 1989). Very good material on conversion and retention rates among new religions.

E.V. Gallagher and W.M. Ashcraft (ed): *Introduction to New and Alternative Religions in America*, 5 vols. (Westport, CT: Greenwood Press, 2006). Essays cover a wide variety of topics.

I. Hexham, J. Townsend, and K. Poewe: 'New Religious Movements'. In *The Canadian Encyclopedia* (2008); available online at www.thecanadianencyclopedia.com.

P. Jenkins: *Mystics and Messiahs: Cults and New Religions in American History* (Oxford and New York: Oxford University Press, 2000). A very good history of new religions in North America.

L. Kliever: 'Unification Thought and Modern Theology'. (*Religious Studies Review* 8, 1982: pp. 214–221).

J.R. Lewis (ed): *The Oxford Handbook of New Religious Movements* (Oxford and New York: Oxford University Press, 2004). Good collection of academic articles.

J.G. Melton: 'Toward a Definition of "New Religion"'. (*Nova Religio* 8(1), 2004: pp. 73–87). Frames 'new religions' in terms of social marginality.

C. Partridge (ed): *New Religions, A Guide: New Religious Movements, Sects and Alternative Spiritualities* (New York and Oxford: Oxford University Press, 2004). Excellent introduction containing brief articles on a wide array of new religions.

R. Stark: The *Rise of Christianity: A Sociologist Reconsiders History* (Princeton, NJ: Princeton University Press, 1996). Uses new religions theory to understand the origins of Christianity.

R. Stark and W.S. Bainbridge: *The Future of Religion: Secularization, Revival, and Cult Formation* (Berkeley, CA and Los Angele, CAs: University of California Press, 1985). Seminal collection of essays by two pioneers in the field.

R. Stark and W.S. Bainbridge: *A Theory of Religion* (New Brunswick, NJ: Rutgers University Press, 1987). A difficult read, but well worth the effort.

T.A. Tweed: 'Introduction: Hannah Adams's Survey of the Religious Landscape'. In H. Adams: *A Dictionary of All Religions and Religious Denominations: Jewish, Heathen, Mahometan, Christian, Ancient and Modern* (Atlanta, GA: Scholar's Press, 1992), pp. vii–xxxiv.

R. Wallis: *The Elementary Forms of New Religious Life* (London: Routledge and Kegan Paul, 1984). Early attempt to theorize the emergence and significance of New Religious Movements.

L.A. Young (ed): *Rational Choice Theory and Religion: Summary and Assessment* (New York and London: Routledge, 1997). Currently a popular theory attempting to explain a variety of religious phenomena.

Membership careers

E. Barker: *The Making of a Moonie: Choice or Brainwashing?* (London: Basil Blackwell, 1984). Classic work on new religious conversion choices.

D.G. Bromley (ed): *The Politics of Religious Apostasy: The Role of Apostates in the Transformation of Religious Movements* (Westport, CT and London: Praeger, 1998). An excellent collection of essays on the nature of new religious leave-taking.

D.G. Bromley: 'Affiliation and Disaffiliation Careers in New Religious Movements'. In E.V. Gallagher and W.M Aschcraft (eds): *Introduction to New and Alternative Religions in America*, vol. 1 (Westport, CT: Praeger Press, 2006), pp. 42–64.

E.V. Gallagher: 'A Religion without Converts? Becoming a Neo-Pagan'. (*Journal of the American Academy of Religion* 62(3), 1998: pp. 851–867). Good discussion of the ways new religious adherents understand their faith choices.

J. Lalich and M.D. Langone: 'Characteristics Associated with Cultic Group – Revised' (2006); available online at www.csj.org/infoserv_cult101/checklis.htm. Anticult checklist of new religious indicators.

J. Lofland: '"Becoming a World-Saver" Revisited'. (*American Behavioral Scientist* 20(6), 1977: pp. 805–818.

J. Lofland and R. Stark: 'Becoming a World-Saver: A Theory of Conversion to a Deviant Perspective'. (*American Sociological Review* 30(6), 1965: pp. 862–875. Seminal article on new religious conversion.

J.T. Richardson (ed): *Conversion Careers: In and Out of the New Religions* (Beverly Hills, CA: Sage, 1978). Very good collection of essays on the processes of new religious affiliation and disaffiliation.

S.A. Wright: *Leaving Cults: The Dynamics of Defection* (Washington, DC: Society for the Scientific Study of Religion Monograph Series, 1987). Why people leave new religions and what that means to and for them.

Cult controversies

C. Barner-Barry: *Contemporary Paganism: Minority Religions in a Majoritarian America* (New York: Palgrave Macmillan, 2005). Excellent discussion of the challenges faced by modern Witches and Wiccans.

D.G. Bromley and J.G. Melton (ed): *Cults, Religion, and Violence* (Cambridge: Cambridge University Press, 2002). Seminal collection of essays by top scholars in the field.

G.H. Combs: *Some Latter-day Religions* (Chicago, IL: Fleming H. Revell, 1899). Early attack on new religions, principally Christian Science, the Latter-day Saints, and the Millennial Dawn (Jehovah's Witnesses).

F. Conway and J. Siegelman: *Snapping: America's Epidemic of Sudden Personality Change* (Philadelphia, PA: Lippincott, 1979). Journalistic account sensationalizing the brainwashing hypothesis.

R. Hoshowsky: 'Cults, The Next Wave: Almost Everyone is Vulnerable'. (*Homemaker's Magazine* March 1998: pp. 54–60).

E.D. Howe: *Mormonism Unvailed* (Painesville, OH: Author, 1834). One of the first published attacks on the Church of Jesus Christ of Latter day Saints.

W.C. Irvine: *Heresies Exposed: A Brief Critical Examination in Light of the Holy Scriptures of Some of the Prevailing Heresies and False Teachings of Today* (New York: Loiseaux Bros., 1935). An evangelical Christian critique of numerous new religions.

W.R. Martin: *Rise of the Cults: A Quick Guide to the Cults*, third ed. (Santa Ana, CA: Vision House, 1980). Critique of new religions by one of the founders of the Christian countercult movement.

R. Ofshe and M. Singer: 'Attacks on Peripheral versus Central Elements of Self and the Impact of Thought Reforming Techniques'. (*Cultic Studies Journal* 3, 1986: pp. 3–24).

R. Rhodes: *The Culting of America* (Eugene, OR: Harvest House, 1994). Conservative Christian critique of new religions.

J.T. Richardson and M. Introvigne: '"Brainwashing" Theories in European Parliamentary and Adminstrative Reports on "Cults and Sects"'. (*Journal for the Scientific Study of Religion* 40(2), 2001: pp. 143–168).

A.D. Shupe, Jr., and D.G. Bromley: *The New Vigilantes: Deprogrammers, Anti-Cultists, and the New Religions* (Beverly Hills, CA: Sage Publications, 1980).

M. Singer and R. Ofshe: 'Thought Reform Programs and the Production of Psychiatric Casualties'. (*Psychiatric Annals* 20, 1990: pp. 188–193).

J.K. van Baalen: *The Chaos of Cults: A Study in Present-Day Isms* (Grand Rapids, MI: Wm. B. Eerdmans, 1938). One of the earliest encyclopaedic critiques of new religions.

J.R. White: *The Fatal Flaw: Do the Teachings of Roman Catholicism Deny the Gospel?* (Southbridge, MA: Crowne, 1990). Conservative Protestant argues that Catholicism is not truly Christian.

B. Zablocki and T. Robbins (ed): *Misunderstanding Cults: Searching for Objectivity in a Controversial Field* (Toronto: University of Toronto Press, 2001). Collection of essays dealing with various topics, including the brainwashing hypothesis.

New religions and social control

D.G. Bromley and D.E. Cowan: 'The Invention of a Counter-Tradition: The Case of the North American Anti-cult Movement'. In J.R. Lewis and O. Hammer (eds): *The Invention of Sacred Tradition*. (Cambridge: Cambridge University Press, 2007).

D.G. Bromley and J.T. Richardson (ed): *The Brainwashing/Deprogramming Controversy: Sociological, Psychological, Historical, and Legal Perspectives* (New York and Toronto: The Edwin Mellen Press, 1983). Important collection of essays examining the brainwashing controversy from a variety of perspectives.

D.E. Cowan: *Bearing False Witness? An Introduction to the Christian Countercult* (Westport, CT: Praeger Publishers, 2003). The only book-length study of the evangelical Christian countercult movement.

D.R. Groothuis: *Confronting the New Age: How to Resist a Growing Religious Movement* (Downers Grove, IL: InterVarsity Press, 1988). Conservative Christian critique of the New age Movement.

I. Hexham and K. Poewe: '*Verfassungsfeindlich*: Church, State, and New Religions in Germany'. (*Nova Religio* 2(2), 1999: pp. 208–227).

D. Hunt: *A Woman Rides the Beast: The Catholic Church and the Last Days* (Eugene, OR: Harvest House, 1994). Conservative Protestant critique of Roman Catholicism.

D. Hunt: *In Defense of the Faith: Biblical Answers to Challenging Questions* (Eugene, OR: Harvest House, 1996). Countercult defence of conservative Christianity.

R. Rhodes: *Reasoning from the Scriptures with Catholics* (Eugene, OR: Harvest House, 2000). Conservative Protestant critique of Roman Catholicism.

The significance of New Religious Movements

H.A. Berger and D. Ezzy: *Teenage Witches: Magical Youth and the Search for the Self* (New Brunswick, NJ: Rutgers University Press, 2007). Very good study of how and why teenagers explore Wicca and Witchcraft.

D.G. Bromley (ed): *Teaching New Religious Movements* (Oxford and New York: Oxford University Press, 2007). Excellent collection of essays by top scholars in the field.

P.B. Clarke: *New Religions in Global Perspective: A Study of Religious Change in the Modern World* (London and New York: Routledge, 2006). Excellent compendium of short articles about a vast array of new religious movements from around the world.

D.E. Cowan: *Cyberhenge: Modern Pagans on the Internet* (New York and London: Routledge, 2005). In-depth study of how modern Witch and Wiccans create religion online.

L. Festinger, H.W. Riecken, and S. Schachter: *When Prophecy Fails* (Minneapolis, MN: University of Minnesota Press, 1956). Seminal study of failed prophecy.

P.C. Lucas and T. Robbins (eds): *New Religious Movements in the 21st Century: Legal, Political, and Social Challenges in Global Perspective* (New York and London: Routledge, 2004). Another excellent collection, this one addressing the various political and legal ramifications of new religious belief and practice.

S.J. Palmer: 'Caught Up in the Cult Wars: Confessions of a Canadian Researcher'. In B. Zablocki and T. Robbins (eds): *Misunderstanding Cults: Searching for Objectivity in a Controversial Field* (Toronto: University of Toronto Press, 2001), pp. 99–122.

Chapter 16

Religion and globalization

David Lehmann

Introduction

When we talk of modernity we refer to many things, of which one is secularization and another is the use of rational, impersonal criteria to decide, allocate, adjudicate and evaluate (see the Introduction to this volume). One sense of secularization is the application of these criteria to the religious field: modern culture does not necessarily encourage disbelief, but it is said to encourage rational belief, that is belief based on doctrine, on principles, on texts. This is one way of depicting secularization. Yet religion, for most people, is not a set of beliefs at which they arrive by reflection from first principles, but rather a symbolic system which confers identity and marks out social and ethnic and other boundaries, and whose rituals mark crucial moments in the life cycle, and in the daily, weekly and annual cycles, as well as providing powerful emotional and meta-social mechanisms for the resolution of psychological and social tension.

We see in an institution like the Church of England an example of religion borrowing the rationality of modern democratic culture: bureaucracy, an elected synod, separation of finance from religious office, and even – up to a point – equal opportunities for members of both sexes. As an institution it sits well with a secular state, yet even this established church does not possess a monopoly of the ritual life of its society. Where there is institutionalized religion like this there is usually an undercurrent or counter-current of 'popular' religion which takes care of the sacred outside the impersonal culture outlined above. In these counter-currents authority is embodied in persons to whom special powers are attributed: they are not Anglican clergy or Catholic priests, but rather *charismatic* leaders who have sprung as if from nowhere, and who exercise the prerogatives of their office not as long as a Church recognizes (and pays) them, but as long as they retain a following. Theirs is an embodied authority. That is one manifestation among many of the deep tension in the religious life of the West and of Europe's former colonies, between the institutional or erudite and the popular. Another version of popular religion, but without charismatic leadership, is seen in the devotion to particular saints or shrines to which supernatural powers are attributed, especially powers to heal and to dispel misfortune. On the whole such devotions do not contest institutional authority which looks on them with benign indifference, save in high-profile cases of co-option such as Lourdes and other sites of religious tourism or pilgrimage.

In an era of colonialism and globalization these issues of authority can be seen in a distinctive light. If we allow that ritual cycles of festivals and feasts and the symbolic representation of the forces of health and illness, good fortune and misfortune, are markers of identity and difference separating peoples, ethnic groups and primary collectivities of different kinds, and if we also allow that rituals and symbols are the outward manifestations of embodied, as distinct from impersonal, authority, we can begin to see why it is that conquest and colonialism, have almost invariably been associated with religious expansion and conflict. For to establish domination it is necessary to embody power, and to do so in a form which is comprehensible to the subject people. Since conquerors have no 'legal-rational' grounds for legitimizing their power over the conquered, religious/symbolic methods, which confer authority on their persons (independently of a set of principles) are a useful resource for its imposition.

But what then of that contemporary form of multi-dimensional, kaleidoscopic conquest and colonization which is globalization? Unlike the empires of the past, we have here a model in which all manner of frontiers (political, economic, cultural, religious) are apparently breached and even reduced to nothing in the creation of a seamless web of market relations and of the legal and humanitarian institutions of capitalist democracy and global rules of governance. In a globalized world of democratic capitalism, all authority is expected to be rational and impersonal, all economic agents to be optimizing automata, and religion a matter of private personal choice experienced in an institutional setting governed by the same democratic principles as the state itself.

The starting point of this chapter is that this picture of public religion's place (or non-place) in globalization is misleading. And the reason why it is misleading is not that the advance of this impersonal secularized culture is merely taking its time, or that it is penetrating some parts of the world at a slower pace than others, or even that the threats it poses to ways of life produces a flight into 'fundamentalism', irredentism and similar all-embracing loyalties. Rather the reason is that the life of ritual and symbolism which is at the heart of popular religion is itself redrawing frontiers all the time, that innumerable forms of popular religion are themselves active globalizers, straddling or violating cultural, ethnic and national frontiers, and in the process are redrawing new frontiers, because ritual or religious communities cannot exist without drawing frontiers.

Globalization is therefore by no means a process which moulds all the cultures which meet within its dynamic into a single homogeneous whole. Indeed it is equally plausible to claim the contrary: globalization may bring about the unpacking of local cultural complexes, but in the process it creates multifarious local identities and criss-crossing frontiers, so that diversity comes to rule more than ever before in local spaces, even while similarities and links across social and spatial distances also become ever more evident. To illustrate with examples in the religious field: although millions of Africans came under the influence of English, Scottish and American missionaries in the nineteenth and twentieth centuries, that is not to say that they exchanged one religious package for another: on the contrary, the packages themselves were reshaped, and not only in Africa. That is why African Christianity, re-exported to the colonial metropolis by postcolonial migrants, is so different from any British religious institution – as witness the numerous Caribbean Pentecostal Churches, Nigerian 'Aladura' Churches or branches of the Zimbabwe Assemblies of God Africa (ZAOGA) in Britain and Ghanaian Pentecostal churches in Britain and elsewhere (see Chapter 10 on Religion in Africa).

Religion breaks through frontiers and in the process throws up new frontiers because religions ancient and modern, monotheist, polytheist and totemic, with their apparatus of ritual practices and internal, proprietary codes, are demarcators, markers. When religion crosses frontiers or breaks through barriers, even when it does so in the most violent manner, the outcome cannot be the abolition of one set of religious beliefs and practices by another, just as attempts to promote a universal God encompassing all religions never make headway, however tolerant and inclusive that vision may be.

Side by side with violence and economic spoliation, with slavery and enserfment and political subjugation, European colonization was also a venture in mind and cultural management. Political systems were first decimated and then moulded with elaborate internal and external mechanisms of boundary creation and maintenance. So if the phrase 'religion as globalizer' is to have any analytic force, it must be underpinned by a concept of religious conquest and encounter which involves more than massacres and the destruction of temples and idols, and by a concept of globalization rooted in contemporary experience which, as sketched above, evokes not homogenization but rather the redrawing, and the multiplication, of social boundaries. When the first Spanish *conquistadores* arrived in the Americas they could barely imagine that the beings they encountered were human at all. It is a distinctive feature of the modern world – the world to which those very conquerors gave birth – that these rearrangements and reinventions are historicized, that is to say that the people involved, victims and perpetrators of colonialism in its many forms, are made aware that they themselves have a place in history (origins) and a location in space (roots) as do the peoples with whom they enter into alliance or confrontation, and it is this location in time and place which contributes to the make-up of identity, in sociological terms. Likewise, in the process of borrowing, imposing and appropriating rituals, taboos, healing procedures, music, through religious conquest and encounter, a 'theory' is transmitted. The transmission of the apparatus of religion is accompanied by a contest of wills to appropriate and even domesticate the powers and virtues born of the invading, and of the conquered, other, and this requires a set of interrelated foundational ideas, about who the 'others' are, their origins and roots, where they come from and whence they derive their powers or their uniqueness, and by acquiring this concept of history, of this-worldly origins and of social causation, the victims of necessity join modernity.

Background: The study of religion and globalization

This chapter's approach to religion and globalization starts with an understanding of how the exercise of authority varies in religious contexts and with a firm grasp of the interplay of the erudite and institutional, and the popular, in religious life. It views religion as, among many other things, a means of boundary maintenance. These elements interact in the religion–globalization nexus: the complementary coexistence of secularism with dominant institutional churches in Europe and Latin America is disrupted by charismatic movements and migration; inherited religious sources of authority lose ground to state

FIGURE 16.1
Jesucristo
es el Señor

The Lima branch of the Brazil-based Universal Church of the Kingdom of God. The first two inscriptions say 'Jesus Christ is God' and 'Put an end to your suffering!' The white dove in the red heart is a worldwide UCKG logo.

intrusion (in education and healthcare for example); popular religion goes global; and religion, like ethnicity, creates new boundaries at an accelerated pace, breaching ancient frontiers of nation, culture, language and religion itself through migration, communication, conversion campaigns and political commitment.

This approach differs from that of Roland Robertson, perhaps the foremost, and certainly the first, student of religion and globalization, because it analyzes globalization at the grassroots, rather than deducing social change from broad-brush characterizations of society or societies 'as a whole'. Robertson's work (1992), and that of Peter Beyer (1994), who has continued in Robertson's theoretical footsteps, can be thought of as the first stage in the evolution of our understanding of globalization's interaction with religion. It is based on assumptions drawn from the classical sociological tradition:

- the understanding that globalization is an extension across national boundaries of the process of Western modernization;
- the use of 'societies' as basic units of analysis whose boundaries coincide with those of nation states;
- the assumption that religious revivals are an expression of 'traditional' identities and a reaction against modernity.

This current of writing marked the beginning of a shift away from static assumptions about modernity and tradition/premodernity, and about the unified character of modern culture and society, and was a first pioneering venture into a less parochial sociological study of religion. But it gives no account of the sorts of ambiguity and mechanisms of domination and resistance which can be seen once one takes account of the dialectic between popular and erudite religion, nor of the alternately devastating and highly creative changes which the clash and mutual assimilations of religious practices and rituals have wrought over the long history of colonialism and its postcolonial sequel.

The multifarious character of these forces is more evident in the next stage in the interpretation of the interaction between religion and globalization which came with the flowering of ethnohistory, notably in the work of the Comaroffs in Africa (Comaroff and Comaroff, 1991), grounded in both contemporary ethnography and historical documentation, and with studies of Pentecostalism in Africa, among others by Maxwell (2006), and pioneered in Latin America by David Martin (1990). Both of the latter place Pentecostalism firmly in the context of its international dissemination and emphasize its modernity. Subsequently the prominence of Political Islam on the world stage has inspired different models, notably that of Olivier Roy (2004) which turns the tradition–modernity contrast around by insisting on the modernity of Islamic funda-mentalism, or at least of its variant in Political Islam, despite its proclaimed restoration of the *umma* worldwide. All these approaches question whether the forms of religious resurgence in the modern world which others saw as the reassertion of 'tradition' are really as traditional as all that, and show how modern they are in many respects.

Religion and globalization: The cosmopolitan pattern

The institutionalization of religion draws a boundary between official and popular practices, for example between the regulated procedures at a Catholic mass or Anglican service led by a qualified and certified priest, and less regulated or even unregulated rituals and festivities. These latter are equally symbolic and liminal (i.e. boundary-maintaining), including festivities at local saints' days, pilgrimage sites, or at the Christmas season. Among contemporary highly institutionalized religions, Catholicism is distinguished by the proliferation of popular forms of celebration and worship, especially in Italy, the Iberian peninsula and Latin America. It is noticeable, at least to the casual observer, that English (not Irish!) religion, whether Catholic or Anglican, has hitherto been somewhat impoverished in this respect, though that may be changing with the growth of evangelical and Charismatic forms (see Chapter 8 on Christianity). Yet still, even in England, the popular version, the version unregulated by the church hierarchy, is there, if only embedded in commercial life, as in the ritual of exchange at Christmas which as an annual family ritual retains at least a vestige of its religious character.

In Islam, especially in the Middle East, institutional religious rhythms centred on mosques and their personnel exist in tension with an infinity of curers, seers, and mystics (or *sufis*). In North Africa, the Islam of the interior, centred on the cult of saints, coexists with the more text-based, professionally-led Islam of the cities. In South Asia, in the twentieth century a more political divergence has developed between the doctrinally-oriented Deobandis and their less stringent Barelwi rivals in South Asia and among South Asian Muslims in Europe (see Chapter 9 on Islam). Destabilization, which in Christianity comes from exponents of an anti-intellectual Charismatic religiosity, comes in Islam from educated people producing unregulated readings of sacred texts. The crisis of authority, deeper and more pervasive than in Christianity, has many causes, but this globalized educated dissidence is certainly one of them.

In Protestantism, evangelical (popular) tendencies have a history of breaking away, in innumerable, often fissiparous sects, while the Church of England itself is today divided between the erudite (or 'liberal') element which controls the establishment and an increasingly vociferous evangelical movement rising from the pews of the more comfortable parishes in England, as well as from the dioceses of Nigeria, Rwanda and Uganda. In Christianity and Judaism the institutionalized and the popular influence one another over time: the mystically inclined hasidic Jewish sects have had enduring influence on other ultra-Orthodox tendencies and also on forms of Judaism which temporize more easily with the secular world, through their emphasis on a Jewish way of life even over and above issues of doctrine and learning (see Chapter 7 on Judaism). Christian Pentecostal practices such as effusive singing, healing and speaking in tongues, are gaining ground among Catholics in the form of the Charismatic Renewal, illustrating how popular forms spread and cross boundaries with little attention to the sensibilities of hierarchical or nominal authority – and the Catholic Church has a 2000-year history of co-opting or accommodating the popular within its ample purview.

In the context of contemporary globalization, this Pentecostalism and the Charismatic Renewal together form a vast multinational charismatic movement which transcends inherited religious boundaries and bypasses the institutional–popular divide in a historically new shift. They are able to dispense with the institutional, episcopal patronage which has in the past blessed popular Catholicism. Globalization allows popular movements access to resources independently of hierarchies on a scale unknown hitherto, and secularization has undermined the monopoly of institutional religion and thus its ability to co-opt popular religion. The very definition of religion becomes a subject of controversy in a world where longstanding institutional apparatuses for the administration of the sacred can no longer command respect for their view of what is acceptable and what is not, while the officially secular character of many state apparatuses essentially excludes them from claiming final authority on the matter. In Europe however, the state, through the executive or the courts, and in the USA the courts, can decide on what counts as a religion when disputes arise over education, for example, or entitlement to charitable status or (in France) to the status of a religious association.

To return to Catholicism, we now relate the dialectic of the erudite and the popular within its vast and elaborate institutional edifice to the global reach of Catholic culture. The Church's strategies in dealing with 'the other' – an 'other' which the Church successfully made into its 'own' – have been quite different from the corresponding experience of Protestantisms of all kinds. Papal defensiveness has prevented the Church from explaining its complicity in the oppression of the indigenous populations of the Americas, which was real, but not the whole story, while the Pope's defence of the sixteenth-century campaigns of destruction against indigenous religion in Latin America as 'evangelization' (notably during a 2007 visit to Brazil) is disingenuously presented as if it was the whole story. For us, it is important to recognise that syncretism persisted, and was tolerated and co-opted in Latin America. As Catholicism established its institutional presence, the conversion of indigenous peoples produced a vast array of festivals and local lay fraternities under whose auspices there developed cults of saints not dissimilar from those which already existed in the Iberian peninsula, while pre-existing beliefs in spirits and in supernatural entities governing peoples' lives were incorporated into a semi-Christian cosmogony in spite of the Church's purification campaigns. Attempts to convey Christian doctrine via popular depictions of animals and spirits to people who spoke little if any Spanish – save the elites – have been described as 'a sort of semiological blind man's buff' in which for example the 'communion of saints' would become 'the game of saints' and the Trinity would be represented, among other attempts, as three Christs by artists trying to depict 'three in one and one in three' without risking misinterpretations (Saignes, 1999). This linguistic fumbling accompanied all sorts of coercion exercised by the authorities, and also by the often grasping indigenous intermediaries, but eventually it settled into a pattern of inventive syncretism which endures to this day. Accounts such as these are repeated in similar terms in studies of West Africa, such as Meyer's *Translating the Devil* (1999) which describes similar hit-and-miss linguistic exchanges between German pietist missionaries and their potential converts among Ghana's Ewe people.

Already in the sixteenth century dissidents within the Church claimed that if different peoples practised different religions, this was their way of worshipping the same universal God. The greatest of all 'defenders of the Indians', the Dominican friar and Bishop Bartolomé de las Casas (1484–1566), had gone so far as to say that the indigenous Mexicans' practice of human sacrifice, far from being the work of the Devil, was their way of worshipping the same God as the Christians, and to denounce the Spanish conquerors who were massacring them in the name of Christianity as violators of God's laws. A century later, in 1648, the Mexican Church laid the basis for what was to become the most popular cult in the Americas, that of the Virgin of Guadalupe, based on the apparition of the Virgin to Juan Diego, a humble Indian, said to have taken place in 1531, in the aftermath of the Conquest of Mexico (1519–1521). The core of the story of the vision is twofold: that the Virgin appeared not to a Bishop or priest or to a Spaniard, but to an unlettered Indian, and that the same Indian was able to show convincing evidence of a miracle to the sceptical Archbishop of Mexico. The Indian overcame the Spaniard and the illiterate overcame the educated, in a story which has several hallmarks of a myth of origin: extreme brevity, the establishment of a quasi-kinship relationship between a human and a divine being, and both the contestation and the confirmation of a politico-religious institution. This is the founding myth of the Mexican Church – one of the most thriving in the world in terms of the devotion and religious participation of its followers – and of the Mexican nation.

This pattern in which boundaries are erected and then perforated – a pattern combining boundary-crossing and co-option under elite auspices – has fed into globalization through multiculturalism's cult of the authentic and of course through migration. In Mexico and Peru we observe 'neo-Indian' cults whose practitioners would not claim to be indigenous themselves but who re-enact rituals from a pre-Columbian past at sites of archaeological interest and in the forecourts of museums and cathedrals. In the global migration of Africans and – more importantly – of images and idealizations of Africa, we see how postmodern projections and theories of cultural authenticity have carried local disputes into a global arena. In Brazil different possession cult tendencies compete for recognition as truly African, or as representing a superior and purer version of one or another African culture. Now, in the USA, in the wake of competing African importations not from Africa but from Cuba, Puerto Rico, Haiti and Brazil itself, cult leaders set out to discredit others by vaunting their own African purity, legitimated by sojourns in Yorubaland, but also bolstered by claims to a universalism derived, for example, from 'the African wisdom that that gave birth not only to Egypt and Ethiopia but to human life in the Rift Valley' (from the apologetic book by Joseph Murphy: *Santería: An African Religion in America*, 1988). Note that in the USA the claim to purity of African heritage also signals an exclusivist black identity, whereas in Latin America the racial divide is blurred, and Africa is often claimed, musically, artistically and spiritually, as a shared heritage.

We also observe how the history of Europe's relationship with India has shaped the overseas implantation of versions of Hindu religion, but this time in social milieux far removed from the vast South Asian diasporas of Europe and North America. Wrenched from their original context of caste society, transformed by a completely new concept of a guru who is leader of a movement or organization rather than a personal guide, the neo-Hindu cults also focus on this-worldly concerns derived from modern Western technologies of self-healing, highlighting transcendental meditation and yoga, as distinct from the focus on reincarnation and karma in South Asian religious cultures. Like the apologist for Santería quoted above they may claim a very post-Enlightenment universalism, encompassing all religions and sometimes incorporating Jesus Christ into their pantheon (Altglas, 2007). Neo-Hindu gurus and their organizations are thus involved in developing a Western-style religion, albeit one with more affinity to the New Age than to the Abrahamic traditions. Yet all the while their unique selling point is their identification with a distant other and a remote history in South Asia.

The interaction of religion and globalization seems to change the location of boundaries in two ways: one, which I call cosmopolitan, brings old practices to new groups in new settings – it is a variant of disembedding, of which one example is the conversion of Spanish America, already mentioned, and others are seen in the transplantation and reshaping of Eastern religions outside Asia. The other variant, which I call global, extends and intensifies transnational links among groups similar in their practices, and creates networks and sometimes even tightly-knit communities of people straddling vast distances and also straddling non-religious boundaries of language, ethnicity and race, such as Pentecostals, the pietist Muslim revival movement Tablighi Jama'at and ultra-Orthodox Jewish sects and cultures. Whereas the cosmopolitan variant combines conversion with a receptiveness to other rituals, such as the indigenous, the global variant conducts conversion as a zero-sum, even confrontational affair, very hostile to the indigenous.

The implication is that we have to distinguish between the observation of similarities across boundaries and the interpretation of shifts in the boundaries themselves. It is fairly clear that the Catholic Charismatic Renewal engages in very similar practices and supernatural invocations to those of Pentecostals, yet thus far one hardly ever hears of preachers' congregations merging or cooperating or even taking any notice of one another – although it will not be surprising if in the future this statement becomes less accurate. On the other hand, the shifts in 'geo-political' spheres of influence, for example in favour of the Pentecostal movement, bring about redrawings of geographic boundaries together with substantial change within those boundaries. Different traditions, and different currents within them, attach varying importance to the thickness of boundaries. The Catholic Church has thin social boundaries, allowing intermarriage and syncretism, whereas Pentecostals, though little concerned by intermarriage, tend to be stricter on sex, decorum and alcohol. Jews and Muslims emphasize barriers to intermarriage, but different currents enforce them with varying strictness and conditions. What is clear, though, is that religion – in the sense of the word consecrated by centuries of usage in Europe – resembles ethnicity in its preoccupation with boundaries, marked out in many ways. Indeed, one of the difficulties faced by Western versions of Hindu traditions in achieving recognition is that they are so open and tolerant, making few demands on those who frequent their centres, and thus often regarded as providing a service more like counsellors or practitioners of alternative medicine than ministers of religion.

Religion and globalization: The global pattern

Here I consider global religious movements and cultures which create strong transnational ties of belonging and similarity while emphasizing the boundaries between their followers and their social environment. They accentuate transnational homogeneity. This can apply to Political Islam, to the innumerable evangelical and Charismatic churches, sects and tendencies descended from the Protestant tradition and associated with names such as the Assemblies of God as well as with the Prosperity Gospel or Gospel of Health and Wealth, all of which build transnational organizations exhibiting varying degrees of centralization, but also to diasporic cultures such as ultra-Orthodox Judaism. They stand out as prime bearers of religious globalization because they straddle vast political, linguistic and geographic frontiers, creating transnational communities and networks of affiliation and togetherness. These movements and cultures benefit from, and take advantage of, globalization in order to strengthen or maintain boundaries and in order to run conversion campaigns. In the case of diasporic situations, where once migration led to a cutting off of migrants from their kin and their landscapes of memory, globalization has enabled religious and ethnic populations to preserve their ties through, for example, marriage, holidays, transfers of religious personnel, property investment and education, while at the same time, diasporic religious leaders look to adapt to their host environment through political connections, commercial development, or educational innovation, as observed among ultra-Orthodox Jews and Muslim ventures in institution-building.

The Pentecostal churches, although they are a movement, not a centralized international organization, exhibit an extraordinary degree of similarity of liturgy, organization, ideology and ethic in the most widely varying contexts – from Chile to China. This is counter-intuitive because religion as a cultural phenomenon is supposed to 'fit in' with inherited cultural traits ('tradition' in 'traditional' jargon), not to impose a unified model worldwide. The unity of the model is the product of a century of experimentation and communication: it is observed in styles of preaching, in a common message about the temptations of the world and salvation through submission to Jesus. But there is also local adaptation of specific features like the names of devils and dangerous spirits. Pentecostals use imagery and symbolism drawn from local cultures, especially *possession cults*, and especially when adopting an 'adversarial approach' to them. In Brazil and West Africa this is particularly in evidence. Where the cults deal with possession by spirits and entities who dictate a person's life, and with elaborate esoteric cures and procedures to summon or dispel spirits of varying kinds, the Pentecostal preachers will conduct procedures to deliver people from these same spirits, and from the diabolic influence of the purported cures offered by mediums. This is not to say that both are 'the same' for they are not, but it does show that these Pentecostals recognize the efficacy of those spirits, that from spirit possession and being possessed by the devil, or from imprecation to exorcism, is not such a long step. The difference is that the Pentecostals, like other evangelicals, call upon individuals to change their lives, to adopt a life of austerity and devotion to the church – by for example attending service daily, giving up drinking, smoking and 'licentious living' – whereas in possession cults the medium or sorcerer retains control of the communication between the spirits and the humans whose destiny they oversee, and require gifts in recognition of their services.

Even in its early days, in what was then the seething frontier town of Los Angeles, Pentecostalism was a multicultural, multi-ethnic movement, attracting black Americans, and Mexican, European and Asian migrants to its following. Today one of its most striking features worldwide is its cross-class appeal, though in the USA it divided along racial lines, in Africa it is strong among the desperately poor, among the aspiring middle classes, among urban and rural populations, and among the African diaspora in Europe. Indeed, it may simply be good at niche marketing, as in Brazil where one Church (*Déus é Amor* – 'God is Love') seems to target the very poor and the very elderly. In addition to their proclaimed thaumaturgic powers, Pentecostal preachers are also very adept at ingratiating themselves with politicians because they can reliably deliver their followers' votes.

The culture of evangelical Christianity was carried first by missionaries from England and Scotland to Africa in the early nineteenth century, and from the beginning this transfer was marked by continuing attempts on the part of Africans to wrest the symbols and meaning of their symbolic and ritual apparatus away from missionaries and colonial authorities. For example, impressed by the medical skills of missionaries, some Africans preferred to cast them in the role of healers – much to the dismay of missionaries who wanted them to be convinced of the truth of their message on its own merits. But the missionaries had, so to speak, only themselves to blame, as they propagated the Bible and its innumerable stories of visions, miracles, Virgin Birth, incarnation, the resurrection of the dead and so on. For indigenous Africans, conversion also represented an upward social move and an aspiration to join the colonials' society, yet in Southern Africa especially they found themselves barred from high office in the church, and it is not surprising therefore that in the early twentieth century they established their own Christian or semi-Christian movements, either in messianic form, in which rituals and taboos from the Old Testament were incorporated (as in the South African Zionist churches), or in churches inspired by Black American missionaries who had broken away from churches which discriminated against them in the United States. Preachers have used the lessons and resources from expatriates and colonial churchmen to set themselves up independently and for example, recently, to Africanize the Bible by vociferously recalling that Jesus was not a 'white man', and had been taken to Egypt to escape persecution by the Romans. The Bible is nowadays treated as a vast storehouse of uplifting stories which are mixed-and-matched by preachers who do not need the legitimacy of an academic or theological qualification. It is a vehicle which helps the colony to 'strike back' and claim a commanding position in global Christianity.

The global spread of churches originating in poor and middle-income countries requires a more elaborate type of organization than Pentecostal churches' classic grassroots approach. For example an admittedly committed source (Adams, 1997) claimed that already in 1994 there were 16,000 full-time missionaries from Africa, Asia and Latin America in the USA, and the Health and Wealth (or Prosperity) Gospel, which in the 1990s might have been despised as a sort of 'McDonalds of religious life', now seems to be the dominant force in Pentecostal expansion. This variant combines an emphasis on witchcraft and exorcism (playing on indigenous themes of possession and healing) with the promise of a healthy and prosperous lifestyle. Among the urban poor it fills an institutional vacuum in slums where there are more churches than latrines (in Nairobi for example), or in neighbourhoods where the only rival 'institution' is the drugs mafia (as in Rio de Janeiro). Small churches can benefit from twinning or sponsorship arrangements with North American counterparts or link in to multinational federations which can help provide training and education in religious institutions abroad. Besides proliferating small churches, the Prosperity Gospel is also borne by large-scale centralized and multinational organizations with a multi-class appeal, which are known as neo-Pentecostal, exemplified by the Brazil-based Universal Church of the Kingdom of God. This organization is now present in at least Argentina, Chile, Peru, Mexico, Portugal, England, Switzerland, Mozambique, Angola and South Africa, where it reproduces exactly the same repertoire of ritual and symbolic devices – such as the red heart enclosing a white dove – across the world, so that the symbols act more like a logo. Only the names of demons change to adapt to the local language. Africa-based or originated churches include the Ghana-based Lighthouse Chapel International and Royalhouse Chapel International, or the Church of the Embassy of God in the Ukraine, which is led by a Nigerian pastor.

Conversion-led movements

Both Islamic and Jewish fundamentalists engage in activities and campaigns to bring secularized or non-observant Jews and Muslims 'back' to strict observance. The largest of the Muslim movements of this kind is Tablighi Jama'at, which counts millions of followers worldwide and has thrived not only in India and Pakistan but worldwide among diaspora populations. Tablighi followers are apolitical and quietist, and establish mosques and schools of their own. Although their male followers are recognizable in public places, with their distinctive style of beard and dress, little is known of their organizational structure. Like Pentecostalism, Tabligh assigns priority to missionary and preaching activity and spreads through the interstices of society by friendship, word of mouth and affinity.

Among Jews the modern pioneers of what is known as the movement of 'return' or 'repentance' are the hasidic Lubavitch sect, also known as Chabad. Under the leadership of its charismatic and highly innovative 'Rebbe' Menachem Mendel Schneerson, Chabad grew from a small group on the verge of extinction in the early postwar period to one of the largest hasidic sects and one of the most influential forces in contemporary Jewish culture. Using a formula similar to the Pentecostals, the Rebbe started a system whereby missionaries are dispatched to far-flung places, to university campuses, to communities bereft of guidance or teachers, where they are expected to become self-sufficient after two or three years. They emphasize the idea of changing one's life, abandoning frivolity, and above all of adopting a way of life attuned to Jewishness. If the process is followed through, 'reverts' change jobs, renounce old friendships and may even distance themselves from their families, becoming heavily reliant on the sect. If they are young they may well be pressed to marry under the auspices of the sect and their many children will be fully socialized into the hasidic way of life. The Lubavitch idea of bringing people 'back' is now widely replicated, but the sect's worldwide network of individuals and institutions is unrivalled in its openness to Jews of all stripes.

At first sight it might appear that Tabligh and Lubavitch are quite different from Pentecostals because they operate among Muslims and Jews who are to be brought 'back' to their heritage, whereas Pentecostals are in the business of converting people who are not Christian at all (Pentecostals do not regard Catholics as Christian). On the other hand, like Pentecostals, both movements operate by crossing frontiers and straddling the most varied social and cultural environments. In the case of Tabligh from India and Pakistan across Europe and North America, and in that of Chabad everywhere from Moscow to Katmandu via Europe and the Americas. It is more or less impossible to know in any detail how their core organization works: Chabad missionaries may seem to have a close link to the headquarters in Brooklyn, New York, where they gather from around the world every year in November, but on the other hand they have to become rapidly self-sufficient. In Russia Chabad emissaries have gained control over the recognized Jewish institutions, including the Chief Rabbinate of Russia, becoming the leading force in the renaissance of Jewish life thanks to organization and also to support from some high-profile businessmen. One of Chabad's skills is the ability to obtain donations from people who are not themselves always known to be very observant.

FIGURE 16.2
Rabbi Menachem Mendel Schneerson

Rabbi Menachem Mendel Schneerson: charismatic leader of the Jewish Chabad Chassidim, who inspired the modern movement of *t'shuva* (return), bringing secularized Jews back to 'Jewishness', to a way of life which is only sustainable in close proximity to the ultra-Orthodox. His portrait is a ubiquitous feature of Chabad households, and is also widely recognized in the public sphere. © chabad.org.

This is more or less comparable to Pentecostals especially now that there are so many centralized, multinational neo-Pentecostal churches. In all these cases – Tabligh, Chabad, neo-Pentecostals – followers are stratified into different levels of participation, and in Chabad and neo-Pentecostals one can clearly distinguish different 'circles': the spinal cord of fulltime cadres, who are deployed by a central nucleus of authority and resources; local fulltime activists who teach, preach and listen; numerous volunteer activists who give time to the movement and are strict, true believers; regular participants who take part in religious services and celebrations; and visitors who drop in from time to time. Pentecostals too seem adept at raising funds, though primarily from their followers and sometimes from politicians, but rarely from wealthy individuals.

In all these cases we observe how leaders manage extensive resources across the world and across cultural frontiers while maintaining a unified core of ritual, of lifestyle, and of symbolism. Thus they have absorbed much of globalization and modernity even to the extent of grasping the management of logos and brand names.

Serious fundamentalism, messianic nationalism and Islamism

The issue of fundamentalism does, however, distinguish Chabad from Pentecostals, and within Islam, between Political Islam and those who some call neo-fundamentalists (Roy, 2004). Definitions of fundamentalism usually point to an insistence on textual inerrancy as a core feature: to this should be added a personalized concept of legitimate authority in which the authority to interpret the text is deposited only with certain persons. In the case of Islam, the worldwide crisis of authority has permitted all manner of local leaders to claim to correctly interpret the text, but since they do not recognize impersonal academic-style scholarly evaluation, they need a following who will accept their interpretation simply because it is theirs. Close attention to creating and thickening symbolic and social boundaries delimiting the group or following, and thus to rules of sexual behaviour, reinforce personalistic authority by predisposing followers to accept the rulings of a leader. As with Chabad, the way of life is prior to the acceptance of doctrine.

Whereas scholars reject labelling Tabligh fundamentalist, neo-fundamentalist Islamism and its cousin Political Islam surely do count as such. In both these cases organizations have established themselves as solely empowered to interpret tradition, norms, rules and texts. Sharia law is often said to be context-dependent and flexible, but nevertheless sharia judges in the lands where Islam has been established for centuries have enjoyed respect and prestige, as have imams and mullahs, so the relatively stable social environment protected the law and religious doctrine from deeply divisive challenge. The crisis of authority brought about by massive social change in the twentieth century started with the founding of two lay organizations which gave birth to Political Islam. One of these was the Muslim Brotherhood, founded in Egypt in 1928 to promote an Islamic revival which would be able to rival and resist the West after the decline and eventual collapse of the Ottoman Empire. By now, it has spawned numerous offshoots and imitations, including the Palestinian Hamas and Al-Qaida, while remaining an influential, illegal, but non-violent force in Egypt itself. The other was the Jama'at-Islam founded in India in 1941 by Maulana Mawdudi – again an organization which has spawned offshoots and imitations in Pakistan, where it is a political party, and elsewhere, including the Taliban.

Fundamentalist organizations and sects in Islam speak a language which in some ways is characteristically modern and definitely global. It is modern because they reject both established but ossified authority – that is, authority operating under the aegis of a state including official sharia judges – and many customs associated by other Muslims with their religion but regarded by fundamentalists as pagan or mere cultural appendages, such as elaborate marriage ceremonies, or indeed family-arranged marriages. Neo-fundamentalists are in pursuit of what Roy (2004) calls the 'global umma', a utopia which is rooted in modernity, fuelled by the diaspora situation in Europe, and removed from the historic lands and cultures of Islam and their accompanying customs and traditions. Tabligh is a pietist version of this. In principle one can perhaps draw a distinction, as Roy does, between this disembedded global imaginary and the (political) Islamist movements and sects which are trying to overthrow governments in Muslim countries and elsewhere; although in practice the two overlap and interchange ideas and modes of behaviour.

The evolution of Political Islam into a global phenomenon is most shockingly illustrated by the case of the Aïn el-Heloué refugee camp in Lebanon, described in a rare grounded ethnography of a Palestinian refugee camp (Rougier, 2007). The camp is home to a population originating in the expulsion of their parents and grandparents from

Palestine in 1948, but its political complexion has evolved away from once-dominant Palestinian nationalism to global jihad. Local leaders of indistinct provenance who have been schooled in Afghanistan notably, but also elsewhere, hold violent sway over the life of what is now a town, albeit one that is not recognized as such because its inhabitants have no citizenship status. The jihadist leadership is manipulated by secularist Syria and Shi'ite Iran, which may sound strange because the Syrian government is fiercely hostile to Islamism. However its hostility is to Islamism in Syria: in Lebanon and Palestine its main enemy is Al-Fatah and it deploys its efforts to prevent the creation of any independent Palestinian entity not controlled by Syria, so the global jihad is a useful ally. This also explains Syrian and indeed Iranian support for Fatah's enemy Hamas, which is otherwise puzzling since Hamas is Islamist and Sunni.

This is but one example: the crisis of authority in Islam, especially Sunni Islam, is repeated in the European diaspora where, for example, imported imams from Bangladesh or Pakistan are unable to communicate with young British-born Muslims, by now even children of British-born parents, who speak no Bengali or Urdu. Here globalization can work to reinforce tradition, because wives, husbands and imams can be brought across from Asia to renew social habits resistant to a secular way of life; but it can also work to undermine tradition as the movements contesting authority and proclaiming a more militant but also more global Islam, campaign among the young.

Neo-fundamentalism is more a matter, in Islam, of the control of personal morality. However, the theme of hostility to the West, to democracy and to any form of public female bodily expression has melded with Political Islam and so its influence will tend to reinforce that of the more political variant. Both are, in different places, to different degrees and at different times, beneficiaries of funding from the Saudi regime which spends vast sums of money funding mosques, madrassas and schools for example in Europe, where bitterly anti-Western preaching passes unquestioned. Thus the global *umma*, the reform of personal life and Political Islam are overlapping, though not necessarily always mutually reinforcing, forces. Like Pentecostalism, they are all constantly evolving so that clear-cut typologies are unlikely to be valid for long.

The interaction of Islam with globalization, to use the terms elaborated above, follows both cosmopolitan and global patterns. On the one hand globalization enables Muslim diasporas to resist the influence of Western secularism, of Western scholarship, and of Western sexual mores, because habits, norms and rituals from the homeland are not lost in the way they might have been in the days when migrants left their homelands behind and lost contact for ever. This is visible in the urban enclaves of the North of England and in areas of London such as Slough and the East End. Linked to distant locations, still, perhaps misleadingly, called 'homelands', these are homogeneous cultural complexes stretched across the globe, holding on to traditions of dress, food, music and marriage. In contrast, the reaffirmation or revival of Islam among educated and professional Muslims is built on the doctrinally based idea of a global *umma* in which national and regional cultures are erased in favour of a unified creed and lifestyle which brings together Muslims of the most varied ethnic and geographic origins – though still divisions such as that between Sunni and Shia will not be blurred.

Among ultra-Orthodox Jews we find not dissimilar patterns in terms of values and attitudes to sacred texts, but we find a very different pattern with respect to the building of institutions, a more concerted effort on the part of authority figures to adapt so as to survive, and a much more marginal political extreme. For example the Lubavitch encouraged women's education, and other hasidic sects and ultra-Orthodox milieux more generally have followed their lead in the creation of outreach programmes directed at secularized Jews. None of this is at the expense of softening the boundaries surrounding ultra-Orthodoxy. Liberal, Reform or Conservative variants which account for the majority of Jews in North America and the UK; are scarcely recognized by the ultra-Orthodox as Jewish at all. Since Reform and Liberal Judaism are perfectly compatible with an understanding of Hebrew and of ancient and Rabbinic texts, to place intellectual grasp ahead of adoption of the lifestyle would be to admit that ultra-Orthodoxy has grey borders and allows for half-measures, and that would be anathema.

The common core of ultra-Orthodoxy is today much more stable in Judaism than in Islam. Newcomers or returnees can rarely attain positions of great influence until the second or even third generation, and leadership is in the hands of the heirs to Rabbinic succession among Yeshiva (study centre) heads, or dynastic families drenched in tradition and surrounded by courts and bureaucracies. Despite the appearance of one-man rule in hasidic sects, institutional (non-religious or non-Rabbinical) decisions are made by committees, in a manner which goes back to the early modern period in Poland. The leadership has adapted to the challenges of the late twentieth and twenty-first centuries by creating an entirely new ideal of very high natality and deep disdain for the values of the permissive society or even secular life in general. In prewar Eastern Europe most of the followers of ultra-Orthodoxy worked for a living and only the most talented studied fulltime and taught, but today there has arisen the ideal of the 'learning society'. This is very much a global culture, densely networked across five continents: marriages are routinely contracted between people in far-flung places, young people are dispatched across the world to complete their education in missions (as in Chabad) or in Israeli seminaries; a high birth rate and the accompanying endless round of rites of passage bring people together – if they can afford it – from across the world. To sustain this way of life leaders have become very adept at extracting funds from the state, especially but not exclusively in Israel, at political lobbying to obtain subsidies for projects like schools, low-cost housing, care homes and the like, and at fundraising among Jews of all persuasions.

This could be thought of, in a loose sort of way, as the counterpart of Islam's diasporic networks. Ultra-Orthodoxy is an extremely efficient vote-bank, obviously in Israel but also to some extent in London and New York, just as diasporic Islamic organizations in Britain are now entering into a relationship with the state in the context of programmes of social integration and combatting violent extremism run by the UK government's Department for Communities and Local Government.

Beyond this institutionalized ultra-Orthodox Jewish culture, we have witnessed since the 1967 war a messianic nationalism within Judaism which is something quite new, because it focuses on a divine entitlement to a stretch of land enshrined in the unerring word of God in the Bible. This is contrary both to classic secular and social democratic Zionism, but also to the tradition of Rabbinic learning which has treated the sacred text for centuries as a source of law and as a basis for unending hermeneutic debate among experts, but never as a set of concrete political prescriptions to be proclaimed by novices and newly religious returnees. The movement has come to dominate the once-tame National Religious Party and to exercise very strong influence in Israel's leading rightwing party, Likud. It is a grassroots movement which has spearheaded West Bank settlement, creating 'facts on the ground' which politicians are pressured, successfully, to recognize. Over time the settler movement has adopted, in an allusive, unprogrammed sort of way, all sorts of ultra-Orthodox paraphernalia from certain detailed but very visible aspects of male and female dress such as egregiously visible fringes hanging out of fatigues for men or calf-length skirts and headscarves for women, mixed in with a self-consciously dishevelled dress code designed to exhibit a lack of care for the body. The movement is not easy to study but it seems to have a disproportionate number of activists who are either recent immigrants to Israel or recent returnees to strict observance, or some combination of the two, highlighting the weak connection with Israeli society and the concomitant globalism of the movement. The features in common with the global *umma* are worth remarking on: the movement is only incidentally implanted in a particular state context – since for these ideological settlers land is of paramount importance and the Israeli state is a mere detail, an irritant. Indeed, seeing that it does not follow religious law and that for them only the return of the Messiah will herald the foundation of a Jewish state deserving of the name, Israel as a state is barely legitimate in their eyes.

Conclusion

It is important, in concluding, to remind the reader that this chapter focuses on only two aspects of a vast, almost limitless, subject. A fuller treatment would require, among other things, a history of the spread of religions worldwide and of the differences between the ways Eastern and Western religions (among which I include Islam as an Abrahamic faith) plus an account of Orthodox Christianity in Russia and the Balkans. It would also have to explain the enormous variations in Islam across Europe, Africa, the Middle East and Asia. From the theoretical point of view, a global coverage would have to question, or at least contextualize, the social science definition of religion, indelibly marked as it is by a polarity opposing monotheism and accompanying assumptions about texts and doctrines to paganism and possession as in the African and Latin American examples used here. Would this concept help us to understand how Eastern religious strands have spread, absorbed and mutually influenced one another?

The focus, then, has been on two of the most prominent political concerns of our time – the politics of identity and fundamentalism. The first part of the chapter had two purposes. One was to remind readers of the need to see contemporary problems in an historical perspective, both to understand what is really new and what is a recurrence of ancient phenomena, and to understand the extent to which contemporary phenomena bear the weight of the history which precedes them, especially in the field of religion and identity which is so deeply marked by heritage and origins. Second, taking globalization to be a process of creating and redrawing boundaries of various kinds – political, linguistic, religious, and ethnic – it outlined the role of religion in creating, thickening and perforating social boundaries, and thus its contribution to sometimes dramatic realignments of affiliation. This analysis is based on the assumption that social boundaries often criss-cross one another – the ethnic, the religious, the national and the linguistic are not usually superimposed, and the religious in particular can change, and this is more and more evident in the contemporary context in which international migration is more multi-directional than before, and where conversion-led religious movements have acquired a qualitative and quantitative importance which has made them the agenda-setters of religious life in many parts of the Western world including Africa. In many cases religion has changed in a context of war and conquest – and although the examples given are post-1492 there could have been innumerable others from earlier periods of history. Examples from the colonial histories of Latin America and Africa contrasted two traditions which manage the relationship of the institutional to the popular in different ways: the more cosmopolitan character of Catholicism is contrasted with a Protestant tradition which is much less inclined to syncretism and to a projection of the other. Yet in both traditions the exchange of rituals and doctrines across boundaries is unending. Despite an inauspicious beginning (to say the least) Catholicism eventually found creative accommodations with indigenous cultures giving rise to a varied and institutionally differentiated presence which permeates society even today. In this process the indigenous people themselves were as much protagonists as objects, a point which comes through with even greater force in Africa, where indigenous preachers built their own churches from the early twentieth century, and in more recent times have brought them to Europe and sometimes also 'gone global', becoming the most dynamic forces in European Protestantism – a phenomenon we described as 'the colony strikes back'. This latter pattern we have called 'global' in contrast to cosmopolitan because it downplays and even abhors cultural distinctiveness – yet at the same time it is suffused with possession, exorcism and healing, which have distinct resonances with indigenous African and Afro-Brazilian cults.

After this first section with its focus on the imaginary, the second section came 'down to earth' with accounts of religious cultures and movements which transcend national and geographical frontiers and distances and clearly draw strength from a more material aspect of globalization – the revolution in travel and communications. It focused on fundamentalist and conversion-led (evangelical) movements because (a) they embody so much of the modernity which globalization promotes, and (b) while globalization has found much of institutionalized Christianity, especially in the institutional Protestant tradition, in a state of almost numb confusion, and Sunni Islam in a massive crisis of authority, the preachers and pastoral entrepreneurs in these movements have taken advantage of the opportunities it offers among the poor and disinherited, among migrants, and among the disoriented Muslim youth of Western Europe, Pakistan and the Middle

East, and also among an intelligentsia uneasy with issues of identity and religion. Once again, the theme of boundaries emerges, since all these movements pay careful, sometimes obsessive, attention to drawing symbolic frontiers – in the form of dress codes, language use, marriage codes – and also material frontiers in the form of rules governing the use of one's time, the classification of employment in terms of its acceptability, the pressure to contribute financially or in kind. Ultra-Orthodox Judaism is the most elaborate example of boundary-maintenance, and although only some of its sects are evangelical in vocation, bringing secularized Jews 'back', they have all undergone a process of retraditionalization in the period since the Holocaust, making rules ever more stringent and using the resources of modernity to consolidate their position, with remarkable success.

Finally, we came to the most straightforward cases, namely of transnational movements, and we saw in the example of the Aïn El-Heloué refugee camp in Lebanon the extremes of several features of the religion–globalization nexus: a deracinated population – the second and third generations of Palestinians in exile; a movement with no territorial base whatsoever, but devoted to a pure politico-religious cause – the global jihad; and, finally, the manipulations of state powers.

Modernity and globalization are changing the definition of religion itself, at least the definition which has been assumed in Western Europe, of a heritage, a culture imbued in childhood and a stable and undemanding set of arrangements governing the rites of passage but also as a set of consensual values. Maybe that was always a myth – but today claims to a possession of doctrinal religious correctness are at the centre of some of our most intractable conflicts and culture wars. This is not to blame religion – for as we have seen religion itself is a multiple concept and only the most superficial and misguided notion of agency or causality would attribute anything much to religion in general.

Summary

- Some theories of religion and globalization think of recent religious resurgence in terms of the reassertion of 'traditional' religion in the face of secular modernity. It is suggested here that it is possible to think of interactions between religion and globalization in other ways.

- A starting point is to emphasize religion's role in creating, upholding, permeating, and puncturing boundaries – between groups, societies, ethnicities, etc.

- It is possible to distinguish between a cosmopolitan globalization of religion in which institutional and popular forms of religion cross-fertilize one another (e.g. Catholicism in Latin America) and a global dynamic in which global religious movements and cultures create strong transnational ties of belonging and similarity, while emphasizing the boundaries between their followers and their social environment. They accentuate transnational homogeneity (e.g. Political Islam and innumerable evangelical and Charismatic churches).

■   There are examples which combine elements of both these patterns of religious globalization.

Key terms

dialectic Interplay between two or more elements, which are shaped in and through the interplay by one another.

Hasidism A mystical, revivalist branch of Ultra-Orthodox Judaism, which emerged from Eastern Europe in the eighteenth century.

heterogeneity Diversity.

Homogeneity Sameness.

Iberian Peninsula The land mass occupied by Spain and Portugal.

legitimizing Rendering something or someone legitimate, authoritative.

Rebbe Term meaning 'my rabbi', used to designate the leader of a Hasidic community.

umma (h) Community.

Zionism The political movement established in the nineteenth century with the aim of building a Jewish homeland in Palestine.

Further reading

The best way to deepen understanding of this subject is to read in history and anthropology, since that provides a sense of social processes behind or beyond the more general or theoretical pronouncements of sociologists. The following texts will be particularly stimulating.

For a historical and anthropological account of the religious encounter between colonialism and African indigenous culture, and the subsequent interweaving of them:
D. Maxwell: *African Gifts of the Spirit: Pentecostalism and the Rise of a Zimbabwean Transnational Religious Movement* (Oxford: James Currey, 2006).

For Latin American syncretism the following is a standard text, though focusing mostly on the history of ideas rather than on the cult of the Virgin of Guadalupe itself: D.A. Brading: *Mexican Phoenix: Our Lady of Guadalupe: Image and Tradition across Five Centuries* (Cambridge: Cambridge University Press, 2001).

The best book on popular religion in Latin America is unfortunately untranslated (Carlos Rodriguez Brandão: *Os Deuses do Povo* ('The people's gods'), republished in a complete edition by the Editorial da Universidade Federal de Uberlandia (2007). A summary can be found in David Lehmann: 'Religion in contemporary Latin American social science'. (*Bulletin of Latin American Research* 21(2), 2002: pp. 290–307).

For studies of Pentecostalism:
A. Corten and R. Marshall-Fratani (eds): *Between Babel and Pentecost: Transnational Pentecostalism in Africa and Latin America* (London: Hurst & Company, 2001) is a very good account of its subject, with case studies.

D. Lehmann: *Struggle for the Spirit: Religious Transformation and Popular Culture in Brazil and Latin America* (Oxford: Polity Press, 1996).

D. Martin: *Tongues of Fire: The Pentecostal Revolution in Latin America* (Oxford: Blackwell, 1990). Despite the apparent concentration on Latin America, this also offers the best panoramic account of the spread of evangelical Christianity across the globe from its nineteenth-century English origins.

D. Martin: *Pentecostalism: The World Their Parish* (Oxford: Blackwell, 2005) is a good update on his earlier book.

Accounts of ultra-Orthodox Judaism tend to be written in ways that are not easily approachable for outsiders, but the following are good ethnographies:

M. Friedman: 'Jewish Zealots: Conservative versus Innovative'. In E. Sivan and M. Friedman (eds): *Religious Radicalism and Politics in the Middle East* (Albany, NY: State University of New York Press, 1990).

D. Lehmann and B. Siebzehner: *Remaking Israeli Judaism: The Challenge of Shas* (London: Hurst and Co, 2006).

H. Soloveitchik: 'Rupture and Reconstruction: The Transformation of Contemporary Orthodoxy'. (*Tradition* 28(4) 1994: 64–129) is a classic text on the postwar reconstruction of Ultra-Orthodox Jewish culture.

The standard sociological approach to globalization and religion is to be found in P. Beyer: *Religion and Globalization* (London: Sage, 1994) and R. Robertson *Globalization: Social Theory and Global Culture* (London: Sage, 1992).

See also J. Comaroff and J. Comaroff: *Of Revelation and Revolution, Volume One: Christianity, Colonialism and Consciousness in South Africa* (Chicago, IL: Chicago University Press, 1991).

On global Political Islam the standard text is now Olivier Roy: *Globalised Islam: The Search for a New Ummah* (London: Hurst and Co., 2004). But the case study by Bernard Rougier: *Everyday Jihad: The Rise of Militant Islam among Palestinians in Lebanon* (London: Harvard University Press, 2007) is indispensable. An excellent study of Political Islam and religious resurgence in Islam, based on the recent history of Iran and Egypt is: A. Bayat: *Making Islam Democratic: Social Movements and the Post-Islamist Turn* (Stanford, CA: Stanford University Press, 2007).

An interesting, if over-enthusiastic, presentation of the internationalisation of Cuban possession cults (*santería*) is found in: J. Murphy: *Santería: A Religion in America* (Boston, MA: Beacon Press, 1988).

The theoretical basis for the present chapter can be found in: D. Lehmann: 'Fundamentalism and Globalism'. (*Third World Quarterly* 19(4), 1988: pp. 607–634).

Also cited in this chapter:

A. Adams: (1997). 'Jumping the Puddle: A Case Study of Pentecostalism's Journey from Puerto Rico to New York to Allenstown, Pennsylvania. In E. Cleary and H. Stewart-Gambino (eds): *Power, Politics and Pentecostals in Latin America* (Boulder, CO: Westview, 1997).

V. Altglas: 'The Global Diffusion and Westernization of Neo-Hindu Movements: Siddha Yoga and Sivananda Centres'. (*Religion in South Asia* 1(2), 2007: 217–237).

B. Meyer: *Translating the Devil: Religion and modernity among the Ewe in Ghana* (Edinburgh: Edinburgh University Press, 1999).

T. Saignes: 'The Colonial Condition in the Quechua-Aymara Heartland'. In F. Salomon and S. Schwartz (eds): *The Cambridge History of the Native Peoples of the Americas, volume III: South America, Part 2* (Cambridge: Cambridge University Press, 1999).

Chapter 17

Religion and politics

Jeffrey Haynes

Introduction

Though it will glance back as far as the nineteenth century, the focus of this chapter falls on the recent past, particularly the latter part of the twentieth century and the early years of the current one. The period is generally characterized by particularly interesting developments in the relations between religion and politics across the world, developments still in train at the present time. The 1980s, 1990s and early 2000s were, globally, an era of fundamental political, social and economic change. Many changes stemmed from, or were at least galvanized by, the ending of the Cold War (involving the Soviet Union and the USA from the late 1940s to the late 1980s). Others were associated with the multifaceted processes known collectively, if somewhat vaguely, as 'globalization' (for clarification of the term see the previous chapter, Chapter 16, Religion and globalization). Key developments in the period included not only the consolidation of a truly global economy and, some would argue, the gradual emergence of a 'global culture', but also a number of fundamental political developments including the steady if uneven advance of democracy – from Latin America to Eastern and Central Europe, Asia and Africa. There have also been myriad examples of the political involvement of religious actors around the world – to the extent that some claim that a global religious revitalization, a 'de-secularization' of the world, is a third characteristic of the period (see Chapter 21, Secularization and secularism). As this chapter will show, this does not imply only an apolitical respiritualization, but also widespread contemporary interaction of religion and politics.

This interaction between religion and politics has not been uniform across the globe. Religious actors with political goals were especially prominent in – though not restricted to – Third World countries. Encouraged by the Iranian Islamic revolution of 1978–79, widespread Islamic militancy developed in the Middle East and elsewhere. Turning to Asia, an explosion of militant Hinduism in officially secular India helped to transform the country's political landscape. During the 1990s and early 2000s, Hindu fundamentalists, focused in the Bharatiya Janata Party, were politically highly important. In Thailand, new Buddhist groups and parties emerged with political concerns, while in Africa there were numerous examples of religion's political involvement, including in Nigeria (a country politically and socially polarized between Muslim and Christian forces), in Somalia (which may well soon have an Islamist government), and in Sudan (a nation politically divided between Muslims and non-Muslims).

The list of examples could be extended, but hopefully the point is clear: at the end of the first decade of the twenty-first century it is rather difficult to find a country, especially in the Third World, where religion is not somewhere near the top of publicly

FIGURE 17.1 Babri Masjid mosque

Hindu fundamentalists celebrate atop the Babri Masjid Mosque, Ayodhya, 6 December 1992. The mosque was reduced to rubble at this disputed holy site in the city. Courtesy Douglas Curran, Getty Images.

expressed socio-political concerns, even in states that have followed secular principles and practices for a long time.

This chapter will examine the extent and nature of religion's interaction with politics, and assess its contemporary political significance across the globe. It will look at the interaction of religion and politics in both Western and non-Western areas in the twentieth century and early years of the twenty-first, following a brief discussion of colonization and its impact upon the current political scene in the Third World. It will also discuss the concept of secularization and its relevance for an understanding of the interaction of religion and politics around the world.

Church–state relations

To begin to understand the current political importance of religion, it is useful to start from an understanding of what religious actors say and do in their relationship with the state. Here more is meant than mere government when referring to the state: it is the continuous administrative, legal, bureaucratic, and coercive system which aims not only to manage the state apparatus but also to structure relations between civil and public power and within civil and political society. Almost everywhere, modern states have sought to reduce religion's political influence, to privatize it and hence significantly reduce its political and social importance. But this has not been the whole story. In countries at differing levels of economic development – for example, rich Western countries, such as the USA, economically middle-ranking countries, like Israel and Poland, and poor Third World countries including Nigeria, Tanzania, Indonesia, and Burma – states have also recognized the importance of religion for politics by seeking to create 'civil religions' that is, bodies of state-designated religious dogma. The purpose was to engineer consensual, corporate religious forms that could claim to be guided by general, culturally appropriate, societally specific religious beliefs, not necessarily tied institutionally to any specific religious tradition. The development of civil religion was often part of a strategy not merely to avoid social conflicts but also to try to promote national co-ordination in countries with serious religious and/or ideological divisions. But seeking to develop civil religions had a danger: minority religious persuasions tended to perceive it as part of an attempt to perpetuate the hegemony of a dominant religious tradition at their expense.

Whilst the interaction of church and state has historically been tense and problematic in many Western countries, to compare the situation with non-Christian contexts necessitates some preliminary conceptual clarifications – not least because the very idea of a prevailing state–church dichotomy is culture bound. Not only is the concept of 'church' a Christian rooted notion; the modern understanding of 'state' is also deeply rooted in the post-Reformation European political experience. In terms of their specific cultural setting and social significance, the tension and the debate over the church–state relationship are uniquely Western phenomena, present in the ambivalent dialectic of 'render therefore unto Caesar the things which be Caesar's and unto God the things which be God's' (Luke 21:25). The consequence is that because they are heavily rooted in the West's cultural history, the two concepts cannot easily be translated into non-Christian terminologies.

Among Third World regions, it is only in Latin America that it is pertinent to speak of church–state relations along the lines of the European model. This is because of the historical regional dominance of the Roman Catholic Church in that region, and the widespread creation of European-style states after colonization. However, the traditional Eurocentric Christian conceptual framework of church–state relations appears alien within and with respect to nearly all African and Asian societies. Some religions – notably, Hinduism – have no ecclesiastical structure at all; consequently there cannot be a clerical challenge to India's secular state comparable to that of, say, Buddhist monks in Burma or Shi'ite mullahs in Iran. On the other hand, political parties and movements energized by religious notions – particularly those of Hinduism and Sikhism – are of great importance in India.

The differences between Christian and other cultural conceptions of state and church are well illustrated by reference to Islam. In the Muslim tradition the mosque is not a church in the European-Christian sense of the word. As a concept, the closest Islamic approximation to 'state' (*dawla*) has the sense of a ruler's dynasty or administration. Only with the specific stipulation of 'church' as the generic concept for 'moral community', 'priest' for the 'custodians of the sacred law', and 'state' for 'political community' is it fully appropriate to use these concepts in Islamic and other non-Christian contexts. On the theological level, the 'command-obedience' nexus that constitutes the Islamic definition of authority is not demarcated by conceptual categories of religion and politics. Life as a physical reality is an expression of divine will and power (*qudrah'*). There is no validity in separating the matters of piety from those of the polity; both are divinely ordained. Yet, although both religious and political authorities are legitimated Islamically, they invariably constitute two independent social institutions. They do, however, regularly interact with each other.

Until recently it was widely believed that modernization would, ineluctably, lead both to religious privatization and to a more general secularization of society. But when Iran's Islamic revolution erupted it suggested not only that there was more than one interpretation of modernization, but also that religion might play a leading role. Since then, religion in politics seems to be everywhere. What have been the political consequences of religion's intervention? The short answer is: they are variable. Religion sometimes appears to have had a pivotal influence on political outcomes – for example, when leading church figures strongly urged the introduction of democracy in Africa, Latin America and Eastern Europe in the late 1980s and early 1990s. However, elsewhere – for example, when Algerian Islamist party the Islamic Sahation Front (FIS) won a convincing electoral victory and the government nullified it and then banned the party from political activity – religion seemed unable definitively to influence political outcomes (despite a civil war in Algeria in the 1990s which cost as many as 150,000 lives).

Defining the 'West' and the 'Third World'

The West

A dictionary definition of the term states simply: 'Europe, or Europe and America'. However what is commonly meant by the term implies more than a statement about geography. It is also about science and ideas. In the guise of the Enlightenment the modern West was arguably born as a reaction against religious and cultural diversity (which had led to war across Europe) in the face of which absolute, universal truths were upheld in scientific, philosophical and religious domains. In the West, science came to provide the model for modern rationality in the form of abstract and general axioms, principles and theories. In this development there seemed little room for historical religion. Consequently, it is surprising to many that religion's political involvement continues to occur in at least some Western areas – that is, where it was long thought to have left the public arena.

Recent examples abound. In Europe, a region long thought to be inexorably secularizing, civil war in the early 1990s in Bosnia-Herzegovina between Croats, Serbs and Bosnian Muslims was a de facto religious conflict. Each combatant identified religious and cultural (not ideological) allies, respectively, in Germany, Russia and the Arab-Muslim world. In the late 1990s civil war in Kosovo was fought between ethnic Albanians and Serbs, a conflict between Muslims and Christians, with the former allegedly aided by co-religionists from the Middle East. The declared independence of Kosovo from Serbia in 2008 led to a renewal of the conflict, with religious differences one of the issues dividing the two sides. In the USA, sustained attempts by a New Christian Right to mould and drive the political agenda underline religion's growing socio-political significance. In Israel, the growing political significance of religiously orientated groups, such as the Ultra-Orthodox Shas Party, is manifested in their appearance in Ehud Olmert's ruling coalition government. There has also been a political role for religion in former communist Eastern Europe. In Poland, Catholic priests achieved considerable political importance in the late communist and post-communist order, while the late Pope John Paul II, who died in 2005, was a Pole, who involved himself in political and social issues such as the campaign to reduce Third World debt as well as fierce denunciations of birth control. In Russia, the Orthodox Church emerged from communism as an actor of major social and political importance, while various constituent republics, including Chechnya and Dagestan, have been subject to serious attempts at Islamicization from Islamist radicals, fought against by the Russian government which devoted thousands of troops to try to thwart them. In Northern Ireland, on the other hand, a conflict with foundations in religious differences finally came to an end in 1998, following a peace deal known as the 'Good Friday Agreement'.

The conflict in Northern Ireland, which came to an end in the late 1990s, lasted for well over a century. However, what was at the root of the conflict was unclear. While many theories were put forward, no theory on its own could, it seemed, adequately describe the contours of the complex struggle. The conflict could be described and accounted for in many ways: ethnically between the British and the Irish, geographically, between the North and the South of Ireland, and religiously between Protestants and Catholics. Different theories point variously to causes when attempting to define the conflict, including: land claims and competing nationalist ideologies; ethnicity and culture, and, perhaps most frequently, religion. In fact, what is more likely is that elements of all of these issues lie at the root of what was commonly referred to as 'The Troubles'.

BOX 17.1 Conflict in Northern Ireland

The Third World

The term Third World, a shorthand expression embracing more than 100 non-Western countries, was invented in the 1950s to refer both to the large group of economically underdeveloped, then decolonizing countries in Africa, Asia and the Middle East, as well as to Latin American states; the latter were mostly granted freedom from colonial rule in the early nineteenth century, but were still economically weak over a century later. However, despite a shared history of colonization there are notable differences between Third World states. For example, such economically diverse countries as the United Arab Emirates (GNP per capita of US$23,950 in 2006), South Korea (US$17,690) and Mozambique (US$340), or politically singular polities such as Cuba (one-party communist state), Pakistan (military dictatorship between October 1999 and February 2008), and India (multiparty democracy), are all classified as Third World countries. To many observers the economic and political – not to mention cultural – differences between such countries outweigh their purported similarities.

While the blanket term 'Third World' obscures important cultural, economic, social and political differences between states, it does however have certain advantages over alternatives like 'the South' or 'developing countries'. The expression 'the South' is essentially geographic and ignores the fact that some 'Western' countries (Australia, New Zealand) are in the geographical South. The idea of the 'South' does, however, have the advantage of getting away from the connotation of developing towards some preordained end state or goal which is explicit in the idea of 'developing countries'. It is by no means clear, however, what the idea of a 'developed' state looks like: does it connote only a certain (high) degree of economic growth or is there an element of redistribution of the fruits of growth involved? And what of widely divergent social conditions in a 'developed' country? In this chapter I will (somewhat hesitantly) use the term Third World in the absence of a clearly better alternative.

Secularization

Secularization, implying a significant diminishing of religious concerns in everyday life, is seen by many as one of the main social and political trends in Western Europe since the Enlightenment (1720–1780). It was long believed that as a society modernizes it inevitably secularizes and differentiates – that is, in becoming more complex, a division of labour emerges in society whereby institutions become more highly specialized and, as a consequence, are increasingly in need of their own technicians. To many, secularization was the most fundamental structural and ideological change in the process of political development, a global trend, a universal facet of modernization. As Western societies modernized there would be a demystification of religion and a gradual yet persistent erosion of religious influence. The end result of secularization, a secular society, is where the pursuit of politics takes place irrespective of religious interests.

Secularization has gone hand in hand with separation of power between church and state in much of Europe. This situation developed over time, an important symbolic moment being the 1648 Treaty of Westphalia, an agreement which not only brought to an end the Thirty Years War between Protestants and Catholics, but also saw the end of religious wars which had followed in the wake of the Reformation. The Westphalian settlement established the rule that it was for secular political leaders to decide which religion would be favoured in their polity. What this amounted to was that the emerging states of Western Europe often tended to become more or less monopolies of one religion or another, as well as increasingly the homes of self-conscious national groups. Autocratic rulers saw religious conformity as an essential underpinning of their rule, necessary to maintain the existing social political order in their favour.

The tendency towards rulers' absolutism and the growth of nationalism were both greatly affected by the French Revolution of 1789. In France itself the Catholic Church, which had retained much of its wealth, social influence and political power after the 1648 treaty, came under attack from the radicals and revolutionaries. The division between them and the church was not bridged during the nineteenth century, and by the end of that period the rise of socialism and communism helped to diminish further the church's influence in the political battles fought between socialists, social democrats and conservatives in Western Europe. While this simplifies a complex situation (for example, the church retained much power in Italy, Ireland and elsewhere), the overall effect of the growth of nationalism and secular political mobilization in Europe was effectively to diminish the church's political power in relation to secular rulers.

Colonialism

As the institutions of church and state separated in Europe during the nineteenth century, the region became increasingly involved in colonizing Asia and Africa. As a result, the vast majority of countries constituting the contemporary Third World underwent the experience of European colonial rule. Now, however, virtually no such colonies remain. By World War II (1939–1945) there were a few European colonizing countries and a large number of colonized areas. The colonizers were not especially interested in the nature and characteristics of the areas that they ruled, despite the diversity of political and social systems, other than in terms of quiescence at their rule and maximization of economic gains.

Most colonies, including some with large populations and extant religious conflicts (for example, India, Indonesia and Nigeria), became independent after 1945. In South Asia there was a rush to independence shortly after World War II, while in Africa there was a similar movement towards independent statehood around the year 1960. Other former colonies have been politically independent for much longer: most Spanish and Portuguese colonies in Latin America achieved independence in the first quarter of the nineteenth century. In some former colonies, however, political independence was attained by European communities which continued to dominate populations of non-European descent. In this way a colonial situation was both internalized and until recently 'frozen' in, for example, South Africa; at an earlier period the independence of Brazil and other South American countries may be seen in a somewhat similar light. To this day, there is a socio-political hierarchy in much of South America and the Caribbean, even in socialist Cuba, in which one's skin colour is often an accurate guide to one's status. This situation is a legacy of European colonialism.

To many Europeans, the spreading of Christianity was an important element in the extending of Western civilization to supposedly godless, benighted native populations; as a result, Christianity made substantial headway in many Third World areas in the nineteenth and twentieth centuries. However, the post-1945 emergence of the Third World, the contemporaneous decline of war-weakened European powers and serious rivalry between the nuclear weapons-endowed superpowers, the USA and the Soviet Union, emphasized the changing nature of the international system.

Religion and politics since the 1960s

To take the analysis further it is convenient to divide the world into three parts, on the one hand, the West (especially North America and Western Europe) and, on the other, the former 'second world' (the erstwhile Soviet Union and its Eastern European communist allies) and finally the Third World. The second world is treated apart from the West not least because of attempts at state-imposed secularization in the former during the communist era (typically, from the late 1940s to the late 1980s/early 1990s). In recent years, there has been a claim that the world is divided by a 'clash of civilizations', with religion playing a significant role.

An academic, Samuel Huntington, has claimed that, after the Cold War, radical Muslim-majority countries dissatisfied with the existing international order were poised en masse to enter into a period of conflict with the West. From that time, successive United States governments (led by George H.W. Bush [1989–1993], Bill Clinton [1993–2001] and George W. Bush [2001–2009]) collectively put much effort into combating Islamic fundamentalist groups and movements around the world, as their main goal was to undermine the stability of friendly regional governments; successive US presidents were also energized by a desire to minimize the perceived threat from 'rogue states' – including the Islamic Republic of Iran – judged to be a key threat to international order. Iran's government, successive US administrations have claimed, is a sponsor of transnational religious terrorism.

For some, the unprecedented acts of transnational terror on 11 September 2001 ('9/11') represented the definitive emergence of what Huntington referred to as new 'civilizational' cleavages, centrally informed by expressions of radical transnational Islam attaining prominence in Western political and security concerns. Since 9/11, much has been written both in the West and elsewhere about the emergence and international impact of a new 'transnational' and 'militant' Islam. This trend is said to encapsulate the rise of a new network of jihadis – that is, groups of militant Muslims engaged in 'holy war' against non-Muslims – who are said to organize and operate independent of state control, gaining followers from many countries, and acting in a global context, where operations are not focused upon any single country. The most infamous example, al-Qaeda, has recruited fighters from numerous Muslim countries – such as Bosnia, Chechnya, Egypt, Morocco, Pakistan, Saudi Arabia, and Yemen – as well as non-Muslim countries, including: Australia, Britain, France, and the Philippines.

BOX 17.2 Clash of civilisations

The West

Two phenomena are simultaneously taking place in many Western countries at the current time, and both challenge prevailing theories of inexorable secularization: (1) an increase in various forms of spirituality and religiosity (see Chapter 12, Spirituality and Chapter 15, New Religious Movements); and (2) more readily and openly than in the recent past, mainline churches articulate their views on political and social issues. It seems that the latter is occurring because churches are no longer willing to be sidelined as states' jurisdictions have expanded into areas historically under their sole control. In relation to the first issue, the question is: are people becoming personally more religious while their societies are becoming collectively more secular? Three main arguments have been offered in support of this contention: (1) religion is replacing secular ideologies which have lost appeal for many people; (2) religion achieves enhanced popularity cyclically; and (3) New Religious Movements are a response to the impact of modernity and/or postmodernity. Let us look at each argument.

First, people are said to be turning to religion in response to a decline in the attraction of secular ideologies such as communism and socialism. As people need to believe in something, especially in the context of the post-Cold War 'new world disorder', the decline of radical secular ideologies has meant that people have (re)turned to religion to (re)discover a religious dimension of group identity, for example in the USA. While superficially attractive, the main problem with this explanation is that religion has not returned only in the 1990s. Rather, in some countries (the USA is the archetypal example) politicized religion has been important since the 1960s.

Second, some argue that a periodic collective thirst for religion is a cyclical phenomenon. That is, religion has been a significant factor in a number of socio-political mass movements in the West over the last 40 years, including the American civil rights movement, the Northern Irish struggle for dominance between Loyalists and Nationalists, and the so-called 'moral majority' in the USA. To many people, it is claimed, this-worldly answers to the meaning and purpose of life periodically appear alienating and unsatisfying and, as a result, religious beliefs intermittently find fresh relevance and power, perhaps within new structures and patterns of belief. However, what needs to be explained is why religion should enjoy a periodic resurgence. What set of factors needs to be in operation to trigger this development? These questions are difficult to answer and are not satisfactorily dealt with by the proponents of the cyclical theory of religious resurgence.

The 'New Christian Right' (NCR) in the USA attacks liberalism as the engine of moral decay. The NCR is dominated numerically by white Protestants – around 20 to 22 per cent of the adult population, that is, some 35–40 million people. There has been a remarkable upsurge in the disaffection and politicization of such theologically conservative Protestants over the last 30 years; many seem to act on their beliefs – especially in relation to attempts to prevent legal abortion – with growing militancy. It is the voice of theologically conservative Christians, united by a shared 'born-again' experience, who regard America's travails (Vietnam, abortion, drug addiction, etc.) as punishment for alleged departure from traditional Judeo-Christian morality. The Christian conservatives strive to uphold what they perceive as desirable 'traditional values', regarding as anathema manifestations of unwelcome liberalism – legal abortion, the absence of prayers in state-run schools, and science teaching which adopts a rationalist, as opposed to a 'creationist' perspective (that is, one believing explicitly in the literal truth of the Biblical creation story).

BOX 17.3 The New Christian Right in the USA

Third, the contention is that Western people are becoming more religious, not less; that is, secularization is being reversed. The argument here hinges partly on surveys purportedly showing both growing attendance at religious services as well as increased sales for religious books. It is also dependent on the fact that large numbers of New Religious Movements have emerged, including the fast growing 'Charismatic' Christian phenomenon unattached to any strong doctrinal tradition. (Charismatic Christianity is a widespread non-denominational tendency offering devotees spiritual excitement, with belief in divinely inspired gifts of glossolalia (speaking in tongues), healing and prophecy; see Chapter 8 on Christianity.)

While, for many Charismatics, religion and politics should be kept separate, they are not alone in eschewing political involvement. Various manifestations of new religious and spiritual phenomena, such as sundry kinds of New Age spirituality (Chapter 13), sects, including the Scientologists (Chapter 15), 'exotic' Eastern religions like the Hare Krishna cult, 'televangelism', renewed interest in astrology, and so on, may not be particularly relevant for the social and political sciences and the self-understanding of modernity insofar as they do not present major problems of interpretation. For in many ways they seem to fit within sociological expectations and can be interpreted within the framework of established theories of secularization. The point is that such religious manifestations are normal phenomena, examples of private religion which do not challenge – nor do they wish to – dominant political and social structures. Because such religious phenomena are, typically, rather apolitical, all they really show is that many people are interested in spiritual issues at the present time. In sum, it is correct to stress that the contemporary multiplicity of extant religious phenomena belie the claim that there has been a widespread loss of interest in religious meaning, even in apparently highly secular countries, and that innovative religious forms are gaining ground, often at the expense of traditional religions. But from a political perspective new religions are rarely very important.

The non-Western world

Given that one of the areas in the throes of an apparent religious revival, Eastern Europe, is a region where religion was, until the early 1990s, strongly controlled and reduced in importance by the state, it is perhaps unsurprising that once the state's restraints diminish it would assume a higher profile than before. However, does it mean that religion necessarily assumes a higher political profile simply because there are more openly religious people than before? Not necessarily: for example, the Russian Orthodox Church does not involve itself extensively in political controversies at the present time despite a popular shift to religion in Russia in the post-communist era. In other words, Russian society may now be highly religious at the level of individual belief, but this has not led to an institutionalized political role for the Orthodox Church. This may be because the Church has not found it easy to change its behaviour after an 80-year period when it was in thrall to the communist state. During communist domination, the

Russian Orthodox Church was compelled to withdraw to its core area of expertise: the spiritual realm.

Before the overthrow of communist governments, the countries of Eastern Europe were characterized by church-state relations where the latter dominated the former. Following the example of the Soviet Union, after World War II the new communist regimes made serious attempts to reduce drastically the social status and significance of religion. Such regimes were 'anti-religious polities', making serious attempts to throttle religion. No religious organizations had the right to be actively engaged with matters of public concern or to play a role in public life. Churches were to be confined to liturgical institutions alone, that is, their only permitted role was the holding of divine services. The point is that the communist regimes saw that it was impossible to get rid of religion completely so they begrudgingly allowed people to retain their religious beliefs – but only as a private concern. On the one hand, this constituted a kind of promise that the authorities would respect the privacy of people's religious faith and practice. On the other, it was normally no more than a camouflage for a policy of aggressive religious privatization.

Before the democratic revolutions of 1989–1990, church-state relations fell into two broad categories – 'accommodative' and 'confrontational'. Church and state were in confrontational mode when they argued over the premiss for their mutual relations and operated in the absence of a modus vivendi; neither side felt able to make serious compromises. In this situation, state hostility towards religion was overt and scarcely disguised. Consequently, churches would often be thrown into postures of defensive defiance. Czechoslovakia and Poland offer perhaps the best examples of prolonged confrontation between state and church. In Czechoslovakia, after a communist-led coup d'état of 1948, there was bitter confrontation between the state and the Catholic Church. In Poland, the authorities had to proceed with considerable caution against the Church because it enjoyed a great deal of popular support: over 90 per cent of Poles are Catholic.

The accommodative style, on the other hand, involved compromise on both sides; in other words, there were rules of the game to which each side adhered. One important factor on the part of the church was that religious officials would strive to avoid criticizing government policies in order to be left in peace. Another aspect was that the majority of priests and high-ranking church officials (with the exception of Poland and to a degree Hungary) consistently failed to confront the state on a variety of issues. Some religious officials actively collaborated with state security.

More frequently, however, state–church relations oscillated between confrontation and accommodation. For example, in East Germany they were confrontational from 1948 until 1971; after that there was more accommodation. In the USSR, the Russian Orthodox Church also experienced periods of both accommodation and confrontation. State policies of repression were apparent between 1917–1943, 1958–1964 and 1975–1985. They were interspersed with periods of relative church–state harmony.

Turning to the Third World, opinion surveys over time indicate that there is a high proportion of religious believers in such countries. It is sometimes argued that social upheaval and economic dislocation, connected to the processes of modernization, have stymied the development of secularization. In particular, the 1980s and 1990s were, for many people, a prolonged period of social, economic and political transition. The consequence, it is claimed, is that many Third World peoples are rediscovering the religious dimension to group identity and politics. There is, in other words, a contemporary 'return' to religion which may be the consequence of various developments, including: (1) inconclusive or unsatisfactory modernization; (2) disillusionment with secular nationalism; (3) problems of state legitimacy; (4) political oppression and incomplete national identity; (5) widespread socio-economic grievances; and (6) perceived erosion of traditional morality and values. It is the simultaneity of these crises that is said to provide an especially fertile milieu for the growth of religion with political goals.

Such factors no doubt provide an enabling environment for religion's political prominence in many Third World countries. Put another way, such unwelcome developments no doubt prod many people to look to religion to provide answers to existential angst. However, it could be argued that religion has often fulfilled such a role; it is highly unlikely that there is 'more' religion now than in the past. Why then do religious groups with political goals seem more common? Is it possible that they are simply more visible due to the global communications revolution? Put another way, there are not necessarily more of them, perhaps we can observe them, and their consequences, more easily than before.

It is important to understand that there were numerous historical examples of political religion in the Third World, especially during and after Western colonization. During colonization European rulers often sought to introduce secularism which, in many cases, led to a religious backlash with Hinduism, Buddhism and Islam, in various countries, all exhibiting periods of intense political activity. Before and after World War I (1914–1918), for example, religion was widely employed in the service of anti-colonial nationalism in Africa, Asia and the Middle East. For example, political Islam was the spearhead of anti-colonial activism in various parts of Africa, as in El Hadj Oumar's campaign against the French in West Africa. Later, for example, in India, Hindu appeals and symbolism popularized the nationalist message, as it did among Buddhists in Southeast Asia. The end of the colonial era was also marked by a political role for religion. For example, Pakistan was founded as a Muslim state in 1947, religiously and, to some extent, culturally distinct from Hindu-dominated India. In addition, Buddhism was of great political importance in Burma and Vietnam in the struggle for liberation from colonial rule. During the 1960s in Latin America, Christian democracy and Liberation Theology were also of widespread political significance in many regional countries. Political religion was also of great importance in Iran, Afghanistan and Nicaragua from the 1970s. What this all points to is that political religion in the Third World has a long history of opposition to unacceptably secular regimes; it is not *ab initio* in the contemporary period. It should be understood as a series of historical responses to attempts by the state to reduce religion's (political) influence.

In the aftermath of independence, modernizing politicians, often influenced by Western ideologies, filled the void left by colonial administrators. However, the modernization process promoted by nationalist leaders, such as Kwame Nkrumah in Ghana or Sekou Toure in Guinea, did not bring the degree of development they looked for. Instead, modernization, also involving secularization, resulted in the attempted transplantation of alien Western institutions, laws and procedures which collectively aimed to erode, undermine and eventually displace traditional, holistic religio-political systems. Because putative modernizers saw their countries as politically, socially and economically backward they believed that what was needed was to emulate the secular model of progress pursued so successfully by Western countries. Consequently, policies and programmes of modernization were pursued. However, over time, the credibility and legitimacy of both secular socialism and secular capitalism often became seriously undermined. This was because such ideologies widely failed to deliver on promises of economic and political development and national integration.

Poorly implemented modernization programmes proved incompatible with traditional religious practices, as growing numbers of people left rural areas for urban locales because of land and employment shortages. While the social, political and economic impact of displacement and urban migration is extensive and complex, it is highly likely that dislocations of large numbers of people from rural communities, and the reforming of personal relations in urban areas, opened the way to renegotiation of allegiances to traditional institutions. Where modernization was particularly aggressively pursued, for example in Iran, India, Thailand, Egypt, Algeria, and Brazil, religious backlashes occurred.

FIGURE 17.2 Ayatollah Khomeini

Ayatollah Khomeini speaking from a balcony of the Alavi School in Tehran during the country's revolution in February 1979. Courtesy IRNA Reuters, Getty Images.

Because of Islam's pivotal role, the overthrow of the Shah of Iran in 1979 was one of the most spectacular political upheavals of recent times. The outcome of the revolutionary process was a clerical, authoritarian regime. The Shah's regime was not a shaky monarchy but a powerful centralized autocratic state possessing a strong and feared security service (SAVAK) and an apparently loyal and cohesive officer corps. Unlike earlier revolutions in Muslim countries, such as Egypt, Iraq, Syria, and Libya, Iran's was not a secular, left-wing revolution from above, but one with massive popular support and participation. The forces which overthrew the Shah came from all urban social classes, different nationalities and ideologically varying political parties and movements, but an Islamic Republic was eventually declared. Shi'a religious leaders (*mujtahids*) organized in and by the Islamic Republican Party came to power, established an Islamic constitution and dominated the post-revolutionary institutions.

Iran's revolution was internationally significant in a number of ways. It was the first time since the French Revolution of 1789 in which the dominant ideology, forms of organization, leading personnel, and proclaimed goals were all religious in appearance and inspiration. The guide for the post-revolution Iranian state was the tenets of the Muslim holy book, the Qur'an, and the *sunna* (the teachings of the Prophet Muhammed and those of the twelve Imams). While economic and political factors played a major part in the growth of the anti-Shah movement, the leadership of that movement (the clerics) saw the revolution's goals primarily in terms of building an Islamic state in which Western materialism and political ideas would be rejected. Over time, this was to be of major importance in the context of Iran's generally poor international relations with the West.

The radicals within Iran's ruling post-revolution elite began to lose ground following the death of Ayatollah Khomeini, the revolution's charismatic leader, in June 1989, just months after the end of the bloody Iran–Iraq war (1980–1988). As it became clear that Iran's government was in dire need of Western investment, technology and aid to help build its revolution, the pragmatic state president Hashemi Rafsanjani and his political allies seemed to gain ascendancy. The lesson of this was that even a successful Islamic revolution cannot succeed in splendid isolation. Iranians, like people everywhere, hoped for improving living standards and were not content with increased Islamicization of state and society, which many perceived as little more than political and social repression behind a religious façade.

BOX 17.4 Iran's revolution

In summary, postcolonial governments often followed policies of nation building and expansion of state power, equating secularization with modernization. However, by undermining traditional value systems, often allocating opportunities in highly unequal ways, modernization produced in many ordinary people a deep sense of alienation, stimulating a search for an identity that would give life some purpose and meaning. Many believed they might deal with the unwelcome effects of modernization if they presented their claims for more of the 'national cake' as part of a group. Often the sense of collectivity was rooted in the epitome of traditional community religion. The result was a focus on religiosity, with far reaching implications for social integration and political society, which many perceived as little stability. This was not just a return to religion, but the mobilization of religious belief in pursuit of social, political and economic goals.

The Hindu nationalist Bharatiya Janata Party (BJP) is the most successful contemporary political party in India, the mainstay of various coalition governments from the mid-1990s. This was surprising to many observers as, during the 1960s and 1970s, Hindu nationalism was merely one of the diverse currents in the ebb and flow of Indian politics. However, by the late 1980s electoral support for the BJP was rising swiftly: between 1989 and 1991 its share tripled to 20 per cent. Many observers linked the rise of the BJP to India's economic turmoil during this time, with popular support for the BJP at least in part a manifestation of ordinary people's disquiet at unwelcome economic developments under the aegis of various Congress (I) governments.

By 1991, it had become the strongest official parliamentary opposition to the Congress (I) Party. Between 1990 and 1995 the BJP won power in the National Capital Territory of Delhi and in six of India's 25 states – four in the Hindi-speaking belt of north India and two on the west coast. Of the 119 BJP members in the 545-seat Lok Sabha (Parliament) in 1995, 106 came from these areas, while only eight of the 220 seats in the eastern and southern regions of India were held by the party. On the other hand, the fact that the BJP's share of the vote in the 1996 general election did not increase much above the 1991 figure, only to 23.5 per cent, suggests that there were definite limits on its appeal. Nearly a quarter of the popular vote was, nevertheless, enough to give it and its allies 188 seats, that is, more than one-third of the total on less than a quarter of the vote.

The 1996 result confirmed both the BJP's rise and a steady polarization of Indian society. The traditionally dominant Congress (I) Party (the party of Indira Gandhi and her son, Rajiv) lost seats heavily in the north, west, and south, although it managed to maintain its position in the east of the country, hanging on to 36 seats. The result was that the share of the vote for Congress (I) declined from 48 per cent in 1984 to just over 28 per cent in 1996. The fading of Congress (I) was hastened because of the failure of India's Muslims to do what they traditionally did: vote for the Party. In the 1995 round of state elections, most Muslims voted against both the BJP and Congress (I) – in favour of candidates or parties with secular credentials. This helps explain the rout of the ruling Congress (I) Party in 1996 and again in 1999: many Muslims identified the party with pro-Hindu sentiments, particularly because of the demolition of the mosque in Ayodhya in 1992 (see Chapter 2 on Hinduism).

However, this was not enough to prevent the BJP's relentless electoral progress. But, like Christian Fundamentalists in the USA or Islamists in Turkey, the BJP was not able to achieve power on its own. The BJP's chief difficulty lay in persuading those unimpressed by its nationalistic agenda that its political aims had a wider applicability in India's pluralist society. The BJP failed to stitch together a coalition government, with the result that the second largest party – Congress (I) – managed to put together a ruling coalition that survived into 1997.

The late 1990s saw the electoral dominance of the BJP: it dominated the political landscape of north and west India. In these regions, its communalistic programme, perceived by many Indian secular intellectuals as the expression of primordial sentiments indicative of the underdeveloped nature of the people concerned, was nevertheless highly appealing to millions of Indians. On the other hand, the BJP found the south and west of the country a tougher nut to crack. This is because it was widely regarded in these regions as a northern-dominated party, intent on imposing its own narrow version of the Hindu tradition at the expense of alternative regional traditions. The result was that the BJP and its allies only managed to acquire a handful of seats in the south and east in elections in the late 1990s. The geographical unevenness of the Hindu nationalist support reflected the plural character of the Indian political scene. For example, many Muslims and Christians found it hard to support the BJP because of its uncompromising message of Hindu domination. Patchy electoral appeal for the BJP was made clear in May 2004, when it lost power to a resurgent Congress (I) Party.

BOX 17.5 The Bharatiya Janata Party (BJP)

A consequence has been that most states in the Third World have sought to prevent, or at the least make it very difficult for, political religion to organize. In most Muslim countries, for example, Islamist parties are either proscribed or, at least, infiltrated by state security services. Algeria's Islamic Salvation Front (FIS), the Islamic Tendency Movement of Tunisia, Hamas and Islamic Jihad in Palestine, the Islamic Party of Kenya, and Tanzania's Balukta were all banned in the 1990s. Others, including the Partai Persatuan Pembangunan of Indonesia, the Parti Islam Se Malaysia and Egypt's Muslim Brothers, were controlled or infiltrated by the state. On the rare occasions when Islamist parties were allowed openly to seek electoral support they were often reasonably successful. Examples include the FIS's electoral victories in 1990–1991 and that of Turkey's Welfare Party (Refah Partisi). The latter won the largest share of the vote (21 per cent) of any party in the 1995 election. Later, in 1996, Refah achieved power in coalition with a rightwing secular party, the True Path. Parties like the FIS and Refah are electorally popular because they offer the disaffected, the alienated and the povertystricken a vehicle to pursue beneficial change.

On the other hand, in India, there is strong electoral support for Hindu nationalist parties – and not only from the poor and marginalized. Shiv Sena jointly rules Mumbai and Maharashtra state with the Bharatiya Janata Party (BJP). Nationally, the BJP has emerged as the largest political party in recent years, eclipsing the country's traditionally dominant Congress (I) Party. In Buddhist Thailand, on the other hand, a Buddhist reformist party, Santi Asoke, had some electoral success in the early 1990s. The point is that parties like Shiv Sena, the BJP and Santi Asoke all have a wide appeal as viable alternatives to ruling parties characterized as both corrupt and inefficient. In sum, when people lose faith in the transformatory abilities of secular politicians, religion often appears a viable alternative for the pursuit of beneficial change. It has widely re-emerged into the public arena as a mobilizing, normative force.

Conclusion

Globally, the recent political impact of religion falls into two, not necessarily mutually exclusive, categories. First, if the mass of people are not especially religious, as in many Western countries, religious actors seek a renewed public role believing that society has taken a wrong turn and, as a result, requires an injection of religious values to put it back into equilibrium. In other words, religion will try to deprivatize itself, so that it has a voice in contemporary debates about social and political direction, aiming to be a significant factor in socio-political deliberations. Religious leaders seek support from ordinary people by addressing certain crucial issues, such as the perceived decline in public and private morality and the insecurities of life, the result of an undependable market where, it is argued, greed and luck appear as effective as work and rational choice. In sum, religion's return to the public sphere is moulded by a range of factors, including the proportion of religious believers in society and the extent to which religious organizations perceive a decline in public standards of morality and compassion.

In many Third World societies, on the other hand, most people are already religious believers. Attempts by political leaders to pursue modernization led religious traditions to respond. Following widespread disappointment at the outcomes of modernizing policies, religion serves to focus and co-ordinate opposition, especially, but not exclusively, that of the poor and ethnic minorities. In the Third World religion is often well placed to benefit from a societal backlash against the perceived malign effects of modernization.

And what of the future? If the issues and concerns that have helped stimulate a return to religion continue (socio-political and economic upheavals, patchy modernization, increasing encroachment of the state upon religion's terrain) – and there is no reason to suppose they will not – it seems highly likely that religion's political role will continue to be an important one in many parts of the world. This will partly reflect the onward march of secularization – which will continue in many countries and regions, perhaps linked to the spread of globalization – which will be fought against by religious professionals and followers, albeit with varying degrees of success.

Summary

- Religions in the more secularized West are 'deprivatizing' and attempting to influence the political process and issues of moral conscience.

- There is widespread rejection, especially outside the West, of the secular ideals which still dominate most national policies.

■ Religions appear as champions of alternative confessional options and values, challenging both the legitimacy and autonomy of the main secular spheres: the state, political organization and the market economy.

Key terms

Bharatiya Janata Party India's leading religious-nationalist party. By 1991, it had become the strongest official parliamentary opposition to the Congress.

Charismatic Christianity A widespread non-denominational tendency offering devotees spiritual excitement, with belief in divinely inspired gifts of speaking in tongues (glossolalia), healing and prophecy.

Islamic Salvation Front During the late 1980s and early 1990s, the Islamic Salvation Front was a popular political party in Algeria.

Islamicization This occurs when a political party or the state wishes to introduce or impose an array of values in society which are ostensibly linked to what are described as Islamic values.

New Christian Right The voice of theologically conservative American Christians, united by a shared 'born-again' experience.

Qur'an The holy book of Islam.

Refah Partisi (Welfare Party) Turkey's banned Islamic party.

Santi Asoke A Buddhist reformist party in Thailand.

secularization When the pursuit of politics takes place irrespective of religious interests. The end result is a secular society.

sunna The traditions of the Prophet Muhammad, comprising what he said, did and approved of.

Further reading

Peter Berger (ed.): *The Desecularization of the World. Resurgent Religion and World Politics* (Washington, DC: Ethics and Public Policy Center, 1999). This volume challenges the belief that the world is increasingly secular, showing that while modernization does have secularizing effects, it also provokes a reaction that more often strengthens religion.

Peter Beyer: *Religions in Global Society* (Abingdon, Oxon: Routledge, 2006). Beyer presents a way of understanding religion in a contemporary global society – by analysing it as a dimension of the historical process of globalization. Introducing theories of globalization and showing how they can be applied to world religions, Beyer reveals the nature of the contested category of 'religion': what it means, what it includes and what it implies in the world today. Written with exceptional clarity and illustrated with lively and diverse examples ranging from Islam and Hinduism to African traditional religions and New Age spirituality, this is a fascinating overview of how religion has developed in a globalized society. It is recommended reading for students taking courses on sociology of religion, religion and globalization, and religion and modernity.

S. Bruce: *Politics and Religion* (New York: Polity, 2003). Islamic fundamentalists wreck the financial heart of New York; Hindus destroy a mosque at Ayodhya; Orthodox Jews battle Palestinians for possession of holy sites; in Egypt, Israel and India political leaders are murdered by religious zealots. In many parts of the world, religion combines with ethnic and national conflict to stimulate political militancy. The collapse of Communism and the failure of Western secular models of development have stimulated the revival of religiously inspired nationalisms. Even in stable affluent democracies, religion is a powerful influence on political preferences. It affects lifestyle concerns such as abortion, gender roles and gay rights. It influences economic attitudes. It shapes the alignments of political parties. Believers try to influence governments and, although most governments in principle tolerate religious diversity, many still attempt to regulate religious behaviour, particularly that of New Religious Movements. Steve Bruce draws on material from all over the world and from all religious traditions to explore the complex links between religion and politics.

Jose Casanova: *Public Religions in the Modern World* (Chicago, IL and London: University of Chicago Press, 1994). In this seminal text, Casanova makes the case that religious 'deprivatization' is a key development marking the political 'return' of religion to the public realm in countries around the world.

Jeffrey Haynes: *An Introduction to International Relations and Religion* (Harlow: Longman, 2007). The book starts with a close reading of the many theoretical and analytical concepts – notably Huntington and the clash of civilizations – that have grown up around this area and then concludes with a summary of the issues under discussion and attempts to put into context what it means to live in a world that is increasingly shaped by a whole host of diverse religious groups.

Mark Juergensmeyer (ed.): *Religion in Global Civil Society* (Oxford: Oxford University Press, 2005). The essays in this volume explore the difficulties and possibilities of a diversity of religious groups occupying the same civil society.

Rolin Mainuddin (ed.): *Religion and Politics in the Developing World: Explosive Interactions* (Aldershot: Ashgate, 2002). This book examines a number of key religio-political interactions in the developing world.

Pippa Norris and Ronald Ingelhart: *Sacred and Secular: Religion and Politics Worldwide* (Cambridge: Cambridge University Press, 2004). This book develops a theory of secularization and existential security and compares it against survey evidence from almost 80 societies worldwide.

David Westerlund (ed.): *Questioning the Secular State: The Worldwide Resurgence of Religion in Politics* (London: Hurst, 1996). Westerlund examines the question of a global religious resurgence. While the book is now rather dated, it is still useful as a global survey.

Chapter 18

Religion and violence

Charles Selengut

Introduction

Religion is often thought to be the antithesis of violence and a force for peace and reconciliation. The ethical teachings of the world's religions condemn violence and the Hebrew Bible, the Christian Gospels and the Qur'an all talk about the life of faith as a way of love, kindness and peace. In Christianity, Jesus counsels turning the other cheek and, suffering on the cross, he seeks forgiveness for his oppressors. Islam venerates the prophet Muhammad as a messenger of peace and the Qur'an describes the harmoniousness of Islamic society and the importance of hospitality and welcoming the stranger with warmth and dignity. The Hebrew Bible talks about world peace when all peoples will live together in harmony and 'nation will not take up sword against nation, nor will they train for war any more' (Isaiah 2:4). In many places all over the world, religion has been a force for equality and morality and has championed the rights of minority peoples, the disadvantaged and the world's poor. And religion has been a voice sensitizing us to the excesses of technology and inequality.

We know, however, that despite being a force for charity and ethical sensitivity, religion also encourages and promotes war and violent confrontation all over the globe. The fervently faithful, acting in the name of religion, have in the last decades murdered hundreds of thousands of people, and groups of militants in various religious communities are organized into terrorist networks whose avowed goal is to destroy all those who oppose their religious aims. In the Middle East, toward the close of the of the twentieth century, militant believers among Jews and Muslims assassinated their political leaders, President Anwar Sadat of Egypt and Prime Minister Yitzhak Rabin of Israel, because these leaders were willing to make religious compromises between Islamic and Jewish claims to what the believers on both sides considered sacred land. On 11 September 2001, the Pentagon in Washington DC and the World Trade Center in New York City were attacked by the militant Islamic al-Qaeda network, thousands were killed and the World Trade Center towers completely destroyed. Religious violence in the Middle East has become particularly incendiary after the American invasion of Iraq and the removal of Saddam Hussein and his regime, with many Islamic militant groups seeing the invasion as a Western Christian incursion into Muslim lands. The Iraq War and the removal of the Hussein dictatorial regime brought to the fore the sectarian religious conflicts within Islam and resulted in a religious civil war between Sunni and Shi'ite Muslims with bombings, suicide attacks and murders taking place all over the country in the name of religious faith.

In Europe, Orthodox Christian Serbs and Muslims have been in violent confrontation for centuries and tens of thousands on both sides have been forcibly

FIGURE 18.1
World Trade Center

Smoke rises from the site of the World Trade Center terrorist attack in New York City. Rescue and recovery work continues but hopes of finding survivors are fading. Courtesy Getty Images.

removed from places their people had lived for centuries in campaigns of ethnic and religious cleansing to ensure that a particular town or area would be populated solely by members of one group. Perhaps the most dramatic violence among these groups occurred in Chechnya where a school was attacked and dozens of children and adults were killed in the confrontation. On the continent of Africa, religious battles between the Muslim and Christian communities have taken place in many countries with particularly violent encounters in Nigeria. Between Hindu India and Muslim Pakistan, two nations with nuclear capacity, continued tensions over the area of Kashmir have resulted in violent confrontations as the religious faithful on both sides claim religious rights to the territory. In the United States as well, a nation of great religious diversity, religious violence has emerged as Christian fundamentalist extremists have attacked abortion facilities and murdered physicians working in these clinics. Some extreme American Christian militant groups, known as Christian Identity, have proclaimed America an exclusively white Christian nation and advocated the expulsion and killing of non-white minorities and non-Christian communities.

The problem of religious violence has greatly increased in the current era of globalization. Religion is no longer limited to a specific geographical location where most if not all people grew up in the same religion and shared the same religious values, sentiments and rituals which were considered normal and taken for granted. In our global world, people of differing and conflicting religious faiths and lifestyles live together in the same towns, cities and nations, creating communities of great variety and excitement, but also making conditions for conflict and strife. Religious beliefs are no longer taken for granted and what is normal, desirable and considered divine law in one community can be viewed as immoral and profane in another community. This situation has enormously expanded the possibilities for religious conflict with the result that people living in the same society find themselves in conflict over the basic issues of social, political and economic life. Issues of gender equality, family and marital life, freedom of the media, holiday rituals, even clothing have become contentious issues in many parts of the world.

In this chapter we will consider why religion and violence are intertwined in so many conflicts. What is it about religion that results in violent confrontation? How do religions, which call for peace and love, condone murder, suicide and destruction? Why is religious violence spreading in the contemporary world and why is there increasing violence among members of the same religion? And, finally, we will consider whether what is often referred to as *religious* violence is really 'religious' or whether religion is a way of legitimating violence in pursuit of secular, political, sociological or economic goals.

Defining religious violence

Defining violence, particularly religious violence, is a complex issue. The conventional definition tends to treat violence as observable physical injury. The problem with this definition is that it ignores the various forms of non-physical, psychic violence in which religious beliefs, holy personages, and sacred places are desecrated or destroyed in religious battles. Religious violence, however, can entail physical as well as psychological and symbolic injury. Thus our approach to religious violence includes any hostile activity leading to (1) physical injury or death; (2) self-mortification and religious suicide; (3) psychological injury; and (4) symbolic violence causing the desecration or profanation of sacred sites and holy places. This is a relativistic approach to religious violence in which no judgment is made about the objective or realistic events that take place. Religious violence is a category and event defined by a particular community and its religious culture. The experience of psychic violence will depend on the religious sensitivities, beliefs, and values of a religious community. Destroying imagines of Hindu deities in a South Indian temple would be, in this definition, an act of desecration, while some monotheistic fundamentalists might claim the destruction of an image of a sacred deity is no violation of religion. Desecration of a book of sacred scripture, insulting a religious saint or prophet or treating a religious shrine in a profane and disrespectful fashion would constitute religious violence.

No one interpretive scheme can fully explain the many forms of religious war, terrorism, and violent conflict. Such activity is frequently motivated by religious mandate and religious law, but what passes for religious violence may also be an attempt on the part of one community to utilize religious sentiment in order to gain political or economic advantage, to punish a historical rival, or to maintain power over a subordinate group. Violence against women and minorities and certain types of religious masochism, like extreme fasting, circumcision or bloodletting may be justified by religious texts, but sometimes it is best understood as serving the social and psychological needs of the individual and collectivity. Again, such violence may not ultimately be 'religious' in nature, but rather be the result of historical and civilizational loyalty. Nonetheless, all types of religious violence are motivated and driven by beliefs and faith in ultimate truth and divine reward and the killings and mayhem are fuelled by a particular interpretation of religious history and faith even if the immediate goals are nationalist aspirations or economic empowerment. Many Western political analysts and journalists refuse to recognize the enduring power of religion and, therefore, fail to appreciate the essential religious motivation at the heart of religious terror and violence. At the core of all religious violence is the continuing and sacred conviction that religious warriors are God's willing and faithful servants ready to die. Still, while all religions have beliefs legitimating violence, and while larger numbers are willing to support violence financially and morally, the number of the faithful who actually engage in violence is very small.

The unique relationship between religion and violence

Why is it that religion is so often involved in violent conflict and why is it that religion is used to justify war and violence? The answer lies in the unique nature of religious faith, organization, and leadership. Religious faith is different than other commitments and the rules and directives of religion are understood by the faithful to be entirely outside ordinary social rules and interactions. Religious faith, rules and commitment, as the French sociologist Emile Durkheim explains, are based upon sacred and ultimate truths and are, consequently, viewed by the faithful as absolutely moral, desirable, and good. For the faithful, religious mandates are self-legitimating; they are true and proper rules, not because they can be proven to be so by philosophers, or because they have social benefits, but rather because they emanate from a divine source.

Put simply, religion operates with a different logic and moral order and what is 'rational' and ethical in fervently religious communities may be seen as irrational or without a logical basis among secularized well-educated Westerners. For example, while secularized Americans or Europeans may applaud the significant charitable work and social services performed by the Hamas community in the Middle East, they do not realize that secular motivation has virtually nothing to do with religious charity. The faithful act charitably because their sacred tradition so demands, not because it is necessarily politically correct or socially utilitarian. To the shock and disappointment of many secularized people, that same Hamas community calls for holy war, where persecuting sinners and unbelievers and killing heretics is, similarly, a religious obligation. The critical motivation, then, for the fervently faithful is not utilitarian ethics, secular logic, or government legalities but the requirement to conform to the demands of religious law, whether or not it makes sense to those outside the faith community. The divine imperatives of the religious tradition, including violence, are not open to question by non-believers, and secular legalities can be breached if they conflict with religious truth. I recall a fervent Christian anti-abortion guest speaker, otherwise a gentle and reserved person, telling my religion class that he contributed to and supported violence against abortion doctors and workers. My middle class, suburban students were shocked and pressed him as to the morality of killing. He calmly replied, 'I have talked to my pastor and this is what God wants us to do. We are protecting the unborn.' Mark Juergensmeyer similarly writes of anti-abortion radicals who support violence – some of whom had been actually convicted of murder – telling him that, while they found their activities problematic and burdensome, they had no choice, since it was their religious duty to respond with violence to abortion activity.

Religious violence is also fostered by promises of rewards in an afterlife free of the disappointment and pain of everyday life. The violent actions carried out by the faithful may be considered criminal, entail long prison terms, and even result in one's own death, but the promise of eternal life, which only religion can provide, can break all legal and cultural restraints against crime and violence. Nasra Hassan, a social worker in the Palestinian territories, tells of a conversation with a Palestinian Muslim youth who volunteered and was chosen to be a suicide bomber. 'S', as the prospective bomber was referred to in the report, explained that it was an honour to be chosen from among many volunteers and that this was the way he could be most certain of a perfect afterlife: 'by pressing the detonator, you can immediately open the door to paradise – it is the shortest path to heaven', where one will enjoy an eternity of spiritual and sexual bliss. All religions have versions of an eternal life for their religious martyrs who die a sacrificial death on behalf of the tradition. In Judaism, such martyrs are called *kedoshim*, the 'holy ones' who verify the truth of the faith by their willingness to die for it. Christianity, during its years as a minority and despised religious community in the Roman empire, actually encouraged religious suicide to prove the power and veracity of the Christian faith to the Roman authorities. In Islam, Hinduism, and Buddhism, as well, strong traditions of self-mortification and religious suicide continue. These otherworldly, supernatural rewards for violence and religiously motivated suicide in the pursuit of spiritual goals should not be dismissed, even in a scientific, secular age, for they can never be totally disproved to a believer's satisfaction; they exist in a world that is beyond the scientific and the rational. Rewards in the afterlife continue to be an inspiration and a motivation for millions of traditional believers all over the globe.

All religion is ultimately about infusing the transitory and sometimes baffling experiences of human life with meaning and justification. Social scientists explain that a primary function of religious institutions is to provide social order and normative structure to human existence, protecting society from chaos and assuring the individual that life, with both its blessings and disappointments, has ultimate meaning and value. Religious systems provide a theodicy, an explanation of human suffering which promises an ultimate reward for those who have followed religious teachings and have been faithful and obedient in the course of their lives. These religious frameworks are so essential to believers that, in the hands of charismatic religious leaders, an appeal to faith can be used to demand violent action by committed followers. The faithful, in these instances, are faced with a terrifying logic: if you are a true believer and wish to remain a part of the community and be assured of heavenly reward, you must concur with the injunction to wage violence against the religion's enemies. It is difficult – frequently impossible – to refuse this religious 'logic' in which violence is justified as an essential element of religious life. The cost of refusal is steep, for it means that one is no longer a part of the sacred community with its promises of a wonderful afterlife to which one has dedicated oneself. Many militant religions put the matter starkly when it comes to calling for violent action: 'You are with us or against us'. In this sense, religion is eminently suited to exercise psychic, if not physical, coercion on members and followers.

The desire to remain connected to the religious community, to continue in the warmth of its fellowship, and to submit to the security of its particular theological understandings, results in acceptance of, if not outright participation in, the violent actions carried out on behalf of the group. The actual violence in any group is usually carried out by small cadres of zealots, as is the case with American militia groups or with Islamic or Jewish militants. However, the larger group supports such movements with financial help, safe houses, transportation, and respectability in the wider religious community. This is the case in the Middle East conflict, in the Catholic–Protestant conflict in Northern Ireland and in the Hindu–Muslim clashes over Kashmir, where powerful and respectable members of these communities, on both sides of the divide, aid, abet, and provide capital for the violent outbursts.

Hence, while it is not necessarily the case that religion is involved in violence, nevertheless, its ability to sacralize human activity and its great power to infuse life with meaning, order, and security, can lead the faithful to engage in what it sees as 'sacred terror' in defense of God and religious truth.

Scriptural imperatives and holy war

The earliest and still most elemental call for religious violence is found in sacred writings, which urge the faithful to wage war in an attempt to destroy those who are believed to be the enemies of God and divine truth. This holy war perspective on religious violence highlights, as perhaps no other one does, the close affinity between religion and violence found in many of the world's great religions. It is not easy for religious leaders, theologians, and ordinary believers to admit that, at the centre of the most sublime religious texts, there is the obligation to wage war and to maim others in the service of God. The scriptures and sacred traditions of the world's religions prescribe violence.

From a holy war perspective, religious violence is not an aberration or tangential to the religious life, but at its very core. This perspective insists that religious violence is not a cover-up for economic or cultural disputes or group competition and envy but a spiritual and theological essence of religious organizations. What this perspective teaches is that religious conflict and violent encounters are, above all, sacred struggles on behalf of religious truth and divine revelation. Holy wars are encounters between good and evil, between truth and falsehood, between the children of God and the offspring of Satan. In this encounter, pious believers are not free agents permitted to choose between violence and non-violence, but are drafted into God's infantry to fight the Lord's battles and to proclaim his message throughout the world. This is, of course, not a mantle easily borne. The burden is heavy and the dangers great, but if believers are to be consistent and faithful to their God, they must answer the call to arms and use every means possible, including murder, assassination, bombings, arson, and collective punishment, to fulfill God's mandate for war. Holy war is a serious business and the protagonists are aware of the stakes involved. There is a kind of brutal honesty in holy war rhetoric and religious warriors do not deny the death, suffering, and destruction that their violence will bring.

The most helpful way to understand holy war is to appreciate how the violent faithful conceive, interpret, and explain their behavior. Firstly, through *theological reinterpretation*, these religious battles, involving violence and killing, are redefined as supernatural undertakings which cannot be explained through human logic and secular reasoning. The violence in holy war is not conventional human violence, where individuals or groups contend with one another for secular goals such as money, power, or status; they are sacred events. Indeed, they are, understood from this theological perspective, not violence at all. It may look like violence, but these are struggles to bring truth and redemption, to inspire truth and faith for which even the fallen enemies will eventually be grateful. Hence, religious battles are never defined in sacred texts as events of violence. Rather, they are battles for justice. The God of the Hebrew Bible, for example, though portrayed as a warrior God demanding warring action from his people, is above all a God of mercy and justice who uses battle to create a peaceful and just world. In the case of Islamic holy wars, similarly, the religious conflict and the violence and killing that follows are carried on in the name of Allah and are meant to instruct and inform those who dwell in idolatry and ignorance. The violence against 'infidels' is actually a call to those living in sin and ignorance to acknowledge the superiority and truth of monotheism.

Hence, for example, for the religious community engaged in religious battles, violence is not a challenge to the Golden Rule, 'love thy neighbor as thyself' or of the commandment, 'thou shalt not murder', for they are situational moments of divine–human co-operation in the furtherance of the divine plan for justice and human redemption. In religious thinking, holy wars are manifestations of what Peter Berger (1967) refers to as 'cosmization' (activities that occur in the ordinary routine world of human existence, but are simultaneously enacted in a supernatural realm, the significance of which transcends all human understanding). Holy wars, as terrifying and violent as they may be, are among the most profound experiences of religious awe and divinity, for they link the religious warrior with God and the divine mysteries of the universe.

Western religions have a particularly strong Holy War tradition which has its basis the biblical narratives of the Hebrew Bible, which tell of God's covenant with Israel. God promises the land of Israel to the Israelites as an eternal possession and commands them and their leaders and prophets to wage war against the indigenous inhabitants of the land (i.e. Canaan). God tells the Israelites to annihilate all the inhabitants and destroy all the Canaanite cities, leaving no trace of their civilization. Because the Canaanites were understood to be evil and idolatrous, they had to be removed from the Holy Land:

> But from the cities of these peoples that Hashem your God, gives you as an inheritance, you shall not allow any person to live. Rather you shall utterly destroy

them; the Hittite, the Amorite, the Perizzite, the Hivvite, and the Jebusite, as
Hashem your God has commanded you, so they will not teach you to act according
to their abominations that they performed for their gods, so that you will sin to
Hashem your God.

(Deuteronomy 20: 16–18)

The wars went on for generations and the Book of Joshua describes in great detail
the various battles for the conquest of the land of Canaan and the necessary killing and
obligatory nature of extermination decreed by God as a way to root out the evil and
idolatrous culture of the local peoples. Israel's periodic loss of will and lapses into mercy
for the indigenous population are derided by God and Joshua and are seen as only leading
to greater and more pernicious evil. Total destruction, as in the case of the Canaanite cities
of Ai and Jericho, is applauded and shown to be a true sign of religious fidelity, while
mercy for the Canaanites, occasionally shown, is derided as moral weakness and infidelity
to the Lord. The Bible records that residents of entire cities were to be killed, leaving no
person alive. After the final destruction of the prominent city of Ai, special sacrifices were
brought on behalf of the community to Hashem and the entire Torah, the extant
scriptures and traditions, was read in reverent and joyous celebration. The destruction
of the city of Ai is a milestone in the holy war quest of the Holy Land.

All who fell on that day, both men and women, were twelve thousand, all the
people of Ai. Joshua did not withdraw his hand that he had stretched out with the
spear until he had destroyed all the inhabitants of Ai. Only the animals and booty
of that city Israel took as spoils for themselves, according to the word of Hashem,
which he had commanded Joshua. Joshua burned Ai and made it a wasteland until
this day.

(Joshua 8:25–29)

These narratives describe the essential biblical understanding of holy war, namely, war
ordained by God to conquer or restore Jewish sovereignty to the land of Israel, which
has been covenantally promised by God to the Jewish people. This original motivation
for holy war has been enshrined in Jewish history and jurisprudence as *milchemet mitzvah*,
an obligatory war, and has come to mean that whenever feasible, a religious war must
be fought for the maintenance of Jewish sovereignty over the land of Israel. In the course
of Jewish history other categories of holy war evolved, including holy wars of defense
and religious wars fought in honor of religious teachings, referred to in Jewish theology
as wars for the 'sanctification of God's name', *kiddush Hashem* wars. However, all these
later versions of holy war are based upon the original Biblical formulation for the conquest
of the Holy Land in ancient Israel.

The Christian approach to holy war is based, in large measure, on earlier biblical
traditions and, although Christian theology has preferred the term 'just war', the just war
doctrine has, in earlier periods, functioned effectively as holy war doctrine. The Christian
understanding argues that war and violence are justified to defend threats to Christian
religion and to punish heretics. 'The enemies of the church', wrote the authoritative

Christian jurist Gratian, 'are to be coerced even by war'. Although it can be argued that Christianity has its roots in pacifism and should be theologically opposed to violence (as it is in some Christian traditions, such as Quakerism), it could be argued that only as long as Christianity was a sectarian and minority religion, could it hold on to its pacifist sensibilities. When Christianity became identified with the Roman state and involved in politics and statecraft, it was forced to defend its doctrines and articulate a holy war doctrine to justify violence in the name of religion.

Christianity as a world religion had to protect its doctrines from theological contamination, and the use of war and violence was understood as a way of preserving the genuine and authentic Christian faith. As a universalistic and therefore exclusivist faith, it claimed to offer the sole possibility of salvation for humanity. Consequently, all other religions were viewed as false and, therefore, as dangerous to the spiritual well-being of the faithful. Enemies of Christianity came to mean, over the course of Christian history, not only those who represented an alien religious threat to the faith, but also sectarians and heretics who rejected conventional and official Christian orthodoxy. The underlying idea in justifying Christian violence was that the church had the sacred obligation and divine mandate to oust evil and champion the true word of God and, in this way, continue as 'God's obedient and faithful servant'. The various wars, persecutions, and inquisitions throughout Christian history need to be viewed in the context of the church's self-understood obligation to defend 'correct faith' against the dangers of heresy and alien faith.

The Crusades, while surely influenced by a variety of economic factors, were essentially holy wars for Christianity to maintain theological and social control and to stop alien religions and heretical sects from gaining power, economic influence and converts. On the way to conquer the Holy Land from the Muslims by force of arms, the crusaders destroyed dozens of Jewish communities and killed thousands because the Jews would not accept the Christian faith. Jews had to be killed in this religious campaign because their very existence challenged the sole truth espoused by the Christian church. The Jews, in the words of the traditional liturgy, were 'perfidious' and were seen by the masses as responsible for the Christian saviour's death. Their very existence amidst Christendom was seen as a challenge and threat to Christian faith and intermittent violence pursued them throughout the medieval and early modern periods of Christian history. Muslims were, likewise, seen as a threat to the Christian faithful and violence against them was, therefore, religiously justified. Christian–Muslim wars were frequently fought over territory, but an underlying motivation, as historians have shown, was the religious goal to remove their alien spiritual presence from Christian lands.

Islam's approach to holy war can be traced to the pre-Islamic polytheistic religious culture of Arabia. In the view of Islam, Arabian society at that time was living in an age of *jahiliyya* (an age of ignorance and a culture bereft of ethics and morality). It was a time of indiscriminate violence and immorality, an age of barbarism where no person was safe. This state of *jahiliyya* was encouraged by the prevalent pre-Islamic religious cults. The message of the Qur'an constituted a call by Allah to reject such practices and immorality and to establish an ethical and moral order, a faith community (*ummah*) in accordance with the divine will as delineated in the Qur'an. This meant that considerable effort and struggle (*jihad*) would have to be expended to transform a pre-Islamic society living in *jahiliyya* into an Islamic state governed by laws and authority which emanated from Allah. Practically, this meant that the struggle or *jihad* fought on behalf of Allah might have to involve violent battles in order to destroy the culture of *jahiliyya* and achieve the goals and society ordained in the Qur'an. *Jihad* could involve political or ideological battles, but *jihad* also could be a holy war resulting in death and destruction in order to obliterate an immoral social and political order and replace it with a Muslim community governed by divine law, *sharia*, as interpreted by Muslim clerics.

The Qur'anic mandate to establish a global Muslim *ummah* has led Islam to divide the world between the lands and states under Muslim control, referred to in Muslim jurisprudence as *Dar al-Islam*, the domain of Islam, and those lands and territories not under Muslim jurisdiction, called *Dar al-Harb*, the domain or abode of war. The faithful Muslim's duty is to engage in religious struggle, *jihad*, to transform non-Muslim lands, the *Dar al-Harb*, into *Dar al-Islam* lands, governed by Muslim law. The goal of *jihad* is not to force individual conversions, but to bring about the transformation, by force and violence if necessary, of non-Muslim areas into Muslim-controlled states, whereby they become part of the Islamic world, the *Dar al-Islam*. Islam from its earliest periods permitted monotheistic religions like Christianity and Judaism to maintain their religious institutional life within Muslim societies, but these communities, known as *dhimmi* communities, while permitted religious and economic rights, were expected to conform to the basics of Islamic morality and law. Islamic teachings emphasized that once a territory was inhabited by Muslims and governed by Islamic law, it was the duty of faithful Muslims to maintain control over these lands which are seen as Islamic lands in perpetuity. Holy war could be fought to main control if these lands were taken over by non-Muslims.

These classical traditions are not merely theological injunctions in the past, but rather they are, to some of the fervently faithful, religious imperatives which are to be carried out in contemporary times. Perhaps the most powerful current religious conflict invoking war, murder, suicide and extreme suffering is the Middle Eastern conflict between Jews and Muslims over the Holy Land. Both religious communities are convinced of their sole rights to the Holy Land and can find proof for this in their scriptures. Religious Zionist Jews appeal to the Torah and consider themselves to be God's chosen people to whom God has given the land of Israel in perpetuity. Palestinians and many within Islam, however, view the State of Israel as usurping Muslim lands, sanctified by Muslim occupancy and sacred history. Indeed, both Jews and Muslims can find very powerful religious texts exhorting them and demanding a holy war. Hence, while some see the Israeli–Palestinian conflict as a political struggle over land and resources, for many of those involved sacred truth and divine promises lie at the heart of the conflict. As such, they are not matters easily compromised.

Although most Christians strongly disagree and distance themselves from violence, radical Christian anti-abortion opponents consider the bombing of abortion clinics and the planned murder of abortion providers to be a religious obligation for faithful

Christians. For them, mere protest and political action are an avoidance of the Christian's responsibility to create a Christian society faithful to the gospel. These Christians are members and followers of an informal confederation of ministers, churches, and anti-abortion groups, some of which are committed to a 'reconstructionist theology', which teaches that it is a Christian's duty to transform secular materialistic society into a Christian theocracy that will eventually be able to properly welcome Jesus Christ when he returns in triumph. That is to say, reconstructionism teaches a postmillennial view of history, believing that Jesus will return to earth only after Christians have reconstructed society to make it conform to the social and political morals and standards compatible with Christ's teachings.

The murder of abortion providers and the destruction of abortion clinics are all part of a self-understood holy war which Christians are fighting to create a Christian society. In the United States, Paul Hill, a former Presbyterian minister who shot and killed an abortion doctor and his escort in 1992 in Pensacola, Florida, was executed for the killings and spoke shortly after the killings of 'the inner joy and peace that has flooded my soul since I have cast off the state's tyranny'. Hill, who willingly surrendered to police after his double murder, explained that the happiness and contentment he experienced on death row was the result of his willingness to kill in the name of God and his willingness to sacrifice his life in obedience to what he saw as God's commandment to engage in

FIGURE 18.2 Paul Hill protest

Anti-abortion protesters picket outside Florida State Prison where former Presbyterian minister Paul Hill was executed 3 September, 2003 near Raiford, Florida. Hill was convicted in the shotgun murder of Dr. John Britton, an abortion doctor, and his volunteer bodyguard, James Barrett, outside a Pensacola clinic in 1994. Courtesy Getty Images.

violence against enemies of God. Christian anti-abortion killers take their theological justification from their reading of the Bible which they see as calling for self-sacrifice when the society violates religious law.

Religious martyrdom

The apotheosis of the religious obligation to commit violence, to the point of self-annihilation, is seen in the phenomenon of religious martyrdom. The term 'martyr' was first used in connection with the early Christians in the Roman Empire who, at the threat and verdict of death, would proudly announce their Christian faith to Roman officials. The early Christian martyrs would deliberately rush forward in the presence of Roman governors and state officials announcing their fidelity to the new Christian faith (and conversely demonstrating their disloyalty to the official Roman cult) which resulted in these early Christians being beaten, tortured, and killed. The word 'martyr', from the Greek meaning 'witness', reflects the early Christian understanding of it as a witness to the truth of their religion. The term has now been extended from its original use in early Christianity and is now used to refer to all who offer their life and well-being for a cause, particularly a religious cause.

Martyrdom asserts that genuine religious commitment is ultimately about honouring and glorifying God and religious truth and not about self-preservation. An early Christian leader in Asia Minor exhorted his followers, 'Desire not to die in bed, in miscarriages, or in soft fevers, but in martyrdoms, to glorify Him who suffered for you'. The Jewish rabbis speak of *kavod hatorah*, maintaining the honour of God's teachings, as a reason to offer one's life. Life is precious, teaches the Talmud, but at a certain point it is to be surrendered for the higher value of transcendental truth. Likewise, although Islam teaches that life is to be greatly valued and enjoyed, the call to martyrdom emerges when the community is threatened. Martyrdom, then, is never an individual act and is to be fully differentiated from suicide. Martyrs offer their individual corporeal existence for God, but their actions are enmeshed in an elaborate theological and sociological framework of meaning and expectations.

Those outside the sphere of the religious community frequently find it difficult to comprehend the nature and motivation for martyrdom. It highlights the radical otherness of religious violence, in that it is holy, sacred and transcendental and not to be understood in secular categories. One approach used by those outside the martyr's community to make sense of this seemingly incomprehensible act is to see the martyr as a victim of 'brainwashing', as acting in a programmed fashion as a consequence of psychological conditioning. However, the fact of the matter is that martyrdom cannot be explained by brainwashing, coercion or the desire to seek financial advantage for one's heirs. While some of these motivations may be present in certain cases, most martyrs act out of a genuine religious motivation fuelled by the belief in an afterlife with wonderful rewards for their willingness to sacrifice themselves for religious ends. Martyrs are both young and old, single and married, with children or without children, highly educated or with minimal formal education. There is absolutely no evidence showing any general characteristics of martyrs. Some martyrs have difficult life circumstances or may come from a background of poverty, but others are extremely high achievers from respected families. For example, on the one hand, the principal hijacker in the World Trade Center attack, Mohammed Atta, came from a solidly middle class Egyptian family, as did a number of his fellow hijackers. Indeed, he had recently received a Master's degree in urban architecture from the Hamburg Technical University in Germany, where a professor described him as the best student on the programme. On the other hand, the failed English hijacker, Richard Reid, who attempted to bomb an Air France plane in 2001 was an unemployed school dropout. Similarly, among Christian martyrs there is a mixture of highly educated, prominent individuals, simple peasants, and uneducated converts who, though new to the faith, are willing to martyr themselves. Jewish history is replete with the record of the martyrdom of the most distinguished Talmudic rabbis in the community, along with those who were far removed from scholarship, including a number of people and movements who martyred themselves against the will of the official religious leadership.

In the modern world, religious martyrdom is still celebrated. Militant Islam has developed particularly elaborate theological justifications for martyrdom and has argued that suicide bombers, including those attacking civilians and even other Muslims are *shahids* (holy martyrs). While many moderate Islamic thinkers disagree with this view of religious violence, militants can find support for their views in particular interpretations of Islamic history and theology. Contemporary Judaism has likewise elaborated justifications for martyrdom and refer to those who die in terrorist attacks or in defence of the State of Israel, as martyrs and warriors. Some Jewish fundamentalists have gone further calling those like Baruch Goldstein, who massacred 29 Muslims at prayer at a religious site in Hebron, a holy martyr since his action was done in support of Jewish rights to the Holy Land. The Second Vatican Council reiterated the continuing significance of martyrdom and proclaimed contemporary Christian martyrs as exemplifying the highest form of love and Christian witness.

Martyrdom is, of course, a relative concept. What one community considers legitimate martyrdom can be seen as dangerous, illegal, and criminal behavior by other groups. This is the case with some anti-abortion activists who argue that those who kill doctors who provide abortions should be understood as martyrs because, at the risk of their own lives and imprisonment, they are defending the rights and life of the unborn child. In their willingness to kill and be killed on behalf of the unborn, they uphold and defend the Christian message of the sacredness of life. They are witnesses, in this view, to the call of the gospel to sacrifice oneself for Christian truth.

Perhaps the most extreme form of martyrdom is the phenomenon of apocalyptic suicide in which believers decide to end their own lives in order to bring about personal redemption and salvation. However, some also understand their martyrdom to be central to the ushering in of a new age of religious purity, which will transform the modern world. The deaths by members of the Heaven's Gate community in 1997 was an example of apocalyptic suicide as all the members were committed to the belief that a spacecraft, travelling in the tail of the Hale-Bopp comet, was coming to transport them to another level of existence. They killed themselves, believing that in doing so they were simply shedding their 'earthly containers' in preparation for transport to another, better level of existence (see Chapter 15, New Religious Movements).

Civilizational clashes, cultural conflict and religious violence

Some cases of religious violence are so interwoven with cultural, political and civilizational elements that the violent conflict, at its very roots, is both religious and cultural. Each religious civilization constructs a sacred view of its own traditions, cultural heritage, and history which describes its unique origins and its divine mission. These sacred narratives are often in conflict with those of competing religions and civilizations. Consequently, they reinforce a sense of ethnocentrism and the seeds of civilizational misunderstanding and conflict are passed on from generation to generation. Some of the most intractable ethnic conflicts are the result of civilizational clashes between competing religious promises, sacred histories and divine truths. Violence is seen as a justifiable attempt to maintain the integrity of one's own group identity from real or imagined enemies who are seen as seeking to hinder the group from realizing their historical and divine mandate. In civilizational clashes each group sees itself as the inheritor of divine promise and sees its territory and culture as representing divine truth.

Faithful Hindus all over the world, for example, refer to the Indian subcontinent as 'Mother India', a sacred land that cannot be violated by those who do not share the Vedic traditions and destiny. The severe violence, in which over 3,000 people were killed, in the north Indian city of Ajodhya in 1992, came about as a result of Hindu militants destroying the famous Babri mosque, which they understood to be a violation of Hindu sacred space. Similarly, Muslim militants have destroyed Buddhist and Hindu sacred sculptures as examples of idolatry. Again, civilizational clashes involving religion and sacred history are important elements in the conflict between Serbs and Muslims in the Balkan areas that were part of the former Yugoslavia. And, of course, competing religious histories and memories contributed much to violence in Northern Ireland.

Perhaps the most dramatic contemporary religious civilizational confrontation is between traditional Islam and Western culture. Militant Muslim traditionalists fight against the West which they see as an enemy and danger to Islam. American and Western culture is viewed by Muslim militants as satanic, immoral and bent on destroying the values and religious culture of Islamic societies. Islamic traditionalists are opposed to the separation of religion and state and believe that the state is religiously required to have Islamic sharia; it should be an essential element of all public law. Foreign policy and international relations, too, must be under the authority of religious scholars, and the truly Islamic state may not, even for national economic or political advantage, do anything that challenges Muslim teachings. In the Muslim view, morality, dress, and popular culture, including films, literature, and leisure activities, are not matters for individuals to decide upon but are matters which come under religious legislation and custom. Again, Islamic religious culture holds that sexuality, courtship, and marriage are not matters to be decided by the individual, but rather activities to be guided by religious law and Islamic tradition. Consequently, Muslim traditionalists believe they must fight and defeat the United States and challenge European culture as well in order to protect Islamic culture from the corrosive effects of Western civilization. The 9/11 attacks on the World Trade Center and the attacks in England and Madrid were all part of a religious, civilizational clash between Islamic traditionalism and Western secularism. At the heart of this conflict is a wholly different and competing civilizational view of individual autonomy, morality and what constitutes legitimate behavior.

Some cases of religious violence are the consequences of colonialism, economic exploitation and political conquest. The European domination in the nineteenth and much of the twentieth century over much of the Islamic world, particularly in Egypt, Iraq and Saudi Arabia, was certainly economic, but it had also been encouraged by a Christian sense of mission to uplift and at times convert the indigenous populations to a more, in the view of the West, progressive and superior Christian religion. Colonialism always involves cultural and economic exploitation and the ensuing violence between those under colonial domination and the colonial powers is frequently expressed in religious conflict and violence. It is an error to see this type of violence as just economic or political because the underlying issues are religious, civilizational and a defence of cultural identity. The violence of the Muslim Brotherhood in Egypt, of the Hamas movement in the Holy Land, of the Zionist Irgun militant underground in Palestine, and the violence between Muslims and Hindus in colonial India have at their roots religious faith and a sense of sacred destiny.

Psychological perspectives

Most explanations for religious violence focus on belief and religious culture. However, generally speaking, the psychological perspective focuses on religious violence as a way that a religion collectivity deals with envy, anger, and frustration. The accumulated aggression, envy, and conflict within any society must find an outlet or the group itself will be destroyed by internal conflict and personal rivalry. According to this interpretation, the people in every society have 'mimetic envy' of their fellow citizens. That is to say, individuals want to achieve the high status, wealth, personal attractiveness and power of others. Such feelings of envy lead to aggression and eventually to violence, in that there is a desire to hurt, destroy and kill those whom we want to emulate. The point is that, religion is a way a society takes these collective feelings of envy and aggression (which if left unchecked will destroy a society) and expresses them symbolically or through religious aggression against outside enemies.

The leading theorist to explain religious violence in such psychological terms is René Girard, a French literary theorist who argued that religious institutions are important for the well-being of societies because religion functions to defuse the anger and aggression that inevitably emerges within them. Religion does this by providing rituals that serve as an outlet for actual and real anger and fury. Through ritual sacrifice and relived myths, religion encourages the expression of 'safe' and controlled anger and aggression so that violence is not expressed against members of one's own group but against victims who cannot fight back. Likewise, aggression might be acted out in symbolic rituals in which aggressive emotions are acted out but no one is actually injured or killed. Indeed, 'sacrificial rites' are critical to avoiding war and ethnic violence. The classical example of a sacrificial rite is the killing of the scapegoat as part of the ancient Israelite Yom Kippur ritual. As described in the Hebrew Bible (Leviticus 16:2–30), one male goat was chosen by the high priest during the holiest service of the Jewish year in the Jerusalem temple to serve as an atonement for the sins of the community. After a complex ritual in the temple, the designated sacrificial goat was dispatched to the Judean desert, where it was thrown from a cliff to its death. When news of the death reached the temple, the high priest announced that all sins for that past year were forgiven, and the masses congregated in the temple precincts to rejoice and celebrate their good fortune to have been forgiven. In Girardian terms, the scapegoat ritual serves as an outlet for the collective anger and aggression that accumulates in social settings. Through the collective expression of ritualized sacrifice, violence is removed from the group and directed against a safe 'victim'. Some form of ritual expression of aggression is part of every religion. Greek mythology and the Christian Gospels all partake of symbolic means of expelling violence through religion and myth.

What happens, however, if symbolic rituals do not work to defuse the violence engendered by mimetic envy? In such cases, Girard argued, a severe societal crisis ensues and the society must look for a real-life enemy against whom to vent the pent-up aggression and fury. Religious violence and wars are sometimes conscious but almost always unconscious ways that a social group scapegoats another group in order to rid itself of the accumulated aggression. Hence, while ostensibly religious wars are fought for presumably sacred goals, it can be argued that religious violence is a basic way of legitimating the destruction of others with whom one is competing. It is important to emphasize that, from this psychological perspective, what makes religious violence so functional is that those who engage in such violence see it as divinely ordained and feel no taint of shame or guilt. Religious violence is self-legitimating because it is based on sacred truth and does not need to be justified by secular or political logic or rationality. Religious warriors, for Girard, are motivated by what Marx identified as a 'false consciousness' because they are unaware that by killing their enemies they are actually engaging in repairing and strengthening bonds of social relationships that make society possible.

Some theorists see the current enmity, wars and tensions between Islam and the Christian West, between Israelis and Palestinians, between Shi'ites and Sunnis, or between Muslims and Hindus as not so much a matter of theological difference, but as a way of venting and relieving internal social tension, aggression, hatred and discord. Hence, while the conflict is ostensibly about religion, the goal is actually internal social order. For example, some researchers have found that two competing Muslim Shi'ite militant groups, Hezbollah and Amal, who had a history of mutual violence, ceased feuding and attacking each other during periods of alliance in unified terrorist activity against Western targets. However, when the religious leaders in both groups ended their mutual operations, the violence and killing between the two groups recommenced. Similarly, Israeli researchers have noted that both Jewish militants and peace activists have come together during wars with the Palestinians.

Some theorists have drawn attention to the role of humiliation and victimization, real or imagined, in religious violence. Many religious wars have deep elements of anger over historical wrongs and indignities. The civil wars in Bosnia and Nigeria and the Sikh attacks on Indian public sites share the experience of historical wrongs which violence will somehow redress. Suicide bombers particularly, who kill themselves and untold innocent civilians in crowded public spaces, are seen by the many of their religious compatriots as having restored honor and dignity to the group. Many of these acts of violence do not change things in any practical fashion for the groups who feel so victimized. What they do provide, however, is a symbolic empowerment and a sense of potency, however fleeting, in the face of the hated enemy. This is the case with Muslim suicide bombers, just as it was with the militant Zionist physician Baruch Goldstein who murdered 29 Muslims at prayer in a holy site in Hebron.

Religion as an expression of ethnic, political or social conflict

There does not appear to be a region in the world immune to religious strife and violence. A critical issue, however, is whether these conflicts are truly *religious* or, as some distinguished religious scholars have maintained, merely attempts to use religion as a vehicle to champion or justify secular, political, military or nationalist goals. Put simply, it can be argued that, rather than religion causing violence, what passes for religious violence is simply a marker for wider social, political or ethnic conflict. In this view, religion and religious organizations are being used in the pursuit of nationalist and often distinctly secular goals. Leaders of political movements are aware of the potency of religious language, history and symbols to justify and exacerbate conflict, even in situations where religion was not initially an element.

Some researchers reject the thesis that it is religion itself which causes violence and maintain that in many conflicts considered to be religious, a closer examination reveals them to be enmeshed in a web of historical, economic and identity issues. Hence, for example, while the disputes in Bosnia and in the former Yugoslavia have very strong nationalist elements, religious identity has been used to encourage violence and justify ethnic animosity. In this view, religion was co-opted to serve distinctly secular goals. Similarly, the longstanding disputes and violence in Northern Ireland between Catholics and Protestants, often viewed as an example of a religious conflict, was at root a political conflict. Religion was used to solidify both groups and to justify the continuing struggles by appealing to religious identity. The serious and continuing battles between predominantly Hindu India and Muslim Pakistan also need to be seen through the prism of international politics relating to the disputed area of Kashmir and not as a religious war between Hindus and Muslims. The wars in Lebanon between Christians and Muslims can also be understood in this way. The two communities had lived for years in reasonable harmony and it was the economic distress of civil strife in the 1970s which resulted in an outbreak of religious violence with each side organizing under a religious banner.

In some cases, political or ideological groups have consciously manufactured religious justification to support a movement's programme. The Ku Klux Klan is an American example of the use of religion in support of racial oppression and violence. The Klan claimed to be doing God's work in furthering the interest of the 'superior' white race and also that the violence and persecution it engaged in was religiously sanctioned. Contemporary heirs to the Klan, like the Christian Identity movement, have likewise adopted a religious rationale to support their racist agenda. Some extreme and violent environmental and animal rights groups with distinctly secular platforms have progressively become more 'religious', using religion and religious texts to champion their programme. While some conflicts are inherently religious, other cases highlight how religion can be manipulated for political and secular goals.

Violence and exogenous pressure

Some religious violence is certainly 'endogenous', in that it is encouraged and sometimes prescribed by the particular religious tradition and scripture, in other cases it is 'exogenous', the result of persecution and conflict with the government or police. Some groups want to be left alone to follow their unconventional religious beliefs and lifestyle which governmental authorities may consider criminal and dangerous to the larger society. In protecting and defending their religious community and lifestyle, such unpopular religions find themselves in conflict, sometimes violent conflict, with the established government agencies. Indeed, this type of violence is often a mixture of internal instability, endogenous factors, and exogenous pressure. Certainly, this seems to have been the case concerning the violence involving the Branch Davidian community in Waco, Texas. Pressure exerted by law enforcement officials in 1993 resulted in the deaths of both Branch Davidians and United States marshals.

Conclusion

Religious violence is a continuing reality all over the globe; each event has its own history and each conflict is embedded in its own unique context of theology, politics and culture. No one theoretical perspective can explain the variety of religious motivations for violence. Some cases are exclusively religious, while others utilize religious rhetoric for distinctly secular goals and still other cases may be a composite of both religious and secular motivation. What is central and critical, however, to understanding and responding to religious violence and terror is the recognition that those who do engage in religious violence are motivated by their conviction that their violent activities and killings are necessary and justified by divine mandate. The secularization so prominent in European Christianity has not occurred in most parts of the world and the religious symbols, sacred texts and traditions continue to hold the pious allegiance of peoples all over the globe. The history of religion and faith shows that so long as religion is about commitment to an absolute truth and a commitment to a sacred history, faithful women and men will be willing soldiers in battles for God.

Summary

- Religions and their sacred texts teach peace and reconciliation, but religious history is one of conflict and violence.

- Claims to provide absolute truth and eternal salvation and these beliefs can encourage and legitimate holy war and martyrdom on behalf of a faith.

- Religiously motivated violence can also become an important element in political, civilizational and cultural conflicts.

- Religious violence can be used to maintain social solidarity by creating a common enemy and can be used to express historical grievances.

Key terms

Christian Identity An American Christian extremist group proclaiming a theology of racism and white supremacy.

Dar al-Islam An 'abode of Islam', referring to a country under Muslim sovereignty where the rules of Islam are legally established.

jahiliyya The 'age of ignorance' in Islamic theology, referring to the immoral culture in Arabia before the teachings of the prophet Muhammad. Also used to describe any society believed to be living with the absence of an ethical and moral code.

jihad An Islamic religious obligation involving a 'struggle' for faith and overcoming evil. *Jihad* can be a psychological or political struggle but it can also involve war and violence on behalf of religion and faith.

martyr An individual who is willing to die in defence of his or her religious beliefs or religious community.

milchemet mitzvah An Jewish obligatory war ordained by God in which killing and destruction are sanctioned by divine command.

mimetic desire A term used by René Girard to describe the human experience of envy and the desire to have the admirable and desirable characteristics of another person or collectivity. Girard believed that mimetic desire was a central feature in understanding human violence.

scapegoating Blaming the troubles of an individual or society on an innocent victim and in this way avoiding responsibility. The term is taken from the Hebrew Bible, which describes a sacrificial ritual in which a goat is sacrificed as an atonement for the sins and transgressions of the community.

sharia Islamic religious law based upon the Qur'an and the authoritative religious traditions as interpreted by Muslim scholars and religious teachers.

ummah The worldwide Muslim community following Islamic teachings.

Zionism The religious and political movement which supports the establishment of the state of Israel.

Further reading

R. Scott Appleby: *The Ambivalence of the Sacred: Religion, Violence, and Reconciliation* (Lanham, MD: Rowman & Littlefield, 2000). An analysis of religion's role as peacemaker and as a force for violence.

Karen Armstrong: *The Battle For God* (New York: Alfred A. Knopf, 2000). A popular historical and sociological study of the rise of fundamentalism and religious extremism.

Peter L. Berger: *The Sacred Canopy: Elements of a Sociological Theory of Religion* (New York: Doubleday, 1967). A classic work dealing with the sociological functions of religion.

Yossef Bodansky: *Bin Laden: The Man Who Declared War on America* (New York: Random House, 2001). A study of the history and theology of extremist Islam. Also contains important biographical material.

David Bukay: *Total Terrorism in the Name of Allah: The Emergence of the New Islamic Fundamentalists* (Sharei Tikvah, Israel: ACPR Publications, 2002). A study of the new radical Islamic theology.

John L. Esposito: *The Islamic Threat: Myth or Reality?* (New York: Oxford University Press, 1983). A sensitive study of the meaning and context of Islamic radicalism.

René Girard: *The Scapegoat.* Translated by Yvonne Freccero (Baltimore, MD: Johns Hopkins University Press, 1986). A classic work on the psychology of religious violence.

Ariel Glucklich: *Sacred Pain: Hurting the Body for the Sake of the Soul* (New York: Oxford University Press, 2001). An excellent study of self-inflicted suffering for the sake of religion.

Samuel P. Huntington: *The Clash of Civilizations and the Remaking of World Order* (New York: Simon and Schuster, 1996). A major study of religious and ethnic conflict.

Mark Juergensmeyer: *Terror in the Mind of God: The Global Rise of Religious Violence* (Berkeley and Los Angeles, CA: University of California Press, 2007). An excellent introduction to the rise of religious violence in the modern world.

Meir Kahane: *Listen World, Listen Jew* (Jerusalem: Institute of the Jewish Idea, 1978). The famous manifesto by the assassinated Jewish extremist outlining his radical ideas.

John Kelsay and James Turner Johnson: *Just War and Jihad: Historical and Theoretical Perspectives on War and Peace in Western and Islamic Traditions* (New York: Greenwood Press, 1991). A study of holy war doctrine.

Charles Selengut: *Sacred Fury: Understanding Religious Violence* (Lanham, MD: Rowan & Littlefield, 2008). A study of religious violence in the contemporary world.

Ehud Sprinzak: *Brother Against Brother: Violence and Extremism in Israeli Politics From Altalena to the Rabin Assassination* (New York: Free Press, 1999). An insightful study of religious violence in Judaism and in Israeli society.

Catherine Wessinger: *How the Millennium Comes Violently: From Jonestown to Heaven's Gate* (New York: Seven Bridges, 2000). A study of martyrdom and apocalyptic suicide.

Chapter 19

Religion and gender

Linda Woodhead

Gender and the study of religion

For most of its history the study of religion has been gender-blind. This neglect of gender often had the effect of privileging the dominant, male, standpoint. For example, male-led forms of religion might be treated as 'real' religion, whereas forms of religion in which women were more prominent might be ignored or dismissed as magic or superstition.

Gender has come onto the agenda of religious studies in two main phases. In the first, which began with the influence of first-wave feminism in the late nineteenth century, and continued under the influence of second-wave feminism in the 1970s and 1980s, particular attention was paid to the ways in which religion might either oppress and restrict or liberate and empower women. Although some important work was inspired by this approach, the lens of 'women's liberation' proved a very narrow one through which to view religion, and it often failed to do justice to the complexity of both religion, and women's appropriations of religion.

A second, more recent, phase has been inspired by third-wave feminism. The latter questions a sharp distinction between women and men, and lays more emphasis on the many ways in which gender is constructed, and the variety of gender positions which may result (similarly, it resists 'heteronormativity', and pays attention to gay, lesbian and bisexual identities, as well as heterosexuality). Gender is viewed as a complex of identity positions which are 'performed' as well as imposed upon people. Much greater emphasis is also placed on gender *relations*, i.e. on the fact that gender does not exist in isolation, but is constructed by way of similarities and differences with other gender positions. So far as the study of religion is concerned, one result is to shift the emphasis away from an exclusive concern with women and religion, to look more deeply at how religion is implicated in the construction of masculinity and manhood. Another is to give greater attention to the ways in which masculinity and femininity are often constructed in relation to one another. Finally, a theoretical focus on religion as oppressive or liberating gives way to a wider range of questions, categories and themes.

Gender and religion in modern Western societies

One of the characteristic features of modernization in Western societies was a division of labour between men and women. Industrialization created a range of new jobs – from factory labour to office work to the new professions – which were reserved almost exclusively for men. In this way men came to dominate the 'public life' of nation states, towns and cities, whereas many women were confined to the 'private life' of the home.

This was particularly true for middle and upper class women, but even domestic working class women who had to work for money would often be engaged in domestic labour or work from home.

The confinement of women in industrial society was challenged by first-wave feminism, which campaigned for women to be admitted to universities and the professions, to be treated equally in law (e.g. to be allowed to own property in their own right), and to be granted the vote. Such campaigning had some notable successes, including changes in legislation allowing women to own property and to vote. The real change, however, came later in the twentieth century as a result of wider social changes. The two World Wars allowed women more of a role in public life; the impersonal and unregulated effects of a competitive market have undermined protectionist strategies which favoured male employment; the massive expansion of non-manual occupations and the rise of knowledge-based work opened up new opportunities for women; the invention of more effective forms of contraception gave women greater control over their reproductive lives; some countries introduced state-supported childcare and nursery schooling. Men have also been affected by these changes. Just as women have taken on jobs and roles previously reserved for men, so men have taken on roles previously reserved for women, including a greater share of domestic work and childcare. On average, however, women still perform a much greater proportion of domestic and caring work than men, and this results in a double burden of work for many women – both in the home *and* in paid employment.

The consequences of all these changes for religion are profound, and religion has played a central and important role both in supporting and resisting the 'modernization' of gender relations. Indeed, the development and internal differentiation of religion in modern times is often bound up with the different positions taken by religion with regard to modern gender relations. The development of conservative and 'fundamentalist' forms of Judaism, Christianity, and Islam, for example, is bound up with the way in which these kinds of religion support a very clear differentiation between men and women, the 'headship' of the male, and the confinement of women to domestic roles and private space. (In other words, such religion is supportive of the gender roles associated with industrial modernization.) By contrast the 'liberal' wings of the same religions have tended to stress the similarity rather than the difference between men and women, and to stress their equality and 'common humanity'. And more 'radical' forms of religion – like some New Religious Movements – have provided spaces for gender and sexual experimentation. We can illustrate this variety by looking in some depth at a number of case studies.

Women converting to Orthodox Judaism in late modern America

Conservative, Orthodox and Fundamentalist forms of Judaism, Christianity and Islam are characterized by a sharp assertion of difference not only between God and the world, but between men and women. The divine hierarchy is taken to be a reflection of a gender hierarchy, in which woman obeys man, just as humanity obeys God. This inscription of hierarchical difference tends to be bound up with a reassertion of the value of the 'traditional family', which is seen as a bulwark against the ills of the modern world.

The appeal of such religion to men may seem obvious; it gives them a clear, powerful, and divine status, a clear identity, and a strong sense of purpose. But why should women be attracted? This is the question that Lyn Davidman (1991) set out to answer in her study of educated, middle class women who convert to Orthodox Judaism in the USA. What she found was that such religion *also* offered wives and mothers considerable status and a role that was considered to be 'equal but different' to that of men. Their exclusion from public life did not seem a loss to them, given that major religious rituals in which they play a central part take place in the home, and given that the home has enormous power and prestige in the Orthodox scheme of things. What is more, women benefited from the fact that Orthodox Jewish men are taught to be closely involved in home and family, and deeply respectful of their womenfolk. As a result, a significant number of women convert to Orthodoxy.

Femininity and masculinity in Fundamentalist and Evangelical christianity

In her classic study of a Christian Fundamentalist church in the USA, Nancy Ammerman (1987) found that although women give formal acknowledgement to male authority in the home, in practice they often exercise considerable power over their menfolk. Moreover, the fact that men are enjoined to respect and cherish wives, children and home, and to honour Christian values of love, peaceableness, faithfulness, cleanliness, decorum, sobriety and relationality, can easily be turned to women's advantage. Both men and women have much to gain from such clear role differentiation, in which each knows his and her place, and each co-operates with the other for the good of the family unit.

Many forms of Evangelical Christianity also seem to offer women a space for the articulation of desires and frustrations. Evangelicalism often prohibits women from teaching in public (teaching men), but it offers them free access to the Holy Bible and the Holy Spirit (see Chapter 8 on Christianity). What is more, there is no prohibition on their teaching one another. Thus many Evangelical women belong to some form of small group – for Bible study, prayer, healing, and so on. Such groups have characterized Evangelicalism from its origins, and have flourished in recent times. They offer a safe space in which women can articulate their deepest desires and concerns – prayer groups, for example, are a natural setting in which to share fears, hopes, desires and personal experiences. Such institutions offer a forum for healing not only by God, but through the love and support of one's sisters.

An important example of a small group movement with international reach is the Charismatic-Evangelical 'Women's Aglow' movement which is the subject of a study by R. Marie Griffith (1997). Griffith finds that meetings are dominated by women's concerns, concerns that they would probably be unable to articulate in other social spaces, particularly with men present. Appropriating the traditional genre of the Evangelical testimony in which an individual describes in public how being born again as a child of God has effected a break between their past (unredeemed) and their present (saved) lives, women in Aglow meetings spend a great deal of time describing domestic strife and woes – childhood abuse, unhappy marriages, unresponsive husbands, wayward children. They then go on to testify to the way in which surrender or yielding to God has effected dramatic change for the better. In other words, their religion provides a means by which their apparent powerlessness is turned into power. By obeying the injunction to obey God and their husbands they actually win what they desire.

Griffith also notes that since the 1980s, the stress in Aglow literature has been shifting away from submission to men, to more active partnerships with men. Equally, more emphasis is being given to the power of prayer in relation to the world as a whole, and not just to domestic settings. This is most evident in the way in which Aglow meetings now devote time to praying for the conversion of particular parts of the world, and for victory over the powers of evil. Women are waging spiritual warfare, and becoming aware of their spiritual power. This religion of the powerless thus offers woman a power they might not otherwise have, and increasingly it is offering possibilities for exercising it – at least in spiritual forms – in public as well as private.

Women's Aglow Fellowship provides support, education, training, and ministry opportunities to help women worldwide discover their true identity in Jesus Christ through the power of the Holy Spirit.

We believe that:

All women and men are created equal in the image of God, each with dignity and value.

God has a unique purpose for all of us and equips us for that purpose.

We can reach our full potential only after finding identity and restoration in Jesus Christ.

(*Affirmation of Faith*, Women's Aglow)

Jesus, thank You for showing me that housework is sacred. Help me to realize while I am cooking and cleaning that I am doing them for You because You are living here and my husband is Your representative.

(Sacred housework, from *Aglow in the Kitchen*, a cookbook for Christian wives)

(Both passages cited by Griffith, 1997: 64, 182)

BOX 19.1 Women's Aglow

The closing decade of the twentieth century also witnessed the rise of Evangelical movements and groups specifically devoted to men and to the development of appropriately Christian forms of masculinity. The most notable of these, the Promise

Keepers, was founded in the USA in 1990 'for training and teaching on what it means to be godly men'. This movement organized several large gatherings, and inspired the formation of many small groups for men, often attached to Christian churches. Such groups provided space for men to explore what it means to be a man in the context of late modernity, and the changing and confusing gender roles of the time. It addressed these by re-affirming a vision of 'gentle' male headship and leadership of the household, in an attempt to reinscribe a clear, powerful masculine identity which was felt by some to be under threat.

The core beliefs of the Promise Keepers, outlined in the *Seven Promises*, consist of the following:

1. A Promise Keeper is committed to honoring *Jesus* Christ through worship, prayer and obedience to God's Word in the power of the *Holy Spirit*.
2. A Promise Keeper is committed to pursuing vital relationships with a few other men, understanding that he needs brothers to help him keep his promises.
3. A Promise Keeper is committed to practicing spiritual, moral, ethical and sexual purity.
4. A Promise Keeper is committed to building strong marriages and families through love, protection and Biblical values.
5. A Promise Keeper is committed to supporting the mission of his church by honoring and praying for his pastor and by actively giving his time and resources.
6. A Promise Keeper is committed to reaching beyond any racial and denominational barriers to demonstrate the power of Biblical unity.
7. A Promise Keeper is committed to influencing his world, being obedient to the *Great Commandment* (Mark 12:30–31) and the *Great Commission* (Matthew 28:19–20).

BOX 19.2 The Promise Keepers

Gender and liberal religion

Most of the world's religions have liberal wings, which stress not difference but similarity and equality between men and women. Such religions tend to be humanitarian, both in the sense that they emphasize the value of human beings and their natural affinity with the divine, and place stress on what is common to human beings rather than what differentiates them. Both elements may be very appealing to women: the latter because it allows them to compete on equal terms with men, and the former because it reinforces their esteem in a way that religions which only affirm male divinity may not. In addition, liberal forms of religion tend to have a strongly ethical and relational stress: humanitarian deeds – particularly loving kindness – are more important than dogma. Not surprisingly, it tends to be the more liberal wings of traditional religions which have been the most willing to grant women leadership roles – as in Reform Judaism, and the more liberal Protestant Christian denominations.

FIGURE 19.1
Campaigning for and against the Ordination of Women

Women and men gather to campaign outside a General Synod meeting which is deliberating whether women should be ordained in the Church of England, 12 November 1992. The first women were ordained in the Church of England in 1994. Courtesy E. Hamilton West/ Guardian News & Media Ltd. 1992.

As yet, research has not been carried out to determine whether or not liberal forms of religion attract professional women to a greater degree than conservative forms of traditional religion. What research has shown, however, is that many women tend to favour more relational and less steeply hierarchical understandings and pictures of God, that they value community and connectedness in religion, and that their religion often has a relational flavour. Thus Ozorak (1996) found that women's responses to religious community depended heavily on the extent to which they found it to be 'supportive, cooperative, and emotionally open', and that satisfaction in these areas more than compensated for dissatisfaction with male-dominated leadership and organization. Men who are attracted to liberal religion may also be attracted by the way in which it authorizes forms of masculinity which can be gentle, loving, and even feminine. As such, it may provide a refuge from the demands of more 'macho' and aggressive forms of masculinity, and may allow men to develop forms of identity which have less support in the secular world.

It would be wrong to give the impression that liberal forms of religion have merely accommodated themselves to gender equality in modern societies. On the contrary, liberal religion has played an important role in fighting for various forms of equality, including women's equality, and greater acceptance of homosexuality.

Women and spirituality

The second night out was a full moon and we waited impatiently for the moon to crest the tall pines so that the ritual could begin. Finally, we saw two flames winding down the mountain path. As they neared, we saw that these were torches, held by priestesses in silver gowns which caught the light from the flames and glittered like pieces of the moon herself. The priestesses paused in the south, and then I noticed the enormous

continued

shadow thrown against the hill. It is Diana who comes behind them. Rationally, I know it is Hypatia [a witch and priestess], but I also know it is Diana. A heavy green cape is swept over her shoulders and matches her baggy pants. Her huge breasts are bare, and her chest is crossed with the leather straps that hold her cape and the quiver of arrows on her back. She carries a large bow and her face is hidden behind a mask of fur and dried leaves. Deer horns spring from her head. There is no face, not a human one, anyway . . . The Goddess pauses between the torches and fits an arrow to the bow. She draws it back and with a 'twang' shoots it into the darkness. The sound is like a catalyst. We are released like the arrow and begin to cheer.

> A description of a ritual performed by a coven of feminist witches in North America, 24 August 1991 in Griffin, 1995.

BOX 19.3 The embodied Goddess

So far our case studies have shown that contemporary forms of religion in the West can be shaped by trying to preserve clear forms of gender difference and male domination, or by affirming equality between the sexes. There are also forms of religion which provide a space for experimenting with a wide range of gender relations, including forms of identity and practice which would be stigmatized in wider society. As Chapter 15 shows, New Religious Movements offer a wide range of possibilities for gender experimentation. Some, like the Jesus People, Hare Krishna and Unification Church (Moonies), have tended to assert traditional gender roles. Others have provided space in which women have been able to explore their gendered identities much more freely than in traditional religion (and, perhaps, more easily than in secular feminism). Palmer (1994) argues that NRMs offer women the opportunity to occupy a whole range of gender roles – from the conservative to the radical – thereby developing a more mature gendered identity than might otherwise be possible (an identity which often takes them outside NRMs later in life).

As we have seen in Chapter 12, the varied world of spirituality also takes gender very seriously, and offers many possibilities for experimenting with gender identity. Many Mind, Body, Spirit practices are run by women for women, and some provide a space in which women try to reconcile their roles and duties of care and domesticity on the one hand, and of paid employment and individual assertion on the other. Goddess-focused forms of paganism are sometimes all female, and focused around veneration and imitation of a number of different goddesses. As Box 19.3 shows, such imitation allows women scope to perform forms of femininity which may give them a new sense of identity and empowerment. Other forms of paganism place more emphasis on gender complementarity, often venerating both gods and goddesses, and striving for harmony between a 'male' and 'female' principle in the universe. Still others, including some forms of reconstructionism, may be male-dominated and seek to reconstruct worlds and rituals which revive supposedly ancient forms of masculinity.

Gender and religion outside the West

The path of modernization taken by Western industrial societies, which involved a sharp division of labour between men and women followed by attempts to break down that division, is not necessarily followed by other societies. By looking at a number of different case studies, we get a sense of the variety of pathways into the modern world, the role of religion in shaping these pathways, and the different implications for gender relations.

Negotiating social change: indigenous religions

In premodern societies, religion may infuse all aspects of social life. It provides the means by which individuals are integrated into wider society and by which that society's values are articulated and reinforced. In addition, it marks boundaries between one society and another, one social group and another, different genders, and different stages of life. Since such societies range from chiefdoms to less hierarchical and non-centralized communities, it is hard to generalize about religion and gender, but in most cases the official religion of a tribe or society could be expected to support existing hierarchies of power. For example, as Chapter 10 on Religion in Africa shows, ancestor worship often underpins the authority of male elders, who ritually mediate the ancestors.

However, as Chapter 10 also shows, indigenous religions do not just support the status quo. Because such religions tend to have oral rather than written traditions, and because they focus upon living relations between the spirit world and the human world, they have considerable flexiblity and potential for change – in many ways they may be more flexible than tradition- and text-bound world religions. They can also serve as effective resources on which less powerful members of society, including women, can draw, and they may be potent agents of social change. For example, as Chapter 10 shows, Tonga women who are constrained within a domestic environment may be possessed by marginal non-ancestral spirits known as Masabe who demand gifts bought out of the wages of their husbands from a cash economy from which they would otherwise be excluded. Likewise, Kaiabari women of the Niger delta gain much influence through divining, in which they are possessed by water spirits that reside in the creeks and which bring economic success in return for human devotion. In these examples, religion helps women adapt in advantageous ways to new money-based trading economies, whilst keeping them within the ambit of existing society.

Religion may also serve to control women's power. This may occur in relation to women's sexual and reproductive power, which may be ritually controlled in indigenous religion, just as it is in the world religions – for example, by moral and ritual laws surrounding sexual intercourse, menstruation and childbirth. Similarly, witchcraft may serve as a form of female power, since the threat of witchcraft activity is a way in which society is regulated, and a disincentive to the infliction of injuries, wrongs and inequalities. But it can also be used as a way of controlling that power, with the accusation of witchcraft and the sanctions used against it serving as a powerful form of control. As

Box 19.4 shows, witchcraft today often has close connections with the tensions generated by modernization.

Africa has been drawn inexorably into the world of capitalist production. And while it has hardly been made over entirely in European image, it has been subjected to forceful social change – of which the marginalization of the domestic, the rural, the 'primitive', and the female has been a crucial, if complex component. This process of marginalization has many sides to it. Perhaps the most poignant is the fact that those displaced along the way quickly tend to become signs and ciphers with which others make meaning. [. . .] In its late twentieth century guise, witchcraft is a finely calibrated gauge of the impact of global cultural and economic forces on local relations, on perceptions of money and markets, on the abstraction and alienation of 'indigenous' values and meanings. Witches are modernity's prototypical malcontents. They provide – like the grotesques of a previous age – disconcertingly full-bodied images of a world in which humans seem in constant danger of turning into commodities, of losing their life blood to the market and to the destructive desires it evokes. But make no mistake: these desires are eminently real and mortal. And some people are indeed more vulnerable than others to their magic allure. Nor, it should be stressed again, are witches advocates of 'tradition', of a life beyond the universe of commodities. They embody all the contradictions of the experience of modernity itself, of its inescapable enticements, its self-consuming passions, its discriminatory tactics, its devastating social costs.

(Jean Comaroff and John Comaroff: 'Introduction'. In Jean Comaroff and John Comaroff (eds): *Modernity and its Malcontents: Ritual and Power in Postcolonial Africap* [Chicago, IL and London: University of Chicago Press, 1993, pp. xxviii–xxix])

BOX 19.4 Witchcraft and modernity in Africa

Defending national and sexual integrity: religious nationalism in India

Whilst contemporary forms of nationalism in the West tend to be secular, the last part of the twentieth century saw the rise of religious nationalisms in several parts of the world. The Indian subcontinent offers a good example. Despite having a nominally secular state, Hindu nationalism has become a powerful force in India, as has Islamic nationalism in Pakistan. The vitality of these neighbouring nationalisms is related, in part, to the fact that both are attempting to define and defend themselves not only against one another, but against the West which had colonized the region until independence was achieved in 1947.

This situation is interlinked with issues of gender. In religious nationalism, women often become living symbols of the integrity of the defended faith and nation. They are often spoken of in highly exalted terms by male leaders of these movements. They are the guardians of the purity of the nation who raise children in the faith, and guard the sanctity of the home. Such women may be contrasted with Western women who are seen to be libertarian, sexually loose, morally degraded, and lacking in essential femininity. Just as it is necessary for men to guard and protect the integrity of the nation state against its enemies, so it is necessary to protect female bodies. Thus in Pakistan, the institution of female seclusion and veiling becomes a sign of the integrity of both women and the nation. It preserves honour and protects against violation. The result is that women are firmly located within a private realm, and dissuaded from entering into the male spheres of religion and politics.

Mawdudi was a major theorist of the Islamic movement in Pakistan, and his writings influenced the development of Islamism more generally. He developed a systematic socio-political programme for Islam. As this extract shows, he believed that women should be largely confined to the domestic sphere in modern Islamic society. What is also notable, however, is that Mawdudi gives women a central place in his programme: he is well aware that successful social reform cannot take place without their co-operation.

> Family is the first cradle of man. It is here that the primary character-traits of man are set. As such it is not only the cradle of man but also the cradle of civilization. Therefore, let us first consider the injunctions of the Shari'a (Islamic law) relating to the family . . .
>
> To make the household a well-managed and well-disciplined institution, Islam has adopted the two following measures:
>
> The husband has been given the position of head of the family. No institution can work smoothly unless it has a chief administrator . . . There must be someone as head of the family so that discipline can be maintained. Islam gives this position to the husband and in this way makes the family a well-disciplined primary unit of civilisation and a model for society at large.
>
> . . . Islam therefore effects a functional division of labour between the sexes.
>
> But this does not mean that the woman is not allowed to leave the house at all. She is, when necessary. The law has specified the home as her special field of work and has stressed that she should attend to the improvement of home life. Whenever she has to go out, certain formalities can be observed . . .
>
> When women have to go out of their homes, they should wear simple dress and be properly veiled . . . Through this directive Islam aims to cultivate in its followers a deep sense of modesty and purity and to suppress all forms of immodesty and moral deviation.
>
> (Abul A'la Mawdudi: *Towards Understanding Islam*
> (Leicester: The Islamic Foundation, 2000: pp. 108–9, 112)

BOX 19.5 Abul A'la Mawdudi

A safe route into public space: veiling in Islam

The covering of women in Islamic societies does not have just one meaning. Whilst it can be used to symbolize and enforce the seclusion and restriction of women, it can equally be appropriated by women and used to negotiate their way into public space. Thus in many Islamic societies today, covering is understood by women as an option which allows them to avoid both libertarian Westernization on the one hand, and a neo-traditionalism which would confine them solely to the domestic realm on the other. Far from being merely reactionary and traditional, the veil and its meanings are being reinvented in order to allow women new freedoms in modernizing societies. Those who veil are often daughters of first-generation immigrants to the city, cutting free from traditional roles and seeking social advancement. Analysis of their views suggests that they desire education to the highest levels, along with jobs and political rights; they divide only on the issue of gender equality in marriage.

For these reasons, it is possible to argue that contemporary Islamism serves many Muslim women as an indigenous form of feminism – not a Western borrowing, but an indigenous liberation movement. Indeed, it may be viewed as a superior option to what is available in the West, where women can enter the public world only on male and rationalized secular terms, and are forced to leave behind vital aspects of their identity including religion. Some Muslim 'feminists' thus interpret the veil as a revolutionary sign, for it symbolizes the entrance of the previously marginalized (women and the poor) into spheres which were previously closed to them (see, for example, Ahmed, 1992). It marks the triumph of the urban and rural poor over a Westernized elite, and a system of inclusion over one of exclusion. For many, the veil represents an attempt to combine religious belief and values with desired social change. It is part and parcel of the process in which Muslim women have become catalysts for change, entering the professions and public life, becoming scholars and spokespersons for Islam, and establishing women's professional and campaigning organizations.

For many Muslim women, the veil thus represents an attempt to combine religious belief and values with desired social change. It can also be important for Muslim women who have migrated to the West, or been born into migrant families. In this context veiling may be a marker of distinct identity in the midst of a secular society, and a signal that the sort of gender relations which pertain amongst the majority (including the sexualization of women) will not pertain in this instance.

> We became Muslims not to follow previous values, but to follow our new values. And we are not forcing anybody to follow our values – we will not impose them on Christians, on Western life . . . What I say is right, they will say is wrong. I say that this dress is to protect my dignity as a woman; Simone de Beauvoir will say that it is an attack against women and a violation of her dignity. I will not go and force Simone de Beauvoir to put on Muslim dress. And I refuse Simone de

Beauvoir to tell Imam Khomeini with rudeness, 'Don't apply this Muslim rule on Muslim women.' By God, this is very strange. [Simone de Beauvoir was a pioneering French feminist writer and philosopher.]

(Safinaz Kazim, Egyptian journalist and drama critic. Quoted in Francis Robinson (ed.): *Cambridge Illustrated History of the Islamic World* (Cambridge: Cambridge University Press, 1996, p. 204))

BOX 19.6 Second-wave feminism and Islam

Entering sacred space: Buddhist and Hindu monastic traditions

An important traditional form of religious space for both men and women is the monastic community. Characteristic of several of the world's religions, monasticism has declined in Western societies but persists elsewhere.

Solitary asceticism is a traditional, and prestigious, element of Hinduism, but social monasticism represents a modern development in the tradition. So too does the appropriation of asceticism/monasticism by women. An influential form of modern monasticism in Hinduism was founded by Swami Vivekananda (1863–1902), who founded a monastic order named after his teacher and guru, Ramakrishna. The Ramakrishna Math and Mission was part of Vivekananda's attempt to revivify Hinduism and turn it into an agent of indigenous modernization. Monasteries were founded for women as well as men, since Vivekananda recognized women's social importance in Indian society.

Whilst these monasteries for women continue to exist in contemporary India, a recent study shows that some are struggling to attract and retain nuns (Sinclair-Brull, 1997). At the time of independence their aim of charity and uplift was supported by high-caste families, and they provided a social space for women who were unable to find a suitable husband. But modernization has engendered a crisis in the monastery, since in an increasingly affluent society in which middle class women are now expected to be educated and to have jobs, the appeal of the ascetic ideal has waned considerably. Where once monasticism offered women who might not otherwise have a choice an option about the course of their lives, such women are now offered many choices. What is more, modern middle class Indians are also increasingly alienated from the strongly hierarchical order of the monastery, which is seen as a relic of a hierarchical caste and gender system with which many are now dissatisfied. The traditional duties of a woman (*stridharma*) such as loyalty to husband, self-sacrifice, and forbearance in the manner of the goddess Sita are waning in influence, and forms of contemporary femininity wander far from such models.

The situation in Buddhism is rather different. In part this is due to the fact that social monasticism has always been integral to Buddhism, in a way it has not to Hinduism. The sangha (monastery) is the primary social space in which the Buddha's teachings can be followed. Set free from worldly concerns, monks are thought to be in a privileged position to concentrate on the path of enlightenment. In both theory and practice, the sangha exists in close relationship with both nuns and lay people. Reciprocal duties exist between the two: nuns and lay people are to serve the material needs of the monks, whilst the monks will in turn nourish them with spiritual teachings and enable them to attain better rebirths through their merit-making activities.

Just as Buddhist teachings on the place of women are ambiguous, so too is women's position in relation to monasticism. Stories of Buddhist nuns date from the earliest phases of the religion. Yet the organization of the sangha formally relegates women to a subservient status, and restricts them from taking part in the decision-making processes of the Buddhist community. Given the continuing importance of the sangha in Buddhist societies, it is not surprising that the modern period has witnessed campaigns and attempts to raise the status of women's monasticism and to introduce or revive women's monastic orders alongside and on equal terms with men's. As Chapter 3 on Buddhism shows, these campaigns have had some success in both northern and southern Buddhism, but have also had to contend with considerable opposition. Such opposition has come not only from Buddhist monks, but from lay nuns who are not fully ordained – and whose ambivalent status gives them a freedom and power they fear would be lost if full ordination brought them under the control and direction of monks.

Renegotiating gender identities: Charismatic Christianity outside the West

With its roots in the Pentecostal movement of the beginning of the twentieth century, Charismatic Christianity combines an Evangelical emphasis on the authority of scripture (the Word) with an emphasis on the authority of direct experience of the Holy Spirit. As such, it helps both men and women to renegotiate their identities and relations in situations of rapid social change, where a single generation may move from a stable rural setting to a precarious urban, industrial existence.

As Chapter 8 on Christianity shows, Charismatic forms of the religion are typified by their emphasis on a combination of Word (the authority of the Bible) and Spirit (the inner inspiration which comes from the Holy Spirit). Word is often symbolized as male, Spirit as female. Correspondingly, men often occupy positions of power as preachers, teachers and leaders, who interpret God's word. But women are also empowered by virtue of the fact that they can receive the Spirit on the same basis as men, and gain considerable authority in the process. Rather than adopting a Western form of feminism which asserts women's rights, equalities and freedoms in opposition to patriarchal oppression, Charismatic Christianity attracts both men and women by affirming some elements of traditional, patriarchal religion and society (male leadership, a sovereign male God, women's domestic roles), whilst at the same time subjecting them to the transforming powers of charismatic rebirth. Under the influence of the Holy Spirit, all that was solid can melt into new forms. Traditional hierarchies and gender roles undergo a gentle revolution, as a social world is partially recast.

Thus the male, authoritative, transcendent, divine 'Word' of God is complemented by the insinuating influence of the gentle, loving, dove-like 'Spirit' of God. Such emphases serve not only to exalt the feminine, but to challenge machismo. Space is created for women not only by offering them divine power, but by converting men to less macho postures. The validation of male leadership in church, world and home may persist. But the process whereby men take more responsibility for their families, and learn Christian virtues of love, gentleness, kindness, faithfulness, leaves women as major beneficiaries. Both the home and the church become spaces in which women can place their fears and sufferings into the hands of God, and fulfil their desires for a new life of divinely inspirited power and love.

Conclusion

Modernization involves profound changes in gender relations, changes which are often mediated by religion. Industrialization in modern Western societies involved a division of labour which relegated women to the private sphere. Whilst some forms of conservative and fundamentalist religion have supported and reinforced such gender hierarchy, other forms of liberal and radical religiosity have supported alternative, more egalitarian, patterns of gender identity and relations. Modernization outside the West has often taken different pathways, with correspondingly different implications for gender. As we have seen in relation to Islam and Charismatic Christianity, for example, women may become important agents of modernization, where modernization involves not the abandonment of religious tradition in favour of secularism, but its careful and reverent transformation into new forms. Likewise, the transformation of gender roles takes place in a way which respects traditional sensibilities, whilst reshaping gender relations in significantly new ways.

Summary

■ Modernization in the West involved a sharp differentiation between men and women and their respective roles, a differentiation which was supported by conservative forms of religion. The rejection of such roles by feminism often led to the rejection of religion, and feminism was seen as a secular movement.

■ Nevertheless, liberal and radical forms of religion in the West have helped men and women renegotiate their identities and relations, and continue to do so.

■ Outside the West, modernization has often been as much a religious as a secular development. One consequence is that even 'feminist' women have not always had to choose between being religious and being modern. On the contrary, religion can serve as a powerful agent of modernization and gender transformation.

Key terms

androcentric Focused around the male; taking men and masculinity as the norm.

Charismatic Christianity An offshoot of Evangelicalism which has spread rapidly across the world throughout the twentieth century. Places particular emphasis on the gifts of the Holy Spirit.

Evangelical Christianity A pan-denominational movement within modern Protestant Christianity which emphasizes the authority of the Bible and experience of the Holy Spirit.

femininity That which is taken to be feminine.

first-wave feminism Nineteenth-century feminism in the West which championed the equal rights and dignity of women on the grounds of their common humanity with men.

gender The differences between men and women.

gender relations The relations between men and women, and sometimes the relations within the different genders, insofar as gender is central.

heteronormativity The imposition of a norm of heterosexuality (which excludes homosexuality).

liberal religion The tendency within a religious tradition which stresses the value of individual human freedom.

masculinity That which is taken to be masculine.

patriarchy An overarching concept used by feminists to refer to a system of male dominance which extends to both social and ideological spheres, and which ensures a hierarchical ordering of society in which men dominate women.

second-wave feminism The resurgence of feminism after the 1960s which continued to campaign for women's equal rights, whilst developing a critique of androcentric and patriarchal society, and placing more stress on male–female difference and the importance of reform which takes account of gendered difference.

third-wave feminism From the 1980s, a new wave of feminism developed, which is sometimes called 'third-wave' or 'postmodern'. It interrogates the notion of 'gender', and suggests that there are many gender positions and relations, not just a simple 'male' and 'female' binary. More attention is given to gay, lesbian and bisexual identities, as well as to 'intersectional' identities, i.e. the ways in which gender identity intersects with other forms of identity, including ethnicity and class.

Further reading

General/Introductory

Darlene M. Juschka (ed): *Feminism in the Study of Religion: A Reader* (London and New York: Continuum, 2001).

Linda Woodhead: 'Gender Differences in Religious Practice and Significance'. In James Beckford and N.J. Demerath III (eds), *The Sage Handbook of the Sociology of Religion* (Los Angeles, LA, London, New Delhi, Singapore: Sage, 2007, pp. 550–570).

Women and religion in Western societies

Conservative

Nancy Ammerman: *Bible Believers. Fundamentalists in the Modern World* (New Brunswick, NJ, and London: Rutgers University Press, 1987).

Lyn Davidman: *Tradition in a Rootless World: Women Turn to Orthodox Judaism* (Berkeley, CA: University of California Press, 1991).

R. Marie Griffith: *God's Daughters: Evangelical Women and the Power of Submission* (Berkeley, CA: University of California Press, 1997).

Liberal

E.W. Ozorak: 'The Power but not the Glory: How Women Empower themselves through Religion' (*Journal for the Social Scientific Study of Religion* 35(1), 1996: pp. 17–29). Argues that women look for relational and connective satisfaction in religion.

M.T. Winter, A. Lummis and A. Stokes: *Defecting in Place: Women Claiming Responsibility for their own Spiritual Lives* (New York: Crossroad, 1994).

Radical

M. Adler: *Drawing Down the Moon: Witches, Druids, Goddess-Worshippers, and Other Pagans in America Today* (Boston, MA: Beacon Press, 1986).

Wendy Griffin: 'The Embodied Goddess: Feminist Witchcraft and Female Divinity'. (*Sociology of Religion* 56(1), 1995: pp. 35–48).

S.J. Palmer: *Moon Sisters, Krishna Mothers, Rajneesh Lovers: Women's Roles in New Religions* (Syracuse, NY: Syracuse University Press, 1994).

Women and religion outside the West

Leila Ahmed: *Women and Gender in Islam: Historical Roots of a Modern Debate* (New Haven, CT, and London: Yale University Press, 1992).

Salvatore Cucchiari: 'Between Shame and Sanctification: Patriarchy and its Transformation in Sicilian pentecostalism'. (*American Ethnologist* 18, November 1991: pp. 687–707).

Bernice Martin: 'The Pentecostal Gender Paradox: A Cautionary Tale for the Sociology of Religion'. In Richard K. Fenn (ed.): *Blackwell Companion to the Sociology of Religion* (Oxford, UK and Malden, MA: Blackwell, 2001, pp. 52–66).

S.S. Sered: *Priestess, Mother, Sacred Sister: Religions Dominated by Women* (Oxford and New York: Oxford University Press, 1994).

Wendy Sinclair-Brull: *Female Ascetics: Hierarchy and Purity in an Indian Religious Movement* (London: Curzon Press, 1997).

Religion and masculinity

Dane S. Claussen (ed.): *The Promise Keepers: Essays on Masculinity and Christianity* (Jefferson, NC: McFarland & Co., Inc., 2000).

Rhys H. Williams: *Promise Keepers and the New Masculinity: Private Lives and Public Morality* (Lanham, MD: Lexington Books, 2001).

W. Bradford Wilcox: *Soft Patriarchs, New Men: How Christianity Shapes Fathers and Husbands* (Chicago, IL and London: University of Chicago Press, 2004).

Chapter 20

Religion and popular culture

Christopher Partridge

Introduction

Over the last couple of decades there has been a rapidly increasing flow of books, articles, journals, doctoral theses, university courses and conferences examining the relationship between religion and popular culture. While much of this has tended to focus on theology and film, and while most of the more interesting analysis has been undertaken from a Christian theological perspective, as the area has matured there has been a growing breadth of discussion from a range of disciplinary and methodological perspectives looking at popular music, computer games, popular literature, soaps, and so on. This recent flowering of interest has not, of course, made the task of providing an overview an easy one. Not only do scholars have distinct reasons for analyzing popular culture, but they focus on a widening spectrum of media and genres and use a range of theories and methods from different disciplines, including theology, religious studies, media studies, cultural studies, sociology, anthropology, psychology, history and literary criticism.

As to the reasons for this contemporary interest by scholars of religion in the study of popular culture, following bell hooks, Gordon Lynch (2005) has suggested that it might simply be because it is perceived to be 'cool'. At a time when interest in religion appears to be declining and much theological debate appears arcane, not to say archaic, the focus on popular culture might be viewed as an attempt to 'rebrand' what many perceive to be a tired product. However, while there may be some truth to this, and while scholars aren't immune to the desire to appear 'cool', arguably there are more substantial reasons for their interest. Influenced by work done in the social sciences and cultural studies, some recognise the social and political importance of popular culture. For example, popular culture is central to our relationships and social lives, in that it provides an emotive vocabulary which can communicate with that which has particular meaning for us. Indeed, our popular cultural preferences reveal something about who we are as persons.

It has also been argued that theology in particular has a contribution to make to the study of religion and popular culture by virtue of the fact that it is a *normative* discipline. Theorizing in terms of an absolute reference point, theology's analysis of popular culture is concerned with issues relating to the nature of truth, what it means to live a good life, the value of relationships, the maintenance of well-being, the establishment of justice, the protection of human rights, and so on. Such analysis helps a given religious community think through issues from the perspective of their own theological commitments and may even provide insights for those working outside their particular community.

Some, however, have taken a further step and argued more generally for an evaluative approach to popular culture. Lynch, for example, bemoans the neglect of evaluation and argues the case for a 'theological aesthetics' of popular culture. He is, in other words, keen to see the study of religion and popular culture include aesthetic judgement. Is this film or piece of music good, bad, spiritually uplifting, degrading, morally weak and so on? Other scholars, however, would argue that the lack of such judgements in the analysis of popular culture is less a matter of neglect and more a recognition that this type of evaluation is inappropriate and, indeed, not possible in any meaningful sense. The reception of popular culture is just too fundamentally subjective. What is spiritually uplifting to one person is trivial to another and what may be beautiful to me is ugly to you. An individual's encounter with popular culture has to be understood in personal, social, historical, and genre contexts – it is a personal encounter. Consequently, it might be argued that the development of a theological aesthetics is not only a backward step towards prescriptive elitism, but an intellectual cul-de-sac, a dead end of arguments over personal preferences. Although Lynch acknowledges these problems, he believes that they can be overcome. Others will be more sceptical about the desirability, if not the possibility of a theological aesthetics and, indeed, any form of evaluation of popular culture. These are important issues and it is likely that they will stimulate debate as the discipline matures.

This chapter is an overview of the emergence of the concept of popular culture and its importance as an area of analysis. It is also an introduction to the way cultural theorists, scholars of religion, and theologians are thinking about it. However, because many of the most useful critical tools which are increasingly used by theologians and scholars of religion have been developed within cultural studies, the chapter will also examine the work done within that broad area.

Defining popular culture

Cultura popularis

Raymond Williams (1921–1988), a key figure in the development of the study of popular culture, makes the point that the word 'popular' was 'originally a legal and political term, from *popularis*', meaning 'belonging to the people'. In the modern period, 'popular' came to mean that which was 'well-liked by many people' (1988: 236). Although it was eventually invested with other related meanings, this seems a good place to begin. Popular culture is that which is available to, accessible to, and appreciated by the people. It is the culture of the people – *cultura popularis*.

But what is meant by 'the people'? For example, a quantitative index might be used, according to which The Beatles, Coldplay, soap operas, *Grand Theft Auto*, books by John Grisham, Harry Potter, football and Hollywood films are identifiably *popular* culture, in the sense that *many* people find them accessible and enjoyable. However, although it should be fairly straightforward to decide what is and what is not popular on the basis of, for example, sales and viewing figures, problems emerge when determining the level of sales required in order to establish 'popularity'. Does an artist have to sell a certain number of CDs or downloads to be considered 'popular'? Alternatively, if a piece of classical music becomes 'popular' because of, for example, its use in an advertisement, does that make it 'popular music'? When 'popular music' is so idiosyncratic that it is appreciated by only a small number of devoted enthusiasts, such as some forms of extreme metal or avant-garde electronica, is it *popular* music? Hence, while some theorists argue that any definition of popular culture requires, at least, quantitative data to be taken into account, to rely solely on sales and viewing/listening figures is problematic.

The above distinctions, such as that between *popular* music and *classical* music, raise another important issue in defining popular culture. In thinking of popular cultural artifacts and activities, some readers may have understood them, as some scholars have done, in terms of cultural alterity. That is to say, 'popular culture' is that which is *other*. It is, for example, *other than* 'culture'. Popular music is *other than* classical music. In other words, 'the popular' is understood to be, not simply that which belongs to the masses, the culture of the populace, but rather that which is *other than* more sophisticated, 'high brow' forms of culture. It is a residual category, an umbrella term for *that which is left over* once the parameters of 'culture' have been defined. Clearly, therefore, the terms 'culture' and 'popular culture' are very often loaded, in that they are inherently hierarchical and evaluative, with popular forms often being understood, not simply as *different*, but as *inferior*. 'Culture', on the other hand, has often been understood as the sum total of morally and spiritually superior human accomplishments. Hence, to drive this point home, 'culture' is often labelled '*high* culture', over against '*popular* culture', which is understood in terms of '*low* culture'. The term '*mass* culture' is also used for that which is motivated by financial profit. That is to say, because mass culture refers to that which is mass produced to satisfy consumer demand, it must also be *popular* and *low*.

As with 'art', while most people will feel that they know what 'popular culture' is when they encounter it, the task of actually defining it is not as straightforward as it might first appear and is often informed by other interests.

As far as this chapter is concerned, the definition is inclusive. The meaning of *popularis*, we have seen, concerns that which is of the populace, of the people, rather than of any elite group within a given society. Indeed, following the lead of 'culturalism' (see p. 508), the term 'culture' is used to refer, not to 'high culture', but to the everyday lives of the people, their social and cultural contexts, their work, their entertainment, their relationships, their daily rituals, their discourse, including their ideas about religion, spirituality, and the paranormal. This is important, because while much valuable work has been done by theologians and scholars of religion in terms of analyzing the content of 'texts', such as books and films, more needs to be done in terms of interrogating the *cultura popularis* – the meanings, discourses, patterns, and structures of *everyday life*. That is to say, in studying popular culture as part of everyday life, the focus widens from particular artifacts (films, CDs, books, etc.) to take in larger social, religious and political contexts within which the artifacts are located. While studies of popular culture can sometimes be little more than a geek's mind in print (e.g. detailed analyses of the topography of other planets in Star Trek or songs by The Beatles beginning with 'I'), if these contexts are kept to the fore, the analysis of religion and popular culture will include important discussions of the nature of the human self and society. In other words, the study of religion and popular culture can help us to understand something about ourselves, our values, and our beliefs. It can have an important critical function in exposing structures of power and the ideological influence of the media. Through such a reading of popular culture, we can observe the values and ideas embedded within apparently neutral artifacts. This is an important task which will allow scholars of religion and theologians to expose, challenge and resist that which is oppressive and dehumanizing in contemporary society. Again, we will see that the tools developed within cultural studies are enormously helpful in assisting us to do this.

Culture and civilization

The notion of popular culture as the debased *other* is central to the emergence of the concept itself. It is particularly evident in the writings of perhaps the first modern theorist of popular culture, the influential poet and literary critic Matthew Arnold (1822–1888) who inaugurated what has become known as 'the culture and civilization tradition'.

For Arnold, popular culture, religion and politics were inextricably related. The son of Thomas Arnold, the Headmaster of Rugby and the principal architect of the public school system in England, he inherited his father's deep sense of Christian morality and his commitment to education as a force for social improvement. In his book *Culture and Anarchy* (1869), he identified culture as knowledge, 'the best that has been thought and known in the world'. More specifically, culture makes 'reason and the will of God prevail'. Indeed, there is a sense in which, for Arnold, the process of becoming cultured is similar to the process of sanctification within Christian theology. It is part of an individual's progress towards 'perfection', in that the very process of becoming cultured has a 'moral, social and beneficial character . . .'. Consequently, when he spoke of those who were 'cultivated' and 'cultured', he referred not just to those who were well-versed in the arts, but also to those who were morally and spiritually superior. Moreover, because it is closely linked to God's purpose in creation, people should be encouraged to become cultured, for in culture we see that which is able 'to minister to the diseased spirit of our time'. This is an important point as far as popular culture is concerned. For, while he never actually uses the term, it is clear that what we would now understand to be 'popular culture' is literally opposed to all that he invested in the term 'culture'. Popular culture is 'anarchy' and has its origins in human sin.

Arnold's theologically informed understanding of culture and anarchy is, of course, profoundly political. Culture is largely the preserve of the educated and the wealthy, a core characteristic of good breeding. Anarchy, however, is manifested in the working class masses and is a destabilizing threat to decent society and to the progress of Christian civilization. The social function of culture is, therefore, to resist anarchy, to challenge that which is 'raw and uncultivated', hedonistic, banal, and vulgar. On the other hand, culture will inoculate the aristocracy and the middle classes against 'the diseased spirit of our time'. It will protect the carriers of culture and transform the uncultured.

As always, the context is significant, in that Arnold was concerned about the threat of anarchy because of certain changes that were taking place in nineteenth-century Britain. In general, the industrial revolution had witnessed the creation of a new industrial urban civilization. In particular, Victorian industrialization and urbanization had created a space within which popular culture was able to flourish. As well as clear lines of class segregation forming in the cities, with whole areas being populated solely by the working class, there were new work relations in industry. Together these led to a cultural shift, in that the working class began developing an independent culture uninfluenced by the culture of the dominant classes. Hence, as well as the emergence of new cultural entrepreneurs, it became the culture of radicals, forged in dire circumstances and intended to inspire political agitation. Consequently, working class culture threatened the social cohesion and stability of the past (from which the dominant classes benefited) and challenged political and cultural authority.

It is little surprise, therefore, that Arnold, as a member of the privileged classes, concluded that Britain was in peril. Along with the decline of the aristocracy, the growing political organization of the working class had led to an erosion of attitudes of subordination and deference. Moreover, working class people, who he referred to as the 'unsound majority', were uneducated and, therefore, wholly unfit for the power they were beginning to assume. Consequently, Arnold concluded that there was a clear role for the authority of the State, which, through culture and coercion, would bring an end to working class thinking and political agitation and, through education, would introduce the masses to the culture of the elite. This culture would, in turn, have the effect of suppressing the appetite of the masses for the vulgar and uncivilized entertainment that inspired such anarchic thinking. However, while he argued that culture would always be good for society, in that it inhibited the tendency towards anarchy, he could not free himself from a fundamental elitism that insisted on bourgeois superiority. In the final analysis, he believed that the masses would always be uneducated, rude and vulgar, and that the bourgeoisie would always be the locus of culture. Again, for this reason, he insisted that the privileged in society must be protected by the State from the proletariat and that popular culture must be suppressed.

The Arnoldian perspective is important, not only because religion, politics, and culture are so closely related, but also because of its influence on the elitist core of modernism and, in turn, on subsequent understandings of 'popular culture' – which have inhibited its study in academia. This is evident in the initial twentieth-century discussions of popular culture, which began in the 1930s. Following Arnold, there was a hostility to any cultural manifestation outside of the traditional, educated, and elitist class. For example, in America, the influential art critic Clement Greenberg (1909–1994) was scathing in his analyses of popular culture or what he referred to as 'kitsch' produced 'without effort'. A similar opinion was expressed in Britain by one of the twentieth century's most important literary critics, Frank Raymond Leavis (1895–1978). For Leavis and his wife, Queenie Dorothy Leavis (1900–1982), the cultural crisis Arnold had identified was continuing apace. 'Mass culture', particularly evident in the rise of Hollywood, was not only a poor imitation of elitist culture, but it was designed to appeal to the uneducated tastes of the working class. It taught nothing, it conveyed no worthwhile messages, and it communicated no laudable values. Instead, mass culture had the effect of lulling its audience into a false perception of reality, deadening them to the true difficulties of life. Hollywood films, for example, 'involve surrender, under conditions of hypnotic receptivity, to the cheapest emotional appeals, appeals the more insidious because they are associated with a compellingly vivid illusion of actual life'. Similarly, popular fiction 'is the very reverse of recreation, in that it tends, not to strengthen and refresh the addict for living, but to increase his unfitness by habituating him to weak evasions, to the refusal to face reality at all'. As with Arnold, he understood culture to belong to the privileged minority. The problem in the twentieth century, however, was that the cultural elite was being challenged. There had been a 'collapse of authority', an erosion of deference, and a serious questioning of the standards previously set by the privileged minority. Since the industrial revolution, prior to which 'there was . . . a real culture of the people . . . a rich traditional culture', a 'folk culture', the masses had systematically revolted against their cultural masters and destroyed all that was culturally positive.

Although Arnold and Leavis were shaped very much by their contexts, which helps us to make sense of their ideas and concerns, nowadays their reasoning seems archaic. Elitist categories such as 'high' and 'low' culture appear arbitrary, particularly when they are also mapped onto class distinctions. To make a fixed division between high and popular cultures, and then to argue that cultural taste is linked to class, ignores the fluidity and complexity of contemporary cultural life. For example, in 1969 the rock band Deep Purple released their *Concerto for Group and Orchestra*, composed by Jon Lord (the group's Hammond organist) and performed with The Royal Philharmonic Orchestra, conducted by Malcolm Arnold. Is this popular culture or high culture? Is this, perhaps, how the upper classes prefer to listen to working class music? Of course not! Similarly, the tenor aria 'Nessun Dorma', from the final act of Puccini's opera *Turandot*, sung by Luciano Pavarotti, achieved success in the UK singles chart following its adoption as the theme of the BBC's television coverage of the 1990 World Cup in Italy. Again, there have been dance and ambient musical interpretations of classical music, such as *Pieces in a Modern Style* (2000) by William Orbit and *Aria* (1999) by Paul Schwartz and Mario Grigorov. Is this popular culture or high culture? Is this perhaps how the working classes prefer to listen to upper class music? Of course not! The attempt to divide culture in this simplistic way is inevitably artificial and clumsy, in that, even if we were to accept the categorization of 'high' and 'low' cultures, they are not stable. Not only is there considerable fluidity between 'the high' and 'the low', but there is significant migration. For example, in different ways the work of Peter Blake, Roy Lichtenstein, and Andy Warhol vividly illustrate how pop art can become high art (and vice versa) within a relatively short period of time. Hence, there is much to be said for abandoning the use of the term 'popular culture' altogether, in that it tends to perpetuate this type of either/or thinking. Indeed, we will see that, to some extent, a far more inclusive and adequate use of the term 'culture' was developed within the discipline of cultural studies in the 1970s.

Religion, theology and popular culture

A helpful typology of the differing relations between religion and popular culture has been produced by Bruce David Forbes and Jeffrey Mahan (2000). While all such typologies have their weaknesses, it does provide a useful framework for our discussion. They identify four broad categories: (1) religion in popular culture; (2) popular culture in religion; (3) popular culture as religion; (4) religion and popular culture in dialogue.

Religion in popular culture

Until relatively recently, much analysis of the relationship between religion and popular culture fell into this category, in that it discussed the articulation of religious ideas and values within popular culture. Popular cultural artefacts were interrogated in order to expose and analyse themes of interest to scholars of religion. Film, in particular, has been the subject of much discussion. For example, Christopher Deacy's *Screen Christologies* (2001) and Clive Marsh's *Cinema and Sentiment* (2004) argue that cinema can provide a context for the exploration of theological questions. In so doing, it replaces the role of the church, becoming a significant setting for the articulation of hopes and values. For example, not only does Marsh find four images of salvation within Frank Darabont's 1994 film *The Shawshank Redemption*, but he argues that it raises issues for theologians to consider, notably, the relationship between salvation and violence. The significance of the rhetoric of violence in popular culture has been discussed at some length by scholars of religion (e.g. Christianson and Partridge, 2009; Mitchell, 2007). To what degree does violent rhetoric shape belief and values? How might we understand the social function of violence in popular discourses? How might we understand audience empathy with violent protagonists in popular narratives? What is the significance of violence being associated with particular religious groups or ideas in the media? Can violence be interpreted less in terms of destruction and disruption, and more in terms of that which is potentially liberating? Even if it is potentially liberating, ethically, what is one to make of those films which appear to glorify antagonism and those that are graphically sadistic, manifesting a pornography of gore? Such questions became particularly acute for Christian theologians when Mel Gibson's *The Passion of the Christ* was released in 2004. Although containing extended scenes of extreme violence, Christian groups actively promoted the film. Indeed, while Christians have been strongly critical of filmic violence, it is interesting to note that letters of complaint were written to the British Board of Film Classification (BBFC) arguing that the 18 certificate should be lowered to 15 because of the importance of the film's religious content. Although these requests were rejected by the BBFC, in 2007 a re-edited, less violent version of the film was awarded a 15 certificate. Such attitudes raise questions about the nature and reception of filmic violence. For example, in what sense is the extreme violence against Jesus in *The Passion* distinct from the violence in, say, Quentin Tarantino's *Pulp Fiction* (1994), which arguably has

FIGURE 20.1
The Passion of the Christ

Still from *The Passion of the Christ*. © Icon Prod. / Marquis Films / The Kobal Collection / Antonello, Phillipe.

a strong theme of redemption? What does the promotion of violence in *The Passion* and the condemnation of violence in a film like *Pulp Fiction* reveal about the reception of those films?

Deacy (2001) has argued that, in a way analogous to Christian thought, films can expose the brokenness of the world, prior to exploring the hope of redemption. Moreover, in some films, particularly those of the 'film noir' genre, not only are the themes of grace and damnation dealt with, but the protagonists are often messianic, in that they undertake a soteriological role of redemption from sin, guilt and alienation, the benefits of which are then imparted to other characters in the film. Similarly, although critical of some interpretations, Marsh (2004) notes that often the characters played by Robin Williams can be understood as 'Christ figures', in that they enable the transformation of others.

Thinking of Christ figures in film, the analysis of which is often clumsy and contrived, Deacy has creatively employed the classical distinction between Alexandrian and Antiochene christologies, the former emphasizing the divine nature of Christ and the latter his human nature. Hence, a good example of an Alexandrian screen christology would be *The Greatest Story Ever Told* (1965), as well as films which portray the protagonist as superhuman. In other words, the redeemer as superhero is more Alexandrian. However, audiences, he argues, tend to identify with a more human, Antiochene redeemer, a typical example of which is the Jesus portrayed in Martin Scorsese's *The Last Temptation of Christ* (1988).

Equally interesting are the recent studies of horror and demonology in popular culture. From German Expressionist films between 1913 and 1933 to contemporary Satan films, the Devil and his minions have not lost their appeal, being regularly summoned to challenge and frighten. Indeed, Douglas Cowan's *Sacred Terror* (2008), which explores religious themes and values within horror films, argues that much of the success of supernatural horror is linked to some understanding of the sacred and, therefore, to a survival of the sacralized self within supposedly secular societies. They depend on the acceptance of religious and paranormal demonologies.

Concerning the reception of film, it has been argued that emotional triggers can be a catalyst for the transformation of viewers. Again, *The Shawshank Redemption* (1994) is a good example, in that, while not an explicitly religious film, it had an extraordinary impact on viewers (see the quotation from the film critic Mark Kermode in the text box)

. . . when I was asked to write and present a Channel Four documentary to accompany the screening of *The Shawshank Redemption*, it was toward the audience reaction that I turned my attention, convinced there must be some reason why such an apparently innocuous film was having such a profound effect on so many disparate viewers. It was during the course of making that documentary . . . that I first encountered the quasi-religious interpretation of Frank Darabont's movie . . .

BOX 20.1 Mark Kermode quote

Hence, again, as well as examining the content of films, scholars are urged to consider their reception. What are films doing to viewers?

Popular culture in religion

Popular culture is increasingly appropriated by religious groups and institutions. Although, as we will see is the case with Christianity, it is not uncommon for conservative religion to reject all forms and styles of popular culture, many do borrow. For example, particularly within the 'emerging church' movement (which seeks to respond to contemporary cultural shifts), there has been an adoption of certain club cultural elements. This was particularly evident in the controversial ministry of the Nine O'Clock Service (NOS) in the 1990s. While drawing on the work of well-known theologians, such as Matthew Fox and Jürgen Moltmann, this Anglican Church in Sheffield, UK, made particular use of multimedia arts and culturally relevant music in its attempt to articulate 'a postmodern agenda' for a new generation of Christians. The leader of the community, Chris Brain, was even ordained, at some considerable cost, in the cassock worn by Robert De Niro in *The Mission* (1986). The point is that religion is here making use of popular culture in order to attain some level of cultural relevance. This, of course, might be interpreted as an explicit attempt to rebrand Christianity as 'cool' by transforming its image in accordance with popular culture.

Interestingly, many Pagans recommend fiction, such as Terry Pratchett's Discworld series and Alan Garner's *The Owl Service* (1967), as an introduction to their tradition rather than more formal manuals (see Chapter 14 on Paganism).

Popular music, of course, is often used within religion. For example, although reggae is very closely identified with Rastafarianism, so successful has it become as a musical genre, that other faiths have used it to communicate their own religious ideas. The band Christafari delivers a mainstream Christian message, while Matisyahu communicates Orthodox Jewish teaching. Although there are those within Judaism and Islam who seek to convey religious ideas through popular music, particularly rock music, it is the contemporary Christian music industry that has been most successful in pressing popular culture into the service of religion. With origins in the Jesus Movement of the early 1970s, which sought to offer an alternative to 'the devil's music', Christian popular music has evolved from poorly produced Bible-based music with an explicit evangelistic rationale and marginal appeal, to a major industry with numerous genres, its own celebrities and, in some cases, mainstream appeal. Indeed, few genres or subcultures evade baptism. For example, thinking of its criticisms of 'the devil's music', it is interesting to note the evolution of 'Christian black metal' or 'unblack metal' as it's sometimes called. This is interesting because black metal is an extreme subgenre of heavy metal, the signification of which is explicitly misanthropic, anti-Christian and, in some cases, Satanist. Black metal musicians have been linked to church burnings, mutilation, and even murder. The intention of Christian black metal appears to be explicitly apologetic, as is evident from perhaps the first unblack metal recording, a demo tape entitled *The Defeat of Satan* (1991) by the Norwegian band Crush Evil, who were later to become Antestor. Again, the context within which unblack metal emerged is significant in that it was in Norway that black metal became most associated with Satanism, extreme rightwing politics, church burnings, and murder.

The appropriation of aspects of popular culture by religious individuals, groups, and institutions has caused some concern about the effect it has on religion. For example, drawing on Neil Postman's influential thesis in *Amusing Ourselves to Death* (1985), Forbes and Mahan (2000) note that in 'the television era' entertainment has become the highest value. Hence, anything that appears on television (or, indeed, in films and popular music) is perceived to be entertainment. Consquently, when religion appears on television, regardless of the intentions of the producers, it is received by its viewers as entertainment. Moreover, television has socialized us into expecting everything to be similarly entertaining. This, in turn, puts enormous pressure on religions to be entertaining and to provide spirituality in a way that their members have been taught to expect by popular culture. This raises important questions about, not only whether the fundamental character and content of religion is altered when received as entertainment, but also whether religion *per se* is being shaped by the media and popular culture.

Popular culture as religion

Some forms of popular culture can function in ways that are implicitly or even explicitly religious. In examining popular culture *as* religion most discussions utilize a 'functional' definition of religion. That is to say, religion is defined, not in terms of what it *is* (a 'substantive' definition), but in terms of what it *does*. Hence, a social or cultural phenomenon can be identified as 'religious' if it fulfils certain functions normally ascribed to religion, such as the provision of purpose in life, hope in the shadow of death, and meaning in the face of suffering and injustice. Clearly, examining human society and culture from this perspective encourages the view that religion is not unique in providing strategies to overcome fear, despair and hopelessness. Indeed, it is possible to view a wide range of activities in this way. For example, it is not difficult to understand various forms of fandom as implicitly religious. In football, devotion can be seen in the regular attendance at weekly rituals (football games which include ritualized behaviour of fans), commitment to pilgrimage (linked, perhaps, to significant moments in a football club's history), the collection of sacred artifacts (such as turf from a particular pitch or the shirt of a revered player), and the discourses of fans which suggest the provision of meaning in life.

Similar levels of commitment can be seen in the significance of celebrities for fans. Elvis is a particularly good example: his home, Graceland, has become a shrine; some believers claim to have had visions of him; theological links are made between Elvis and Christianity; there are both serious and spoof religious organizations devoted to the worship of Elvis, such as 'The First Presleyterian Church of Elvis the Divine' and 'The First Church of Jesus Christ, Elvis'. The same, of course, is true of other musical celebrities such as Jim Morrison (of The Doors) whose grave in the Père Lachaise cemetery in Paris receives a regular stream of pilgrims and functions conspicuously as a shrine for many devotees.

Religion and popular culture in dialogue

There is a sense in which this is a superfluous category. Forbes and Mahan (2000) consider it necessary because it includes 'interactions between religion and popular culture [which] do not fit well in the three categories thus far'. However, a more flexible understanding of the first three categories must include some form of dialogue. Hence, while Forbes and Mahan intend that debates surrounding, for example, filmic violence should be included in this category, we have seen that analyses of religion and values in popular culture should be attending to such issues. Indeed, some form of dialogic engagement is central to the analysis of popular culture in all of the above categories.

Occulture and popular culture

In 1972, the British sociologist Colin Campbell argued that cultic organizations arise out of a general cultural ethos, a 'cultic milieu'. The concept of the cultic milieu is helpful for understanding, not only contemporary commitment to alternative spiritualities and the paranormal, but also the religious significance of popular culture. Having said that, for various reasons, key themes within the cultic milieu suggest that the term 'occultic' is a more precise adjective than the older sociological term 'cultic'. This is certainly the case if one considers, not only the contemporary alternative religious milieu in the West, but much of the content of popular culture, whether film, literature, music, or computer games. More particularly, thinking of 'culture' in terms of the meanings, discourses, patterns, and structures of everyday life, it is evident that what we are witnessing is the emergence of an 'occulture'.

Occulture refers to those social processes by which spiritual, paranormal, esoteric and conspiratorial meanings are produced, circulated and exchanged. As such, it includes an enormous, constantly expanding and recycled range of ideas and practices, from extreme rightwing religio-politics to radical environmentalism, from angels to ghosts and demons, from spirit guides to astral projection, from a fascination with ancient and mythical civilizations to the tarot and the Kabbalah, from *feng shui* to eschatological prophecies, from the Holy Grail to Wicca, and from alternative science to UFOs and alien abduction. Popular self-help literature, for example, demonstrates the way such fungible ideas are utilized, understood and disseminated. For example, some years ago two very popular series of books were published: '*Principles of . . .*' (published by Thorsons) and '*Elements of . . .*' (published by Element). Overall, they constituted a general introduction to the more 'respectable' occultural beliefs and practices. Although some of the books, such as *Principles of Numerology*, *Principles of Wicca*, *Principles of Tarot*, and *Principles of Your Psychic Potential* could be described as 'occultic' in the narrower sense of the term, others, such as *Principles of Colonic Irrigation*, discuss subjects that are not 'occultic' in themselves but have, nevertheless, become occultural. In other words, within occulture, the interest in colonic irrigation – a procedure for removing waste and toxins from the bowel – is part of a broader interest in well-being and the self. Again, key ideas and practices of religious traditions, such as Buddhism, are de-traditionalized. That is to say, such consumers of occulture are not particularly interested in becoming devout Buddhists, but rather want simply to acquaint themselves with some *principles* of Buddhist belief and practice, which can then be merged with some *elements* from other systems in the service of the self. Hence, the meaning of certain Buddhist beliefs and practices, as well as those of procedures such as colonic irrigation, shifts. However, the point is that, subjective spiritualities, focused on a personal journey, rather than a commitment to a particular tradition, find in occulture a rich resource for new ways of thinking and being.

Popular culture is central to the efficacy of occulture, in that it feeds ideas into the occultural pool, develops, mixes, disseminates those ideas, and thereby suggests new lines of occultural thought. Indeed, occulture, particularly visual occulture, animates ideas and practices. Concepts and theories such as the manipulation of energies, the efficacy of spells, the existence of faeries, and the probability of alien intelligences have life breathed into them by visual occulture. Intriguing avenues of possibility are opened up. Hence, the theory of occulture argues that *popular occulture* is, in various ways, sacralizing the Western mind – introducing it to new spiritualities, mainstreaming older esoteric theories, championing the paranormal and often challenging traditional, particularly Christian, forms of religion. Indeed, as well as popular culture being used as introductory material within Paganism, it is not difficult to find new religious groups and spiritualities that have their origins in popular culture, from the Church of All Worlds (Robert Heinlein's *Stranger in a Strange Land*) to spiritually oriented vampire belief (vampire fiction) and the Jedi faith (*Star Wars*).

A good recent example of the relationship between occulture and popular culture is Dan Brown's *The Da Vinci Code* (2004), the enormous success of which is itself an indication of the appetite for occulture in the modern world. It very clearly introduces people to alternative spiritual theories, challenges traditional authorities and rationalizes everything with conspiracy. Reflecting the occultural zeitgeist, it is not difficult to trace occulturally important streams of thought in the book, from Indian spirituality to Paganism and Earth mysteries, and from secret societies to a range of conspiracies relating to ideas of global domination. Indeed, Brown's earlier book, *Angels and Demons* (2000), which first introduces his protagonist, Robert Langdon, concerns one of the most enduring and widespread modern conspiracy theories relating to world domination, namely that of the Illuminati. *The Da Vinci Code* simply develops this popular conspiracist approach in relation to traditional forms of religion generally, and to the Church, Opus Dei, the Prior of Sion and the Knights Templar in particular. It is, in other words, an explicitly occultural attack on organized religion. However, the point is that it is a good example of popular *occulture* because, not only does it draw on occulture for many of its ideas, but it weaves these together in a distinctive way, thereby creating a new occultural narrative, and then disseminates that narrative within occulturally curious societies. More specifically, for many readers it raised questions about the church by introducing them to new occultural theories, which will, almost certainly, be merged with other theories introduced elsewhere in popular culture. The net effect of this process is occulturation (increased occultural curiosity). For example, a 2005 survey of the Danish adult population found that the Harry Potter stories, Tolkien's *The Lord of the Rings* and Dan Brown's *The Da Vinci Code* and *Angels and Demons* all increased interest in 'magic and fantasy' for about a third of respondents. Indeed, 53.5 per cent of respondents stated that Dan Brown's novels had increased their interest in 'religious issues'.

Christ, culture and apologetics

Most recent approaches to the study of popular culture from the perspective of religious studies seek to be theologically disinterested and draw on methodologies developed within cultural studies and the social sciences. Theologically interested approaches, on the other hand, usually explicitly articulate confessional and often apologetic and missiological perspectives. That is to say, they have a faith investment in the analysis of popular culture and seek to defend a particular understanding of that faith as the absolute source of goodness and truth.

A classic and still influential discussion of the relationship between theology and culture is *Christ and Culture* (1951) by H. Richard Niebuhr (1894–1962). This analysis of what he calls the 'double wrestle' of the church (i.e. the Christian's struggle with what the Bible teaches and the culture 'with which it lives in symbiosis') argues that there has never been a consensus concerning the relationship between Christ (i.e. Christian faith and theology) and 'culture' (i.e. 'the world'). Historically, there have been a variety of theological responses to culture, which can be gathered together in five broad approaches: Christ against culture; the Christ of culture; Christ above culture; Christ and culture in paradox; Christ the transformer of culture.

The first approach, *Christ against culture*, dismisses engagement with culture as theological disobedience. Typical of highly dualistic conservative theologies, it argues that the 'world', determined by 'sin', is intellectually and spiritually opposed to the absolute truth of the Christian revelation. Hence, because culture contradicts revelation, the individual is presented with a choice between light and darkness, truth and falsity. Extreme examples of this approach include 'world-rejecting' new religions or communities such as the Amish, which physically seek to separate themselves from the surrounding culture. However, even those that do not go to the trouble of physical separation, do make a rigid distinction between 'Christ' and 'culture' and seek to limit exposure to popular culture as much as possible. They are, therefore, particularly critical of 'popular culture *in* religion'.

A good example of this approach is John Blanchard's *Pop Goes the Gospel* (1983), which views popular music through a narrow theological lens. While pretending to 'take a calm, balanced, thorough and biblical look at the whole subject', he provides a negative assessment of popular music which claims to uncover explicit and subliminal occult messages, blasphemy when songs are played backwards, an encouragement 'to get turned on to drugs', and the ubiquitous promotion of 'filth' (i.e. sexual promiscuity) in 'masturbatory rock'. However, his principal argument is that 'the case against the use of pop music in evangelism is overwhelming'. Popular music is simply incompatible with Christian faith.

Similarly, within Orthodox Judaism, an approach that might described as *Torah against culture* has been responsible for debate over the use of non-kosher musical styles. Lipa Schmeltzer, for example, although a devout and popular Haredi singer, who sings in Yiddish and derives his lyrics from sacred texts, is severely criticized by some rabbis for producing music that is indecent and unfit for the Jewish public. According to Rabbi Efraim Luft of Israel's ultra-Orthodox Committee for Jewish Music, such musicians 'are leading the public astray and are causing a great negative influence on the young generation'. However, while he is, like Blanchard, critical of the lyrical content of secular popular music, his concern is more to do with its instrumentation: 'The main part of the music should be the melody. Percussion should be secondary. They should not bend notes electronically and should not use instruments like electric guitars, bass guitars or saxophones in Jewish music.' To do so is inherently corrupting. For example, in 'Rules for Playing Kosher Music' (published by the Committee for Jewish Music) we are told that 'the saxophone has replaced the clarinet in [Haredi] rock music because it produces . . . indecent sounds . . . When the saxophone was adopted for use in jazz bands in the 1920s it received the name "the Devil's flute" because of its indecent seductive tones'. Indeed, the 'purpose of modern music', insists Rabbi Luft, 'is to distract young people and change good characters into bad'. This is why, even well-intended Jewish popular music, 'where the dangerous beat plays more of a part than the melody, has no place in a society where people are trying to keep their moral standards high . . .'. Such is the influence of bodies like the Committee for Jewish Music and the Guardians of Sanctity and Education within the Haredi community that their criticisms have led to most public concerts by ultra-Orthodox musicians being banned in Israel. Even, Menahem Toker, an award-winning disc jockey, was dismissed from a radio show as the result of pressure from Haredi activists.

The second approach identified by Niebuhr, *the Christ of culture*, stands at the opposite end of the spectrum to 'Christ against culture'. This culturally positive approach assumes that theological truth can be discovered within culture. That said, while much theologizing from a 'Christ of culture' perspective is of the 'religion *in* popular culture' type, it understands the relationship to be dynamic. In other words, Christ is actively *revealed* through both culture and faith. Hence, for example, human institutions or systems of government, such as democracy, embody theological truth. Whereas the first approach operates with a strong doctrine of *special* revelation (which understands the divine to be revealed through a particular individual or text) this approach might be understood to operate with a strong doctrine of *general* revelation (which understands the divine to be revealed through nature, the conscience, or a human artefact). In this sense, God can be understood, not only to be working within popular culture, but also to be revealed through specific forms of popular culture, such as films. Hence, in reflecting on popular culture theological truth is revealed.

The final three approaches provide mediating positions between these two poles and, according to Niebuhr, offer more mature theologies which can inform a non-revolutionary faith that seeks the gradual transformation of cultures. Perhaps the most popular of these is his final approach, *Christ the transformer of culture*. While it adopts a similarly negative understanding of culture to the first approach, it seeks positive engagement. Christian truth is understood to be a resource with which to challenge and, indeed, to convert contemporary culture. In other words, this is an essentially missiological approach to culture, in that theological engagement with culture is motivated by the desire to transform it according to Christian truths and values. One might, for example, take an apologetic approach that critically scrutinizes popular culture in order to find aspects which reflect divine truth and goodness, which can then be commented on. It is 'apologetic' because it engages with popular culture in order to commend and defend a particular theology. For example, Brian Godawa's *Hollywood Worldviews* (2002) argues, as the title suggests, that films are a source of cultural myths that inform viewers' worldviews. They introduce ideas about salvation, evil, the good life, truth, and so on. In so doing they familiarize audiences with alternatives to the Christian worldview, such as, he argues, Paganism and postmodernism. Once analysis of a film exposes these perspectives, they can then be challenged and compared to Christian theological ideas. This is understood to be the groundwork for the articulation of particular theological and cultural assumptions aimed at the transformation of culture.

Applicationist and correlational approaches

Much theological analysis of popular culture adopts what has been referred to as an applicationist approach, which seeks to apply certain predetermined theological beliefs and values critically to popular culture. The beliefs and values of popular culture are compared to theological 'truth'. In other words, there is little room for meaningful dialogue, in that the observer views popular culture with a particular set of beliefs and values in place and judges it accordingly. Godawa's *Hollywood Worldviews*, noted above, is a good example of a Christian applicationist methodology.

In the film, *Shirley Valentine*, Shirley's brief adulterous affair on holiday is represented in this story as a constructive and helpful part of her journey towards a more liberated and authentic life. Yet from a conservative, applicationist perspective, this would tend to be seen as an inappropriate celebration of an inherently sinful act.

(2005: pp. 101–102)

BOX 20.2 Gordon Lynch quote

The correlational method, on the other hand, seeks to move beyond applicationist analysis. As a form of what Niebuhr identified as 'Christ above culture', it can be found in early Christian writings, such as those of Clement of Alexandria, who challenged Gnostic teaching, arguing that Christ is 'the true gnosis'. However, in the modern period, it is Paul Tillich (1886–1965) who developed it as an important method. Essentially, Tillich's (1959) correlational method incorporates dialogue into a formal theological structure by seeking to 'correlate' analyses of the human condition produced in modern culture with 'answers' provided by 'the symbols used in the Christian message'. However, because it is an 'answering' methodology, its attempt to be truly dialogical is undermined. That is to say, while the correlational method listens to popular culture, and while it remains open to the possibility that wider culture has something to teach the theologian, in the final analysis it is convinced that the source of truth and goodness is to be found within a particular religious tradition. At a popular level, this type of thinking is evident in, for example, Connie Neal's analyses of the Harry Potter books and films. Distancing herself from the numerous Christian attacks on the Harry Potter phenomenon, she argues that it introduces certain important moral and spiritual themes (2002). Nevertheless, she is clear that Harry Potter must be read through a Christian theological lens and the issues should necessarily be addressed from a 'biblical perspective'.

Recognising the limits of Tillich's correlational approach, it has been revised by the Roman Catholic theologian David Tracy (1939–). His 'revised correlational method', which analyses theology's relation with the modern situation, seeks to be both mutually illuminating and mutually critical (1975, 1981). In other words, whereas the correlational method brings the questions raised by culture into dialogue with the answers revealed within the Christian tradition, the revised correlational method looks to cultural analysis to provide answers as well. That is to say, revised correlational analysis forces the theologian to go beyond providing an *answering theology* to engagement in a *listening theology* that genuinely searches for answers within culture – answers which may well challenge established religious truth claims. For the scholar of religion and popular culture, this provides a genuine attempt at openness and dialogue, in which popular culture becomes an important resource for truth and goodness in its own right. A good example of a theologian who has taken this approach in his analysis of popular culture is Tom Beaudoin (1998). Christianity, he argues, has much to learn from popular culture and might even be transformed by listening seriously to the concerns, questions and answers articulated by it.

In developing a cogent revised correlational approach to popular culture, theologians would learn much from their colleagues in cultural studies.

Learning from cultural studies

The above approaches will take us some way towards understanding the relationship between religion and popular culture. However, they can only take us so far. Convinced of the value of interdisciplinary research, some scholars of religion (including some of those already mentioned) are turning to cultural studies to provide a theoretical perspective and critical tools which will enable a more comprehensive understanding of the production of meaning and the mutual influence religion and popular culture have on each other. What follows is a brief introduction to some of the ideas developed within cultural studies that are relevant to the study of religion and popular culture. It will also help the reader to situate the study of religion and popular culture within a wider cultural and intellectual context.

The culture industry and the opium of the masses

The Frankfurt Institute for Social Research was founded in 1923 by a group of German intellectuals, most of whom were upper and middle class, leftwing, and Jewish. As far as the study of popular culture is concerned, the key theorists at the School were Theodor Adorno (1903–1969), Max Horkheimer (1895–1973), Herbert Marcuse (1898–1979), Leo Lowenthal (1900–1993), and Walter Benjamin (1892–1940). When Hitler rose to power in the 1930s, the School relocated from Frankfurt to Columbia University, New York, with some members moving to Los Angeles. In 1949 the School moved back to Germany, although some members remained in the United States. These geographical, political and cultural contexts are important, in that they informed the School's analysis of popular culture. For example, not only was the School greatly occupied with the significance of the influence of the Hollywood film industry, but Adorno's influential work on popular music was shaped to some extent by his experience of Tin Pan Alley compositions and the emergence of jazz in America. More importantly, directly affected by virulent anti-Semitism and the rise of totalitarian regimes in both Germany and Italy, their work was shaped by a deep concern for human freedom. In America, Adorno felt that this freedom was being threatened by a more subtle form of totalitarianism, namely a cultural system over which people had no control and which shaped their understanding of the world. Indeed, his experience of the 'authoritarian irrationalism' of fascism and anti-Semitism led to a concern about the prevalence of the irrational in American popular culture. For example, he produced a lengthy and insightful content analysis of the astrology column in the *Los Angeles Times*.

While much could be said about all the members of the Frankfurt School with an interest in popular culture, not least Benjamin, whose thought departed in several respects from that of his colleagues, this section will focus primarily on Adorno. In particular, it will introduce what he called 'the culture industry', a term he and Horkheimer coined to refer to the products and processes of 'mass culture'.

While Adorno viewed the culture industry and popular culture in a similarly negative way to Arnold, he thought quite differently about its effects. Rather than it being an agent for 'anarchy', it actually appeared to inhibit social change. Central to Adorno's thinking was the idea that the masses were operating with what Karl Marx (1818–1883) had identified as a 'false consciousness' imposed on them by the ruling class. That is to say, not only are the dominant ideas and values in a society those of the ruling class, reflecting and maintaining their interests, but they shape the way all the members of that society think about the world and their place in it, including the subordinate classes, who simply accept it as an accurate reflection of reality. This 'false consciousness', this false view of reality, is circulated through the culture industry, which convinces the masses that this is the way things are and this is the way they should be. However, rather than simply stating this explicitly, the culture industry insinuates its ideology into people's minds and undermines the desire for change in a far more subtle way. This type of analysis and the issues it raises are, of course, directly relevant to scholars of religion seeking to understand the role of popular culture in the construction of values and the maintenance of power relations in society.

Adorno's work on popular music is a good example of how he understood the culture industry to operate. To begin with, however, we should note that Adorno's interest in what he clearly understood to be a debased and inferior form of music cannot be divorced from his own circumstances, just as Arnold's analysis of popular culture was shaped by his privileged position in society and just as the criticisms of rock music by conservative religious commentators are informed by their particular cultural and theological presuppositions. Not only was Adorno an accomplished composer, musician and musicologist, but he was a highly educated, upper-middle class intellectual.

Adorno argued that popular music was determined by two processes: 'standardization' and 'pseudo-individualization'. Popular music is standardized in that the songs are actually structured in much the same way. This is, he argued, typical of the way the culture industry undermines originality and authenticity with 'patterned and pre-digested' products that erode any intellectual stimulation which might lead workers to question the mechanisms of oppression that underpin the capitalist mode of production. However, because listeners desire novelty and become bored quickly, there is a continual need for perceived change. This is why, says Adorno, 'the necessary correlate of musical standardization is pseudo-individualization'. Pseudo-individualization, through various superficial and stylistic changes, makes each piece of music appear unique and different. The worker is beguiled by 'the veneer of individual "effects"' that make the 'patterned and pre-digested' product look interesting and novel. The signficance of all this in a capitalist economy is that, along with other forms of mass-produced entertainment, it distracts the workers and ensures their passivity. Popular music offers relief 'from both boredom and effort simultaneously' and can be produced on demand in a way that guarantees the relaxation of the workforce. It calms workers' minds, pacifies them, and erodes any desire to transform their conditions. Likewise, he argued that dancing to popular music uses up energy that might be better spent on social transformation.

In this way, popular culture has a narcotic effect on the masses, undermining the desire for social change and, thereby, preserving conformity to the basic structures of capitalism. As Marx said of religion, so, in effect, the Frankfurt School concluded of popular culture, it is 'the opium of the masses'. Indeed, for Adorno, the culture industry had effectively replaced religion's role in this respect. Those who submit to its beguiling influence are lulled into accepting a false consciousness. Its narcotic effects ensure that the workers are cultural dopes by providing superficial and temporary pleasure, rather than genuine wellbeing and fulfilment.

Again, there are obvious lines of continuity between Adorno's concerns and those of scholars of religion and popular culture, particularly theologians. For example, popular culture, far from providing truth and insight about the human condition, as we have seen some scholars claim that it can, might simply offer that which is deceptively superficial, and, in so doing, undermine genuine questioning, analysis and theological enquiry. Indeed, Adorno himself effectively established a link between the culture industry and secularization, popular culture and a spiritually disenchanted age within which myths and images of the divine lack potency. He saw a vibrant religious culture being replaced by a 'pseudo-culture' which, in turn, supported a pseudo-enchantment. If this is true, then occulture needs to be understood as central to the process of disenchantment, not re-enchantment.

Interestingly, in recent years, such concerns about popular culture and the manipulation of the masses have been made with reference to *The Matrix*, a film in which humanity is enslaved in a virtual reality world that limits real freedom by providing superficial pleasures. That said, the fact that *The Matrix* raises such questions suggests a counterargument to Adorno's thesis, in that film can challenge viewers to question the status quo and has encouraged significant theological and philosophical speculation. Indeed, against Adorno, there are too many examples of political protest, philosophical analysis, theological discussion, and (apparently) genuine spirituality articulated within and inspired by popular culture, too many examples of people using mass culture in ways that subvert its intended meanings, to be able wholly to accept his arguments uncritically. Nevertheless, his work does raise significant questions about the nature of popular culture that are of concern to scholars of religion and culture.

Culturalism

As the 1960s dawned, so did a new approach to the study of popular culture that would challenge the patrician elitism championed by Arnold and Leavis. Furthermore, although Marxist analysis continued to be important, gradually the Frankfurt School's suspicion of popular culture gave way to far more sympathetic neo-Marxist analyses.

This new approach to popular culture, which became known as 'culturalism', began its ascendancy in the 1950s with the work of the British scholars Richard Hoggart (1918–) and Raymond Williams and reached its apotheosis in the founding of Birmingham

University's Centre for Contemporary Cultural Studies (CCCS). If one were to identify a key moment in this history, it would be the publication of Hoggart's *The Uses of Literacy* in 1957. This book is important because, anticipating the subsequent progress of British cultural studies, it provides a thoughtful, if rather idiosyncratic account of the everyday lives of ordinary working class people, which attends in detail to diet, speech patterns, décor, family relations, popular fiction, newspapers, magazines, song lyrics and much else. A year later, in 1958, Williams produced another foundational text of culturalism, *Culture and Society*, followed, in 1961, by *The Long Revolution*. While Williams was not as concerned as Hoggart with the details of working class life, his attention to the very concept of 'culture' was also enormously important for the emerging discipline, in that he shifted the focus away from Arnold's understanding of culture as 'the best that has been thought and known in the world' to 'culture as a whole way of life'. In so doing, he stressed the importance of an ethnographic approach to the study of culture. Indeed, Hoggart's work and E.P. Thompson's (1924–1993) enormously influential text, *The Making of the English Working Class* (1963) are excellent examples of the kind of analysis Williams had in mind. Hence, whereas Arnold and Leavis had, so to speak, written their analyses of culture 'from above', operating with an aesthetic ideal of what they understood 'culture' to be, Williams, Hoggart and Thompson insisted on writing 'from below', on simply observing everyday working class life as it was being lived. While this early focus on the working class has since been significantly broadened, and while the interpretation of popular culture became increasingly positive (Hoggart's being, like Adorno's, generally negative), their overall approach has had a formative influence on subsequent cultural analysis.

Unarguably the most significant institution to promote and develop this paradigmatic shift in the study of popular culture was the CCCS at Birmingham University, founded in 1964. Although initially directed by Hoggart, it wasn't until his departure for a post at UNESCO in 1968 that it entered its most important period. Under the leadership of Hoggart's successor, Stuart Hall (1932–), the work of the CCCS was increasingly informed by three premises of Marxist analysis:

1. Cultural processes are fundamentally connected to social relations, particularly class relations and class formation;
2. Culture concerns power. As such, it affects the ability of individuals and groups to define and realize their needs;
3. Related to the first two premises, culture is a site of social difference and struggle. Indeed, because popular culture in particular came to be understood as the primary terrain of struggle, it emerged as the principal focus of cultural analysis.

While the work of several Marxist theorists influenced the analyses of the CCCS, the principal theoretical influences, particularly in the 1970s, were Louis Althusser (1918–1990), a French structuralist Marxist, and Antonio Gramsci (1891–1937), an Italian political theorist imprisoned by Mussolini. While Althusser's work shaped much of the thinking at the CCCS, particularly notable was Gramsci's understanding of 'hegemony'. For Gramsci, Marxism had traditionally placed too much weight on the significance of the economic and the industrial, neglecting the ideological and the cultural. Hence, in his reflections on why socialist struggles consistently failed, he argued that it was because bourgeois hegemony had remained in place. Indeed, the culture and civilization tradition can be understood as an explicit attempt to preserve hegemony. Arnold wanted the state to suppress 'anarchy' through both the explicit use of force and through the imposition of a particular form of 'culture'. Hegemony theory exposes the processes by which this happens.

Hegemony theory complemented the CCCS's use of Althusser's concept of 'ideological state apparatuses' (ISAs). It was argued that ISAs, which included political and educational systems, the media, the family and so on, while not *overtly* coercive, in the sense that the police, the military and the judicial system were, they were nevertheless *covertly* coercive. That is to say, while individuals felt as though they were acting as free agents, in actual fact, they were being socialized into behaving in particular ways that conformed with the dominant ideology. There are clear lines of continuity between Gramsci and Althusser here. For Gramsci, within capitalist societies there is the state, which is responsible for *overt* coercion, and there is 'civil society' which is responsible for hegemony, or *covert* coercion. In mature Western, capitalist, liberal democracies, hegemony typically operates through the groups and institutions of civil society. These groups and institutions are essentially those identified by Althusser as ISAs, particularly the mass media and those responsible for the production of popular culture. That is to say, popular culture becomes a tool of deception, oppression, and the maintenance of hegemony.

It is also important to understand that, because the coercion is covert, operating through ISAs, including the media and popular culture, hegemony is 'consensual'. Because we are socialized into thinking in certain ways, we willingly adopt the dominant worldview. This, of course, serves the interests of the powerful, in that it ensures their continued dominance. The key point, however, is that there need not be *overt* physical coercion or indoctrination involved in the consent of subordinate groups to the hegemony of the dominant group. (Again, we might think of this with reference to *The Matrix*.)

Central to this hegemonic process is the granting of concessions in order to secure consensus. For example, this can quite easily be observed in histories of colonialism, such as that in Jamaica, where the British sought to secure control over the slaves transported from West Africa by the imposition of the English language and Christianity. However, what actually emerged from this political and cultural struggle was not merely English and Christianity, but Jamaican Creole and Afro-Christianity. This new African-influenced language and religion is the consequence of a hegemonic 'negotiation' between dominant and subordinate cultures. While the religion and language allowed some separation from the dominant culture, expressing resistance, and asserting the dignity of the African slave in an oppressive context, they nevertheless constitute an expression of incorporation into the dominant culture. They are not wholly English, Christian or African, but rather occupy a negotiated position. The struggle took place, but the hegemony remained. It did so largely because the subordinate groups were allowed to incorporate something of their own culture in the dominant culture. A concession was made to the subordinate group.

Hegemony, therefore, is the result of negotiations between dominant and subordinate groups, rather than the simple imposition of power by the dominant group. Analysing popular culture from this perspective helps us to understand that it is never simply imposed from above or created from below, nor is it wholly commercial or wholly authentic, or fully an act of resistance to or incorporation into dominant culture, but rather it is always negotiated. There is always what Gramsci referred to as 'a compromise equilibrium' between competing elements.

To continue the focus on Jamaica, a good example of a compromise equilibrium or negotiation between acts of resistance and incorporation into the dominant system is the profit reggae began to make for the music industry. On the one hand, devout Rastafarians, such as Winston Rodney (Burning Spear) and Bob Marley sang about an imminent apocalypse which would bring the destruction of Babylon (i.e. Western capitalist societies) – they wanted to 'chant down Babylon'. On the other hand, many of them were signed to labels such as Island and made enormous profits. In other words, there was a negotiation between the anti-capitalist religio-politics of Rastafari and the capitalist interests of the record labels and promoters, for which Rastafarian revolutionary discourse was a commodity circulated for profit. The more success they achieved in getting their message across and the more people they converted to their

FIGURE 20.2 Burning Spear

Winston Rodney, 'Burning Spear', performs during Day One of the New Orleans Jazz and Heritage Festival at the Fair Grounds Race Course, 25 April 2008, in New Orleans, Louisiana. Courtesy Getty Images.

cause, the more Babylon, the dominant culture, benefited. There was a compromise equilibrium between Babylon and Zion; an uneasy relationship between religion and the popular music industry. The problem for the Rasta, of course, was that the hegemony of Babylon remained in place.

Structuralism and semiology

Structuralism has its roots in the ideas of the Swiss linguist Ferdinand de Saussure (1857–1913) who sought to establish a 'science of signs' in his posthumous *Course in General Linguistics* (1916). Of particular note is a distinction he makes between the 'signifier' and the 'signified', the two parts of a linguistic 'sign'. The signifier is a sound, a phrase, or a word, indeed anything which produces meaning. The signified is the image, object or idea evoked by the signifier. However, the signifier and signified have no necessary relationship. For example, the relationship (or signification) between the signifier 'church' (a sound or word) and the signified 'church' (a building with a steeple) is the result of cultural convention. We have learned to think of a particular type of building when we hear that sound or read that word. While this may seem rather obvious, semiology has become an illuminating and important area of analysis.

This is particularly important in popular culture because signification is often not straightforward. For example, a swastika worn by a German soldier and a swastika worn by a 1970s punk rocker should not be understood in the same way. Although the signifier is the same, the signifieds are different, in that the appropriation of Nazi symbolism by punks was an attempt to shape a new identity which challenged the values and interests of the dominant postwar generation, which was often nationalist and sometimes racist. In other words, this is a case of symbols being adopted and given new meanings as an act of resistance against the prevailing hegemony. The punk use of Nazi symbolism was simply 'semiotic resistance' rather than an indication of Nazism. The same might also be said of Satanic discourse and the use of inverted crucifixes in extreme metal music. It is often less an expression of committed Satanism and more a case of semiotic resistance to religious hegemony. Not to understand this leads to misunderstanding and the assumption that such music is evidence of explicit religious Satanism and, perhaps, demon possession. There is a failure to appreciate what Roland Barthes (1915–1980) referred to as 'the level of myth' in signification.

The work of Barthes has been enormously important for the development of cultural studies. In his influential book *Mythologies* (1957), a collection of essays on French popular culture, he analyses 'signification' or, more broadly, the way meanings are produced and circulated in society. In his discussion of numerous everyday examples of popular culture, from toys to soap powder and from a cover of the magazine *Paris-Match* to the face of Greta Garbo in the film *Queen Christina* (1933), he seeks to expose implicit meanings embedded in everyday 'texts'. Things are rarely what they seem. There is more going on under the surface of these 'falsely obvious' texts. In the Preface to the 1957 edition of *Mythologies*, he states that he 'wanted to track down, in the decorative display of *what-goes-without-saying*, the ideological abuse which . . . is hidden there'. In other words, Barthes's analysis of popular culture was fundamentally political, in that he sought to get beneath the *apparently* 'what-goes-without-saying' statements of the media and popular culture to the underlying ideology. The point is, again, that popular culture is, in Gramscian terms, hegemonic, in that it promotes the values and interests of the dominant groups in society and the job of the cultural theorist is to expose them. This type of analysis is, we will see, enormously important in the study of religion and popular culture.

In order to understand 'myth' in Barthes's work, we need to note his development of the Saussurean model. He closes *Mythologies* with a theoretical section entitled 'Myth Today', which takes Saussure's approach and expands it to include a second level of signification. So, for example, the signifier 'rat' produces the signified 'rat', a large rodent associated with sewers. For the second level of signification, the sign of primary signification becomes the signifier. In this case, the large rodent associated with sewers becomes the signifier and the signified might become, for example, a self-serving, morally weak man (e.g. 'a love rat'). Barthes refers to primary signification as 'denotation' and secondary signification as 'connotation'. The point is that, if denotation indicates what might be referred to as 'real meanings' (e.g. dictionary definitions), the connotative process of secondary signification takes us away from these meanings and onto the levels of meanings constructed for a particular purpose (e.g. a punk's use of the swastika). These are the levels of 'myth'. For example, in *Mythologies* he discusses a photograph on the cover of the French magazine *Paris-Match* of 'a black soldier saluting the French flag'. This is primary signification/denotation. The various colours and shapes denoted a particular image which he recognised to be a black soldier saluting a French tricolour. However, immediately the connotative process of secondary signification got to work and other thoughts began to form in his head. While at the level of denotation a black soldier salutes the French flag, at the level of connotation it is a positive statement about French imperialism. Connotatively, the picture is an imperialist 'myth'. However, it is important to understand that a mythical system operates within a particular context. For example, the context of this issue of *Paris-Match* was shaped by the recent defeat of the French in Vietnam in 1954 and their current conflict in Algeria (1954–1962). Hence, the myth of military success and ethical colonialism was important. However, for Barthes, the problem is more acute, in that myths 'naturalize' signs. Drawing on the context to assist the process of interpretation, myths make it difficult not to immediately read off secondary signification. French readers of *Paris-Match* in the mid-1950s will, quite naturally, read the picture of a black soldier saluting a French flag in terms of a positive message about French imperialism. Myth ensures that the conceptual segue is seamless. Indeed, myth sanitizes, inoculates, simplifies, and naturalizes ideology by transforming it into a simple statement of fact. There are no complexities; no discussion is required; this is how it is.

Again, for the scholar of religion and popular culture, this approach to texts assists in understanding how certain kinds of meanings are generated and what values are endorsed. For example, it is interesting to analyse the use of the crucifix in vampire literature and films. At the level of denotation, throughout Bram Stoker's *Dracula*

(1897) the crucifix is revered as a source of significant protective power against evil. Connotatively, this is a Christian hegemonic myth, which needs to be understood in the context of late-Victorian London where it was written. It supports the dominant symbols of religious authority and sacred power. However, over the years the efficacy of the crucifix in vampire fiction has been eroded. Indeed, there has been a shift towards new symbols of purity. For example, in the film *Blade* (1998), we are told that, while 'crosses don't do squat', natural, organic products such as silver, sunlight and garlic have a powerful effect on vampires. Again, the contemporary context is important in understanding this shift. At a connotative level, at the level of myth, vampire fiction affirms a shift in the locus of sacred authority towards the natural world and, in some cases, towards nature spirituality. Hence, the rules of sacred authority, purity and pollution are still operating, but the understanding of that authority, purity and pollution has been redefined. Of course, the wider argument is that, if myths naturalize ideology by transforming them into simple statements of fact, then, as the occulture thesis argues, popular culture is an enormously important factor in determining the future trajectory of religion and spirituality in the modern world.

Finally, in his essay 'The Television Discourse: Encoding and Decoding' (1974), Stuart Hall drew on Barthes's work to expose discrete messages – 'signifying practices' or 'discourses' – within popular culture. The producers of popular culture, he argued, 'encode' it with particular meanings, which the viewers/listeners then 'decode'. For example, if an advertisement links an aftershave to an image of a handsome, athletic man sailing a large yacht, its encoded message is probably seeking to connote a particular idea of masculinity, sexual appeal, material success, and freedom. However, depending on one's context, prior experiences and beliefs, the message will be decoded differently. While some viewers will decode this message favourably, in that they find the values appealing, others will adopt a 'negotiated code', accepting some aspects of the message and rejecting others. Still others will read an 'oppositional code' and wholly reject the advert as, for example, the crass use of a banal stereotype of masculinity in order to sell them something they don't want. Again, it is interesting to examine the way national awards are perceived. In Britain, for example, the Order of the British Empire (OBE) is understood by many recipients to be a significant personal honour. These individuals fully accept the OBE's encoded message. For example, the television and radio presenter, Terry Wogan, declared that he was 'surprised and delighted that Her Majesty has given me this honour . . . I hope I can prove worthy of it'. On the other hand, the celebrated Rastafarian poet Benjamin Zephaniah adopted an oppositional code when he publicly rejected the award in protest at some of the British government's policies, including the decision to go to war in Iraq. More pointedly, because of his particular context, history, and identity the word 'empire' was decoded in a distinctly negative way. Openly dismissing the award as a legacy of colonialism, he declared that the very title, 'Order of the British Empire', reminded him of 'thousands of years of brutality. It reminds me of how my foremothers were raped and my forefathers brutalized'.

Summary

■ The modern period has witnessed the growing importance of popular culture in everyday life.

■ The study of popular culture is interested in the meanings, discourses, patterns, and structures of everyday life. Hence, the study of religion and popular culture can help us to understand something about ourselves, our values, and our beliefs, as well as the structures of power and the ideological impact of the media.

■ Defining popular culture highlights some key issues and debates, such as the elitist distinction between '*high* culture' and '*low* culture', which is clearly articulated in the Christian, class-based analysis of Matthew Arnold, who understood popular culture to be sinful and politically dangerous. Similar understandings of popular culture have shaped the responses of conservative religious groups.

■ There are three relationships between religion and popular culture that repay analysis: religion in popular culture; popular culture in religion; and popular culture as religion.

■ Narrowly theological approaches to the study of religion and popular culture can only take us so far. There is a need for interdisciplinary studies.

■ Some of the most interesting and insightful analyses of popular culture have been developed within cultural studies. While not all scholars of religion and culture will be comfortable with the neo-Marxist theorizing informing the research of the Centre of Contemporary Cultural Studies in the 1970s, the critical tools and theoretical perspectives that were developed there can help us understand the place of popular culture in contemporary societies, particularly in terms of social and cultural transformation. Is popular culture, for example, a communicator of healthy values or does it contribute to and maintain a 'false consciousness'? Does it liberate or oppress? Is it, perhaps, a little more complex than either of these positions?

■ The theory of occulture has emerged out of research into both contemporary religious belief and the relationship between religion and popular culture. It identifies a constantly changing reservoir of ideas, images and narratives that provides a resource for new spiritual thinking. Popular culture is central to occulture, in that it contributes, develops, disseminates and animates ideas.

Key terms

apologetics The systematic articulation of a rationale for and a defence of the teachings of a religious tradition.

black metal A subgenre of heavy/extreme metal, it articulates a misanthropic and anti-Christian ideology, often espousing Satanism and, in some cases, far right politics. Some musicians and fans have been associated with church burnings and murder. Some of the more important bands include, in the 1980s, Venom (whose 1982 album *Black Metal* gave the genre its name), Bathory, Merciful Fate and, in the 1990s, the Norwegian bands Mayhem, Burzum, Emperor, and Darkthrone.

Haredi/Haredim   Sometimes referred to as 'ultra-Orthodox', this model of Orthodox Judaism is particularly hostile to modernity. Their concerns about the corrupting influence of popular culture are related to a more general opposition to pluralism and relativism in the modern world and a rigorous commitment to the protection of Jewish culture.

hegemony   The dominance, especially political, of one group over another. Particularly associated with the Italian political theorist Antonio Gramsci, hegemony theory seeks to understand why one group in society remains dominant. He argued that we are socialized into thinking in certain ways that serve the interests of the dominant group by, amongst other things, popular culture. Hegemony is maintained this way without any physical coercion being necessary. Cultural hegemony has been discussed by several influential theorists, most notably Michel Foucault.

Marxism   A political philosophy based on an interpretation of the work of Karl Marx and Friedrich Engels, with whom Marx developed communist theory and co-authored *The Communist Manifesto* (1848).

missiology   The study of mission. It is that branch of applied theology that analyses the work of the missionary. It is fundamentally interdisciplinary, involving theology, communication theory, cultural anthropology, and linguistics.

occulture   If 'culture' refers to those social processes by which meanings are produced, circulated and exchanged, 'occulture' refers to those social processes by which spiritual, paranormal, esoteric and conspiratorial meanings are produced, circulated and exchanged. Occulture embraces ideas, images and narratives that resource new spiritual thinking and popular culture. Indeed, popular culture is central to its efficacy, in that it contributes, develops, disseminates and animates occultural content.

plausibility structure   Introduced by the sociologist Peter Berger, it refers to the socio-cultural context for systems of meaning. Whereas in earlier historical periods, societies tended to operate with a single framework for determining what was plausible or believable, in contemporary, pluralistic societies characterized by rapid social change, numerous plausibility structures are forced to coexist. Hence members of religions are aware of alternative truth claims. This leads to a relativization of meaning systems and the erosion of confidence in the plausibility structure of one's own group.

Rastafari   Originating as a black liberation movement in Jamaica, Rastafarianism is indebted to the political thought of Marcus Garvey (1887–1940). Central to Garvey's teaching was the return of Africans to Africa, the only place, he believed, where black people would feel at home and be respected as a race. It was widely believed that Garvey had made the following prophecy: 'Look to Africa for the crowning of a Black King; he shall be the Redeemer.' In November 1930, Ras (meaning 'Prince') Tafari Makonnen (1891–1975) was crowned Negus of Ethiopia. Declaring himself to be in the line of King Solomon and taking the name Haile Selassie I, many believed him to be the Messiah. Ras Tafari was God and had come to lead Africans out of white society and back to the promised land of Ethiopia (often used as a synonym for Africa).

semiotics The study of signs, initially developed by the Swiss linguist Ferdinand de Saussure in his posthumous *Course in General Linguistics* (1916). A sign is anything that produces meanings. Hence, semiotics is concerned with the production of meaning.

Further reading

Media studies, cultural studies and social theory

Theodor Adorno and Max Horkheimer: *The Culture Industry* (London: Routledge, 1991) is the best collection of Adorno's most important essays on the concept of 'the culture industry'.

Matthew Arnold: *Culture and Anarchy* (London: Cambridge University Press, 1971), first published in 1869, is his famous series of essays debating key questions about the nature of culture and society.

Roland Barthes: *Mythologies*, tr. A. Lavers (London: Jonathan Cape, 1972 [1957]) is his collection of enormously influential essays on semiology and popular culture.

Colin Campbell: 'The Cult, the Cultic Milieu and Secularization' [1972]. In Jeffrey Kaplan and Heléne Lööw (eds): *The Cultic Milieu: Oppositional Subcultures in an Age of Globalization* (Walnut Creek, CA: AltaMira Press, 2002, pp. 12–25). This seminal early essay identifies a 'cultic milieu' which stands in opposition to the social mainstream. The book in which it's reprinted is an important collection of articles exploring the contemporary significance of the theory. However, since then the more inclusive theory of 'occulture', which builds on Campbell's thesis, has been developed.

Ferdinand de Saussure: *Course in General Linguistics* [1916]. Trans by Roy Harris (Chicago, IL: Open Court, 1986). Arguing that language is central to the human understanding of reality, this is the foundational text of modern linguistic theory and what became known as Structuralism.

John Fiske: *Understanding Popular Culture* (London: Routledge, 1989), although a little dated now, is still a useful introduction to the study of popular culture.

Ann Gray and J. McGuigan (eds): *Studying Culture: An Introductory Reader*, second edition (London: Arnold, 1997). This is a good collection of key texts from the history of cultural studies.

Raiford Guins and Omayra Zaragoza Cruz (eds): *Popular Culture: A Reader* (London: Sage, 2005). This is an excellent collection of key texts that provides an overview of the study of popular culture.

Stuart Hall: 'The Television Discourse – Encoding and Decoding' [1974]. In Ann Gray and J. McGuigan (eds): *Studying Culture: An Introductory Reader*, second edition (London: Arnold, 1997, pp. 28–34). A seminal and much discussed paper proposing a model of mass communication.

Richard Hoggart: *The Uses of Literacy: Aspects of Working-Class Life, with Special Reference to Publications and Entertainments* (London: Chatto & Windus, 1957) is a foundational text in British cultural studies, which discusses the lived culture of the working classes.

F.R. Leavis: *Mass Civilization and Minority Culture* (London: Minority Press, 1933) is another seminal text, arguing that culture can only be appreciated and judged by a minority and that 'mass culture' is the antithesis of 'culture'.

Jim McGuigan: *Cultural Populism* (London: Routledge, 1992) provides an important critical discussion of the emergence of cultural studies.

Neil Postman: *Amusing Ourselves to Death: Public Discourse in an Age of Show Business* (London: Heinemann, 1985) is an interpretation of Marshall McLuhan's dictum that 'the medium is the message', which offers an influential critique of television and its effect on viewers. Insisting that it represents an attack on literate culture, he argues that its ascendancy along with the decline of the printed word has led to the demise of public discourse.

John Storey: *An Introduction to Cultural Theory and Popular Culture* (London: Prentice Hall, 1997) is an excellent introduction to key theories, debates and issues.

Dominic Strinati: *An Introduction to Theories of Popular Culture*, second edition (London: Routledge, 2004) is another excellent introduction to key theories, debates and issues.

E.P. Thompson: *The Making of the English Working Class* (London: Gollancz, 1963) is a seminal historical analysis of the lived culture of the working classes and an important early text in cultural studies.

Raymond Williams's three early books are seminal texts in the development of cultural studies, all of which focus on the cultural significance of language and literature: *Culture and Society: 1780–1950* (London: Chatto & Windus, 1958); *The Long Revolution* (London: Chatto & Windus, 1961); *Keywords: A Vocabulary of Culture and Society* (London: Fontana, 1988).

Theology, religious studies, and popular culture

Tom Beaudoin: *Virtual Faith: The Irreverent Spiritual Quest of Generation X* (Chichester: Jossey-Bass, 1998) is a positive appreciation of popular culture, which argues that it can play an important role in the formation and expression of an individual's spiritual journey.

Tom Beaudoin: *Consuming Faith: Integrating Who We Are Into What We Buy* (Lanham, MD: Sheed & Ward, 2003) examines branding, consumerism and spirituality in the shaping of personal identities.

Eric Christianson and Christopher Partridge (eds): *Understanding Religion and Violence in Popular Culture* (London: Equinox, 2009) is a collection of studies by scholars from the disciplines of religious studies, biblical studies, film studies and sociology exploring the relationship of violence to religion in popular culture, from the discourse of terrorism to the spectacle of worldwide wrestling.

Lynn S. Clark: *From Angels to Aliens: Teenagers, the Media, and the Supernatural* (New York: Oxford University Press, 2003), which is based on significant qualitative research with teenagers, explores their fascination with the supernatural in popular culture, arguing that, whilst traditional, institutional religion may be declining, interest in alternative spiritualities and the paranormal is increasing.

Lynn S. Clark (ed.): *Religion, Media and the Marketplace* (New Brunswick, NJ: Rutgers University Press, 2007) is an interesting collection of interdisciplinary essays exploring the confluence of religion and consumer culture.

Kelton Cobb: *Blackwell Guide to Theology and Popular Culture* (Oxford: Blackwell, 2005) is an excellent overview, which provides a particularly thoughtful critical introduction to the theological analysis of popular culture.

Bruce D. Forbes and Jeffrey H. Mahan (eds): *Religion and Popular Culture in America* (Berkeley, CA: University of California Press, 2000) is not only a useful collection of essays on a wide range of subjects, but it is helpfully organized according to the typology of the differing relations between religion and popular culture produced by Forbes and Mahan: (1) religion in popular culture; (2) popular culture in religion; (3) popular culture as religion; (4) religion and popular culture in dialogue.

Stig Hjarvard (ed.): *Northern Lights: Film and Media Studies Yearbook* 6 (2008). This volume on 'the mediatization of religion' includes several important essays of interest to scholars of popular culture and religious change.

Stewart M. Hoover: *Religion in the Media Age* (London: Routledge, 2006). Persuaded that we live in an age which has seen a shift away from traditional institutional religion toward more subjective forms of spirituality, this is a thoughtful analysis of how mass media might relate to this process.

Stewart M. Hoover and Lynn S. Clark (eds): *Practicing Religion in the Age of the Media: Explorations in Media, Religion and Culture* (New York: Columbia University Press, 2004) is a collection of studies examining a range of manifestations of the confluence of the sacred and the secular in the modern world.

Gordon Lynch: *Understanding Theology and Popular Culture* (Oxford: Blackwell, 2005) is one of the most accessible and stimulating recent introductions to the field.

Gordon Lynch: *Between Sacred and Profane: Researching Religion and Popular Culture* (London: I.B. Tauris, 2007) provides a helpful collection of essays addressing a range of questions central to the study of religion and popular culture. Indeed, it is an excellent book for students needing to acquaint themselves quickly with the key issues and debates.

Eric M. Mitchell and Kate McCarthy (eds): *God in the Details: American Religion in Popular Culture* (New York: Routledge, 2001) provides a collection of largely stimulating essays on a range of subjects from Bruce Springsteen to Burning Man and from apocalyptic themes in films to *The Simpsons*.

Jolyon Mitchell: *Media Violence and Christian Ethics* (Cambridge: Cambridge University Press, 2007) examines Christian and secular critiques of media violence, including audience responses. It is particularly useful for thinking through ways of theorizing media violence.

Jolyon Mitchell and Sophia Marriage (eds): *Mediating Religion: Conversations in Media, Religion and Culture* (London: Continuum, 2003). This is a comprehensive resource for students of media, religion and popular culture, including annotated bibliographies.

H. Richard Niebuhr: *Christ and Culture* (New York: Harper & Row, 1951) is, as discussed above, an influential critical overview of theological approaches to culture.

Christopher Partridge: *The Re-enchantment of the West: Alternative Spiritualities, Sacralization, Popular Culture and Occulture*, 2 vols (London: T & T. Clark International, 2004, 2005) makes the case for Western sacralization/re-enchantment in relation to the occulture thesis. As such, it discusses the significance of popular culture for religious belief in the West.

Christopher Partridge and Eric Christianson (eds): *The Lure of the Dark Side: Satan and Western Demonology in Popular Culture* (London: Equinox, 2009) is a collection of multidisciplinary essays analysing the demonic in popular music, film and literature.

Adam Possamai: *Religion and Popular Culture: A Hyper-Real Testament* (Brussels: Peter Lang, 2005) includes an interesting sociological analysis of the way spiritualities emerge out of an engagement with the myths disseminated through popular culture (i.e. hyper-real religions).

Paul Tillich: *Theology of Culture* (Oxford: Oxford University Press, 1959) is a good place to begin reading his thought in the area. However, it has to be said that, not only did he begin formulating his thinking on culture and correlation very early in his career, but it can be found throughout his work, most notably in his *Systematic Theology*, 3 vols (Chicago, IL: Chicago University Press 1951, 1957, 1963).

David Tracy: *Blessed Rage for Order* (New York: Seabury Press, 1975) and *Analogical Imagination* (New York: Cross Road, 1981) provide, along with much else, a systematic articulation of his 'revised correlational method'. These, however, are seminal works in a major methodological project and, as such, require a good level of theological literacy.

Music

John Blanchard: *Pop Goes the Gospel* (Welwyn: Evangelical Press, 1983). This was a popular and typically Christian fundamentalist treatment of popular music.

Mark Evans: *Open Up the Doors: Music in the Modern Church* (London: Equinox, 2006). A thoughtful discussion of the issues and debates surrounding the use of contemporary music styles in Christian worship.

Michael J. Gilmour: *Tangled Up in the Bible: Bob Dylan and Scripture* (New York: Continuum, 2004). A study of Dylan's reading of the Bible, particularly the way he makes use of biblical images, concepts, and themes.

Michael J. Gilmour (ed.): *Call Me the Seeker: Listening to Religion in Popular Music* (New York: Continuum, 2005). This is one of the first collections of essays devoted to religion and popular music.

Keith Kahn-Harris: *Extreme Metal: Music and Culture on the Edge* (Oxford: Berg, 2007) is an important and revealing analysis of the global extreme metal scene, based on studies in Scandinavia, Israel, the USA and the UK. It includes discussions of key themes of the genre such as violence, the occult, neo-fascism and Satanism.

Anthony Pinn: *Noise and Spirit: The Religious and Spiritual Sensibilities of Rap Music* (New York: New York University Press, 2003) excavates the spiritual dimensions of rap and its relationship with religions, notably Christianity and Islam.

Gregory Reece: *Elvis Religion: The Cult of the King* (London: I.B. Tauris, 2006) is an enjoyable discussion of devotion to Elvis.

Graham St. John (ed): *Rave Culture and Religion* (London: Routledge, 2004). This is a thoughtful collection of articles on the spiritual dimensions of rave culture.

Robin Sylvan: *Traces of the Spirit: The Religious Dimensions of Popular Music* (New York: New York University Press, 2002) is an examination of the relationship between religion and poplar music, which focuses on subcultures and the religious significance of their experiences and rituals.

Robin Sylvan: *Trance Formation: The Spiritual and Religious Dimensions of Global Rave Culture* (London: Routledge, 2005) explores the spiritual and religious dimensions of global rave culture, arguing that the rave scene is a significant source of spirituality for many people.

Film

Eric Christianson, Peter Francis, and William Telford (eds): *Cinema Divinité: Religion, Theology and the Bible in Film* (London: SCM, 2005) is an excellent collection of essays, which, apart from discussing the nature and application of film theory to theology and introducing various critical approaches to the study of film and theology, provides a helpful overview of much of the recent literature on the film and religion.

Douglas E. Cowan: *Sacred Terror: Religion and Horror on the Silver Screen* (Waco, TX: Baylor University Press, 2008) focuses specifically on the relationship between horror and religion.

Christopher Deacy: *Screen Christologies: Redemption and the Medium of Film* (Cardiff: University of Wales Press, 2001), as discussed above, explores christological and soterological themes in film.

Brian Godawa: *Hollywood Worldviews: Watching Films with Wisdom and Discernment* (Downers Grove: IVP, 2002) is, as discussed above, a Christian apologetic engagement with film.

Christopher Grau (ed.): *Philosophers Explore* The Matrix (New York: Oxford University Press, 2005). This is an interesting collection of essays examining philosophical themes explored in *The Matrix*.

Gerard Loughlin: *Alien Sex: The Body and Desire in Cinema and Theology* (Oxford: Blackwell, 2004) is a detailed theological analysis of human sexuality that draws liberally on not only Western critical theorists but also Western popular culture.

John Lyden: *Film as Religion: Myths, Morals, Rituals* (New York: New York University Press, 2003) is an interesting analysis of the viewer's reception of the film 'as religion'.

Clive Marsh: *Cinema and Sentiment: Film's Challenge to Theology* (Milton Keynes: Paternoster Press, 2004), as discussed above, provides several theological analyses of particular films, as well as arguing the case for studying the reception of film by viewers.

Clive Marsh: *Theology Goes to the Movies: An Introduction to Critical Christian Thinking* (Abingdon, Oxon: Routledge, 2007) argues that film helps people to reflect on their lives, rather than simply being 'escapism'. Hence, Marsh insists, it can become an important theological resource.

Clive Marsh and Gaye Ortiz (eds): *Explorations in Theology and Film: Movies and Meaning* (Oxford: Blackwell, 1997) is an older, but nevertheless worthwhile collection of essays.

Jolyon Mitchell and S. Brent Plate (eds): *The Film and Religion Reader* (Abingdon, Oxon: Routledge, 2007) is the best currently available and indispensible for students of film and religion.

S. Brent Plate (ed.): *Representing Religion in World Cinema: Filmmaking, Mythmaking, Culturemaking* (Basingstoke: Palgrave Macmillan, 2003). This collection of essays is an excellent introduction to the relationship between religion and film beyond Hollywood and the West.

Melanie J. Wright: *Religion and Film: An Introduction* (London: I.B. Tauris, 2006) is not only arguably the best introduction currently available, but it provides a good example of the value of inter-disciplinary scholarship.

Popular literature

Giselle L. Anatol (ed.): *Harry Potter: Critical Essays* (Westport, CT: Praeger, 2003). While not a volume concerned specifically with issues relating to religion and culture, it has several important studies that are of relevance to the field.

Amy Frykholm: *Rapture Culture: Left Behind in Evangelical Culture* (New York: Oxford University Press, 2004) is perhaps the best analysis of the Left Behind phenomenon.

Crawford Gribbin: *Writing the Rapture: Prophecy Fiction in Evangelical America* (New York: Oxford University Press, 2008) is an important study of the subject, including, of course, Left Behind.

Connie Neal: *The Gospel According to Harry Potter: The Spiritual Journey of the World's Greatest Seeker* (Louisville, KY: Westminster John Knox Press, 2002). An accessible introduction to the books and films from a conservative Christian theological perspective, which argues that they articulate important spiritual and moral issues.

Journals

Most theology and religious studies journals will publish articles of interest to the scholar of religion and popular culture. Likewise, journals publishing research in cultural studies, film studies or popular music studies will also include relevant articles. A particularly good journal is the *Journal of Popular Culture*. However, specifically in the area of religion and popular culture, the following online journals are useful resources:

Journal of Religion and Popular Culture, <http://www.usask.ca/relst/jrpc/>

Journal of Religion and Film, <http://www.unomaha.edu/~jrf/>

Chapter 21

Secularization and secularism

Grace Davie and Linda Woodhead

in modern societies. Their interest, however, is in the way pluralism leads to religious growth and vitality. The theory postulates that individuals have a natural need for religion, and will make religious choices in a 'rational' way, so as to maximize their gains and minimize their losses. Where there is an abundant supply of religious choices – a rich religious marketplace – individuals will be more able to make satisfying choices which meet their needs, than where there is little choice. Applying this to Europe and America, RTC theorists claim that they can explain why religion has declined in the former (because monopolistic churches meant there was little choice) whilst remaining vital in the USA (where there is a lively religious marketplace, with offerings to suit every religious customer). RTC attacks secularization theory head on, and a battle has ensued between proponents of these two very different approaches. Irrespective of who is right, the controversy illustrates, once again, the difference between Europe and America, and the way in which the different cases can give rise to very different theories.

What it is safe to say, is that European forms of religion are less and less frequently seen as the global prototype (other than by hard theories of secularization, like Steve Bruce's). Or to put the same point in a different way, the relative secularity of Europe is not a model for export; it is something distinct, peculiar to the European corner of the world. As Grace Davie puts it, Europe comes to be seen not as the norm and pioneer in its secularity, but as 'the exceptional case'. Thus the long-established idea that there is a necessary connection between modernization and secularization is increasingly challenged not only by fresh evidence, but by new and different ways of looking at the world which do not assume that Europe offers the only possible model of modernity and modernization.

Summary

- Secularization theories attempt both to describe what is happening (religion is declining in the modern world), and to explain it.

- 'Hard' versions of secularization maintain that modernization inevitably involves the decline of religion.

- 'Soft' versions try to isolate the factors which may lead to the decline of certain kinds of religion in certain circumstances – secularization is seen as contingent not inevitable.

- Multidimensional models of secularization try to isolate the several different senses of secularization.

- Secularization is more evident in Europe than elsewhere, and the hard theories take Europe as their model.

- Challenges to hard secularization theory have come from theorists who treat European secularity as the exception not the norm.

■ Secularization may be a normative aspiration as well as a neutral description of reality. In this case, secularism and secularization go hand in hand.

Key terms

differentiation/functional differentiation (sometimes also called 'social differentiation') The distinctively modern process whereby social activities become split between different social institutions (like law, education, healthcare).

exceptionalism The view that one country or region (e.g. Europe) is exceptionally secular (or religious).

sacralization The growth of religion.

secularism The view that religion should be opposed or restricted.

secularization The decline of religion.

secularization theory A theory which describes and explains the decline of religion in terms of some wider factor(s).

pluralism The simultaneous existence in a single social arena of a number of different world views, ideologies, cultures or religions.

Further reading

Introductory

Linda Woodhead and Paul Heelas (eds): *Religion in Modern Times: An Interpretive Anthology* (Oxford, UK, and Malden, MA: Blackwell, 2000, pp. 307–341 and 429–474) draws together classical and contemporary readings on secularization and sacralization.

Secularization

Peter L. Berger: *The Sacred Canopy: Elements of a Sociological Theory of Religion* (Garden City, NY: Doubleday, 1967). In the course of a wider discussion of the relation between religion, society and knowledge, Berger develops his early argument that pluralization is the missing causal link which explains the connection of secularization and modernization.

Steve Bruce: *Religion in the Modern World: From Cathedrals to Cults* (Oxford, UK and New York: Oxford University Press, 1996) and *God is Dead: Secularization in the West* (Oxford, UK and Malden, MA: Blackwell, 2002) offer strong versions of the secularization thesis.

José Casanova: *Public Religions in the Modern World* (Chicago, IL and London: University of Chicago Press, 1994) offers a multidimensional analysis of the ways in which religion retains public and political significance in the modern world.

Grace Davie: *Europe: The Exceptional Case. Parameters of Faith in the Modern World* (London: Darton, Longman and Todd, 2002) examines European exceptionalism and the ways in which religion maintains a vicarious and precarious presence in Europe.

Karel Dobbelaere: *Secularization: An Analysis at Three Levels* (Frankfurt am Main: Peter Lang, 2002) offers a multidimensional approach to secularization.

David Martin: *On Secularization: Towards a Revised General Theory* (Aldershot: Ashgate, 2005) offers an explanation of the geographical variability of secularization.

Sacralization

Peter L. Berger (ed.): *The Desecularization of the World: Essays on the Resurgence of Religion in World Politics* (Washington, DC: Ethics and Public Policy Center; Grand Rapids: William B. Eerdmans, 1999) considers how contemporary religious resurgence counts against universal theories of secularization.

Grace Davie: *The Sociology of Religion* (London: Sage, 2007, pp. 67–88) offers an introduction to Rational Choice Theory.

Index

Note: References to captions and tables are indicated by *italics* (*9, 39t*). Definitions of key terms are in **bold** type (**294**).

Related titles from Routledge

Religious Studies
A Global View
Edited by Gregory D. Alles

Religious Studies: A Global View is the first book of its kind to survey the field of Religious Studies from a global perspective. In ten chapters focusing on specific geographic regions, a team of international contributors explore the work that is being done in religious studies around the world. They particularly focus on the work done in the last fifty years, and invite readers to rethink their conceptions of what that study involves: its history, structures, leading figures and key issues. Regions discussed include:

Western Europe Eastern Europe North Africa and West Asia Sub-Saharan Africa South and Southeast Asia Continental East Asia Japan Australia, New Zealand, and the Pacfic Islands North America Latin America

Key topics and themes discussed include the emergence of a global community of Religion scholars, the influence of technology, the history and institutionalization of the discipline, objects, methods and theories in the study of religion, and the demarcation of the field.

Religious Studies: A Global View challenges the assumption that serious thinking about religion is solely a Western undertaking and aims to foster global cooperation in the study of religions. It is the ideal resource for students, researchers, lecturers and teachers interested in how the field of Religious Studies is developing in contemporary academia.

Gregory D. Alles is Professor of Religious Studies at McDaniel College, Westminster, MD, USA. He is co-editor of *Continuum Advances in Religious Studies*.

ISBN13: 978-0-415- 39743-8 (hbk)

Available at all good bookshops
For ordering and further information please visit:
www.routledge.com

Religion: The Basics
Second Edition
Malory Nye

From the local to the global level, religion is - more than ever - an important and hotly debated part of modern life in the 21st century.

From silver rings to ringtones and from clubs to headscarves we often find the cultural role and discussion of religion in unexpected ways.

Now in its second edition, Religion: the Basics remains the best introduction to religion and contemporary culture available.

The new edition has been fully revised and updated, and includes new discussions of:

- The study of religion and culture in the 21st century
- Texts, films and rituals
- Cognitive approaches to religion
- Globalisation and multiculturalism
- Spirituality in the West
- Popular religion

With new case studies, linking cultural theory to real world religious experience and practice, and guides to further reading, Religion: the Basics is an essential buy for students wanting to get to grips with this hotly debated topic.

978-0-415-44947-2 (hbk)
978-0-415-44948-9 (pbk)
978-0-203-92797-7 (ebk)

Available at all good bookshops
For ordering and further information please visit
www.routledge.com

Related titles from Routledge

Introducing World Religions
Victoria Kennick Urubshurow

Introducing World Religions offers an exciting new approach to the study of the world's religions. Taking its inspiration from performance studies and using an innovative dramatic metaphor, it enables students to explore religious ideas and culture in terms of the players (key figures), the script (foundational texts) and performance (religious practices). The discussion of key players treats human and non-human figures on the world stage, including the principle (God, Dharma, Dao), imaginal figures (angels, baals, bodhisattvas), exceptional persons (founders, prophets, gurus), and historical personas (significant players in the drama of religions).

The discussion of the foundational texts includes materials that balance or challenge mainstream texts with an alternative perspective. The section on performance explores non-verbal religious activities such as pilgrimage, icon painting, dance, divination, and meditation.

Specially designed to assist learning, it includes:

- chapter timelines showing key persons, events and dates
- maps, charts and photographs
- glossary of key terms and concepts
- key reading, a comprehensive bibliography and index
- a support website at www.routledge.com/textbooks/9780415772709

Ideal for one-semester or modular introductory survey courses on the world's religions, *Introducing World Religions* will be essential reading for any student of religions, worldwide.

ISBN13: 978-0-415-77269-3 (hbk)
ISBN13: 978–0–415–77270–9 (pbk)

Available at all good bookshops
For ordering and further information please visit:
www.routledge.com